Human Rights Education for the Twenty-First Century

Pennsylvania Studies in Human Rights
Edited by Bert B. Lockwood, Jr.

A complete list of books in the series is available from the publisher.

Human Rights Education for the Twenty-First Century

edited by George J. Andreopoulos and Richard Pierre Claude

Foreword by Shulamith Koenig

PENN

University of Pennsylvania Press

Philadelphia

10   9   8   7   6   5   4   3   2   1

Published by
University of Pennsylvania Press
Philadelphia, Pennsylvania 19104-6097

Library of Congress Cataloging-in-Publication Data
Human rights education for the twenty-first century / edited by George J. Andreopoulos and
    Richard Pierre Claude ; foreword by Shulamith Koenig.
        p.   cm. — (Pennsylvania studies in human rights)
    ISBN 0-8122-3388-3 (alk. paper). — ISBN 0-8122-1607-5 (pbk. : alk. paper)
1. Human rights—Study and teaching.   I. Andreopoulos, George J.   II. Claude, Richard Pierre, 1934–   .
III. Series.
JC571.H769442   1997
232'.071—dc21   96-40949
                                                                                      CIP

To Giuliana Campanelli
Christopher Michael Claude
Elena Alexandra Andreopoulos
and
Timothy Andrew Claude

This book was made possible by the initiative and support
of the Organizing Committee,
People's Decade of Human Rights Education

Contents

Foreword

Shulamith Koenig

All of the contributors to this book are pioneers in the new, vast, and broadly defined field of human rights education. They believe that such education offers hope
for the future of our children and the destiny of humanity as a whole. They form a
community of concern with a program for action. Their program promotes people
learning to safeguard and hold fast to their dignity and freedom—women, men, and
children engaged in learning about human rights in the context of their struggles
and their daily lives. I invite you to join this community which sees human rights as
a fully comprehensive, holistic value system capable of guiding our lives beneficially
and preventing abuses of our human rights. Human rights education is essential to a
genuine process of global social change, and it should be included in educational and
cultural activities in every society throughout the world.

The chapters in this volume supply many reasons—social, legal, and political—
for promoting human rights education. There are personal reasons as well. People
often come to human rights education because of a transforming personal experience. For me, it all began in Israel in agonizing conversations with my dearest friend,
the late Achi Yotam, an Adlerian psychologist. Achi, my husband and friend Jerry,
and I often discussed the questions of how and why the oppressed turn into oppressors. One night we talked until the morning light appeared over the far mountains.
We shared our deep distress over recent developments in our community, including
abuses of the human rights of Palestinians. With idealism and perhaps some naiveté,
we sought to find Archimedes' fulcrum, the distinct leverage point which, when discovered, can effect genuine and lasting change. In human terms, we agreed, that
point is dignity. If we take human dignity seriously, we must join forces to reject, remove, and fully eliminate the gap of dignity between people in all societies across
the globe, beginning with our own community. As a result of this clarifying analysis,
I resolved to work with Palestinians for a two-state solution. At the time, while the
Intifada pitched stones against bullets competing in a deadly game, I saw clearly that
human rights education may be a way to learn to look at our lives from the perspec-

tive of compassion and social justice and with the humility needed to break through the vicious cycle of humiliation in which we all participate.

Humiliation is the enemy of human dignity. Humiliation is a powerful experience, the impasse to being human. In defending our dignity, we refuse to be humiliated. We must recognize this in others. Unless we learn to live a life in which we do not degrade, disgrace, demean, or violate the dignity of the other on any level, personal or communal, the cycle of violence, oppression, and abuse will go on ad infinitum.

Value clarification, at once a process and one of the central objectives of human rights education, must allow each person so involved to draw upon her and his own lights and experience. I draw commitment to human rights education from the prophets Isaiah and Micah, Mohammed, Jesus, and Buddha, as well as Karl Marx, Martin Buber, Alfred Adler, Mahatma Gandhi, and Eleanor Roosevelt. My parents, Daniel and Malka Zechory, taught me that all human beings are born equal in dignity, and my husband and three sons taught me how to make my voyage of promoting of human rights education without concessions. Many friends encouraged me in the founding and development of the Organizing Committee for the People's Decade of Human Rights Education: Betty Reardon, Richard Claude, Stephen Marks, Clarence Dias, Mado Spiegler, Tara Krause, Donna Hicks, Elsa Stamatopoulou, Fatma Alloo, Susana Chiarotti, Loretta Ross, Suhier Azzuni, Orli Lubin, Walter Lichem, Ivanka Corti, and Upendra Baxi, to mention just a few whose energies joined the walk toward human rights education. We invite you to accompany us in this journey, encouraging your own communities to engage in dialogue about human rights as inalienable, indivisible, and interconnected guide markers in the struggle for justice.

At the Fourth UN World Conference on Women in 1995, the People's Decade of Human Rights Education organized a nine-day Institute for Human Rights Education. Twenty women from twenty countries presented their own human rights education training manuals. They focused on women's human rights and gender equality, and they shared the conviction that if all people understood social, economic, and civil injustices as human rights violations, then a path toward justice could be developed at the community level for women, men, youth, and children.

Our Beijing Institute asked one question in many forms, reflecting the cultures of the participants:

How do we learn to belong and how do we learn to behave?
How do we dance our lives in step with human rights?
How do we find techniques to weave a human rights culture?
How do we learn to love our neighbor as we love ourselves?
Can we start with dialogue, and if so, with whom?

Of course, these questions help to open dialogue, but they only begin the process. We must press on tenaciously, keeping our own experiences in mind. For example, how do we start, even in our own families, to learn about equality and that differences between women and men are not liabilities but the joy, inspiration, and celebration of uniqueness that simultaneously define and unite us? Human rights education has many more questions than answers. This is because the answers must come from the people themselves as they become empowered to identify their problems, define their needs, and invoke human rights norms around which they find answers and formulate plans of action.

Identifying problems, defining needs, clarifying norms, formulating and undertaking plans of action: this is the process of human rights education for empowerment. Those who by now have undertaken it in more than one hundred countries can testify that it is a powerful process. Human rights education for empowerment can help to mobilize people in their own communities to use the space created by the UN Decade of Human Rights Education (1995–2005) in the same way the UN Decade of Women was used to enrich and strengthen the women's movement.

The Women's Decade helped millions of women to see their problems as interconnected with the struggles of others elsewhere. Can human rights education in a Bangladesh village, where authorities promote farming for export instead of for local consumption, help its residents respond to the hurtful impacts of globalization plans that leave human lives out of the equation? And more challenging, can ties of solidarity be built whereby Bangladeshi issues may be seen as linked to the struggle against racism and poverty in other areas of the world, including the United States? Can human rights education help bring sanity to those who speak of sustainable development yet forget that sustainability is impossible unless sustained by people's potential both to participate in the realization of their human rights and to enhance their creative potential to contribute to their own progress?

In Copenhagen, in a meeting with 120 representatives from nongovernmental organizations, we were told: human rights education is development. In my view, several important notions are entailed in this statement and have important implications for human rights education. While these notions may seem abstract, I will share a concrete illustration of each flowing from actual human rights education projects.

The first notion is that human rights constitute the common heritage of all humankind. Human rights are a legacy passed from one generation to the next, and as such this heritage should be a central subject of education. It is available from childhood onward to share in the energy and life force of a world where human rights norms should become the underpinnings of social change, breaking through the vicious cycle of humiliation and the imposition of suffering on humans by fellow humans that so ruthlessly and shamelessly dwells among us.

In a rural county in Georgia in the United States, a teacher working with mentally disabled children participated in a group assembled to learn about human rights. Typically human rights standards were contrasted with a listing of specific human rights violations affecting mentally disabled children. At the end of the first discussion, one teacher rose and spoke with great passion. He said that his training was steeped in the culture and tradition of the Deep South, but that in learning about human rights he had to see some of his training and practices as parochial and narrow. He said, "I now realize that for the last twenty-five years I have been violating the human rights of the children with whom I have been working. I want to know more so that we can stop these practices."

Second, human rights should frame human discourse and dialogue. Human rights calls for a dialogue that recognizes that freedom without law is anarchy and law without freedom is tyranny. The task of human rights education, in this context, is to provide dialogue about the fine balance among culture, law, and freedom and the point of intersection of these three where we are denied our dignity, and where we learn actively to solve the concerns of individuals and communities about class, gender, and race by committing ourselves without compromise to a human rights way of life.

In Natal, South Africa, as part of a project of human rights education on women's human rights and gender equality, rural women decided to enter into a dialogue with their chiefs, with whom they spent many months discussing equality and the imperatives of women's participation in the decisions that determine their lives in the private and public arenas. In December 1995 the local government held regional council elections. Of those who participated in the dialogue with the chiefs, twenty-two women ran for office, and eight of them were elected to the fifteen seats.

Third, human rights are needed to protect people from harm and to help them protect themselves. Viewing human rights as preventives to human rights violations and as mechanisms for protection and the redress of grievances is an essential quality of human rights standards. As a consequence, we must come around to seeing that human rights education means people, individually and in groups, acquiring the knowledge and perspectives to protect themselves from human rights violators and to remedy the wrongs they endure.

As a direct result of human rights education in Israel, the Arab community with the aid of human rights activists brought together forty Arab mayors who agreed about the importance of grievances on the issue of land and housing. They presented these grievances to the UN Human Rights Subcommission in Geneva and to the Committee on Economic, Social and Cultural Rights. Some of these actions, in fact, initiated a process to overturn discriminatory practices against Arabs in Israel.

These three examples illustrate but a few of the kinds of activities associated with effective programs of human rights education. One of the reasons why such education is taking hold all over the world is that it brings people around to speaking the common language of human rights which has become a global lingua franca addressing social, political, cultural, and economic issues worldwide. One of the contributors to this volume, Upendra Baxi, has written that "perhaps no single phrase in recent human history has been privileged to bear the mission or burden of human destiny more than 'human rights' in the last fifty years." In his book *Inhuman Wrongs and Human Rights: Unconventional Essays*, he adds: "the great gift of classical and contemporary human thought to culture and civilization is the notion of human rights. The struggle to preserve, protect and promote basic human rights continues in every generation in each society." From this premise, we should understand that human rights education will fulfill its mission if it joins in this struggle.

A Hebrew word I carry in my heart is *Sha've*, one word with two meanings that are one: "equal" and "worthy." *Sha've* in my human rights dictionary is the message contained in the Universal Declaration of Human Rights. *Sha've* is the hope we have lost in our transgressions. *Sha've* is the meaning we discover in human rights education in the context of struggle to overcome all injustice. Human rights is truth limited in words but bewitched by its own expectations, a tension never to be resolved but with the nourishment of hope. Those who join us in human rights education join us in an exciting voyage where real hope lies.

Preface

Human rights education (HRE), which includes teaching people about their rights, is a difficult task. It is made somewhat easier because endorsements for human rights education have been proclaimed in various global and regional legal instruments ever since 1945 when the Charter of the United Nations called for cooperation "in promoting and encouraging respect for human rights and fundamental freedoms." Reaffirmed in 1993 in Vienna at the United Nations World Conference on Human Rights, this foundational premise of "promoting and encouraging" creates responsibilities at the state level (formal education) and among social institutions, including nongovernmental organizations (nonformal education).

To help interested groups meet these obligations, we have developed a book of previously unpublished essays addressing problems and challenges that are both conceptual (Part I) and practical (Parts II–V). The book is designed to be useful to practitioners, offering not only theoretical guidance but also "nuts-and-bolts" advice regarding planning and implementing programs of formal (or school-based) and nonformal (or out-of-school) human rights education.

In October 1992, with support from the Organizing Committee of the People's Decade of Human Rights Education, the Columbia University Center for the Study of Human Rights sponsored a meeting of representatives of groups worldwide who had begun or were planning programs of human rights education. The meeting was charged with excitement about the need to fill a "values gap" in the post–cold war period and to focus on values-based educational programs appropriate for emerging and reemerging democracies as we move toward the twenty-first century. Sharing experiences and raising questions about how to promote such work globally, the meeting was titled "The Conference on Goals and Strategies of Human Rights Education." It was organized by Shulamith Koenig, director of the Organizing Committee, and funded by the Friedrich Ebert Foundation with the full support and participation of its director, Pia Baumgartin.

Participants included educators, activists, policymakers, and human rights victims concerned with preventive strategies addressed to human rights abuses. A Working Group reconvened in June 1993 at the Yale Law School under the auspices of the

Orville Schell Center for International Human Rights. The Working Group decided to undertake the development of a multiauthored volume, co-edited by George Andreopoulos (Yale University) and Richard Pierre Claude (University of Maryland), in combination with an international editorial committee consisting of Jennifer Green (Human Rights Program, Harvard Law School); Abraham Magendzo (Programa Interdisciplinario de Investigaciones en Educación, Santiago); Stephen P. Marks (Center for International Studies, Princeton University); J. Paul Martin (Center for the Study of Human Rights, Columbia University); Betty Reardon (Teachers College); Peter Juviler (Barnard College); and Cosmas Gitta (Fellow at the Columbia University Center for the Study of Human Rights). With their active participation, the project was three years in development.

This book is directed toward a global audience of educators, scholars in all disciplines, research specialists worldwide, nongovernmental organizations (NGOs), foundation officers, and others concerned with formal and nonformal education. Participants were advised by the editors to compose their essays addressing readers and users involved in the human rights movement—principally activists in the initial stages of HRE development and others who are concerned with initiating programs for teaching people about their human rights and fundamental freedoms and also bringing these lessons to potential abusers such as the police and military.

The book is very much a collective effort of editors and authors. We try to address the need and justifications for HRE in the new post–cold war world, analyze HRE as a strategy for development, present relevant information about human learning processes, deal with issues of pedagogy in this new field, and supply a basis for advocacy favoring HRE as a part of the international human rights movement. The book is designed to be forward-looking and to anticipate people's needs as we look toward the future. Thus we seek to contribute to ever livelier efforts to bring HRE to previously excluded groups and specific community-based arenas: women, labor, adult education, and so on.

This is a multiauthored volume consisting of essays by experienced activists, educational experts, and a small number of involved officials of international governmental organizations. The call for papers for this volume was announced at the United Nations World Conference on Human Rights (Vienna, 1993), where numerous planning meetings were held with experienced NGO teachers and human rights educators. Through this and other channels, authors have been successfully recruited from around the globe who share their experiences, offer critical perspectives, and lay out constructive practical suggestions for others, especially those newly embarking on HRE programs.

Having announced plans for this volume in Vienna in 1993 at the World Conference on Human Rights, it is not surprising that contributing authors and their essays reflect the objectives for human rights education specified at the Vienna Conference. For example, Section IV of the Vienna Declaration and Programme of Action states that the purpose of human rights education, training, and related public information should be the promotion and achievement of stable and harmonious relations among communities and fostering mutual understanding, tolerance, and peace. To these ends, the World Conference called "on all States and institutions to include human rights, humanitarian law, democracy and rule of law as subjects in the curricula of all learning institutions in formal and non-formal settings."

Each author and teams of co-authors in this volume have been advised to supply an essay that may be widely viewed as practically and conceptually useful to others in thinking through theoretical issues and in making choices as they initiate and undertake HRE programs. Usefulness to the audience should be a hallmark of the volume. Authors have been instructed to avoid self-advertising and merely descriptive presentations of existing programs. Where actual programs are described, we have sought to supply critical discussion of the utility, constraints, and planning objectives linked to prospective models for emulation. Thus descriptions of specific programs serve as the basis for general advice for others with recognition of the problems of and possibilities for program transferability.

While not mandatory for all authors, we have urged authors, where appropriate, to address some theoretical issues which the Editors' Introductions denote as thematic concerns. These are (1) *problems of normative theory* (why is HRE a preventive strategy in relation to human rights violations? how does HRE serve as the transmission of information as well as toward the transformation of society? toward the development of civil society and democracy?); (2) *issues of impartiality and objectivity* (what evaluative criteria are identifiable for HRE? how are responsibilities related to rights? how should facts and values be clarified and distinguished in HRE?); (3) *pedagogical strategies and methodologies* (what theories of learning should inform HRE? how are the many diverse objectives of HRE distinguishable, such as the development of cognitive skills, attitude change, behavior change, empowerment, and so on?); and (4) *research needs and opportunities* (what can universities contribute to the training of teachers in HRE? and how can they cooperate with NGOs and activists in this effort? how can universities assemble accessible resources helpful to scholars and activists in their efforts to develop programs of human rights education?).

Finally, we have tried to take into account that resource constraints and institutional limitations may impede the immediate realization of the objectives of human rights education. Devising human rights educational activities and curricula is not a project for the impatient or the fainthearted. We are concerned with nothing less than developing human rights education appropriate for the present and to carry us into the twenty-first century when we hope that education will be aimed at strengthening the respect for human rights and fundamental freedoms.

Human rights education is a long-term strategy with sights set on the needs of coming generations. Such education for our future may be unlikely to draw support from the impatient and the parochial, but we believe it essential to construct innovative educational programs to advance human development, peace, democracy, and respect for the rule of law. Reflecting these aspirations, the UN General Assembly proclaimed a United Nations Decade of Human Rights Education (1995–2005) (Res. 49/184). In so doing, the international community referred to human rights education as a unique strategy for the "building of a universal culture of human rights" and emphasized that "human rights education should involve more than the provision of information but should rather constitute a comprehensive, life-long process by which people at all levels in development and in all strata of society learn respect for the dignity of others and the means and methods of ensuring that respect in all societies." In committing the international community to these objectives, the Declaration and Programme of Action of the Decade of Human Rights Education, proclaimed by the General Assembly, summons and endorses a movement for human rights education. The editors and authors of this volume hope that our efforts serve some catalytic purpose in furthering the movement to infuse educational efforts with respect for the human dignity of all, without distinction of any kind such as race, sex, language, or religion.

Each of the five sections of our book are preceded by an Editors' Introduction, which lays a foundation for the essays that follow and ties contributions together. Relying on the five-part organization of the book, bibliographies are consolidated in a topically divided general bibliography at the end of the volume. Finally, J. Paul Martin, who has been involved with human rights education for twenty years at the Columbia University Center for the Study of Human Rights, has carefully reviewed the entire work and written an Epilogue appropriately entitled "The Next Step: Quality Control."

It is certainly true, as Martin concludes, that no existing guide or accessible source supplies so substantial and wide-ranging a set of suggestions, reports, and "how to do it" recommendations as this volume. Given the global array of participants, the editors and authors of the volume hope our work furthers international dialogue on the problems and challenges of initiating, planning, and implementing human rights education. In this task, many books and projects will follow. But most simply, to justify human rights education, it is unlikely that the compelling words of Haim Ginott will ever be surpassed: "Dear Teacher: I am a survivor of a concentration camp. My eyes saw what no man should witness: Gas chambers built by learned engineers. Children poisoned by educated physicians. . . . So I am suspicious of education. My request is: Help your students become human."

Acknowledgments

This project could not have come into being without the assistance, encouragement, and unfailing support of a number of friends, colleagues, and organizations. In particular, we would like to thank the European Human Rights Foundation, Jaimi Aparisi, Achene Boulesbaa, Timothy R. Clancy, Vienna Colucci, Mercedes Contreres, David R. Davis III, Drew S. Days III, Marie Serena Diokno, Nicholas Evageliou, Richard Falk, David P. Forsythe, Felice Gaer, Tara Krause, Bert B. Lockwood, Jr., Alice Marangopoulos, Elisa Muñoz, Joan Paquette-Sass, Kristi Rudelius-Palmer, Cristina Sganga, Thomas Stevenson, Eric Stover, the Reverend Richard W. Timm, Felicia Tibbits, Thongbai Thongpao, Padre Juan Vesey, David Weissbrodt, Claude E. Welch, Jr., Richard Alan White, Laurie Wiseberg, and Felice Yeban. A special note of thanks must go to Marge Camera, who patiently typed successive drafts of this manuscript without losing her sense of humor. We owe her more than we can ever express in words.

Above all, our thanks go to the contributors to this book, who brought this project to fruition. We sincerely hope that the end result lives up to their endorsement.

List of Acronyms

AAAS	American Association for the Advancement of Science
AAASHRAN	AAAS Human Rights Action Network
ACRI	Association for Civil Rights in Israel
AI/B	Amnesty International, Bratislava
ALDHU	Latin American Association of Human Rights
ANA	Aid Norway Albania
ANC	African National Congress
APAP	Action Professionals' Association for the People, Addis Ababa
APC	Association for Progressive Communications
APRODEH	Association for Human Rights, Lima
ARC	American Refugee Committee
AZADHO	Zairian Human Rights Group
BALD	Educational Project with Germans and Foreigners, Dortmund
BRAC	Bangladesh Rural Advancement Committee
CDR	Centre for Documentation on Refugees, Geneva
CEALL	Latin American Adult Education Commission
CEDAW	Convention on the Elimination of All Forms of Discrimination Against Women
CELS	Center for Legal and Social Studies, Buenos Aires
CHHRA	Cambodian Health and Human Rights Alliance
CIDA	Canadian International Development Agency
CIS	Commonwealth of Independent States
CLC	Community Law Centre, South Africa
CODEHUCA	Commission for the Defence of Human Rights in Central America, San José
CPDR	Committee for the Protection of Democratic Rights
CPJ	Committee to Protect Journalists
CRC	Convention on the Rights of the Child
CSW	Commission on the Status of Women
DGB	Federation of German Labor Unions

DHRE	United Nations Decade of Human Rights Education
DIANA	Direct Information Access Network Association
ECOSOC	United Nations Economic and Social Council
ECOWAS	Economic Community of West African States
EDICESA	Ecumenical Documentation and Information Centre for Eastern and Southern Africa, Zimbabwe
EFDR	Ethiopian Federal Democratic Republic
EIMET	Expanded International Military Education and Training
EU	European Union
FIDA	International Federation of Women Lawyers
FRG	Federal Republic of Germany
FWCW	Fourth World Conference on Women
GDR	German Democratic Republic
HBV	Union for Trade, Banking, and Insurance, Germany
HRAP	Human Rights Advocacy Project
HRE	Human rights education
HRI	Human Rights Internet, Ottawa
HURIDOCS	Human Rights Information and Documentation System, International
IAEWP	International Association of Educators for World Peace
ICCPR	International Covenant on Civil and Political Rights
ICPD	International Conference on Population and Development
ICRC	International Committee of the Red Cross
IDASA	Institute for Democracy in South Africa
IDERA	International Development Educational Resource Association
IDRC	International Development Research Council, Ottawa
IHEU	International Humanist and Ethical Union
IHRLC	International Human Rights Law Clinic
IIDH	Interamerican Institute for Human Rights
ILO	International Labour Organization, Geneva
IMET	International Military Education and Training
INDIX	International Network for Development Information Exchange, Ottawa
INHURED	International Institute for Human Rights, Environment and Development, Nepal
IPRA	International Peace Research Association
INSEAD	European Institute of Business Administration
IRDO	Romanian Institute for Human Rights
IWRAW	International Women's Rights Action Watch
LADO	League for the Defense of Human Rights, Romania
LHR	Lawyers for Human Rights

LRF	Legal Resources Foundation, Zimbabwe
MEDH	Ecumenical Movement for Human Rights, Argentina
NDI	National Democratic Institute for International Affairs
NED	National Endowment for Democracy
NETC	U.S. Navy, Naval Education and Training Center, Newport
NGOs	Nongovernmental organizations
NICEL	National Institute for Citizen Education in Law
NJS	U.S. Navy, Navy Justice School, Newport
OAS	Organization of American States
OECD	Organization for Economic Cooperation and Development
OSCE	Organization for Security and Cooperation in Europe
PDC	Partners for Democratic Change, Slovakia
PDHRE	People's Decade of Human Rights Education
PDSR	Social Democratic Party of Romania
PHR	Physicians for Human Rights
PIIE	Program for Interdisciplinary Research on Education, Chile
PROCESS	Participatory Research, Organization of Communities, and Education Towards Struggle for Self-Reliance
RCT	Research Centre for Torture Victims, Copenhagen
RFE	Radio Free Europe
RL	Radio Liberty
SADCC	South African Development Coordination Conference
SAFHR	South Asian Forum for Human Rights
SCCPR	Slovak Center for Conflict Prevention and Resolution, Comenius University
SERPAJ	Peace and Justice Service in Latin America
SIM	Netherlands Institute of Human Rights, Utrecht
SIRDO	Romanian Independent Society for Human Rights
TOES	The Other Economic Summit
TTF	Thongbai Thongpao Foundation, Thailand
UDHR	Universal Declaration of Human Rights
UNAMIR	United Nations Assistance Mission in Rwanda
UNBIS	United Nations Bibliographic Information System
UNDP	United Nations Development Program
UNDPI	United Nations Department of Public Information
UNDW	United Nations Decade for Women
UNESCO	United Nations Educational, Scientific and Cultural Organization, Paris
UNHCR	United Nations High Commission on Refugees
UNICEF	United Nations Children's Fund, New York
UNITAR	United Nations Institute for Training and Research

UNTAC	United Nations Transitional Authority in Cambodia
USAID	United States Agency for International Development
USIS	United States Information Services
WCHR	World Conference on Human Rights
WHO	World Health Organization, Geneva
WILDAF	Women in Law and Development in Africa
WOLA	Washington Office on Latin America
ZDWF	Documentation Center for Voluntary Social Work with Refugees, Bonn

Part I
Theories and Contexts

EDITORS' INTRODUCTION

Human rights education is not a passing teaching fad. It is not a whimsical invention from designer seminars mulling over dreams for the twenty-first century. Human rights education is an international obligation with a half-century history.

In 1946 the United Nations Charter specified one of the organization's goals as the promotion and encouragement of human rights. That objective was clarified in 1948 when the UN General Assembly, with no dissenting vote, adopted the Universal Declaration of Human Rights. It was proclaimed as "a common standard of achievement for all peoples and all nations," who were directed to "strive by teaching and education to promote respect for these rights and freedoms" (Preamble). Thus education is identified as instrumentally connected to the Charter task of promoting human rights. Additionally, the preambular language of the Declaration announces that "teaching and education" are not simply new, post–World War II state functions, among the governmental duties attending membership in the United Nations. Rather, as if to acknowledge popular action at the grassroots level and the work of nongovernmental organizations (NGOs), "teaching and education" are announced as the obligation of "every individual and every organ of society."

Education is not only a means to promote human rights. It is an end in itself. In positing a human right to education, the framers of the Declaration axiomatically relied on the notion that education is not value-neutral. In this spirit, Article 30 states that one of the goals of education should be "the strengthening of respect for human rights and fundamental freedoms" (Sec. 2). The human rights covenants (later developed by the United Nations and coming into effect in 1976 to formalize the basis in international law of the rights declared in 1948) also elaborated upon those rights. In this vein, the International Covenant on Economic, Social and Cultural Rights placed the educational objective of strengthening respect for human rights in a cluster of related learning objectives. For example, Article 13 of the Covenant says that "education shall be directed to the "full development of the human personality" and to the person's own "sense of dignity" (Sec. 1). Thus education that promotes such full development of the human personality also promotes human rights.

There are larger goals addressing social concerns as well. The Covenant also says that the States Parties "further agree that education shall enable all persons to participate effectively in a free society, promote understanding, tolerance and friendship among all nations and all racial, ethnic or religious groups, and further the activities of the United Nations for the maintenance of peace" (Article 13, Sec. 1).

Complementing these positive formulations of the objectives of education are the negative proscriptions of the International Covenant on Civil and Political Rights. It tells us that once a state adopts the system of international human rights, it may not stand in the way of people learning about them. Everyone has "the right to hold opinions without interference" (Article 19, Sec. 1). Insomuch as education is a process involving the sharing and dissemination of ideas, the enterprise is bolstered by this Covenant, which sets forth the proposition that "Everyone shall have the right to freedom of expression; this right shall include freedom to seek, receive and impart information and ideas of all kinds, regardless of frontiers, either orally, in writing or in print, in the form of art, or through any other media of his (or her) choice" (Article 19, Sec. 2).

The International Bill of Rights, consisting of the Universal Declaration of Human Rights and the two Covenants, gave prominence to the importance of education in today's world. Consistent with the tendency of international instruments to use repetitious language and to repeat cardinal principles, it is not surprising to find echoes elsewhere of the standards noted above. Thus the stipulations of everyone's right to education and the goal of education in furthering respect for all human rights as well as corresponding government duties to supply such education, are all found in numerous other international instruments. Examples of such agreements include the Convention on the Rights of the Child (1989),[1] the Helsinki Final Act (1975),[2] and the American (1948),[3] European (1953),[4] and African (1986)[5] regional agreements on human rights standards and institutions.

1989 was a landmark year in world history: the UN General Assembly requested the secretary-general to see if support existed among member states to convene a world conference on human rights. When that conference took place in Vienna in 1993, Secretary-General Boutros Boutros-Ghali commented on the "historical intuition" shown by the General Assembly in 1989 because, as the secretary-general said, "Two months earlier, the Berlin Wall had fallen, carrying away with it a certain vision of the world, and thereby opening up new perspectives. It was in the name of freedom, democracy and human rights that entire peoples were speaking out. Their determination, their abnegation—sometimes their sacrifices—reflected then, and still reflect, their commitment to do away with alienation and totalitarianism."[5]

The first chapter in Part I of this volume supplies an overview of the post–cold war context in which we now begin anew to take human rights education seriously. George Andreopoulos's chapter gives extended exposition to the changing nature of the linkages between international security and humanitarian concerns, and highlights some of the main tasks confronting the human rights education agenda as a result of these developments. At the core of this effort lies the fundamental assumption that unfulfilled basic human needs constitute, in the words of the UN secretary-general, "the deepest causes of conflict."[6] According to Andreopoulos, human rights education is a global task, the time for which has come, unencumbered by the ideological vagaries of the cold war. In this new context, human rights education must reaffirm the universal character of human dignity and the failure of all collective identities to capture the uniqueness of each human being and satisfy all needs essential to his or her welfare.

In the absence of the cold war, the United Nations has taken new initiatives regarding human rights education. A firsthand report on one such action comes from Ambassador Jorge Rhenán-Segura, permanent representative of Costa Rica to the United Nations in Geneva:

At the 1993 session of the UN Commission on Human Rights, the Costa Rican Delegation proposed a resolution on human rights education which was adopted on March 9, 1993. In that resolution, the commission recommended "that the understanding of human rights both in its theoretical and practical applications should be established as a priority in educational policy. At the General Assembly, intense negotiations were necessary before achieving consensus on a resolution of the "Proclamation of a decade for human rights education." Opposition came mainly from Western countries, including the United States, who felt there were already too many decades with little practical results to show for them. In addressing these objections before the Commission, I expressed my government's profound attachment to the idea of a Decade of Human Rights Education and our willingness to contribute to the early implementation of a program of action for the Decade, drawing on the experience already gained in many countries and the new opportunities offered by the changing world social and economic conditions.[7]

In December 1994 the General Assembly of the United Nations proclaimed 1995–2005 as the United Nations Decade of Human Rights Education.

The role of the United Nations in specifying educational objectives for member states has been substantial. If we return to the founding principles on which the United Nations was originally based, we see that the intergovernmental organization, of course, has multiple objectives beyond promoting human rights. First, it seeks to foster friendly relations among nations, helping to maintain international peace and security; second, it works to facilitate economic, social, and cultural cooperation and development; third, the United Nations should achieve international cooperation in pursuing "fundamental freedoms for all without distinction as to race, sex, language, or religion." These objectives—peace, development, and equality—are all interconnected with education and human rights in ways that are explored in the essays in Part I.

Peace. Betty A. Reardon's chapter on "Human Rights as Education for Peace" provides an important critical perspective on the decades of development that have been invested in various formats for "peace education." She complains that, by and large, peace education has suffered from a lack of theory at its center, failing to display "the elements of prescription and holism" needed for our emerging planetary social system. Reardon carefully elaborates the recommendation that peace educators add human rights at the core of their work to make peace education "not only more comprehensive but also more comprehensible." One compelling reason is that the conceptual core of peace education is violence—a negative concept, and the conceptual core of human rights is human dignity—a positive concept. No undertaking has sought to integrate education and human rights more comprehensively than UN efforts at post-conflict peace building. This concept refers to "comprehensive efforts to identify and support structures which will tend to consolidate peace and advance a sense of confidence and well-being among people."[8]

In a very informative chapter, Stephen P. Marks addresses the challenges of developing a human rights education component as part of the most ambitious so far peace-building effort conceived under UN auspices: the United Nations Transitional Authority in Cambodia (UNTAC). Marks outlines the six-step strategy that the component devised in order to implement its mandate and assesses its impact. Despite the severe time constraints under which the strategy was conceived and carried out, important lessons have been learned which "can be applied elsewhere, if the political will exists to make use of the methods developed by UNTAC in Cambodia." A key lesson, according to the author, is that "the concept of democratic empowerment is helpful as a criterion for conceiving and implementing human rights education projects."

Development. The conceptual relationships between human rights and development—social, political, and economic—are analyzed in the essay by Clarence Dias. He ties human rights and development together with education, explaining very succinctly how human rights education can influence development. He notes the reaffirmation of the human right to development, articulated in the Vienna Declaration of 1993. In that light, he specifies what human rights education about development should encompass in conceptual and practical terms. His expectation is that effective human rights education about development has significant strategic value: it offers a method of breaking the vicious cycle of poverty and powerlessness to replace it "with a much-needed cycle of empowerment." Likewise, in a brief comment on education on the rights of the child in Nepal, Gopal Siwakoti stresses the importance of human rights NGOs in rendering policymakers sensitive to the need for effective domestic implementation of conventional obligations (in this case, the UN Convention on the Rights of the Child). According to Siwakoti, "human rights educational seminars and workshops, held in conjunction with upcoming treaty reporting obligations of States Parties, can very practically help to implement . . . the right to development."

Human rights education directed toward the empowerment of participants is unique as a pedagogical objective and differs markedly from the goals of other areas of education, conventionally defined. "Human Rights Education as Empowerment: Reflections on Pedagogy" by Garth Meintjes discusses this important thematic topic which arises at many points throughout the volume. Meintjes acknowledges that human rights education designed to empower people is a unique educational objective with inherent political risks. These flow from the fact that human rights education devised to empower people at the grassroots level may be seen as dangerous to elites, subversive to the "powers that be," and potentially antagonistic to rulers and government institutions. But Meintjes follows the views of Paulo Freire in arguing that human rights education for empowerment can be liberating to the oppressed as well as to their oppressors.

The next chapter, "Conflict Resolution and Human Rights Education: Broadening the Agenda" by Donna Hicks, builds on Reardon's observation that "conflict resolution" methodologies have emerged from academic peace studies. Hicks then addresses the relevant issues in the context of development studies. She reports on her field research showing how "interactive problem solving" worked in the Cambodian setting, with special reference to women's groups and their largely neophyte efforts to identify unmet needs and to explore notions of equality. Hicks's work was done in 1992 when UNTAC organized the aforementioned operational effort to implement human rights education on a nationwide basis.

Equality. Dorota Gierycz's chapter on "Education on the Human Rights of Women as a Vehicle for Change" eschews discussion of methodology in favor of a very substantive review of the equality standards and human rights provisions of various international instruments, including the Convention on the Elimination of All Forms of Discrimination Against Women (CEDAW). Gierycz analyzes the recent conflicting trends in women's rights as exemplified in the preparatory process to the 1995 Fourth World Conference on Women in Beijing, in particular the controversy over the term *equality*, which was used by certain forces in an attempt to slow down the progress achieved in the 1993 World Conference on Human Rights in Vienna. Although the timely intervention of the High Commissioner for Human Rights prevented a major showdown over the issue and led to a positive outcome in Beijing, formidable challenges yet remain. According to Gierycz, the human rights of women should be integrated into the mainstream of formal education and such teaching should be informed by international norms.[9]

Ellen Dorsey's chapter introduces an important informal mode of human rights education, that involved in "participatory research." The focus is on the grassroots-based "charter campaigns" conducted in South Africa in anticipation of constitutional innovation. The charter campaigns Dorsey describes involve women, children, and the disabled. She concludes that the participative methodologies used in each instance offer the best hope for the creation of a "nonhierarchical process of dialogue." The aim of such dialogue is "not simply to foster awareness of rights" but to generate a "societywide discourse about rights" and to promote individual and communal diversity through the establishment of "political space for competitive values." The latter is of major importance if societies beset with long-standing cleavages along racial, ethnic, gender, and socioeconomic lines are to create the preconditions for peaceful coexistence. To this end, human rights education should contribute to the spreading of a global human rights culture.

The concluding chapter in Part I addresses some key theoretical issues associated with the construction of a credible and empowering human rights discourse. Upendra Baxi stresses the historical continuity of popular struggles "for rights and against injustice and tyranny." In this context, what he calls "the endless normativity of human rights standards" has led to the "continuing confrontation between emergent cultures of rights and entrenched cultures of power." Baxi challenges the notion that human rights education should be viewed as a means to a designated end such as "peace," "justice," or "dignity"; on the contrary, its importance lies in the fact that it is an end in itself. This is the only perspective that can sustain the role of human rights education as that of a critical component of "the processes of empowerment of every human being . . . to experience freedom and solidarity."

Notes

1. On the delicate matter of children's rights vis-à-vis parental/guardian duties, States Parties "shall provide direction to the child on the exercise of his or her rights in a manner consistent with the evolving capacities of the child" (Article 14, Sec. 2). Education of the child shall be directed, among other things, to "the development of respect for human rights and fundamental freedoms" (Article 29, Sec. 1b).

2. Final Act of the Conference on Security and Cooperation in Europe, Helsinki, 1975, 14 I.L.M. 1292–1325 (1975): the participating states "confirm the right of the individual to know and act upon his (or her) rights and duties in this field" (Principle VII).

3. American Declaration of the Rights and Duties of Man, May 2, 1948, Ninth International Conference of American States: "Every person has the right to an education, which should be based on the principles of liberty, morality and human solidarity" (Article 12).

4. European Convention for the Protection of Human Rights and Fundamental Freedoms: "No person shall be denied the right to education" (First Protocol, Article 1).

5. Secretary-General Boutros Boutros-Ghali, "Human Rights: The Common Language of Humanity," Opening Statement for the World Conference on Human Rights, published with the Vienna Declaration and Programme of Action (June 1993), 5.

6. UN General Assembly, Report of the Secretary-General on the Work of the Organization, *An Agenda for Peace: Preventive Diplomacy, Peacemaking and Peace-Keeping*, U.N. Doc. A/47/277/S/ 24111 (June 17, 1992), 4.

7. Memorandum by Dr. Jorge Rhenán-Segura to the Organizing Committee of the Decade of Human Rights Education, June 16, 1994.

8. *Agenda for Peace*, 16.

9. Cf. Lea Flaster, "Human Rights Education: A Context for Teaching About Women's Lives," *Feminist Teacher* 3, no. 3 (1988): 14–18.

Chapter 1
Human Rights Education in the Post–Cold War Context

George Andreopoulos

The end of the cold war has brought little intellectual comfort. On the one hand, it has dispelled the ghost of the "clear and present danger" to which our thinking had been conveniently conditioned. On the other hand, it has witnessed the resurgence of a troublesome array of unconventional challenges, and in the process has unmasked the poverty of our conceptual tools. The often-asked question of whether we are in a transitional period or at a dead end is reflective of a false dilemma. More than anything else, it is the very nature and quality of our response that will determine the outcome.

Recent developments place a great burden on the advocates of the growing importance of humanitarian concerns. For the first time since the creation of the United Nations, they have the opportunity to challenge the excessive preoccupation with the maintenance of international peace and security at the expense of the other fundamental goal of the UN system: in the words of Article 1, Section 3 of the Charter, "To achieve international co-operation in solving international problems of an economic, social, cultural or humanitarian character, and in *promoting and encouraging respect for human rights and for fundamental freedoms for all* without distinction as to race, sex, language, or religion" (author's emphasis). The latter goal was reaffirmed in the Vienna Declaration and Programme of Action (the concluding document of the World Conference on Human Rights), which states in Part I, paragraph 4 that "The promotion and protection of all human rights and fundamental freedoms must be considered as a priority objective of the United Nations in accordance with its purposes and principles, in particular the purpose of international cooperation. In the framework of these purposes and principles, the promotion and protection of all human rights is a legitimate concern of the international community."

The earlier reference to the preoccupation with the maintenance of international peace and security *at the expense* of the promotion and protection of human rights raises the question of the nature of the linkages between these two goals. The simplistic traditional dichotomies between matters of domestic jurisdiction and those of international concern are becoming increasingly unsustainable. The same fate awaits the concomitant assessment that human rights issues are irritants at best and destabilizing factors at worst in the quest for world peace. Yet it is one thing to discredit the past and another to articulate a credible alternative, in particular, an alternative that, in the words of Article 55 of the Charter, considers the promotion of "universal respect for, and observance of, human rights and fundamental freedoms" as related "to the creation of conditions of stability and well-being which are *necessary* (author's emphasis) for peaceful and friendly relations among nations."[1]

This essay explores some of the key challenges facing the quest for security in the post–cold war context, assesses the changing nature of the linkages between security and humanitarian concerns, and highlights some of the main tasks confronting the human rights education agenda as a result of these developments.

Any attempt to redress the balance between the quest for security and the quest for humanitarianism and explore the resulting linkages must confront what Richard Falk has aptly called the "challenge of the weak state," namely, a state "that is in the grips of a war of internal fragmentation or that is in any sense ungovernable, either as a consequence of civil strife or overwhelming humanitarian crisis."[2] It is a challenge that reflects the growing strains between the concepts of *regime security* and *societal security*.[3]

Traditionally, this distinction has reflected two concerns: the identity of the forces that articulate the security needs of a certain unit, and the extent to which these forces can coexist with (or tolerate) the articulation of alternative security needs that can question and even challenge their own perceptions of the security needs of the said unit.[4] The underlying assumption of this distinction is that groups and individuals that live within the boundaries of a unit must be secure against the rulers of the unit, as well as against the enemies of the unit.

The recent prominence of the "weak state" compounds the already existing strains. The main problem that the international community has to confront, especially in instances of massive civil strife, is the capacity of subnational actors (ethnic, religious, cultural groups) to question not only the legitimacy of the rulers of a certain unit (nation-state), but the integrity of the said unit as a frame of reference for the resolution of the conflict. More ominously, subnational actors have challenged the possibility of coexistence with other forces within the same public space (however defined) even when the resulting framework guarantees their privileged access to power. But, regardless of specific outcomes, one trend is clearly emerging: *micro-level behavior*, in the form of the choices that individuals and small groups make, can produce *macro-level effects* more easily than in the past.[5] As the ongoing crises in the former Yugoslavia and Somalia have shown, subnational insecurity (the main legacy of weak states) challenges both the relevance of the unit (nation-state) and the modalities of a credible response on the part of the international community.

So far there has been a noticeable verbal shift in the security discourse of the

"New World Order." This shift was reflected at the conclusion of the UN Security Council's first heads-of-state summit. The statement issued emphasized that "The absence of war and military conflicts amongst states does not in itself insure international peace and security. The non-military sources of instability in the economic, social, humanitarian and ecological fields have become threats to peace and security. The United Nations membership as a whole . . . needs to give the highest priority to the solution of these matters."[6] This concern with the "non-military sources of instability" was carried a step further in the secretary-general's *Agenda for Peace* document. Noting that "fierce, new assertions of nationalism and sovereignty spring up, and the cohesion of states is threatened by brutal ethnic, religious, social, cultural or linguistic strife,"[7] he concludes that the aims of the United Nations in this changing context must include

*To stand ready to assist in peace-building in its differing contexts: rebuilding the institutions and infrastructures of nations torn by civil war and strife; and building bonds of peaceful mutual benefit among nations formerly at war;
*And in the largest sense, *to address the deepest causes of conflict: economic despair, social injustice and political oppression.*[8] (author's emphasis)

The reference to the "deepest causes of conflict" is suggestive of an important assumption: that *unfulfilled basic human needs are sources of conflict*; such sources relate to all societies and cultures irrespective of the type of regime and level of development. And it is the very same unfulfilled needs that render the concern for post-conflict peace building of critical importance to this new vision, particularly in the aftermath of widespread civil strife. More than interstate conflict, civil strife necessitates a long-term approach to conflict containment since it has to confront the existential variety of subnational challenges.

Are there any trends in recent UN case law that sustain this verbal shift in the security discourse? A closer examination of two prominent cases—Operation Provide Comfort and Operation Restore Hope—suggests an increasing willingness on the part of the international community to link humanitarian crises with threats to international peace and security. Operation Provide Comfort involved the potentially forcible protection of persecuted Kurds in the immediate aftermath of the Gulf War.[9] Operation Restore Hope involved the attempts to establish a secure environment for humanitarian relief operations in Somalia, in the aftermath of massive civil war that had rendered the country ungovernable.[10]

Although this is a welcome development, there are two main caveats to be borne in mind.[11] First, the linkages are being developed on an ad hoc basis, rather than within a conceptual framework that ensures a consistent and coherent response on the part of the international community.[12] In the Iraqi case, it was the transboundary impact of the Kurdish refugee flows (on neighboring Turkey and Iran) that seemed to form the consensual basis for Security Council action.[13] In the Somali case, Secretary-

Figure 1.1. Secretary-General Boutros Boutros-Ghali presents an educational volume, *The United Nations and Apartheid, 1947–1994*, to President Nelson Mandela of South Africa. The secretary-general said that in the post–apartheid, post–cold war world, the "international community must ask fundamental questions about humanity and about how, by protecting humanity, it protects itself." (UNPHOTO/E Edbebe 9410–035/10)

General Boutros Boutros-Ghali cited the "repercussions of the Somali conflict on the entire region[14] "as constituting a threat to the peace and thus justifying enforcement measures under Chapter VII of the Charter (which was eventually invoked in Resolution 794) to achieve the aforementioned goal of a secure environment for humanitarian relief operations.

However, a closer look at the Security Council debate and the text of Resolution 794, would indicate the absence of any acknowledgment of a clear transboundary impact of the humanitarian tragedy unfolding in Somalia, akin to the transboundary impact created by the Kurdish refugee flows in the Iraqi case; rather, the potential threat to the peace is linked to the "magnitude of the human tragedy caused by the conflict . . . further exacerbated by the obstacles being created to the distribution of humanitarian assistance."[15] Thus it is the very magnitude of the humanitarian crisis per se coupled with the continuing frustrations of the UN relief efforts (looting of relief supplies, attacks on ships and aircraft bringing in humanitarian relief supplies, and attacks on the Pakistani contingent in Mogadishu, among others) that seemed to form the consensual basis for Security Council action.

Second, the question of the forcible delivery of humanitarian assistance against a government's expressed wishes, especially if the humanitarian crisis does not produce discernible crossborder effects, is yet to be tested. In the Kurdish case, the legal basis for their protection came as a result of the aforementioned crossborder impact of refugee flows. However, it has also been argued that Resolution 688 cannot be delinked from the Gulf War experience since it constituted an unfortunate by-product of a very traditional breach of the peace (Iraq's invasion of Kuwait); and that the mandate of the allied forces "to restore international peace and security in the area" entitled them to use whatever means to deal with both Iraq's aggression and its consequences.[16] In the Somali case, the initial UN engagement came at the behest of all Somali faction leaders for a UN role in bringing about national reconciliation.[17] Moreover, the launching of Operation Restore Hope (with Resolution 794) was premised on both the lack of government in Somalia and the earlier request by all faction leaders for UN assistance.[18] Yet these first steps, albeit inconsistent and partial, point to a critical direction: *the need to legitimize international responses to humanitarian crises in terms of human suffering per se, irrespective of its crossborder implications and the presence (or absence) of a responsive government.* To be sure, a significant corpus of international human rights law has developed since 1945 which has legitimized noncoercive action in response to human rights violations (primarily in the form of fact-finding missions, reports, recommendations, and in the state and individual complaints procedures of the regional human rights systems, especially the European and Inter-American ones). In addition, the international community has been legally empowered to intervene in certain cases of extreme and massive human rights violations, but the response has not been consistent with the enormity of the problem.[19] However, there is a gray area ranging between noncoercive action and massive human rights abuses amounting to genocidal massacres, for which the international community has at best a precarious legal basis for action. In the past, responses in this gray area have been determined on the basis of geopolitical considerations, with human rights concerns featuring only in cases of substantive overlap.

Recent events have generated expectations that the perennial subsumption of the humanitarian under the geopolitical would terminate. In United Nations Charter terms, it is the aforementioned idea that the promotion and protection of human rights would acquire a status consistent with its formal standing as one of the main goals of the UN system. Yet, as we have seen, both the verbal shift in the security discourse and UN case law point to the direction of articulating the linkages between the two goals with the quest for peace and security remaining the international community's most important norm.

Despite its shortcomings (especially the ad hoc nature of the approach), this is a welcome development for a very basic reason: as long as the United Nations espouses a state-centric concept of security, any serious discussion of the promotion and protection of human rights will draw its sustenance from its normative links to the hierarchical primacy of global peace.[20] These vertical links, however, do not and should not reflect a one-dimensional undertaking. As the discourse on human rights raises its profile, the security discourse is conceptually enriched by fine-tuning its tools to the growing challenge of subnational insecurity. In fact, only by taking the human rights factor seriously can the UN system begin to tackle the growing complexity and unpredictable consequences of subnational challenges. Thus both discourses are locked in a hierarchically structured symbiotic relationship: the human rights discourse needs the security discourse to enhance its credibility in the international community, while the latter needs the former in order to cope with the macro-level effects of micro-level behavior.

What are some of the key tasks that this changing context poses for human rights education? Although the following list is by no means exhaustive, it highlights some of the key issues relating to the preceding observations.

First, the growing importance of subnational insecurity renders indispensable the articulation of security threats in terms of groups and individuals. As we have seen, there have already been some attempts in that direction: Boutros Boutros-Ghali's underlying assumption that unfulfilled basic human needs constitute "the deepest causes of conflict" in the *Agenda for Peace* document, as well as the increasing use of the term *human security*, whose precise conceptual contours and analytical use are yet to be examined fully. In a 1993 article assessing the status of the *Agenda for Peace* recommendations, the secretary-general came the closest in trying to capture what such a task would entail: "Everywhere we look we see the clash of absolutes: self-determination and sovereignty; interdependence and non-intervention; the State and social change; common purposes and diversity; the United Nations in a fragmented world. Our task is to find the balance—not as an act of compromise for its own sake, but with creativity."[21] The quest for a creatively balanced approach toward human security suggests the need for pedagogical strategies that will integrate *cognitive* (growing awareness and understanding of the complexities of weak states/fractured societies), *attitudinal* (the development of a greater sensitivity to the linkages between the fate of these weak entities and the welfare of the international community), and *empowerment* objectives (enabling members of these entities to define their own individual and collective identities in the new context as a way of meeting their needs and those of their respective communities).

Second, education strategies about human security must be premised on two key notions: the common features of intolerable practices which violate essential aspects of human dignity, and the multifaceted nature of the human being which no group identification—no matter how comprehensive—can capture. The first points to the remarkable continuity of human suffering throughout history: tales of oppression, exploitation, denial of basic needs, persecution, and extermination to which every society can relate in the evolution of its popular traditions. The second points to the varied roles that each human being is expected to assume during his or her lifetime, roles that are essential to the formation of the individual's unique identity and welfare. The issue is beautifully stated by Eric Hobsbawm in his discussion of the transformation of nationalism during the later nineteenth century:

Men and women did not choose collective identification as they chose shoes, knowing that one could only put on one pair at a time. They had, and still have, several attachments and loyalties simultaneously, including nationality, and are simultaneously concerned with various aspects of life, any of which may at any one time be foremost in their minds, as occasion suggests. For long periods of time these different attachments would not make incompatible demands on a person. . . . It was only when one of these loyalties conflicted directly with another or others that a problem of choosing between them arose.[22]

Thus to heal the wounds on the aftermath of widespread civil strife, human rights education programs must reinforce the commonality of suffering among different ethnic/religious groups. In such a context, those features of the suffering which stress the multiplicity of human attachments may well be the ones with the greatest chance of success. In the Yugoslav conflict, for example, tales of Croatian suffering at the hands of Serbs and vice versa should stress the common features of the victims and their survivors: tales of fathers and mothers losing their offspring, rather than tales of Serb/Croat parents losing their sons and daughters; the importance here lies in the universally recognizable (and easily identifiable with) *parental* role rather than the particularistic and divisive ethnic identity.

What renders such a perspective imperative is that the facile labeling of people on the basis of their ethnic/religious identity fails to capture the complex and unexpected alliances and enmities that often develop during these conflicts.

In the Yugoslav conflict, we have witnessed the alliance between Bosnian Serbs and rebel Muslim forces in their attacks against the UN-designated safe area of Bihac in northwest Bosnia, which was defended by the Bosnian V corps.[23] In Rwanda, after the recent genocidal acts committed by Hutu elements against the Tutsi ethnic group,[24] we have witnessed the sheer terrorization of Hutus by fellow Hutu elements in the refugee camps in Zaire in order to prevent their voluntary repatriation.[25]

The third point follows from the second. Education strategies must target the selective use and interpretation of cultural practices that sustain oppressive institutions and discriminatory policies. The importance of this task can hardly be over-emphasized. At a time when subnational groups are frantically examining, analyzing, and (re)evaluating their traditions in search of clues as to the contours of their submerged identities, the quest for identity is becoming coextensive with the quest for security. To be sure, it is a well-known fact that cultures are constantly "evolving internally, as well as through interaction with other cultures"[26] and that cultural traditions exhibit conflicting practices of both tolerance and intolerance in all shapes and forms. In this vein, the main focus should be to challenge oppressive cultural practices on the grounds of both their *accuracy* and their *representative character* within the cultural discourse in question.[27] But for this enterprise to be constructive, it is imperative that the alternative to the contested cultural practices is articulated in terms of both its internal legitimacy and its consistency with existing international human rights norms.[28] Relevant here are tales of prior peaceful cohabitation among groups in conflict: for example, tales of the rather harmonious coexistence of different ethnic and religious groups in the territory of the former Yugoslavia until 1918 (thus debunking the myth of "ancient ethnic hatreds"), as well as tales that challenge stereotypical demonizations of the "other" and point to traditions of tolerance and inclusion rather than those of intolerance and exclusion (intermarriages between Serbs and Croats are a case in point). Needless to say, the enormity of the challenges will necessitate a concerted and long-term commitment on the part of the international community.

This brings us to the fourth point. Comprehensive human rights education must be a key component of post-conflict peace building. In his *Agenda for Peace* document, the secretary-general has stressed that the term refers to "comprehensive efforts to identify and support structures which will tend to consolidate peace and advance a sense of confidence and well-being among people."[29] Thus if preventive diplomacy lies on the one end of the spectrum of ways in which the UN system can strengthen its response to potential/actual threats to the peace, post-conflict peace building lies on the other end; in the secretary-general's own words: "Preventive diplomacy is to avoid a crisis; post-conflict peace-building is to prevent a recurrence."[30]

Herein lies a major challenge for human rights education. All recent attempts to link international security with basic human welfare will be severely tested in assessing the effectiveness of peace-building strategies in fractured societies. The comprehensive approach that peace building necessitates, sometimes indistinguishable from nation building, suggests two things: the instrumental role of creating a normative framework respectful of basic human rights and freedoms and capable of sustaining remedial action in cases of unmet basic needs, and the commitment on the part of the international community to stay the course. The fact that certain mandates of recent UN operations have included provisions about human rights education is a first step in the right direction.[31] To be sure, assessments concerning the effectiveness of these programs, the "lessons" learned, and their relevance for other case studies will be hotly debated. Yet what matters at this stage is the tendency toward the institutionalization of human rights education programs in UN peace-building activities.

Finally, a key task of human rights education is to transcend the simplistic dichotomies between humanitarian assistance providers and recipients.[32] Much current discussion portrays the interaction as a one-sided flow of material resources, information, and manpower. Very little thought is given to the potential for a mutually beneficial interaction, an interaction capable of transcending the superficial "feel-good" reactions of the donor communities in order to reflect an understanding of the fundamental baseline of human welfare that binds providers and recipients together. Nothing exemplifies this problem better than the international community's mixed response to the crisis in the former Yugoslavia.

On the one hand, international and regional organizations (United Nations, European Union, Organization for Security and Cooperation in Europe) have been trying and failing to deal with the worst excesses of the conflict, a conflict that has witnessed serious and well-documented violations of international humanitarian law.[33] In the process, western publics have become aware of the enormity of the humanitarian crisis unfolding before their very eyes. On the other hand, that awareness has yet to result in a more determined response to the crisis.[34] The reason for that failure is instructive: the Yugoslav conflict is not perceived as having an adverse impact on the national security interests of the major western states. This detached (or limited) expression of interest signals not simply the continuing primacy of traditional perceptions relating to the maintenance of international peace in the UN system, but, more critically, how little western publics and elites have learned the "lessons" of the Yugoslav tragedy. Thus any attempt at devising human rights education strategies to deal with similar situations must emphasize the potentially enormous benefits of a better understanding (and thus of a prompt and concerted response) by the international community. To put it bluntly, western publics have, in certain ways, as much to learn about the ramifications of the Yugoslav tragedy as the citizens of the former Yugoslavia themselves.

Conclusion

Few guides and many perils await the charting of the new course. For the first time since the Charter's inception, the international community seeks to articulate unfulfilled basic human needs as an international security issue. On the one hand, this is a reflection of the continuing primacy of the maintenance of international peace and security in the UN system. On the other hand, the (admittedly) improvisational response to this undertaking does suggest the potential for a paradigmatic shift: a shift whose parameters are determined by the growing realization that the security discourse is in need of the insights of the human rights discourse to cope with the existential variety of subnational challenges. Human rights education constitutes a critical catalyst in that realization. Unencumbered by the ideological vagaries of the cold war, human rights education "must seize the moment." In the process, it must re-affirm a very basic message: the universal character of human dignity and the failure of all collective identities, no matter how comprehensive, to capture the uniqueness of each human being and satisfy all needs essential to his or her welfare.

Notes

1. This was also reaffirmed in Part 1, paragraph 6 of the Vienna Declaration: "The efforts of the United Nations system towards the universal respect for, and observance of, human rights and fundamental freedoms for all, contribute to the stability and well-being necessary for peaceful and friendly relations among nations, and to improved conditions for peace and security."

2. Richard Falk, "Human Rights, Humanitarian Assistance, and the Sovereignty of States," in *A Framework for Survival: Health, Human Rights, and Humanitarian Assistance in Conflicts and Disasters*, ed. Kevin M. Cahill (New York: Basic Books and the Council on Foreign Relations Press, 1993), 27.

3. For a discussion of this issue, see Richard Ullman, "Some Notes on the Continuing Problem of Security" (unpublished essay, August 26, 1991).

4. George Andreopoulos, "Confronting the 'New World Order': Challenges for International Peace and Security," in *International Rights and Responsibilities for the Future*, ed. Kenneth W. Hunter and Timothy Mack (forthcoming, Greenwood Press).

5. John Lewis Gaddis, "Fault Lines, Forecasting, and the Post–Cold War World: An Experiment in Geopolitical Tectonics" (unpublished paper), 18–19.

6. United Nations Security Council Summit Statement, UN Doc. S/23500, January 31, 1992.

7. UN General Assembly, Report of the Secretary-General on the Work of the Organization, *An Agenda for Peace: Preventive Diplomacy, Peacemaking and Peace-Keeping*, UN Doc. A/47/277/S/24111 (June 17, 1992), 3.

8. Ibid., 4.

9. The key resolution in Operation Provide Comfort is Security Council Resolution 688, adopted on April 5, 1991. For a discussion of the operation, see Jane E. Stromseth, "Iraq's Repression of Its Civilian Population: Collective Responses and Continuing Challenges," in *Enforcing Restraint: Collective Intervention in Internal Conflicts*, ed. Lori Fisler Damrosch (New York: Council on Foreign Relations Press, 1993), 77–117. Lawrence Freedman and David Boren, " 'Safe Havens' for Kurds in Post-War Iraq," in *To Loose the Bands of Wickedness: International Intervention in Defence of Human Rights*, ed. Nigel S. Rodley (London: Brassey's 1992), 43–92; and Nigel S. Rodley, "Collective Intervention to Protect Human Rights and Civilian Populations: The Legal Framework," in *To Loose the Bands of Wickedness*, 14–42, especially 28–34.

10. The key resolution in Operation Restore Hope is Security Council Resolution 794, adopted on December 3, 1992. For a discussion of the operation, see Jeffrey Clark, "Debacle in Somalia: Failure of the Collective Response," in *Enforcing Restraint*, 205–39; Francis Deng, *Protecting the Dispossessed: A Challenge for the International Community* (Washington, D.C.: Brookings Institution, 1993), 51–63; and United Nations Department of Public Information (UNDPI), *The United Nations and the Situation in Somalia*, April 1995.

11. For the following remarks, see Andreopoulos, "Confronting the 'New World Order.' "

12. For example, there is no sound legal basis for the international community's failure to deal with the Sudanese civil war, which has witnessed the widespread use of food as a weapon of war and has generated huge refugee flows in neighboring countries, as well as flows of internally displaced persons. The humanitarian tragedy continues despite the limited success of Operation Lifeline Sudan. For the latter, see Francis M. Deng and Larry Minear, *The Challenges of Famine Relief: Emergency Operations in the Sudan* (Washington, D.C.: Brookings Institution, 1992).

13. But even that was not problem-free. Several states expressed concern over the use of an international aspect of the crisis (the refugee flows) to deal with what was primarily an issue of domestic jurisdiction (the human rights situation in Iraq). Moreover, when the decision was taken to send armed UN police forces to protect the humanitarian relief effort, including the "safe haven" areas, Iraq objected on the grounds that Security Council Resolution 688 did not expressly authorize the use of force; and the secretary-general indicated that a new resolution was necessary to justify the forcible deployment of UN peacekeeping forces. On the other hand, the United States and its allies felt that Resolution 688 (a) by characterizing the consequences of Iraqi repression as a threat to international peace and security and (b) by insisting on immediate access for international humanitarian organizations, allowed for possible enforcement action to deal with the crisis in case of continuing Iraqi resistance.

14. Boutros Boutros-Ghali, letter to the Security Council, November 29, 1992, p. 3.

15. From the preambular provisions of Resolution 794, *The United Nations and the Situation in Somalia*, 47.

16. Adam Roberts, "Humanitarian War: Military Intervention and Human Rights, John Vincent Memorial Lecture, Keele University (February 26, 1993), 11. The wording of the mandate is taken from the text of Security Council Resolution 678, November 29, 1990.

17. The opening paragraph of Security Council Resolution 733, January 23, 1992, clearly states: "The Security Council, considering the request by Somalia for the Security Council to consider the situation in Somalia"; *The United Nations and the Situation in Somalia*, 39.

18. Ibid., 1, 39, and 47. In its preamble, Security Council Resolution 794 reaffirms Resolution 733. See also the letter of the secretary-general to the Security Council, November 29, 1992.

19. On the positive side, witness the precedent-setting Security Council Resolution 418, November 4, 1977, which imposed an arms embargo against South Africa in response to the Council's determination that the acquisition by South Africa of arms and related material constituted a threat to international peace and security because of the regime's apartheid policies and its attacks against neighboring states. Thus the domestic factor (the apartheid regime) is per se constitutive of a threat to peace and security. On the negative side, witness the—until recently—moribund Genocide Convention, which empowers (under Article VIII) any contracting party "to take such action under the Charter of the United Nations as they consider appropriate for the prevention and suppression of acts of genocide." It is the first time since the Genocide Convention's entry into force that its provisions may be invoked in judicial proceedings relating to cases of serious violations of international humanitarian law committed in the territories of the former Yugoslavia and of Rwanda; see Article 4 of the statute of the International Tribunal for the Former Yugoslavia and Article 2 of the Statute of the International Tribunal for Rwanda. See also Rodley, "Collective Intervention," 23–24, 27–28.

20. For a useful discussion of the linkages between peace, democracy, and human rights, see Thomas M. Franck, "The Emerging Right to Democratic Governance," *American Journal of International Law* 86, no. 1 (1992): 46–91, especially 87–90.

21. Boutros Boutros-Ghali, "An Agenda for Peace: One Year Later," *Orbis* 37, no. 3 (Summer 1993): 332.

22. *Nations and Nationalism Since 1780: Programme, Myth, Reality* (Cambridge: Cambridge University Press, 1990), 123–24.

23. "UN Chief Rebuffed by Bosnian Factions," *International Herald Tribune*, December 1, 1994, p. 1. See also the thoughtful remarks of Charles G. Boyd, "Making Peace with the Guilty: The Truth About Bosnia," *Foreign Affairs* 74, no. 5 (Sept.–Oct. 1995): 32–33.

24. United Nations Security Council, Letter dated 9 December 1994 from the Secretary-General Addressed to the President of the Security Council including in its annex the Final Report of the Commission of Experts established pursuant to Security Council resolution 935 (1994), S/1994/1405, December 9, 1994.

25. This is one of the main factors impeding voluntary repatriation. The other is the refugees' fear of reprisals by the current government in Rwanda; United Nations Security Council, Report of the Secretary-General on Security in the Rwandese Refugee Camps, S/1994/1308 (November 18, 1994), especially 2–4.

26. Abdullahi Ahmed An-Na'im, "Introduction," in *Human Rights in Cross-Cultural Perspectives: A Quest for Consensus*, ed. Abdullahi Ahmed An-Na'im (Philadelphia: University of Pennsylvania Press, 1992), 4.

27. See also relevant remarks in the Editors' Introduction to Part IV of this volume.

28. An-Na'im, "Introduction," 2–6. Internal legitimacy means that the alternative interpretation must be in harmony with the main tenets of the culture in question.

29. *Agenda for Peace*, 16.

30. Ibid.

31. For example, in the cases of Namibia, Haiti, Cambodia, and El Salvador. On the Cambodian case, see the chapter by Stephen P. Marks in this volume.

32. Humanitarian assistance is used here generically to cover both coercive and noncoercive forms.

33. United Nations Security Council, Report of the Secretary-General Pursuant to Paragraph 2 of Security Council Resolution 808 (1993), S/25704, May 3, 1993.

34. Since these lines were written, the presidents of Serbia, Croatia, and Bosnia-Herzegovina have signed the U.S.-brokered Dayton Peace Accord in Paris, in December 1995. It is too early to say whether this agreement will hold. A key component of the accord is the certification by the Organization for Security and Cooperation in Europe (OSCE) that Bosnia can carry out free and fair elections by September 14, 1996. Recent OSCE internal reports have questioned Bosnia's ability to do so. Given that an OSCE recommendation about the elections must be made by July 14, the peace accord is at a critical juncture; see Chris Hedges, "Report on Bosnia Questions Ability to Hold Elections," *New York Times*, June 2, 1996, A1.

Chapter 2
Human Rights as Education for Peace

Betty A. Reardon

Peace education, a worldwide movement, is a diverse and continually changing field, responding to developments in world society and, to some extent, to the advancing knowledge and insights of peace research. As practiced in elementary and secondary schools and presented in the university programs that prepare classroom teachers, peace education goes by various names: conflict resolution, multicultural education, development education, world order studies, and, more recently, environmental education. Each of these approaches responds to a particular set of problems that have been perceived as the causes of social injustice, conflict, and war. Each could also be classified as "preventive education education" as it seeks to prevent the occurrence of the problems that inspire it.[1] More important, each is conceived as *education for peace* and thus acknowledges that it is intended to be a means to the realization of a set of social values. Although each relates to peace in the sense of social cohesion and the avoidance of the form of violence to which it responds, none of them displays the elements of prescription and holism so essential to understanding the increasingly conflictual interdependent, planetary social system from which peace is to be wrought. Each is primarily responsive, particularistic, and problem focused.

Peace Education Needs Human Rights Education

Even that strand of peace education that sees itself devoted specifically to learnings about "peacemaking" has been primarily problem-centered, focusing on "negative peace," the reduction, avoidance, and elimination of warfare. As such, it has been devoted more to a study directed toward eliminating the causes of war than to creating the conditions of peace, more to negative circumstances of *what should not be* than to the positive possibilities of *what could be.* So it is that peace education and peace studies (as the field is known in universities) have been a bit of a "downer" for all but those students who are either "positive thinkers" by nature, drawn to social action fields, or simply curious about the study of the "impossible." Thus peace education as such is less visible in American secondary and elementary schools than the other approaches enumerated here, which have more immediate relevance to community concerns. And only a small fraction of university students ever pursue courses in peace studies, even though they are now offered in several hundred institutions of higher education. While not entirely attributable to its responsive, particularistic, and problematic nature, the fact that it is a minority, not a majority, of students who receive peace education may well be a serious obstacle to the peacemaking capacities of this country and any country that does not actively educate its citizens *for peace*. This assumption underlies the central argument put forth here that human rights education is not only a corrective complement to education for peace but that it is essential to the development of peacemaking capacities and should be integrated into all forms of peace education. It is through human rights education that learners are provided with the knowledge and opportunities for specific corrective action that can fulfill the prescriptive requirements of education for peace.

Human rights education, fast becoming another global educational phenomenon, appears to be developing along equally varied, but more substantively focused and prescriptive lines. It comprehends some of the same normative goals espoused by peace education, provides a dimension of concrete possibilities for alternatives to current world conditions, and offers a constructive action dimension to complement and apply to all the diverse forms of peace education. Many recent world developments similar to those that have produced the existing approaches to peace education have been articulated as human rights issues and problems, so that some peace educators are adding human rights to the list of approaches. While the addition is certainly necessary, it is far from sufficient and fails to exploit the essential contribution that human rights can make to peace education, namely, providing the basis for a prescriptive, holistic yet particularized approach that would make peace education not only more *comprehensive* but also far more *comprehensible*. The actual human experiences that comprise much of human rights education are more readily understood than the theoretical and analytical content of peace education.

The conceptual core of peace education is violence, its control, reduction, and elimination. The conceptual core of human rights education is human dignity, its recognition, fulfillment, and universalization. As I have argued elsewhere, human rights are most readily adaptable to the study of positive peace, the social, political, and economic conditions most likely to provide the environment and process for social cohesion and nonviolent conflict resolution.[2] This essay contends that education for peace should be primarily prescriptive and that human rights offers the most appropriate route through which to move from problem to prescription in all the various approaches to peace education. Positive peace, conceptualized by the peace research community to extend the definition of peace beyond the limitation, avoidance, or absence of war to include issues of justice, poverty, and freedom, is the concept of peace that is the foundational principle of the Universal Declaration of Human Rights. The inextricable relationship between human rights and peace is articulated in the very first sentence of the Preamble to the Declaration, "recognition of the inherent dignity and of the equal and inalienable rights of all members of the human family is the foundation of freedom, justice, and peace in the world." Since the core and seminal document for all current standards of human rights, to which all members of the United Nations are assumed to assent, acknowledges this principle, surely education for peace should also do so. Certainly, both peace researchers and activists and human rights scholars and advocates can agree that violence in all its forms is an assault on human dignity.

Peace research now recognizes several particular forms of violence as the conceptual rubrics under which data are gathered and knowledge derived: *physical* or *behavioral violence* including war and other uses of direct force to destroy or weaken or otherwise harm another nation, group, or individual; *structural violence*, which refers to the poverty and deprivation that results from unjust and inequitable social and economic structures; the *political violence of oppressive systems* that enslave, intimidate, and abuse dissenters as well as the poor, powerless, and marginalized; and *cultural violence*, the devaluing and destruction of particular human identities and ways of life, the violence of racism, sexism, ethnocentrism, colonial ideology, and other forms of moral exclusion that rationalize aggression, domination, inequity, and oppression. All these forms of violence can be made most apparent and comprehensible within a human rights framework. Analyzing these forms of violence as violations of particular human rights standards provides a constructive alternative to presenting them as abstract concepts, as is often the case in peace education. It is for just such reasons that some educators teaching in the fields of conflict resolution, multiculturalism, development education, and world order studies and a limited number of environmental educators are now integrating human rights issues and standards into their curricula as subject matter content, as perspectives for the development of critical capacities, and as areas for experiential learning. To each of these forms of peace education, human rights brings not only the element of concrete experience and observable social conditions but also a much-needed normative and prescriptive dimension.

Each has acknowledged a concern with values formation and ethical decision-making processes that have been problematic in an educational system, somewhat ambivalent on the subject of values and ethics, alternately purporting to be value-free and/or to encourage consideration of contending values and value systems, while in actuality conveying the unarticulated and unexamined prevailing values of the society, mainly ignoring the ethical questions imbedded in social issues. This confusion in education is readily reflected in the contradictions in public policy and in the limited capacities of citizens to make policy judgments.

It is contended here that each and all approaches to peace education can make a significant contribution to the clarification of this confusion and to the development of judgment-making capacities through the integration of human rights content and perspectives.

Conflict Resolution

Conflict resolution is probably the most widely practiced approach to peace education in American elementary and secondary schools. The approach is mainly one that emphasizes processes and techniques for dealing with small group and interpersonal conflict. Teachers of these techniques, often introduced to overcome problems of classroom discipline, playground fights, and some of the more serious forms of violence that now plague our public education systems, try to communicate the values of fairness and demonstrate the efficacy of nonviolence. However, like the wider field of dispute resolution, the orientation of the instruction tends to be pragmatic rather than explicitly normative or ethical.

Specific and often very effective skills are taught which enable a third party or the disputants themselves to reach a resolution acceptable to both or all parties to the dispute. The emphasis is on the achievement of an acceptable resolution in terms of the particular elements of the immediate dispute. It is rare, at least, in elementary and secondary education that consideration of the roots or the long-range consequences of the conflict are brought into the process. Most conflict resolution education, as generally practiced, does not teach students to understand structural and systemic aspects of conflict, and only in a few cases comprehends the cultural elements of conflict, thus overlooking value issues.

Yet this lack in no way devalues the skills that are taught. They are of lifelong relevance to all forms of experience, interpersonal as well as social and political. Conflict resolution training certainly has had dramatically positive results in the schools where it is offered. And these results argue well for such skill development to be a required instructional goal of all our schools if we truly desire them to be peaceful and democratic learning environments. It does, however, indicate that while necessary to peace education, the study of conflict resolution is not sufficient to its purposes of providing learnings that will contribute to fundamental and long-range change to reduce violence substantially by increasing social justice and respect for human dignity.

Were this skills training and its attitudinal bases, which incorporate the values of reason, open communication, and fundamental fairness, to use principles of human rights as the criteria of fairness, conflict resolution could offer a more integrated and comprehensive approach to peace education. For example, examining causes and long-range effects of conflicts in terms of violations and fulfillment of human rights would provide an excellent basis for the clarification of the values of equity and fairness and the application of principles of justice. Some of the most severe and violent conflicts are caused by actual or perceived violations of human rights. In looking at whatever conflict or conflict process that is being studied in the framework of the recognition, fulfillment, and universalization of human dignity, students can come to understand the differences between constructive and destructive conflicts; to appreciate how nonviolently conducted conflict has often been the means to overcome injustice and achieve more truly peaceful social orders; and to understand that conflict is a significant process in all social change[3]. For peace education, the purpose of teaching the skills of conflict resolution is to widen the possibilities for preventing conflicts from erupting into violence and for assuring efforts to achieve just resolutions that honor human dignity.

In this regard, the theme and principles of nonviolence, the focus of some peace education, could be used as a conceptual framework for conflict resolution and as a normative approach to teaching about social change, political strategy, and modern history. It could also illuminate how the commitment to human dignity that is the essence of nonviolence inspires the struggle for human rights as the basis for overcoming the many forms of violence that impede a viable, just peace. This commitment requires consistency between means and ends. Violence, the ultimate insult to human dignity, is not a suitable means through which to struggle for its realization. Human rights, "the how and the who" of potential violations that could result from a given means, are an excellent tool for determining whether those means are truly nonviolent.

Multicultural Studies

The study of various ethnic groups and cultures has become a major focus in education at all levels, producing certain controversies as it seeks to respond to others.[4] There are two major wellsprings of this stream of peace education. The first was in the recognition of the need for understanding other cultures resulting from the realities of international interdependence and the necessity of international cooperation to address global problems. This source emphasized the study of the cultures of other parts of the world, giving little attention to the variety of cultures within nations. This omission, particularly as it did little to challenge the Eurocentrism of most American curricula, was one impetus for the second wellspring, the ethnic consciousness movements of the 1970s and 1980s, which became the social equivalents of the civil rights movements of the 1950s and 1960s. As conflict resolution was a response to communal and school disturbances (often caused by ethnic tensions and conflicts), multicultural studies was a response to changes in immigration patterns and the reawakening of cultural identities long presumed to have been subordinated to one common national identity. The "hyphenated Americans" included the recently arrived from Asia, Latin America, and Eastern Europe and the descendants of European and African peoples many generations in the United States. In an essentially racist society, few of these groups were fully at peace with or adequately acquainted with the values and traditions of others. As the interests of groups came more openly into conflict, the necessity of such understanding proved to be as essential to *domestic tranquility* as *international understanding* was deemed to be to world peace. Experiences similar to this were evident, as well, in the former socialist countries where ethnic conflicts produced armed

Figure 2.1. The opening session of the General Assembly at the United Nations headquarters in New York. Foreign Minister Humayun Rasheed Choudhury of Bangladesh (at the podium) stated: "Let us rededicate ourselves to working together for a world of peace, not only where war is merely absent, not only where human survival is just possible, but also where justice prevails and human dignity is upheld." (UNPHOTO 168302 John Isaac)

conflicts (e.g., Yugoslavia and Armenia), some of them, like those in Africa and Asia, of genocidal proportions.

Cross-cultural ignorance and the hostilities it helps to maintain and exacerbate argue strongly for multicultural education as an essential element of education for peace. The atrocities that characterize the conflicts fed by ethnic hostilities demand that human rights be central to any education directed toward intercultural understanding. Indeed, some educators would argue that respect for and knowledge of other cultures are essential to the realization of human rights, and that concepts of human rights should be the essential ethical core of such understanding. This relationship in turn makes evident the necessity of intercultural understanding not only to prevent violence but to assure an adequate and effective process of peacemaking.

Indeed, ethnic conflicts demonstrate perhaps more clearly than any other conflicts that human rights should be guiding criteria not only for conflict resolution but for all aspects and phases of a peace making process. Particularly in the negotiations of settlements and the establishment of the terms of peace among conflicting ethnic groups, human rights principles should be used to assure the parties of the fairness of the agreements. Within the peace processes of peacekeeping, peacemaking, and peace building outlined by the secretary-general of the United Nations,[5] human rights standards would be an invaluable tool in all phases. They could be used in decision making about peacekeeping actions, and guide peacemaking negotiations toward outcomes that would be inherently more just and thus most significantly viable. It is in the area of peace building, creating the conditions for peaceful relationships, that preparation in multicultural understanding informed by human rights concepts could make a significant contribution to the formation of the peacemakers and the publics that must support their efforts. These specific aspects of the most significant recent proposals for a peacemaking process demonstrate that multicultural education fused with human rights education is essential not only to those charged with carrying out the process, but to the citizenry who will in the end determine when, where, and if such processes should be undertaken. While citizens of all nations need such education in these years when the United States is the major "player" in peacekeeping, it is an urgent necessity.

Human rights concepts and principles can also be used to achieve what has been the major instructional goal of multicultural education: developing the capacity to understand, clarify, and appreciate similarities and differences among cultures. Such comparisons are not intended to judge one culture as ethically superior to any other or others. Aversion to the notions of cultural superiority and cultural relativism, combined with an acknowledged commitment to equity among peoples, makes peace educators sensitive to such judgments. Yet the field is a value-centered one and has been much in need of a value system that does not do disservice to the value of pluralism fundamental to cultural equity and diversity. Human rights, as enumerated in the Universal Declaration and the international standards, provide the framework for comparisons and assessments of the human condition on the basis of the most global criteria available. Although primarily western in origin, these standards have a sufficient degree of authentic universality to have been generally accepted as human values, the core principles of which are adaptable to most cultures. Indeed, such was a major conclusion of the 1993 Vienna World Conference on Human Rights. Although disputed by authoritarian governments, the principle of universality is globally recognized by human rights movements and, more significantly, by most UN member states, even some of those in contention with the movements.

Study of the myriad modes cultures use to implement rights could provide concrete instruction about the variety of possibilities a culturally diverse world has for honoring human dignity, pursuing human values, and fulfilling human needs. This in itself is an essential lesson in peace education which seeks to develop the consideration of multiple alternatives in an effort to determine which among various policies, proposals, and behaviors are most conducive to the achievements of peace and justice. Cross-cultural study of human rights concepts could be the vehicle for learning about how cultures vary in the structures of human and social relationships and ways of according respect to the human person: how human identity and dignity is experienced in different contexts, both individual and communal. A major purpose of such inquiry is to demonstrate not only variety and differences, but the possibilities of what cultures can learn from each other about what it is to be human.

Using human rights concepts and standards in multicultural education can provide the essential basis for teaching reasoned valuing and judgment making. The standards in their derivation and application involve both principles that are universal and practices that are culturally and contextually particular. Learning to recognize and differentiate between principle and practice involve skills as important to peacemaking capacities as are the skills of conflict resolution. By observing how some principles can be practiced in a variety of ways, students can gain not only lessons about how cultural diversity could flourish within a system of common social ethics, but also within what contexts and circumstances value judgments regarding cultural practices are valid and defensible.

The use of the standards in such study is intended to provide reference points and general principles. Each of the general principles of the Universal Declaration of Human Rights can provide a basis for searching out cultural norms and practices that implement or deny the principles. Distinctions could be made between the actual social institutions, practices, and conditions and the cultural beliefs and values in which they are embedded. Such learning includes, of course, tolerance of differences and cross-cultural understanding, but also the limits of the acceptability or tolerability of social conditions that cause any human suffering that can be classified as violence. The legal standards of the covenants and conventions can be used to assess tolerability: how the societies, particularly the political and economic systems in which the peoples of the various cultures live, measure up to the standards.

Here is another major point of inseparability between human rights and the forms of peace education intended to contribute to their achievement. It is in the assessment of tolerability and acceptability that the notion of *violence* converges with that of *human dignity.* Violence, for the purposes of peace education, has been defined as unnecessary, avoidable, or intentional harm. When human dignity is assaulted in any way by social institutions, norms, or behaviors that are, or purport to be, sanctioned by the values and worldviews of the culture, the resulting harm is described as *cultural violence.*

It is readily evident from the limited study of this form of violence that peace research has thus far conducted that few cultures are free of it. While the degrees of severity may vary from one society to another, it is a global phenomenon. It is one factor that enables us to conceive of human rights as universal aspirations and "common standards of achievement for all peoples and all nations."[6]

The notion of a "common standard of achievement" provides avenues for the consideration of international cultural change as a long-range, comprehensive strategy for the universal fulfillment of human rights, the kind of strategy that has informed the women's and antiracist movements. Inquiry into such change and the requisite strategies has long been pursued in peace education. Although the areas for remedial action on behalf of human rights are primarily legal and political, it is becoming evident that the most egregious violations are often the consequence of deep-rooted cultural beliefs and traditions. The most vivid and, to many women, the most apparent of these are the beliefs and traditions of patriarchy. Clearly sexism, racism, and various other forms of authoritarian oppression have been rationalized over centuries by appeal to particularistic interpretations of the most revered authority sources of the cultures of the societies in which they have flourished. Yet both have been universally denounced as antithetical to human dignity in international instruments drafted by the United Nations and accepted by most world cultures. These denunciations, it needs to be emphasized, have been for the most part the consequences of social movements organized and carried out by victims of the indignities and their advocates, not governments. Such movements are the consequences of social learnings we would now classify as human rights education. Although some governments may come into power as a consequence of human rights initiatives and movements, they are not the initiators or the movers, they are the moved. States have crafted and agreed to human rights standards under the pressure and inspiration of other forces. For the most part, states are still major obstacles to the fulfillment of human rights, being primarily and sometimes exclusively motivated by their obsessions with their own perpetuation.

Thus human rights standards can be taught as the concepts of dignity and justice that identify and acknowledge social wrongs and cultural faults, as the guidelines through which societies can conceptualize and pursue cultural change, and as the impetus to governmental action to defend the dignity of citizens, action that requires that governments, too, receive human rights education.

It is especially important in the study of cultures to provide an understanding that cultures, like all things human, evolve and change. They respond to their environments and adapt to survive. In the global age, in which the unity of humankind is as much a pragmatic necessity as an ethical imperative, the universal standards of human rights provide the most obvious and effective guidelines for cultural change. Here it is to be underlined that such change, while it can be influenced, even inspired, by other cultures and international society, is only legitimate and actually effective when embraced and propelled by the peoples of the cultures concerned. It is necessary that those peoples intend to change their cultures. Intentional cultural change can result only from education. The relationship between such change and education is the foundation upon which the People's Decade of Human Rights Education is built. The people themselves should determine if, when, and how their cultures should be changed, and design the learning strategies to devise the changes deemed necessary.

Here, too, women's issues, especially such culturally sensitive questions as marriage and reproductive rights, are good cases in point. Whereas specific global standards are both necessary and useful, the ways in which they are implemented need to be decided and applied by those directly concerned. Such issues offer excellent instructional opportunities for reflection on how principles that respect the unity of humankind, the integrity of the various and distinct human cultures, and the dignity of the human person could be formulated and applied in a global society. They also show how *all* those involved in the designated social wrong must be educated to change themselves and the situations that violate rights. For example, both women and men must be involved in such education relating to women's rights.

Development Education

Development education as an approach to education for peace has focused on the economic inequities between the rich nations and the poor.[7] The systematic undermining of the well-being of the peoples of the poor nations imposed by the present global economy are classified as *structural violence*. The structures, institutions, and policies of the present economic system limit the length and debase the quality of life of the majority of the human family that inhabits the poor countries of "the South."

Peace-oriented development education inquires into the consequences of these structures and potential alternatives to them, placing special emphasis on the responsibilities of the nations of "the North," whose wealth and power enable them to virtually control the system. In that these states are "representative democracies," their citizens also bear responsibility. Social and personal responsibility are key notions of human rights education. As peace education has addressed this issue with regard to war crimes and crimes against humanity, so, too, development education might address it in relation to the violation of economic and social rights that are life-and-death questions for millions.

All forms of development education could be enhanced by the incorporation of human rights as goals and standards. They can be used as the basis for reflection on the needs for and the efficacy and desirability of modes and purposes of economic and social development and the roles of the North and South in carrying them out. A major drawback to development education has been what some educators have claimed is a stance of "noblesse oblige," reinforcing the stereotypes of northern nations as "advanced" or "developed" and therefore superior to the "less-developed" or "underdeveloped" nations. The core questions put to students are about how much and under what circumstances the "developed" nations should "contribute" to the "developing" nations. There are few or no questions as to the source and justice of the North's control over the resources from which they make their contributions to the South.

Even those curricula and programs that are presented in terms of global social justice rather than charitable sharing of bounty tend toward motivating learners in the North to want to "help" and those in the South to want to "progress." Were development education to be presented primarily in the context of issues related to facilitating the equitable fulfillment of social and economic rights, these attitudes of condescension and "boot strapping" might be avoided. The inquiry could look into the origins of economic and social rights in such a way as to demonstrate how the recognition of the rights of industrial workers was a contributing factor to the development of the industrial capacities that led to the North gaining control of the South. The future of these rights and changes in human rights concepts could also be explored. The concept of the "right to development" is an excellent introduction to the notion that communities of people as well as individuals are the subjects of rights. In that the evolution of these standards is current and highly political, the concept of group rights can also be used to teach the dynamics of the ongoing process of identifying and remediating obstacles and insults to human dignity that constitutes the global human rights movements.

Human rights can bring to development education the notion of development as a process of the evolution of a society based upon normative principles that call for the fulfillment of economic, social, and cultural rights through the elimination of avoidable poverty and the equitable distribution of whatever benefits a society may possess. Some refer to this process as "social development," a process through which societies become more responsive to the needs and dignity of all their members. This is the concept of development most consistent with the principles of the universality and indivisibility of human rights, a concept best communicated by a holistic or comprehensive approach to education for peace.[8]

World Order Studies

World order studies, developed from inquiries into war prevention and concern with *physical*, particularly armed, *violence* is the approach to education for peace that has included explicit study of human rights since its inception. Human rights has been one of the major substantive areas of world order studies which defines itself as an inquiry into the realization of a set of global values. It focuses on the possibilities for alternative security systems and international institutions more adequate to the realization of the values and the resolution of multiple global crises. It pays special attention to interlinkages among and between world problems and to the capacities of international law to resolve them. Thus it has considered the relationships between militarism and political repression, between arms expenditures and the deprivation of social and economic well-being, and more recently the coincidence of ecological destruction and the plight of indigenous people. The international law of human rights has relevance to this field because of the institutional problems it addresses and the normative nature of the approach.[9] These are characteristics that confine it to the upper secondary and university levels of formal education.

World order studies pioneered the integration of the concepts of "alternative futures" and "relevant utopias" into peace curricula, and introduced a problem-solving approach that emphasized the application of the "world order values" to the assessment of alternative institutional and policy proposals for the prevention of war and achievement of positive peace. Because of this value framework, the approach can be even further enriched by the development of human rights education, just as it has something of significance to offer to that development.

One of the barriers to the involvement of secondary and nonspecialist students in world order studies is the abstract and theoretical nature of most of the discourse, particularly as it pertains to actual and potential international institutions. Human rights issues can bring an element of the lived human experience to the consideration of institutional issues. Case material on human rights abuses and specific struggles for justice presented as challenges to be met in the design and pursuit of institutional changes can enliven the study with factual knowledge of what needs to be changed, and with concrete examples of how present institutions actually affect people's lives.

Introducing the institutional issues is a contribution that world order studies can make to human rights education. Both the world order and human rights movements find national sovereignty to be a major impediment to the achievement of their espoused goals. Human rights education, however, has yet to exploit the pedagogical possibilities of "relevant utopias," proposals for institutional and systematic change that could alter the present system of sovereign nation-states so as to increase the possibilities for the fulfillment of human rights. And little attention is given to the institutions' processes for remediation of human rights abuses. For example, students might be called upon to consider how nation-states or human rights organizations and activists should respond to human rights abuses, but not how international standards and legal remedy could be applied, or how to change or transform the international system in which the abuses take place. Questions about how to assure an order that upholds human rights, an order called for by Article 28 of the Universal Declaration of Human Rights, still receive inadequate attention in human rights education. Human rights education could be made more adequate to the needs of educating to make judgments on international institutions and policies by adapting this leaf from the world order studies book.

The inquiry that might be derived from bringing together the structural issues of world order and the ethical questions of human rights presents a core question from which a significant new dimension can be brought to each field. What are the possible structural and institutional changes that might effectively reduce violence and promote human dignity in the world social system? The questions that follow could serve to guide the development of curricula that could achieve the purposes of both fields of study. These questions would address indicators of violence and dignity. Study of these indicators would, of course, involve the international human rights standards. Further questions to explore the kinds of political processes and citizens' movements that could promote institutional change would include study of human rights organizations and initiatives throughout the world. Thus the range of agents capable of acting for human rights and peace beyond nation-states and international organizations would be included, promoting a fuller and more accurate picture of the present system and the possibilities to change it. Such an inquiry would also open to secondary and university students opportunities for action, specific ways in which they could exercise the responsibilities of global citizenship.

Environmental Education

Finally, a few comments on an approach only a few consider to be education for peace, yet one that may present the greatest opportunity of an integrated, comprehensive education for peace. Environmental education, developed by those who view the problem from planetary and ethical perspectives has much in common with comprehensive peace education in its systemic analysis and its value-based inquiry. Perceived by many as "nonpolitical," it provided a convenient and fruitful basis for educational collaboration among educators who might otherwise have been deterred from direct cooperation on more apparently political topics. Such a collaboration between American and Soviet educators in the waning years of the cold war produced a new approach to comprehensive peace education, "ecological and cooperative education."[10]

This is an approach that brings an ecological or living systems perspective to the study of global problems, and applies the pedagogy of cooperative learning to develop urgently needed capacities for social integration. It also brings up possibilities for the application of human rights principles to subjects even wider than social, ethnic, or national groups. It provides a way of considering the possibility that the human species as a unit has rights, a possibility implied in the designation of some human rights abuses as "crimes against humanity." The question of who may claim the right to a healthful environment has stymied those who would make such a claim for individuals or even for groups in class actions. There are no ways to separate or draw borders between "sections" of the environment. It is an organic unity and can only be effectively addressed as such. A claim made to environmental rights would of necessity have to consider the whole environmental system, the planet and the living systems that comprise it. (The failure to recognize this imperative has been a factor that obstructs reason and clarity in environmental debates.)

The claim would also require consideration of responsibility that would, given our knowledge of how unregulated individual behaviors cumulatively affect the environment, need to be defined just as comprehensively. If humankind has rights, does it not also have responsibilities, and through what agents might that responsibility be exercised? Such is a question of proportions which can only be addressed by the planetary generation, those born to an Earth seen from space as a whole and living planet. It is a question that, more than any other, will determine their future. From teaching experience, I know that they recognize and respond to that question.

Ecological and cooperative education points to the direction in which education for peace is now moving, and, it can be argued, *should* move. If that direction is to lead to a humanly viable and ethically tolerable (even if temporary) destination, should not the movement be guided by the principles and standards of human rights? If each approach can be made more effective by the inclusion of human rights, then human rights must be central to any comprehensive, integrated approach. Peace education and human rights education in their present forms are but different starting points to the same intended destination, a more just and peaceful world.

Notes

1. "Preventive Education," *Unesco Sources* 57 (April 1994), monthly dossier, pp. 7–16.

2. Betty Reardon, *Educating for Human Dignity: Learning About Rights and Responsibilities: A K–12 Teaching Resource* (Philadelphia: University of Pennsylvania Press, 1995).

3. Morton Deutch, *The Resolution of Conflict: Constructive and Destructive Processes* (New Haven, Conn.: Yale University Press, 1973).

4. James Banks, *Multiethnic Education: Theory and Practice* (Boston: Allyn and Bacon, 1988).

5. UN General Assembly, Report of the Secretary-General on the Work of the Organization, *An Agenda for Peace: Preventive Diplomacy, Peacemaking and Peace-Keeping*, UN Doc. A/47/277/S/24111 (June 17, 1992).

6. Universal Declaration of Human Rights, para 1.

7. The materials and approaches to development education most appropriate to a human rights perspective have been and are being devised by the United Nations Children's Fund (UNICEF).

8. Betty Reardon, *Comprehensive Peace Education* (New York: Teachers College Press, 1987).

9. Richard Falk, Robert Johansen, and Samuel Kim, *The Constitutional Foundations of World Peace* (Albany: State University of New York Press, 1993).

10. Betty Reardon and Eva Nordland, *Learning Peace: The Promise of Ecological and Cooperative Education* (Albany: State University of New York Press, 1994).

Chapter 3
Human Rights Education in UN Peace Building: From Theory to Practice

Stephen P. Marks

United Nations "peace-building" operations offer new and promising opportunities to develop and apply a general approach to human rights education. An example of this potential is the education, information, and training program of the Human Rights Component of the United Nations Transitional Authority in Cambodia (UNTAC). The peace plan, under which the United Nations went to Cambodia in 1992–93, provided a broad mandate that called for a concentrated and intense effort to carry out human rights education at all levels and of all types. The experience is instructive not only for other possible peace operations under UN auspices, but also as a test case for conceiving a strategy for human rights education and carrying it out under severe time constraints. It is thus a case of a comprehensive approach toward human rights education in both theory and practice.

A new direction of operational support for human rights education emerged with the Security Council's decisions to implement comprehensive political settlements to regional conflicts and its recognition that human rights could provide the normative framework for institutional modifications and constitutional reform, as well as self-determination through free and fair elections. There are three recent examples where education about human rights was given an explicit place in the mandates of UN operations, namely, those in El Salvador, Cambodia, and Haiti. This is a new dimension of UN peacekeeping since human rights was absent from peacekeeping as traditionally practiced before the late 1980s. Peacekeeping operations did not include either monitoring human rights or informing populations about these rights. With the end of the cold war and the greatly enhanced expectations placed on the United Nations, unfettered by the veto that had blocked so many possible responses to complex emergencies, the Security Council referred more and more frequently to human rights.[1]

The framework for UN peace operations is set out in *An Agenda for Peace*, produced in response to the historic summit of heads of state and government on January 31, 1992. The report defines and reviews the three traditional areas of preventive diplomacy, peacemaking, and peacekeeping, plus a fourth, called "post-conflict peace-building." Whereas preventive diplomacy seeks to avoid the outbreak of a violent conflict, peace building seeks to prevent its recurrence. Designed for situations like El Salvador and Cambodia, where warring parties agree to end hostilities and work toward reconciliation and rehabilitation, but remain suspicious of each other and politically ambitious, peace building should include, in the words of the secretary-general, "disarming the previously warring parties and the restoration of order, the custody and possible destruction of weapons, repatriating refugees, advisory and training support for security personnel, monitoring elections, advancing efforts to protect human rights, reforming or strengthening governmental institutions and promoting formal and informal processes of political participation."[2] This function also can entail "support for the transformation of deficient national structures and capabilities, and for the strengthening of new democratic institutions," in short "the construction of a new environment."[3] Human rights education within the framework of peace building has been tested in several major UN operations, especially in UNTAC. This chapter examines the application of peace building through human rights education as practiced by the United Nations in Cambodia and suggests some general guidelines for human rights education as part of peace building.

UNTAC was an experiment in implementing a broad mandate to reach all levels of society during a brief period. The official duration of the transitional period was just under two years,[4] but the effective period for implementing this mandate was approximately one year. It was an impossibly short period to transform a society, yet a degree of democratic empowerment occurred and is continuing to affect the political process in Cambodia. To review this experience, I begin with the mandate, that is, what the parties and the UN Security Council asked UNTAC to do, and then discuss how, on the basis of that mandate, a strategy for a countrywide human rights education program was implemented. With this mandate and strategy in mind, I make some general observations about the opportunities and obstacles facing internationally managed human rights education through the formal and informal structures.

UNTAC's Human Rights Education Mandate and Strategy

The mandate of UNTAC's human rights education program is set out in the Paris Peace Agreement of October 1991 and the Report of the Secretary-General of February 1992. The secretary-general's report to the Security Council on Cambodia says that "The development and dissemination of a human rights education program is foreseen as the cornerstone of UNTAC's activities in fostering respect for human rights."[5] This statement is based on UNTAC's responsibility as set out in Article 16 of the Paris Agreement for "fostering an environment in which human rights shall be ensured" and Section E of Annex I, which says that UNTAC shall make provision for the "development and implementation of a program of human rights education to promote respect for and understanding of human rights." The meaning of "education" is broad; it implies "teaching" in formal and informal learning environments, as well as "training" and "information." With respect to formal teaching, the secretary-general's report envisaged "that UNTAC would also work closely with existing educational administrative structures in Cambodia to ensure that human rights education is appropriately included in the curriculum at all levels, including children, adults and special groups" (para. 13). Significantly the report states that

Cambodians must fully understand both the content and the significance of those rights and freedoms in order to be in a position to know when and how to protect them properly. This is especially important in an environment in which the framing of a new Cambodian Constitution containing human rights guarantees will be on the national agenda. . . . Such a civic education program would be developed in a manner that is culturally sensitive and generally "accessible" to Cambodians. Its dissemination would reply upon all channels of communication available in the country, included printed materials (words and pictures), cultural events and presentations, radio and television media, videocassette distribution, mobile teaching units, etc. (paras. 12–13)

"Training" is also used in the human rights section of the secretary-general's report in four places: "complementary training" to civic education (para. 14); "some training" in the application of guidelines and materials targeted to civil servants (para. 16); "supplementary training" for law enforcement officials and the judiciary, "especially in the areas of fundamental criminal procedure" (para. 17); and "training" of UNTAC personnel in the areas of law enforcement and judicial functions (ibid.) The term "training" is intended in these passages in the proper sense of imparting skills necessary for the performance of certain specialized tasks.

Thus while the secretary-general's report does not make the distinction between types and levels of education, it does provide guidance on training and information, and target groups for these educational activities. The implementation of these broad guidelines required a more specific strategy and plan of action.

After determining that the mandate included all levels and types of education, the Human Rights Component devised and implemented a six-step strategy. Step one was to identify the target groups to whom educational activities would be directed, on the basis of studies of Cambodian society made by specialized agencies and programs (such as the United Nations Educational, Scientific and Cultural Organization [UNESCO], the United Nations Children's Fund [UNICEF], and the United Nations Development Programme [UNDP]), consultations with international NGOs with experience in Cambodia, and Cambodian staff members and indigenous NGOs. The fifteen groups thus targeted included two from UNTAC (UNTAC Civil Police and electoral staff), seven from the existing administrative structures (police, teachers, university students, ministerial officials, other civil servants, political party representatives, judges, and prosecutors); and six from the civil society (defenders, human rights associations, women's associations, journalists, monks, and health professionals).

Notably absent from the target groups within the civil society were trade unions. The reason was that, as confirmed by consultations with the International Labour Organisation and the Asian American Free Labor Association, the labor movement was neither independent nor sufficiently organized to provide a context for learning activities. The military, both UN forces and those of the existing administrative structures, was initially included. The Cambodian troops were to be cantoned in special sites where courses would be organized. However, the failure to implement the demobilization and cantonment phase of the peace plan excluded this possibility. Nevertheless, in cooperation with the dissemination unit of the local delegation of the International Committee of the Red Cross, several provincial human rights officers set up ad hoc training for the military.

The second element of this strategic planning was to determine the specific expectations with respect to each group and in light of the secretary-general's report. In most cases, the main goal was a basic understanding of the concepts of human rights, the content of the international standards, their applicability to Cambodia, and their relation to the lives and work of the learners.

The third step was to assemble the necessary human and financial resources beyond the initial staff of four in the Education, Training, and Information Unit in Phnom Penh (a training officer, an information officer, an NGO relations officer, and a unit chief). Eventually the Phnom Penh staff assigned to the Education, Training, and Information Unit was increased by five (two police trainers, one education officer in charge of women's projects, a training officer to head the mobile teams, and a senior advisor for media projects), eventually aided by four training assistants and two UN volunteers. A major staffing addition, not foreseen in the secretary-general's report, was the appointment in late 1992 of twenty-one provincial human rights officers, whose responsibilities included education, training, and information, and twenty-one training assistants, Khmer-speaking educators, trained by the Component and assigned to each provincial human rights officer, working full time on training at the provincial level. Such staffing is relatively small compared with other components of the mission, but is significant compared to what is normally available for human rights education.

To supplement the financial resources, UNTAC launched an appeal to governments in October 1992, which resulted in a Trust Fund for a Human Rights Education Program in Cambodia, with about $1.8 million eventually expended to contract services among local and international NGOs having specialized staff and experience to target groups that Component staff were unable to train directly.

The fourth and fifth steps consisted in setting a timetable for each of the projects and implementing them. There was a sense of urgency to proceed with the implementation because of the extremely short time available to the mission, and the conviction that such resources and political will were not likely to be found again. Moreover, bureaucratic delays to obtain approvals from administrative and financial services in

Phnom Penh and New York shortened even more the effective time for project implementation.

The sixth and final step was project evaluation, which varied from one project to
the next and often took the minimal form of questionnaires completed by participants
or a self-evaluation session. Evaluation was more systematic with the police training,
law school, health professionals, teacher training colleges, and women's groups. In
general, the degree of assimilation of concepts and skills appears directly proportional to the links established between the content of teaching and the daily lives
of the learners. Statistics were maintained of the various training activities, although
this should be done more systematically in future operations and outside evaluators
should be employed.

This six-step strategy was implemented in both formal and informal education.

Formal Education

When UNTAC arrived, education in Cambodia was at a virtual standstill, 75 percent
of the teachers, about 67 percent of primary and secondary level students, and almost
80 percent of higher education students having been eliminated or fled the country.
Formal education facilities had all been closed down or put to other use.[6] It was in
this context that UNTAC sought to develop teaching and training on human rights in
the schools and universities, using a slightly different approach for each.

Even where formal education is grossly deficient, the development of human
rights education requires working through existing structures. Thus UNTAC obtained
from the Ministry of Education a decree making human rights part of the official curriculum of civic education in the primary and lower secondary schools and instructing
the provincial education directors to cooperate with provincial human rights officers
in setting up programs in the schools. UNTAC printed teaching materials, conducted
briefings and courses for teachers in the schools and in the teacher training colleges,
sent mobile teams to the various provinces to give courses of one to two weeks to
various groups, and supported several projects directed at primary and secondary
education through the Trust Fund.

The university audience was highly receptive to human rights teaching.[7] UNTAC's
human rights education efforts focused primarily on law and medical students. At the
country's only law school, UNTAC prepared and taught a four-hour-a-week course for
a three-month period for some 242 students, culminating in an examination. Student
motivation and learning curve were both remarkably high, in spite of their low level of
preparation. Students were particularly receptive to teaching methods that employed
critical thinking (not typical in the university) that they could apply to other subjects
in the law school, rather than the exegesis of abstract international texts. To succeed,
this method has to place the academic value of free inquiry ahead of the diplomatic
propensity to avoid controversial political issues. Teaching, even through the United

Nations, has little impact if it is based on cautiously worded official positions. It requires a willingness to link human rights concepts to real-life situations. By taking on an issue on which passions run high in Cambodia (such as the presence of ethnic Vietnamese), students were trained in a four-step mode of analysis: (1) establish the facts impartially and thoroughly; (2) identify the human rights issues involved; (3) analyze each human rights issue in light of the fact situation; and (4) make appropriate policy recommendations. The most difficult step was the first, since Cambodian students have very little experience with critically assessing sources of information, in part because impartial and reliable information is scarce and in part because "facts" are often created to fit preconceived conclusions.

Dr. Allen Keller and his colleagues had similar experiences at the Medical Faculty and the College of Nursing during the project described in Chapter 21 of this book.

Informal Education

The strategy for "informal" education[8] had to be tailored to meet the needs and circumstances of each of the target groups. Part of the training, especially in the first months of the mission, was directed at UNTAC itself, through briefings for civil police and district electoral supervisors. However, the Component's main human rights education effort was directed toward the Cambodian population. In particular, efforts were made through *training* to reach the key categories of the emerging civil society and public officials and through *the media* to reach all segments of the population.

The mandate stated that "UNTAC would also work closely with . . . special groups, [including] those individuals best placed to be further disseminators of information, such as teachers and community leaders."[9] This section of the mandate was interpreted to mean that human rights education should be directed toward democratic empowerment of the emerging *civil society* and *public officials.*

The principal forces of civil society in Cambodia are the Buddhist clergy, the free press, and NGOs, mainly those focusing on human rights, women, and development.

The *Buddhist clergy* constitute a particularly effective vehicle for reaching the public at large, especially in remote areas. Buddhism and the monks were severely victimized during the Khmer Rouge period. According to a leading authority on the period, "Khmer Rouge policy toward Buddhism constituted one of the most brutal and thoroughgoing attacks on religion in modern history."[10] The population of monks was reduced from about sixty thousand to less than one thousand.[11] The Vietnamese-installed government in Phnom Penh tolerated the monks, although the National Front for Construction and Defense, an organ of the party, supervised them closely.[12] After the arrival of the United Nations, Buddhism flourished and several monks who returned from exile became leaders in the human rights movement. For example, the Venerable Maha Ghosananda, the Supreme Patriarch and co-founder of the Inter-Religious Mission for Peace in Cambodia, is an inspirational figure among NGOs.

He and his fellow monks found full compatibility between the teachings of the Buddha and international human rights. The following meditation typifies his view that human rights are universal:

During his lifetime, the Buddha lobbied for peace and human rights. We can learn much from a lobbyist like him. Human rights begin when each man becomes a brother and each woman becomes a sister, when we honestly care for each other. Then Cambodians will help Jews, and Jews will help Africans, and Africans will help others. We will all become servants for each other's rights. . . . Any real peace will not favor East, West, North, or South. A peaceful Cambodia will be friendly to all. Peace is nonviolent, and so we Cambodians will remain nonviolent toward all as we rebuild our country. Peace is based on justice and freedom, and so a peaceful Cambodia will be just and free.[13]

Through marches, teaching, lobbying with governmental and parliamentary leaders, and spiritual guidance to the population, which is 90–95 percent Buddhist, the clergy has popularized constitutionalism and human rights, even in remote areas. During the first year of UNTAC, the Phnom Penh authorities resisted the Component's attempts to set up systematic training for this category. The active participation of monks in the human rights associations, including regularly providing meeting and office space in the Wats (pagodas), nonetheless allowed the Component to work with them in human rights education. In early 1993 it became possible to implement a more systematic strategy through a Trust Fund project that trained "master trainers" who in turn prepared hundred of monks to teach human rights to their congregations.

The experience with the monks has implications for human rights education in other peace-building contexts. With the exception of societies where organized religion is subservient to repressive government, the main religions provide both a source of understanding of prevailing values and a cultural context which must be integrated into teaching. Religion is thus a vehicle for reaching widely and deeply into society. It is unfortunate that this book does not contain a chapter dealing with human rights education through religious values, although several chapters illustrate its importance. No doubt, certain intolerant interpretations of major religions and practices of most religions are problematic for human rights, but there is support for the claim that "faith in human rights reflects a convergence of the religious wisdom of the world."[14] The potential for human rights education through religious beliefs is enormous.

Journalists were already receiving training through a UNESCO program, funded by the Danish government, as well as through the University of Phnom Penh under an arrangement with the French government. The Component integrated human rights teaching significantly into these programs. The UNESCO program was primarily aimed at skills development for the journalists from all three factions and representing both print and broadcast journalism. The most common substantive theme of their sessions was human rights, including issues of freedom of expression and human rights aspects of current events in Cambodia. Freedom of expression was generally respected during the transitional period, and there was hope that it would continue to thrive under the new Constitution of September 23, 1993, which guarantees freedom to express opinions and to publish (Article 41). Some twenty newspapers are published in Khmer, English, French, and Chinese, some of which criticize the government and its leaders freely.[15] Subsequent developments relating to a new press law, the closing of a newspaper, and the murder of a journalist have placed these accomplishments in jeopardy. Nevertheless, the international and domestic preoccupation with such incidents is a sign that serious debate over freedom of the press is taking place.[16]

The Cambodian experience illustrates two dimensions of the relation between human rights education and journalism that are more generally relevant. First, regarding the status and freedoms of journalists, it is essential that human rights education activities that reach journalists, civil servants, the police, politicians, and NGOs focus attention on the distinction between protected and prohibited speech, and on the rights and responsibilities of journalists. In this field the accusation of imposing Western values should be a matter of open discussion rather than an inhibiting factor. Examples abound to illustrate how, in nonwestern societies, a free press can be the rampart of the civil society against authoritarian rule and a critical element of democratic empowerment.

The second dimension of the relations between human rights education and journalism is that journalists themselves have much to learn about how to report a human rights story. UNESCO had it right in Cambodia by bringing human rights concepts into skills training. The persistent lack of professional ethics and skills among Cambodian journalists demonstrates the need to sustain this effort well beyond the short duration of the peace mission. A comprehensive human rights education program should not tell journalists to preach human rights but rather equip them to identify the rights and remedies relevant to a story. It should always be remembered that these issues are literally matters of life and death in most countries where peace building takes place.

According to the secretary-general's report, "UNTAC would also expect to collaborate with *non-governmental organizations* (NGOs) operating in Cambodia for this purpose as well as to encourage the establishment of indigenous human rights associations."[17] The proliferation of NGOs, independent of the state and party structures, was described by the special representative of the secretary-general on human rights in Cambodia as the "first step towards a civil society in Cambodia after its destruction between 1975 and 1978."[18] During the transitional period, UNTAC handled the registration of associations and was quite liberal in accepting applications. Indigenous human rights association and women's organizations were both partners and learners in the Component's human rights education effort.

Five human rights groups were functioning in Cambodia during the transitional period, with combined membership claimed to be in the hundreds of thousands. The Component focused its efforts on capacity building so that these groups could become effective advocates and defenders of human rights. Members of these associations were trained as human rights educators, defenders, and monitors. They were provided with materials to conduct their own educational work and participated in Component-sponsored conferences, seminars, and discussion groups where they could refine their policies and strategies. The key organizations were allocated substantial grants from the UN Trust Fund to organize their own education and training programs and to send delegations to the UN Commission on Human Rights and the Bangkok preparatory conference for the World Conference on Human Rights. A major objective of this support was to mobilize international and regional NGOs to work with their Cambodian counterparts. One of the Trust Fund projects, the Human Rights Task Force for the Cambodian Elections, was under the responsibility of one U.S.-based and six Asian-based human rights groups. The Task Force prepared human rights activists from each of the main indigenous human rights associations to monitor human rights during the election. As a result, these associations provided by far the largest numbers of election observers registered by the Electoral Component. The Task Force facilitated planning and coordination of activities of these groups and was so successful at this effort that it was continued after the elections as the Cambodian Human Rights Task Force, with additional funding from the Trust Fund.

Women's NGOs were also active partners in human rights education. Women constitute more than 60 percent of the Cambodian population as a result of mass murder and civil war. The lack of equal educational and employment opportunities had deep cultural roots, which required special efforts in human rights education. Courses were run by the Component in Phnom Penh and in the provinces, providing both basic education (introduction to concepts) and in-depth "training-of-trainers" for these associations. They were also provided with Trust Fund grants to conduct their own human rights education activities or to work with international NGOs. For example, an innovative project was conduced with support from the Trust Fund by the Decade of Human Rights Education. (This program is described in the chapter by Donna Hicks in this book.

After UNTAC's departure, human rights associations continued to be a vital part of Cambodian social and political life. Seven more human rights NGOs have emerged. UNTAC had supported the creation of a coalition of fourteen human rights, women's, and development NGOs, called Ponleu Khmer, which was particularly active during the drafting of the constitution. Ponleu Khmer continued after the proclamation of the constitution and the departure of UNTAC to educate the population about participatory democracy and to push for a sense of accountability on the part of elected officials and civil servants. In June 1994, nine human rights NGOs founded the Cambodian Human Rights Coordination Committee in order to strengthen links and improve exchanges of information. In 1994 the Cambodian Institute of Human Rights finalized and obtained official approval of the new human rights curriculum for grades 1 to 11 and organized four month-long constitutional workshops for profes-

Figure 3.1. Sin Kim Horn, a medic and coordinator of the Health and Human Rights Education Project of the American Refugee Committee in Phnom Penh, Cambodia, speaks on UNTAC and the health impacts of human rights violations in prisons. He is shown speaking at the annual meeting of the François Xavier Bagnoud Center for Health and Human Rights, Harvard School of Public Health. (Londa Hirsch)

sors at the law school, government leaders, members of the Assembly, persons trained in law, and judges, in an effort to help them better understand the constitution and take it more seriously.

Specific reference was also made in the secretary-general's report to officials of existing administrative structures, and in particular *police, judges, prosecutors, and civil servants.*[19] The Component's strategy was to make officials aware of the obligations the parties had accepted in the peace process and their specific responsibilities as public servants. The second objective was to prepare them for a more responsible and accountable public service under the government to be created following the adoption of the constitution. The strategy was implemented by provincial and Phnom Penh staff of the Component rather than through the Trust Fund. Two police trainers were added to the staff, as was one person experienced in working with civil servants.

With respect to *judges and prosecutors*, the Component worked with UNTAC's Civil Administration Component on joint training activities following the adoption, in September 1992, of the Provisions Relating to the Judiciary and Criminal Law and Procedure Applicable in Cambodia during the Transitional Period (Transitional Provisions). Component staff took part as instructors in courses held for the judges and prosecutors and developed a special series of judicial training activities. In July 1993 a three-week, all-day program on the judicial functions and independence of the judiciary was organized by the Centre for the Independence of Judges and Lawyers of the International Commission of Jurists, supported by the Trust Fund. The learners were judges who had been or were likely to be appointed to the Court of Appeals and the Supreme Court.

Complementing the training of judges was the preparation of persons to represent the accused in court. The near total elimination of all lawyers during the 1975–78 period and thirteen years of one-party rule from 1979 to 1992 left Cambodia without anything resembling a bar association. No private attorneys or public defenders had practiced in the country in any capacity since 1975. The Transitional Provisions guaranteed the right to legal assistance for any persons accused of a crime or a misdemeanor. Because of the dearth of attorneys, the Transitional Provisions stipulated that anyone with a secondary school diploma, or a family member of the accused, regardless of level of education, may represent the accused in court. In order to provide a minimal level of competency for these potential "defenders," the Defenders Training Program was created, which has continued as a project of the International Human Rights Law Group

Civil servants participated in the two-week courses run by the mobile teams. Many were employed by the local administration without being party members and, in fact, were sympathetic to indigenous human rights NGOs, although they did not reveal this fact to their employers. Separate and specialized courses were developed for the *police*, who were surprisingly receptive to the training. Interactive and student-centered teaching methods worked well with this group. Of course, police training can only have an impact when conducted over the long term where there is the political will and the institutional infrastructure to sustain a professional police accountable to elected representatives.

The experience of human rights education for public officials in Cambodia suggests three considerations of more general relevance. The first is that local authorities are likely to accept training of their officials only if it is handled by international officials. Trainers should be UN staff, even if on temporary status. Second, civil servants relate human rights to their professional work when there is an official code of professional conduct. Of course, the UN *Code of Conduct for Law Enforcement Officials* is the appropriate reference for police training. Other codes should be used for other categories of public officials, such as *The Basic Principles on the Independence of the Judiciary* and similar texts for prosecutors and the legal profession. Third, especially in societies that have undergone years of civil war and political repression, human rights education during the presence of a UN mission can only be the first step in a much longer process of systematic training. Therefore, human rights education should seek, during the mission, support for the planning and financing of training institutes, in particular a judicial training institute and a civilian police academy.

A common feature of human rights training in both the civil society and among public officials was a hunger for knowledge about human rights. Past experience with violent conflict and a genuine conviction that the peace building will bring about a more just society undoubtedly contributed to this enthusiasm. Moreover, a clear mandate and a minimal amount of deference contributed to the ready acceptance of major human rights education initiatives by local officials. These conditions, which are likely to exist in other peace-building operations, suggest that those in charge of implementing human rights education should act rapidly and develop ambitious projects that take full advantage of the opening provided by the existing administrative structures.

In developing a strategy for human rights information, the Component's task was to develop a culturally relevant human rights information campaign using all possible media. Cultural relevancy meant that the message to be disseminated would be consonant with concepts and principles of Cambodian society today. These concepts and principles were found in the Buddhist religion, which provides a spiritual basis for human rights action. The Component, in close collaboration with the TV and Graphic Design units of UNTAC's Information and Education Division, developed a human rights information campaign on two pillars, printed materials and audiovisual media.

As regards *print media*, Khmer artists were used to develop a logo representing a Cambodian landscape with the sunlight of human rights illuminating all aspects of Cambodian life in peace. It was used on T-shirts, posters, and book covers, such as the cover of a special Khmer edition of the Universal Declaration of Human Rights.

The production and distribution of printed material served three purposes. Several items were used for teaching, such as the four hundred thousand training leaflets. The compilation of Khmer translations of official UN texts, a four hundred-page book of which 100,000 copies were distributed, served as legal reference for NGOs, defenders, and public officials. Most of the materials were aimed at creating a positive image of the expression "human rights" in Khmer and relating it to the peace process, including 500,000 basic leaflets, 200,000 stickers, 100,000 copies of the Universal Declaration, 100,000 balloons, and 82,000 posters. Specifically, the message of these materials was that peace in Cambodia must be built on respect for human rights.

The strategy for *broadcast media* covered both television and radio, which are particularly important in light of the low level of education and literacy in Cambodia. The human rights "message" was simplified as much as possible and made attractive by using symbols, stories, and popular actors. The dissemination of audiovisual materials was done through all existing channels. Video and audiocassettes were offered to all Cambodian broadcast authorities as well as those outside Cambodia with Khmer programs directed at Cambodia. In addition, five hundred cassettes with a human rights video were distributed through district electoral supervisors, provincial human rights officers, and indigenous human rights groups. Feedback from these circles indicates that frequent showings were organized even in the remotest areas. UNTAC's radio and television production units ran into numerous delays but eventually had considerable reach. Radio UNTAC, for example, began in October 1992, producing only one thirty-minute program of "news" (i.e., excerpts from the UN spokesman's daily briefing), but by election time in May 1993 managed to broadcast fifteen hours a day for seven days a week.[20] Remote areas were reached by twice-daily transmission from Voice of America from Bangkok and by distribution by the Electoral Component in the provinces of a hundred copies of each Radio UNTAC program.

The presence of a peace-building mission generates high expectations among the general population, virtually guaranteeing enthusiastic participation in special events organized for them. International Human Rights Day offers an ideal opportunity for massive public participation, as was the case on December 10, 1992, when the Component organized celebrations throughout Cambodia, with songs, drama productions, speeches by human rights organizations, and distribution of Khmer-language banners, stickers, posters, leaflets, and the brochure containing the Universal Declaration. A poster contest was organized for children under fifteen on "What human rights means to me," resulting in ten thousand posters, the best of which were published, along with selected texts in English and Khmer on children's rights, in a book called *A Dream of Peace.* The role of culture is essential to transmission of knowledge and understanding, and traditional means of cultural expression should be a part of a human rights education strategy. UNTAC, with UNESCO, produced a series of traditional musical performances, a comic book, and a series of posters.

The impact of informal training activities and of the mass distribution of printed materials and of television, video, and radio productions has not been tested scientifically. UNTAC estimated that approximately 120,000 people directly benefited from education and training and that the figure for mass communication, considering the population of more than 9 million, the wide availability of radios, the area covered by transmission, and the dissemination of cassettes of the programs, is probably several million. There are many signs that the basic message that people in Cambodia have certain rights that must be respected by all has penetrated. One year after UNTAC's departure, observers in Cambodia note that the concept and the primacy of human rights have become part of the public discourse in Cambodia to a degree previously unknown.

Conclusions: Lessons Learned

The lessons of approximately one year of implementing a program of human rights education, training, and information in Cambodia are relevant more generally to human rights education as a component of peace building. These lessons concern primarily: (a) the definition of target groups; (b) the relationship between human rights as taught and practical realities of daily life; (c) relations with the existing administrative structures; (d) methods of teaching; (e) administration of extrabudgetary funds for educational projects; and (f) long-term impact of education and training.

The strategy described above proved to be successful insofar as the principal elements of Cambodian society were identified and constituted the major transmitters of knowledge and understanding. What is important to consider in developing strategies for other contexts is to persevere whenever a key target group has been identified but program actions have been difficult to implement. For example, it was not until fairly late in the mandate of UNTAC that the Component found appropriate implementing agencies to bring human rights education to health professionals and the Buddhist clergy on a significant scale. Had this not been done, there would have been major gaps in the program.

Teaching, especially at the beginning of UNTAC's human rights program, tended to describe the relevance of Buddhist principles and then explain the content of the Universal Declaration and the International Covenants. Students' questions led the instructors to realize that effective education must be linked to the lives of the learners. Moreover, the brevity of the courses meant that this newly acquired knowledge had little chance of being consolidated and transformed into appropriate actions to protect and exercise those rights. Real case studies of violations, for example, have a greater impact than abstract examples. The Women's Training Project, in which training was based on women using drawings and drama to bring out aspects of their daily lives, was the prototype of this approach. The defenders' course is another example of an educational activity that is effective when the students are exposed to real courtroom situations.

The local authorities manifested a general willingness not to interfere with practically any educational plans of the Component. The Component was perhaps not fully prepared for such openness, and similar operations should be prepared to move massively into intensive educational activity. In practice, the opportunities were limited by the availability of staff and funds. Had these two matters been resolved earlier, greater advantage could have been taken of this openness.

There is no doubt that this Component's program and other similar ones conducted by the Cambodian human rights associations were successful in that they introduced large numbers of people for the first time to basic human rights concepts. Support for these groups and retraining of their trainers are essential to the long-term effectiveness of their efforts. The use of mobile teams is an effective mechanism for mass education at a basic level, but they did not have a systematic inbuilt mechanism for ensuring that the critical follow-up work with course participants would be carried on. Video should be used more frequently, especially in villages, where literacy is low. The most important lesson regarding teaching methods is that, even in a society like Cambodia where people, especially women, are not generally demonstrative, interactive methods work best. This requires more preparation by the teachers, but the results are worth it.

The availability of resources through the Trust Fund was a vital element in the effectiveness of the program. It would have been considerably more effective if funds had been available sooner and if the administrative procedures were not as heavy as they were. The availability of such a fund at the beginning would have made a considerable difference.

Finally, human rights education, like all other aspects of peace building, is primarily a means of laying long-term foundations for humane governance. The concept of democratic empowerment is helpful as a criterion for conceiving and implementing human rights education projects. This concept is based on a concern for the degree to which the beneficiaries of the project acquire knowledge and skills they can use to participate effectively in decisions affecting their lives. Democratic empowerment of indigenous human rights associations requires the constant improvement of their educational programs and protection from harassment and abuse by the authorities. Democratic empowerment of the new government requires assistance in the preparation of key legislation and development and strengthening of national institutions. This has been the direction of the successor to the Component, the Phnom Penh Office of the UN Centre for Human Rights.[21] In sum, human rights education was tested as part of United Nations peace building in Cambodia on a scale that was unprecedented. Many of the lessons of that experience can be applied elsewhere, if the political will exists to make use of the methods developed by UNTAC in Cambodia and to adapt approaches identified elsewhere in this book to the harsh realities of societies in transition from civil war and political repression to democracy and the rule of law.

Notes

1. See Philip Alston, "The Security Council and Human Rights: Lessons to Be Learned from the Iraq-Kuwait Crisis and Its Aftermath," *Australian Year Book of International Law* 13 (1992): 107–76.

2. UN General Assembly, Report of the Secretary-General on the Work of the Organization, *An Agenda for Peace: Preventive Diplomacy, Peacemaking and Peace-Keeping*, UN Doc. A/47/277/S/24111 (June 17, 1992), 32.

3. Ibid., 33–34.

4. According to the Paris Agreement on a Comprehensive Political Settlement of the Cambodia Conflict, the transitional period extended from the signing of the agreement (October 23, 1991) to the transfer of authority from the Constituent Assembly to the new government (September 24, 1993).

5. Report of the Secretary-General on Cambodia, UN Doc. S/23613, para. 12. This document is the principal source, after the text of the Paris Agreements, of UNTAC's mandate.

6. UNESCO, *Inter-Sectoral Basic Needs Assessment Mission to Cambodia, 15 January–8 February 1991*, Report, Bangkok (February 1991), 10.

7. Part of the explanation for the intense interest of university students in human rights is the brutal repression of student demonstrations in 1991, shortly before the arrival of UNTAC.

8. Sometimes a distinction is made between "informal" and "nonformal" education. For simplicity, I use "informal" for all types of learning that takes place outside the official schools and universities.

9. Report of the Secretary-General, S/23613, para. 13.

10. David Hawk, "The Photographic Record," in *Cambodia 1975–1978: Rendezvous with Death*, ed. Karl D. Jackson (Princeton: Princeton University Press, 1989), 212.

11. Ibid.

12. Eva Mysliwiec, *Punishing the Poor: The International Isolation of Kampuchea* (Oxford: Oxfam, 1988) 47.

13. Maha Ghosananda, *Step by Step* (Berkeley, Calif.: Parallax Press, 1992), 70–71.

14. Robert Traer, *Faith in Human Rights: Support in Religious Traditions for a Global Struggle* (Washington, D.C.: Georgetown University Press, 1991), 219.

15. Report of the Special Representative of the Secretary-General, Mr. Michael Kirby (Australia), on the Situation of Human Rights in Cambodia, Submitted in Accordance with Commission resolution 1993/6, UN Doc. E/CN.4/1994/73 (February 24, 1994), para. 159, p. 41.

16. See Bala Chandran, "Cambodia-Media: Free Press Blurs as Editor Goes to Jail," Inter Press Service, July 27, 1994; Derek Francis, "Noun Pledges to Revive Morning News," *Phnom Penh Post*, July 29–August 11, 1994, p. 15.

17. Report of the Secretary-General, S/23613, para. 13.

18. Report of the Special Representative, para.165, p. 42.

19. Report of the Secretary-General, para. 6.

20. Zhou Mei, *Radio UNTAC of Cambodia: Winning Ears, Hearts and Minds* (Bangkok: White Lotus, 1994), 28.

21. Report of the Secretary-General, *Situation of Human Rights in Cambodia*, UN Doc. A/49/635/Add. 1 (November 3, 1994), paras. 10–33, pp. 4–10.

Chapter 4
Human Rights Education as a Strategy for Development

Clarence Dias

It is commonly accepted that a vicious cycle of poverty and powerlessness breed grave, continuing, and widespread human rights violations. Development can help break this vicious cycle because it is supposed to help alleviate (and ultimately eliminate) poverty. Moreover, human resource development enables greater participation, especially by the marginalized and excluded sectors of society. It is not surprising, therefore, that development is vital to eliminating the structural causes of human rights denials, violations, and abuses.

Nevertheless, increasingly, development as currently practiced has itself become a significant cause of human rights violations. A brief review of development practices in Asia reveals why this is so.

Human Rights Education and Development: A Cycle of Empowerment

All too often, development policies, programs, and projects in Asia involve

profligate resource exploitation and consumption which convert hitherto renewable resources into nonrenewable resources;

expropriation of the survival resources of the poor and of the public commons, such as communal forests and pasturelands;

chemically intensive agriculture creating problems of soil and water destruction and, at times, poisoning of the food chain;

accelerated industrialization through which hazardous technologies, products, and wastes are exported in the name of development;

tourism development projects such as golf courses and five-star hotels which displace communities and drain scarce resources such as water; promotion of tourism has also led to an alarming rise in prostitution, including child prostitution;

imposition of risks, burdens, and often forced resettlement on powerless and vulnerable groups and communities;

mega-development projects creating serious national indebtedness which, in turn, prompts the adoption of structural adjustment programs, historically leading in several instances to food and job riots.

We may call these the symptoms of "perverse development." Even as such perverse development has been increasing worldwide, the past decade has witnessed a remarkable achievement by the international community. Development has been redefined and given a normative framework drawn from the field of internationally defined human rights. The very objective of development has been reoriented toward the realization of human rights and not economic growth alone. The economic growth generated by development must be directed toward the progressive realization of *all* human rights of *all*.

The United Nations Declaration on the Human Right to Development unequivocally asserts that development is an inalienable human right, that the human person is both the central subject of development and the beneficiary of the right to development, and that international human rights must be seen as essential, interdependent ends and means of development. But long before the Declaration on the Right to Development, the UN Charter itself reiterated that a fundamental purpose of the United Nations is to promote social progress and development and to promote universal respect for human rights and fundamental freedoms (Article 55 and 1(3)–(4)). By joining these twin objects together in a single article and obligating member states to promote them (Article 56), the Charter stresses the complementary relationship between human rights and development. Various international human rights instruments such as the Covenant on Economic, Social and Cultural Rights, the Covenant on Civil and Political Rights, the Convention on the Elimination of all Forms of Discrimination against Women, and a number of International Labor Organization conventions all reiterate the realization of human rights in and through development.

In short, human rights provide the rationale for development, the normative framework for development, and criteria by which those who undertake development can be held accountable. Given this premise, human rights education thus becomes extremely important in ensuring that genuine development takes place. Such development in turn fosters empowerment and the realization of human rights. Hence the vicious cycle of poverty and powerlessness can be replaced by a cycle of empowerment.[1]

Human Rights Education to Foster Development That Protects and Promotes Human Rights

Human rights education can influence development in several ways. First, it can help the more effective *monitoring* of existing development activities in terms of their human rights impacts. Thus a halt can be called to illegitimate and perverse development which violates rather than promotes human rights. Such development can be redesigned to limit the human, social, and environmental damage caused. For example, in the Narmada dam project in India, redesign of the project to reduce its height, and thereby lessen the area submerged and the number of people displaced, has been presented to the governments involved for their serious reconsideration.

Second, human rights education is vital to the struggles for *justice* for development victims. Human rights education can help the public rally behind such victims in their arduous struggle for rehabilitation, redress, and justice. For example, the ten-year struggle of the Bhopal victims for justice has been successful in changing the perceptions of the general public in India of the Bhopal chemical spill tragedy. At first, the world's worst industrial disaster was perceived as an unfortunate accident. But today it is being clearly recognized that Bhopal also represents a case of mass and grave human rights violations as well.

Third, human rights education can *promote* understanding of the rationale of development (as the betterment of the human condition). This in turn can help catalyze people-initiated development. For example, fishing communities around Laguna Lake in the Philippines were made aware of the proposed impact of drastically reducing the water level, all resulting from the Calaba zone project as a result of "mining" the waters of the lake for industrial activities. Local people are successfully challenging the project and suggesting alternative development uses of the lake emphasizing its aquatic resources.

Fourth, human rights education can help secure more effective *participation* in all stages of development processes: of project design, initiation, management, monitoring, evaluation, and redesign. For example, NGOs in Bangladesh are developing training programs to enable those communities first to be affected by Project Flood to participate in the environmental impact assessment hearings to be conducted in connection with that project.

Fifth, human rights education can help secure the *accountability* of development actors with respect to projects, policies, and budgets and to acts of both commission and omission. For example, the ARUN Concerned Group, a coalition of NGOs in Nepal opposing the ARUN project to develop major hydroelectric dams to use the waters flowing down the Himalayas, are campaigning around issues relating to the cost of the project. The ARUN Concerned Group points out that the amount to be raised by the loan for the project equals the entire budget of the government of Nepal for one year.

Figure 4.1. Nepali citizens gather around a Sherpa who has delivered cheese to be weighed and inspected at the dairy plant at Kathmandu. UNHURID used these occasions to inform people of the "National NGO Workshop and Children's Seminar." (UNPHOTO PB/mh)

Nepal's Experiment in Education on the Rights of the Child
Gopal Siwakoti

Human rights education in pursuit of development objectives has been widely used in Asia, especially among transitional democracies in the region. The region is sometimes regarded as more complex than others in dealing with human rights issues because of its historical, political, religious, and cultural diversity. Nepal, a landlocked Himalayan kingdom situated between China on the north and India on the south, is a unique country where all political ideologies (monarchical, liberal, and communist) work together under the parliamentary democratic system established in the Nepali Constitution of 1990.

Before 1990, Nepal operated as an absolute monarchy which banned political parties, but today one can find human rights education and training activities sponsored by NGOs among all sectors and in many parts of Nepal. This came about, in part, because human rights groups supplied forums in the predemocratic struggle of Nepal to press demands for the restoration of multiparty democracy. As soon as elected government came to power under the new constitution, officials realized that human rights education organized by NGOs supplied a mechanism for the consolidation of democracy and for enlisting popular participation in pursuit of development objectives. Nonformal education on the rights of the child supplies an example that may be of interest beyond our Himalayan boundaries.

After the success of the Nepali democracy movement in 1990, the interim government ratified the Convention on the Rights of the Child (CRC), along with those on Torture and on Women and the International Covenants. Of course, these treaties cover a wide range of human rights and oblige states to undertake effective legislative, judicial, administrative, and other measures of implementation.

For example, Article 42 of the Convention on the Rights of the Child says: "States Parties undertake to make the principles and provisions of the Convention widely known, by appropriate and active means, to adults and children alike."[1] With this and other treaty duties in view, and mindful of challenges facing newly emerging democracies, in 1991 NGOs organized a conference in Kathmandu on "Human Rights Law-Making and Transition to Democracy."[2]

---

1. Convention on the Rights of the Child.
2. *First International Conference on Human Rights Law-Making and Transition to Democracy*, International Institute for Human Rights, Environment and Development (INHURED International) (1992), P.O. Box 2125 Putalisadak, Kathmandu, Nepal. In addition to indigenous NGO representatives, experts attended from many international groups, including Amnesty International, Human Rights Advocates, Human Rights Watch, the International Human Rights Law Group, SOS Torture, and the Congressional Human Rights Foundation.

Among the many follow-up meetings spawned by this conference was a national-level workshop on children which focused on the provisions of the CRC and prospects for national implementation measures. It quickly became evident that this kind of NGO activity had multiplier effects involving concerned government officials facing policy planning and budgeting responsibilities; the media, newly sensitized to issues relating to Nepali children; and Nepali society generally. Moreover, the program eventually became more participatory and result-oriented as Nepal faced up to its treaty-reporting duties under the Convention on the Rights of the Child. Article 44 of the Convention says: "States Parties undertake to submit to the [United Nations] Committee [on the Rights of the Child], through the Secretary General of the United Nations, reports on the measures they have adopted which give effect to the rights recognized herein and on the progress made on the enjoyment of those rights . . . within two years of the entry into force of the Convention." This treaty obligation supplied the pretext for organizing workshops and programs of education on the rights of the child, among other things, to lobby for implementation measures and to give input to the government report to be submitted to the UN Committee on the Rights of the Child. For example, in 1992 the International Institute for Human Rights, Environment and Development (INHURED International) in Kathmandu, along with UNICEF, Redd Barna/Norway, and many Nepali NGOs, participated in a workshop on the Children's Convention. It supplied educational opportunities to inform policymakers, to prompt questions from members of the media, and to raise the consciousness of the general public regarding children's issues. Moreover, it was replicated in similar workshops in five administrative regions of the country, leading to such meetings in all seventy-five districts.

Indeed, children also participated in the National Seminar of NGOs, after which they went back to their communities to share their learning and return to the Capitol with friends. The resulting Children's Seminar discussed the status of children and their responsibilities as well as the duties of parents, the community, local government bodies, and political parties.

As an outcome of this process, the government's National Planning Commission, with responsibility to prepare Nepal's treaty report, did so by forming a joint committee with NGO representation from Child Watch and the children representatives of the Child Awareness Group. Thus the National NGO Workshop and the Children's Seminar, as well as various declarations and plans of action developed in their wake, became the basis for NGO input in the national report to the United Nations. The NGO-led process of education on the rights of the child has certainly been as important as the resulting report.

This remarkable achievement involving the CRC has supplied Nepali NGOs with a model. They now use similar methods and organize educational modules in preparation for the monitoring of other international human rights instruments requiring state reports. In this process the nonformal educational activities directed toward treaty obligations take on structure and clear focus as NGOs consider the development of alternative reports (vis-à-vis government reports) under other human rights instruments. Relevant are the Convention on Civil and Political Rights and its Optional Protocol and the Convention on Economic, Social and Cultural Rights, especially as reporting obligations bear on issues of importance in Nepal including racial discrimination and untouchability, torture, and discrimination against women.

In a transitional democracy, Nepali experience shows that human rights NGOs can effectively use nonformal educational techniques to make lawmakers, policy analysts, government officials, and the public familiar with international commitments to human rights and responsibilities for effective domestic implementation. In doing so, Nepali NGOs have pursued three educational objectives: (1) to build up confidence in the existing political process by which all political forces can work together toward a common goal; (2) to promote the achievement of basic needs for all through recognition of the right to development; and (3) to develop a socioeconomic, political, and cultural infrastructure for making hard-won democracy sustainable.

Finally, human rights educational seminars and workshops, held in conjunction with upcoming treaty reporting obligations of States Parties, can very practically help to implement the right to development through monitoring and action. The seminars alert the government to popularly perceived obstacles to development by highlighting problems, for example, affecting the rights of the child, particularly regarding exploitation of child labor, child prostitution and trafficking, and denial of health care and education. All of this is consistent with steps called for in the Declaration on the Right to Development adopted by the UN General Assembly in 1986. Article 6 of the Declaration says that "States should take steps to eliminate obstacles to development resulting from failure to observe civil and political rights as well as economic, social and cultural rights."

Sixth, human rights education can help *remedy* existing defects of development policies, projects, and practices. It can help fight practices of racial and gender discrimination in development. It can help build pressure for remedying historic neglect, for example, of indigenous peoples or ethnic minority groups in development. It can help challenge skewed development priorities, for example, showpiece cardiac centers that were constructed at great expense in the Philippines by President Marcos while infant health and mortality issues and the provision of basic health care in the rural areas were ignored.

In sum, human rights education about development has much to offer, both for the promotion and progressive realization of human rights and for the protection and prevention of human rights abuses in the process of development.

Human Rights Education About Development

The United Nations World Conference on Human Rights in 1993 produced some important results. The resulting Vienna Declaration and Programme of Action provide an ideal international impetus for sustained human rights education about development. The Vienna Declaration "reaffirms" in emphatic terms the concept of the "Human Right to Development." It calls for "implementation of the right" at the "national level" (Article 5). It declares that "democracy, development and respect for human rights are mutually interdependent and reinforcing" (Article 8). Democracy, in this context, means empowerment of people to "full participation" in all transactions that affect "their lives." It links the concept of "sustainability" to human rights in development (Article 1). It emphasizes the "people-centered" goal (Article 25) and "participation by the poorest people in decision making" which affects their community. It emphasizes the role of nongovernmental organizations (NGOs) in "implementation" of "the right to development (Article 73). It calls upon the UN development agencies "to also assess the impact of their policies and programmes on the enjoyment of human rights" for the purpose of assessing protection of those rights (Section II, para. 2).

Moreover, human rights education clearly figures prominently in the Vienna Programme of Action. But what does human rights education about development encompass? There are both conceptual and practical aspects.

The Conceptual Level

In terms of sorting out the ideas connected to human rights education about development, three important propositions need to be the subject of focus.

1. *The right to development is itself a human right.* The Universal Declaration of Human Rights declares that "Everyone is entitled to a social and international order in which the rights and freedoms set forth in this Declaration may be realized" (Article 28). Development is not a matter of benign charity or of administrative discretion. It

is an obligation cast upon all member states, developed and developing alike. For the developed states, the obligation takes the form of a pledge, unfortunately not often honored, to contribute one percent of the country's gross domestic product to development assistance. But despite the failure to meet this obligation, the existence of the human right to development is no longer in question. Such a right has been reaffirmed in the United Nations Covenant on Economic, Social and Cultural Rights and a number of other international human rights instruments. The contours and content of the right to development have been elaborated in the UN General Assembly Declaration on the Right to Development.

Human rights education must carefully draw upon the various provisions of the UN declarations and international human rights instruments that have established development as a human right. This is essential to enable those presently denied development to assert their right to development successfully.

2. *Human rights provide both the rationale for development as well as criteria for securing the accountability of development actors.* Here again, human rights education must draw upon UN declarations and international human rights instruments which clearly establish that "international human rights are essential and interdependent ends and means of development" and that participation by the poorest people" in the development process is an "inalienable human right."[2] This is essential if people are successfully to press for equitable distribution of the benefits and burdens of development. Otherwise development tends to degenerate into the aggrandizement and self-perpetuation of an elite and privileged few.

3. *All human rights must be protected in the process of development.* Various international human rights instruments and the UN Declaration on the Human Right to Development recognize and reiterate several human rights that must be respected, protected, and promoted. *All these* human rights, be they economic, social, cultural, civil, or political, *must* be respected in the process of development. The argument is advanced by several authoritarian governments that there needs to be a trade-off between development and human rights: "development now, human rights later."[3] Such an argument has been unequivocally rejected in international human rights law. Human rights education on this issue can help ensure against development and human rights for the rich only and neither bread nor freedom for the poor and marginalized. In order to achieve this, a careful identification of such rights in the development process will need to be made and human rights education materials developed around each such right. These rights include freedom of information and transparency, non-discrimination, participation, accountability, and the right to redress if such rights are denied or violated.

The Practical Level

At a practical level, human rights education could focus on at least two initial entry points. These are human rights impacts of specific categories of development projects upon specific categories of victims, and human social and environmental impact assessment.

With regard to the first point, specific development projects (euphemistically described by the World Bank as "risk-prone") have inevitably produced development victims (once again euphemistically described by the World Bank as "project-affected people"). Human rights education materials need to be developed, through a participatory methodology involving development victims (e.g., women, children, indigenous peoples) about the specific human rights impacts of particular development projects (e.g., tourism development, mining, mega-dam building).

Regarding the need for human, social, and environmental impact assessment, the World Bank and several bilateral development agencies as well have made EIA (environmental impact assessment) an essential first step in their development project cycle. EIA serves an important dual function. First, it enables preventive action to be taken (through project redesign) to minimize the adverse environmental impacts of a proposed development project. Second, it becomes a mechanism for participation whereby those likely to be affected by a proposed development project can intervene to secure a more equitable distribution of the benefits and burdens of such a project. In recent years, development agencies are increasingly recognizing the need to move from environmental impact assessment to human rights impact assessment as well.

Human rights education materials need to be prepared detailing the policies and procedures of development agencies in respect of EIA. Such material will facilitate increased participation by NGOs and affected communities and groups in environmental impact assessment hearings on specific projects. Often such EIA hearings, without such NGO and community participation, tend to be tokenistic and formal. Through the impact assessment process, project-affected people can intervene preventively and press for project redesign or abandonment as appropriate.

Human Rights Education About Development: The Need for Active and Participatory Methodologies

Conventional human rights education methodologies do have a role to play in human rights education about development. There are mundane tasks that need to be undertaken. A whole host of international treaties, declarations, and resolutions of international institutions and conferences, national constitutions and law, and development agency policy statements and operational directives need to be carefully mined as a resource for rights assertion. These dry, legal statements articulating or elaborating specific rights need to be simplified and translated from legalese to a more user-friendly language. Moreover, these rights need to be rearranged and clustered so as to be meaningful to real-life people in real-life situations. Such a task, for example, is being undertaken presently by the International Center for Law in Development, where work is in progress on a Draft Charter to Secure Human Rights in Development Processes.

Such a charter is far from enough, and there is a clear need to move to more active and participatory methodologies. As a next step, we plan to engage in a series of dialogues, built around the Draft Charter, with project-affected people and the NGOs working with them. The Draft Charter will be used as a device for awareness raising about human rights in development. The dialogue will also undertake an assessment of the strengths and limitations of existing human rights norms and standards and remedies in light of the specific realities experienced by project-affected peoples. The Draft Charter will undergo constant revision and redesign as its content is invoked by grassroots communities in specific advocacy or action campaigns for the assertion, promotion, or protection of their human rights. The Draft Charter will also undergo constant revision by way of further elaboration of component rights responsive to the specific development realities of project-affected peoples.

The importance of interactive, participatory processes in human rights education can hardly be overstressed. Four examples will serve to show the significance of pedagogy for human rights about development and for participation as a form of education involving human rights.

(1) Responding to an awareness-raising effort about the UN Declaration on the Right to Development, Maori groups successfully raised claims in New Zealand courts based upon the right to development. The judgment of the court, reinterpreting the Treaty of Waitangi to uphold Maori claims to ancestral land, in turn, has become an invaluable precedent for the incorporation of the human right to development into national law.

(2) Several Asia-Pacific NGOs meeting in Fiji decided to launch a "dirty dozen" campaign singling out the twelve "dirtiest" development projects in the Asia-Pacific region. The projects would be chosen on the basis of their blatant disregard of human rights and environmental standards.

(3) At its Houston meeting, TOES (The Other Economic Summit) adopted a "people's conditionalities" campaign. It involves the formulation and assertion of people's conditionalities with respect to specific, typical categories of development projects (e.g., large dam and infrastructure building, tourism development, export-processing zones, industrial zones, aquaculture, reforestation by multinational corporations). The conditionalities, which would be invoked as preconditions for future projects, are drawn from international human rights standards and seek to protect the human rights of people affected by risk-prone development projects. The protective conditionalities are to be based upon the experiences of risks and harms actually experienced by project-affected peoples in past or existing development projects.

(4) Recently several Philippine NGOs, working with more than eighty organizations of subsistence fisherfolk around the country, catalyzed their communities into a process of drafting a fisheries code for the Philippines. At the end of a year-long process, the organizations of subsistence fisherfolk (assisted by legal resource NGOs) drafted a comprehensive model fisheries code for the country. Over the last two years they have been engaged in a process of lobbying their congresspersons and senators

to adopt the code. As a result, their bill is pending in the national legislature and the fisherfolk are continuing to participate, vigorously, in the political process, setting for themselves the goal of campaigning until their bill becomes a law. This has entailed negotiating political compromises, redrafting provisions of the code, and forging new political coalitions and alliances. In this example, the symbiotic interaction between participation and empowerment is quite evident. As participation led to empowerment, the grassroots organizations became confident and sought to participate at ever more complex levels; this in turn led to further empowerment.

Human Rights Education About Development:
A Matter of Urgent Priority

There is, at present, an urgent need for human rights education about development because forces and events are combining to make development, as practiced, a major cause of serious and mass human rights violations. Accelerated zonal industrialization (such as the Eastern Seaboard Project in Thailand and the Calabarzon Project in the Philippines) has become the linchpin of development strategies for many Asian countries. But this is happening at a time when stringent environmental and health and safety standards adopted in the developed countries are pushing multinational corporations offshore. Industrialization is thus becoming a mechanism for the dumping of hazardous technologies, substances, products and wastes in the countries of the developing world—all this, too, in the name of development!

Economic recession in the developed countries has prompted their governments to relax their standards (and accountability controls) with respect to the overseas acts of their corporations to ensure that such corporations can maintain their international competitive edge. The adoption of economic liberalization and privatization policies by developing country governments, as core elements of structural adjustment programs, has been creating fresh human rights problems, especially for the poorer sections of society. This has also been raising the need for more effective accountability mechanisms with respect to the human rights impact of the private corporate sector.

Much has been said about the benefits of the global communications revolution, but in developing countries it is spreading the cancer of conspicuous consumption—a Coca Cola culture. People are being taught that development is about *having* more and more rather than about *being* more. In such an overconsumption scenario, ironically, all too often more proves to be less (when overconsumption of resources leads to their depletion and exhaustion), and less may well prove to be more (especially from perspectives of intergenerational equity and justice).

The oft-proclaimed shift of development, not through aid but rather development through trade and investment, has serious environmental and human rights implications which are evident today, for example, in the newly and rapidly industrializing provinces of China. The new world order panacea of globalization, trade and economic liberalization, and privatization is converting development into a process of social Darwinism, producing hordes of development victims and development-displaced persons and growing numbers of marginalized peoples whose very rights of subsistence are being denied. Now, more than ever before, there is an urgent need for human rights education about development to break the vicious cycle of poverty and powerlessness and replace it with a much-needed cycle of empowerment. Only then can development help protect and promote that most cherished of all human rights—the right to be human (of which the right to be woman is, of course, an essential and integral part).

Notes

1. These concepts are also developed in Clarence J. Dias, *Development, Democracy and Human Rights: An Asian NGO Perspective* (New York: International Center for Law in Development, 1993).

2. United Nations Declaration on the Right to Development, and the Vienna Declaration and Programme of Action.

3. For a political and economic response to this view, see Robert E. Goodin, "The Development-Rights Trade-Off: Some Unwarranted Economic and Political Assumptions," *Universal Human Rights* [succeeded by *Human Rights Quarterly*] 1, no. 2 (1979): 31–42.

Chapter 5
Human Rights Education as Empowerment: Reflections on Pedagogy
Garth Meintjes

The idea of human rights education as empowerment may be approached from two very different perspectives. On the one hand, one could adopt a very general and abstract approach and focus upon the fact that in 1948 the UN General Assembly proclaimed the "Universal Declaration of Human Rights as a common standard of achievement for all peoples and all nations, to the end that every individual and every organ of society, keeping this Declaration constantly in mind, shall strive by teaching and education to promote respect for these rights and freedoms and by progressive measures, national and international to secure their universal and effective recognition and observance."[1]

On the other hand, one could adopt a very specific and personal approach and focus upon concrete and practical experiences in which the relevance and value of human rights can readily be demonstrated. For example, in 1989, the day after South Africa's last all-white parliamentary elections, I volunteered to join a group of black lawyers and students who were collecting sworn statements from the residents in a racially segregated township called Elsie's River. During the previous evening, the witnesses claimed, the police drove armored vehicles up and down every street and randomly fired tear gas into innocent people's homes. Apparently, with this show of force, the police were reasserting their power and letting off some of the steam that had accumulated during an election campaign in which their actions were heavily criticized.

As I approached one of the numerous state-constructed apartment complexes, I sensed a glare of hostility from above. I slowly looked up. On a balcony two floors above me, I saw a boy about fourteen years old. He stared menacingly at me, while his hands continued carefully to sharpen the ten-inch blade of a knife. Instantly my whole body froze as my mind desperately grasped for something to say, yet nothing seemed appropriate. None of the words I could think of could counter the power in his hands. In the end I said nothing. I knew that we were both trying to fight apartheid, but that we had chosen different means.

Half an hour later, after I had begun to take a statement from a family whose cramped apartment still reeked of tear gas, a crowd of angry students began to stone the passing vehicles at a nearby intersection. As I watched from a window, a police unit dressed in riot gear arrived within about ten minutes. A moment later, a new wave of tear gas canisters started to rain upon the crowd. But before the first canister even struck the ground, the crowd was gone.

Deprived of a physical encounter, the frustrated police began to drive slowly away from the intersection. And then, unexpectedly, they came upon two students approaching from the opposite direction. They abruptly stopped their vehicle, leaped out, and simply started to beat them. The horror of their cruelty and their inhumanity filled me with such contempt and anger that I could not bear to watch. I wanted to scream—to cry out—to demand that they stop! But again words escaped me.

Today when we think of human rights education as empowerment, and the ways in which it might be taught, it is important that we always keep both these perspectives in mind. For real empowerment can occur only if we succeed in integrating the knowledge and experiences of both.

With this in mind, this chapter offers some reflections on the central pedagogical issues underlying the idea of human rights education as empowerment.[2] The first part addresses the meaning and nature of empowerment, along with the following two primary considerations. First, human rights education directed toward the empowerment of participants is unique as a pedagogical objective and differs markedly from the goals of other areas of conventionally defined education. Second, human rights education designed to empower people at the grassroots level is sometimes viewed as threatening to elites and potentially antagonistic toward certain types of government institutions. The second part attempts to offer some tentative reflections on the following questions: (1) Given the unique objective of human rights education as empowerment, how can appropriate pedagogies be designed? (2) How can the optimum conditions for their success be created? (3) How can the efficacy and results of such human rights education be evaluated?

The Meaning and Nature of Empowerment

Empowerment

Meaning

"Empowerment is a process through which people and/or communities increase their control or mastery of their own lives and the decisions that affect their lives."[3] Although this definition by Seth Kreisberg admittedly still requires further elaboration and explanation, it should already be evident that the nature and dynamics of an empowering pedagogy will be dramatically different from the kind of teaching that Paulo Freire termed "banking" education.

In the banking concept of education, knowledge is a gift bestowed by those who consider themselves knowledgeable upon those whom they consider to know nothing. Projecting an absolute ignorance onto others, a characteristic of the ideology of oppression, negates education and knowledge as a process of inquiry. The teacher presents himself to his students as their necessary opposite; by considering their ignorance absolute, he justifies his own existence. The students, alienated like the slave in the Hegelian dialectic, accept their ignorance as justifying their teacher's existence—but unlike the slave, they never discover that they educate the teacher.[4]

The critical difference between empowerment and banking education is the psychological impact each is likely to have. To treat students simply as receptacles to be filled with useful ideas and information, is to deprive them of their critical consciousness and to deceive them into believing that knowledge is an object to be received rather than a continuous process of inquiry and reflection. Students who are empowered, however, become conscious of their own participation in the creation of knowledge and of their own critical ability to conceptualize and reconceptualize their experiences of reality.

Accordingly, human rights education as empowerment requires enabling each target group to begin the process of acquiring the knowledge and critical awareness it needs to understand and question oppressive patterns of social, political, and economic organization. It should be noted, however, that this dynamic process is only potentially liberating. Its eventual success will depend upon the ability of those who have been empowered to transcend the previously oppressive power relations. This will require the ability to envision, develop, and function within new nondominating patterns of organization in which the human dignity of everyone is protected and promoted.

For example, the teenaged boy I described in the above narrative was probably engaged in a very real and painful struggle for control over his life and the decisions that affect him. Unfortunately the kind of empowerment upon which he seemed forced to rely may not be very useful to him today. In fact, if he is still alive, he may well be part of a group now commonly referred to as South Africa's "lost generation." In other words, it is likely that he is still part of a group that remain "disempowered"* because they are unable to adjust and adapt to the functioning of a new social and political reality. For them, the internalized walls of apartheid are still very real.

Static Versus Dynamic Conceptions

The idea that teaching about human rights can be empowering obviously presupposes that one's target group is somehow in need of empowerment. Whether this

---

*Throughout this chapter I refer to those who are in positions of relative powerlessness as being "disempowered." By using the term *disempowered* I intend to emphasize that oppression is an institutional or structural position that is *externally* determined and imposed. To describe the oppressed as being "powerless" would only be further to deny or ignore our *inherent* power, worth, and dignity as human beings.

supposition is in fact correct depends largely on the context and the nature of one's conception of empowerment. In my view, it is necessary to distinguish between what I would call "static empowerment" on the one hand and "dynamic empowerment" on the other. As explained below, this distinction has a significant impact upon the pedagogical approaches and methods one may adopt.

The notion of static empowerment implies a fixed, rigid, and ahistorical conception focuses upon the present structural or institutional disparities of social, political, and economic power. By using such a conception of empowerment, one will be viewing the space-time[5] position of a potential target group without any reference to the dimension of time. In other words, one will be overlooking the significance of historical changes in the factors that determine social, political, and economic power. Under such a conception, human rights education as empowerment need only be directed at those who are presently viewed as being alienated, marginalized, silenced, or oppressed.

Moreover, those holding a static conception would tend to focus their emancipatory efforts on finding ways of making the existing, often hierarchical and undemocratic, institutions and structures more accessible. Such efforts might include: teaching the disempowered those particular social, political, or economic skills they presently lack; providing them with important or useful information about the functioning of the oppressive institutions under which they are living; and offering material or other assistance with which institutional access may be secured. In my view, such efforts can be more accurately described as paternalistic helping, or even as "assistencialism," rather than as real empowerment. And "the greatest danger of assistencialism is the violence of its anti-dialogue, which by imposing silence and passivity denies men conditions likely to develop or to 'open' their consciousness."[6]

Perhaps the most detrimental effect of a static conception of empowerment, however, is its tendency to exclude or ignore those who are presently empowered, particularly if they are also viewed as contributing to the present oppression. For example, it may be very easy for human rights educators to become partisan and to overlook the empowerment needs of the police officers described in the above narrative. The danger of this approach is that it may perpetuate marginalization by adopting the same "us and them" distinctions that it is seeking to overcome.

Therefore, instead of adopting such a fixed, rigid, and ahistorical conception, I believe that empowerment ought rather to be viewed dynamically. This means that one must recognize the importance of the dimension of time when determining the empowerment needs of a particular target group, given its position in the evolution of space-time, that is, its position in the overall context of its historical, social, political, and economic circumstances. To do so leads to the recognition that everyone may over time become either vulnerable to disempowerment or amenable to empowerment.

Absolute Versus Relative Conceptions

If viewed in absolute terms, the line between those who are empowered and those who are disempowered would likely be drawn rather arbitrarily, possibly resulting in an unfair and unnecessary exclusion of many who, although only partially disempowered, would potentially still benefit from empowerment education. Moreover, reliance upon absolute conceptions of empowerment and disempowerment may also cause one inadvertently to disempower further those who are at present only partially empowered.

Therefore, rather than adopting an arbitrary, absolute, or unqualified perspective, I believe it would be more reasonable and accurate to view disempowerment in relative terms as a variable position upon a continuum spanning the extremes of absolute power and complete oppression. In other words, by viewing disempowerment in relative terms, one is more likely to recognize that a particular target group can, to some degree, be simultaneously empowered and disempowered in relation to various other groups or individuals.

For example, I believe it is quite possible that the police officers described above are also, in spite of their Draconian powers, in need of empowerment education. Most of them were drawn from a social sector (class) in which few children ever progressed beyond the level of secondary education, and many did not even complete their final years at this level. Furthermore, judging from my own experience—my brother was a police officer—it is very likely that some of them may be having great difficulty with their social and family relationships. In my view, if human rights education as empowerment can be used to address not only political but also social problems, then it would be wrong to exclude a group such as this.

Two further implications of this relative conception are worth noting. First, it suggests that human rights educators must be sensitive to those aspects of the existing social, political, and economic institutions that have the potential to contribute to the further development and maintenance of a rights culture. And second, they should be careful not to overlook the extent to which a history of struggle against particular institutions may have given rise to a language and culture that already enshrines the ideals of human rights. For example, Kader Asmal recently noted this about the struggle against apartheid: "Commentators at home and overseas have not really grasped the extent to which the liberation movement, throughout its history, has used the language of rights as part of its vocabulary of protest and action."[7] And further: "This emphasis on universal values associated with human rights standards, the urgent need to replace apartheid structures . . . by democratic ones and active opposition to racism in all its forms . . . counterpose the basic values of human rights as understood in international law to the illegitimate doctrine of institutionalised racism."[8] It is, therefore, this combination of a dynamic and a relative conception of empowerment that will be relied upon throughout this chapter.

The Unique Pedagogy of Empowerment

Professional literature on the development of educational programs stresses that the first step in the planning of teaching and curricular activities requires the sorting out of ends, objectives, and means. As far as the goals or ends of human rights education are concerned, several formulations exist, not all of which necessarily entail empowerment. For example, a Council of Europe publication offers this list of goals which is nearly devoid of any but the most elliptical reference to empowerment as an end:

(i) Knowledge of the major 'signposts' in the historical development of human rights.

(ii) Knowledge of the range of contemporary declarations, conventions, and covenants.

(iii) Knowledge of some major infringements of human rights.

(iv) Understanding of the basic conceptions of human rights (including also discrimination, equality, etc.)

(v) Understanding the distinctions between political/legal and socio/economic rights.

(vi) Understanding the relationship between individual, group, and national rights.

(vii) Appreciation of one's own prejudices and the development of tolerance.

(viii) Appreciation of the rights of others.

(ix) Sympathy for those who are denied rights.

(x) Intellectual skills for collecting and analyzing information.

(ix) Action skills.[9]

The objectives associated with these goals are largely cognitive and attitudinal, although "action skills" may imply learning for behavioral change. In my view, groups concerned with human rights education may appropriately pursue a number of objectives through a variety of different means. These could include: (1) attempts to bring about *attitudinal changes* (e.g., teaching tolerance among the politically influential toward Ethiopian tribal groups not well represented in Ethiopia's government structures, or tolerance toward refugees among British and German "skinheads"); (2) dialogue and reflection exercises aimed at *value clarification* (e.g., critically exploring the negative implications of the common use of "manmade" language relating to gender references in formal writing as well as in everyday conversation); (3) learning and understanding the *substantive provisions* of the Universal Declaration and other international human rights instruments; (4) the promotion of *attitudes of solidarity* (e.g., African-American Studies programs that engender concern and respect for the peoples of Africa and their problems related to food distribution, health, and welfare); and (5) teaching programs and techniques directed toward the *empowerment* of participants (e.g., enabling people to define and meet their own needs). No doubt, this list of human rights educational objectives is not exhaustive.

In addition to the diverse goals and objectives specified for human rights education, the problem of analysis is compounded by virtue of the fact that the objectives and means used to attain them, such as those listed above, will differ in relation to the various target groups involved: for example, children in primary schools, adults in literacy programs, peasant farmers involved in subsistence agriculture, police and military units, government officials and bureaucrats, health professionals involved in programs of continuing education. Careful consideration needs to be given not only to the relative disparities in their respective levels of empowerment, but also to the important differences in format or context in which each group may have to be addressed.

As noted further below, it is also important to recognize that certain formats or contexts may have preexisting goals or characteristics that differ sharply or even conflict with the goals, objectives, and means of human rights education as empowerment. For example, in an empirical analysis of British secondary schools, Pat O'Shea notes that civic education designed to promote democratic values is presented with three different justifications: (1) most often as if political education were a form of cultural enrichment providing "civilizing influences on the citizen"; (2) sometimes such education is said "to improve the efficiency with which learning about society happens"; but (3) "more rarely the intention is empowerment, or the clearer articulation of participants rights."[10]

The danger here for human rights education is the possibility that, while the rhetoric of empowerment may gain increased acceptance, the ends and means will remain those of conventional education. It is for this reason that some may even wish to question the wisdom of attempting to integrate human rights education into the curriculum of any formal educational program. For example, Russell A. Butkus raises essentially similar questions regarding the merits of John Dewey's vision of democracy and education: "I am not certain to what extent justice education can be done with children and I am even less certain that authentic justice education can occur through institutionalized schooling."[11] And further: "He misunderstands the powerful negative influences that society exerts upon the school . . . he is unwilling or unable to recognize the deep and serious political/economic interests that underlie North American democracy and education."[12] This issue will be discussed further below.

The Threat of Empowerment

Empowerment objectives when effectively met may sometimes appear threatening to entrenched elites. Accordingly, human rights educators must bear the responsibility of foreseeing such consequences and developing the means to counteract them. However, the opposite may also be true in cases where the governing elites, either out of ignorance or sheer cunning, so enthusiastically endorse human rights education that the idea itself becomes discredited or questioned by the disempowered. The challenge, therefore, is to ensure that community-based programs enjoy widespread legitimacy without at the same time unwittingly exposing those who are beginning to assert or exercise their rights to any undue hazard or unnecessary risk of repression and regression. Nevertheless, to assess such risk, a certain amount of political realism may be necessary.

A sense of such realism, indeed the political grounding of Paulo Freire's innovative work, is well stated in Richard Shaull's "Foreword" to Freire's classic book *The Pedagogy of the Oppressed*: "There is no such thing as a neutral educational process. Education either functions as an instrument which is used to facilitate the integration of the younger generation into the logic of the present system and bring about conformity to it, or it becomes 'the practice of freedom,' the means by which men and women deal critically and creatively with reality and discover how to participate in the transformation of their world."[13]

Implicit in this passage are two important observations. First, it suggests that the threat of empowerment appears to be inversely proportionate to the degree to which a particular regime is willing or able to tolerate or even encourage unconventional ideas and thinking. Put differently, it is those regimes that are inflexible and static, and whose preservation is dependent upon the maintenance of the status quo, that are most likely to resist or repress the efforts of human rights education programs. Second, it is important to note that the claim that "no educational process can be neutral" should not be taken to mean that all education is or must be inevitably partisan. In other words, while it calls upon educators to recognize the political nature of all knowledge, it does not, and should not, require that they necessarily be committed either to a particular party or to a static set of ideas, values, or beliefs. Indeed, human rights educators should strive to do the very opposite when seeking to awaken each student's own critical consciousness. It is in this context that the distinction, suggested earlier, between a static and a dynamic conception of empowerment is once again of critical importance. For it is only by viewing knowledge as a dynamic and liberating process that a truly empowering pedagogy can be developed.

In my view, this distinction is implicit in the pedagogy of the late Christian Bay's approach to empowerment education. His book, *Strategies of Political Emancipation*, is substantially a call for "problem-posing education" based on Freire's goals and techniques. Bay argues that despite Freire's disclaimers, the first world can learn from the third world. As advanced technological societies tend to render citizens more passive and promote conformity, we all take on some aspects of disempowerment. Speaking, therefore, of the need for educational empowerment, Bay writes: "By 'political education' I mean liberating education that focuses on [present] political problems and on posing new political problems."[14] He relies here on Freire's notion of education aimed at confronting conventionally limited situations by posing questions about justice and about the possibility of transcending traditionally accepted patterns of domination and deprivation.

Bay proposes that emancipative education should aim at the implementation of human rights in practice and not just learning about human rights. And the implementation of human rights in practice rests not only on the government but also on each and every individual. To achieve this goal, human rights education requires that the teacher-student relationship evolve from a diagonal to a horizontal relationship, in which hierarchy is removed from the education setting. As a consequence, Bay says, "students begin to trust the strength of their own minds, built up through experience in discussion in dialogue, and in dialectical encounter, sufficient to enable the person to choose his or her own answers to all the searching questions, regardless of the pressures of conventional wisdom."[15]

Bay concluded that, in his view, "massive results can be achieved at a minimal risk or cost, when many more educators catch on to the promise of work of this kind."[16] His optimism about minimizing risks associated with human rights education for empowerment rests on faith that people can devise strategies premised on the expectation and insistence that both government and the individual must be committed to the understanding and respect for such rights. But the individual must learn through experience to eschew "democratic make believe" and avoid the language of "democracy achieved" in favor of the best antidote to alienation: "democratic self-government in fact."[17]

If human rights education for empowerment presents risks in various political settings because it appears to compete with governmental control, such education also presents risks to teachers accustomed to classroom control. Educators professionally involved in formal education are seldom familiar with or comfortable in a classroom with a human rights ethos. This is a learning environment in which direct instruction by a teacher is minimized and in which respect for student views is symbolized by the absence of a clear hierarchy of knowledge.

Reflections

Design of Empowerment Pedagogies

The literature on education for empowerment, while not extensive, is philosophically rich and politically grounded. Yet, as the Council of Europe objectives cited above suggest and O'Shea's characterization of civic education in British schools concludes, education for empowerment is seldom central to the concerns of professional educators in the industrially developed democracies of the first world. It is best known and used with some exemplary results in various third world countries.

Pedagogy directed toward the goal of empowerment and seeking the objective of reinforcing political efficacy on the part of participants has been successfully used in various third world countries relying primarily upon the methods of Paulo Freire. As Butkus notes:

Freire proposes a method of problem-posing education in contrast to banking education. Problem-posing education dissolves the teacher/student dichotomy. The educational process is seen as a partnership of mutual cooperation between teacher and students. Problem-posing education is based on Freire's anthropological vision: Human beings are knowing subjects committed to naming and transforming the world through dialogue with one another.[18]

It is in this light that the connection between Freire's epistemology and a dynamic conception of empowerment must be understood. "Freire understands humans as relational, dynamic beings who can intervene in reality in order to change it."[19] Accordingly, knowing must be seen as a process of continuous interaction between different individual subjects and their objective world. In this way, "human beings come to be and know themselves through their interaction with the world."[22]

Education for empowerment, however, must go even further and recognize that humans not only have the ability to know reality, but that they also have the capacity for critical reflection and action. Therefore, education aimed at developing this capacity must enable students to analyze the underlying structure of an action or experience, to unveil and apprehend its causal relationships, and to discover the hidden motives or interests it conceals. Freire describes this process of "conscientization" as follows: "Conscientization refers to the process in which men, not as recipients, but as knowing subjects, achieve a deepening awareness both of the socio-cultural reality which shapes their lives and their capacity to transform that reality."[21]

Perhaps paradoxically, Freire himself avoids claims about the utility of his methods outside the cultural framework of Latin American peasant populations in which he has shown that significant advances in literacy skills are possible in the context of continual political-educational dialogue. In any event, Freire's techniques have been adapted for use as empowerment pedagogies in other third world settings, most prominently in Asia where John Clark,[22] Clarence Dias,[23] and R.W. Timm[24] have linked human rights education aimed at empowerment to allied economic, political, and legal development objectives.

For example, empowerment is the stated objective of the nonformal human rights educational work of PROCESS (Participatory Research, Organization of Communities, and Education Towards Struggle for Self-Reliance, Inc.), a Philippine nongovernmental organization set up to help people learn and act upon their economic and social rights, particularly in rural settings. The group's planning usually takes place on site, where they conduct community organizing activities. They may typically focus upon a small fishing village where people are encouraged by PROCESS organizers to meet and define their local needs and problems.[25] At some point when maximum possible consensus is achieved, the group introduces what they call their barefoot lawyers who help to reinterpret needs in terms of rights, relating, for instance, to the unfair use of fishing licenses by absentee licensees. Having conceptualized needs in terms of rights, the group then begins to talk about, devise, and select remedial strategies that include the systematic collection of information and action plans, for example, the formulation of petitions, the drafting of new legislation, as well as litigation and presentations by lawyers to administrative boards. The open-ended planning process involved in this example yields a bonus that formal education too seldom does: it reaches the grass roots and involves people in a community context in acquiring control over their own fates and meeting their own needs on their terms.[26]

As this example illustrates, any attempt to design an empowerment pedagogy must begin by transcending the relationships of domination that so frequently form part of conventionally designed education. Moreover, it is entirely inappropriate and contradictory to teach students about human rights in a context where "The teacher talks about reality as if it were motionless, static, compartmentalized and predictable. Or else he expounds on a topic that is completely alien to the experiences of the students. His task is to fill the student with contents which are detached from reality."[27]

The importance of this observation for the design of empowerment pedagogies can hardly be overstated. First, human rights are inherently about relationships; and whatever their nature, whether they concern the power relations between individuals, groups, society, and/or the state, they are inevitably always dynamic and relative. To ignore this important aspect of human rights knowledge would be to distort their social and political functions. In other words, to teach students about human rights is to teach them about concepts and values aimed at enhancing their social and political choices. Second, the range of relations affecting human rights is potentially unlimited. Any attempt, therefore, at establishing boundaries between it and other areas of human knowledge is likely to be arbitrary and imprecise.

Third, as the empowerment pedagogy employed in the PROCESS program illustrates, it is important that human rights education be contextual in nature, that is, it must focus upon the specific experiences, needs, and problems of its participants. For it is their relationships with each other, their community, their environment, and their government that must be transformed or enhanced. Not only does such an approach avoid the danger of being viewed as foreign, abstract, or irrelevant. It is also, as Butkus points out, "the only legitimate point of entry in the pedagogical process. To begin elsewhere is to negate the significance of the concrete, existential reality in which people find themselves. Any hope of sponsoring people to critical consciousness and social action is directly related to their capacity to reflect on experiences and situations that deeply touch their lives."[28] Moreover, by relating human rights education to the concrete experiences of each target group, one enables them to make their own evaluation of the normative validity, accuracy and professed universality of international human rights laws.

Creating Optimum Conditions for Empowerment

In any effort to analyze and define empowerment objectives for education, we must finally be attentive to another obvious dimension of the educational enterprise: the diverse formats that are employed. These include: *formal* education (primary, secondary, and higher education); *nonformal* education (organized training for population subgroups outside the structures of formal education); and *informal* education (unsystematic education acquired in daily exposure to cultural symbols, the media, the workplace, and so on). After briefly describing some of the differences between each of these formats, I offer some general comments about creating the optimum conditions for empowerment.

Formal

As noted earlier, many empowerment educators would question the wisdom of trying to incorporate human rights education into the formal educational setting. For example, Charles P. Henry states: "Obviously, such an idealistic goal collides with the reality that schools are designed to socialize students into the existing social structure. From the earliest grades, students are taught to respect authority and revere the nation's founders and their successors."[29]

On the other hand, it would be a mistake to overlook the extent to which a culture of resistance or struggle may already exist within most formal educational settings. This point is well noted by Kreisberg, who points out that research in the field of critical pedagogy has found that "domination in schools and society does not function as a seamless web."[30] Instead it appears that schools function as "contested public spheres" not only to produce domination, but to produce resistance to domination as well.

Indeed, in schools students resist doing homework and delay the beginnings of classes. They develop intricate systems of cheating and psyching out teachers. . . . They refuse to participate in some classes and organize to change unfair rules. In fact, there seems to be no imposition of domination that does not simultaneously create forms of resistance. Hegemony is never complete. In the moment of rejection of domination lies the seeds of transformation and liberation.[31]

How uniform and pervasive these forms of resistance are in different societies and cultures is a question that merits further inquiry. What is already evident, however, is that it would be wrong to assume that all areas of formal education are inevitably unsuitable for human rights education programs aimed at empowerment.

Nonformal

This format offers many advantages for human rights education, and, not surprisingly, it is the one most often employed in empowerment programs. Some of the advantages of nonformal education include the following: (1) educators do not have to confront the obstacle of having to adapt their pedagogy to the predetermined goals and methods of formal education; (2) it readily allows for a multidisciplinary approach in which knowledge may be drawn from the fields of history, philosophy, sociology, law, politics, economics, anthropology, and so on; (3) target groups can be identified and organized in accordance with their specific needs and interests; (4) the format's inherent flexibility affords educators more freedom in curriculum innovation by allowing them, for example, to draw upon the rich and creative possibilities of experiential education; and (5) it can easily be adapted to fit within the practical constraints of each target group's particular political and social environments.

The main disadvantage of this format is usually its lack of recognition and resources. Because of its nonformal nature, program organizers and educators often earn little public recognition beyond the circle of their participants. As a result, they are continuously dependent upon support from voluntary and charitable resources.

Informal

Informal sources of information are possibly the most pervasive means of education and communication. However, the unsystematic nature of this format tends to restrict its pedagogical utility. In my view, therefore, informal education will be pedagogically useful only if one either succeeds in integrating it into a more systematic format, such as in an experiential education program, or if one's target group has already developed a pedagogical orientation (i.e., critical consciousness) with which this information can be understood and conceptualized. In these circumstances, the potential may be substantial for interactive learning on the "communications superhighway," described by Lloyd S. Etheredge in this volume. In the absence of such circumstances, educators must always be conscious of this format's inherent potential for abuse as a means of indoctrination and propaganda.

General Comments

The most suitable educational environment for a pedagogy aimed at empowerment is one in which the traditional relationships between both students and educators, on the one hand, and students and knowledge, on the other, are transformed. There are several implications that flow from this general observation.[32] First, it means that any preexisting hierarchy of instruction must be replaced by horizontal relationships of dialogue. Without this precondition, it is unlikely that students will be empowered to take possession of their own education. Second, flowing from this need for dialogue is the further requirement that educators be good listeners. This is necessary for students to become both directly and effectively involved in the continuous process of acquiring knowledge. Third, to enhance further this process of dialogue, it is important that the physical learning environment be democratically structured and nonthreatening. Students who feel dominated or stifled by the rules and structure of the educational setting will not feel comfortable or encouraged to participate in the learning process.

Fourth, in an effort to transform the relationship between students and knowledge, it is probably more effective to begin with their own concrete experiences of reality, and to use a process of induction to conceptualize and evaluate their significance or importance. As suggested earlier, abstract or general ideas and concepts are important, but only to the extent that they can meaningfully be integrated into the specific and personal experiences of students. Finally, students should never be expected to accept any experience or idea without reflection and critical evaluation. To do so would be to deny both the epistemological significance of their own experiences and the importance of their participation in the pedagogical process.

Evaluating Human Rights Education as Empowerment

> Imagination is more important than knowledge.
> Albert Einstein[33]

> Education is that which remains, if one has forgotten everything which he learned in school.
> Anonymous Wit[34]

If one merely views empowerment statically, then there would be relatively little difficulty in measuring the effectiveness or importance of any particular human rights education program. Such an approach would, for example, primarily seek to establish the degree to which a particular group of students has successfully learned about the history, nature, and content of a given set of human rights principles, and then to search for signs of any behavioral changes, such as an assertion of one's rights, recognition of the rights of others, or protest or concern over any apparent violation of these rights.

The problem with such a static conception, however, is that it reduces empowerment once again to a technique for the effective delivery of educational services, albeit one with a human rights content. This means that a particular education program is only as good as the substantive human rights knowledge that has been taught. More important, however, this approach totally ignores the development of an authentic critical consciousness, that is, of a truly liberated mind.

In contrast to such an approach, we should accept the more difficult challenge of identifying and assessing the development of each student's *own* critical, conscious, and creative thinking in which a strong respect for human rights is consistently reflected. In other words, the dynamic conception of empowerment which informs this pedagogical approach requires that we try to establish criteria which effectively evaluate the development of a critical human rights consciousness.

Tentatively, I would suggest that the following criteria be considered: (1) the ability of students to recognize the human rights dimensions of, and their relationship to, a given conflict- or problem-oriented exercise; (2) an expression of awareness and concern about their role in the protection or promotion of these rights; (3) a critical evaluation of the potential responses that may be offered; (4) an attempt to identify alternative or creative new responses; (5) a judgment or decision about which choice is most appropriate; and (6) an expression of confidence and a recognition of responsibility and influence in both the decision and its impact. No doubt this list is not exhaustive, nor is it intended to be; it is merely offered as a point of departure, which I hope others will build upon, criticize, and revise.

Perhaps the most vital question we as educators must address, then—given the terrible reality of human history, of our continuous struggle for domination over one another, and of the danger of increasingly destructive conflict—is whether it is enough for people merely to live within the limits of what they have been taught. If our answer is negative, then how can we as human rights educators continue to ignore the need to design more empowering pedagogies?

Notes

1. Universal Declaration of Human Rights, 71.
2. In October 1992 the Organizing Committee of the Decade of Human Rights Education and the Columbia University Center for the Study of Human Rights Education sponsored the "Conference on Goals and Strategies of Human Rights Education." Participants set up working groups, including one on "University Level Education." Members of the group made various commitments including a promise by Richard Claude (University of Maryland, College Park) to develop a brief concept paper on human rights pedagogy, and to do so in draft form for circulation among members of the working group. The idea was to present a paper for critical assessment by other members and for their contributions to its further development by editing, subtracting, and adding directly to the draft. The present chapter elaborates upon that draft but also introduces further issues which were not originally raised. Furthermore, these reflections are in part also a response to a challenge laid down by Abraham Magendzo, director of the Programa Interdisciplinario de Investigaciones en Educación, Santiago, Chile. At the conference he urged participants to begin to identify the problems associated with, and to think through the implications of, human rights education directed toward the objective of empowerment.
3. Seth Kreisberg, *Transforming Power: Domination, Empowerment, and Education* (Albany: State University of New York Press, 1992), 19.
4. Paulo Freire, *Pedagogy of the Oppressed* (New York: Continuum, 1990), 59. Freire now acknowledges the importance of using inclusive language; see Freire, *Pedagogy of Hope* (New York: Continuum, 1994), 67.
5. Cf. Paulo Freire, *Pedagogy of Hope*, 41.
6. Paulo Freire, *Education for Critical Consciousness* (New York: Continuum, 1987), 15.
7. Kader Asmal, "Democracy and Human Rights: Developing a South African Human Rights Culture," *New England Law Review* 27 (1992): 287–304, at 291.
8. Ibid., 292–93.

9. Derek Heater, *Human Rights Education in Schools: Concepts, Attitudes and Skills* (Strasbourg: Council of Europe, 1984), 7–10. See also Hugh Starkey, "The Council of Europe Recommendation on the Teaching and Learning of Human Rights in Schools," chap. 2 in *The Challenge of Human Rights Education*, ed. Hugh Starkey (London: Council of Europe, 1991).

10. Pat O'Shea, "Creeping Democratization, Peers School," chap. 7 in *Towards Democratic Schooling, European Experiences*, ed. Knud Jensen and Stephen Walker (Philadelphia: Open University Press, 1989), 88–102.

11. Russell A. Butkus, "Christian Education for Peace and Social Justice: Perspectives from the Thought of John Dewey and Paulo Freire," in *Education for Peace and Justice*, ed. Padraic O'Hare (San Francisco: Harper and Row, 1983), 141–71, at 153.

12. Ibid.

13. Richard Shaull, "Foreword," in Freire, *Pedagogy of the Oppressed*, 13–14.

14. Christian Bay, *Strategies of Political Emancipation* (South Bend, Ind.: University of Notre Dame Press, 1981), 76.

15. Ibid., 77.

16. Ibid., 78.

17. Ibid., 56.

18. Butkus, "Christian Education," 150.

19. Ibid., 148.

20. Ibid.

21. Paulo Freire, "The Adult Literacy Process as Cultural Action for Freedom," *Harvard Educational Review* 40, no. 2 (1970): 27, cited in Butkus, "Christian Education," 149.

22. John Clark, *Democratizing Development: The Role of Voluntary Organizations* (London: Earthscan Publications, International Institute for Environment and Development, 1991).

23. Clarence J. Dias, ed., *Initiating Human Rights Education at the Grassroots, Asian Experience* (Bangkok: Asian Cultural Forum on Development, 1991).

24. R. W. Timm, *Working for Justice and Human Rights: A Practical Manual* (Dacca, Bangladesh: Hotline Asia/Oceania and Commission for Justice and Peace, 1989).

25. Clarence J. Dias, "Alternative Law for People's Empowerment," in *Law as Weapon*, ed. José Ventura Aspiras (Manila: Participatory Research, Organization of Communities, and Education Towards Struggle for Self-Reliance [PROCESS], 1990), 19–26.

26. Richard Pierre Claude, "Civil Society and HRE," in his *Human Rights Education in the Philippines* (Manila: Kalikasan Press, 1991), 44–59; and Claude, "Human Rights Education: The Case of the Philippines," *Human Rights Quarterly* 13 (1991): 453–524, at 487–500.

27. Freire, *Pedagogy of the Oppressed*, 57.

28. Butkus, "Christian Education," 155.

29. Charles P. Henry, "Educating for Human Rights," *Human Rights Quarterly* 13 (1991): 420–23, at 420.

30. Kreisberg, *Transforming Power*, 16.

31. Ibid., 17.

32. Cf. Butkus, "Christian Education," 154–55.

33. This statement is generally attributed to Albert Einstein, although I was unable to find a citation to support it.

34. Cited with approval by Albert Einstein in *Albert Einstein: Out of My Later Years* (New York: Citadel Press, 1990), 36.

Chapter 6
Conflict Resolution and Human Rights Education: Broadening the Agenda

Donna Hicks

This chapter attempts to integrate two social and political change processes that have traditionally been both conceptualized and practiced separately: human rights education and conflict resolution. Human rights education evolved in reaction to the need to take action against the dehumanization and annihilation of peoples witnessed all too frequently in recent history. One of the goals of human rights education, therefore, is to intervene in the dehumanization process by making people aware of their rights as protected by international human rights law.

It is argued that education alone is not enough to produce the kind of change necessary to end the potentially life-threatening process of dehumanization that robs people of their ability to develop and flourish as human beings without the burden of threat to their existence. There needs to be a change in the relationship that gives rise to the destructive and inhumane interactions. Those who are perpetrating the dehumanization need to be brought into the change process. Changing the awareness of the violated by informing him or her as to how he or she "should" be treated is necessary but not sufficient to guarantee dignified treatment.

What is needed is a complementary intervention approach that addresses the need to change the *existing* conditions that perpetuate and legitimize destructive and dehumanizing interactions. There needs to be a change in the relationship, that is, a change in both the awareness of the violated and the attitudes and behavior of the violator. Interactive Problem Solving, a social psychological approach to conflict resolution, directly addresses this level of intervention: intervention at the level of human interaction.

The Interactive Problem Solving (IPS) method of intervention involves examining the way people interact with each other in dehumanizing conflict relationships. The central focus of the work addresses the human needs that are sacrificed in these relationships as well as transforming the destructive relationships into ones that are mutually tolerant; that is, relationships that allow for the acknowledgment and recognition of each other's right to existence (identity) while reducing the felt experience of threat that the differences in those identities tend to elicit. The transformation of relationships is accomplished, in part, by bringing people together, face to face, to hear directly how the destructive conflict relationship is affecting their fundamental needs as human beings.

A human rights education project undertaken in Cambodia in the summer of 1993 will be summarized and critiqued as a way of demonstrating the rationale for and need to incorporate conflict resolution practices into the human rights education agenda. The IPS approach to conflict resolution will then be introduced along with the theoretical assumptions that could potentially link the two processes. Finally, a model of the integration of human rights education and the IPS approach to conflict resolution will be proposed in addition to exploring the implications of the model for the practice of both disciplines.

Cambodia Project: A Case Study in Human Rights Education

After surviving four years of a political regime responsible for the massacre of approximately 1.4 million Khmer men, women, and children and nearly twenty years of ensuing civil war, on October 23, 1991, a peace accord was signed in Paris by all of Cambodia's warring political factions, bringing the hope for peace to this politically, culturally, and psychologically ravaged country. The peace plan included the temporary establishment of the United Nations Transitional Authority in Cambodia (UNTAC) to oversee elections to be held in June 1993 and generally to assist in the process of change necessary for rebuilding the country's political and civil infrastructure.

After being shut off from the outside world for nearly twenty years, Cambodia was faced with profound political and social challenges. It was the task of UNTAC to assist the Khmer people in developing a political system and democratic institutions that addressed both the particular needs of the Khmer culture and the need for safeguards of personal and individual rights that would prevent the kind of abuse of power that made genocide possible only two decades ago.

After its tragic recent history under the Pol Pot regime, Cambodia was left with an unprecedented distortion in demographics: 65 percent of the population are women, and adding their dependent children increases the figure to a startling 75 percent. Khmer women have been burdened with maintaining the production of their predominantly rural agrarian economy as well as, in many cases, assuming the role of head of household. In spite of these shifts in roles, Khmer women are kept in an extreme state of poverty and hardship with no political experience or social authority to change their circumstances.

For a culture that is historically and traditionally patriarchal, the shifts in roles and identity of women that have occurred in response to the shifts in demographics have created conflicts within the culture, forcing the remaining men, and the society as a whole, to examine some of the fundamental values on which the patriarchal system rests. How can the culture come to grips with the reality that the unequal treatment of women in Khmer society can no longer be tolerated, for pragmatic reasons alone? How can the culture be made aware of the fact that improvement of the status and skills of women is of benefit not only to the well-being of women but to the survival of the entire community?

It was in this context that UNTAC commissioned the Decade of Human Rights Education (DHRE) to train a number of Khmer women to become human rights trainers, who in turn would travel throughout the countryside to make as many women as possible aware of their legally protected human rights. Because Cambodia is a signatory to all UN conventions (a stipulation of the Paris Peace Accord), the rights of Cambodian women are protected by the Convention on the Elimination of all Forms of Discrimination Against Women (CEDAW).

It is important to note at the outset that the purpose of the project was not only to make Khmer women aware of their human rights as an end in itself, but more broadly to help facilitate the change process necessary to prevent the kind of unspeakable violations of their dignity experienced most blatantly under the Pol Pot regime, and more insidiously as an unequal member in a patriarchal social order.

In two months, approximately 120 Khmer women were trained as women's human rights trainers. The women were chosen as participants on the basis of their affiliation with indigenous human rights groups and other nongovernmental organizations (NGOs), both local and international, in Cambodia. Most of the women had a background in human rights; however, some did not, particularly the participants from the rural areas.

Five week-long workshops were planned, three in Phnom Penh and two in the rural provinces, one in Stung Treng in the northeast and the other in Battambang in the northwest. Due to heightened Khmer Rouge activity in the northwest provinces, the training in Battambang was canceled.

There were thirty women in each of the five workshops. Their ages ranged from eighteen to sixty, but the mean age was approximately twenty-five. There were only two women over the age of fifty because so few in that age group survived the Pol Pot massacre.

The challenge presented to the two international trainers sent by the DHRE was to introduce to the Khmer women trainees their rights as women as articulated in CEDAW but to do so in a way that drew on their own life experiences of having their dignity violated. A participatory methodology was therefore used to incorporate input from the participants actively into the training—not only their personal stories but their feedback regarding the effectiveness and cultural relevance of the training itself.[1]

Several activities were planned in order to use the women's life experiences to understand their rights as specified in CEDAW. The first involved asking the women to reflect on a time when they felt that their dignity as a woman had been violated.

Each woman was given the opportunity to tell her story first to a small group, then to the large group.

The content of the stories varied, but familiar themes emerged from all the workshops. Many of the older women told of their unspeakable torture by the Khmer Rouge. Some related their experience of the undignified and often physically threatening treatment they endured by their husbands. Some of the younger women told of being treated like slaves by their employers. A few young women described situations in which they were made to feel inferior in the school setting, ranging from not being encouraged by their teachers to blatant exclusion from educational opportunities. What was common to all of the stories told by the women across all ages was having survived an experience of humiliation, being made to feel something less than human at one extreme, and, to a lesser degree, to feel that one's place in the world was less than equal to that of their male counterparts, at all levels of the social hierarchy.

In another exercise, the women were asked to discuss their role in Khmer society. Lists of roles were generated to include the role of wife, mother, daughter, and worker (outside the home). The women were then asked to discuss each role from the perspective of what society expected from them in that role. They were then asked to examine how they felt about the societal expectations. Did the expectations seem agreeable to them? Was there anything about their roles that they would like to see changed, and, if so, how?

These exercises were performed in preparation for the next activity, which was to ask the trainees to come up with a list of rights for women they would like to see protected by Cambodian law. This was a particularly relevant question, for the Cambodian constitution was being written during the time of the workshops, and women's groups (including some of our trainees) were actively lobbying the Constituent Assembly in order to have women's issues considered and included in the constitution. They were asked to generate a "wish list" of ways they would like to be treated as women in Khmer society. They first worked together in small groups to generate their list jointly, then the large group was assembled and each of the groups reported their ideas, which were recorded on newsprint by the trainers.

In the second part of the exercise, the trainers compared the articles in CEDAW to the lists of rights generated by the women. In all four groups of women trained, there was nearly complete overlap in the lists generated by the women and the rights specified in CEDAW, with only a few exceptions.

The method of using the women's life experiences to make them aware of their human rights needs was a powerful and empowering exercise for the women. One unanticipated consequence of the exercises was the extent to which the women experienced validation and acknowledgment of their suffering in the telling of their stories. For many of the women, it was the first time they had had an opportunity to speak aloud about their traumatic experiences. Since the culture does not support this kind of "emotional openness," hearing each other's stories allowed them both to empathize with each other and validate their own trauma, reducing the isolation they felt from having silently endured their suffering for so long. This gave them an emotional point of connection that, by the end of the workshop, provided the basis of a strong solidarity among the women.

Another empowering aspect of the workshop for the women was when, on the fourth day of the training, a number of Khmer men were invited for the day. The trainees led the men through a series of exercises in order to make them aware of their human rights as Khmer women. The trainees asked the men to come up with a list of rights they would like to see protected by the constitution for a significant woman in their lives. Once the men's list was completed, the trainees compared it to the lists they had generated the day before. As might be expected, in each workshop the list generated by the men was much less comprehensive than the lists generated by the women. In order to make the men aware of why they wanted other rights guaranteed, the women performed dramatic presentations of everyday situations common to women in which their dignity was routinely violated. For example, one of the plays enacted a common experience of how abusively a woman is treated at home by her husband after he has been drinking with his friends. Others dramatized what it was like for a young girl who was forced into marrying someone she would not have chosen herself in a marriage arranged by her father. Treatment of women in the workplace was another theme.

What was particularly empowering about the day with the men was that not only did the women have the opportunity to become trainers for a day, but their audience was Khmer men. The structure of the workshop provided the security they needed to be able to "tell their stories" to men, to those who had significantly contributed to their unequal and unfair treatment in Khmer society. This opportunity gave hope to many of the women that a change in their status was possible.

In the debriefings of the workshops, the trainees consistently reported feeling encouraged and empowered in learning about their human rights. However, they also felt that a major part of the task of realizing their rights could not be addressed without educating the men. It was apparent that the day spent with the men in the training was a first step, but the women agreed that much work needed to be done to facilitate a genuine change in the attitudes of Khmer men toward women.

It became clear that this project, as successful as it was in making the women aware of their human rights, was only a step in the direction of the change that was necessary to see those rights implemented in the daily lives of Khmer women. What was needed was a way to bring men into the process so that their contribution to the conditions that were giving rise to the undignified treatment of women could be addressed.

It also became clear that educating the women and men of the human rights of women was not enough to produce the kind of change necessary to make Khmer women equal citizens within the Khmer culture. There needed to be a way to explore the attitudes and beliefs about women that were perpetuating the unequal treatment of women and thwarting their development. There needed to be a way to change the nature of the relationship between men and women so that women would be allowed to participate as equal citizens in their culture.

The Interactive Problem Solving Approach to Conflict Resolution

The IPS approach to conflict resolution maintains a number of assumptions derived from the human needs theory of conflict, upon which the model of intervention was developed.[2] Among these assumptions are:

1. Conflict arises between groups when ontological needs, fundamental to human development, are unmet or suppressed. These include

- the need to *belong* to a group from which one's *identity* is (partially) derived;
- the need to feel a sense of *security* and *esteem* in the expression of one's identity;
- the need to have one's identity *recognized* and *acknowledged.*

2. No amount of force or type of coercion can suppress the drive to fulfill these needs; it is a developmental imperative.
3. The perception of threat to these needs can provoke a reaction of violence by the individuals or group feeling threatened.

The "human needs" theory of conflict was first developed by John Burton in response to the traditional "realist" theory of international relations proposed by Hans Morgenthau and others, who viewed conflict as an inevitable consequence of power politics.[3] In the "power politics" frame, it is necessary for states to pursue and protect their self-interest, given the anarchic structure of the international system. This conceptualization results in relationships between states that are competitive and adversarial. Conflicts resulting from the pursuit of competing interests are considered a sometimes necessary and rational consequence, given the reality of limited resources and each state's freedom to promote its interests virtually unrestrained. The "victors" in such a competition are those who exert the most power and can secure their borders from invasion by competitors. National authorities, therefore, maintain the control of national interests by using "policies of threat" ranging from deterrence strategies to military intervention if necessary, to eliminate the threat.

Conflict resolution, in this framework, consists of strategies that suppress the threat to the state by the use of power in the form of force and coercion. At the level of negotiation, power bargaining combined with adversarial strategies are employed. When negotiation fails, the use of force is justified and, indeed, a rational choice.

Burton's critique of power politics centers around the fundamental idea that conflict arises when individual ontological needs (needs driven by the process of human development) are not met. This conceptualization "humanizes" conflict in the sense that its source is embedded in the quality of relationship between peoples and how these relationships either promote or thwart the satisfaction of basic human needs of development, not the quality of relations between states, governed by the dictates of power.

Arising out of this conceptualization is a fundamental difference in which conflict is analyzed and resolved: within the power politics frame, conflict can be stopped by the use of deterrence or, if necessary, force; within the human needs frame, resolving conflict requires an analysis of the unfulfilled human needs that are at the root of the struggle, through the use of an analytic problem-solving methodology.

The problem-solving approach to conflict resolution, at its core, maintains an assumption about human nature that guides the practice: there are fundamental needs of development (identity, belonging, security, and recognition) that cannot be suppressed with any degree or kind of force. The crucial point is that political strategies designed to overcome, by force, individuals or groups that react, violently if necessary, to have those needs met, are inherently flawed. The strategies are flawed because human beings cannot be forced or socialized out of these developmental needs. It is like trying to stop a child from learning to walk. The fulfillment of these needs is a developmental imperative. Their inherent force is greater than any external power that attempts to control them.

Given the assumption that developmental needs for identity, belonging, recognition, and security cannot be externally socialized out of human beings, the IPS approach to conflict resolution focuses on an analysis of the roots of conflict, that is, the unmet human needs that are not being satisfied.

The characteristics of the approach can be understood by examining *what* is being addressed, *how*, and by *whom* when attempting to resolve intergroup conflict. The Interactive Problem-Solving Workshop, developed by Herbert Kelman, will be described as an illustration of a specific model of intervention that incorporated Burton's human needs approach with principles from social psychology.[4]

"What" Is Being Addressed in Interactive Problem Solving

Unlike official negotiations where the political, economic, and historical factors that give rise to the conflict are examined, the IPS approach (often categorized as "unofficial" or "second track" diplomacy") focuses on the dynamics of the relationship between the conflicting parties that maintain and escalate the conflict.[5] In particular, what is examined is the experience of threat, real or perceived, to the fulfillment of the fundamental human needs of both parties. It is argued that the reduction of the experience of threat is a contributing factor in changing a relationship between two parties from one that is mutually tolerant of each other's identities to one that is characterized by mistrust and suspicion where both parties desire some form of annihilation of the other.

In an effort to reduce the threat, the problem-solving approach *examines the norms* that typically govern interactions between conflicting parties that justify and maintain the violent behavior that threatens each other's existence. The approach, therefore, tries to create a *context for learning* where new norms of interaction are established which could potentially *transform the relationship* to one where both parties are free to develop and flourish as human beings, without the threat to their existence. According to Kelman, the problem-solving workshop "seeks to create an alternative normative context, encouraging genuine interaction, an analytic approach, and collaborative problem-solving, which are conducive to the emergence of new ideas for conflict resolution."[6]

"How" Interactive Problem-Solving Addresses Unmet Needs

Underlying the basic assumption that unmet human needs must be addressed in relationships of conflict is another fundamental belief that *human needs are not negotiable.* Therefore, the conflict resolution process that addresses the level of needs cannot be based on compromise or bargaining which often characterizes negotiation techniques that address each party's "interests." Instead the process involves taking an "analytic" approach whereby the environment is set up to "problem-solve" by getting at the root causes of the conflict. The purpose is to analyze each party's needs without debate, in order to gain insight into the perspective of the other. Often in conflict relationships, the information that each party has of the other is based on bias and stereotypes, as the parties usually do not have an opportunity to talk to each other face to face.

One of the key aspects of the IPS process is that the "solutions" to the conflict are generated by the participants themselves. After the "needs analysis" has been completed, both parties work together to arrive jointly at ways in which each other's needs could be met.

"Who" Conducts the Interactive Problem-Solving Workshop

As explained above, the participants are responsible for the "work" that is accomplished in the workshop. Any solutions or agreements that emerge come from the two parties themselves. The third party acts to *facilitate* the process, not to mediate or push for agreements. This facilitative component is what sets interactive problem solving apart from traditional mediation techniques where it can be the responsibility of the mediator to see that an agreement is made between the conflicting parties.

It is the role of the third party to keep the needs analysis and joint thinking on track, intervening when discussions turn into debate rather than an exploration of each other's perspective. In addition, the third party provides the norms and ground rules for the discussion, and in general creates an atmosphere of safety in which the difficult and often emotionally charged exchanges can take place.

The Complementarity of Approaches

Having experienced the roles of both human rights educator in Cambodia and third party facilitator in several IPS workshops, it became clear to me that the two approaches could be strengthened by an integration of each other's principles and practices. What became clear in the Cambodian case was that education alone was not enough to produce the kind of change necessary in order for Khmer women to become equal citizens in their community. It was the women's strong plea that men be brought into the process so that the attitudes and behaviors that perpetuate their undignified treatment be addressed. At this juncture the idea to incorporate the IPS practices into the human rights education agenda became apparent. The IPS approach addresses the "human" level of conflict and examines the way parties in conflict interact with one another. It explores ways in which the dynamics of the conflict relationship impede the fulfillment of fundamental needs of development of both parties.

One of the strengths of the IPS approach is that it provides an opportunity for groups in conflict to confront each other directly in order to address their unmet needs. A destructive consequence of conflict is the alienation and isolation of the parties from each other, creating the distance and lack of communication that give rise to the dehumanization process. Accurate information about the other is replaced by distortions and stereotypes which fuel and escalate the conflict. The other becomes "less than human," which justifies the impulse to humiliate and annihilate. The IPS approach provides not only the opportunity but the safety for conflicting parties to break the alienation and isolation and address each other while within the throes of conflict.

Interactive Problem Solving's Contribution to Human Rights Education Methods

In the Cambodian case, if the men and women were brought together in the structure of an IPS workshop, both groups would have the opportunity to address directly the human needs that are being sacrificed, given the existing dynamics of the relationship between Cambodian men and women. As in any IPS workshop, the dialogue would begin with a "needs assessment" and would be followed by a period of joint thinking during which the participants themselves come up with ways to address the needs expressed by both and the constraints under which both parties would be operating. The cultural constraints in implementing women's human rights could be explored in this session. The final aspect of the workshop could focus on a plan of action to be taken by both parties in an effort to work together in improving the status of Khmer women.

What would remain a significant aspect of this intervention from human rights education methodology is using the daily life experiences of the participants in order to understand each other's human rights needs. Hearing personal stories from participants, to the extent that they feel comfortable in revealing them, is a powerful exercise in that it enables the person who has lived through humiliation to have that experience validated and acknowledged. In addition, it initiates the process of "humanizing" the interactions between the groups, as it is difficult to listen to someone who has suffered a violation of one's dignity without stirring one's own humanity that has been repressed in order to perpetrate the indignity. In this way, both parties "unfreeze" their humanity, which can facilitate the transformation of the relationship.

The act alone of bringing parties in conflict together is not enough to change the relationship. The quality of interaction, that is, the extent to which the parties are able to experience each other's and one's own humanity, can significantly change the nature of the relationship between them. The motivation for mutual dehumanization shifts to mutual tolerance, enabling the development of a way of being in relationship with each other that is respectful of each other's needs and integrity as human beings.

The Human Rights Education Contribution to IPS

It is my view that one of the contributions human rights education could make to the IPS workshop is in incorporating the exercise of using the participants' life experiences of being personally violated as a way to develop the "human connection" between the parties, making it easier for the relationship to change. At present, the model addresses only the needs of both parties. However, beneath the "needs" are the personal stories of the deprivation and humiliation that gave rise to the articulated needs. There are no needs, or rights for that matter, disconnected from experiences of human suffering.

The most serious consequence of separating the discussion of needs from the personal indignities that have given rise to the articulation of those needs is that it can easily, if not inevitably, turn into political rhetoric, locking the parties into intractable political positions, with no progress toward mutual understanding. On the contrary, this type of discussion feeds the alienation and fuels the fears of both parties.

More important, a discussion of the experiences of indignity that are the basis of each party's stated needs enables the connection to be made between the "personal" and the "political." For example, in many of the problem-solving workshops with Israelis and Palestinians, self-determination was expressed by the Palestinians as one of their fundamental needs. However, this need, as stated, often fueled the deepest fears of the Israelis, who viewed Palestinian autonomy as a threat to their fundamental need for security. The discussion of these seemingly interlocking needs quickly becomes polemical, with each side adhering to its political positions and often resorting to historical debate in an effort to justify them.

It is suggested that if each party had the opportunity to express to the other their experiences of humiliation and suffering brought on by not having their needs met, it could create the connection between their personal life experiences and their political demands. The separation of the personal from the political is inherently dangerous as it can justify (and there is no lack of historical evidence to support this idea) the most egregious acts of inhumanity imaginable. Pol Pot's justification of the massacre of nearly 1.4 million Khmer in order to realize his political vision of the development of a purely agrarian, Maoist state in Cambodia is only one of numerous examples.

There are certainly no guarantees that the perpetrator of violations of human needs will be transformed by being face to face and hearing the personal stories of those who have suffered the indignities. The degree of denial of one's own humanity and repression of one's own ability to empathize with and experience the human suffering of another can be so profound that nothing can activate the "unfreezing" of the inability to connect with others. For this reason it is imperative to have laws that protect individuals from abuses of power. There is no question in my mind that bringing Pol Pot face to face with his victims in an effort to unfreeze his humanity would be an act of futility.

There is one last point to be made on the benefits of relating personal life experiences of indignity in the problem-solving process. The act of "telling the stories" not only fosters the potential for a human connection to be made between the parties in conflict but, equally important, serves to legitimize publicly the suffering of those whose dignity has been violated. This kind of recognition is a significant step in the healing process of the victimized, and can contribute to the reconstruction of their self-esteem as a member of a disenfranchised identity group.

Another contribution that human rights education methodology could make to IPS is to expand on the "norms" established that govern interactions during the workshop. The workshop setting creates a "context for learning" in which new ways of interacting with one another are established. An analytic approach to understanding the perspective of the other is taken so that both parties can work together in order to arrive jointly at ways to satisfy their unmet needs.

The "norms of interaction" should thus be expanded to include additional norms of behavior that are guided by human rights principles. How this expanded list of norms would become manifest in behavior would require further reflection and analysis. However, the basic idea is to use the problem-solving workshop as a "testing ground" for learning new ways of relating to each other so that one's own dignity and the dignity of the other remain intact.

Interventions by the third party could be made when the norms of interactions are violated. The interventions would have to be carefully crafted so that the third party does not compromise its neutrality and take on the role of the "teacher." These norms would have to be agreed upon by both parties and gone over in detail in a preworkshop session with each party separately so that all are fully aware of their purpose and content before the workshop begins. In this way the third party would be "authorized" by all participants to uphold the agreement to interact with each other according to these preestablished norms.

The suggestions made for the incorporation of each other's methods in human rights education and the IPS model of conflict resolution assume that the practices of both will continue on related but separate paths. The final section of this chapter explores a new framework in which both human rights education and conflict resolution can be integrated into a broader agenda, which responds to the current needs of the world community for a new approach to achieving global peace and security.

Broadening the Agenda

The latest UN *Human Development Report* makes a strong statement regarding the relationship between international peace and human development.[7] The report states that the two agendas must be integrated, for "without peace, there may not be development, and without development, peace is threatened." It claims that peace and security will not be achieved except in the context of sustainable development that leads to "human security."

What is required is a reconceptualization of security away from power politics' focus on conflicts between states and the traditional military strategies designed to protect them, to one that places its emphasis on the fulfillment of basic human developmental needs. Security, conceptualized in "human" terms, seeks to ensure the satisfaction of fundamental needs and ways in which potential threats to those needs can be avoided. The unit of analysis in the explanation and conceptualization of "conflict" shifts from the behavior of states and its institutions to the behavior of people and identity groups in pursuit of the fulfillment of their needs for development.

This reconceptualization is consistent with Burton's human needs theory of conflict, which states that the deprivation of the fundamental human needs for identity, security, belonging, and recognition is at the core of conflict and that no amount of force or coercion can suppress these developmentally driven needs. People will resort to violence, if necessary, to seek satisfaction of their needs. Conflict, therefore, is the inevitable consequence of the suppression or arrest of the fulfillment of these needs. Needs, conceptualized as such, cannot be negotiable. They are driven by the indomitable force of development and cannot be compromised without consequence. Avoiding conflict, therefore, requires a means by which the fundamental human needs of all peoples can be met. Guaranteeing the fulfillment of basic needs of all identity groups becomes a fundamental objective of states and their institutions.[8]

In his *An Agenda for Peace*, UN Secretary-General Boutros Boutros-Ghali brings to the attention of the world community the need for "preventive diplomacy," defined as "action to prevent disputes from arising between parties, to prevent existing disputes from escalating into conflict and to limit the spread of the latter when they occur."[9] The implication of Boutros-Ghali's call, in part, suggests the broadening of objectives of conflict resolution professionals to include that of the prevention of conflict. But how do we begin to answer this call? What is the theoretical basis for action to be taken to prevent conflict? Specifically, what theory of conflict can address the current security needs?

Finally, the Vienna Declaration and Programme of Action, the outcome of the

World Conference on Human Rights in 1993, considers human rights education training and public information "essential for the promotion and achievement of stable and harmonious relations among communities and for fostering mutual understanding, tolerance, and peace."[10] Once again, what theories will be used to guide policy decisions in order to achieve "mutual understanding, tolerance, and peace"? How should the human rights education agenda be designed to best achieve these goals?

What appears to be needed is a comprehensive plan of action, designed to incorporate the objectives of several interrelated efforts described above, driven by the superordinate goal of peace through the protection of the diversity of human expression and the fundamental needs that are required to enable such diversity to develop and flourish without threat. The rationale for the comprehensive action plan would derive from a theoretical model based on Burton's theory of conflict: unmet human developmental needs are the root causes of conflict, and peace cannot be achieved until fundamental needs are fulfilled. This is not to say, however, that ideological differences, along with political and economic factors, are not significant contributors to the causes of conflict. According to Burton, even if the political and ideological factors are resolved, bringing an end to the conflict, if fundamental human needs are not met, the struggle will persist, resulting in a threat to a long-term settlement.

The model would include three interdependent components of intervention in order to achieve the stated goal of peace through the protection of the diversity of human expression: *political and legal elements*; institutionalized *means by which to address the threat to human needs*; and establishment of *norms of interaction* based on principles of equality and dignity that allow for the unique expression of identities, along with *educational strategies* designed to incorporate them into the daily lives of all people. It is argued that each of the three components is a necessary but not sufficient means to achieve the common goal of peace through the protection of the diversity of human expression. What is needed is the integration of resources and skills so as to produce the synergistic effects that are greater and more effective than any one component acting alone.

Political and Legal Elements

The objectives of this component include the development and improvement of institutions based on the principles of a democratic form of governance worldwide where both individual and minority needs are recognized and fulfilled. In addition, actions must be taken to allow for the growth of a vibrant civil society which engages the active participation of citizens in the decision making that affects their lives.

In order to ensure that human needs are met, legal articulation of those needs and laws enacted to protect them are essential. The major work in this area has been accomplished in the development of international human rights law. The debate continues, however, as to which "needs" should be considered basic and fundamental to human development. It is hoped that by including the conflict resolution perspective into the needs-rights debate, particularly Burton's ideas regarding the relationship between unmet human needs and conflict, that a greater depth of understanding of the issues will be achieved. Further analysis of this topic is necessary and is part of the author's ongoing research.

Means by Which to Address Threats to Human Needs

Since the IPS model was designed to address unmet human needs, it seems logical that an adaptation of the model (as detailed above) might be developed to be used in the broader campaign to address the threats to the fulfillment of the needs that allow for the diverse expression of human identities. Programs could be designed and institutions created to train teachers at all levels of education, clergy, law enforcement officers, health care providers, the military, business executives and managers, government employees and officials, policymakers at all levels, and any other socializing agents who could incorporate the problem-solving methods into their daily lives and the lives of those with whom they interact.

The skills required to manage the differences that arise between and among peoples do not come naturally and need to be taught. There is no lack of evidence to demonstrate what happens in a society that does not include methods to resolve conflicts in its socialization processes. In fact, the unsocialized impulse is to distance oneself from the person with whom we are in conflict; this sets the stage for the sometimes subtle and often violent process of dehumanization. There must be ways in which people can be in conflict and still maintain an ethic of civility toward each other.

What is needed, however, is a theoretical base that is grounded in the human experience, from which the norms of civility are derived. There needs to be a way for people to connect the norms to experiences in their daily lives in order to make them meaningful guides to behavior. For this reason, teaching conflict resolution skills to people at any age should involve a process in which the daily life experiences of being treated in an undignified manner are aired in order to explain and justify the norms that are being taught.

Establishment of Norms of Human Interaction and Educational Strategies

One of the goals of human rights education is the establishment of human rights principles as the value base for a civil society. Much work has already been done by the Decade of Human Rights Education in promoting this idea. What is needed, however, is a thoughtful analysis of how the principles of human rights can be translated into the day-to-day behaviors that promote human dignity. What will it look like to treat each other in a way that does not violate each other's or one's own humanity? How will these behaviors be taught? What are the best methods to accomplish the successful integration of these norms of behavior into our daily lives?

Further research and analysis are needed in order to answer these questions.

However, one suggestion, as detailed above, is to devise a method that combines the practices of both human rights education and conflict resolution: integrating the "content" of human rights education, using both the human rights norms and the exercise where the personal stories of the violation of one's dignity are told into the IPS process. The process by which groups in conflict are brought together, face to face, in order to arrive jointly at ways to address unmet needs could be an effective means not only to learn but to "try out" the norms of interaction. The participants, however, would not necessarily have to be in conflict. They could be brought together in a problem-solving environment where issues could be addressed before they have reached the level of active conflict. These ideas require further elaboration and should be considered an "outline" for the development of an integrated model from which a comprehensive action plan could derive.

Conclusion

It is difficult to imagine what it would be like if all identity groups were allowed to develop and flourish to the full extent of their respective capacity without the need to defend the right to their existence. What would the consequences be of achieving social integration through mutual understanding and tolerance of different ways of being in the world? Where would this spirit of "integration" lead us? What is certain is that we will never move beyond the imagining of such a world until a "campaign of cooperation" is initiated now that coordinates the contributions of several intervention strategies in an effort to approach holistically the unrelenting challenges that face the world community.

It cannot be understated how important it is to establish means by which peoples and groups can be in conflict with one another while maintaining their dignity and the dignity of the other. What is imperative is the development of skills that allow the expression of anger and the voicing of our fundamental needs that are not being met in a way that does not lead to violence and threaten the integrity of those in conflict. The impulse to distance oneself from the other and to attack either psychologically by verbal abuse or physically with bodily damage needs to be contained. At present this impulse has gone awry where violence can be observed at all levels of human interaction: in the family, schools, communities, and between states. We need to understand the "impulse to humiliate and annihilate" before we can develop ways to address it.

The efforts required to arrest the impulse toward violence are dauntingly immense, and effective strategies to implement the changes necessary are perhaps outside the limits of our understanding. However, it is certain that we need to begin with a well-thought-out theoretical base. We need to start with a theory of human behavior that can explain the impulse toward violence. There needs to be an understanding of the relationship between the individual and propensities toward violence and the "triggering mechanisms" or external conditions in the environment that give rise to the violent impulses.

At present it appears that Burton's theory of conflict can address many of these unanswered questions. It is also apparent that the power politics theory of conflict has failed as a guide to policy decisions, primarily because it ignores the human dimension of conflict and views coercion through the use of power as the answer to threats to the security of the state. Human needs are considered irrelevant to state security.

Policy decisions guided by the theoretical assumptions of human needs theory could be an effective new approach to addressing the violence and social disintegration that is threatening the developmental needs of many peoples worldwide. However, because of the complexity of the task alone, a collaborative effort is needed to effect the change and to promote the learning necessary to accomplish the change.

It has been demonstrated that human rights laws are not enough to stop violence and threats to one's dignity. Human rights education, with its normative focus, is also not enough to guarantee the internalization of a "code of conduct" that guides human interaction. Nor have conflict resolution practices been able to effect the change necessary to prevent conflicts from emerging. The only strategy that stands a chance of achieving the changes that allow groups freedom from threats for expressing their respective identities is one that integrates all the resources available from different approaches while recognizing the uniqueness of each contribution. This "experiment in collaboration" could be a model of what the world could be like if the "impulse toward humanity" reigned.

Notes

1. For a description of the participatory methodology used in the trainings, see M. Suarez and R. Arroyo, "Tough Challenges for Women's Rights Educators," in *Human Rights Education: The Fourth R* 3, no. 3 (1993): 1–5.

2. For a history of the evolution of the human needs theory of conflict and its assumptions, see John Burton, *Conflict: Human Needs Theory* (London: Macmillan, 1990).

3. For a discussion of the realist view of conflict, see Hans Morgenthau, *Politics Among Nations: The Struggle for Power and Peace* (New York: Knopf, 1948); G. Schwarzenberger, *Power Politics: A Study of World Society* (New York: Stevens, 1964); and Kenneth Waltz, *Theory of International Politics* (Reading, Mass.: Addison Wesley, 1979).

4. H. C. Kelman and S. P. Cohen, "The Problem-Solving Workshop: A Social-Psychological Contribution to the Resolution of International Conflicts," *Journal of Peace Research* 13 (1979): 79–90.

5. H. C. Kelman, "Informal Mediation by the Scholar/Practitioner," in J. Bercovitch and J. Ruins, eds., *Mediation in International Relations: Multiple Approaches to Conflict Management* (New York: Macmillan, 1992).

6. Kelman and Cohen, "The Problem-Solving Workshop," 99.

7. United Nations, *Human Development Report* (New York: United Nations Publications, 1994).

8. John Burton, *Conflict: Resolution and Prevention* (London: Macmillan Press, 1990).

9. Boutros Boutros-Ghali, *An Agenda for Peace* (New York: United Nations Publications, 1992), 11.

10. *The Vienna Declaration and Programme of Action,* from the World Conference on Human Rights, Vienna, Austria (New York: United Nations Publications, 1993), 66.

Chapter 7
Education on the Human Rights of Women as a Vehicle for Change

Dorota Gierycz

In proclaiming the UN Decade of Human Rights Education, General Assembly Resolution 49/184 stated that "human rights education constitutes an important vehicle for the elimination of gender-based discrimination and ensuring equal opportunities through the promotion and protection of the human rights of women." This chapter seeks to demonstrate how the knowledge of the human rights of women, resulting from various forms of human rights education and awareness raising training can improve the de jure and de facto situation of women and can influence the development of international legal standards aimed at the protection and promotion of those rights.

Introduction

Legal literacy, encompassing the knowledge of the rights and freedoms of individuals and the existing national and international laws and regulations, is a necessary condition for their implementation and for the ability of all individuals to apply them in practice, address their violations, restore justice through proper legal proceedings, and demand compensation for damage whenever it occurs. Legal literacy is also essential for the development of a legal culture, which in turn is indispensable for the harmonious development of societies, for democracy building, and for the well-being of individuals and their sense of citizenship.

Among all fields of law, literacy in human rights, as that most directly touching upon people's lives, is probably the most needed. Furthermore, among human rights, the human rights of women occupy a special place and require particular attention and educational efforts. Although the human rights of women have gained considerable visibility in recent years, including recognition as an integral part of human rights, public knowledge of them is inadequate. There is still much opposi-

The views expressed by the author do not necessarily represent those of the United Nations.

tion, both active and passive, to full acceptance of the equality between men and women in all spheres of life and efforts to eradicate de facto violence and discrimination against women.

Thus, despite the fact that women constitute half the world's population and that their de jure rights are recognized in most countries of the world, discrimination and violence against women prevail in daily life and have detrimental consequences not only for women, but for societies deprived of the full contribution of women, as citizens, to social development and to the resolution of key national and international problems. The insufficient implementation of the human rights of women not only violates international standards of human rights, but also deprives humanity of distinct and badly needed human resources and values.

The lack of equal applicability of human rights to women is far from being generally acknowledged and properly addressed by legislation, systems of justice, and education at national and international levels. The legacy of ages of discrimination cannot be overcome without educational and awareness raising efforts in societies, and in particular among the decision makers and women themselves. Therefore, in order to apply all human rights and fundamental freedoms to women, literacy in the human rights of women is essential. This requires continued and comprehensive education in the human rights of women—formal and informal—at all levels, including training, advocacy, and information campaigns. Only through conscious and continuous activities aimed at the identification and eradication of all forms of discrimination and violence against women, correction of discriminatory laws and practices, and proper understanding of existing laws, legal standards, and terminology can the objectives of equality and enjoyment of all human rights be achieved by women. That goal cannot be reached without the concerted efforts of educators, experts in the field, nongovernmental organizations (NGOs), representatives of the legal profession, administration and the mass media. Thus education in the human rights of women is both particularly important and particularly difficult to achieve, as it constitutes a very comprehensive task requiring cooperation at all levels of society.

Evolution of the International Standards of Equality and Their Applicability to Women

International standards of human rights and the equal rights of men and women, although well established in international law, have been applied only to a limited extent at national and international levels. At the creation of the United Nations, its Charter, which now binds its 185 member states, reaffirmed "faith in fundamental human rights, in the dignity and worth of the human person, in the equal rights of men and women and of nations large and small" (Preamble). The Charter lists among the main purposes of the United Nations the achievement of "international co-operation in promoting and encouraging respect for human rights and for fundamental freedoms for all without distinction as to race, sex, language or religion" (Article 1, para. 3).

The Universal Declaration on Human Rights (1948), which states that "everyone is entitled to all the rights and freedoms set forth in this Declaration, without distinction of any kind, such as race, color, sex, language, religion, political or other opinion, national or social origin, property, birth or other status," provides for equality between men and women. Specifically, Article 7 states that "All are equal before the law and are entitled without any discrimination to equal protection of the law. All are entitled to equal protection against any discrimination in violation of this Declaration and against any incitement to such discrimination."

The provisions of the Declaration are further developed in Article 26 of the International Covenant on Civil and Political Rights (1966), which states that "All persons are equal before the law and are entitled without any discrimination to the equal protection of the law. In this respect, the law shall prohibit any discrimination and guarantee to all persons equal and effective protection against discrimination on any ground such as race, color, sex, language, religion, political or other opinion, national or social origin, property, birth or other status." This formulation is generally recognized as a nondiscrimination provision in international law.

In adopting the Charter, the Universal Declaration of Human Rights, both International Covenants on Human Rights, and subsequent international human rights instruments, no country has ever argued against the principle of equality between men and women or considered it inconsistent or in conflict with national tradition, culture, or religion.

On the other hand, since the early days of the United Nations, it has been obvious that thousands of years of historical discrimination against women could not be overcome overnight and that this legacy called into question the practicality of those general and gender-neutral standards. Thus, owing to pressures from the women's lobby and its prominent representative, Eleanor Roosevelt, the Commission on the Status of Women (CSW) was created in 1946 as the UN Economic and Social Council (ECOSOC) subsidiary body. Its main objective was to implement the principle of equality between women and men and to ensure de facto observance of the human rights of women.[1] For a long time the commission was the only visible international body working toward the implementation of the human rights of women. Its main role concentrated on the preparation of new legislation to protect the human rights of women[2] and on governmental dialogue regarding the situation of women in various parts of the world.

The climate of the cold war and the lack of political interest in a majority of countries in women's issues, as well as in the applicability of the commission's decisions, diminished its practical impact on the protection and promotion of the human rights of women and made its achievements barely known to the public. The UN's human rights agenda was overshadowed by other, more politically vital issues related to East-West disputes: socioeconomic versus political rights, collective versus individual rights, and often spectacular cases of political dissidents.

Besides, the work of the United Nations was viewed then as strictly governmental, very limited as to direct interaction with NGOs. That, together with the human rights movement's relatively low level of interest in the human rights of women, kept the legislative achievements of the commission largely unknown and highly underutilized by women at the grassroots level. Regretfully, even today the record of the CSW remains little known and applied in practice, although it could serve as the most valid source of education on the human rights of women and as a point of departure for the critical assessment of the commission's activities and subsequent strengthening.[3]

Efforts Toward Equality and Eradication of Violence Against Women During the United Nations Decade for Women and Beyond

Increased interaction between the CSW, governments, and NGOs in the area of the human rights of women began in 1975 with the proclamation of the International Women's Year and the 1976–85 United Nations Decade for Women (UNDW): Equality, Development and Peace. In that context, various aspects of the human rights of women began to gain more attention and visibility, although neither the term "human rights of women" nor the holistic approach to the issue had yet emerged. The struggle for women's equality has centered on two key issues: actions directed toward the disclosure and eradication of all forms of violence against women, and the struggle for the recognition and implementation of all human rights and fundamental freedoms in relation to women, without discrimination. Since then, the activities of governmental and nongovernmental organizations, as well as many human rights activists and educators, individuals, and organizations have been channeled into those separate, although closely linked, aspects of the protection and promotion of the human rights of women. Thus, in order to record the change to which all of them have contributed since 1975, each sphere has to be analyzed.

Historical Evolution in Addressing Violence Against Women

Traditionally, violence against women was kept out of public agendas at both the national and international levels. Even during the UNDW, while feminist writers, scholars, and female human rights activists increasingly reported on the shocking incidents of violence against women[4] perpetrated by individuals, institutions, and states, there was a consistent effort on the part of law enforcement and justice institutions, legislators, and large sectors of public opinion to deny the existence of violence against women. Incidents of violence were considered mainly as private, domestic, and family matters, and treated as such "in privacy," outside the realm of public scrutiny or interference. Those incidents were often justified by cultural tradition, custom, or a social code of conduct, and therefore not considered to be criminal offenses.

Feminist claims that all forms of violence are interconnected, regardless of whether the violence is manifested within the home, in the family, in personal relationships, or at the state level, in structural violence or in warfare, have long been ignored. Also largely ignored have been the studies and analyses which contend that all forms of violence, whether expressed through dominance and exploitation, authoritarianism and coercion, or unequal power relations between rich and poor, stronger and weaker, men and women, share common roots. In addition, feminists have noted that violence against women, as a manifestation of control and power, increases in times of war, armed conflict, or social crisis, such as internal upheaval, economic recession, or high unemployment. This link supported the claim that all violence was interconnected.[5]

Those approaches to violence were first incorporated into the governmental debate at the Third World Conference on Women held in Nairobi in 1985. The Forward-Looking Strategies placed violence against women in the "Peace" section and considered it "a major obstacle to the achievement of peace." The strategies also stated explicitly that "Violence against women exists in various forms in everyday life in all societies. Women are beaten, mutilated, burned, sexually abused and raped."[6] The statements were unique at the time. Never before had an intergovernmental document confirmed the existence of daily and universal violence against women, cited examples, and recognized its public nature through its link to peace.

Convention on the Elimination of All Forms of Discrimination Against Women

Content

The issues of sex equality and the elimination of discrimination against women in all its forms developed new dynamics at the 1975 World Conference on Women in Mexico, which accorded them high priority on its agenda. Equality was specified as one of three main goals of the UNDW and, consequently, was integrated into the discussions of intergovernmental bodies in succeeding years.

In that atmosphere, the CSW, assisted by experts, elaborated the Convention on the Elimination of All Forms of Discrimination Against Women. The Convention, the central and most comprehensive treaty on the human rights of women, was adopted by the General Assembly on December 18, 1979. It constitutes not only the international bill of rights of women, which already existed in international customary law, but also an agenda for action for countries to achieve it. In view of its holistic and comprehensive nature, the Convention represented a legislative milestone that went beyond the established framework of discussion on the human rights of women at the time of its adoption.

The Convention explicitly acknowledges in its Preamble that "extensive discrimination against women exists"; it defines discrimination in Article 1 as "any distinction, exclusion or restriction made on the basis of sex which has the effect or purpose of impairing or nullifying the recognition, enjoyment or exercise by women, irrespective of their marital status, on the basis of equality of men and women, of human rights and fundamental freedoms in the political, economic, social, cultural, civil or any other field"; and it includes a commitment to eliminate it through a set of legislative and other measures (Article 2).

The Convention obliges States Parties to undertake "all appropriate measures, including legislation, to ensure the full development and advancement of women, for the purpose of guaranteeing them the exercise and enjoyment of human rights and fundamental freedoms on a basis of equality with men" (Article 3), and encourages the adoption of special temporary measures aimed at accelerating the equality between women and men, and the establishment of special measures protecting maternity (Article 4).

In its substantive Articles 6 to 16, the Convention develops a detailed agenda for equality which covers practically all spheres of life: political rights (Articles 7–8); the rights to education, employment, health, and economic and social activities (Articles 10–13); civil capacity and business matters (Article 15); marriage and the family (Article 16); nationality (Article 9); and family planning (Article 16e). The Convention pays special attention to the situation of women in rural areas (Article 14) and calls for the suppression of trafficking in women and of the exploitation of women through prostitution (Article 6). The Convention also takes a stand on the impact of culture, tradition, stereotypes, and images in restricting women's rights and fundamental freedoms.[7] That interrelationship, already noted in the Preamble, is further addressed in Article 5, in which the States Parties are called upon to work toward changing the traditional roles of men and women in society and in the family, in order to eliminate prejudices and customary practices based on the idea of inferiority of either sex or on stereotyped roles.

Various articles of the Convention combine obligations of means (e.g., parts of Article 2) and, predominantly, obligations of results,[8] which are, for example, stated in Article 3. The obligation of results provisions are also specified under subsequent articles of the Convention (Articles 4–16). Many see as a major weakness of the Convention the fact that it does not impose on the States Parties any specific deadlines or means to be applied, and leaves them too much freedom as to how (and in practice, whether) they are to fulfill their obligations under the Convention. The Convention also does not provide for any complaints procedure enabling individuals to submit communications in case of violation of their rights under the Convention. Other shortcomings relate to the Convention's lack of universality; weaknesses in the work of the Committee on the Elimination of Discrimination Against Women (CEDAW) monitoring the implementation of the Convention; and the insufficient, although improving, involvement of human rights activists, educators, and other representatives of civil society in implementing the Convention.

Universality of the Convention

The universality of the Convention can be defined in terms of the universality of its ratification or the adherence to it, and in terms of its scope. The number of States Parties to the Convention has been on the increase and reached 139 as of June 1995, but still more than 40 UN member states were not parties to it, of whom 7 (including the United States) have already signed the Convention. Most of the countries that did not sign or ratify the Convention have incorporated Muslim law in their civil or family codes and have large Muslim populations (e.g., Algeria, Bahrain, Brunei, Darusalaam, Comoros, Iran, Kuwait, Lebanon, Malaysia, Mauritania, Niger, Pakistan, Qatar, Saudi Arabia, Sudan, Syria, and the United Arab Emirates), or are strongly influenced by religious and customary laws and practices (e.g., Botswana, Mozambique, São Tomé and Principe, Burma, the Democratic People's Republic of Korea, Singapore, Fiji, Kiribati, Papua New Guinea, the Solomon Islands, Tonga, and Vanuatu).

Similar reasons are behind reservations or declarations based on religious law or cultural tradition[9] which accompanied the ratification, signature of, or adherence to the Convention by some countries (e.g., Bangladesh, Brazil, Egypt, Iraq, Libya, Malta, Morocco, the Republic of Korea, Maldives, Mauritius, Thailand, Tunisia, and Turkey). Although specific reservations varied from country to country, they generally considered Articles 2, 9, 15, and 16 as conflicting with national laws or customs and therefore not binding. As those articles constitute the essence of the Convention and touch upon crucial areas in the discrimination against women in many parts of the world, many other States Parties to the Convention have declared that the reservations "are incompatible with the object and purpose of the Convention" and as such incompatible with the international treaty law."

Another weakness of the Convention related to its scope, namely, the lack of explicit reference to violence against women, was overcome through the adoption by CEDAW of general recommendation number 19, which defined violence against women as an extreme form of discrimination and as such linked it to the appropriate provisions of the Convention. The adoption of this recommendation in 1992, prior to the adoption of the Declaration on the Elimination of Violence Against Women by the General Assembly, enabled the Committee to take up that issue in spite of the lack of specific provisions in the text of the Convention, and to request that the States Parties deal with the issue of violence in their periodic national reports.[10]

The Mandate and Work of CEDAW

Articles 17 to 30 of the Convention define the mandate and functioning of the Committee on the Elimination of Discrimination Against Women monitoring the implementation of the Convention.[11] The committee is composed of twenty-three experts in the field covered by the Convention, nominated by Governments and elected by the States Parties for a period of four years, with the possibility of reelection. The States Parties are obliged under the Convention to submit to the committee every four years a national report on progress in the implementation of the Convention and the measures applied. The committee meets once a year for a period of three weeks (which was originally limited to two weeks) in order to discuss the national reports with the representatives of the governments and to make recommendations to States Parties with regard to the reports or to the situation of women in the country concerned.

As the provisions of the Convention are not directly incorporated into the national laws of the respective countries which have ratified the Convention, the review of national reports by the committee constitutes the only official mechanism of control over its implementation. There is a general feeling that this basic role of the committee could be performed better, through, for example, more focused demands for concrete data and information; more consistency in evaluating progress and setting deadlines for the reporting countries to substantiate their information as to how the actions and policies envisaged in their national reports have been implemented in reality; and more use of independent data and nongovernmental sources in assessing the situation of women in the reporting countries.

Other factors impeding the Committee's functioning include an insufficient amount of time allocated to its sessions; a shortage of staff and budget; weakness of the secretariat servicing the committee; insufficient working cooperation with other human rights treaty bodies; uneven involvement of individual experts in the committee's work and their often insufficient knowledge of the situation in the reporting countries; and the criteria for the submission of candidates to the committee by governments, which exclude many outstanding women advocating human rights at the grassroots level who will never obtain the nomination of their respective governments.

In order to improve its record, the committee in recent years has undertaken some actions aimed at closer cooperation with NGOs and human rights experts. It also began the policy of designating from its composition experts responsible for gathering information on countries whose reports were under consideration, in order to be prepared better for the debate. Moreover, the committee undertook some other functions going beyond the monitoring process. For example, it contributed to UN World Conferences; it instituted cooperation, mainly through meetings of chairpersons, with other human rights treaty bodies; it was represented at the key nongovernmental human rights seminars, educational events, and other meetings; and, last but not least, it elaborated, in the period 1986–95, twenty-one general recommendations on various provisions and aspects of the Convention. The new functions of the committee, however, were criticized in some quarters as not in conformity with its primary responsibility. Whatever the criticism, the activities undoubtedly gave the committee some visibility and ensured its long-denied position among human rights treaty bodies.

The Impact of NGOs and Human Rights Experts on the Implementation
of the Convention and the Work of CEDAW

Preparation of the periodic report, its presentation to the committee by the national delegation, and the committee's analyses and appraisal of the report and of the situation of women in the country should be subject to scrutiny by national and international civil society represented by nongovernmental experts and activists in the area of the human rights of women. This was not the case in the early years of the committee's work. Knowledge of the Convention and the resulting obligations for the States Parties was very low. Most governments did not fulfill their duty to translate the Convention into their national languages and to publicize it widely. They also did not take sufficiently seriously their obligations to report under the Convention, assuming that the whole process could remain in "closed circulation" between national bureaucracies and the United Nations. During the cold war, the access of the public and NGOs to governmental reports prepared for international organizations was rather restricted. The public's lack of knowledge even of the existence of the Convention and the functioning of the monitoring mechanism, CEDAW, allowed many governments, for years, to produce one-sided, self-congratulating reports, which all too often were praised by the committee without being contested. That situation has not yet changed sufficiently even now, despite the progress in democratization and development of civil society. Owing to lack of information and legal education, citizens of many countries are not aware that it is their right to know how their governments fulfill their international commitments and that they should not only be informed about the content of reports for CEDAW, but should participate in their preparation.

The importance of the Convention was also underestimated by many human rights groups, including some women's groups, at least in the early years of its adoption. Again, lack of awareness and knowledge were among the main reasons. Skepticism about the Convention resulted partly from the fact that it was considered to be just one more UN agreement, bound to remain on paper. This feeling about UN agreements prevalent until now, was particularly pronounced in the cold war period, when many international human rights standards were violated without even being addressed at international forums, in order not to upset the existing balance of power. Another a priori rejection of the Convention originated in some feminist quarters and was based on the conviction that laws, like all power structures from which they emanated, were products of patriarchy and male domination and that as such they could not serve the cause of women. Thus in the first years after the Convention's entry into force there was no impetus to give it due prominence and ensure the best possible implementation.

The situation began to change gradually after the 1985 Nairobi Conference with the creation of the International Women's Rights Action Watch (IWRAW), the first global organization focused on supervising the implementation of the Convention.

IWRAW, a network of scholars and activists, began to report systematically on the activities and legislation that promoted or impeded the implementation of the Convention.[12] It also held international meetings and educational seminars centered on the Convention, prepared a guide to reporting under the Convention, supported and monitored the work of CEDAW, and provided independent data on the status of women and on cases where their rights had been violated.

In 1986, shortly after its creation, IWRAW published its first report on the five sessions of CEDAW (1982–86), based on analyses of UN records. Soon afterwards, IWRAW introduced the practice of observing CEDAW's sessions. The proceedings of the 1988 session were covered by Andrew Byrnes, a lawyer from Australia, and reflected in a IWRAW report. The report, soon known as the Byrnes report, was extremely well received and became a model for the NGO's reporting and monitoring of the committee's sessions. The systematic reporting and monitoring of CEDAW by IWRAW encouraged both better governmental compliance with the reporting requirements and nongovernmental monitoring of the Committee's sessions. Thus IWRAW played an important educational role in promoting knowledge and critical analysis of the Convention and its monitoring body, CEDAW.

The possibilities of using the reporting mechanism for monitoring governmental commitments with regard to the human rights of women is still much underutilized, although awareness of its existence and the involvement of NGOs in the supervision of the work of the committee and governments has been increasing recently because of the inclusion of the Convention and CEDAW into the human rights education and training programs organized by human rights advocacy groups.

Developments Toward Eradication of Violence Against Women and Recognition of the Human Rights of Women at the World Conference on Human Rights

The major breakthrough in terms of governmental approaches to violence against women and to the human rights of women occurred in 1993. Extensive changes were instituted as a result of the concerted efforts of NGOs, which demanded a clear governmental stand on those issues during the preparations for the World Conference on Human Rights (WCHR) held in Vienna in 1993.

The participation of women's groups and NGOs in the WCHR was well prepared and preceded by a global campaign for recognition of women's human rights, with a focus on violence against women. The campaign began in June 1991, when the Center for Women's Global Leadership convened a meeting of twenty-three women from different parts of the world working to end gender violence. That group developed a strategy of "sixteen days of international activism against gender violence," calling for worldwide recognition that violence against women violates women's human rights. The first sixteen days campaign in 1991 resulted in a petition that urged the preparatory committee of the WCHR to include women's rights and gender violence as central concerns of that forum. The petition was sponsored by the International Women's Tribune Center and the Center for Women's Global Leadership, as part of the Decade for Human Rights Education. During the sixteen days campaigns in 1991 and 1992, women's groups conducted meetings on a worldwide basis and collected signatures on the petitions. The signed petitions were delivered to the UN's preparatory meetings to the WCHR and to the conference itself. They also reached the UN secretary-general, Boutros Boutros-Ghali.

The reaction of the UN Secretariat, as well as of most governments, was reluctant, and in the case of some, clearly negative. However, consolidated action by NGOs, and particularly the hearings of the Tribunal on the cases of violations of the human rights of women during the conference, could not be ignored. Well-documented testimony of women from all parts of the world who had been victims of violence, and had been deprived of their basic rights, forced governments to take a stand on the issue; they could no longer claim that those violations constituted individual and extreme events, nor could they pretend that, for example, "kitchen accidents" related to dowries were incidental and private because they took place within homes or families. It was impossible to argue in front of TV cameras that trafficking in women or rape could happen only to women of "dubious conduct," who were thus themselves guilty.

The overwhelming evidence on the violations of the human rights of women shown and debated in public could no longer be denied by governments calling themselves democratic. In the atmosphere of the officially proclaimed victory of democracy in international relations and the emphasis on the need for creation of free and democratic society at the national level, it was increasingly difficult to argue against the right to full enjoyment of human rights and democracy by women.

A Methodology for Women's Human Rights Education
by Maria Suarez-Toro and Roxana Arroyo

The object of human rights education by, for and about women, is to contribute to civil society's movement toward transformation, deeply rooted in respect, promotion and protection of the rights of all. Specifically the objectives are to:

identify the main rights that have been denied, hidden, and disregarded in women's daily lives, and which have no expression in national and international legislation;

identify rights gained by women through their struggles, strengths and support from others;

build a new pedagogy on human rights education where women appropriate and reconceptualize human rights legislation as "instruments" of the people to fulfil their needs; and

develop strategies that rebuild a body of women's rights of prevention, protection, and promotion of dignity and the qualitative transformation of society.

Step 1

Exercise: Reconstruct the first time women remember feeling a right was denied them due to their gender.

Example: *A 62-year-old Costa Rican urban dweller in San José told us that at age 13, her father made her marry a man, 10 years older, who had raped her. She had 11 children, with this man, and said her life had been on hold since the marriage.*

Insights: (a) Most experiences women recall involve the "private" sphere of their lives and are not, in classical human rights terms, human rights matters. (b) Many first experiences of denial of rights arise from comparing the socialization process of boys and girls. Women learn early that men have rights that women do not, making evident a double standard of rights and discrimination based on differences.

Step 2

Build each woman's story of being the subject of rights, the empowerment to act on it, and the support of others to do it.

Exercise: Reconstruct the first time women remember when they gained a right out of the process of recognizing needs, dignity, and power.

Example: *The same Costa Rican woman gained her first right two years before, at age*

60, when she graduated from 6th grade in night school. Had she not been forced by her father to marry her rapist, and by the rapist immediately to have children, she would have been able to achieve this at age 14.

Insights: (a) A woman's initial experience of rights often gives her a sense of self-determination to fulfill a need denied because she is a woman. ("The first time I wore pants and dared to leave the house in them"; "The first time I dared say no when I did not want to make love with my husband"; "The first time I ate when I was hungry, instead of doing so after all the rest had eaten.")

(b) Many address bridging the gap between private and public, going beyond the domestic sphere and the roles demanded of women.

(c) Others demonstrate the indivisibility of self-determination and the guarantees of social, economic, and cultural rights. For the Costa Rican woman, the degree was an act of self-determination which could only be achieved in the context of social conditions that made education possible.

(d) Many demonstrate the process of learning to say no to others, and yes to women's needs.

Step 3

Have students examine the international human rights instruments—and their interpretations—to see if their rights are accurately reflected.

Exercise: Different techniques can be used to study the international legislation: film, video, drama, short stories, or excerpts from novels, and so on. Women then are asked to compare the rights described with their own stories. This is followed with a discussion in which experiences are compared and contrasted. Encourage comments and questions. Everyone contributes their knowledge and reactions on all issues raised.

Example: *A group of students of international human rights law went through the process and were asked to find their rights expressed in the Universal Declaration. They spoke of mothers being battered, their own sexual harassment as children, and about different sexual standards applied to their brothers and themselves. If they found their rights in the documents, it was a product of the interpretation of the text to the domestic sphere but not explicit as human rights.*

Insights: (a) Women study and look into international legislation not as a formal, cognitive exercise, but as related to their needs.

(b) The center and core is not "the rights," but "the life" and how it is reflected in international human rights legislation.

(c) This process helps women understand the limitations of dichotomies that stem from the androcentric view of rights, the separation of private and public, and divisions between the different generations of rights.

Step 4

Out of the previous discussion, suggest actions and strategies to overcome limitations and to work with others engaged in similar efforts.

Exercise: The group drafts a list of the limitations identified. Devise actions and strategies at different levels (daily lives, local, national, and international) to transform society and build women's human rights. Compile a list of all groups known to defend, promote, protect, and reconceptualize human rights at all levels. Discuss how they do it and how they can be contacted.

Example: *In a workshop in Guatemala in 1991, indigenous women mentioned the women on human rights commissions as their possible support group. In Costa Rica, women human rights activists have appealed for the support of women's groups in facing domestic violence themselves.*

Insights: (a) Strategies that help women develop self-sufficiency through productive projects such as battered women's houses and support groups.

(b) Nonformal strategies of survival used by victims of abuses.

(c) Suggested changes in international law which overcome the separation between the private and public, reconceptualize human rights to include women's experiences and rights, and affirm the indivisibility of human rights.

Step 5

This step includes sharing women's fears about implementing new strategies, discussing where the fears come from, who perpetuates them, and who supports women in overcoming them. This augments the initial strategies by including action plans.

Exercise: The strategies and actions that have been developed are written on a blackboard or large poster. The first emotional reaction to each is registered. Participants then present their reaction to the group, explaining how to overcome them.

Example: *One human rights activist said that her experience of overwhelming discrimination against women in the human rights movement evoked deep sadness. This stemmed from the realization that, despite being a just cause, it will take many years to overcome these many problems.*

Insights: (a) Women appropriate the strategies only after fears have been dealt with as an integral part of the process.

(b) This exercise empowers women personally and collectively. It promotes the creation of group support emanating from the workshop groups.

(c) The process helps identify actions to overcome the obstacles that perpetuate gender roles and the victimization of women.

All these factors decisively contributed to the critically important outcome of the conference. The conference finally challenged cultural relativism with regard to violence against women and stated in its Declaration that "Gender-biased violence and all forms of sexual harassment and exploitation, including those resulting from cultural prejudice and international trafficking, are incompatible with the dignity and worth of the human person and must be eliminated" (para. 18). It also considered violations of the human rights of women in situations of armed conflicts as a violation of the fundamental principles of international human rights and humanitarian law and stated explicitly that in particular "murder, systematic rape, sexual slavery, and forced pregnancy require a particularly effective response" (para. 38). In order to follow up on those decisions, the conference suggested the appointment of a special rapporteur on violence against women by the Commission on Human Rights at its fiftieth session in 1994.

In addressing the human rights of women, the conference stressed the holistic nature of those rights and the need for their integration and recognition in all spheres of life. It also stated explicitly in its Declaration that "the human rights of women and of the girl-child are an inalienable, integral and indivisible part of universal human rights" (para. 18).

The conference also made an attempt to strengthen the existing regime for the protection of the human rights of women in the UN system. It requested CSW and CEDAW to examine quickly the possibility of introducing the right of individual petition through the preparation of an optional protocol to CEDAW. The Declaration also urged universal ratification of the Convention by the year 2000, and the withdrawal of reservations that are incompatible with and contrary to the object and purpose of the Convention or which are otherwise incompatible with international treaty law (para. 39).

The results of the conference also indicated basic changes in public attitudes to the human rights of women, achieved through the years of work of human rights activists and advocates, and the untiring efforts of human rights educators. They proved to the public that existing human rights standards contained in international instruments have not been equally applied to women; that women were discriminated against in all spheres of life and in all countries, although to different degrees; that discrimination against women and the lack of observance of their human rights was a social issue; and that these historically formed inequalities could be redressed only through prompt de jure and de facto implementation of the human rights of women at the national and international levels.

The Human Rights of Women Between Vienna and Beijing: Conflicting Trends

The major breakthrough in Vienna in 1993 opened a new period in the struggle for the human rights of women, with focus on the eradication of violence against women and the strengthening of the implementation of the Convention on the Elimination of all Forms of Discrimination Against Women. Consequently those issues strongly marked the preparatory process of the 1995 Fourth World Conference on Women (FWCW) in Beijing and the conference itself. The preparatory process, however, was also characterized by the reverse trend to redefine the existing standards of the human rights of women and to slow down the pace of change accelerated in Vienna.

Progress in Combating Violence Against Women

In Legislation, Through Adoption of the Declaration on the Elimination of Violence Against Women

The results of Vienna sped up efforts toward elaborating a comprehensive governmental approach to the issue of violence against women through the negotiation and adoption of the Declaration on the Elimination of Violence Against Women.[13] The Declaration, which had originated within the CSW, was adopted by consensus on December 20, 1993 by General Assembly Resolution A/48/104. The Declaration clearly defines violence against women as "any act of gender-based violence that results in, or is likely to result in, physical, sexual, or psychological harm or suffering to women, including threats of such acts, coercion or arbitrary deprivation of liberty, whether occurring in public, or in private life" (Article 1). The definition of violence against women encompasses, but is not limited to, physical, sexual and psychological violence occurring in the family (including battering, sexual abuse of female children, dowry-related violence, marital rape, female genital mutilation, nonspousal violence, and violence related to exploitation); in society (including rape, sexual abuse, sexual harassment and intimidation at work, in educational institutions, and elsewhere, trafficking in women, and forced prostitution), as well as physical, sexual, and psychological violence perpetrated or condoned by states, wherever it occurs (Article 3). Thus the definition clearly breaks with the interpretation of violence against women as a private matter and makes states accountable for protecting their female citizens against violence.

The scope of the Declaration moves beyond punishment of perpetrators and victims' assistance. It explicitly calls for proper education and awareness-raising activities in order to modify social attitudes and patterns of conduct of both women and men, with the ultimate goal "to eliminate prejudices, customary practices and all other practices based on the idea of the inferiority or superiority of either of the sexes and on the stereotyped roles of men and women" (Article 4j).

In addition, in a clear echo of the feminist ideology, the Preamble of the Declaration states correctly that "violence against women is a manifestation of historically unequal power relations between men and women, which have led to domination over and discrimination against women by men, and to the prevention of the full advancement of women, and that violence against women is one of the crucial social mechanisms by which women are forced into a subordinate position compared with men." This passage clearly identifies violence against women as a major impediment to the advancement of women and their equality, and links it to the social order and to the human rights of women. It also explains, at least in part, why the world for so many years has refused to recognize violence against women as a public and criminal matter and has historically insisted on noninterference in that sphere as private, protected by culture, customs, and traditions that should not be disputed: simply because the rejection of violence against women as an acceptable norm of conduct challenges the established social order based on women's subordination and undermines the existing power structures, which many would like to preserve.

. . . and in Reality

In implementing the decisions of the WCHR, Radhika Coomaraswamy, a national of Sri Lanka, was appointed as the first special rapporteur on violence against women. Her initial report, issued in 1995,[14] provides a comprehensive analysis of the issue of violence against women, its roots, and incidents that have occurred throughout the world. Like other recent studies (e.g., the UN publication *The World's Women 1995: Trends and Statistics*),[15] the report confirms that violence against women persists at all levels and in all parts of the world. It is difficult to obtain complete and accurate data on violence against women, as the information is fragmented, based on small, ad hoc studies lacking consistent methodologies and techniques. Data on sexual assault is particularly limited. Although the studies confirm that violence against women is ever-present and that it penetrates all spheres of life, all social strata, cultures, and regions, they point to some forms of violence that are particularly alarming due to their high incidence and their continual increase and because of their political or cultural nature. These facts merit particular attention from human rights advocates and educators.

The most common and persistent type is violence against women at the personal level; it takes place in the home and is perpetrated by male cohabitants. The existing samples, which showed that, for example, in Bangladesh, killings of women by their husbands account for 50 percent of all murders, and that 60 percent or more of the women in Africa, Latin America, and Asia have been abused by their intimate partners, are still valid as indicators of the prevailing trend.[16]

Another area of discrimination, which has been officially acknowledged only recently and which is particularly critical in some parts of Asia and Africa, is the treatment of the girl-child. The preference of parents for male children often manifests itself in neglect, deprivation, or discriminatory treatment of girls to the detriment of their mental and physical health. In extreme cases, girls in the family are treated as market commodities to be given away or sold in order to increase family income.[17]

Women domestic servants, migrant workers, and refugees are increasingly ex-

ploited, discriminated, and abused. They often face various forms of sexual intimidation and exploitation. For example, they are confronted with "additional" conditions
related to their employment, refuge, or integration into a foreign country, namely,
sexual favors to the men who can influence those decisions. Young girls seeking jobs
as domestic servants or in the entertainment business, or who migrate abroad following job/marriage advertisements are often driven into the "sex industry." Recent
reports indicate a continuing increase in trafficking in women and abuses of female
migrant workers. For example, there is a growth in trafficking of sex workers from
east European countries to western Europe. There has also been an increase, between
1982 and 1994, in the number of Filipino women migrating as "entertainers." Most
of them are between sixteen and twenty-three years of age. The majority were tricked
into working as prostitutes or in sex-related businesses.[18] With the increasing gap between the worlds of rich and poor, and the tendency of the latter to emigrate to the
"better world" at any price in order to survive, the issue is bound to become even
more pressing.

Added to this is the recent and ever-increasing effect of the AIDS epidemic on
women. The explosive rates of expansion of the disease among women results from
their lack of access to education, information, and means of proper protection as well
as subordinate and powerless position in society, within their marriages, and in other
sexual relationships.[19]

Other forms of violence against women, which continue despite the results of
Vienna, although often masked as "acceptable" forms of traditional practices or customs, include, among others, female circumcision and strict dress-behavior codes
imposed on women by society, often even codified by law. Resisting these societal
norms and laws threatens not only women's social position but often their well being
and lives.

Female circumcision and other traditional practices harmful to women's health
continue to be inflicted on girls and women in many parts of the world, mainly
in Africa. For many years, international governmental organizations, including the
World Health Organization (WHO), refused to recognize and address the problem,
claiming that such acts were based on "social and cultural backgrounds." Fortunately
this policy has changed, in large part because of the work of national committees on
traditional practices in a number of African countries and women's networks. They
have focused on female genital mutilation as a crime and demanded its eradication. They also called for awareness raising and educational campaigns to tackle this
problem within the context of health and human rights education. Despite gradually changing attitudes toward female genital mutilation and its gradual elimination,
at least among educated, urban communities, official authorities in many countries
continue to protect it as a "private" ritual. Estimates of the total number of women
subjected to female genital mutilation in Africa and in some parts of Asia reached
100 million in 1994. At the current rate of population increase, the estimated number

of girls eligible for this practice will amount to 2 million every year.[20] There is also a dangerous trend to "institutionalize" this practice through its performance in hospitals in order to avoid immediate health risks. Thus it is very difficult to assess whether any visible progress has been made toward eradication of female genital mutilation in recent years.[21]

Although the past few years have brought to light many cases of women being persecuted through violent measures for resisting traditional codes of conduct or behavior, they also marked the first changes in the attitudes of governments and law enforcement agencies to those issues. Those codes apply to women only and differ from country to country. They are defined either de jure or de facto as binding customs. What they have in common is severe restriction imposed on women's personal rights and freedoms, such as freedom of movement, free choice of domicile, style of life, and equal rights within the family and marriage, including its conclusion and termination. Thus these laws and customs create a state of "gender apartheid" which contradicts human rights and in particular the human rights of women. Still, despite the existence of "gender apartheid" laws and practices in some countries, very little has been done at the international level to challenge this system. Even the extreme cases of abuse and violence did not "make the news," nor have they figured prominently in national political campaigns.

However, progress is finally, albeit slowly, being made. Recognition of gender-related violence as grounds for asylum is being gradually instituted, thanks to the steady efforts of women activists. The first case in which a woman was granted political asylum due to sexual persecution occurred in Canada in 1993. Since the alteration of Canada's official asylum guidelines, two hundred women have been granted asylum based on those rules. Similar rules were recently issued in the United States, and in April 1995 political asylum was granted to a Jordanian woman on the basis that her government had failed to protect her from her husband's physical assaults. Progress can also be witnessed in the case of a Haitian woman, who was refused political asylum in the United States, although she had been raped by soldiers because of her support for President Jean Bertrand Aristide. Her case is now under consideration. The guidelines for women asylum seekers in the United States give examples of the types of violence that constitute grounds for political asylum, including infanticide, genital mutilation, slavery, forced marriage, and opposition to traditions such as wearing a veil. The changes in approaches of these two countries are welcome first steps toward the official recognition that so-called traditional cultural practices and customs are, in fact, violations of the human rights of women. As their lives are put at risk, they should be eligible for political asylum.

Some progress can also be noted with regard to the issues of war-related violence against women, which emerged so strongly at the WCHR. War-related violence against women, including rape, has been known throughout history. However, the extent of violence against women during the recent armed conflicts in the territory of the former Yugoslavia, and, afterwards in Rwanda and Haiti, and in particular the rape of women used as a means of terror, intimidation, and as a tool of war, have shaken public opinion. Unfortunately the disclosures and testimonies by women victims of such violence, most of them from Bosnia and Herzegovina, have been only recently, and to a limited extent, followed by proper legal inquiry by the United Nations Tribunals for the former Yugoslavia and for Rwanda. The disclosure of war-related violence against women, however, in particular in the former Yugoslavia, has brought worldwide visibility and attention to these issues.[22]

Work on an Optional Protocol to the Convention on the Elimination of All Forms of Discrimination Against Women

Following the decisions of the WCHR, both CSW and CEDAW took up the issue of new procedures to strengthen implementation of the Convention through examining the possibility of introducing the right to petition through the preparation of an Optional Protocol to the Convention.[23] In pursuance of the best tradition of cooperation with governmental bodies, two nongovernmental organizations, the Women in the Law Project and the Maastricht Center for Human Rights, organized an Expert Group Meeting on the Adoption of an Optional Protocol to the Convention on the Elimination of All Forms of Discrimination Against Women at Maastricht in 1994. The meeting, attended by international legal experts and three members of CEDAW, adopted a draft optional protocol (CEDAW/C/1995/WG.1/WP.1). The draft will be further discussed and the issue will be taken up by the CSW at its forthcoming session.

Controversy over "Equality" as Indication of the Difficulties That Emerged in the Preparatory Process for the FWCW in Beijing

The success of the Vienna Conference led to the quick consolidation of those forces that did not support the concept of equality between men and women as reflected in the human rights standards or that have their own understanding of those issues, not necessarily shared by most of the international community. The preparatory process for the FWCW in Beijing, in 1994–95, revealed this phenomenon. The controversy centered around such terms as *equality* versus *equity, dignity,* and *gender.*

Paradoxically, the word "equity" was inherited from the preparatory discussions for the International Conference on Population and Development (ICPD) in Cairo in 1994, in which it had been injected by some women's groups. They considered "equality" insufficient, as forcing women to be equal with men on their terms, in the world of values and institutions established by men only, and therefore not reflecting women's contributions. The result of this "improvement" opened the gates for undermining the principle of equality throughout the process of the negotiations. The opponents of "equality," representing countries with strong religious-fundamentalist

Figure 7.1. An ad hoc planning committee discusses how to organize an education forum on the theme "Women's Rights Are Human Rights." Shown here at the NGO Forum on Women meeting in China in 1995, each participant wears a button saying "I am a Human Rights Educator." (Organizing Committee for the People's Decade of Human Rights Education)

tendencies, tried to replace it with "equity" and "dignity." While the equality of men and women [24] in terms of all rights and fundamental freedoms is measurable and belongs to accepted standards of democracy and human rights, "equity" and "dignity" can always be defined by those who have power, in accordance with their own understanding of what is "undignified" or "inequitable" for women. There was a risk that if such language was adopted, the issue, for example, of the participation of women in decision making or of women's reproductive rights would fall into the category of "undignified," at least in some countries and in accordance with the views of male political, religious, and spiritual leaders.

Similar reasons were behind the "misunderstanding" related to the term *gender*. Although gender analysis and gender studies have been developed for many years in all parts of the world, including the United Nations, the term became suddenly unacceptable.

The problem of terminology was finally resolved mainly through the contribution of the High Commissioner for Human Rights, Ayola Lasso. In his comments on the Draft Platform for Action for the Fourth World Conference on Women (A/Conf.177/L.1), he referred to the existing standards of protection of the human rights of women and warned against the danger of opening them to misinterpretation. He emphasized the importance of the legal principles of equality and nondiscrimination, which provide the foundations for the enjoyment of human rights, and the applicability of these principles to all aspects of women's lives by the Convention on the Elimination of All Forms of Discrimination Against Women. He further stressed that the appearance in some parts of the draft text of "equity," which is conditioned by subjective criteria, could not replace "equality," as it would serve to undermine this fundamental principle enshrined in the United Nations Charter and other subsequent documents. Similar reference was made to the "dignity of women" as different from the original formulation enshrined in the Preamble to the Universal Declaration of Human Rights stating "the dignity and worth of the human person and the equal rights of men and women."

The positive outcome of the Beijing Conference, as reflected in its final document, the Beijing Declaration and Platform for Action, resulted from the forceful participation in the debate of many delegations from both the developed and developing countries. These countries were concerned with the risk of lowering the existing standards of equality and protection of the human rights of women. NGOs also played an important role, but their presence was less visible and focused than at the WCHR in Vienna.

Special recognition, however, should be given to the High Commissioner for Human Rights for the critical role he played in defending the human rights of women by using his legal expertise and knowledge. Thus he proved in practice the point that education on the human rights of women is essential for the promotion of gender equality and equal participation of men and women in combating gender bias and stereotypes.

Notes

1. Commission on the Status of Women, doc.E/90, July 1, 1946.

2. Among others, Convention on the Political Rights of Women (1952), Convention on the Nationality of Married Women (1957), Convention on the Elimination of All Forms of Discrimination Against Women (1979), Declaration on the Protection of Women and Children in Emergency and Armed Conflict (1974), and Declaration on the Elimination of Violence Against Women (1993).

3. *The United Nations and the Advancement of Women, 1945–1995*, UN Department of Public Information (New York: United Nations, 1995), sales no. E.95.129, 686.

4. For example, Govind Kelkar, "Women and Structural Violence in India," paper presented at the 10th International Peace Research Association (IPRA) Conference, Gyor, August 25–28, 1983; Erin Pizzey, *"Scream Quietly or the Neighbours Will Hear"* (London: IF Books, 1974); Eve Burton, "Surviving the Flight of Horror: The Story of Refugee Women," *Indochina Issues* 34 (February 1983).

5. See, for example, Suzanne Steinmetz and Murray Strauss, eds., *Violence in the Family* (New York: Dodd, Mead and Company, 1974); Susan Brownmiller, *Against Our Will: Men, Women and Rape* (New York: Simon and Schuster, 1975); Betty Reardon, "Militarism and Sexism," paper presented at the 9th IPRA Conference, Toronto, June 21–26, 1981; Brigitt Brock-Utne, *Educating for Peace: A Feminist Perspective* (New York: Pergamon Press, 1985).

6. The Nairobi Forward-Looking Strategies for the Advancement of Women, United Nations, DPI/926–41761, September 1993, 10M, p. 8.

7. Marsha A. Freeman, "Women, Development and Justice: Using the International Convention on Women's Rights," in *Ours by Right: Women's Rights as Human Rights*, ed. Joanna Kerr (London: Zed Books, 1993).

8. See Rebecca J. Cook, "State Accountability Under the Women's Convention," in *Human Rights of Women: National and International Perspectives*, ed. Rebecca J. Cook (Philadelphia: University of Pennsylvania Press, 1995).

9. For detailed information on the matter, see Rebecca J. Cook, "Reservations to the Convention on the Elimination of All Forms of Discrimination Against Women," *Virginia Journal of International Law* 30, no. 3 (Spring 1990): 643–716.

10. See Elizabeth Evatt, "Eliminating Discrimination Against Women: The Impact of the UN Convention," *Melbourne University Law Review* 18 (December 1991): 435–49.

11. See Andrew Byrnes, "The 'Other' Human Rights Treaty Body: The Work of the Committee on the Elimination of Discrimination Against Women," *Yale Journal of International Law* 14, no. 1 (Winter 1989): 1–67.

12. *The Women's Watch*, IWRAW's serial publication reporting on law and policy change in accordance with the principles of the Convention, is a unique source of information on the human rights of women analyzed from the perspective of the Convention.

13. See "Violence Against Women: A Crime Prevention and Criminal Justice Perspective," Crime Prevention and Criminal Justice Branch / UNOV, EGM/VAW/1991/WP.9, November 7, 1991; Jane Connors, "Government Measures to Confront Violence Against Women," Commission on the Status of Women, Working Group on Violence Against Women, Background Paper no. 3, August 1992.

14. Preliminary Report Submitted by the Special Rapporteur on Violence Against Women, Its Causes and Consequences, Ms. Radhika Coomaraswamy, in accordance with Commission on Human Rights Resolution 1994/45 (E/CN.4/1995/42).

15. *The World's Women 1995: Trends and Statistics* (New York: United Nations, 1995), sales no. E.95.XVII.2, p. 158.

16. Reported by the Special Rapporteur; *The World's Women*, 158; IWTC/UNIFEM Resource Center: Fact Sheet on Gender Violence, 1992.

17. "Born Unequal: The Plight of the Girl Child," in *A Time for Action: Girls, Women and Human Rights* (New York: UNICEF, 1991), sales no. E.93.XX.USA.4, p. 3; by the Special Rapporteur, chapter on "Son Preference and Gender Difference in Nutrition," paras. 154–59; *The World's Women*, 160–61.

18. *The World's Women*, 161–62; see also Report by the Special Rapporteur, chap. 3, "Prostitution and Trafficking."

19. Second review and appraisal of the implementation of the Nairobi Forward-Looking Strategies for the Advancement of Women, Report of the Secretary-General, Addendum, E/CN.6/1995/3/Add.3, p. 11.

20. Report by the Special Rapporteur, chapter on "Female Genital Mutilation," paras. 146–53; see also Nahid Toubia, *Female Genital Mutilation: A Call for Global Action* (New York: 1993).

21. World Health Organization, *Female Genital Mutilation — the Practice* (Geneva: WHO, July 1994).

22. Report by the Special Rapporteur, chapter on "Violence Against Women in Situations of Armed Conflict," paras. 261–92.

23. See Cees Flinterman, "Draft Optional Protocol to the Convention on the Elimination of All Forms of Discrimination Against Women," *Netherlands Quarterly of Human Rights* 6 (1995): 85.

24. Anne Bayefsky, "The Principle of Equality or Non-Discrimination in International Law," *Human Rights Law Journal* 11 (1990): 1–34.

Chapter 8
Charter Making and Participatory Research
Ellen Dorsey

Previous chapters in this volume deal explicitly and implicitly with the role of human rights education (HRE) in the construction and consolidation of democracy or broadly as a mechanism for empowering communities traditionally oppressed or disenfranchised. Other chapters discuss different models of HRE. This chapter provides an example of a participatory approach to human rights education as central to securing human rights guarantees and fostering a human rights culture in a newly evolving democracy.

As South Africa struggled in transition to transcend its repressive past and a climate of intense violence, simultaneous and spontaneous campaigns to draft charters of rights claims for historically voiceless communities were launched. They all adopted similar models of participatory education to draw communities together, to create a nonhierarchical process of dialogue, and to foster a perception of efficacy that their rights can be recognized. Such dialogue is designed not simply to foster awareness of rights but to create a new space for their particular rights claims.

It is this goal that makes the participatory approach so important to study as a form of human rights education and as a crucial step toward creating a human rights culture. Under the mandate of drafting a charter of rights (for women, workers, children, the disabled, religious people, prisoners, and gays and lesbians, among others), those who have traditionally been denied a voice, even within the voiceless black majority, had the opportunity to draw together to discuss their needs and articulate their rights claims, perhaps for the first time. This dialogue crossed divisions within each group across race, class, gender, ethnic and religious groups, and geographical location that have traditionally precluded access to and knowledge of others' perspectives.

The charter campaign itself serves as a channel for these rights claims to be incorporated into the larger political process of transition, with the document that is produced from the dialogue serving as a legitimate representation of the demands of that community. These documents will not only become a source for interpretation of rights disputes in the future, if they are addended to a future Bill of Rights as proposed. But the campaigns to draft the charters immediately elevated the claims of these communities in the national political discourse, ensuring that their agenda was at least heard in the process of crafting the institutions of governance for the future. As these communities were typically represented in the transition negotiations only by the leadership of the central political parties, the creation of a space for the articulation of the needs of these communities is particularly important.

Taken together with a massive human rights education campaign in the workplace, schools, places of worship, and so on (see the chapter by Edward O'Brien in this volume), the charter campaigns represent an alternative human rights socialization, breaking the cycles of inefficacy and norms of intolerance and fear. Such alternative socialization is an integral component in fostering a human rights culture for a post-apartheid South Africa. In South Africa a rights culture requires that political voice be given to all previously oppressed segments of the society. It is one where an acceptance of the legitimacy and viability of human rights norms guaranteed by new democratic institutions would be ingrained throughout society and upon which standards of rights accountability for public and social institutions would be created.

The primary goal of these rights socialization efforts is *not to instruct* society about the nature of democratic institutions or even of global human rights norms, but to generate a societywide discourse about rights. The short-term goal of such discourse is to facilitate debate about the transitional process and the nature of rights that should be entrenched in a new constitution. But there are several long-term goals. The first is to produce a perception in the legitimacy of the rule of law and to foster a belief in the effective functioning of a representative system of government, where those previously denied access to the law will develop expectations about their rights under law and capacity to use the new political institutions for the redress of their grievances. In South Africa this goal is a critical one. The historical denial of legitimate access to the law for the majority population has not only eroded general belief in the concept of justice as administered by the state, but has contributed greatly to the violence plaguing the country. Some of the alternative systems of justice that were constructed in the apartheid years are certainly antithetical to the production of universal norms of human rights in the future.

The second long-term goal of such a discourse is to foster a societal norm of tolerance for individual and communal diversity and to establish a political space for competitive values. Again, given the levels of political violence occurring in South Africa currently and the history of extreme political polarization, fostering a norm of tolerance is the single imperative in laying the foundation for a democratic society and human rights culture. Such educational and participatory programs of rights realization are based on the assumption that the interaction produced through debate over rights will most directly break down the stereotypes that preclude tolerance.

Thus the long-term goals of these charters, as conceived by their originators, parallels that of the goals of formal educational programs for human rights: to create a perception of the efficacy of the political institutions for guaranteeing the protection

Figure 8.1. Before South Africa's first democratic election in April 1994, human rights education took place in many forms, including charter writing and the voter education programs sponsored by the South African Street Law Project. (National Institute for Citizen Education in Law [NICEL])

of rights in the future. These campaigns are also directed toward fostering a degree of societal tolerance for the realization of the rights of all segments of society, specifically those that have historically been most neglected. It will be argued further that the transformative potential inherent in this model of HRE is profound, far beyond the goals of those who launched the campaigns. After examining the evolution of the campaigns and how they should be evaluated as a model of HRE, I give broad assessments of the concerns and implications the South African case evokes as a model to be followed by other societies.

The Charter Campaigns for Human Rights in a Post-Apartheid South Africa

The history of the human rights charter campaigns in South Africa is the story of a long tradition of democratic participation by individuals and organizations in the liberation struggle, the precedent of drafting documents to outline the demands of the oppressed, the confluence of initiatives by different groups of minority communities in the initial stages of the transition process, and the influence of one individual. Much has been written on the democratic character of the liberation movement in South Africa as embodied in the 1955 Freedom Charter and as reflected in the efforts of the African National Congress (ANC) at participatory practices of decision making, which were employed even in exile. While sometimes failing in application, standards of accountability and consultation were initiated in the early years of the struggle. In recent years, as transition was inevitable, debates over how representative institutions and participatory democracy could be merged were the focus of much intellectual and political concern. When the African National Congress first began its efforts to draft a set of constitutional proposals, this concern over retaining the participatory character of the movement intensified. And it was from this concern, and from efforts by various sectors of the liberation movement to sustain their own practices of consultation, that the idea of the charters for human rights evolved.

In the internal debates of the ANC over the utility of a bill of rights, the idea of expanding the concept of a bill to be a people's document was advanced by Albie Sachs, a professor of law in exile in Mozambique. He argued that a bill of rights would have legitimacy in the eyes of the people if it was not perceived as being a document produced by a small committee of experts. It could not represent mere duplication of constitutional initiatives of other countries, with all the biases and inappropriateness in application that that would imply. Instead, he argued that

it should emerge from extensive popular input and participation. All the people in the different areas most directly affected should have a central role in determining what the formulation should be. People in the religious spheres representing the different religious communities themselves should help to write a charter of religious rights with an outline of both rights and responsibilities. The women's movement should itself be making the major input in relation to human rights for women. Workers should be determining, formulating, and agreeing upon the basic terms of a charter of rights for workers.[1]

The specific idea of the charters came from the experience that the leaders of the liberation movement had in drafting the Freedom Charter in the mid-1950s. The Freedom Charter stood, over time, as the People's document, the vision of emancipation upon which resistance activity had been sustained and demands for liberation were legitimated and given organic unity. As Sachs maintained, the Freedom Charter had stood the test of time because it had been drafted in a participatory manner and had emerged from the real lives of the people whose aspirations it represented.[2] It was this experience that precipitated the idea of a People's Bill of Rights within the ANC. From there, the idea of drafting charters for the rights of the voiceless rapidly gained strength within various special interest groups. There was historical precedent in the workers' and women's movement for drafting charters outlining their political claims.

By the late 1980s and early 1990s, there emerged simultaneous, spontaneous, and corresponding efforts to produce drafts of charters to give voice to the rights of communities of people traditionally excluded from the political process. They were marginalized by their membership or participation in groups of particularly powerless people subjected to grave discrimination in the past, a discrimination that may or may not have included racial discrimination. Whether because of stereotypes about their communities or ignorance about the practices or characteristics of their communities, their fundamental rights had been denied by society and the political institutions of the Apartheid regime. Consciously or unconsciously, these communities were routinely subjected to broad and sustained discrimination.

The absolutely extreme form of racial oppression that was the apartheid system placed other forms of discrimination and other categories of rights violations in the shadows. Additionally, a typical hierarchy of the oppressed had developed in society, whereby many individuals were subjected to several levels of oppression, such as Muslim women or gay black men. With the opening of political space provided by the initiation of the transition to a democratic South Africa, the opportunity was created to organize those so discriminated against and to elevate their claims to protection in a future political order.

Because of the democratic norms of participation that existed in the liberation struggle, the imperative of broad consultation led to the use of participatory research methods to conduct the campaigns. The participatory method was a vehicle to generate information about the perceptions the disenfranchised had of their historical and contemporary discrimination, to outline the demands they had for the future and to sketch policy prescriptions.

It was clear to all the organizers of the campaigns the communities that they represented would be at different stages of consciousness about the structures of domination that they exist under, different levels of organization within local communities and across racial lines, and in terms of the relative power that could be potentially mobilized at the national level. It was increasingly clear to the organizers that they also had a powerful organizing mechanism at their disposal in the form of national consultation around rights claims.

There has been a proliferation of campaigns to construct charters by different groups. Four of the most visible and far-reaching of the campaigns are for women's rights, the rights of the disabled, workers' rights, and the rights of children. Other campaigns were initiated for the rights of religious people, gays and lesbians, and the mentally handicapped. A charter for the rights of people that are HIV positive was also completed shortly before the elections, and other efforts were made to draft a charter for the aged. A land rights charter, an education charter, and a prisoners charter were briefly debated and later abandoned.

Ultimately what is occurring is the creation of human rights. It is a process of the *articulation of claims* that arise from discrimination and oppression, the process of *developing consensus* about what those claims mean in terms of the structure of the political regime and institutions for protection in the future, and an organizational effort to *empower those claims and elevate them to the status of recognized rights* in the new political order.

Methodology

Common to the charter campaigns and essential to their uniqueness as a human rights education initiative is the application of participatory research methods (PR).[3] The work of Paulo Freire laid both the conceptual and philosophical foundations for the development of the participatory research methodology. As the chapter by Garth Meintjes in this volume illustrates, it is Freire's basic hypothesis that only in directly confronting social contradictions can a person (he unfortunately refers only to the gender "neutral" man) actually engage in their transformation. The key to the transcendence of domination is active reflection by the powerless. This becomes dialectically linked to successful action for social change and true emancipation. "Attempting to liberate the oppressed without their reflective participation in the act of liberation is to treat them as objects which must be saved from a burning building; it is to lead them into the populist pitfall and transform them into masses which can be manipulated."[4]

It is this essential crux of Freire's broader philosophy that is fundamental to the participatory research methodology and is particularly appropriate to our focus on fostering a human rights culture. A human rights approach presupposes the establishment of a norm of tolerance while ensuring that the realization of human dignity is accessible to all, whether the formerly oppressed, the oppressor, or the marginalized within the oppressed.[5] It also demonstrates the shortfalls in establishing mechanistic guarantees for rights without a concomitant sense of representation, ownership of the institutions, and a generalized perception of their potential efficacy.[6]

The right to speak may not only be essential as the transformative act, but as *the* foundational right. As Richard Falk has argued, the right to express your rights may be *the* human right. All other rights are necessarily contextually (that is *not* to say, hierarchically) contingent. The process of dialogue becomes one that fosters a sense of efficacy, that can resolve potential or inherent tensions in sets of claims of rights, and that can act as the catalytic event in elevating those claims to powerful demands challenging the wielders of political power. In the end, after the claims have become recognized as rights themselves, the communities in turn have a sense of ownership in the institutions designed to foster their protection, promotion, and enforcement.

What is the utility of the PR methodology as a human rights education instrument for societies undergoing social transformation, grappling with the problem of developing human rights cultures? The case study of the charter campaigns in South Africa presents an excellent study for simultaneously explaining general principles of the application of PR to the human rights area. As efforts grow to use PR in HRE, such as in the global women's movement, such data will yield important insights.[7]

Examination of the Origins, Evolution, and Methodologies of Sample Charter Campaigns

Although they are rich in unique data and thought provoking problems, a review of each campaign cannot be provided here.[8] Nonetheless it is important to discuss briefly how the campaigns were different at their inception or in design according to the unique characteristics of the communities they represent. It is also important to look at the similarities in application of PR methodology as well in the goals of empowerment for the various communities.

Inception

The origins of the campaigns are as unique as the communities they represent. Several of the campaigns started at the beginning of the transition through the organizing efforts of key individuals; others were the culmination of previous efforts by particular communities to catalogue their claims. The disabled people's and children's charter campaign are examples of the first pattern. Several key individuals and organizations adopted the charter idea at the onset of the transition process as the focus of their efforts to organize their communities and elevate their place in the new political dialogue.

The Disabled People's Charter is unique in origin. It emerged from the interaction of a dynamic and growing movement for the rights of the disabled with the personal involvement of one of the foremost voices for human rights in South Africa. Albie Sachs, as mentioned earlier, is in many ways the midwife of the charter campaigns both through his inspiration and as architect of the idea of the charters as a device to ensure that the new constitution would be a people's document. Upon returning to South Africa, Sachs, who was disabled by a car bomb blast a few years earlier, was asked to speak to a disabled people's organization. From that meeting was born the idea of a charter to catalogue an inclusive set of demands of disabled people to guide future policy formulation.

In the case of the Children's Charter, the paucity of voices for children's rights in the face of devastating conditions served as the catalyst. The most basic steps of defining what children's rights are had yet to be taken before a charter could even begin to be written. Efforts to secure the rights of children in the past had been profoundly inadequate or only a product of the machinations of the apartheid state to legitimate itself.

In April 1990 a consultative conference was held in Botswana to begin a process of sketching strategies for alleviating abuses against South African children. An interim national council was elected from delegates representing progressive organizations working with children. The National Children's Rights Committee, one of the most active of these organizations, outlined four critical areas of children's rights to be addressed in constructing a new social and political order: child survival, protection, development, and participation in effecting social change. The Children's Charter campaign has figured prominently in the committee's initiatives and has acted as a vehicle for political participation, for educating children about their rights to security and development, and especially for creating a sense of possibility that children can be agents in transforming the conditions in which they live.

The workers' and women's charters represent a very different tradition. Long-standing efforts to catalogue the political demands of their communities coincided in the early days of the transition with the initiation of a "charter movement" for all marginalized people's rights. In both of these communities there was historical precedent for drafting, in consultative ways, statements of the political demands for the rights of the group. Previous efforts at drafting charters were not as extensive as the recent participatory campaigns that reflect the new and corresponding drive to advance their communities' rights. However, these older efforts did mutually reinforce the newer efforts, spurring and giving impetus to each, and each reflects the history of organizing that previously existed within each group.

Target Communities

As varied as the origins of each campaign were, so too are the constituents for which each campaign speaks. Each of the charter campaigns confronted similar challenges in bringing together their communities across race, class, gender, religion, ethnicity, and rural/urban and geographical divisions. The apartheid system was masterful, if not largely successful, in imposing a rigidity of physical barriers that were rooted in social patterns. But each particular community of the disempowered has its own structure of differences embedded within it. For the disabled, the challenge is the diversity in their categories of the disabled. For example, the needs of the hearing impaired are markedly different from those of the physically, mentally, or visually impaired. For women, philosophy, tradition, and cultural practices sharply define perspectives on the salience of different rights issues. The mere act of labeling a right is contentious. The right to have control over land and economic decision making is fundamental to the rural African woman, whereas for urbanized white women, equality in the workplace is most important. The differences are much more profound and subtle than this brief analysis suggests. Simply recognizing the effects of patriarchal structures of domination divide women in South Africa across educational levels, cultural experiences, and perceptions of efficacy for the future. Similarly, where the disenfranchised are culturally and economically situated within their larger communities creates differences in their realities of oppression. In the gay community, the experiences of white lesbians are profoundly different from those of African gay men, whose communities historically shun any sign of homosexuality.

Such complexity in concentric and crosscutting currents of oppression provides another set of challenges for the design of a PR human rights initiative. While the central objective of the campaigns is to use participatory methods to create dialogues designed to break down such divisions and to advance common claims, these permutations will differentially impede the progress of any such campaigns. Some will be affected in terms of organizational difficulties; others may be shattered by philosophical differences or an inability to allow their common concerns to transcend differences in experiences.

Design of the Campaigns

Although the different applications of participatory HRE methods to the design of each campaign cannot be analyzed here, several of the campaigns will be given a particular focus as examples. For activists or practitioners, such an analysis could prove instructive if they attempt to replicate this model. What can quickly be seen in the uniqueness of each application is the inherent need to create a model appropriate to the characteristics of the community itself: the level and history of organization within the community, the potential divisions demographically and philosophically, the access and receptivity within the group that can be gauged beforehand, and the availability of resources, time, and energy to conduct the campaign. It is interesting to note that there will be an almost natural tendency for a campaign to emerge that is appropriate to its community and the resources of its organizers, as the different charter campaigns suggest. But the space for creativity and strategic vision of what is possible should not be underestimated. Thus the charter campaigns range from modest to ambitious: far-reaching in vision for the movement's future to short-term in their concern with creating a document for use in the present.

The Women's Charter

The participatory research plan for the Women's Charter is the most comprehensive, thorough, and novel for any of the charter campaigns. In fact, and as conceived, to date it represents the largest PR project ever conducted globally. In April 1992, following months of formulation and strategic planning, the Women's National Coalition was launched with a specific mandate to unify women by drafting and adopting a charter outlining demands for equality in the new constitution. It was hoped that through the consultative process, a clear consensus would emerge regarding the positions of all women of South Africa on issues of gender oppression in the family, unpaid labor within the household, abortion and control over family planning, and questions of violence against women and protection against it. It was also hoped that the divisions of South African women would be bridged by concentrating on specific concerns relevant to all women, "gender relations in the household and on social relations that perpetuate gender subordination."[9]

Ten regional centers covering the entire area of South Africa have been planned both for the research program and to serve as administrative bases for regional coalitions of the Women's National Coalition. The sites were chosen to ensure the easiest access for women and to correspond to the differing groupings of women in the country. A regional campaign coordinator was appointed to work with the regional coalition and those women's organizations in existence in that area, to bring them together and to facilitate ongoing alliances. The regional coordinators would help chose field workers for the research campaign, lay the logistical foundation for their deployment, and work out language, communication, and outreach problems for the collection and processing of data.[10]

Given the conscious goal that women own the project, careful efforts were made not to leave women feeling that they were the objects of a study. Using focus groups within organizations and by classification on socioeconomic and demographic lines, questionnaires were prepared for in-depth interviews of individuals, while public tribunals, meetings, and hearings were planned to canvass women broadly. A community report card "What do women want?" was also employed. Other appropriate participatory research activities were to be determined by the regional coordinators to reflect the unique characteristics of their target communities, the ideas of the regional participants in the coalition, and logistical factors such as time and resources.

The campaign was designed to retain an organic mix of unified national goals and strategic objectives with a particularistic concern for preserving the uniqueness of the different characteristics that exist within the women of South Africa. This would serve to give legitimacy and validity to the project and would create greater opportunity for women, long denied the belief that they can shape their destinies, a place to transform them creatively.

It was planned then that the data would be collected from the diverse sources and from the different regions, collated, analyzed, and made public in different ways to facilitate further consultation within the regions and by the coalitions of women that they represent. The range of consultation activities was as broad as imagination itself, from forums in grocery parking lots to teams of charter representatives canvassing rural areas in the homelands. From there, the catalogue of critical issues and demands could be carried into the national debates.

In response to a series of political, organizational, and philosophical crises that nearly destroyed momentum toward the Women's Charter, a set of major strategizing workshops were held in the summer of 1993. The first workshop brought representatives from the regional coalitions together to foster coordinated strategies to solidify the campaign. The regional representatives canvassed their local women's affiliates to compile a general assessment of activity in their region. They also sought to outline five key issues that the women in their region felt were the most essential to their rights efforts. From these discussions a Programme of Action was outlined and referred back to the regions.

It was then determined that these five issues would serve as the basis of group discussions each month from July through November 1993. The idea was that each theme was to become a common point for the women to transcend their particularistic perspectives. "It was felt that the five issues will provide a unifying force that can mobilize women, ensure maximum participation of women, will allow us to collect the demands of women for the charter, and to ensure effective equality for women in our country," reported the Women's National Coalition News (March–June 1993).

The five issues defined were: women's legal status, women and land resources, women and violence, women and health, and women and work. The national office would prepare materials to frame the dialogue for the focus groups and to suggest activities to create an effective environment for debate, while commonalities could be abstracted. The focus group would serve as one forum through which a dialogue could be constructed. But the forums were only one component in the multimethod, participatory strategy. In addition to a timetable for compiling the information, the campaign was timed to have short-term, medium-term, and long-range goals. The short-term goal was to have an impact upon the national debates about constitutional principles and to conduct voter education specifically targeting women. The medium-term goals were focused on the lead-in to the elections, to use the campaign and the charter document to influence political parties and lobby candidates to incorporate the women's agenda fully into their policy platforms. The long-term focus is on ensuring effective implementation of the provisions and guarantees of a constitution responsive to women's rights.

The data collected from the campaign was collated into a final research report, from which the language for the final Women's Charter for Effective Equality has been drafted. It is a catalogue of oppression and reflects a complexity of understanding by the women of South Africa of the forces that subjugate them, deny them access to political power, wreak disproportionate economic havoc upon them, and make them victims of some of the highest levels of violence felt by women in the world.

The majority of needs, as outlined by the charter, fall within the classification of second generation rights or those rights essential to humane development. Health, education, decent housing, and employment concerns figured prominently in the charter. Black respondents were more concerned with issues of social provision, whereas white respondents were more concerned with questions of equality under the law and the right to a clean environment. But protection from violence and sexual harassment, maternity benefits and adequate child care, control over their own bodies, and equality in the political arena, the work force, and the family were also central themes. A large percentage of the women indicated that they do not enjoy freedom of political expression, fearing reprisal outside their homes—a result that only highlighted the importance of the charter campaign in providing a channel for expression in the transitional process.

The Disabled People's Charter

In early 1991 the Disabled People of South Africa, under the direction of Michael Masutha of Lawyers for Human Rights, launched the charter of disabled people's rights to be an inclusive set of the demands and objectives of the disabled in a new political order and a document to guide policy formulation on issues that affect the diverse community of the disabled.

The campaign had several stages. The first step created several workshops around the country with organizations representing disabled people. The workshops had several goals, fostering discussions for a better understanding of the basic human rights issues as perceived by the participants, providing a forum to share experiences of oppression and discussion of common concerns for the future, and operating as a mechanism to coordinate those claims and foster consensus on strategy for the transition.

Workshops were held throughout the country. One national workshop was even held specifically to address discrimination and the demands of disabled women. The workshops typically had forty to eighty participants, ranging in age from teenagers to the aged, from diverse race and ethnic groupings, from all classes, and, most important, from all categories of disability. The parents of disabled children, mentally handicapped persons, victims of stroke and head injuries, and the hearing impaired were among those consulted and brought into workshops where possible.

The enormity of logistical and communications difficulties presented by transcending these inherent divisions among the range of disabilities presented unique challenges for the application of a participatory model. Compilation of demands was facilitated by the national magazine of the disabled in South Africa, *disAbility*, which placed a questionnaire investigating the range of political claims of its readership in one of its quarterly issues.

The second stage of consultation followed the compilation of demands. A drafting seminar evaluated the results of consultation and canvassing. The seminar was divided into two parts: a drafting workshop for the charter and an investigation of the specific demands contained within the newly formed document. Thus the first section dealt specifically with the concepts of socioeconomic rights and capacity for enforcement. Expert speakers discussed how the charter could be used as a legal document and what effect the incorporation of socioeconomic rights would have for enforcement.

The second part of the seminar was a report back from ten commissions assigned the task of studying categories of political claims: self-representation, employment, education, social security, disabled children's rights, independent living, disabled women, sport and recreation, and communication. Participants from twenty-five different disabilities rights organizations were encouraged to offer input into the assessment of problems and goals associated with each category of claims and to present policy prescriptions.

At the conclusion of the seminar, a six-person drafting committee was charged with the responsibility of disseminating a final draft to all participating organizations. Each organization would then carry the charter through an additional stage of consultation with its membership, whose reactions could be incorporated six months later at the congress that would adopt the final Disabilities Rights Charter of South Africa.

In September 1992 the draft charter was adopted. It was decided that a sustained consciousness raising campaign would be launched for the popularization of the document. Regional structures were established to conduct a campaign of popularization. The regional steering committees are charged with assisting local organizations in identifying their particular priorities for the promotion of the rights of the disabled in that region. In addition to the unique needs of each region, each of the regions would adopt its own consciousness raising campaigns with the mainstream media and public to highlight the plight of the disabled and to articulate their demands for a new political order.

Each region also undertook a campaign of outreach to public officials and governmental agencies. They challenged local authorities for the protection of the rights of the disabled, using the legitimacy of the charter campaign and the draft document. Each region determined the method by which it would conduct these campaigns, whether through lobbying, mass action, or seminars and workshops. The combined effort of direct action and consciousness raising provided an opportunity to test the viability and applicability of the charter on the ground, thereby opening a space for the reformulation of the charter before it was officially accepted as a formal document nationally.

Already there have been concrete successes associated with the campaign for the rights of the disabled. Beyond the organizational successes that the mere drafting of the charter represented, and the level of support given to all initiatives by the larger disabled community, there were clear signs of how the campaign influenced the national political debates in transition. While they were frustrated with the pace and nature of national negotiations, disabled people found some optimism in the reconfiguration of mainstream political discourse to incorporate the rights of the disabled. While the first six drafts of the Interim Bill of Rights did not make specific mention of the rights of the disabled, the seventh report tabled on July 29, 1993 did include one particular clause for the protection of their rights. While a small gain, it highlighted the growing leverage that the movement could wield.

Examples abound of the educational and empowerment effect of the campaigns on the transition process as well. Communities of disabled people were challenging social and economic practices that violate the broad terms of the charter, right alongside their lobbying of public officials. Again, the noticeable shift in the perception of efficacy and control that the participants began to have of their own environment is a powerful validation of the educatory importance of this type of rights approach.

The Children's Charter

The Children's Charter was drafted at a summit held from May 27 to June 1992. Different groups of children from the ages of 12 to 16 participated, representing seventeen different regions of the country from rural and urban areas and representing all races and social groups. Children drawn from squatter communities, that were homeless, or from histories of exile came together in a forum to discuss their past experiences of oppression and to draft a set of claims for their rights under a new political order. The National Children's Rights Committee was used as a resource to select the participants, reflecting the lack of grassroots youth organizations.

Adult organization was limited to the collection of material and establishing workshops around specific issues relevant to children's rights: the nature of constitutions and bills of rights for the protection of children's rights, health and welfare, homelessness, education, violence, and family life. The goal of the workshops was to inform the children about conditions around the country and existing and proposed mechanisms to deal with those conditions. There was consensus among the organizers of the conference that the children needed some a priori information upon which their discourse could build and from which their own claims and strategies for the future could be articulated.

After the workshops, there was a plenary session in which recommendations were presented by the participants. From each of the issues discussed, a plank would be incorporated into the charter. While the children did not devise the themes of the workshops or the preparatory material used, they advanced the claims to be incorporated into the charter and then made decisions about how it would be used after it was drafted.

Proposals came from the children themselves that they needed to take the completed charter to organizations, political parties, and public officials to advance their claims in the new political order and to protect children's rights in the interim period. Deputations were made to the Minister of Law and Order concerning conditions of violence against children and police harassment. The charter was also presented to delegates at the national negotiating forums, along with being sent to the Inkatha Freedom Party, the African National Congress, and the National Party.

Across the country, children have been coming together to develop creative plans to use the charter as an organizing device among other children and to secure their rights in the public realm. Forums are also being held to discuss their interpretation of the meaning of the document for their own lives.[11] One example of the enhanced sense of efficacy that came from the summit's charter drafting process was reflected in a delegation to the local police force to discuss the problems of street children and their treatment at the hands of the police. The charter document was used in this delegation as the basis of a problem-solving approach to the police. While the children were accompanied by individuals from the child advocacy and welfare organization

Molo Songololo, it was the children that organized the event, petitioned the police officers directly, and sought media coverage in the local and national newspapers.

This one example reflects the impact of the summit at a broader level. It has helped children to deal in an immediate time frame with the conditions of violence in their communities and violence perpetrated by state officials, by giving them the courage to speak up against police brutality in the recognition that they have rights that are being violated by the local authorities. It has also given the children a sense of efficacy in their capacity to shape their political future. It has made the process of political transformation more salient to their daily lives and given them a stake in the successful establishment of functioning institutions in the new order.

While the method of reaching the children may have been limited because of the nature of the community being drawn together, those children that did participate in the summit and those subsequently brought into the dissemination and organizing campaigns have a profoundly new assessment of their stake in the country's future. Many examples were given to me by both the participants in the summit and representatives of organizations working with the children of a politicization that has occurred in novel ways from those traditionally associated with youth resistance of the last decade.

The examples of application of participatory HRE for these campaigns are quite different. The women's campaign is using the drafting of the charter to foster a broad women's movement from a nascent movement with preexisting organizations and coalitions. The *process of creating* the charter is the educational and empowering one. Whereas with the children's campaign, a charter drafted with little real broad representation is *to be used creatively and applied differently* to foster dialogue and debate among children. It will also be used creatively by children to develop awareness of their rights and to begin the process of building a children's movement. The women's charter will reflect the depth of participation, making it more representative and potentially legitimate. The children's charter reflects the problems of the past for organizing around children's rights issues and will likely foreshadow the obstacles in the future for bringing attention to children's issues.

What Can Be Learned from the South African Charter Campaigns? Problems, Successes, and Implications for Forging Human Rights Cultures Globally

It is more than a bit presumptuous to draw lessons from a process that is, as yet, uncompleted. But as process is the goal—to transition, to forging participatory democracies, to organizing communities of people, and to fostering human rights cultures that reflect change and diversity—a summary analysis is warranted. Patterns of problems can be highlighted. Conclusions can also be drawn about the utility, successes, and generalizability of the South African charter campaigns as a novel form of human rights education. The following is an overview of the potential problems that arose in the conduct of the campaigns, some of which are unique to the South African case and others that could be generalizable to similar efforts elsewhere. Several recommendations are advanced that might serve as a basis to analyze the generalizable utility of such initiatives for other societies attempting to foster human rights responsive regimes.

Concerns

No Precedent

There is no historical or legal precedent for the South African charter campaigns. Never before has a project of such magnitude, with similar goals or in a similar context to that of the transition from apartheid rule in South Africa, been conducted. As such, there is a lack of consensus on how the documents that come out of the campaigns can be used in a new constitutional order. There are six or seven different operative assumptions about how the charters might be used, from annexation to a bill of rights, to policy directive, to organizational device. There have been far-reaching debates about legal precedent where different constitutional models and explorations of organic versus statutory law have been examined. Concerns have also been voiced over the potential for the ghettoization of claims that might occur if the charters have no formal status.

Legitimacy of Process

As the success of participatory research as HRE is the legitimacy and validity of the research process, two key issues are sufficient time for thorough consultation and legitimate representation of the demands of the whole community. While the organizers of the various campaigns have consciously tried to leave enough time and to develop legitimate consultation mechanisms, there are serious structural problems involved in the South African case that cannot be overcome simply. While the following points deal with the South African situation, they are surely relevant possibilities for any society undergoing a transition from a repressive past to a rights-responsive future.

Time.

No one involved in organizing the charter campaigns (or, for that matter, in the liberation struggle) has been prepared for the pace of the transition. These charter campaigns simply do not have the luxury of a ten-year period for a thorough and inclusive process of consultation. Nor do they have the capacity for a broad-based testing of the legitimacy and accuracy of the document and an assessment of its generalized acceptance by the community it represents. If the charters were to be addended to a bill of rights drawn after elections for a constituent assembly are held, they had to be completed at the time of elections to maximize their leverage effectively. Some have met that goal, others did not.

Representation.

The historical and institutionalized patterns of oppression effectively preclude a thorough consultative initiative. Communities are fragmented geographically. The rural-urban divide alone presents great problems of access. The homeland system not only contributes to this fragmentation, but has created several no-go areas during the transition in the form of the Bophuthatswana and Ciskei governments and throughout much of the Natal region. Organizing openly in South Africa is itself a new phenomenon. South African activists have only had a three-year experience with it, an experience itself marred by grave levels of violence. There are therefore both logistical and conceptual problems associated with lack of experience in fostering this type of open political discourse. Similarly, individuals from across the country, and particularly in the voiceless communities, have had no experience with access to forums to express their demands free of fear of oppression or retaliation.

Discourse = Discord

While the philosophical foundation of the participatory HRE rests upon the fostering of a process of dialogue, there are inherent tensions in the creation of space for debate. Preexisting divisions within a community can rise to the fore. In the South African case, as with virtually any other that has racial, class, and gender cleavages, goals and objectives can become divisive when they reflect very concrete differences in identity. Tensions within the charter campaigns have emerged philosophically over what rights are considered legitimate and over the long-term implications of endorsing certain sets of rights. Tensions have also emerged over strategy and tactics. Thus . . .

Charters Cannot Substitute for Social Movements

The organizational and consciousness raising dimensions to the various charter campaigns cannot act as a substitute for real social movements. In many ways the effectiveness of the campaigns presupposes at a minimum the existence of a nascent social movement. Even though one of the key goals of the charter campaigns has been to foster a movement for the articulation of the rights of the historically voiceless, for claims to be established there must exist the prerequisite characteristics of a human rights relevant social movement: there must be a broad common ideology, shared experiences of oppression, and a desire to precipitate change.

While it is not *necessary* that these characteristics exist, the absence of these characteristics makes the efforts to draft a set of rights claims very vulnerable to factionalization, loss of coherence, and potential failure in drafting universally endorsed claims with *enough leverage* to be elevated to a rights status.

Broad Acceptability

It will be an empirical question in the case of South Africa whether the idea of the charters or the resulting documents are broadly accepted as having normative stature by society or dismissed out of hand, marginalized, or ultimately watered down in the process of creating the permanent constitution. It is nonetheless quite easy to conjecture in the South African case, or in any abstract model of a human rights charter for a transitional society, that—after consultation, formulation, and drafting of the charters—they could be rendered trivial or supplanted by other forces. The potential for such charters to become simply a rhetorical fix for governments seeking to legitimate their human rights credentials is also not difficult to visualize.

Recommendations

Clearly, in any context in which the model of these campaigns could be applied, any efforts made to maximize participation would serve to give greater leverage to the resulting document, legitimize the process, and strengthen the standards of accountability that come out of the elevation of the claims to that of institutionalized rights. There are several further coordinating steps that could be taken which might help foster greater coherence in each campaign. Consistency across campaigns could exponentially maximize the leverage that could be brought to bear at the national level. A national workshop or forum might be quite useful to bring the campaigns together to share experiences and develop ongoing mechanisms to sustain the campaigns and develop a united strategy.

National and regional representatives of the various campaigns could be brought together to consult on the following issues. They could share their mutual experience in conducting the campaigns. They could discuss and debate the viability and utility of standardizing the claims format of the different charters. Would it be useful to develop some form of consistency in expression and categorization of claims, while retaining the unique nature and particularistic goals of each campaign?

Another issue that might be raised is the level of consistency the articulated claims have with international standards of human rights. Perhaps the participants will discover that there is, in fact, a consistency in the demands with those advanced and protected by international law. The claims then might be heightened in their *particularistic* presentation by parallels drawn to international standards, such as that with the Universal Declaration of Human Rights.

Similarly, the workshops of charter coordinators and regional representatives should discuss the goals and debate the general objectives that each of the charter campaigns have, both in terms of consciousness raising and in regard to the documents that are subsequently produced. Out of these discussions, a common strategy might emerge. If, for instance, there is a common notion of how the charters should be used in the formulation of the constitution and a new bill of rights, then a strategy for introducing, advancing, and generating support for this common goal could be sketched. Pooling resources for a common strategy would exponentially increase the power and leverage that any one campaign could generate. In many ways, the worst case scenario is where one campaign has very clear goals, while the rest have very different and undefined objectives. A coordinating workshop could avoid this occurrence. As well, the delegates to the workshops could debate a variety of mechanisms for the enforcement of rights claims presented in the charters. Some possible options might be a human rights ombudsperson with special offices for each of the charter communities, reporting mechanisms through a human rights commission, and ongoing educational campaigns in schools, businesses, and churches to disseminate the materials of the charters. Just as the efficacy of the voiceless is enhanced by the charter campaigns themselves, the workshop process might stimulate the sense of possibility for the organizers and for regional and local representatives.

Implications

Create a Sense of Ownership in the Constitution, Foster Respect in the New Rule of Law

By making the constitution drafting process a representative one, the new constitution would truly become a people's document. A sense of ownership would develop, not just for the set of demands advanced by the community or political leaders. All of the campaigns taken together would become a method of broadbased, grassroots popularization of the new political institutions that are being negotiated. They would also serve to create an ongoing method of direct participation in the transition.

As well, the campaigns are producing a rights discourse critical to developing mass perceptions of the legitimacy of the rule of law that is to emerge. The campaigns themselves can be seen as alternative socialization devices to reconstruct mass perceptions of what legal institutions imply about justice. If a sense of ownership in the institutions is produced, the rule of law that envelops those institutions will also be granted legitimacy. In South Africa, the disjuncture between formal systems of justice meticulously crafted to perpetuate discrimination and the vast abuses of the state have left a more devastating legacy for efforts to construct a rule of law.

Break Down the Hierarchy of the Oppressed

Within every structure of domination, there is a hierarchy of oppression. As was discussed, black women face twice as much oppression as their white counterparts, and rural black women face triple the obstacles to make their voices heard. The fundamental principles of the charter campaigns are to break down the concentric circles of oppression and to dismantle the structures of domination where rights fall vertically, to one where rights are guaranteed horizontally.

Recall Freire's conception of how domination affects both the oppressors and the oppressed in a dehumanized state. The transformative agenda of the charter campaigns, through their goals and the participatory methods used to realize them, will optimally transform the structures of oppression—not merely invert them or supplant them with a new hierarchical order.

Perhaps most important, by elevating the claims of the historically and particularly oppressed as equal to the status of racial oppression, the charters serve a critical function in overcoming distrust in minority protections. Together they reflect international trends to secure minority rights within the framework of protection of individual rights. Simultaneously, they will demonstrate the balance that can be achieved between individual and group rights, that any new and modern rights culture can produce and must guard.

Catalogue the Claims of the Historically Voiceless

The documents produced by the charter campaigns have become sources of information on the particular experiences of oppression that each community has suffered, on their perception of the rights that they should enjoy in a new political order, and on their conception of the appropriate methods to achieve them. There are three basic and essential usages for such a catalogue of claims:

(1) Through the specificity and precision given by the charters, an accurate depiction of the claims will be representative for any constitutional usage, whether direct incorporation into constitutional statutes or for the language of a bill of rights. As Sachs has said, the charters will allow us to "get the formulation right" in the new constitution.

(2) The terms of the charters will lay the basis for affirmative action policies to be expanded to incorporate all forms of discrimination and the range of communities that have suffered oppression in the past.

(3) Finally, the charters can be used for policy direction and judicial interpretation in the future, depending upon the legal stature that is granted them in the new political order. In any case, they can be used as a gauge to assess the legitimacy of public policy initiatives for the community, those that are either taken on their behalf or directly against their interests.

Sustain a Participatory Democracy

The long-term potential in the charter campaigns is the creation of new methods for political participation befitting a transitional process. From a history of mass politicization and broad-based participation in the liberation struggle, there is near universal consensus within the mass democratic movement that the vitality of civic participation in both institution formation and in public policymaking should be sustained in every way possible.

Create Rights

We can conceive of human rights as the culmination of the following process:

the articulation of political claims
consensus building around those claims
an authoritative method of advancing and presenting those claims for broader, social
    consumption (the process can either be one of a top-down imposition or of a mass-
    based substantiation of broad acceptance)
societal acceptance that the claims have the status of norms or standards by which
    individual, collective, and state behavior is gauged
customary, formal, or legal application, elevation of norms to rights status

After examining the process by which the claims of particular communities of the oppressed, historically disenfranchised, and traditionally disempowered have been articulated through consultation, advanced authoritatively through the weight of legitimacy granted by the participatory process, and established as a norm codified in a document outlining the demands of women, workers, children, the disabled, the aged, and so on, a process of rights construction has been initiated.

It is within the participatory process that political claims become rights, for the consultation generates both consensus and ownership. Participation is power. The greater the participation, the more authority that the demands have to claim rights status. Thus, in terms of constructing rights for a new socioeconomic and political order, the method employed by the charter campaigns has within it two essential and unique characteristics for modern rights construction. First, the levels of consultation and participation bring immediate legitimacy to the process of claims formulation and advancement of policy-relevant demands. Second, the dialogical process of participation is a critical mechanism for overcoming the universalistic versus relativistic tension that has plagued modern constitution drafting and rights formulation. In many ways, the process of debate precipitates a resolution of tensions in the perception of the supremacy and hierarchy of rights. As Richard Falk has often argued, the key to transcending the debates over universalistic claims to legitimacy versus concern over retaining the particularistic character of rights is *discourse*. The dialogue can serve to break down habituated notions of rights and the perception of those who did not believe in their entitlement to rights. As such, one is not simply redefining rights but opening a political space to create rights. Furthermore, a precedent of critical discourse can establish a process by which society can continually democratize itself.[12]

Conclusion

At the end of the process of organizing rights campaigns, constructing a justiciable bill of rights, and drafting a modern and democratic constitution, there is no guarantee that the institutions will work. There is no guarantee that democracy will flourish in a post-apartheid South Africa or even that rights will be guaranteed or enforced in a new sociolegal order. Serious economic and political constraints are operating like a temporal vice on the potential for peace in the future. Whether political parties and representative institutions can channel the demands for reconstruction are, at this point, quite questionable.

But in our effort to understand the relationship of the construction of democratic institutions to efforts to forge a human rights culture, the charter campaigns as a method of HRE have made one critical contribution to South Africa's future by giving a voice to the historically voiceless. They have already produced the one fundamental right—the right to rights. While the growth in the perception of all to have a right is one essential step toward fostering a human rights culture, in the final analysis the charter campaigns have created a sense of efficacy. Perception of efficacy to alter one's destiny is the key to transformation, as Freire has demonstrated.

Can the human rights charter campaigns in South Africa serve as a model for other societies grappling with human rights abuses in the past? There are certain themes that are generalizable. For those societies in transition from an authoritative system of control to a rights-responsive future, similar campaigns could facilitate the creation of space for the articulation of claims from those historically denied such space. Similar campaigns could also serve to mobilize the mass population in participatory mechanisms to develop a sense of ownership in the institutions that are forged and could also serve to break down structures of domination that extend beyond those characteristic of the former regime. Similar campaigns could act as alternative socialization devices for fostering rights awareness and responsiveness and could contribute to the development of a belief in the legitimacy of a rule of law. Finally, similar campaigns could bolster the sense of efficacy for those that have been historically disenfranchised.

Taken together, these possibilities might aid in creating a human rights culture in societies grappling with a repressive past and might also lead to a revitalization of concern for human rights in societies that have long since taken their achievements for granted. The South African human rights charter campaigns, whatever their ultimate fate, could serve as tremendous models to stimulate creative rights education initiatives throughout the world. Each society will have to grapple with its own unique imprint, but the philosophical foundation, participatory methods, and transformative goals for the realization of human dignity are surely exportable.

Notes

1. Personal interview with Prof. Albie Sachs, October 22, 1992, Pretoria, South Africa.

2. For an excellent analysis of the historical and philosophical dimensions and of the political and social legacies of the Freedom Charter, see *The Freedom Charter and Beyond,* ed. Nico Steylter (Community Law Centre, University of the Western Cape, 1991).

3. See Lisa Veneklassen, "The Methodology of Participatory Research and Women's Legal Rights," in Working Paper No. 2, *Perspectives on Research Methodology,* Women and Law in Southern African Research Project, December 1990.

4. See Paulo Freire, *The Pedagogy of the Oppressed* (New York: Continuum, 1986).

5. Ibid., 58.

6. See Richard Claude, *Educating for Human Rights: The Philippines and Beyond* (Quezon City: University of the Philippines Press, 1996).

7. Veneklassen, "Methodology." Margaret Schuler, "Theory and Practice of Participatory Research," unpublished manuscript available at the Institute for Women, Law, and Development, Washington, D.C.

8. See Ellen Dorsey, "The Right to Rights in a New Political Order: Elevating the Claims of the Historically Disenfranchised: The South African Human Rights Charter Campaigns," paper presented at the APSA conference, Fall 1993. The author detailed four of the charter campaigns in this paper.

9. Gay Seidman, " 'No Freedom Without the Women': Mobilization and Gender in South Africa, 1970–1992," *Signs: A Journal of Women in Culture and Society* 18, no 2 (1993). See also Amy Biehl, "Dislodging the Boulder: South African Women and Democratic Transformation," in *South Africa: The Political Economy of Transformation,* ed. Stephen Stedman (Boulder, Colo.: Lynne Rienner Publishers, 1994).

10. Notes on the campaign are taken from an informal sketch of the project provided by the National Campaign Coordinator, Pregs Govender.

11. Interview with Shirley Mabusela on Era program, CCV TV, August 4, 1993.

12. For an interesting analysis of the different dialogical processes toward HRE, see Alicia Ely-Yamin, "Empowering Visions: Toward a Dialectical Pedagogy of Human Rights," *Human Rights Quarterly* 15, no 4 (1993).

Chapter 9
Human Rights Education: The Promise of the Third Millennium?

Upendra Baxi

The better part of the twentieth century has been characterized by a unique innovation: the proliferation of human rights standards, especially in the discursive praxis of the United Nations. Despite the reality of massive and monumental violations, one may say that ours is an Age of Rights. No preceding century of human history has been privileged to witness such a range of rights enunciations as ours. Moreover, never before have we come to a situation in which the language of rights nearly replaces all other moral languages. As the UN secretary-general observed at the Vienna Conference on Human Rights in June 1993, human rights constitute a "common language of humanity." Further, even as the alleged end of ideology is being proclaimed worldwide, a human rights sociodialect emerges as the only universalistic ideology-in-the-making, enabling both legitimation and delegitimation of power and anticipatory critiques of human futures. All these developments have led to continuing confrontation between emergent cultures of rights and entrenched cultures of power. This dialectic between rights and power has never been so vividly persistent and poignant as in the last seven decades of the twentieth century.

The single most critical source of human rights is the consciousness of peoples of the world, who have waged persistent struggles for decolonization and self-determination, against racial discrimination, gender-based aggression and discrimination, denial of access to basic minimum needs, environmental degradation and destruction, and systematic "benign neglect" of the disarticulated, disadvantaged, and dispossessed (including the indigenous peoples of the earth). Thus human rights cultures have long been in the making by the praxis of victims of violations, regardless of how rights are formulated, that is, regardless of the mode of production of human rights standards and instruments. Clearly, human rights education (HRE) must begin by commissioning a world history of peoples' struggles for rights and against injustice and tyranny. The emergence of more contemporary concerns with rights enunciations cannot be understood without a history of everyday moral heroism of diverse peoples asserting the most basic of all basic rights: the right to be human and to remain human.

Nor should the contemporary mode of production of human rights and fundamental freedoms be considered in isolation from the history of these struggles. No doubt the work of the United Nations in promoting and protecting human rights provides its own saga of the triumph of collective human/social imagination. But producing the truths of human rights by governments, diplomats, and statespersons has always been informed and formed by an ever increasing, and persistent, human striving to make states more ethical, governance more just, and power more accountable.

In other words, one may narrate histories of the Age of Rights from two perspectives. First, we see human rights from the point of view of myriad peoples' struggles, attending closely to a large number of narrative voices and to micropolitics ultimately shaping the larger stories of politics of rights and liberation. Second, we can take the other vantage point, which appropriates the narrative voice to national actors: parties, leaders, constitution makers, judicial actors, and the semi-autonomous fields of rights enunciation within the UN system and culture.

As between these two perspectives, the choice of narrative paths offers distinctive starting points for human rights movements. The choice of approaches may have an enduring influence on the movement for HRE in terms of scope, objectives, principles, missions, pedagogies, and constitutional and management strategies (including monitoring). On the eve of the launching of the UN Decade of Human Rights Education, serious engagement with historiographies of human rights movements may be deferred only at the cost of our common future.

For a considerable period, and at least for the last two decades, the received wisdom on human rights promotion and protection has been under the signature of crises from both the standpoints noted above. Rights discourse still emphasizes restraints on the power of the postmodern leviathan state. At the same time, increasingly, a great discovery of the Age of Rights is that civil society, the ensemble of relatively state-free spaces (actors, agencies, and institutions), provides equally and, often enough, more pervasively fertile sites of violations. Thus a common realization is dawning in human rights movements. On the one hand, the need for limiting the overweening power of state operators and hegemonies remains imperative. On the other hand, state action and intervention seem to offer the most reassuring promise of providing chemotherapy to the cancerous growth of culturally rooted, and economically "derived," forms of violations of human rights and fundamental freedoms. Thus arises the great dilemma of the Age of Rights: the rights discourse must both, and in a just and effective measure, simultaneously disempower as well as empower the state. This new dialectic of simultaneous disempowerment and reempowerment of the state (with postmodernist identity and even destiny) must be addressed seriously in fashioning programs and strategies for HRE. I revisit these themes toward the conclusion, after a rapid *tour de horizon* of the UN biography of HRE.

The Universal Declaration and HRE

The origins of notions of HRE, even as itself constituting a human right, can be traced to the text of the germinal Universal Declaration of Human Rights. The Preamble stresses the central importance of a "common understanding" of human rights and fundamental freedoms to the achievement of "freedom, justice and peace in the world." It proclaims that a "common standard of achievement" of these values, nationally and globally, requires, among other things, that every individual and organ of society, keeping this Declaration constantly in mind, shall try by teaching and education to promote respect for these rights and freedoms. "Education" in human rights is thus the individual and collective duty of all, nationally, regionally, and globally.

Read in the context of the Preamble, Article 26 of the Declaration affirming everyone's right to education must, of course, include HRE as a human right in itself. Article 26 conceptualizes education not merely in terms of development of individual personality or even in terms of good citizenship of a nation-state. Education has a global orientation of producing true citizens of the world, imbued with civic virtues of respect for pluralism, peace, dignity, and rights. Nor is education, necessarily, all about rights. Article 29 of the Declaration categorically declares that "free and full development" of human personality also entails fulfillment of duties to the community. Education, including HRE, is a right indeed, but that right is not an end in itself. It is a means to other ends, enumerated above, whose pursuit in totality would contribute to the attainment of "freedom, justice and peace in the world."

The Preamble gives a conscientious raison d'être for HRE as well as a pragmatic justification. The former asserts that: "disregard and contempt for human rights have resulted in barbarous acts which have outraged the conscience of mankind, and the advent of a world in which human beings shall enjoy freedom of speech and belief and freedom from fear and want which has been proclaimed as the highest aspiration of the common people." The pragmatic justification for HRE is that it is "essential, if man is not to be compelled to have recourse, as a last resort, to rebellion against tyranny and oppression, that human rights should be protected by the rule of law."

The references to the "highest aspiration of the common people" and outraging of "the conscience of mankind" indicate that human rights and fundamental freedoms are common properties of human conscience and common moral sentiment. Barbarous practices of power are recognizable and recognized, regardless of whether politicians, statespersons, jurists, and international organizations have produced human rights enunciations commensurate with the power of politics to produce a series of contingent, but monumental, evils. The experience of outrage at flagrant and massive violations *antedates* rights enunciations and survives their well-manicured formulations. The Declaration thus conceives of human rights and fundamental freedoms as a domain of *conscience collective* (almost in the sense in which Emile Durkheim so imaginatively sculpted that notion to understand and analyze social solidarities). HRE strategies have to acknowledge, and build upon, this common human solidarity to promote rights education.

The pragmatic justification of the Declaration is no less striking. Tyranny, defined as an absence of human rights protection under the institutions and structures of the rule of law, signifies *absence or annihilation of human rights cultures, in both civil society and the state.* Such a situation leads to "rebellion," breakdown of social order, civil strife, and repression, disrupting just peace not at a national level but also regionally or globally. HRE as a strategic instrumentality for protection of peace, in all dimensions and on all levels, was wisely and with foresight recognized by the authors of the Universal Declaration. Any *genesis amnesia* on this score will impoverish our enterprise.

The 1974 United Nations Educational, Scientific and Cultural Organization (UNESCO) Recommendation Concerning HRE

The 1974 Recommendation both enlarges and limits notions of HRE. It enlarges the notion of "education" as implying "the entire process of social life" affecting the whole of people's personal capacities, attitudes, aptitudes and knowledge" (Article 1a). Also, the aims of HRE are to promote "international understanding," "cooperation," and "peace" considered as "an indivisible whole" uniting concerns of friendly relations between peoples and states" and of "respect for human rights and fundamental freedoms." This unity finds configuration in the Recommendation as "international education."

This welcome expansion of "education" is, however, accompanied by contraction of HRE itself! Human rights and fundamental freedoms are only those defined in the UN Charter, the Universal Declaration, and the two international covenants. Clearly, in the UN tradition, human rights education extends much further.[1] Of necessity, the present efforts of developing HRE must include a view of human rights larger than those found only in official enunciations and instruments.

In the Recommendation on "international education," HRE emerges as entailing

(1) "intellectual and emotional development"; "a sense of responsibility and of solidarity with less privileged groups" resulting in "observance of principles of equality in everyday conduct" (Article 5)

(2) a culture of "inadmissibility of recourse to war" and understanding of responsibility to strengthen world peace (Article 6)

(3) the incompatibility of "the true interests of people" with interests of "monopolistic groups holding economic and political power, which practice exploitation and foment wars" (Article 15)

(4) "inter-cultural understanding" (Article 17)

(5) meaningful opportunities for "active civic training," enabling cooperative endeavor in "the work of public institutions" imparting competence to political participation (Article 13)

(6) capabilities to eradicate "conditions which perpetuate major problems affecting human survival and well-being" and which enhance "international cooperation" to this end (Article 18)

In many respects, the Recommendation charts out the map of HRE well beyond the Universal Declaration. The markers are of considerable pertinence to our re-imagining HRE. The specificity of clusters of concern and capabilities, purposes and promises, symbolized by the Recommendation puts stress on "appropriate . . . emotional development" (without which solidarities remain incoherently emergent) and "inter-cultural understanding" (without which rights enunciations can be, and have been, unfairly castigated as Eurocentric in their origins and functions). These elements, plus the radical quest for egalitarianism in everyday life, both nationally and globally, ought not be overlooked in future revitalization of notions of HRE in a post–cold war era.

The 1993 UNESCO Montreal Declaration on HRE

Building upon the 1974 Recommendation (and a subsequent set of associated enunciations since 1974[2]), the UNESCO World Plan of Action on Education for Human Rights and Democracy adopted by the International Congress (Montreal, Canada, March 8–11, 1993) unfurled many innovative themes on the eve of the Vienna Conference on Human Rights. Before commenting on the "daring" of the Montreal Declaration, some of its inaugural propositions must be noted.

First, the Montreal Plan explicitly directs the attention of HRE to the *victims* of human rights violations, as well as the *defenders* of "democracy." Second, while reiterating the notion of education as a lifelong process of learning, the Montreal Plan inaugurates the notion of HRE "in difficult situations." Obviously and increasingly, state failures (an amalgam *always* of national *and* global forces) present a testing time for the run-of-the-mill notions of HRE. Third, the Montreal Plan anchors HRE in the harbor of liberal democracy. It declares that all education, especially HRE, should "promote societal transformation based upon human rights and democracy." Fourth, HRE should itself be "participatory and operational, creative, innovative and empowering at all levels of civil society." Fifth, HRE has a prophylactic role and function; HRE must evolve "special and anticipatory strategies aimed at preventing the outbreak of violent conflicts and related human rights violations." Sixth, the "key challenge of the future" confronting HRE is how to "enhance the universality of human rights by rooting these rights in different cultural traditions." Seventh, this endeavor of cultural rooting (implantation) must recognize that "effective exercise of human rights is also contingent upon the responsibility by individuals towards the community." Eighth, the Montreal Plan offers at least three criteria by which "success" of any HRE mission may be evaluated. A HRE mission is successful when it *changes* "conduct leading to a denial of rights," *creates* a climate of "respect" for "all rights," and *transforms* the civil society in "a peaceful manner and participatory model."

The Montreal Plan is, of course, justified in strongly linking human rights and democracy, but it needs to be supplemented by notions of "historic" time. The prevailing liberal democracies in the North emerged from centuries of histories of peoples' struggles with the state and within civil societies. To imagine that HRE strategies in themselves will somehow accelerate historic time for the rest of the world is to arrest meaningful global movement.

It needs to be at least acknowledged that the erstwhile colonial powers aborted conditions of political development and maturation in most parts of the world. It also needs to be acknowledged further that practices of power during the long dark night of the cold war did not enable former colonial powers and their allies to contribute to the decolonized nations' capabilities to "nurture democratic values, sustain impulses for democratization" or to promote "peaceful" democratization of whole civil societies. Nor is the quest to locate, in the post–cold war era, the Other (the Enemy) of a solitary superpower necessarily conducive to the rapid evolution of human rights cultures around the world.

Democracies are processes, never fully formed historic products, or—to put it in a language with which at least professional philosophers will feel at home—democracy is a process of becoming, not of being. From this standpoint, the dilemmas of sustainable democracy, while more acute in the South, are also awesomely present in the North as well. Read thus, the Montreal Plan addresses HRE, both in guiding principles and in strategies of action, to the critical tasks of democratizing and re-democratizing civil society and state formation, *everywhere* in the world.

The Montreal Plan, however, moves close to the heart of contemporary darkness when it refocuses HRE on its inaugural task of transforming civil society. This task is urgent and compelling for both the South and the North, especially for the North where civil societies, while developing and nurturing impassioned cultures of human rights at home, are indifferent to how their elected representatives may often play God abroad, especially in the South.

Finally, the Montreal Plan's teleology of HRE raises an important question concerning HRE: should it be regarded as an end in itself or as a means to some designated end? On possible answers to this question will depend the future legitimation, organization, accountability, autonomy, pedagogies, and performance of HRE.

The choice is between saying that we ought to pursue HRE in itself as a human right to better achieve all other human rights and fundamental freedoms, or that we ought to promote HRE for ends like "good governance," "sustainable development," "economic progress," "democracy," and "transformation of civil societies." The choice is critical, in the sense of the nature of dispensability or expendability of HRE. If we were to regard HRE as a means for "economic" development in societies exposed to structural adjustment programs, for example, only market-friendly rights will be germane to HRE endeavor; similarly, cultures that regard patriarchy as "divinely" ordained may not consider a regendering of human rights cultures as critical to many of the "ends" described above.

The choice has to be clearly made. I believe HRE is important because it is an end in itself. It is conceivable, and a matter of not just ethical but also political judgment, that as and when the HRE mission succeeds, it may ill serve other postulated goals and ends. This is so because, as Roberto M. Unger has reminded us, rights typically have in history a destabilizing function, a "context smashing" tendency."[3] Neither of these features necessarily go so far as to question the integrity or rationale of the nation-state itself but both acutely interrogate all the processes of power and authority within state and civil society. HRE as an end in itself seeks to reinforce the processes of empowerment of every human being in everyday life to experience freedom and solidarity, not fractured by grids of power and domination by the civil society and state. Mohandas Gandhi used to say that *swarai* (independence, that is, just self-rule) brings exercise of freedom in nonthreatening ways to the Other. To my mind, the ability to perceive such freedom as not threatening all that is good, true, and beautiful in human achievement is the *summum bonum* that HRE promises us.

HRE in the Vienna Declaration

Celebrating both, in its germinal preambulatory formulation, "the spirit of the age" and "the realities of our time," the Vienna Declaration on Human Rights marks yet another milestone in human rights lexicon, theory and activism.[4] Section D, Part II of the Declaration and paragraphs 33–36 of Part I focus on HRE. The Vienna Declaration, in brief, *reiterates* the expanded notion of "education" first articulated in the 1974 UNESCO Recommendation; *extends* that Recommendation, making education, and HRE, go beyond select bodies of human rights discourse to inclusion of "peace, democracy, development and social justice"; *innovates* HRE as a gender-specific mission, stressing the "human rights *needs* of women"; *reconstructs* the enterprise of HRE to make it inclusively communitarian; and *focuses* HRE programs and strategies on special state agencies and agents.

Of the Vienna goals and strategies, the most excitingly innovative dimension is, of course, the reference to "human rights needs of women." The phrase invites the suspension of the dichotomy between "needs" and "rights." The concept of "human rights needs" implicit in the motto "Women's Rights Are Human Rights" indicates the ongoing process, in contemporary rights discourse, transmuting *needs* into *rights*. But equally important for HRE pedagogies and strategies, identification of human rights needs must minimally include access to information, to opportunities for the exercise of rights, to modalities and instrumentalities in the identification of violations of human rights, and to public discourse that may contest state/society assertions that either no right exists or, if it does, no violation can be said to have occured.

This listing of human rights needs can and must be expanded with care, the implication being that HRE can never be a static body of given knowledges of rights enunciations but must forever remain a dynamic engagement with these knowledges. In this sense, HRE will be future-oriented as well.

The Draft Plan of Action for the United Nations Decade of Human Rights Education: 1995–2005

The Draft Plan of Action naturally builds upon the lineage of HRE thus far canvassed. Two sets of standards should be recounted here: the "normative bases" of HRE and the guiding principles.

Article 2 of the Draft specifies several normative bases undergirding HRE. These involve a commitment to: "(a) the strengthening of respect for human rights and fundamental freedoms; (b) the full development of the human personality and its sense of dignity; (c) the formation of understanding, tolerance, gender equality, and friendship among all nations, indigenous peoples, racial, ethnic, religious, and linguistic groups; (d) the enabling of all persons to participate effectively in a free society; and (e) the furtherance of the activities of the United Nations for the maintenance of peace."

The General Guiding Principles of the Draft (Part Two) are especially noteworthy. First, HRE should create the "broadest possible awareness and understanding of all the norms, concepts and values" of the foundational texts as well as all other relevant international human rights instruments. Put another way, HRE is not directed merely to literacy concerning human rights texts; their intertextuality also has to be learned and imparted (that is, their cross-connections, reciprocal supplementation, their hermeneutical totality). The ideology-in-the-making of human rights ("all the norms, concepts and values") becomes in the Draft the repertoire of HRE. This is further reinforced by the reference to "universality" and "interdependence of all rights."

Second, HRE has to move from the "universal" to the particular, from the abstract to the concrete, from the global to the local. Effective HRE "shall be shaped in such a way as to be relevant to the daily lives of the learners" and shall "seek to engage learners in a dialogue about the ways and means of transforming human rights from the expression of abstract norms to the reality of their social, economic, cultural and political conditions" (para. 4). This critical formulation summons HRE praxis to tasks of everyday relevance, in micropolitical, microsocial contexts. It formulates the imagination of HRE as *dialogical*. Dialogue, by definition, can best occur under conditions of dignity and equality, and dialogical HRE strategies creatively conflate the distinction between the "learner" and the "learned." Humility is, of course, the hallmark of learning. And dialogical HRE interaction is obviously a confrontation between the "pre-given" ("social, economic, cultural and political conditions") and the future histories-in-the-making.

Third, the Guiding Principles envisage participatory HRE praxis as entailing

Figure 9.1. These children are the adults of the twenty-first century. A Philippine children's shelter regularly holds educational programs on the Convention on the Rights of the Child, to which the Republic of the Philippines is a party. Article 42 of the Convention mandates human rights education: "States Parties undertake to make the principles and provisions of the Convention widely known, by appropriate and active means, to adults and children alike." (Asian Students' Christian Trust, Manila)

"equal participation of women and men of all age groups and all sectors of society both in formal learning . . . and non-formal learning through institutions of civil society, the family and the mass media" (para. 3). HRE endeavors ought thus to cut across hierarchies of formal/informal education systems, gender and age and reach out to realms other than state power.

Fourth, the Draft marks a community of concern between "democracy, development and human rights" (their "mutually reinforcing nature"). Accordingly, it reiterates a prime function of HRE to "seek to further effective democratic participation in the political, economic, social and cultural spheres and [it] shall be utilized as a means of promoting economic and social progress and people-centered sustainable development."

This remarkably imaginative formulation offers to HRE missionaries an embarrassment of riches. HRE strategies have to foster that order of participation that promotes both "economic and social progress" and "people-centered development." In a sense, this formulation leads back to an equally remarkable enunciation in Article 18 of the 1974 UNESCO Recommendation, which rightly insists that all education, including HRE, should address the major problems of humankind, especially "the eradication of conditions which perpetuate" attacks on human survival and well-being: "inequality" and "injustice." HRE, like all education, must ineluctably be "multidisciplinary," as well as global, regional, national, and local *all at the same time* and at all levels of learning.

Critiques of Human Rights as Sites of Resistance to HRE

Recognition of critiques of human rights enunciations is essential to the HRE mission of developing a "universal culture of human rights." There exists in the North a rights weariness and in the South a rights wariness. Neither can be wished away; each has to be grasped in its historical settings and lessons learned through dialogical encounters. Human rights and HRE knight-errantry can lead only to a Quixotic enchantment, leaving the world untransformed at its core. The rights weariness is partly a response to the human rights enunciation explosion. Ethical theorists question the emergent hegemonies of rights languages, displacing *all* other moral languages (of virtue, duty, responsibility, and communitarianism). Pragmatists scoff at the Quixotic character of many human rights formulations, which seem to represent to them *not* a utopia but a dystopia. Rights weariness is an ethical stance that doubts whether the liberal traditions of individual rights can be the privileged bearers of human transformation, especially when the ideals of rights seem to be squandered by an excess of rights talk.[5]

Rights wariness regards it as a duty to raise uncharitable questions concerning the career and future of human rights promotion and protection in the present mold.[6] The critics perceive an immense duality, and even duplicity, in the endless propagation of human rights languages, even to the point of identifying those as "human rights colonialism." Wariness about rights may best be captured by the following (perhaps too simplistic) formulations:

(a) The discourse of human rights ought to be pluralistic, according equal dignity to all traditions of the world; by contrast, it is hegemonically "western."

(b) The classical liberal tradition of rights and justice carries the legacy of the original sin: these traditions are at their best and brightest in justifying/recycling colonialism/imperialism, in both "classical" and contemporary incarnations.

(c) Human rights agendas offer pathways, in different radical idioms, of the White Man's Burden; in other words, they mask the ends of power and domination (political and economic) by the North.

(d) The North is unable, despite its proud boast, to make the world safe for democracy and rights and is unwilling to create conditions within its own jurisdiction to eliminate practices and circumstances that encourage massive and flagrant violation of human rights.

(e) This stands demonstrated (even outside the arena of foreign policy and the making of wars) in the North's pronounced inability and unwillingness to subject its own economic agents to a common human standard of regulation of risk and liability for injury (whether signified by Bhopal, or the dumping of toxic wastes or of injurious drugs in overseas markets proscribed at home, or by gender-aggressive contraceptive devices). Implicit in policies of export of hazardous processes and products is a double standard concerning the value of human life.

(f) The North has betrayed commitments, contained in salient UN declarations, that provided for a global structural adjustment program for promotion and protection of human rights, especially for the South. Some of these declarations also contained promises of reparation for massive and sustained violations of rights of colonized peoples and nations, for example, Social Progress and Development (1969), pledging 1 percent of the gross national product of North for aid to the South and *just*, nondiscriminatory patterns of trade, commerce, and intercourse between the North and the South; eradication of Hunger and Malnutrition (1974); Use of Scientific and Technological Progress in the Interest of Peace and Mankind (1975); and the Right to Development (1986).

(g) Human rights diplomacy of the North has been complicit, during and even after the cold war, with the worst violations of human rights in the nation-states of the South.

(h) The classical model of human rights spread an ideology of possessive market individualism where human rights become rights of *homo economicus* or *homo consumeris* devoid of any communitarian responsibilities and fidelity to age-old spiritual heritages, transcending both the market and the state.

(i) The cosmologies of human rights discourse are based on variants of civic religion and secular nationalism, not cognizant at all of the potential of divergent religious, cultural, and interfaith traditions for promotion of fraternity, solidarity, dignity, justice, and rights.

In all these genres of critiques lies an impulse for rethinking human rights. They acknowledge, indeed, that some human rights and fundamental freedoms are universal and indivisible but interrogate, for example, preferred hierarchies of rights, extolling civil and political rights over economic, social, and cultural rights.

Clearly, no amount of incantation of the mantra of "human rights culture" is going to succeed in the face of these diverse critiques. Nor would it do, even as a gesture, to deny elements of domination or hegemony or to gainsay the ascendancy of one variant of liberal human rights paradigm in most of the contemporary human rights formulations. It would also constitute a serious misrecognition of these genres of critiques to say that all these, put together, constitute merely self-serving resistance to human rights cultures.

The Tasks Ahead

Human rights education begins to gather a global momentum precisely at a historical juncture when fantastically new forces of production (especially digitalization and biotechnology) have begun fostering new international divisions of labor through the rolled-up processes of globalization. If the ideological superstructures are varieties of postmodernist ethics (including rights weariness), the Realpolitik of the emergent world is increasingly rights wary. For once, the discourse is explicit: human rights are instrumentalities of social development, which could best take place through "free trade" whose logic in turn is at odds with *so many* proclamations of human rights—the discursive twist explicitly since the UN summit on social development is clearly in the direction of a market-friendly (or specifically trade-related) human rights paradigm.

To be sure, amidst all these transformations, the core objections of HRE remain, more or less constant in the sense that

- human rights education is, after all is said and done, *education*
- as with other "forms" of "education," HRE ought to contribute to the "full development of human personality"
- HRE contributes to this objective especially by strengthening respect for human rights and fundamental freedoms
- as "education," HRE must contextualize all learning by its focus on world peace, security, and development in ways that nurture human rights cultures everywhere

These objectives have to be attained in a world dizzy with the acceleration of history. The difficulties of HRE are well worth pondering in this context, as a prelude to the identification of the tasks ahead.

No matter how "education" is conceived (formal/informal/adult, continuing, extension education), human rights *education* has necessarily to relate to and deal with educational *formations* already in place everywhere: it has to engage itself with

- education systems as articulations of state policies and national objectives and as hierarchic grids of power within society
- patterns of distribution of access to literacy and to elementary, primary, secondary, tertiary education
- patterns of relationships between educational apparatuses and the economy, national and global

- ideologies, philosophies, epistemologies, technologies, and pedagogies internal to the domain of education and cultivated by its practioners
- histories of education and of entrepreneurship
- traditions of academic freedom (as freedom to teach and as freedom to learn)

HRE conceived as "education" needs to find an exponential entry point at each one of these and related levels. State constitutional policies, as in the Philippines, for example, can do a great deal to facilitate privileged space for human rights education.

Notes

1. As is not self-evident from the two volumes of United Nations bluebooks, *Human Rights: A Compilation of International Instruments* (New York: United Nations, 1996), sales no E. 94, XIV.1.

2. In particular the Recommendations of the UNESCO International Congress on Teaching of Human Rights (Vienna, 1978), the UNESCO International Congress on Human Rights Teaching, Information and Documentation (Malta, 1987), and the International Forum on Education for Democracy (Tunis, 1992).

3. Roberto M. Unger, "The Critical Legal Studies Movement," *Harvard Law Review* 96 (1983): 561.

4. Also discussed in Upendra Baxi, *Mambrino's Helmet? Human Rights for a Changing World* (Delhi: Har Anand Publications, 1994), 1–17.

5. For example, Maurice Cranston says, "once a right is conceived as an ideal, you acknowledge its impracticality; it becomes easier to dismiss it as a right": "Are There Any Human Rights?" *Daedalus* 112 (Fall 1983): 1–17.

6. Alasdir MacIntyre, *After Virtue* (Notre Dame, Ind.: University of Notre Dame Press, 1984), 69.

Part II
Approaches to Teacher-Training, College, and Adult Education

EDITORS' INTRODUCTION

Colleges and universities are critically important to the development of serious efforts to initiate human rights education. It is generally in institutions of higher education where international exchange programs position students face-to-face with their fellow students from overseas, where innovative and experimental courses are inaugurated, where teacher training takes place, and where related research is conducted. Colleges and universities can serve as the incubators for human rights education.

Like any field of education, human rights education cannot flourish without the support of training facilities and specialized research. While the research output of universities is enormous, some research that is important to human rights educators is not undertaken in teaching institutions but conducted at independent centers, such as the InterAmerican Institute of Human Rights (San José, Costa Rica), The Hague Academy of International Law, and the International Institute of Human Rights. The latter organization in Strasbourg also sponsors annual programs of in-service teacher and nongovernmental organization (NGO) training.

Most of the university-based research on problems of human rights is being done in faculties of law, the social sciences, philosophy, and the humanities, often in specialized interdisciplinary centers and institutes. Examples are: the Institute of Human Rights, Essex University; the Centre for Human Rights of the University of Ottawa; the Center for the Study of Human Rights, Columbia University; the Townsend Institute for the Humanities, University of California (Berkeley); and the Human Rights Institute of the University of the Philippines, to name but a few.

To be useful, human rights research and related scientific inquiry must be accessible to others, and, for the investigators involved, it is encouraged and rewarded when there are appropriate publishing outlets, including interdisciplinary scholarly journals. The existence of such specialized journals is a relatively new development. The *Netherlands Quarterly of Human Rights* (University of Utrecht) and the *Human Rights Quarterly* (University of Cincinnati College of Law), as well as the *Harvard Journal on Human Rights* are all products of the 1970s and 1980s when human rights first began to be taken seriously as a subject for formal education beyond the scope of legal studies.

Among the specialized scholarly journals of education which frequently publish articles on human rights education are: the *Canadian Journal of Education, Educational Research Quarterly,* the *International Journal of Educational Reform,* the *International Journal of Political Education, Social Education,* and *Western European Education.* Articles on human rights education and related symposia in these journals often stress the need for teacher training, both pre-service and in-service, as well as curriculum, text, and materials development. These topics are the concern of the chapters in Part II.

The issue of how effective human rights education is to be undertaken, beginning with the professional preparation of teachers, is the subject of the chapter by Nancy Flowers and David A. Shiman. They propound the view that "all prospective teachers should come to see themselves as human rights educators and advocates." With this far-reaching premise in mind, they offer numerous tested suggestions and exercises to help future teachers recognize that most aspects of their enterprise involve human rights. For both teacher training and for the in-service education of teachers, the authors clarify their "5-E framework" of explanation, exhortation, examples, experience, and environment. Additionally, they supply useful sample activities for a training course. This chapter can beneficially be read in combination with that which follows on the "Training of Trainers."

Paul Spector's description of the technical requirements for training human rights trainers carries the thematic view of educators in the field, that participative methodologies are necessary insomuch as "human rights education is done best in the give-and-take of discussion with fellow human beings." The chapter is highly systematic in identifying training strategies and learning objectives, in laying out techniques for stimulating participation, and in calling for evaluation exercises.

Educational programs that include evaluation activities of various kinds are more likely to succeed in gaining support and in meeting their objectives than unevaluated programs. Evaluation techniques are routinely taught in schools, departments, and colleges of education. Thus such techniques may readily be factored into programs of formal education. But training programs, often directed toward the needs of NGOs concerned with nonformal education, should incorporate evaluation training as well. At the most pragmatic level of concern to NGOs who are often dependent on private funding sources, their prospects for externally secured grants are enhanced by building evaluation procedures into their projects.

The evaluation of human rights education can sometimes produce startling insights into the need for such training. For example, consider the seasoned judgment of Jan Martenson, United Nations Under Secretary-General for Human Rights until 1992. He was responsible for the Programme of Advisory Services of the UN Centre for Human Rights. In an interview in July 1991, he noted that over the previous three years the Centre had organized multiple human rights training courses for more than three thousand administrators of justice, government officials, law enforcement officers, and others sensitively responsible for the protection of human rights in various countries around the world. They were trained by qualified international human rights experts. In addition to expressing concern about underfunding for the Programme, Martenson focused on the three thousand trainees and concluded significantly: "The result was invariably the same, the people said: We didn't know, we didn't know that these [human rights] standards existed, that our country had ratified them, and particularly we didn't know that we had to apply them also in our daily activities."[1]

In 1993 the United Nations World Conference on Human Rights issued a Declaration in Vienna lamenting widespread ignorance of human rights and focusing on the need for human rights education. The Vienna strategy for "fostering mutual understanding, tolerance and peace" calls for a reorientation of teaching, learning, and research in the fields of "human rights, humanitarian law, democracy and the rule of law."[2] If this prescription for a reorientation of teaching, learning, and research is to be realized, creative conceptual and planning tasks lie ahead. This is the thesis of Rita Maran's chapter on college-level teaching in the field of human rights. She demonstrates that, aside from legal studies, human rights education has been generally alien to existing structures of higher learning institutions. To give salience to the challenge of the Vienna Declaration, a great deal of planning is in order, much of it, as Maran notes, marked by "puzzles and paradoxes." Few institutions of higher learning have demonstrated greater reluctance to integrate human rights into their curricula than business schools. Yet, as the brief note by Olivier Giscard d'Estaing argues, on both normative and practical grounds, business schools need to take human rights seriously. Citing the experience of the European Institute of Business Administration (INSEAD), d'Estaing stresses the importance of infusing "business training with human rights education, including human and business civic duties."

To be effective, according to the Vienna Declaration, human rights education should include concern for "peace, democracy, development and social justice," as identified in international and regional human rights and related instruments. This is nothing less than a call for a holistic approach. In "Curriculum Development for an Interdisciplinary Minor," Rhoda E. Howard describes such an approach devised by a Canadian university faculty committed to the development of an innovative undergraduate program on "international justice and human rights." The chapter details the planning process, objectives, and thematic content of a creative program of college study which draws on existing college resources and challenges students with field experience in human rights internships.

In recent years, college-level political science courses have increasingly called upon simulations and role-playing as highly motivating learning processes. Bernard Hamilton's chapter focuses on the use of "awareness and skill games" that promote more than student reflections on professorial lectures, but rather enhance participation and invest the efforts to resolve conflict with a sense of efficacy on the part of the student. For example, case studies involving the minority Kurds of Turkey and human rights problems in Haiti should help to improve the capacity of social science students to sort out complex information, analyze it, see alternatives, and make reasoned choices. According to Hamilton, college-level simulations and problem solving linked to case studies provide materials with which students must intellectually struggle, and in the process they wrestle with intricate issues in a fully engaged fashion. Awareness and skill games, applied to human rights issues, can link affective responses to cognitive processes, promote critical thinking, and strengthen problem-solving skills.

The final chapter, by Matthew Cowie, is a pensive reflection on a program that is university-based insofar as it was developed within the law faculty of Nottingham University, but the course is offered in an extramural English community setting for adult learners in the neighborhood work force. The chapter emphasizes that such learning is a participatory process, that access to knowledge should be empowering, and that the learner is also the teacher, and vice versa. Rich in theory and praxis, Cowie's chapter shows how adult education, when carefully planned, can attain the twin goals of problem solving and the liberation of human potential from structures of human domination.

Notes

1. "Interview," *Human Rights Newsletter* (Geneva: UN Centre for Human Rights) 4, no. 3 (1991): 5.

2. Vienna Declaration and Programme of Action, "Human Rights Education," sec. D, paras. 78–82.

Chapter 10
Teacher Education and the Human Rights Vision

Nancy Flowers and David A. Shiman

The United Nations Universal Declaration of Human Rights (UDHR) assigns a crucial role to education. In its Preamble, it calls on us to promote "understanding, tolerance and friendship" and to "strive by teaching and education to promote respect for these rights and freedoms." In addition, Article 26 declares that we must not only ensure every child access to education, but also ensure that education is "directed to the full development of the human personality." The Convention on the Rights of the Child (CRC) expands on this article, making special reference to primary, secondary, and tertiary education, specifying that this right be achieved "progressively and on the basis of equal opportunity" (Article 28).

This human rights vision incorporates far more than the right to an education as presented in these two documents. The education professional is profoundly influenced by other human rights responsibilities addressed in these documents. The UDHR, for example, speaks of the right to life, liberty, and security (Article 3), to food, clothing, shelter, medical care, and needed social services (Article 25), and to rest and leisure (Article 24). The CRC addresses human rights of children related to abuse and neglect (Article 19), disability (Article 23), expression of opinion (Article 12), and health care (Article 24).

Preparing teachers to become human rights educators means addressing the totality of interrelated and interdependent rights found in these visionary documents. This chapter suggests ways to incorporate human rights education themes into both the pre-service and in-service education of teachers at all levels.[1] It provides curriculum resources and offers teaching strategies for creating "human rights moments" in the classroom.

We develop below an approach to human rights education in teacher training that is rooted in a conceptualization of moral education offered by Kevin Ryan.[2] We adapt his "five Es" for moral education to organize our recommendations for teacher education. To be most effective, the education of a teacher sensitive to human rights should involve all five of the following dimensions: (1) explanation, requiring intellectual examination and understanding of human rights issues or themes; (2) example, identifying or serving as models of human rights activists to emulate; (3) exhortation, urging everyone to act in accordance with human rights principles on behalf of those in need; (4) experience, providing opportunities to act to improve a human rights condition; and (5) environment, creating a classroom and institutional culture grounded in human rights principles. Our approach also includes the development of teaching skills, an aspect not present in Ryan's original framework.

Professional Preparation of Teachers

Human rights should be a fundamental organizing principle for professional practice,[3] so that all prospective teachers come to see themselves as human rights educators and advocates. They must know the UDHR and the CRC. This convention, in particular, is the raison d'être for any professional teacher preparation program. It helps to maintain focus on the interrelated tasks of ensuring the protection of the child's well-being, the provision of essential services to the child, and the child's active participation in her or his own development.

We offer the following suggestions with the awareness that some teacher education programs are already engaged in some of these activities. They are seldom, however, placed in the framework of human rights education. We believe it is very important to make this connection to human rights explicit, for it connects professional preparation to a powerful global vision.

Explanation

Prospective teachers need to engage in philosophical and practical discourse that challenges them to consider the human rights dimension of almost every aspect of the teaching enterprise. This process will affect why one teaches, what one teaches, and how one teaches. In particular, these prospective teachers need to explore the justice and equity issues raised by the educational research regarding gender, race or ethnicity, class, disability, and sexual orientation. Doing so will help future teachers make explicit for themselves the value bases that undergird their selection of instructional methodologies. Some actions that educators of teachers might consider are the following.

Engage prospective teachers in critical analysis of the visions and prescriptions for a better world embodied in the "International Bill of Rights"[4] and other principal human rights conventions, particularly the CRC and the Convention on the Elimination of All Forms of Discrimination Against Women. Such an examination requires understanding the history of the human rights struggle, at home and across the globe, and reflecting on the meaning of these human rights principles for their personal and professional lives.

Ensure that prospective teachers critically examine the human rights environment of their own community and society and determine what roles schools do, can, and should play in advancing the goals articulated in the international documents mentioned earlier. This scrutiny will involve identifying those whose rights are violated or unachieved and consider ways school communities can act on behalf of the disempowered.[5]

Assist prospective teachers to develop analytical criteria by which to assess the human rights condition of a classroom and the policies and practices of a school or district. Regarding the classroom, this process will involve being able to generate justice-related questions about the following practices: evaluation, grouping, distribution of teacher instructional effort among students, teacher responses to classroom disruptions, selection and use of instructional materials, curriculum orientation, teacher discipline, questioning modes, establishment of rules, and patterns of student participation in decision making. Regarding the school or district, this process will involve being able to generate justice-based questions about such areas as discipline policy, school-parent relations, extracurricular activities, tracking and retention policies, guidance and counseling, and school governance, to name but a few.

Incorporate a child study activity in which students generate their research questions based on articles in the United Nations CRC. Such a study might compare children's rights identified in the CRC with their needs as described by human development theorists. These prospective teachers can then assess each child with respect to her or his achievement of basic rights and needs.

Ensure that these prospective teachers can adapt the concept of human rights to different age levels. They should be able to select those concepts or themes, such as respect, tolerance, justice, fairness, equality, prejudice, discrimination, caring, that are appropriate for the students they teach and develop learning activities based on each.[6]

Develop in prospective teachers an understanding that serving children requires an increasingly high degree of interprofessional cooperation not only with teaching colleagues but with those in social and health services as well and enable teachers to acquire needed advocacy and collaborative skills.

Expand prospective teachers' conception of human intelligence beyond the linguistic and logical-mathematical modes traditionally valued in schools to include multiple intelligences such as spatial, musical, bodily-kinesthetic, interpersonal, and intrapersonal.[7] By doing so, these future teachers will come to offer a wider range of learning opportunities to their future students, thereby enhancing the "full development of their human personality" described by the UDHR.

Engage these future teachers in the study of the relationships between learning styles and gender, class, or ethnic background and the development of teaching methodologies sensitive to this diversity and effective at engaging learners in a variety of ways.

Ensure that these prospective teachers recognize that being a human rights educator requires addressing the tensions between being an advocate and being a teacher.

Their commitment to equality and justice requires that they learn to create a class-room climate built on open discourse that encourages alternative perspectives and mutual respect. Schools are arenas where values collide, and not all members of the school community will share their global vision and their conception of what it means to be a professional. Therefore, they must learn interpersonal skills that enable them to work collaboratively with a wide variety of people.

Example

A teacher-education program must provide examples for emulation drawn from both present and historical members of the professional community. Obviously these examples should include faculty who are modeling what they espouse. In part, this recognition involves renaming as "human rights work" certain ongoing efforts that traditionally have been described in the language of "community service." Some actions to consider are the following.

Acknowledge publicly educators and social service personnel within your region who actively teach and work for human rights.

Identify famous educators such as John Dewey, Socrates, Emma Willard, Maria Montessori, Jane Addams, Jonathan Kozol, and W.E.B. DuBois who chose to stand for human rights principles in their professional work.

Honor students on campus who perform service to the community that promotes human rights.

Establish a Human Rights Educator award to be presented to students about to enter the profession.

Publicize the human rights work of faculty and staff as exemplars of what the professional program stands for.

Involve your institution in Amnesty International's Educators' Urgent Action Network, which strives to assist colleagues around the world who are in jeopardy for peacefully exercising their human rights.

Involve your institution in ongoing projects to collect and distribute educational resources to needy children here and around the world.

Exhortation

The teacher education program itself must stand for human rights principles in an explicit, public way. It needs to encourage students to see themselves as human rights educators and to urge them to act accordingly. Some actions to consider are the following.

Create and disseminate a mission statement that reflects human rights principles and declares the program's commitment to eliminating injustice of all sorts and to promoting humane relationships. Course syllabi should reflect this commitment, and applicants to the teacher education program should be made aware of this value base.[8]

Compose a Teacher's Code with students and teachers that articulates a commitment to advancing and advocating for the human rights of others. Encourage graduating students to affirm these principles when they leave the university to begin their professional work.

Experience

The teacher education program should ensure that prospective teachers become actively involved "doing human rights." There is no better preparation for becoming a human rights activist than taking action. Some actions to consider are the following.

Involve students in the governance of the institution via participation on committees, particularly those that directly affect the students' lives.

Involve students in the determination of recipients of human rights awards presented by the professional program (see "Example" above).

Require these future teachers to complete a human rights action project which might involve activities such as the following: collaborative action with social service workers, volunteerism at local correctional center, food bank, homeless shelter, battered women's home, or youth center, or collecting educational materials or fund raising on behalf of needy children elsewhere in the world.

Promote and support student efforts to organize university vacation projects, such as house building for Habitat for Humanity.

Encourage prospective students to become involved with Amnesty International's Educators' Urgent Action Network, described in a previous section (see "Example" above).

Engage students in improving the human rights condition within their teacher education program and the larger university. They might examine those classroom justice concerns related to evaluation, teacher-student interaction, or instructional materials, mentioned in the "Explanation" section above. They might explore campuswide justice concerns related to freedom of speech, due process, and student recruitment, admission, and retention policies. Based on their research efforts, these prospective teachers can propose changes aimed at promoting a human rights culture at the institution.

Environment

The teacher education program needs to create a human rights ethos in which its students feel valued, respected, and involved. There is no better form of professional socialization to a culture of justice and respect than actually being educated within

one. Creating and sustaining such a climate is built upon many small, everyday interactions among teachers, staff, students, and administration. Some more programmatic
actions to consider are the following.

Indicate a commitment to the "full development of the human personality" by en-
    couraging students to employ multiple intelligences (see "Explanation" above) to
    show their understanding of the subjects under study.
Establish an atmosphere in which students feel comfortable and safe raising concerns
    about the quality and fairness of courses, programs, and instructors. The profes-
    sional program might even have its own ombudsperson.
Promote student involvement on all appropriate committees within the institution.
Acknowledge publicly (see "Example" above) the human rights accomplishments
    of students and faculty via press releases, newsletters, bulletin boards, and other
    media.

Even though some teacher-education programs are undertaking the kinds of actions described here, the vast majority of teachers have neither been introduced to
human rights concerns nor encouraged to view themselves as working within a human
rights tradition. In most instances, their initial contact with human rights education
begins at in-service sessions.

In-Service Education of Teachers

Legislators may mandate human rights education, and departments of education may
develop strategies to implement it,[9] but unless teachers themselves feel interest and
commitment, the subject will never become alive and important to students. To reach
those primary and secondary teachers who received no formal training in human
rights education during their professional preparation, we must offer dynamic in-
service programs.

Most teachers will agree that everyone ought to know about human rights. Few,
however, feel adequately informed to teach the subject, and even fewer will see how
human rights can fit into their already overprescribed curricula. Some teachers may
also have misgivings about the perceived controversial nature of human rights education. A successful in-service program in human rights must address these reservations,
giving teachers a confident grasp of the basic information and providing practical,
creative answers to their questions about introducing human rights in the classroom.

Structure

Regardless of its length or the grade level addressed, any in-service training on human
rights should include the same components of explanation, example, exhortation,
experience, and environment developed above. A minimal two-hour workshop can

suffice to introduce the UDHR and examine its relevance to teachers, their students, and their communities. Even the most cursory in-service can provide teachers not only with information, but also with opportunities to take personal action and can leave them with ideas and materials to put to immediate use.

An ideal program begins with an introductory workshop of three to five full days. This period allows teachers time to get into the subject, discuss human rights questions, examine international documents, reflect on local-global links, and begin to develop materials for use in their own classrooms. This initial course should extend through the following year by a series of regular follow-up sessions when teachers can come together again to further their learning, renew their enthusiasm, share their successes and failures, and build a network of human rights educators. These meetings are critical to the sustained establishment of human rights education, especially in parts of the world where democracy has been systematically suppressed for generations.

Methodology

All aspects of an in-service session should adhere to the principles of respect, justice, and participation. For example, how are presenters and participants selected, housed, and addressed? Do they reflect the ethnic and racial proportions of the population? Are opportunities provided for everyone to speak? Are opposing opinions respected? How are conflicts resolved? Is confidentiality respected? Are participants asked regularly to evaluate the course, and how do course organizers respond to their suggestions? In fact, the course should model what teachers are being encouraged to do with their own classes.

Passive lecture format should be kept to a minimum. Instead, participants should be engaged in a variety of active methods: small group projects, one-on-one discussions and interviews, and active learning situations where teachers, like their pupils, are out of their chairs and physically involved in problem solving and self-expression. In addition, participants should be offered a range of modes in which to learn, including art, drama, movement, music, and verbal expression.

A program where only the "official" presenters do the teaching invites passivity. At one point or another, every participant should play a leadership role, perhaps teaching a model lesson, demonstrating how a rights concept might be introduced into a particular subject, or analyzing a conflict of rights at school and how it might be solved. One task of in-service leaders is to ensure that this sharing of leadership occurs.

Contents

Inherent in every human rights topic, whether an objective overview of legal instruments or a subjective response to social responsibility, are humanistic values that should also be articulated.[10] This discussion of content incorporates practical ideas for teaching and for encouraging participation in the community. Regardless of the length of the session, the following topics need to be included for teachers of all grade levels.

1. Definition of Human Rights

Participants need to be aware of the global standards for respecting human dignity and promoting justice. To do so they must extend their thinking beyond their own constitution or bill of rights to acknowledge a variety of rights: political, civic, cultural, social, and economic. They not only need to understand that different conceptions of human rights arise from different cultural and historical traditions, but also to recognize the existence of a common core of rights to which almost all subscribe. Inherent in such a discussion is the intersection of moral rights and legal rights.

2. Definition of Human Rights Education

The goals, curriculum content, and teaching strategies for human rights education need to be introduced. Defining human rights education should be done in a manner that treats teachers as colleagues rather than empty vessels needing to be filled. Ideally teachers will recognize as human rights education much of their established practice, such as their respect for the dignity and individuality of each child. At the same time, this act of defining should help teachers to identify areas where they need to change and grow.

3. Human Rights in Historical Context

Participants often need to develop new ways of thinking about history and their part in it. Tracing human rights concepts through history, either through lecture or activities, further helps to broaden the perspective and brings in many different cultures and conceptions of rights. One perspective-changing exercise is to examine a variety of events and developments in human history (e.g., the spread of Islam, the exploration of the western hemisphere, the invention of the printing press or the computer, the French Revolution, the invention of the birth control pill, the partition of India) through a "human rights lens": for example, did these events advance or set back the cause of human rights? What human rights issues were involved? What rights were violated or affirmed?

4. Principal Human Rights Documents

The documents described as the International Bill of Rights and the conventions mentioned earlier (see "Explanation") need to be put in context in relation to history, international law, and the United Nations. Although the UDHR, the primary document for learning about human rights, is written in legal language and not user-friendly to many teachers and students, it can become readily accessible if approached from a variety of methods. There are also several versions of the UDHR written in simplified language available in many languages. Amnesty International's animated video, which illustrates all the articles of the Declaration, provides an excellent intro-duction.[11]

5. Contemporary Human Rights Issues and Events

People think first of human rights in terms of violations because these graphic examples are more readily accessible to the media, and no course should ignore them. However, examples where rights have been affirmed are equally important to include. Participants need also to recognize that human rights abuses result from complex historical, economic, social, and political situations, not simply because of unjust government policies. Contemporary events should also be analyzed in relation to the international documents: what specific rights are involved here? Are rights in conflict? How can rights be protected or promoted? This discussion might involve the participants in a map activity in which they identify human rights concerns around the world. They might also explore local examples of these global rights problems.

Furthermore, a course should select sample cases with a judicious eye to geo-graphic, ethnic, and ideological balance. Every effort should be made to avoid either a *we-they* polarization that implies either that human rights violations only happen abroad (as is often the case in the United States) or undue concentration on past abuses in the home country (as can occur in a country newly emerging from dictator-ship). One effective method is to select a specific issue (e.g., the rights of refugees, indigenous peoples, or women) and trace it through several global situations, com-paring and contrasting the different situations. Another approach to contemporary issues is to examine two or three geographic areas in depth, exploring the factors that have created current conditions. Newspapers and magazines provide the best raw ma-terial for this topic. The Amnesty International Annual Report,[12] which summarizes the rights situation in every country, provides excellent background material. Where possible, area experts and former victims of abuses can provide briefings. These real-life experiences often prove the most memorable examples and strongest exhortation to teach about human rights.

6. Human Rights in the Curriculum

To the perennial question "Where does human rights fit in?" one might begin to answer with another question, "Where is it already taught?" An in-service train-ing needs to help teachers recognize "human rights moments" (e.g., situations where rights are exercised or in conflict) that regularly occur in everyone's teaching day, both in the classroom and in the school community. Such "human rights moments" might serve as building blocks for rights-oriented discussions. These sessions will also help teachers identify ways they can take off from school-based concerns to broader, global ones, for example, censorship of the school newspaper to Article 19 of the UDHR.

Brainstorming among teachers can provide new ways to apply the "human rights lens" to traditional subject areas, especially those beyond history and social studies. Where, for example, might human rights fit into the science, vocational training, literature, sports, or foreign language class? On this topic, participants may prefer to be separated by the grade level or subject area taught, though teachers in wholly different contexts often stimulate new thinking in each other.

In even the briefest in-service session, time should be allotted for teachers to develop human rights lessons they can actually put to use. Teachers then demonstrate these to the other participants, and if possible these lessons are reproduced for inclusion in the packet of human rights resources that all participants take home.

Where logistics permit, children can be effectively incorporated into these in-service sessions, especially in the phase of curriculum development. For most children and teachers, working together on strategies to teach human rights is a human rights lesson in itself. And young people often prove to be excellent teachers for younger children.

7. Human Rights in the Community

Community involvement is clearly at the heart of the "experience" dimension. Whatever injustice and intolerance exist in a community will be present in its schools as well. Teachers are essential in showing students how to examine events in their own lives through a "human rights lens." Students then can see that abusive language, stereotyping, teasing, bullying, and other forms of discrimination have a direct relationship to human rights, as do the social manifestations of intolerance such as sexism, racism, and homophobia. Teachers can also nurture positive practices in social relations, political processes, and cultural observations that demonstrate respect for human rights and dignity and acknowledge and include diversity in background and lifestyle. Many teachers need help, however, to develop strategies for establishing such an environment of respect and inclusiveness in their classrooms.

As the institution principally entrusted with social and character education and in many cases the center for the community, the school can also serve as a laboratory for the practice of nonviolence, tolerance, and human rights. Here, too, educators need opportunities to identify and discuss their school's environment and its successes and failures in this area, as well as to generate ideas for increasing awareness among the whole community.

Faced with some of the grim facts about human rights abuses, members of the school community need to feel that they personally can make a difference, both at home and in the world. Once again participants need to brainstorm together about human rights actions appropriate for their school or classroom. Some useful models are Human Rights Day programs, letter writing on behalf of prisoners of conscience or young people whose rights have been abused, and a variety of community service projects, including having older students teach younger ones about human rights.

Every human rights course must include some opportunity to take personal action, even simply signing a petition or writing a letter. This principle is as important for teachers as for students!

8. The Not-So-Hidden Agenda

No training will be effective without making the participants feel not only able, but also eager to teach human rights. Most teachers are inspired to recognize themselves as participants in a worldwide movement and to realize that they are linked with other teacher-activists across the globe who are trying during the UN Decade of Human Rights Education, 1995–2005, to make rights literacy a part of every person's basic education.

A dose of reality is essential at the conclusion of the course. Each teacher needs candidly to consider and discuss what allies, assets, and obstacles to human rights education he or she will face on return to school. Participants can be very useful to each other in suggesting how to address potential problems, and all will benefit from guidelines for teaching about controversial subjects and suggestions for avoiding conflict with recalcitrant administrators and members of the community. Every participant should be asked to describe at least one concrete way he or she plans to put the course to immediate use. Finally, a role-playing activity in which teachers present and defend their plans for instruction in human rights to a school board or school administrator can help prepare for this return.

Follow-up sessions, as requirements of the course or informal get-togethers, are the best method for providing support and sustaining this commitment, as well as learning from each other's experiences.

Sample Activities for a Training Course

1. HR Tree

This activity employs an artistic medium to generate human rights themes. Participants are asked to respond to two questions:

1. What rights do you believe should be universal?

2. What does society need to ensure that these human rights are nurtured and strengthened?

Using large sheets of paper and magic markers, groups of participants draw a tree with leaves or fruit to represent the rights they decided should be universal. The roots of the tree represent what is needed to nurture and strengthen human rights in the society.

After the groups have had about fifteen minutes to create their human rights trees, each group briefly presents its work of art to the rest, explaining and perhaps defending the inclusion or exclusion of certain human rights.

This activity is an exceptionally good warm-up for an in-service session. It encourages interaction and provides the leader with some awareness of the level of understanding of those participating—and it is fun.

2. Designing a New Country

This is an excellent activity to precede a presentation on the UDHR, allowing participants to respond intuitively and personally to the topic of human rights. It also brings to the surface the difficulties involved in reaching consensus on priorities and moral standards.

Working in small groups, participants draw up a bill of rights for an imaginary new country, for which they also provide a name. Each group then displays and explains the list of rights for its new country. From these lists all the participants generate a consolidated bill of rights, a process that necessarily involves combining similar items from different lists. Discussion should include an examination of the criteria for selection and the underlying value systems such choices imply. In addition, each group should consider the method it used to arrive at decisions: did everyone have a chance to participate fully?

Next, participants categorize rights included on this master list according to whether they are civil, political, social, cultural, or economic rights. Does this bill of rights have a preponderance of one category? If so, how can this disproportion be explained?

At this point participants may be given markers or adhesive dots and asked to cast five or six "votes" for the rights on the master list most important to them personally. The object is not to prioritize rights but to provide a sense of the group's feelings and values: why do certain rights receive many "votes" and others very few?

Later in the course, after the UDHR has been introduced, the group should return to the master list and try to match its rights with corresponding articles of the UDHR. What rights in the UDHR has the group omitted? Have they included rights not mentioned in the UDHR? How can these differences be explained?

3. Rights in the News

This activity is an excellent culmination to an examination of the UDHR.

All participants are provided with sections of recent newspapers, ideally representing a broad spectrum of political position and types (e.g., tabloids, community, regional, national papers, and newspapers for specialized audiences). Working singly or in groups, participants peruse the papers for evidence of the following:

1. rights exercised;
2. rights abused or not yet achieved;
3. rights protected;
4. rights in conflict.

Not only news stories but all aspects of the paper, such as the classified ads, sports pages, editorials, masthead, and letters to the editor, should be examined. Participants clip articles that illustrate each rights situation, mount them on posters, and explain their relevance. These posters should remain in the room during the rest of the course, for with their heightened awareness, participants usually continue to find new articles.

4. "They're All Alike"

This simple game illustrates the importance of individuality with a childlike but profound effectiveness appropriate to any age group.

The leader sets out a pile of rocks (or potatoes, onions, autumn leaves) and declares "You know about rocks. They're all alike—hard, dirty, common, always in the wrong place at the wrong time." However, each participant is then given a "pet rock" and invited to get to know it well and then introduce it to the group. Participants can be relied on to wax eloquent on the individual qualities of "my rock." Finally, all the rocks are dumped back into a heap. The leader declares, "Those rocks, they're all alike," and challenges participants to find their "pet rock," an inevitably easy task that serves dramatically to underscore the dangers of stereotyping.

Resources for Human Rights Education

Each participant should leave a course with enough material to introduce human rights into his or her own school setting. Minimal requirements for such a packet are copies of the "International Bill of Rights," an annotated bibliography, and some sample lessons. Ideally teachers would also be given some of the principal human rights education texts or be able to purchase or obtain them through libraries.[13]

Conclusion

We live in a global community where people clamor for self-determination, assert their freedom, and strive to help those shackled by poverty and discrimination. These are local as well as global struggles that affect us all, but in particular they impact the lives of children. More than ever, teachers are needed who can help students make sense of this complex world and find their roles in creating a humane and just society.

Human rights belong in every teacher's professional education. And every professional program, whether pre-service or in-service, should realize these prime goals, which are central to what we do as educators and essential for the welfare of human beings in our local communities and throughout the world. Interwoven with the traditions of moral, global, multicultural, and peace education, these goals are fundamental to citizenship education in a democracy.

1. PROTECT against future human rights abuses;
2. RECONSTRUCT society in accordance with the principles of justice and human dignity;
3. INFORM and educate about rights as well as the responsibilities that accompany them;
4. MOBILIZE ourselves and others to work on behalf of those in need of support;
5. EMPOWER ourselves with the knowledge, skills, and attitudes necessary to become effective instruments of global justice.

Notes

1. Francine Best, "Human Rights Education and Teacher Training," *The Challenge of Human Rights Education,* ed. Hugh Starkey (London: Cassell Educational Limited, 1991), 120–32), addresses some of the same concerns raised in this chapter. See also Kim Sebaly, "Education About Human Rights: Teacher Preparation," in *Human Rights and Education* (New York: Pergamon Press, 1987), 207–21, for a thoughtful discussion of issues related to concept, content, and methods with examples from teaching about human rights through a comparative education course.

2. Kevin Ryan, "The New Moral Education," *Phi Delta Kappan* (November 1986): 228–33.

3. See Centre for Human Rights, *Teaching and Learning About Human Rights: A Manual for Schools of Social Work and the Social Work Profession* (New York: United Nations, 1992). Teacher educators would benefit greatly from this book. It relates professional practice to international standards of human rights and offers thoughtful ideas for professional education.

4. The United Nations documents entitled the Universal Declaration of Human Rights (1948), the International Covenant on Economic, Social and Cultural Rights (1966), and the International Covenant on Civil and Political Rights (1966) make up what is often referred to as the International Bill of Rights.

5. Stanley L. Witkin, "A Human Rights Approach to Social Work Research and Evaluation," *Journal of Teaching in Social Work* (1993): 239–53.

6. Sebaly, "Education About Human Rights," 210.

7. Howard Gardner, *Multiple Intelligences: The Theory in Practice* (New York: Basic Books, 1993).

8. The Mission Statement of the College of Education and Social Services of the University of Vermont, written by its faculty, declares in closing: "The ultimate purpose of these activities is to create a more humane and just society, free from oppression, that fosters respect for ethnic and cultural diversity, and maximizes human potential and the quality of life for all individuals, families, and communities" (Burlington, Vermont, January 1992).

9. The following states of the United States have mandated human rights education in public elementary, intermediate, and secondary schools: California, Minnesota, and New York.

10. See Betty Reardon, *Educating for Human Dignity: Learning About Rights and Responsibilities, a K–12 Teaching Resource* (Philadelphia: University of Pennsylvania Press, 1995), for a discussion of the interconnection of humanistic values and human rights education.

11. This useful video is available from the Publications Department of Amnesty International, 322 8th Avenue, New York, NY 10001 (212) 807–8400.

12. Available from the Publications Department of Amnesty International.

13. The following bibliography is recommended for teachers in North America, though the starred items are also available in languages other than English. The fact that most of these titles were published in the 1990s illustrates the burgeoning interest in the field as teachers recognize that understanding human rights is essential to world citizenship in the twenty-first century.

*1. Amnesty International Human Rights for Children Committee, *Human Rights for Children: A Curriculum for Teaching Human Rights to Children Aged 3–12*. Alameda, Calif.: Hunter House, 1992. (Preschool-Intermediate). Organized around ten principles derived from the UN Convention on the Rights of the Child, this resource book provides teaching strategies for each principle and activities designed to give it practical application at different developmental levels.

2. David Donahue and Nancy Flowers, *Uprooted: Refugees and the United States*. Alameda, Calif.: Hunter House, 1995. (Intermediate-Secondary). Through classroom activities for many subject areas, this resource curriculum teaches the history of refugees in the United States, international legal standards, and current refugee issues.

3. RoAnne Elliot, *We: Lessons on Equal Worth and Dignity*. The United Nations and Human Rights, 1992. Available from UNA-MN, 1929 South 5th Street, Minneapolis, MN 55454 (612) 333–2824. (Intermediate). This curriculum offers tolerance education through activities that provide students opportunities to discuss issues of race, ethnicity, and religion.

4. David McQuoid-Mason et al., *Human Rights for All: Education Towards a Rights Culture*. St. Paul, Minn.: West Educational Publishing, 1995. (Intermediate-Secondary). Initially written by a team of U.S. and South African lawyers to prepare young South Africans for democracy, this innovative curriculum has now been edited for publication in North America and provides an excellent conceptual introduction to human rights.

5. Betty Reardon, *Educating for Human Dignity* (note 10 above). (Preschool-Intermediate). This book takes a developmental approach to human rights education, discussing the social and developmental levels of each age group and providing appropriate sample lessons.

6. David Shiman, *Teaching Human Rights*. Denver: University of Denver, Center for Teaching International Relations, 1993. (Intermediate-Secondary). This is the most comprehensive curricular resource available for the secondary level, containing more than twenty-five classroom activities.

*7. United Nations, *ABC, Teaching Human Rights: Practical Activities for Primary and Secondary Schools*. New York: United Nations. Centre for Human Rights, 1989. This is a fine guide for practical applications in the classroom; the central theme is that children should experience human rights through active learning.

8. Lucille Whalen, *Human Rights: A Reference Handbook*. Santa Barbara, Calif., and Oxford, UK: ABC-CLIO, 1990. (Intermediate-Secondary). This is the ideal resource for any course on human rights; it offers a history of human rights, useful listings of human rights organizations, publications, and electronic data sources, and the texts of major international human rights documents.

Chapter 11
Training of Trainers

Paul Spector

This chapter discusses the technical requirements for training trainers. Most of the information in it is derived from human rights, cross-cultural, conflict resolution, and economic development training programs conducted over the last three and a half decades. Citizens of most nations of the world participated in these programs, so I believe that the information is valid for most parts of the world. The chapter covers five topics: (1) motivating and inspiring trainers; (2) training strategies; (3) designing training programs; (4) implementing training of trainers; (5) evaluating training.

Motivating Trainers

Although the world thirsts for human rights education, there may be much controversy about its specific content. Many trainers will face proscriptions and discouragement from authorities, or seeming indifference among the people themselves who have been cowed by those for whom human rights spells trouble.

Human rights educators must be enthusiasts who are highly motivated. Trainers need to understand that they will be able to achieve only as much sophistication in their audiences as their political and cultural climates permit. Their task is to teach as much about human rights as they can realistically do without being stopped. They need to be inspired to persist in expanding boundaries despite opposition and limitations, and often in the face of only modest progress.

The first principle is to raise consciousness about human rights as the single most important goal. Human rights educators need to understand that much of the battle is won once consciousness is raised. People thirst for human rights regardless of what authorities are willing to permit. Their own pain and suffering engender the need for human rights. Once people are aware that their suffering is not foreordained, they lend themselves to further human rights education and to the attainment of as much of their rights as they can get. As a rule they will strive for all the human rights they can achieve through peaceful means without plunging their societies into chaos. Once awareness is raised, the remaining educational need is to develop the means for achieving human rights peacefully. The most pacific of methods is talk, the right to discuss with others what they need and want to improve their lives.

Wise educators know that they must work at the razor's edge, always pushing for progress peacefully, always just short of being shut down. To achieve this state and to maintain it in progressive equilibrium, human rights educators need to acquire the backing of powerful members of the established authority who are sympathetic to progress in human rights, or who understand that continually thwarting peoples' rights in the face of modern communications is to court rebellion.

Societies are so complex that there is almost always someone in the establishment who understands the need to make progress in human rights; sometimes it the most established leaders, who understand the continual need to make progress while maintaining balances among conflicting interests in human society. Unfortunately, as is evidenced by the strife and civil turmoil around the globe today, not all societies are so blessed. To survive to teach, human rights educators must not only be inspired to improve their societies, but must also understand the avenues open to them and the limits in their societies.

Inspiration for improvement is all-important because people who know how to deal with their establishments are always in danger of being co-opted by those in power who would use them to pacify the very people whose rights they wish to realize. Human rights educators need to find, or be able to inspire, genuine allies in the continual struggle for human rights.

Human rights educators should understand that diverse beliefs about human rights stem from diverse conceptions of human nature. At an earlier stage in history, the members of most aristocracies believed that they were superior to the slaves, serfs, and peasants who supported them by virtue of intelligence, power, wealth, or divine ordination. They arrogated to themselves not only wealth and dignity, but also the means of controlling those who produced the wealth. That almost always meant the repression and suppression of the human rights of their inferiors. A Hungarian nobleman in the nineteenth century summed it up well when he said, "Humanity begins with barons." Their concern for the lives, well-being, and rights of lesser beings was akin to their concern for their animals; often the animals, being more immediately serviceable, were given preference.

In modern times, people in command often profess to be egalitarians, but generally still act as if they believe in inequality. They believe that their intelligence, education, talent, piety, or better understanding of affairs enjoins them to arrange the order of their nations or the world, but with the one great difference from the past, that they are working for the good of all humankind, or at least for the good of great majorities. Repression and suppression of human rights are now cloaked in the necessity to serve the common good. Sometimes deprivation of human rights is deemed a temporary expedient until enough wealth and productive capacity is generated to enable the common citizenry to enjoy theirs. Sometimes in the face of superabundance, deprivation of the most fundamental rights for some of the citizenry is deemed necessary to maintain the order that has produced the wealth. Witness a pet industry in one of the great western democracies that spends billions on the well-being of animals while millions of human beings are deprived of adequate health care, sometimes life itself, a situation that is defended vigorously as necessary to preserve the full freedom of the marketplace.

Human rights educators need courage to face the reality that, in their own societies, they must struggle against mind-sets permitting the repression of human rights and vie with politicians who may actively support suppression of human rights and human rights education.

Anchoring Human Rights Education in Local Cultures

As a general rule, appeal should be made to local scripture, constitutional foundation, or laws that embody written recognition of human rights. Human rights educators should be, or should become, thoroughly conversant with these written reinforcements. There is a strong tendency to advert to the commonly accepted written word as sacrosanct, perhaps because it represents the contract that permits stable order in society. One can be sure that opponents of human rights education will cite scripture of some form (often mistakenly) in arguing against human rights education.

As soon as possible, human rights educators should recruit persons who are both concerned for human rights and know their anchors in the local religion, constitution, or laws. Even when the initiating human rights educators are well respected and well versed in these matters, it is wise to recruit others who are recognized experts. They should be people who are respected for their authority, learning, wisdom, and probity. The more such people become affiliated with the endeavor to introduce human rights education, or who join as trainers themselves, the better.

Human rights educators should know, and should make known, that as long as fewer than 20 percent of the people in this world own 85 percent of its wealth, given modern communications, there will be a continual struggle for human rights. People in command can be made to understand that it is better to make progress peacefully than to force people to resort to bloodshed to gain the rights that belong to them. What is progress? Progress is relative to the situations in which people find themselves. In a society where women need to spend hours getting and carrying water each day, progress may consist of getting men to share the burden. In a society so rich that more is spent on packaging than on the health care of the poorest fifth of the population, progress may consist of attaining universal health insurance. In a society where 80 percent of the people are disenfranchised, progress is getting universal voting rights. In a society where most of the people do not bother to vote, progress is persuading them to exercise their franchise.

Training Strategies

The most effective general training method for human rights education is a participatory one. People need to be encouraged to discuss human rights concepts, problems, and issues, and to debate how they would attain their rights and the rights of others. Unlike most academic or technical bodies of knowledge, which can be conveyed about equally well by personal or impersonal means, human rights education is done best in the give-and-take of discussion with fellow human beings. Human rights are not abstractions or ideals alone, but in the end are what we accord each other in the context of our cultures and political settings. To make them practical we need to learn them in the context of discussion with others. There are certain ideas and techniques with which all human rights educators should be familiar, which they should be able to adapt to their own situations.

Raising Human Rights Consciousness

Whether audiences are literate or illiterate, I have found it desirable to start with an orientation that captures attention and furnishes a preview or overview of the main human rights concepts or issues that will be discussed. The logic pursued in such an orientation is as follows.

There are human problems or contradictions between basic values and human behavior which the audience can readily recognize.
We have institutions such as governments and families, and mechanisms such as the rule of law, elections, or diwans which help us to cope with such problems.
We have evolved concepts such as equality, social security, and justice which serve to protect human life and well-being. These concepts, taken together as a body of ideas, constitute our belief in human rights.
Our current purpose is to explore how we can improve the workings of our institutions and the other mechanisms for protecting human life and well-being, by learning more about these protective ideas, and agreeing among ourselves how to apply them to our day-to-day behavior.
We will also explore ways to help others to develop concern for human rights as a means of improving the ways we cope with human problems.

The orientation should intrigue and challenge the audience to want to hear and see more. It should engender cognitive dissonance. For example, one might start with statements such as, "We say we believe in equality, but . . . ," or "Most of us say we believe in social justice, but . . . ," or "in democracy, but . . . ," or "order in society, but . . . ," and then go on to point out contradictions in the actual conduct our lives. For example, ". . . we are content to let women do twice as much work as men."

Having raised the audience's curiosity, the speaker can go on to raise awareness of how ideas about human rights such as equality applied to political, economic, civic, and personal arrangements can help to guide thinking and behavior toward the resolution of such contradictions.

The concept of equality generally needs to be defined in such a way that all members of the audience understand and accept it in order to be able to develop the logic for protecting all human lives. I have found that the definition which holds that "each human being wants to stay alive as much as any other person" creates an understanding of human equality that is more immediately appreciated as credibly valid than such relatively abstract and palpably unfulfilled ideas as "equality of opportunity," "equality of wealth," or "equality before the law."

An orientation serves to interest potential trainees, to raise their awareness of human rights issues, and to lay the foundation for ensuing discussions. To emphasize the main points, it is useful to buttress the orientation with a robust set of illustrations that do not depend on the availability of electricity. Posters or lap charts serve very well to illustrate or dramatize each major point. A supplemental set of viewgraphs which can be used when electricity and equipment are available should be kept handy.

A Course of Human Rights Discussions

The orientation should be followed by a course of discussions centered on the issues of how human rights can serve to protect us all, and how they can be promoted in the context of one's cultural, social, and political realities.

Before embarking on a course of discussions about human rights, it is desirable to determine the audience's conceptions about fundamental human values. I have found that in virtually any group, if people are asked to list their five most important values, among them will almost always be some expression of the value of human life. This life value will be expressed in various forms such as "life itself," "my family," "health," "security," "a good job," "education for a better life," "a stable society." Once participants realize that they all value human life, regardless of which aspects of it they deem most important, they usually desire to discuss ways to protect life and well-being. Moreover, they almost invariably include in their conception of human life the idea of human dignity. Most people are willing to consider the best means, in their circumstances, to protect life and dignity for all people, poor as well as rich, women as well as men, children as well as adults. A principal subject of debate in this regard is likely to be the relative importance of individual rights compared to group rights.

The discussions should deal with the major problems that concern the participants. In each case they should explore how human rights can help to ameliorate or resolve the problems. Throughout, it is wise to keep focused on these basic principles—the need to protect human life and equality of human life—when participants stray into tangents, or when arguments become too controversial or emotional to be constructive. The facilitator should refrain from imposing his or her own views on the learners. Participants should be encouraged to voice their views and to draw their own conclusions about the promotion and use of human rights in light of their basic values.

The fact that most governments acknowledge the Universal Declaration of Human Rights helps to legitimize discussions of human rights in the general form described here. Even most dictatorships today recognize, in some measure, that modern governments are instituted to protect the lives and well-being of their citizens.

Training for Various Modes of Human Rights Education

Three main modes of communication are available for human rights education:

Public information using the mass media to disseminate information. All forms of print—posters, newspapers, magazines, bulletins, flyers, and mailings—as well as the electronic media—radio, television, audio and videocassettes and discs, and cinema—can be used in human rights education on a mass scale. Special training in the use of each medium is required to employ it to its best effect. I do not discuss such technical training in this chapter but rather confine myself to the training of trainers with respect to the substance of human rights education, which can then be conveyed to media specialists.

Nonformal methods. These consist principally of exhibits, festivals, commemorative activities, lobbying, conventions, professional meetings, parties, home celebrations, and religious activities with a focus on human rights. This chapter does not cover the techniques required to prepare and implement the activities for such nonformal methods.

Formal in-school and out-of-school learning among groups of participants. I concentrate on the preparation of trainers who can train others to do human rights education in such settings. The substance of this training also informs the other two modes, but must be tailored to each technology. I assume here that the mode of instruction will be either face-to-face interaction between students and teachers, or between facilitators and participants.

The most commonly used method for adult education and training programs, worldwide, is a combination of lecture and discussion, supplemented by case studies, exercises, demonstrations, and readings. The basic tools are still some form of chalkboard, newsprint, and overhead projector or slide projector. In more recent times, audiocassettes, a form of lecture, and videotapes, basically a combination of lecture and demonstration, have become widely used.

In rich countries, computer-assisted instruction, using the enormous storage capacity of CD-ROM to furnish very flexible interactivity, has been used. In this mode the computer program can be very responsive to the needs of learners since it permits learners or the computer to call up a wide array of information as needed to make the learning effective.

In general, computer-assisted instruction can be delivered most efficiently to individuals or to groups as long as each learner has his or her own terminal. For human rights education it might be more effective to use one terminal for two or three learners. This would encourage them to discuss information conveyed by the computer, but as far as I know, this is still an untested medium for this purpose.

Distance learning programs generally use combinations of printed lessons, tests, and face-to-face, or mail- or telephone-mediated tutorial guidance. Often there is also a period of residential instruction. TV, radio, audiocassettes, videotapes, and CD-ROM are generally used as supplements to printed lessons rather than as the main bearers of information. They are most often used to motivate and stimulate students to keep up with their printed lessons and to supplement instruction with demonstrations that are difficult to convey in print. TV and computer-based instruction are extremely expensive for the amount of information they convey. As much as two and a half million dollars per course is spent in preparing first-quality electronic instruction. It must be used by enormous numbers of paying students to defray the upfront costs of production.

Designing Training

It is essential that trainers become proficient both with respect to the substance of human rights education and the techniques for facilitating participation by learners. Pursuing the general strategy described in the last section, training designers should tailor the actual substance of education to the understanding of their participants.

Trainers should know the written expressions of human rights, including both the Universal Declaration of Human Rights and local scriptural or legal versions, so that they can guide discussions constructively. If the would-be facilitator is ignorant of the important fundamentals, he or she must learn them and must learn to help people to apply concepts to life situations. If after trying, the aspirant cannot do this, it is better to participate as an assistant to a more adept facilitator than to attempt to lead discussions themselves.

Specific local training strategies must be chosen in order to accomplish the training within the budget and in the environment in which training must be done. The first task is to define the learning objectives that trainees should achieve. Human rights objectives can be summarized generically as:

awareness or consciousness of human rights
learning about human rights problems
learning about the origins or reasons for the problems
learning about ideal solutions

learning about practical and feasible solutions
commitment to promoting human rights
commitment to expanding human rights education
commitment to sensible actions favoring human rights education and the promotion of human rights in one's cultural, religious, and political contexts.

It is necessary to determine which of these need to be pursued for the learners for whom the training is being prepared. The training prepared for a body of lawyers who have been active in human rights affairs obviously differs from the training for illiterate adolescent girls in a very traditional society.

The first practical step in defining specific training objectives is to determine the characteristics of the learners. This should be done empirically by quick research methods. The simplest is to hold systematic discussions with small groups of representative learners. Topics representing each of the generic objectives should be introduced. Members of the group should be asked to offer their opinions. The forum leader should take pains to elicit the opinions of all group members, as representative information about human rights awareness, sophistication, and commitment is being sought.

A simple technique that can be used in such small groups to determine the group's positions, after some members have volunteered their opinions, is first to ask the members for any additional views, then to ask them by a show of hands to indicate their agreement or disagreement with rephrasing of the opinions that were voiced. If there is reason to believe that members of the group are reluctant to expose their opinions to the others, then a simple form of anonymous ballot should be used. Even illiterates can put a mark in one column or another beside numbers representing the topics in question. The results of such research should be carefully considered in formulating the specific learning objectives.

Learning objectives should be defined in behaviorally observable terms, that is, in sufficiently concrete form to permit one to know whether the objectives have been achieved. This need not be a complicated or mysterious task. Training designers should take the trouble to write a list of objectives. For each one, ask "How will I know whether that has been accomplished?" Distinguish between the behavior of the trainer and the learning of the trainee. You are not asking "What have I done?" but "What has the trainee learned?"

A partial list of learning objectives for trainees might look like this: Trainees will be able to:

identify the conditions of their lives, or the behavior of those who influence them that they believe to be unjust or unfair
know the range of human rights expressed in the Universal Declaration of Human Rights

identify the improvements in their lives that they desire most

identify the improvements they think are feasible in their life circumstances

identify the changes in other people's behavior needed to rectify injustices

specify the changes in one's own behavior needed to get the improvements

specify the investments or sacrifices in time, money, labor, training, and so on that
one can afford and is willing to make to achieve feasible improvements

specify the behavior needed to get others to join in the struggle for human rights

determine orders of priorities in terms of importance, urgency, and feasibility in attaining specific human rights peacefully

specify the activities one is willing to undertake to promote human rights education

specify the preparation one must and can undergo to carry out human rights education

choose the men, women, and children who will be recruited for human rights education

specify the times, locations, and actions one will take to further human rights education

When specific behavioral objectives have been defined, one can choose the program design and the methods and materials that can help trainees learn them. Only
after these are known can one choose the most cost-effective training designs and
methods for training trainers.

Single objectives or logically related sets of objectives should be grouped into
training units which may consist of one or more lessons or discussions. A set of facts,
ideas, or skills should be taught in order to achieve each objective. The form in which
the substance of training is to be conveyed should be determined both by the particular fact or idea and by the characteristics of the learner. For example, the idea of
fairness might be introduced to children by distributing candy unfairly to the various
children in the group, whereas the same idea might be introduced to adults by a discussion of the value of different work tasks.

The designer should take care to sequence units in logical order, making sure that
later work requiring prerequisites has been preceded by the necessary earlier learning.

Learners should be allowed to practice skills until they have become proficient.
For example, a trainee should be required to learn to deliver an orientation lecture
flawlessly.

Learners should be allowed to review and summarize what has been covered, but
not so often or at such length that they become bored.

Certain general training design issues should be settled once the objectives are
known:

What will be done to capture initial attention? A brief lecture? A short film or videotape? A play or puppet show? Posters? A contest or game of chance?

What will the main educative methods be? Lectures? Discussions? Readings? Combinations of lectures and discussions, supplemented by readings? Conduct of research or preparation of role-playing vignettes? Preparation of oral or written reports? The writing of a petition?

Will it be feasible to use practical exercises or demonstrations? For example, can trainees write down their desires and values? Can psychodrama be used? Can case studies be used? Is it feasible to ask trainees to play roles in the cases being studied to vivify the meaning and impact of the contents?

Can discussions be stimulated? Will all persons feel free to participate? Can one encourage participation of reticent persons without violating community standards or personal dignity?

Insuring Effective Education and Training

For each major point in the course of study and for the participant learners, the training designer should ask the following questions:

What is the best way to introduce the theme, topic, or point? By an anecdote, parable, or allegory? By lecture? By a provocative question? By a paradox? By inducing discussion? By calling on participants to introduce the topic?

What is the best way to make sure it is understood by all? Alternative ways to express the same idea? By giving examples? Illustrate with diagrams, charts, or pictures? By using an analogy whose elements are familiar to all? By letting leaders explain it to others? By having the audience play out roles that help them to internalize the idea? By citing a case?

What is the best way to make it memorable? By asking for a show of hands? By citing statistics? By telling a dramatic story? By inducing heated discussion? By giving a dramatic or engaging lecture? By a field trip to make reality overtake or reinforce abstract beliefs?

When the main elements of the ultimate education or training program are known, the training program for trainers can be designed. The trainers and trainers of trainers must learn the same substance as the ultimate learners. They must overlearn the substance in order to train well. They need depth of knowledge that permits them to adapt their material to a wide variety of persons, learning styles, and situations. Beyond this, they must learn the techniques for teaching others the substantive contents of human rights education.

The first of these are techniques for stimulating participation in the first place. The following is a list of simple techniques that are commonly used.

Persons introduce themselves and mention family or organizational affiliation. The trainer should participate in this exercise.

In addition to introducing themselves, persons talk about their work, their interests, or ambitions.

Persons choose or are assigned partners. The partners tell each other about themselves, their families, their work, and their interests. Each person tells the group
about his or her partner.

In some settings, discussions are preceded by a prayer or a patriotic recitation or
salute. A discussion of the meaning and import of such an introduction can stimulate discussion.

Participants write a list of their most important values, or orally volunteer values that
they subscribe to or believe others subscribe to. The facilitator writes these down
on a chalkboard or on paper. The facilitator asks the participants to group these
into similar, perhaps more fundamental categories.

Participants tell about problems or difficulties that they believe need amelioration or
solution. Sometimes it is best to use the partner system or small committees of three
to five individuals to elicit such opinions initially before they report to the group at
large.

After consciousness has been raised, or introductions have been made, it is sometimes feasible to assign the members of the group to formulate questions about
human rights. and to interview each other or members of their committees for answers. The facilitator should give examples of the questions to be formulated. The
questions, for example, may be about human rights problems, about desirable improvements, about ideals or feasible improvements, or about differences between
men and women or children and adults with respect to human rights.

In some settings the group can undertake a research project to get started. They formulate from three to ten questions about human rights. Then each participant goes
into the community to interview householders, housewives, passersby, customers
in stores, workers, students, officials, or others. The participants should try to get
information from different types of individuals, for example, richer and poorer,
students and teachers, men and women. They bring the results back by a stipulated
time. The group lists and categorizes the results and then discusses them.

Sometimes it is best that the trainer conduct this kind of research beforehand. Then
he or she reports what has been asked, and asks the participants to volunteer what
they think the results are for each category of respondent and each question. When
discussion ensues, the facilitator should ask people to say why they think the various findings emerged as they did.

To raise consciousness the trainer may need to deliver an orientation lecture. As
soon as discussion gets under way, the trainer should become a facilitator who is responsible to:

define, determine, or clarify the subject(s) of the discussion, goals of the discussion,
the time available, discussion protocol such as individual time limits and the requirement to permit others to speak

help to maintain order in the expression of individual opinions

draw all individuals into the discussion

tactfully control overbearing discussants

help to define terms used by others

get participants to clarify their own and others' positions

help participants to state their positions more clearly

call the discussion back to the main topic when it begins to go off on unrelated or diversionary tangents

mediate between individuals who are arguing

soothe ruffled feathers or bruised egos

move the discussion to new topics when participation begins to flag

ensure that there are rest breaks to permit people to refresh themselves

Some Critical Practical Matters

Critical political questions must be asked before training is conducted:

Is training legal and condoned by the authorities?

Who will be recruited to back the education effort?

Will the press be alerted and invited to participate? At what stage in the program? in helping to recruit trainees, backing, or funds? while it is going on? after the program has demonstrated success or popularity?

Will notables or influential people be invited to participate in the training? Will they be asked to voice their opinions of training needs? Will they be asked to help in specifying training objectives? in designing training? Will they be trained before others?

Certain mundane questions must be asked and answered in designing human rights education programs:

Are the trainees literate or illiterate?

Is there enough money in the budget to print materials for distribution?

If trainees are illiterate, can someone design illustrations that will help to convey information about issues or to fix issues in memory?

Is electricity available to permit the use of overhead projectors, videotapes, or other electronic training aids?

How much time will the trainees actually be able to devote to learning? if they must travel to the training venue? if they have household, family, or work duties?

When can training be done? How often should it be done? Can the training be done before or after work? in the evenings or on weekends or holidays?

Where can training be done? Is a school, temple, church, or mosque available? someone's home? an outdoor space?

Who can help in the training? How much and what kind of training is needed to prepare them? Do they need to be paid for time or expenses? how much?

Whose permission is needed to conduct the training nationally, provincially, locally?

Institutionalizing Training

It must be borne in mind that there will be a degradation in quality as the training is transmitted from one generation of trainer to the next. Four main principles should be employed whenever it is feasible to do so:

Try to keep the training generations to a minimum. Attempts to spread training rapidly by so-called "Multiplier" or "Cascade" methods have generally failed. Training in each generation of the Cascade is usually too restricted in scope or time to be effective. Changes introduced at each generation often end in very different training between the original and the third or later generations.

Try to create a training institution such as a training school, a training center, a training library, or a college in which the best trainers can train the trainers who are immediately in touch with the final learners.

It is important to recruit inspired and inspiring trainers who can refresh the education with their own creativity. Look for talented trainers who have a flair for ideas and for presenting them. Keep the training as simple as possible consistent with the training objectives. It is not necessary to get every last idea or fact into play. If the participants are moved by the main points, if their awareness is raised, then their own creativity will inform their own understanding and the understanding of others.

The best thing one can do is to create self-learners who are inspired to become teachers. Then one can leave them with materials that they can use to become more sophisticated and expert in what they do. Therefore a distinction should be made early on between what is essential to convey and what can be left to the future in archival form. All trainers and trainers of trainers should learn and use the concept of Training Hammer Blows. With respect to human rights education, the points that are made must be telling, moving, and memorable. It is pointless to go into detail that will obscure main points, lead to diversions, or interfere with memory until the main objectives have been achieved. It is first necessary to orient people toward human rights consciousness and the will to solve human rights problems. Once participants are engaged and are motivated to go further in their learning, they can and should go into the kind of detailed examinations of the rights and wrongs of behavior that the day-to-day exercise of human rights demands.

Implementing Training

Ideally a training course for trainers in human rights education should last at least two months. Its duration should be not less than one month of full-time study.

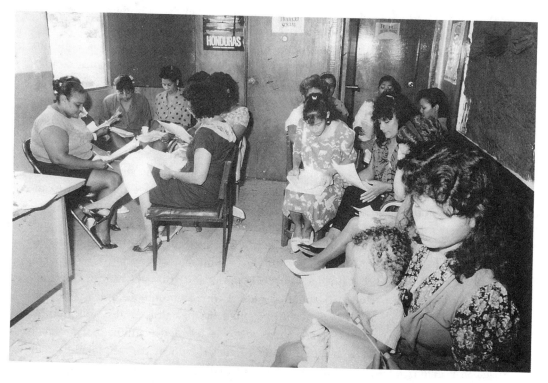

Figure 11.1. *Promotoras* ("promoters") organize curriculum materials. These Panamanian educators were trained to teach human rights to women under the auspices of the Fundación para la Promoción de la Mujer. The UN General Assembly (Res. 49/184), in connection with the proclamation of the United Nations Decade of Human Rights Education, stated its belief that human rights education constitutes an important vehicle for the elimination of gender-based discrimination and for ensuring equal opportunities through the promotion and protection of the human rights of women. (National Institute for Citizen Education in Law [NICEL])

Each course should be offered in the spirit of experimentation. Trainees should be invited to inform it with their own experience, and to offer criticism and suggestions for improvement, which, if sensible, should be used to revise or refine the course.

The most efficacious instructional approach for training of trainers is to engage them in problem solving. This implies that they are heavily involved in practical development activities. First they need to be challenged to learn the substance of human rights education. This is done by assigning readings which all trainees discuss actively in small groups or in plenary sessions.

Trainees are then assigned a topic to research in depth, for example, the historical development of human rights, the status of women's or children's rights, differences in human rights legislation among nations, or differences among local groups. The trainees are required to deliver both oral and written reports about their research and to participate in critical discussions. The purposes of the research and reports are to build a sense of expertise in each individual and to develop a body of knowledge that the whole group acquires in an active mode (not simply by reading).

At the beginning of the training course, each trainee, pair, or triad is assigned to develop a full training program which they will use in training their own students. They are required to define learning objectives, to develop and implement methods for assessing learner characteristics, to design instructional methods suited to various types of substantive contents and learners, to develop classroom materials such as posters and handouts, and to assemble a reading list for their eventual students. They are also required to develop methods for evaluating training.

Each individual trainee or working group is also assigned an exercise to develop one problem case. This requires that the trainees clearly delineate the full scope of the problem and possible methods for solving it. For example, the problem may be a heterogeneous group of learners, some of whom are literate, some illiterate, some educated, and some not; or the problem may be the need to engage people from two or more conflicting factions in human rights education.

In general, each day is divided into four periods with breaks both within and between them. Each period lasts about two hours with a ten-minute break. The first period is devoted to a lecture or panel presented by specialists, and is followed by a question-and-answer period. The second period is devoted to individual or small group development work. After lunch, the third period is devoted either to additional discussion generated by the first period or to small group discussions of readings and ongoing development work. The fourth period is spent on development or other practical exercises.

In order to keep the students motivated and fully engaged, and the program fast-paced and interesting, it is necessary to allow for free periods, individual study and research periods, exercises, and field trips. The last period every other day can be assigned to these activities. Two all-day or half-day field trips a month are usually sufficient. One afternoon a week should be allowed for free time to attend to personal business or to catch up on work that has fallen behind.

Instructors should make themselves available to the trainees at the end of each day to explain missed or obscure points or to clarify issues and deal with criticisms and complaints.

If possible, celebrities should open and close the course. These may be local or national authorities, religious figures, authors or journalists, noted business or professional personages, or the heads of significant institutions. In general, the press should be invited to cover the course at its inception and conclusion or at field exercises.

Evaluation

Training should be evaluated formatively and summatively. Formative evaluation is done to improve the training as it is being designed and developed. Summative evaluation is done at the end of training and after trainees have had an opportunity to apply training in order to determine its value.

Formative Evaluation

In formative evaluation, each presentation should be evaluated by the trainees for clarity, substantive value, organization, and interest. Each presenter should be evaluated for quality of delivery. Evaluation forms should be prepared beforehand. They should give the trainees opportunities to rate the presentations and presenters on four- or five-point scales from unsatisfactory to outstanding. The form should also provide an opportunity for trainees to write specific criticisms and to make suggestions for improvements.

At the end of each day the facilitators should solicit criticism of that day's instruction. One period at the end of each week should be devoted to an evaluation discussion about the week's experiences.

Summative Evaluation

Part of the last day of each course should be set aside for the trainees to discuss their experiences during the whole course in the absence of instructors. They should appoint a secretary to keep notes of the discussion. They should appoint two or three spokespersons to report on the deliberations of this evaluation committee of the whole to the faculty and any outsiders, like donors, who may be interested.

The impact of the training should be followed up at the trainees' sites after a period in which they have had time to implement the training. This period can be anywhere from one week to years after training, depending on when the trainee implements his or her training. Follow-up evaluation is usually expensive. A judgment must be made as to whether it is more important to determine field impact or to invest in further human rights education efforts. The type of follow-up will depend on budgets and other resources available. Follow-up evaluations essentially can be done in three ways:

Trainees and their own trainees can be interviewed or observed in their local settings. Trainees should be interviewed about their recollections regarding training and about the ways in which they have put the training to use in the field. Interview and observation schedules can be constructed to reflect the specific goals of human rights education. This is a relatively inexpensive method because follow-up can be confined to small samples. It is not without cost because interview and observation schedules must be constructed, tried out, and refined. Data collectors must be trained and must travel to the sites where educational activities are being carried out, and qualitative data must be carefully analyzed by people who are sensitive to the biases that lurk in such data.

It may be possible to use statistics that might reflect the impact of human rights education that have already been collected by public or private agencies. This method is apt especially if mass media have been employed. For example, voting statistics or female schooling statistics may reflect the influence of the training program. For such statistics to be meaningful, it is necessary to carry out well-controlled analyses. This may require comparison of measures taken before and after the training, or in regions where the education program was carried out and where it was not. The virtue of this method is that it is relatively inexpensive if statistically sophisticated inexpensive labor is available. However, it should be understood that the method is relatively insensitive. The available statistics may not actually reflect the training and education; therefore, either false positive or false negative effects may be attributed to the training.

If radio or TV has been used, it may be worthwhile to determine the specific impacts of training on a relatively large audience. In this case a new database is generated, that is, new statistics are collected from the field (rather than those collected by others for other purposes). It is possible to collect data by interview, questionnaire, or observation that reflect the specific goals of the human rights training. For example, the number of persons who received training from the trainee, or the number of persons who demonstrate raised awareness about human rights or human rights education can be determined by sampling. Here again, it is necessary to take pains to perform the appropriate statistical analyses which include traditional controls or possibly very sensitive tests of trends over a period of time. The disadvantage of this method is that it is expensive. Appropriate representative samples must be drawn; survey instruments must be constructed, tried out, and refined to ensure that the questions are unbiased, unambiguous, and clear to the respondents; surveyors must be trained to implement the interviews, or large-scale mailings of questionnaires must be made; and appropriate statistical analysis must be done to obtain valid information.

A Final Note

It is becoming fashionable to jump onto the information superhighway. There is a tendency to believe that electronic technology will be the salvation of education, especially where education has lagged in the poorest nations. Educational quality depends on the substance of the information and the cogency of its cognitive expression and organization. The medium over which it is transmitted generally cannot improve these characteristics. It can either enhance or degrade the emotional impact of the information. A good script may have greater impact when it is read than it does if it is badly produced for TV or film. The chief value of the electronic media lies in their potential for reaching enormous numbers of people. Properly used, they can be extremely valuable.

It is necessary, however, to issue a word of caution. There are relatively very few radios and television sets in the poorest nations of the world compared with the industrialized countries. For example, in the least developed countries (LDCs) in 1990, there were only 100 radios, 9 television sets, and 4 telephones per thousand people. In contrast, the industrialized countries had 1,130 radios, 545 television sets, and 590 telephones per thousand persons (including babes in arms).[1] In the LDCs there were 39,390 persons per post office, compared with 4,200 in the industrialized countries. For the foreseeable future, the superhighway will be available mostly to the people of the developed world. The people who need human rights education most will be most deprived even in this regard. It is essential that trainers be well trained, and on a large scale, because they will be the medium for most human rights education for the vast majority of the world's people.

Notes

1. United Nations Development Programme, *Human Development Report 1993* (Oxford University Press, 1993).

Chapter 12
Teaching Human Rights in the Universities: Paradoxes and Prospects

Rita Maran

> Knowing, whatever its level, is not the act by which a subject transformed into an object docilely and passively accepts the contents others give or impose on him or her. . . . In the learning process, the only person who really *learns* is s/he who is able to apply the appropriate learning to concrete existential situations.
>
> Paulo Freire, *Education for Critical Consciousness*[1]

To begin at the relevant beginning, the adoption of the United Nations Charter in 1945 positioned human rights as a foundational organizing principle of our time. Because of the human rights mandate in the Charter, a combined moral-legal order was to emerge over time. That order was to become the point of departure for civil societies the world over, in the struggle for human rights. Thus was the human rights culture born.

Now, as we celebrate the fiftieth anniversary of the Charter, how fares human rights in the academic world, the area on which this chapter focuses? Here I point out certain accustomed features in the landscape of human rights education in the university, along with paradoxes associated with those features. It may be that others among the relatively few who teach human rights in the university have come to accept these paradoxes, or perhaps no longer see them. I then continue with specific methodological approaches and classroom exercises, and conclude with thoughts on where university teaching of human rights can set its sights. At this stage, as we shift gears for even more robust approaches to educating about human rights, this chapter proposes a fresh, practical scrutiny of the human rights education landscape, to see where we have got to and what the terrain ahead looks like—for both old hands as well as newcomers to this field.

Shining a Light on a Few Paradoxes

The uncovering of paradoxes calls more for a questioning mind than a profound study; the paradoxes are not very deeply buried. Closest to the surface is the not unfamiliar query from university educators: "What? Human rights education? In the university?" Such reservations tend to surround the study of human rights, and to undercut the notion that the study of human rights—admittedly a relatively new area of study in academia—constitutes a right and proper subject in higher education.

Ask a half dozen college professors—your choice—whether they support human rights education and get as many different responses. "Issue for issue, human rights is compelling, and it interests me as a concerned member of society, but I am not convinced that there is a developed body of scholarship on the topic." Or: "In these economic times, we can't spare funds for an innovative course that falls between conventional disciplines." Or: "If students want to do something about human rights, I would not stand in the way of their organizing a course." And so on.

A good point of departure then, in academic discourse, is the quite valid question: "What is meant by human rights education in the university setting?" The short answer nominates international human rights law as the starting point. It is the purpose of this chapter to provide a somewhat longer answer, and to present practical ideas for instructors interested in preparing human rights curricula that will satisfy course committees' requirements.

Another paradox: in a profession prone to specialization, teaching and activism are often considered separate and distinct activities. Thus faculty who are—to whatever degree—human rights activists extramurally, have been known to operate on the premise that such activities are best kept separate and apart from teaching. Open support of human rights threatens to transgress the glass wall that maintains the separation of activities outside the classroom from views expressed in the classroom. Although the basic tenets of human rights are unconnected to any political strain, the concern is that an instructor who is visibly supportive of human rights will be identified with particular political factions.

Another familiar statement leading to paradox number three: "Courses that revolve around international law should be confined to schools of law." Human rights education, although indeed frequently taught as a law-based subject and thus when found on a campus is most often listed in law school course offerings, is in fact an interdisciplinary topic. True, international human rights law is a relatively recent comer to the legal domain, having arrived with the advent of the UN Charter, the Universal Declaration of Human Rights (1948), and the remainder of the International Bill of Human Rights. Indeed, it could almost be said that the acceptance of this body of law by jurists has run a parallel course to acceptance of the United Nations itself by governments, leaders, and diplomats—at times waxing, at times waning. Nonetheless, that body of international law devoted exclusively to rights is no more the exclusive domain of lawyers than is the U.S. Constitution or Bill of Rights—documents studied by every high school student in this country before graduation, and yet with students neither urged nor expected to become law practitioners.

Not unexpectedly, and unparadoxically, the first stop along the road to human rights education was in schools of law, since international human rights law is the foundation of human rights education. Prime examples are in the law schools at the University of California at Berkeley, the University of Minnesota, Harvard, Yale, the University of Virginia, Georgetown, and most recently Howard University. That leads faculty in other disciplines—who unabashedly avow a meager formal knowledge of human rights—to consider the topic well located in a school of law. And there, by that reasoning, it should stay. If, in keeping with the goal of rendering to students the best education possible, there is to be expansion beyond the law school's walls, it is up to human rights educators to bring it about. It should be remembered also that while curriculum involving legal studies is an exciting challenge to some students, to others it may be daunting. This should be taken into consideration in class lectures as well as in one-on-one meetings.

Here, again, the instructor is in the seemingly paradoxical position of educating students about a body of law by drawing on many other disciplines in addition to law. Paradoxically but happily, no one agrees with this interdisciplinary direction more heartily than those teaching in the law schools, who hail the advent of non–law school-based courses on human rights. By a curious twist, if any group can be said to problematize this shift of human rights onto a broader academic playing field, it is more likely to be found in disciplines outside the law school.

What Department Does Human Rights Education Call Home?

Identifying a home department for a human rights undergraduate course in the university is no simple undertaking. In theory, departments ranging from the humanities to political science to international studies, from regional and cultural studies to development studies and interdisciplinary field studies, might reasonably be candidates. In some cases, the avenue of least resistance is interdepartmental or interdisciplinary.

Although each human rights instructor calls on her or his own intellectual formation and academic strengths, planning a truly interdisciplinary course calls for incorporating existing and "new" knowledge from numerous fields. A relatively broad body of cross-disciplinary literature has developed within the human rights field over the past dozen years, obviating the need for the human rights educator to search very far beyond the "human rights" shelves of the library to find books interrelating disparate fields of study with the study of human rights.

Once embarked on arousing interest in a joint human rights curriculum, how does the human rights educator proceed? Given the institutional bureaucracy that tends to act as a deterrent to change, the reality is that finding a home department for human rights is likely to occur through collegial working relationships that are already in place. Discussion with a colleague might start from a known shared interest in the growing interdisciplinary nature of studies generally, and proceed to pedagogic approaches for integrating principles, theories, sectoral interests, modalities, and clinical aspects of human rights in course work in various departments.

An interested faculty member in, say, philosophy, can invite her or his home department's examination of a proposed course syllabus incorporating the philosophical foundations of human rights. In other scenarios, the would-be human rights instructor recalls to an interested colleague the guest lectures that she or he has given on human rights in that colleague's class, or their collaboration on a campus or community project — often but not always involving human rights violations.

The human rights instructor might propose a few other pedagogic possibilities: arranging for guest lectures by both instructors in each other's courses; co-teaching the human rights course; and cross-listing interdisciplinary human rights courses in one or more other departments. At the University of California at Berkeley, for example, where peace and conflict studies, in the College of Letters and Science, is the home base for the human rights curriculum, the courses are cross-listed with legal studies.

Curriculum Development

On a different note, human rights instructors will avail themselves of curriculum development funding programs available at most colleges, through which incentives are offered for developing new curricula. Or, with a modest curriculum development grant, instructors can develop a series of "human rights modules" for use in the curricula of disparate disciplines. Each module might offer a week's worth of lesson plans relating human rights to the curriculum in the designated course. The professor in anthropology, would, with the module packet, be able to open a discussion on cultural relativism basing the discussion on international human rights norms and recent developments relevant to them. A course on modern European history might examine the foundations and current practices of the Council of Europe's human rights regime. City planning or engineering students might concern themselves with the right to a healthy and sustainable environment, as enshrined in human rights instruments.

The human rights module is specifically designed to complement the particular course's curriculum, and is developed through collaboration between the course instructor and the human rights educator, with assistance from a willing and able undergraduate or graduate student who assembles and organizes the materials. Nothing more elaborate need be devised for the physical presentation of the module than arranging the materials in a binder which, with the agreement of the course instructor, is then made available on the home department's bookshelf, as well as on reserve in the library.

Human Rights and the Business Community's "Bottom Line"
by Olivier Giscard d'Estaing

The business community cannot escape the challenge of human rights. Whether as small shops in the local community or as multinational corporations in numerous host countries, business enterprises should respect human rights, refrain from interfering in the internal policies of human rights-respecting governments, not collaborate with abusive governments, avoid acting as political vehicles, and respect the employment, environmental, and socioeconomic policies of their places of business in accordance with international standards. As they are reminded of these obligations, a great change should be and already is taking place.

At least that is the experience of the European Institute of Business Administration (INSEAD, Fontainebleau). This French-based alliance of business leaders and educators seeks to initiate serious changes in international business practices. Members of INSEAD know it is possible and have seen corporate leaders undergoing an awakening of conscience as to their new social and civic responsibilities, exceeding the normal framework of their companies' activities. A sense of company citizenship can develop and is needed more than ever in our post–cold war world as business leaders begin to realize the potential of expanding regional markets and envision the implications of prospects for global markets.

Entrepreneurial leaders should not have to learn these lessons the hard way, as some did incurring expensive litigation after disastrous chemical spills in India and as others did in terms of boycotts directed against them for doing business in South Africa during the years of apartheid. It is time for schools of business and professors of business ethics to provide human rights education for business administration majors in our colleges and universities. It is all well and good to teach about global business opportunities, but this is insufficient unless we educate businessmen and women that their responsibilities are also global. This can be done. The contributions of business to human dignity need to be expressed and explained. The way to do it is to infuse business training with human rights education including human and business civic duties drawing on the UN Code of Conduct on Transnational Corporations.[1]

Business schools and entrepreneurial training institutions are the normal places to conduct research and to influence the business community in this broad field. For teaching purposes, cases can readily be developed to show executives both the benefits of good civic behavior and respect for internationally defined human rights, and the risks of misbehavior with potential for

---

1. UN Code of Conduct on Transnational Corporations, E86 II A.15 (1986).

disastrous impacts on corporations and on the image of the free enterprise system.

With many professions, including medicine, law, science, and journalism, now incorporating human rights standards into their curricula, business should not be the last to fall into line. Indeed, it is time for schools of business, at both the undergraduate and graduate levels, to take the lead in human rights education. The promotion of international human rights is clearly not the primary objective of ethical businessmen and women, but human rights norms should certainly be an integral part of their sense of and respect for the standards of professional business responsibility. Making money need not be inconsistent with respecting human rights.

With one or more of these initiatives under way, the instructor's preparatory re-search forms the basis for a well-defined syllabus, which she can then submit to the appropriate committee, department, or other relevant committees on curriculum.

With an approved syllabus, and with a class scheduled to meet, what issues does the instructor face?

Teaching International Human Rights Law to Non–Law Students

Because students—no different in this respect from the public at large—may tend to see human rights largely in the context of abuses and violations, the duality of *promotion* as well as *protection* of human rights needs to be introduced at the outset. The instructor can make it clear early in the course that the issue of stopping human rights abuses—a subject that often is the entry point for students—is fundamentally and integrally linked to strengthening the human rights promotion and protection mechanisms, and that the study of human rights covers not only violations but a great deal more. This concept forms the ground on which more sophisticated discussions can take place as the semester progresses.

Motives for taking a human rights course vary: undergraduate and graduate students who undertake studies on human rights are interested in planning a professional career in human rights. Others are motivated less by career planning than by the search for a means of empowering people somewhere in the world, and enabling redress of people's grievances. For those and others, the instructor's introductory lecture makes clear that a carefully constructed foundation course in human rights constitutes a lifelong tool. Students learn, among other things, to apply this "lens" of international human rights law to the day's news, and to distinguish the cosmeticizing of human rights from Realpolitik. In this relatively benign teaching environment, the instructor's challenge is to maintain the high level of common interest, and to chan-nel that interest into an understanding of basic human rights concepts.

Take, for example, the much-discussed case in 1994 of a young U.S. citizen found guilty of defacing public property in Singapore. The Singapore government's punish-ment was to cane the young man. The case evoked much heat but little light on basic human rights issues. Missing in the public discussion as well as the media treatment was reference to the central role of international human rights treaty law that pro-hibits cruel, inhuman, or degrading treatment or punishment. With the exception of a National Public Radio "Perspective" commentary that referred to the Convention Against Torture, human rights was notably absent in public discourse. Or, for another example, in the media coverage of women fleeing their home countries for the sake of avoiding the "traditional practice" of female genital mutilation, the critical issue of the universality of rights in relation to culture has yet to be raised. Such events offer rich fodder for the classroom mill, concerning as they do the universality of rights. Such discussions go right to the heart of questions about the validity of international human rights law, and furnish the day-to-day quality of reality that engages students' scholarly and political interests.

Student Expectations

When students enroll in a course at their college—anything from calculus to philosophy of linguistics—they may justifiably assume that they have an idea of what the course will cover. For a course labeled "Human Rights," it is entirely possible that none of the students has a clear idea of the course's content. The odds that any two students' ideas will coincide are unlikely. On the other hand, among the obvious positives is that, for whatever reason, students intentionally elected to take the course, and some may have some notion of what they wish to get out of the course.

When there is clear intentionality on the students' part, it raises the ante: the instructor recognizes the added weight attached to instructing students who come seeking concrete solutions and remedies. While it is almost certain that many students bring to class an awareness of injustices, only a few may have learned about the phenomenon of "binding legal obligations." Their experience and background will include some who have spent periods of time in places where violations are a fact of daily life. Most are aware of gross violations seen on television news—genocide, torture, mass killings; those come looking for root causes and remedies. A human rights course can help satisfy the student's socially responsible conscience and intellectually hungry mind.

In a human rights course, certain unvoiced concepts may be present in a shadowy form. By that I refer to notions of nonviolence, morality, peace, social justice, ethics, and human dignity, any or all of which may constitute some students' motivating force. At this time, discourse in this country is directed more toward immorality, violence, war, armed conflict, and other forms of injustice. We need to remember, and to remind students, that more positive strivings also have a rightful place in the curriculum. Carving a place for the positives in class discussions encourages students to think positively about forming linkages between their socially responsible selves and their scholarly selves.

Points of Reference

For a pedagogical point of reference, Paulo Freire's teachings are useful. In a classroom packed with university students of all ages, backgrounds, and languages, Freire's practical methodology uses the student's need-based interest as the mortar that holds the stones of education in place. "Democracy and democratic education are founded on faith in men, on the belief that they not only can but should discuss the problems of their country, of their continent, their world, their work, the problems of democracy itself. Education is an act of love, and thus an act of courage. It cannot fear the analysis of reality or, under pain of revealing itself as a farce, avoid creative discussion."[2]

As for students' varying reactions to working with legal concepts and rhetoric, different pedagogical approaches can be useful here, to ensure a positive learning experience. Each instructor will devise her or his own. One technique, as an example, is to refer back to the Constitution and the Bill of Rights, familiar to every student who, in high school, was required to study "U.S. History." A brief enough discussion on how integrated the notion of rights is to students in this country should succeed in clarifying the analogous nature of the International Bill of Human Rights to people around the globe.

Another practical example is U.S. legislation such as the Americans with Disabilities Act (ADA) of 1992. The ADA was necessitated by the fact that earlier statutes promoting and protecting the rights of disabled persons proved only partially useful. Examples that draw from this country's experiences facilitate getting across an essential fact of political life: rights-protecting laws, whether national or international, may not in and of themselves accomplish what they have been set up to accomplish. More activity may be and usually is required—more monitoring, more legislation drafting, more lobbying, more fact finding—if the full rights of whichever group or individual is at issue are to be secured. This is one of the ways in which the course can maintain a constant balance between the negatives of human rights violations and the positives of human rights protections.

In summary, this new body of information on human rights is presented as a foundation for the knowledge students will continue to acquire during their lifetimes, whether as professionals in human rights or interested and involved citizens in various professions and enterprises. Learning about international law on human rights in this teleological way, and correlating law with a multitude of other disciplines, lead to a pragmatic expansion of the scope and depth of knowledge on human rights.

Nongovernmental Organizations as Part of the Curriculum

Another important body of information to enhance students' understanding of the role of international human rights law deals with the role of nongovernmental organizations (NGOs). NGO activities on behalf of the promotion and protection of human rights have arisen from the establishment of international human rights law and its expanding authority. Students learn that the working base of NGOs in the field of civil and political rights—including such familiar ones as Amnesty International, the Human Rights Watch organizations, Physicians for Human Rights, and Article 19, and the hundreds of other NGOs in countries around the globe concerned with economic, social, and cultural rights—is based squarely in that body of law. Governments everywhere, including the United States, acknowledge the usefulness of the authoritative reports compiled by human rights NGOs. Students can readily examine the latest annual *State Department Country Reports*,[3] and related class discussions help produce an understanding of political processes involving international human rights law in this country, including the significance of Congress's mandate to refer to those reports in determining foreign policy on economic and military assistance.

Creating the Interdisciplinary Syllabus

A syllabus for this interdisciplinary college course can be drawn from various disparate sources: first, the literature available on human rights education generally;[4] second, readings in the human rights and associated literature, certainly including *Human Rights Quarterly*, the comparative and international journal of the social sciences, humanities, and law, published by Johns Hopkins University Press. Scanning one's own files figures usefully, including the fourth-class mail everyone receives from a range of organizations seeking contributions. This category of mail offers a general view of the needs and claims to rights in this country and elsewhere in the world, and can spur another range of research.

The available human rights education literature is not overly abundant with respect to university-level teaching of human rights, but it more than provides an intellectually sound basis for syllabus and curriculum development. Amnesty International and Human Rights Internet's publications—*Reporter, Tribune,* and *Human Rights Education: The Fourth R*—are useful in this respect.

Finally, beyond such searches is the simple approach of contacting the professor teaching international human rights at any of a dozen or so institutions and asking to see a copy of her or his current syllabus. The refusal rate on such requests is extremely low—teachers of human rights are usually glad to exchange views with other members of that community.

Education About the United Nations and Regional Systems

For students to understand the foundations of international human rights law, it is essential that they have a working knowledge of the multilateral system centered in the United Nations and the three regional systems—Europe, the Americas, and Africa. During the past few years when those same students finished high school and entered college, the image of the United Nations as presented through the media was hardly a positive reflection of the organizations's scope and authority. Classroom lectures and discussions that draw on books, journals, and current newspaper and weeklies' reportage of the human rights functions of the United Nations are appropriate settings to bring out the dynamic tension between what member states' obligations are and what their practice tends to be. It is in these classroom settings that students' interests in human rights as justice and fairness can be melded with human rights as law.

A Classroom Exercise

To go from the theoretical to the practical: a particularly effective classroom exercise is one in which the actual reports of States Parties to a treaty body—for example, the Committee on the Elimination of All Forms of Discrimination Against Women—are handed out and discussed. To carry out this exercise in a class of thirty to fifty students, the instructor obtains five or six different States Parties reports, routinely distributed by the United Nations to depository libraries and NGOs. The class is divided up into the same number, five or six groups, each of which is handed one report. Each student has on hand—not just at this session but at every class meeting—the small but useful volume published by the Center for the Study of Human Rights. It is useful, inexpensive ($6), easily portable, and contains twenty-five of the main international human rights instruments.[5] Each group is asked to read the report, discuss it among themselves for ten or fifteen minutes, and do an on-the-spot comparative analysis of the requirements of the Women's Convention with the country's report that they are analyzing. They discuss to what extent their identified country complies with the treaty, article by article. In each group, with luck, there comes a moment when students realize that the report they are examining is the real thing, and that people's claims to rights are the ongoing business of UN professionals who meet regularly for that purpose.

Another kind of excitement comes from the fact that students find themselves able to read and compare complex documents with a growing understanding and sophistication. Demystifying and decoding such texts are lifelong intellectual tools. At such moments, basic tenets of international human rights law, promulgated through the United Nations, are crystallized and become part of students' knowledge bank. Through examining countries' reports, the students come to understand clearly just how differently countries behave in fulfilling their human rights obligations. Students perceive how, as a result of international treaties, alterations are made to domestic law. They see for themselves what governments consider appropriate for inclusion in reports that come under the scrutiny of the international community. Further, students become aware of the concept that international law and national law are meant to be complementary rather than competitive.

Each group's report to the class on their assigned country brings home the scope of rights embodied in the treaty under examination: Does that country consider itself in compliance? What commitments is it willing to make in order to create or amend its national laws for more complete compliance? To what extent does it consider that its national law offers more complete protection than does the international? There is, further, the extreme when a country chooses to thumb its nose at the process, when it states quite boldly that it is not now in compliance nor does it intend to take steps to improve. That sort of contradiction stimulates intense interest; further, it can be used to make the point that even those nations that on the face of it seem to disregard their legally contracted obligations on human rights, nonetheless do continue to submit their reports as mandated under treaty requirements.

Student interest may be expected to run high on the issue of cultural relativism in relation to universality, a topic for which a healthy number of classroom hours should be set aside. Thus the exercise in which they do an analytical reading of States Parties' treaty reporting (the same exercise applies to the two International Covenants, the Convention Against Torture, the Convention on the Elimination of All Forms of Racial Discrimination, and the Convention on the Rights of the Child) is likely to touch off still further in-depth classroom discussions and term papers.

To reiterate an earlier point: the great boon, to teacher and student alike, in offering a course that is cross-disciplinary, is in having at stage center the wide spectrum of knowledge, ideas, and perspectives of students from any and all disciplines. In this setting, students are encouraged to pull together knowledge and ideas they have from their major fields of study, and then to go on to find that under this new heading, "Human Rights," a new and different set of meanings may be generated. Majors in anthropology, development studies, ethnic studies, literature, women's studies, and more, find here a safe testing ground for forays into human rights from those perspectives. For the human rights course, they must seek out different literature and reconceptualize understandings of the meaning of historical and current international relations, including of U.S. foreign policy relative to human rights.

Does the United Nations Support Human Rights Education?

During the Vienna World Conference on Human Rights in 1993, Secretary-General Boutros Boutros-Ghali declared the importance of human rights education, and of integrating human rights education into a wide range of UN bodies.[6] NGOs had voiced the concern that not only might the ordinary citizen be uneducated about human rights and therefore be unlikely to claim or to support claims for rights, but that government officials responsible for the incorporation of human rights into political and economic policy might be short on basic information about human rights. As a result, the Vienna Conference issued a number of specific directives to advance human rights education. Among them were: a resolution by the General Assembly on behalf of the United Nations Decade for Human Rights Education[7] and the interlinking of human rights education within the United Nations, including with UNESCO, the Committee on Economic, Social and Cultural Rights, the Centre for Human Rights, and the Secretariat.[8]

The Vienna Conference called for the United Nations to look inward as well as outward; its Declaration and Programme of Action called for strengthening the United Nations' World Public Information Campaign on Human Rights that offers advisory services and technical assistance programs to states. Further, the Centre for Human Rights in Geneva was called upon to undertake coordination of those initiatives. The

Centre requested, by a letter from the assistant Secretary-General to all NGOs,[9] that NGOs submit proposals for human rights education that would enhance the draft plan of action for the UN Decade for Human Rights Education, in force from 1995 to 2005.

Further evidence of the Centre's new work in educating about human rights are the recent publications in an innovative series entitled "Professional Training Series." The series sets forth principles, theories, and practical means of integrating human rights into identified professions and the training they offer. Number 1 in the series is *Human Rights and Social Work: A Manual for Schools of Social Work and the Social Work Profession'*[10] number 2 is *Human Rights and Elections: A Handbook on the Legal, Technical and Human Rights Aspects of Elections*;[11] number 3 is *Human Rights and Pre-Trial Detention: A Handbook on International Standards Relating to Pre-Trial Detention.*[12]

The series builds on an earlier seminar, "The Teaching of Human Rights," a UN International Seminar held in Geneva in 1988, which aimed at stimulating a comprehensive approach to human rights education. The seminar considered the target groups for human rights education to be law enforcement personnel, lawyers, judges, police academies, and people in their religious, labor, and civic organizations.

In fact, little attention was focused on university education on human rights. Nor was there mention—either in 1988 or in the current professional training series—of plans for studies linking development, economics, and business management with human rights. Attention to professionals in those fields is more than warranted in an age increasingly sensitive to linkages between civil or political rights and economic rights.

At UNESCO, the director-general communicated UNESCO's support not only for the Commission's resolution on Education and Human Rights but also for the UN Decade for Human Rights Education, adding its own action plan for increasing the availability and range of materials.

Representatives of international human rights treaty bodies, of the regional systems, and of the International Labour Office held their own meeting during the Vienna Conference. They focused on the necessity of educating citizens about their rights, and asked governments to ensure human rights training for state and other relevant officials including particularly those "involved in development cooperation, peace-keeping and election monitoring." Similarly, the Committee on Economic, Social and Cultural Rights was asked to cooperate on planning for increased human rights education in general, and on promoting knowledge of the International Covenant on Economic, Social and Cultural Rights in particular.

Teaching Program for University Teachers

At the International Institute of Human Rights in Strasbourg, the summer session each July includes a program for university professors of international human rights law. During the month-long session of the International Centre for the Teaching of

Human Rights in the University, several dozen professors from all continents meet together in lectures, workshops, and informal discussion groups to discuss pedagogical methodology as applied to human rights. The formal daily lectures, and the more informal workshops, are held in French, Spanish, English, and Arabic. This language flexibility makes possible more widespread participation, heightened subtlety of discourse, and a wider range of topics available for discussion. An anecdotal aside: a group of scholars from North Africa met to discuss the issue of compatibility of the Koran with the Universal Declaration of Human Rights. Agreement on the point was not reached, but the process was worth noting: support for the notion of compatibility came from the older male scholars and the (mostly younger) female scholars, while opposition to compatibility and universality was voiced by the younger male scholars.

A major concern among professors from the African and Asian continents is the availability of literature and documents for their students' research and hands-on work. The advent of computer-based on-line documentation may improve this situation, but unless greater funds are allocated for human rights at the United Nations, for example, neither the print nor computer-generated materials tend to be readily available; the poorer countries at greater distance from human rights centers in North America and Europe therefore have greater difficulty in offering students those educational resources.

Conclusions

Human rights education in the university has made important strides toward the desired goal of institutionalization. Faculty inside the academy (who also wear activist hats in the world outside) are creating new interdisciplinary curricula. University instructors in mainstream departments who are ready to teach human rights have their choice of excellent syllabi. As the teaching of human rights is integrated into mainstream university core departments, it acquires the advantages that attach: routine listing of courses in the general catalogue, funding for regular full-time faculty, graduate students working on masters and doctoral theses, and so on. The freer movement of students among the humanities, history, law, rhetoric, the social and political sciences, and the physical sciences will bring a new group of players onto the expanding human rights education playing field.

The global stamp of approval is in place, with the United Nations' declaration of support for human rights education for the coming decade. NGOs (including educators doing hands-on education and research in the field) bring back newly developed model curricula. Faculty welcome colleagues to their home institutions for guest lectures—the UN World Conference on Women certainly furnished just such opportunities for human rights specialists coming vast distances to Beijing in 1995. The basic groundwork has been laid; the openings are there; the field is ready for expansion.

Notes

1. Paulo Freire, *Education for Critical Consciousness* (New York: Continuum, 1969), 88.

2. Ibid., 38.

3. U.S. Department of State, *Country Reports on Human Rights Practices for 1994* (Washington, D.C.: U.S. Government Printing Office, 1995).

4. See, for example, Theodor Meron, *Human Rights in International Law: Legal and Policy Issues* (Oxford: Clarendon Press, 1992).

5. Center for the Study of Human Rights, *Twenty-Four Human Rights Documents* (New York: Columbia University, 1992).

6. Commission on Human Rights; E/CN.4/1994/39, January 4, 1994.

7. Subsequently approved on December 20, 1993. Resolution 48/127.

8. E/CN.4/1994/39, January 4, 1994, Report of the Secretary-General on Action Taken in Relation to the Declaration of a Decade for Human Rights Education.

9. Circulated on July 12, 1994. Ref. No. G/SO 216 GEN.

10. New York: United Nations, 1994. GE.94–15160.

11. New York: United Nations, 1994. HR/P/PT/2.

12. Published jointly by the Centre for Human Rights and the Crime Prevention and Criminal Justice Branch (New York and Geneva, 1994).

Chapter 13
Curriculum Development for an Interdisciplinary Minor

Rhoda E. Howard

McMaster University has about twelve thousand undergraduate students and fifteen hundred graduate students. It is situated in Hamilton, Ontario, Canada, an industrial city of 317,000 people with large immigrant populations. About two-thirds of McMaster's students come from Hamilton and the surrounding area, with one-third from other parts of Ontario and elsewhere. Just under a quarter of its undergraduate students live on campus in residences.

In 1990 the university devised a new Strategic Plan. Two outcomes of this process were the decision to stress interdisciplinary teaching and the decision to stress globalization. The university then called for the establishment of interdisciplinary theme schools to fulfill these dual mandates. Theme schools must be funded by outside donations, some of which are targeted to the schools themselves. The schools last for five years, with student intakes only for the first three, the last group graduating at the end of the five-year cycle. There is some possibility that the schools might be renewed, or that their subject matter might be integrated into the regular curriculum in some fashion at the end of the five years.

The Human Rights School

In May 1991, I joined with Dr. Gary Warner, the director of McMaster International, and eight other faculty members to submit a proposal for a Theme School on International Justice and Human Rights. The proposal was approved in 1992, and the school began in September 1993. As of this writing (July 1995), the school has functioned for two academic years. The Human Rights School is incorporated into the McMaster program as a twenty-four-credit minor, to complement students' major or honors programs. We know of no other undergraduate interdisciplinary program in human rights in Canada: indeed, we know of no other anywhere in the world.[1] While undergraduate law programs frequently incorporate a great deal of material on human rights, the study of human rights requires investigation in many disciplines other than law.

One of the proposers' aims in implementing this school was to attract idealistic young people and help them to channel their idealism rather than discard it. Young people are often told by their elders that their ideals are a function of their immaturity, and that they will fade as adult responsibilities take hold. Yet the international human rights movement is now enormous and involves millions of idealistic citizens all over the world. It seems more appropriate to encourage idealism than to impose cynicism on our students. The faculty members in the Human Rights School want to encourage students to be citizens of the world, whose boundaries of interest and commitment extend far beyond their own hometown or even their own country.

Program Content

The theme school addresses the entire range of human rights listed in the major UN documents, including civil and political rights; economic, social, and cultural rights; and collective "third generation" rights. It especially focuses on international debates about the relationships between development, technological modernization, democracy, and human rights. The school is entitled "International *Justice* and Human Rights" because of the debate about whether the concept of human rights is culturally specific and inapplicable to nonwestern societies. We include "international justice" as a more widely applicable and (to some) more acceptable term than human rights. The concept of international justice also focuses attention on debates about humanitarian intervention, North-South relations, and the human rights obligations of multinational corporations. All of these topics are addressed in the school.

We took as our general starting point the premise that it is both desirable and possible to achieve for all people in the world a society that provides both for their basic material needs and for their personal security against political terror or dictatorship. Part of our focus, then, is the new stress on democratization and the creation of civil society in countries that until recently labored under dictatorial rule. Another focus is the cultural dimension of such democratization and the necessity for western human rights "missionaries" to be sensitive to cultural styles and preferences. Many critics of the concept of human rights argue that it is overly individualistic and reflective of competitive capitalist social ethics. For some communitarian critics of a perceived western bias in human rights discourse, the collective right to national self-determination is the key human right, a prerequisite for all societies still subject to neocolonial or "northern" control.

Yet national self-determination, while in principle a human right, can deteriorate in practice into pressures to close a society off. States frequently impose strong controls on public debate and political participation, and uphold discriminatory social relations among castes, ethnic groups, races, or genders. The role of individual human rights, in such situations, is to defend citizens against abusive state or social practices. Thus our program scrutinizes and critiques human rights practices internal to all societies and states, wherever they may occur and whatever may be their culture, level of development, or colonial history.

We also focus on the question of development and how it intersects with human rights. While in principle there is a right to development that includes all other human rights, in practice development often means economic growth under authoritarian rule. Sustainable development is a key preoccupation of the teachers in this program, who include scientists, an economist, and development-aid practitioners. Yet viable scientific programs for sustainable development are frequently undermined for reasons of power or profit.

The theme school focuses on both international and Canadian human rights issues. We believe that it is important for students to be critical of their own society; otherwise, they may become unintentional cultural imperialists, trumpeting their own society's virtues without considering its failings. As it happens, most of our students are already well aware of Canada's pressing human rights issues, especially the debates about native self-government and about multiculturalism. They are less aware of Canada's human rights history, or of problems of economic rights such as the right to food. Yet a historical context is crucial not only to understand one's own society, but also to make informed comparative judgments about human rights progress elsewhere.

These intellectual challenges make it essential that a program on human rights deal with practice as well as (legal) principle, and that students have an interdisciplinary framework for their analysis. McMaster's program is truly interdisciplinary. Students are recruited from all of McMaster's faculties, and included for the 1993 cohort one student from engineering, one from nursing, six from business, eight from science, twelve from humanities, twenty-one from social science, and five from "Arts and Science," a special interdisciplinary undergraduate program with very high admission standards. Unfortunately there were no nursing or engineering students in the 1994 cohort, owing to scheduling demands. Faculty members are also widely recruited. Over its five-year life cycle, the program will incorporate one teacher from the engineering faculty, three from sciences, two from health sciences, six from social sciences, two from business, and four from humanities. McMaster University does not have a law faculty, and as the Human Rights School must be staffed from internal faculty resources, there are no plans to recruit a law professor.

The interdisciplinary nature of the program has made it extremely difficult to schedule classes. McMaster University's schedules are developed on the basis of program requirements. For the most part, different programs can be scheduled independently of each other because there is no overlap of classes for the student. Bringing together students from many different programs in the theme school has been exceptionally difficult. As of 1994 the theme school became an evening program, with about half its courses scheduled for Thursday evenings. Other university programs are required not to schedule core courses for this time slot, to enable students to register in theme schools.

Many of the students in the program already have a strong background in volunteer activities connected to human rights. Some, despite their youth, have already been involved in politics. There are also a few mature students in the program, including one who worked as a missionary for twelve years in Central America. Although quite a few of the students aspire to become international lawyers, the vast majority wish to incorporate their human rights training into other professions or in careers in the public or private sector.

Students must apply to enter the Human Rights School from within McMaster University, in February of their freshman year. To enter, they must be in an honors program or another four- or five-year program (e.g., in engineering) with a minimum grade average of C+. Once accepted, students must complete a sequence of twenty-four credits in order to qualify for their minor. This includes a six-credit (September to April, or two academic terms in the Canadian system) compulsory core course and the choice of one of three three-credit courses in their sophomore year, and five of nine three-credit courses in their junior and senior years. The courses in the school are closed to students not accepted into the program.

In recruiting the first cohort of students for 1993, we asked for transcripts of grades, statements of interest, and résumés from each applicant, and we weighted the three items equally. In the event, it transpired that a number of students with very impressive statements and résumés did not earn the minimum grade requirement. For 1994, therefore, we reverted to a more customary admission procedure, weighting résumés and statements of interest as far less crucial indicators of eligibility. About sixty students were admitted for each of the 1993, 1994, and 1995 cohorts.

Courses

The aim of the human rights program is to provide breadth of coverage and to cover human rights issues from a variety of disciplinary perspectives. As noted above, all incoming students must take one compulsory core course. In 1993–94 this course was divided into three sections of about twenty students each. I taught one section, while Dr. Patricia Daenzer of McMaster's School of Social Work and Dr. Sam Ajzenstat from our philosophy department taught the other two. We covered the international human rights documents, current philosophical debates on human rights, some key international debates (e.g., whether human rights are culturally relative) and some key Canadian issues. In 1993–94 we used four texts.[2] Because of budget constraints, the core course was offered as one course for all sixty students in 1994–95, taught by me and Dr. Ajzenstat. In 1994–95 we used only two textbooks, supplemented by other readings.[3] In 1995–96 the core course will again be taught as one large group.

Once they have taken the core course, the students may choose among a variety of other courses. In the second term of their sophomore year, three courses are offered. In January 1994 we offered a course on the right to food, taught by Dr. George Sorger, a biologist with a strong activist background in Central America; a course on the disintegration of Yugoslavia, taught by Dr. Stefania Szlek Miller, a political scientist; and a course on the right to development, taught by Dr. Gary Warner, a professor of French who has extensive NGO experience administering development projects in Africa. In 1995 Dr. Warner was on leave and was replaced by Dr. Mary Tremblay, a physiotherapist who taught a course on the rights of the disabled, an area in which she has much experience both as an activist and as a professional.

In their junior year, students can choose three of five three-credit courses. In 1995–96 the topics offered included civil society, taught by a philosopher, Dr. Gary Madison; ecosystem health and human rights, taught by Dr. Douglas Bryant, a biochemist; international children's rights, taught by Dr. Daenzer; indigenous peoples' rights, taught by Dr. Wayne Warry, an anthropologist; and international economic cooperation and human rights, taught by Dr. Ken Chan, an economist. Courses vary from year to year according to faculty availability.

In their senior year, students choose two of four three-credit courses. In 1995–96 I offered a course on international women's rights, while Dr. Miller offered a course on comparative genocide. Dr. Alex Berezin, a professor of engineering physics, offered a course on human rights in technological society, and Dr. Howard Jones, a classicist, offered a course on the "Faces of Intolerance" that will examine the development of civil and political rights through inquiry into some of the great political trials in history (e.g., the trial of Socrates). The senior students also have the option of taking a three-credit independent research course or a six-credit thesis course, if they are not writing a thesis for any other program.

The decision to include a course on comparative genocide is perhaps unusual. Although estimates indicate that far more people have died in the twentieth century as a result of genocide than of war, the subject of comparative genocide is very rarely taught.[4] There are many courses on the Jewish Holocaust in North American universities, but most of them do not generalize to other genocides, whether of the Armenians, the Cambodians, or Burundians. McMaster's theme school faculty members believe it essential that programs on human rights not neglect this important topic, which, with recent tragic events in Bosnia, in several parts of the former Soviet Union, and especially Rwanda, is now very much on the world human rights agenda.

The decision to include a course on women's rights also reflects current international preoccupations. For many years, at least in the opinion of some feminist scholars, women's rights were marginalized from the central human rights discussions.[5] One reason for this marginalization was that violations of women's rights frequently occur in familial or social situations, whereas human rights are classically viewed as protections of the citizen against the state. But with the inclusion of violence against women as a key aspect of the Final Document of the 1993 Vienna World Conference on Human Rights, this distinction has broken down. In addition, activists have long been aware that without recognition of women's roles and their involvement in both production and decision making, development projects can be doomed to fail.

As the variety of courses indicates, professors in the human rights program at McMaster do not necessarily teach within their own disciplinary boundaries: the theme school encourages professors as well as students to step outside the confines of their normal academic experiences. This, however, does raise the problem of professors' and students' having radically different backgrounds. By their senior year, for example, students taking honors degrees in philosophy or political science may well know more about the human rights debates in these fields than do some of their professors. Similarly among the faculty, as became evident in in-house workshops, there are widely varying levels of knowledge. Some have published extensively and explicitly in the field of human rights, while others enter the school more or less as citizens; that is, as experts in their particular academic fields who worry about the human rights implications of what they do.

Such a variety of backgrounds can nevertheless be exciting and result in much intellectual cross-fertilization. I have already found myself obliged to rethink some of my intellectual positions as a result of contact with faculty members outside the humanities and social sciences. As a result of Dr. Mary Tremblay's entrance into the program, I will need to put myself soon through a crash course on the rights of the disabled. In my classroom, the participation of a student from biopsychology proved useful in some debates, for example, over whether there are any physiological differences between men and women. In a collaborative interdisciplinary program such as the Human Rights School, disparities in knowledge should be taken as opportunities to teach, and learn from, each other.

Teaching Methodology

McMaster's policy for all its theme schools is to emphasize self-directed or problem-based learning. This approach means that the teachers in the theme school eschew formal lectures and examinations. Instead, there is a great deal of emphasis on student participation in the classroom, on group work, and on student-initiated projects. In the core course, for example, students hold debates, present assigned reading material to each other, and lead their own discussions. In most other theme school classes, students also present their research findings to each other. In most courses, 30 to 40 percent of the total grade is for class participation. The students appreciate the training in public speaking and group leadership that this experience gives them.

All professors in the theme school have devised interesting ways of promoting self-directed, group, and independent learning, both inside the classroom and out. In Dr. Miller's course on the breakdown of Yugoslavia, students enacted a number of simulations, starting with the 1989 negotiations to help resolve the internal constitutional conflicts in the then Yugoslavia, and ending with a war crimes trial. Each student took the position of a particular actor (e.g., Albania, Bosnian Serbs) and relied her or his arguments on primary documents such as UN records and the Transdex translations of European newspapers. In Dr. Warner's class on human rights and development, students explored a number of scenarios around the general question of appropriate development strategies in the underdeveloped world, especially in Africa: for example, they examined the role of NGOs, the World Bank, and of Canada's International Development Agency. In Dr. Sorger's class on the right to food, students drew up nutrition budgets on minimal (student) incomes in order to test whether their diet could be both affordable and nutritious. In Dr. Roy Adams' course on trade union rights in winter 1995, students enacted scenarios of worker demands and employer responses.

In her course on the rights of the disabled, Dr. Mary Tremblay encouraged students to contact various voluntary organizations as a means of analyzing different strategies for attaining and improving access to human rights. Professor Basanti Majumdar from the nursing faculty taught a course on health and human rights in 1994–95; as a means of examining cross-cultural problems in interpreting health, her students interviewed Canadians who have lived abroad and non-Canadians coming to McMaster to practice or study. Dr. Howard Jones, the classicist who entered the program in 1995, had students give dramatic readings, for example, from Socrates' speech at his own trial, and from the transcript of the trial of Oscar Wilde.

Thus, in general, the teaching methodology stresses hands-on learning, student inquiry, and a great deal of flexibility in the topics the students research. This methodology allows students at this early stage in their lives to gain experience in areas in which they might expect to be professionals or volunteers later on. The disadvantage is that some students tend to focus only on what are well-known issues in Canada. Among my own group of students in 1993–94 there was a great deal of interest, for example, in gay rights, children's rights, and victims' rights. There was less interest in international questions, and very little interest in civil and political rights, which are more or less thought to be nonproblematic in Canada, even though they were attained fairly recently.[6]

After two years of experience, the faculty members of the Human Rights School have also realized that the methodology of self-directed learning is somewhat problematic because it leaves very little room for the teacher to impart her or his knowledge or thoughts to the class. The self-directed learning approach expects professors to act as "facilitators" or "resources" rather than as scholars who make original contributions to knowledge and who have particular points of view that they can impart. Students are very enthusiastic about the self-directed learning style, which allows them considerable freedom in the classroom. It is easy, however, for classroom discussions to degenerate into current issues discussions in which students offer opinions from their own personal experience, not necessarily grounded in serious thought or research. Without examinations of some kind (I favor take-home or open-book essay exams for courses such as this), there is no way to compel students to read their assigned material. The collective pool of knowledge of Canadian 19- and 20-year-olds, even when very enthusiastic about human rights, is quite shallow. The students might be better served by discussions led by professors, into which professors could more easily inject new ideas or theoretical questions, than by student-led discussions that professors merely "referee" as it were.

Problems

Since the program began, there have been many queries from students about the possibility of human rights internships. I managed to arrange one internship at a European human rights institute for a student whose study in Europe was financed by a program that already existed in his faculty. Other inquiries yielded only one or two possibilities for unpaid summer internships in Canada. Given financial constraints, it will not be possible to provide funds for student human rights internships.

In recruiting faculty and in other aspects of the program, I have encountered the problem of the politics of representation, more popularly known as "political correctness." As on many campuses in the United States, there are some people at McMaster University who believe that scholars should not teach about groups if they are not members of those groups themselves: thus, for example, men should not teach in a women's studies program. In January 1994, when the eminent Muslim legal scholar Abdullahi Ahmed An-Na'im visited the Human Rights School, quite a few Muslim students criticized me for inviting Dr. An-Na'im to speak "for" all Muslims. Indeed, they suggested that as a non-Muslim, I had no right whatsoever to invite a speaker on Islam to campus. For people holding such views, a program on human rights that does not concede that only its members may speak about a particular group is in itself a violator of human rights. Here freedom of speech and academic freedom give way to particular interpretations of group rights.

My views on this vexatious question are mixed. I believe that these debates on the politics of representation reflect a conceptual confusion: critics think that if a professor teaches *about* a particular group of people, he or she is speaking *for* that group of people. I do not accept the proposition that one is not permitted to teach about groups of people to whom one does not belong: thus, for example, I would regard as discriminatory an attempt to bar a man from teaching a women's studies course. I also think that there is a very good argument that outsiders can be more detached than insiders. The purpose of university education is above all inquiry, the asking of difficult and often "heretical" questions. Insiders are often too wedded to the dominant ideological perspective of their group to have the detachment they need. Teachers in universities are not supposed to speak for groups, whether they are members or not; they are supposed to teach about, and ask questions about, those groups.

Nevertheless, I have some sympathy with groups suffering discrimination who are tired of being taught about by members of the groups that discriminate against them. In a program on human rights, it is also preferable to have faculty members who do reflect the overall population diversity on campus. The Human Rights School has been able to achieve racial, religious, and gender diversity among its faculty members, though the faculty members do not necessarily teach about their own (minority) groups. In the case of indigenous peoples, given that Canada's treatment of them is probably this nation's greatest shame, it is certainly preferable to have an indigenous person as a professor. Indigenous Canadians can legitimately demand the right to teach as well as to be taught to and about. Unfortunately, because of commitments elsewhere, the program lost the services of Dr. Dawn Hill, an anthropologist and a Mohawk from Six Nations at Grand River Territory, who taught the course on indigenous rights in 1994–95.

The biggest problem facing McMaster's Human Rights School is funding. Even though the theme schools are officially a key part of McMaster University's Strategic Plan, the university expects them to be funded by external donations. The Human Rights School requires about $U.S.700,000 for its six years of operation (one year planning plus five years of teaching). So far this has been difficult to raise, and the budget has had to be cut. One problem here may be that McMaster University is, in effect, ahead of the game. McMaster decided to have a human rights school before UNESCO, the General Assembly of the United Nations, and the 1993 Vienna Conference declared human rights education to be an urgent priority. Yet presumably it will take some time before the large U.S. foundations (and the somewhat smaller Canadian ones) decide to incorporate human rights education in their priorities. With good reason, many government and private donors may prefer to focus their resources on human rights activists in the field rather than students in North America. Another problem is that McMaster is, in effect, asking donors to finance a program that is scheduled to end almost as soon as the donations are made: this is not a very attractive proposition.

The final problem is what is likely to happen to all of the expertise and enthusiasm the Theme School on International Justice and Human Rights has generated. In April 1995 the school was favorably reviewed by two faculty members from McMaster and one external reviewer. The university was expected to decide in September 1995 whether to continue the school for three more years, that is, to permit three more cohorts of students to enter it. Whether or not the school is renewed for three years, it would be a shame if no provision is made for international justice and human rights to be integrated into the general curriculum on a permanent basis.

At the moment there is considerable concern at McMaster University that the theme schools (there is one other school at present) are using funds that might be better used elsewhere on campus. The Human Rights School's faculty-student ratio is quite low and is perceived as a drain on other programs that might have average class sizes of well over one hundred. Although the school is supposed to be funded from outside sources, very little money has been raised specifically for the human rights program so far. Even if the program can pay other departments for faculty members, as is so far the practice, we are drawing senior faculty members whose replacements— often part-time teachers—may not be as knowledgeable as they.

These problems are to a large extent the result of decisions to make the Human

Rights School a special one, with competitive admissions to the program. There is no reason that a human rights program elsewhere would have to follow such a procedure. McMaster University's priority is the generic idea of theme schools rather than a particular desire to set up a human rights program. In other universities, there might be a desire to set up a human rights program, and make courses available to the entire student body, rather than only to the students admitted to a small and expensive program.

An ongoing human rights program would also solve the problem of library redundancy. Our students' independent research is facilitated by the extensive collection of human rights books, journals, and documents acquired for the theme school in the last three years. Under McMaster's plan to end theme schools after their five-year cycle, these books and documents on human rights may well be rendered superfluous by 1998.

Colleagues interested in setting up a human rights program elsewhere might wonder if making it available to students from all faculties on the campus is a good idea. The advantage of this approach is that it permits interaction among students with a wide variety of backgrounds and knowledge. So far our experience with incoming students is that they do not need to have an academic background in human rights: it is enough that they are active, informed citizens willing to work hard. I found to my surprise, for example, that my students were well able to debate the various positions found in their textbook of readings in philosophy, with very little guidance from me. Any student from any part of the campus could be involved in a human rights program, once she or he had taken the core course. For example, if McMaster's human rights program were extended and made available to the campus as a whole as part of the university's regular offerings, students in McMaster's women's studies program or indigenous studies program might choose to take the theme school courses on women's or indigenous rights.

Conclusion

As the director of McMaster's Theme School on International Justice and Human Rights, I often become so caught up in administrative details that I wonder if my effort is worth the result. Every class I conduct convinces me that it is. The students I have the privilege to teach are a wonderful group of fine, committed, serious young people. Despite the misgivings I have reported above, the small group, independent learning format works very well for the program as a whole. Fine-tuning, rather than wholesale abandonment of our methodology, appears to be the appropriate corrective to teaching problems. The time the theme school faculty is able to devote to students' projects and research papers has paid off in notable improvements in their grades.

The students' enthusiasm for the program is remarkable. They report to me that whereas they had previously discussed sex and sports when relaxing over drinks in the evening, they now discuss human rights issues. Other students not in the program overhear these conversations and then are disappointed when they learn that, unfortunately, classes are closed to those not registered in the theme school.

The faculty members involved in the Human Rights School also benefit from it. One of McMaster's objectives in setting up theme schools was to encourage interdisciplinary research. While the faculty members who originally proposed the Human Rights School were not a preexistent research group (and a few of the original proposers have had to drop out of the school), the opportunity for faculty members from all parts of the campus to get to know each other through research and teaching workshops is proving exciting. As philosophers and professors of business who had previously never met get to know each other, the result will undoubtedly be cross-fertilization of ideas and perhaps collaborative research.

Finally, the university community as a whole benefits from the presence of the Human Rights School. Through its program of guest speakers the school has introduced new topics of discussion to the wider university public. Aside from Dr. Abdullahi An-Na'im's controversial lectures, in 1993–94 guests included the late Dr. John Humphrey, the Canadian who helped draft the Universal Declaration of Human Rights at the United Nations in the 1940s; the Honorable Ed Broadbent, president of Canada's International Centre for Human Rights and Democratic Development; and Francis Seow, former attorney-general of Singapore. In 1994–95 guests included Dr. Alan Borovoy, general counsel to the Canadian Civil Liberties Association, and Dr. Jack Donnelly, the noted scholar of international human rights. These events have been reported widely in the student and local press. Such speakers might appear frequently at law schools, but they are less generally found at universities without law programs, nor do undergraduates in their sophomore year generally have the opportunity to meet them.

A human rights program thus serves to introduce to some campuses debate on important national and international issues, in a manner that cuts across disciplines, faculties, and narrow academic specialties. Add to that the enthusiasm and excitement of the students, and it is definitely worth the effort to organize and administer such a program.

Notes

1. On Canada, see Heather Gibbs and Magda Seydegart, "Education and Human Rights in Canada," *ACS [Association for Canadian Studies] Newsletter* 15, no. 4 (Winter 1993–94): 1, 12–35.

2. John Arthur and William H. Shaw, eds., *Social and Political Philosophy* (Englewood Cliffs, N.J.: Prentice-Hall, 1992); Center for the Study of Human Rights, *Twenty-Four Human Rights Documents* (New York: Columbia University, 1992); Richard Pierre Claude and Burns H. Weston, eds., *Human Rights in the World Community: Issues and Action*, 2d ed. (Philadelphia: University of Pennsylvania Press, 1992); and Jean Leonard Elliott and Augie Fleras, *Unequal Relations: An Introduction to Race and Ethnic Dynamics in Canada* (Scarborough, Ontario: Prentice-Hall, 1992).

3. The 1994–95 texts were *Twenty-Four Human Rights Documents,* and Jack Donnelly, *Universal Human Rights in Theory and Practice* (Ithaca, N.Y.: Cornell University Press, 1989).

4. Helen Fein, *Genocide: A Sociological Perspective* (Newbury Park, Calif.: Sage, 1993).

5. Charlotte Bunch, "Women's Rights as Human Rights: Toward a Re-Vision of Human Rights," *Human Rights Quarterly* 12, no. 4 (1990): 486–98.

6. Thomas R. Berger, *Fragile Freedoms: Human Rights and Dissent in Canada,* rev. ed. (Vancouver: Clark, Irwin, 1982).

Chapter 14
Human Rights Awareness and Skill Games in Political Science

Bernard Hamilton

As a teacher of human rights, I want my students to learn about the major concepts and documents in the field, the main processes by which human rights are sustained, including the principal mechanisms available under international law and the skills that achieve success in the practice of human rights. At the same time, I encourage them to develop their academic skills: to analyze, to evaluate, and to argue clearly and concisely. I find that after a few sessions covering the development of human rights, students learn best by being asked to reflect on real-life human rights situations. I encourage them to discuss what they have absorbed from the media, from their observations of human rights agencies at the start of the course, and from a series of games that we play in the classroom. In this chapter I describe some successful classroom games which are consistent with efforts by social scientists to use simulation activities for social justice education.[1]

The Use of Games in Teaching Human Rights

The classroom provides a place where students obtain what few books, films, or internships can offer.[2] Awareness games allow students to develop their sensitivity to human rights and to recognize their importance. Skill games provide students with an opportunity to experience responsibility and test their developing skills. Since the students are operating within the sanctuary of the classroom, they can make mistakes safe in the knowledge that errors will not affect the outcome of an application for political asylum or of an interethnic conflict. In this way, students can be given real and current human rights problems with which to grapple. Because of the students' need to focus on just a few aspects of human rights at one time, scenarios such as those in this chapter should simplify problems. Scenarios can become increasingly complex as the course develops, and they are in that order in this chapter. This is important because students do not want to feel that the situations have been grossly simplified to the point where they are of little relevance. To maintain a sense of timeliness, it is also helpful to construct fresh simulations each year. Always allow a third of the classroom time for postgame discussion since it is in the exploration that most of the learning is achieved. I first describe two awareness games I have created and then discuss three skill games.[3]

Awareness Games

First They Came for the Cyclists

Background:

One of the simplest ways to get students thinking about human rights is to offer them the game called *First They Came for the Cyclists*. The title reflects a joke concerning the early days of Germany's Nazi regime, when two neighbors were discussing the shortage of eggs in the market. The first neighbor said, "I blame the Jews," to which his companion replied, "I blame the cyclists!" "Why the cyclists?" asked the first neighbor. "Why the Jews?" replied the second neighbor. Students are reminded that, to use the words of Pastor Martin Niemoeller's poem, it is as foolish to blame the Jews or the communists or the trade unionists for perceived problems as it is to blame cyclists.

The Game:

Using the 1991 Minority Rights Group Education Pack,[4] I point out how human rights activists, from countries as distant as Nigeria and the United States, have been inspired by Pastor Martin Niemoeller's words to write about situations with which they are familiar. I then invite students to produce their own poems. If they need a useful way to approach the task, I encourage them to think about third generation rights with which they are already familiar, such as the right to air, water, or trees.

Rationale:

This exercise is particularly valuable because it enables students to think about the consequences of destructiveness. They become aware that one act of destructiveness can lead to another with irreversible consequences. Here is an example:

First they came for the trees
but I didn't care
because I wasn't a nature lover.

Then they came for the fish
and I wasn't bothered
because I preferred meat.

Then they came for the water
and I did nothing
because I preferred soda.

Then it got very dark and very cold.
There was no more gas or electricity
and no wood for a coffin
because first they came for the trees.

In the dialogue, it is important to let students discuss the acts of human intervention that have attempted to halt destructiveness. If students seem to be fixated on the negative aspects of human behavior, it is usually possible to modify an awareness game to include positive aspects. For instance:

First they came for the woman
because they thought she had stolen a pear.

But we called the police
who said that way just wasn't fair.

Then we all went to court
where the judge set her free as the air.

A simple method is to ask students to say what they think will happen in a situation, then what they would like to see happen and how that might be brought about. Often this leads to very fruitful discussions of human rights law, humanitarian law, human rights education, or the roles of citizens' groups.

Lexie

Background:

Another useful game to help students develop their awareness is *Lexie*, which is an acronym for the medieval canon "Lex Iniustia Non Lex Est": an unjust law is not law. This exercise shows students much about the relationship between prejudice, politics, and law. First, it acquaints students with the way in which prejudices can become institutionalized when they are allowed to influence legislation. Second, it illustrates how easily the accumulation of prejudicial laws can lead to genocide. Using this exercise, students gain an understanding of one of the ways in which the political give-and-take of democracy can lead to unjust laws obtaining legislative approval. They also learn why there is a clear need for internationally recognized human rights standards to exist in order to counter such tendencies.

The Game:

Students are told that there is no political party with a clear majority in this game. However, their party could gain political control if they were to form a coalition with a much smaller extremist party. These extremists want some rules passed to contain the activities of a particular group within the society. The extremist party is also negotiating with a rival party and would probably align itself to whichever party agreed to pass the largest number of rules against the group.

Students are then given a modern English version of some of the anti-Jewish laws passed by the Nazis between 1933 and 1945, for example: "They may not use public libraries"; "They may only buy food between four and five in the afternoon"; "They may not be employed as judges"; "They may not purchase eggs."

Rationale:

It is highly challenging for students to experience the role of political decision maker and to confront the temptation to make rules that constrain human rights in order to obtain political power. Students often tend to go along with considering the merits of the proposed laws until they gradually yield to arguments that none deserves their support. The value of the game lies in the debate around these arguments.

Skill Games

Students can often grasp a sense of how human rights standards are enforced by tribunals or similar quasi-judicial bodies. To help them comprehend the complexity of adjudicating responsibility, I use a game that seeks to assign degrees of guilt to four citizens of Nazi Germany who were involved at differing levels of complicity in the persecution of minorities.[5] Students are often less aware of the role of conflict resolution, either in the prevention of human rights abuse[6] or within the "friendly settlement" process. "Friendly settlement" is the term used for the attempt to reconcile the plaintiff and defendant without recourse to a judicial or quasi-judicial hearing. It might involve an undertaking by a governmental organization that the conduct complained of will not be repeated. There might be an offer of compensation or other conciliatory gesture. Friendly settlements are employed in both global and regional human rights procedures. Since most human rights complaints are dealt with through such procedures, it is important that students gain some experience of the process.

I spend a session or two teaching the conflict partnership process, outlined in *The Eight Essential Steps to Conflict Resolution* by Dudley Weeks.[7] I then give students some human rights scenarios in which they can apply these techniques. Even though they may not resolve all of the issues because of time constraints, students do negotiate an acceptable solution to a human rights problem. They learn how skilled negotiators can bring about conflict resolution, and how it is often possible to achieve a settlement that leaves all parties feeling they have gained something. Frequently the judicial approach fails to do this. In addition, students learn that human rights problems need not be insoluble and depressing. Such conflict negotiations can provide areas for new understanding and development based on shared perceptions and interests. I give below three games that enhance students' knowledge and skills of evaluation and conflict resolution.

The Kurds of Turkey

Rationale:

The attraction of the Kurdish game is that it is one with which students can easily identify. Many of them do spend some time helping or educating others at some stage of their education, often overseas. They can see how easily a U.S. volunteer might be perceived by foreigners as breaking local rules. They are therefore inquisitive about the procedures available when their human rights, or those of someone they know, appear to have been violated by foreign security forces. The game also gets students to think about the various options available for resolving the problem. They come to learn that an optimal procedure in one country might be hopelessly inappropriate in a neighboring country. Thus they appreciate the value of a diverse range of approaches, and how the use of a number of approaches concurrently might enhance the chances of success. The skills involved are primarily evaluative, but some negotiation is needed.

Background:

The Kurds are one of the largest peoples in the Middle East (22.5 million). They have no state of their own but constitute a significant proportion of the populations of Turkey (19 percent), Iraq (23 percent), Iran (10 percent), and Syria (8 percent). They also live in Georgia and the Commonwealth of Independent States (CIS). The Kurds are thought to be descendants of peoples who settled in the region four thousand years ago. They have a distinct culture, despite differences within the group in language, lifestyle, and economy. Most Kurds are Muslims.

After World War I, a number of new states were created in the region. In seeking to create a national identity, these new states sometimes played down certain elements of their culture while overemphasizing other aspects. In Turkey, for example, Kurdish associations, schools, publications, religious fraternities, and teaching foundations were banned in an attempt to establish a specifically Turkish state. This action had a unifying effect on Kurdish groups from 1925 on. Kurdish resistance was met with large-scale forced migrations. Traditional Kurdish areas near the then Soviet borders were declared a military zone, in part to facilitate the objective of forming a Turkish state.

Following Turkey's first free elections in 1950, properties confiscated from Kurds were restored, public services improved in Kurdish areas, and Kurds were elected into the government. A new constitution in the 1960s allowed the Kurds free expression. By 1965 the separatist Kurdish Democratic Party (KDPT) was formed. The left-wing Turkish Worker's Party also took up the Kurds' case. Fearing major upheavals, the Turkish government banned some publications and sent in security forces to patrol certain areas. Violent confrontations occurred, and the government banned the Turkish Worker's Party for having recognized the Kurds. In 1971 a military coup was followed by reports of the murder and torture of Kurds. In 1979 martial law was declared in Kurdish areas. Clashes occurred between the army and the Kurdistan Workers' Party (PKK), and were followed by mass trials.

In 1984 Turkey returned to civilian authority. The new government applied to join the European Union and agreed to consider a less restrictive approach to Kurdish culture. It also accepted some of the Kurdish refugees who fled there from Iraq in 1988. Additional clashes occurred within Kurdish areas, however, and the government empowered local governors to censure and deport Kurdish people. This repression seemed to arouse popular support for PKK activities. The government's inhumane treatment of Kurdish refugees from Iraq in 1991 further heightened Kurdish resistance to government oppression. In April 1991 the government restored the legal right to use Kurdish speech, song, and music, except for political, educational, publishing, or broadcasting purposes. At the same time, new legislation attempted to define as terrorism even democratic attempts to modify a harsh state. The year 1992 saw the first-ever sustained aerial bombardment of Kurdish guerrilla camps in Turkey. Reports said that military force was being used against civilians and that illegal detention, torture, and extrajudicial killings were occurring amid government attempts to terrorize the Kurds.

Turkey, as a party to human rights treaties of the United Nations, the Council of Europe, and the Conference on Security and Cooperation in Europe (CSCE), is legally bound to respect certain human rights of its citizens, even during states of emergency. UN intervention to monitor and deter attacks on civilians is therefore possible. The United Nations could also try to bring the parties together in order to negotiate a peaceful agreement on the status of Kurds within Turkey. Foreign governments that provide Turkey with military assistance could suspend this aid until human rights are respected in Turkey. Germany did this following the deaths of civilians during Kurdish New Year celebrations in Turkey. If a case were to be brought to the European Commission on Human Rights, it could also influence the Turkish government to move closer to the human rights norms of Europe.

The Game:

Imagine that you have just heard from the sister of someone you know called Ken. Ken is an American citizen who has just completed high school but is not going to college until next year. He has been working for an organization that helps refugees, and recently he has been helping to teach children in a Turkish refugee camp for Kurdish people who have fled persecution in Iraq. The children only speak a local dialect. Ken has learned it and communicates with them in their language.

Recently Ken failed to return from the nearby town where he drives each week to collect the camp's mail. Townsfolk say that he was arrested after he picked up the mail. Some people think that the mail might have contained anti-government material. Others believe that the authorities disapproved of Ken apparently condoning the use of Kurdish speech for educational purposes. Ken's employers have been told by the local police that they know nothing about Ken's arrest. They say that there were military patrols in town at the time Ken disappeared, but that these have now gone up to the mountains.

Ken's sister fears that Ken's human rights might have been seriously abused, and she has requested your advice. Hold a group meeting to decide what you will advise Ken's sister. Write down what you would like to see happen if she follows your advice, and also what you think will actually happen.

Points you may wish to consider in your discussion:

1. Ken is a U.S. citizen and the U.S. has provided overseas aid to Turkey for a number of years;

2. Turkey and the United States are members of the CSCE, which has a High Commissioner for National Minorities;

3. Turkey is a member of the United Nations, which has procedures for considering allegations of gross human rights violations;

4. Turkey is a member of the Council of Europe and a signatory to the European Convention on Human Rights;

5. There are a number of international humanitarian and human rights organizations working in the area;

6. The European Union has made strenuous efforts to maintain peace and stability within the region, and Turkey wishes to strengthen its present links with the Union and its members.

The UN World Conference on Human Rights

Rationale:

This is a useful exercise for students who have had an extended opportunity to see a nongovernmental organization (NGO) at work. They appreciate the chance to play the sort of roles they have observed during their field trip. Students are often surprised to learn about the diversity of goals and methods that exists within the NGO community. The game elucidates more information than does a general discussion of field trip experiences. Students also obtain a considerable understanding of the UN human rights system and the very different ways in which countries relate to it. In their discussions, students often provide some candid assessments of the chances that NGOs, governments, and the media have of influencing international developments. In evaluating possible strategies, students frequently demonstrate a far greater coherence between newly acquired knowledge and critical thinking than they would reveal in a term paper completed at the same stage of the course. The skills involved are evaluation and negotiation.

Background:

In 1993, the United Nations held its first World Conference on Human Rights in twenty-five years in Vienna, Austria. The Vienna Conference was proposed to the UN General Assembly by Jan Martenson, under-secretary-general for human rights. The objectives of the conference which Martenson outlined were:

1. to evaluate programs in human rights since the adoption of the Universal Declaration of Human Rights;

2. to identify obstacles to progress and ways of overcoming them;

3. to examine the relationship between development and the enjoyment by all human beings of economic, social, cultural, political, and civil rights;

4. to examine ways to improve the implementation of human rights standards and instruments;

5. to evaluate the effectiveness of methods and mechanisms used by the United Nations;
6. to make concrete recommendations to improve both the effectiveness of UN activities and mechanisms and the resources needed to achieve those ends.

Under-Secretary Martenson anticipated that these conference objectives would lead to the following human rights outcomes:

1. the reaffirmation of international standards;
2. the universal application of UN norms;
3. improved implementation;
4. a way of mobilizing all sectors of the UN system in the efforts to promote human rights.

The United Nations welcomed recommendations from NGOs, and those submitted three months before the conference started were to be included in the official background documents available to the conference. NGOs were to participate in the conference itself.

Several preparatory meetings were held for the Vienna Conference, but significant disputes arose over:

1. divisions between the northern and southern hemispheres;
2. the right to development;
3. how human rights can take into account religious and cultural differences;
4. the extent to which NGOs should be permitted to participate in a conference organized by governmental organizations.

There were even suggestions that the conference should be canceled.

Nongovernmental human rights organizations were very distressed by this situation. Seeing themselves as impartial experts on human rights, they wished to play a full part in the conference. Some NGOs wanted to see each government reporting to the conference on its precise national plans for implementing human rights, including a timetable and budget for its proposed activities. Many NGOs believed that the United Nations could refine its own human rights activities. They wished to see:

1. human rights given a higher profile within the United Nations and integrated into all of its relevant activities;
2. a rapid response mechanism established to deal with urgent situations;
3. closer cooperation and coordination between those UN bodies responsible for human rights;
4. closer cooperation and coordination between the traditional bodies that deal

Figure 14.1. Political science students from Williams College meet at the United Nations in New York with Jorge E. Illueca (Panama), president of the 38th regular session of the General Assembly. Playing the roles of country representatives, the students raised challenging questions. (UNPHOTO 163 012/SAW LWIN)

with human rights and the greatly increased UN peacekeeping activities, some of which involve unprecedented human rights protection programs;

5. greater impartiality in dealing with human rights, possibly involving the creation of a commissioner or court of human rights, which would lead to action without the necessity to await periodic meetings or obtain a requisite number of votes through lobbying;

6. greater resources devoted to human rights than the current one percent of the UN budget.

The Game:

It is now eight months before the scheduled start of the conference. Some representatives of human rights NGOs have agreed to meet in Washington, D.C. to help focus the conference on its original objectives. Imagine that your group is that meeting.

Jan Martenson is no longer under-secretary-general for human rights. You under-stand that his successor, as well as the new secretary-general himself, are only some-what sympathetic toward human rights. You realize that they cannot completely con-trol the feuding governmental representatives and that strong feelings lurk behind some of the political positions that have been adopted. You know that Washington is the capital of one of the few countries in the world in which legislation may require the protection of human rights to be a part of foreign policy. You also know that the United States ratified the International Convention on Civil and Political Rights in April 1992, and that the United States has been very successful in influencing UN ac-tivities since the end of the cold war. As NGOs, you are well aware that recent U.S. administrations have been criticized for being selective in the issues they seek to ad-dress in foreign policy.

You also know that the world's media has representatives in Washington, D.C. and that the recent world environment conference in Brazil received a great deal of coverage. Sending press statements is within the budget of your meeting, but you are aware that to attract publicity your message must be topical. It should be addressed to potentially interested journalists and, ideally, be presented by a very famous person.

At your meeting, try to prioritize your aims. Select a sequence of methods to im-plement each aim. Record your arguments for and against each step you propose and estimate your chance of success.

Human Rights in Haiti

Rationale:

This is a somewhat sophisticated scenario and therefore more valuable to stu-dents if it is used toward the end of the course. They gain an appreciation of the vari-ous perspectives major human rights players might bring to a specific situation and how these affect their choice of goals and strategies. They perceive that there is no such thing as a "quick fix" for many human rights problems, even among those who can agree that a problem exists. The scenario also offers students an opportunity to review the wide range of mechanisms available under international law for addressing a human rights problem of this type. Because the scenario involves so many differing perspectives, students obtain valuable practice at developing their negotiating skills. They also get an opportunity to see what a conflict resolution approach can achieve.

Background:

Haiti is a Caribbean republic. Among its close neighbors are the Dominican Re-public, Cuba, Jamaica, and the United States. It was governed for many years by dicta-tors supported by the armed forces and an armed civilian militia, known as the tontons macoutes. There have been numerous reports of human rights violations under these regimes. In December 1990 a democratic election was held. An outspoken Catholic priest, Jean-Bertrand Aristide, was elected president. In January 1991 a member of the previous government led an armed coup to prevent Aristide from taking office. This coup failed, and President Aristide took office in February. His government sought to prosecute those responsible for earlier human rights violations. In April, rural police chiefs were placed under civilian authority. They were ordered to turn in their weapons, and known human rights violators were dismissed. In August, a commission was established to investigate human rights abuses that had occurred over the previous four years. On a number of occasions, Aristide's political opponents were attacked by crowds. A senator who was believed to favor a no-confidence motion against the government was beaten. President Aristide appeared to condone such attacks.

On September 29, 1991, President Aristide was overthrown by a military coup and fled to Venezuela. The United Nations and other organizations condemned the coup. The Organization of American States (OAS) sought to mediate between him and the de facto government. This government granted an amnesty to all those charged with or convicted of "political crimes" during Aristide's presidency. Many of those convicted of serious human rights crimes were released. Reports of torture and murder by members of the armed forces have been widespread since the coup, and there have been allegations of beatings and other ill treatments in penitentiaries. Extortion seems to be a motive for some of these activities, but political factors are also evident. Political leaders and popular organizers, including priests, have been singled out for persecution. Judges have reportedly gone into hiding in some areas, and the legal system does not function. The military has absolute power over most Haitians.

As a result of this lawlessness and oppression, many Haitians have fled, cutting themselves off from families, communities, and their economic base. Some are hiding in the overcrowded slums of Port-au-Prince; others have crowded onto boats, in search of refuge overseas. Many of these boats were intercepted by U.S. vessels. At first, Haitian refugees were interned at a U.S. naval base, where they were interviewed by Immigration and Naturalization Service (INS) agents to assess the legitimacy of their refugee status. Later refugees were returned to Haiti, where they would be entitled to apply for assessment at the U.S. consulate at Port-au-Prince.

In an attempt to ensure a return to democracy, the rule of law, and military accountability, the OAS has established an economic embargo. This does not prevent non-OAS states from supplying goods to Haiti, so it has not proved to be an effective sanction on the present ruling group. Canada took a firmer step in June 1992 when it froze all bank accounts belonging to the Haitian government, and there have been calls for others to take firmer sanctions. Some experts predict that poverty, suffering, and civil conflict will escalate unless democracy returns.

The Game:

Imagine that your group is an international commission assembled to consider the problems of Haiti and achieve a negotiated solution. Divide your group into eight teams to represent the eight parties at the commission:

1. Haiti's de facto government, led by Marc Bazin;
2. Haiti's constitutional government, led by Aristide;

3. the Vatican;

4. the United States;

5. the OAS;

6. the UN Commission on Haiti;

7. the UN High Commission on Refugees (UNHCR);

8. the National Council of Churches Caribbean and Latin America Office (NCCCLA), which is an NGO.

Your commission will hold a series of meetings in an attempt to negotiate a solution. Before each round of negotiations, teams meet in private to review their goals, methods, and achievements in light of what was learned about other teams' positions and negotiating strategies. All negotiations must take place during the rounds and be made in a way that ensures that each team is aware of their content. There is to be no secret communication between teams. This simulation is designed to give you an understanding of the complexity of international human rights. For this reason, it is important that each team maintains a careful record of what is said in team sessions and negotiation rounds, so that this can be reviewed by the class at the end of the negotiations. Use as many rounds as you require to achieve a solution. Below are the positions of the eight teams:

1. Haiti's de facto government

You are concerned that a return to constitutional government might bring about further revenge killings. You believe that Bazin could build up better relations between Haiti and the United States if only the world would accept the legitimacy of his rule. You fear that Aristide's return could worsen Haiti's relationship with the Vatican, which does not favor Aristide and is the only state to have recognized the Bazin regime. Because of Bazin's past work at the World Bank and as finance minister under Haiti's Duvalier regime, you are particularly concerned to obtain the confidence of overseas investors. You fear that popular domestic support for Aristide could grow into an increasing demand for the sort of social changes that might dissuade international investment.

2. Haiti's constitutional government

You believe that rule of law must be reestablished in Haiti. You know that Aristide, who obtained 67 percent of the vote in Haiti's democratic election and who is very popular with the peasants, offers Haiti a real chance to move away from rule by force toward a more just society in which the military is accountable to a democratic government. You favor a strengthening of economic sanctions, the denial of entry to Haiti for oil tankers, and a refusal of visas to coup participants who at present are able to go abroad freely. You are ready to compromise in order to achieve a return to constitutional government.

3. The Vatican

You are concerned for the well-being of the people of Haiti, the majority of whom are Catholic. You do not favor Catholic priests taking leadership roles in the national politics of any country. You do not like the recent emphasis placed on liberation theology. In recent years, you have removed from Latin American countries a number of those priests and bishops who have espoused it. There have been conflicts between your office and Father Aristide in the past. The Vatican is the only state to recognize the de facto government of Bazin. You have received a number of reliable reports that the rule of law does not prevail in Haiti, and that a number of priests have been attacked by people carrying guns. It is also known that several leading priests have been convicted at public hearings established by the de facto government.

4. The United States

Your country's interests require peace and stability in the region. You favor democracy and a free market economy. You do not support socialism, and your embassy favored Marc Bazin during Haiti's democratic election in 1990. You know that other OAS members dislike U.S. military interventions in Latin America, although governments value assistance from time to time in dealing with such problems as drug trafficking. You dislike the criticism your country's response to Haitian refugees has received and would like to see the situation end. The U.S. military has some experience of human rights training, and you wonder whether one of your main contributions might be in this area or whether it might be viewed with suspicion by some countries.

5. The OAS

You have participated in a recent civilian democracy mission to Haiti. In recent years you have seen military governments in Latin America give way to civilian ones, and you would like to see Haiti become a democracy. You are prepared to maintain the present economic embargo, which the majority of Haitians appear to want despite the privations it brings them. You recognize that it is they who suffer, rather than Haiti's elite, since goods can be had at a high price from European or African countries who are not eligible for membership in the OAS. You favor a peaceful rather than military solution to the problem since there is great concern among members to discourage the United States from using force in the region.

6. The UN Commission on Haiti

You are extremely concerned about the absence of the rule of law in Haiti. There appears to be little doubt that human rights abuses are widespread, but you know that UN human rights procedures are lengthy. You do not believe that the present OAS embargo will influence the de facto government of Haiti. You wish to avoid any attempted solution involving foreign military participation, and believe that such an intervention could constitute a violation of Haiti's national sovereignty. Your public statement to this effect has been met with assurances from the United States. As a result of your considerable experience with problems of this type, you believe that a negotiated solution offers the best solution. You think that the United Nations could be useful in this, not least because of its ability to publicize both positive and negative actions by governments.

7. The UNHCR

You would like to see the situation improve so that Haitians are not compelled to become refugees. You believe that both political and economic changes are required to achieve this. You also believe that the screening system used by the United States to identify persons at risk of persecution is inadequate. You think that international standards are not being met, such as a refugee's right to have legal advice and an effective case review before being returned to Haiti. High-level correspondence on this issue between your office and that of the U.S. undersecretary of state has been leaked to the *New York Times*.

8. The NCCCLA

Your organization recently returned from a visit to Haiti where it met congregants and pastors throughout the country. You were a part of that mission and had an opportunity to assess the human rights situation, which appeared to be very bad. You observed that the OAS embargo seemed to have no effect on the de facto government. You also examined the U.S. refugee processing procedure and spoke with persons involved. You found the system to be inadequate for similar reasons to those expressed earlier. As a U.S.-based organization, you believe that the United States could play an influential role in Haiti, and you wish to see the following undertaken:

1. a continuous flow of human rights NGO delegations to Haiti in order to support human rights activists (within Haiti) and ensure that current information reaches the U.S. public and policymakers;
2. U.S. public condemnation of human rights abuses by the Haitian military and police, and pressure to restore the rule of law;
3. maintenance of the existing OAS embargo, and additional measures by the United States to freeze assets and restrict visas of perpetrators who have dealings with the United States;
4. support by the United States for multilateral international programs to make the Haitian security services more professional;
5. an ongoing assessment of U.S. refugee processing procedures;
6. highly trained staff from the INS and Department of State to review and adjudicate claims to refugee status;
7. improved accessibility of the U.S. refugee processing staff to high-risk cases;
8. acceptance of asylum applications in person or by telephone.

Conclusion

Students who are attracted to political science frequently want to observe, understand, and develop skills used in the political process. Through a balance of reflection on their everyday experiences, their human rights field trips, and topical scenarios carried out in the safety of the classroom, students achieve these goals. They come away with an understanding of the political complexity of human rights and an appreciation that they possess and can develop the skills necessary to achieve success in human rights work, including legal analysis and conflict resolution. This experiential approach to learning motivates students to reach a high level of achievement in research, argument, and understanding. In short, academic skills are developed as students explore political processes and gain an introduction to the skills and knowledge involved in human rights.

Notes

1. Robert Craig, "Social Justice and the Moral Imagination," *Social Education* 57, no. 6 (1993): 333–36.

2. I give students a lengthy bibliography and filmography dealing with the various topics covered by the course, with a list of useful journals and newspapers. Basic texts for courses of this type are Ian Brownlie, *Basic Documents in Human Rights*, 3d ed. (New York: Oxford University Press, 1992), and Hurst Hannum, *Guide to International Human Rights Practice*, 2d ed. (Philadelphia: University of Pennsylvania Press, 1992).

3. These approaches are based on ones used with my students in the School of Public Affairs at the American University, the Department of Government and Politics at the University of Maryland, and the Graduate School of the U.S. Department of Agriculture. I am pleased to have this opportunity to express my gratitude to them.

4. This pack was devised to introduce students to minority issues and the subject of racism and prejudice. It discusses the background to Pastor Martin Niemoeller's poem and is designed for use in courses in history, the humanities, citizenship, and religious education.

5. Alternatives in Religious Education, *The Holocaust: A Study in Values* (3945 South Oneida St., Denver, CO 80237: 1976). See also Mary Brabeck, "Human Rights Education Through Facing History and Ourselves," *Journal of Moral Education* 23, no. 3 (1994): 333–47.

6. Examples of the role of conflict resolution in the prevention of human rights abuse can be found at both a global and a regional level. Dispute management, resolution, and prevention are part of the program of advisory services and technical assistance of the United Nations Centre for Human Rights. At a regional level, the High Commissioner on National Minorities of the Commission on Security and Cooperation in Europe employs conflict resolution in his highly regarded quiet diplomacy.

7. Dudley Weeks, *The Eight Essential Steps to Conflict Resolution* (Los Angeles: Jeremy P. Tarcher, 1992).

Chapter 15
Toward a Critical Pedagogy for Adult Education

Matthew Cowie

This chapter advocates a partnership among education providers to facilitate adult learning in the field of human rights. Higher educational institutions can learn from nongovernmental organizations (NGOs) and community initiatives in providing appropriate educational opportunities for adult learners. In human rights education, teaching must be imaginative, critical, and utopian. The adult learning experience in higher education should have the mutually virtuous aims of self-development (moral universalism) and the fostering of democratic citizenship (social learning).

The Right to Adult Education

Adult education is of growing importance in western industrialized countries as the demographic shape of the populace ages. Furthermore, trends in long-term unemployment, early retirement, the decline of manual labor, and the technologizing of the workplace all point to epochal change.[1] Although the complexity of social and political change seems to outstrip our ability to keep pace, these changes provide opportunities for participation in learning, leisure, and social activities. Change has brought new challenges as individuals' resources to reflect critically on their situation and to understand modern conditions of societal complexity have diminished in the late twentieth century.[2] Thus one of the pressing questions for western democratic states is how to educate in a society where there is an excess of information.[3]

The importance of elementary education was recognized in the nineteenth century for the training of an industrial work force. State-provided, free, and comprehensive secondary education was central to the postwar welfare state. Traditionally, though, adult education has not fitted this model. Instead of being compulsory, full-time, and state-organized, adult education has typically been part-time and state-assisted or organized in the voluntary sector. It has come to have the image of the poor cousin to mainstream education. It has a similarly marginal place in international human rights instruments.

The recent Bill of Rights for the Adult Learner, drawn up by leaders of the U.S.-based Coalition of Adult Education Organizations (CAEO), underscores the importance of adult learning in the modern world: "A democratic nation is made possible through the efforts of a knowledgeable populace actively committed to the general welfare and alert to the opportunities for personal growth and development. Essential for realizing this commitment is the availability of a wide variety of adult and continuing education opportunities."[4]

State-imposed ignorance has often been a feature of the most oppressive regimes. Denial of learning opportunities is a benign, though effective, political weapon of exclusion from participation in political life. Equally important, it also violates the rights of the majority to self-development. Adult education is the keystone to the full enjoyment of civil, political, economic, social, and cultural rights.

The personal and social benefits of education stated in the Bill of Rights for the Adult Learner are mirrored in Article 26 of the Universal Declaration of Human Rights (UDHR) and Article 13 of the International Covenant on Civil and Political Rights (ICCPR). These instruments highlight the personal implications of education: "full development of the human personality" (UDHR, Article 26) and "the development of the sense of human dignity" (ICCPR, Article 13). The texts also emphasize the wider implications of learning for national and international society: "it shall promote understanding, tolerance and friendship among all nations, racial and religious groups" (UDHR, Article 26) and "enabling all persons to participate effectively in a free society" (ICCPR, Article 13).

The Bill of Rights for the Adult Learner

A democratic nation is made possible through the efforts of a knowledgeable populace actively committed to the general welfare and alert to the opportunities for personal growth and development. Essential for realizing this commitment is the availability of a wide variety of adult and continuing education opportunities. The institutions and agencies of a democratic society will strive to assure that the following rights are possessed by all who have adult responsibilities and who seek to learn in any setting.

- The right to learn regardless of age, gender, color, ethnic or linguistic background, marital status, the presence of dependents, disability, or financial circumstances.
- The right of equal opportunity for access to relevant learning opportunities throughout life.
- The right to education leave from employment for general, as well as vocational or professional, education.
- The right to financial aid and educational services at levels comparable to those provided for younger or full-time learners.
- The right to encouragement and support in learning subject matter that the learner believes will lead to growth and self-actualization.
- The right to a learning environment suitable for adults to include appropriate instructional materials, media, and facilities.
- The right to have relevant prior experiential learning evaluated and, where appropriate, recognized for academic credit toward a degree or credential.
- The right to participate or to be appropriately represented in planning or selecting learning activities in which the learner is engaged.
- The right to be taught by qualified and competent instructors who possess appropriate subject-matter qualifications, as well as knowledge and skill relating to the instructional needs of adults.
- The right to academic support resources, including instructional technology, that can make self-directed learning or distance learning possible.
- The right to dependent care and related structures of social support.
- The right to individualized information and guidance leading toward further study.

These texts do not specifically mention the rights of adults, although they do generally say everyone has the right to education, and so therefore, arguably, they refer to adults by implication. The only text that explicitly mentions adult education is the European Social Charter, which covers careers guidance and facilities for vocational training.

The right to adult education is a precursor and a necessary prerequisite to critical educational opportunities for adult learners, for even literacy is a political issue: "Illiteracy is one of the concrete expressions of an unjust social reality. Illiteracy is not strictly a linguistic or exclusively pedagogical or methodological problem. It is political, as the very literacy through which we try to overcome illiteracy."[5]

Paulo Freire and Donaldo Macedo have argued that the opportunity of reading and hence rewriting the world is a form of personal enrichment and an act of political reconstitution. Though made in the context of illiteracy in the developing world, Freire's point is equally applicable in the context of poverty in developed countries. Research shows an alarming level of black American and Hispanic illiteracy.[6] Education in the black community has often failed even to provide elementary skills for ordinary tasks, let alone critical tools for the learners' empowerment.

Theory of Communicative Action and Adult Education

Freire's radical pedagogy has had enormous influence in adult education in both the developing and developed world.[7] However, criticism has been made of Freire's undifferentiated critique of politics and class. A more politically sensitive paradigm of adult learning using Jurgen Habermas's theory of communicative action is emerging as a rival theory.[8]

Similarly to Freire, Habermas would argue that teaching and action are not polar opposites but that teaching can encompass "reflective action." This can be achieved in practical terms by encouraging "discourse ethics" which promotes moral development, responsibility and democratic citizenship in the public sphere. Habermas's project will form the theoretical grounding for practical speculations on the form, content, style, and prospects for adult education and human rights.

Although it is impossible to do justice to the richness and complexity of Habermas's later work in the *Theory of Communicative Action* and *Moral Consciousness and Communicative Action*, I can, for the purposes of adult education in human rights, draw a number of important lessons.

Concepts of Adulthood and Education or Learning

The questions of who is an adult and when does adulthood begin are problematic and paradigmatically constitutive of adult education as a discipline. The defining feature of adulthood is independence and of infanthood, dependence. Maturity is a process of acquiring skills and knowledge which promote independence.

Some cultures mark adulthood with formal ceremonies, sometimes at a particular age. Within the western school system, adulthood is marked by the transition from the world of school (graduation or school leaving) to the search for work. However, I argue that, although adult education has generally been perceived as "nonformal" education which occurs after a period of set formal instruction, it should not be so narrowly construed.

Peter Jarvis[9] has defined education as institutionalized learning, in the sense of a ritualized, regular, geographically situated learning experience directed toward participant(s) learning and understanding. Thus an educational institution—whether school, university, or college—will be judged by whether it promotes or hinders learning capabilities. However, as a criterion of educational quality, "learning" is a problematic indicator given its nonquantitative nature. It is not easily measured by testing and may at first sight appear synonymous with the word *education*. It is not tautologous to replace *educate* with *learn*. I believe that it is possible to separate these concepts and to use the latter, in a moral and cognitive sense, as a critical yardstick for adult education in the field of human rights.

In the legal instruments that define "the right to education" discussed above, a number of different knowledges are posited as the "purpose" of education. The legal texts do not generally differentiate forms of knowledge production (learning) in education. In fact, some texts are wedded to what can be called an instrumental or technical view of learning: "Every person has the right to an education that will prepare him to attain a decent life, to raise his standard of living, and to be a useful member of society."[10] A technical or instrumental interest in knowledge is structured by what it can achieve for you. It is a means to a specific end. It promotes the acquisition of skills that enable the learner to manipulate and control his or her environment.

The model I seek to develop is the encouragement of communicative knowledge, which mirrors to a degree the approach taken by the UDHR, the ICCPR, and the Bill of Rights for Adult Learners. In those instruments the purpose of learning concerned the improvement of interpersonal relations by creating an environment in which understanding of others is rendered possible. Furthermore, although Habermas has ceased to speak in terms of emancipatory knowledge interests, the UDHR and ICCPR also make the assumption that education can enlighten and transform personal presuppositions that structure thought and action.

The distinction between instrumental and communicative knowledge interests underpins Habermas's project and is crucial to a critical reflective practice in adult education teaching. Although practical skills such as reading and writing are important in developing a critical human rights program, it is the development of communicative competence and moral reasoning that has to be encouraged as the primordial value and yardstick.

The dangers of instrumental rationality in an increasingly technological and complex society have been a recurrent theme in Habermas's work. This theme of the "scientisation" of social practices such as education is a constant fear: "the cult of efficiency refers to a growing, and seductive, tendency to make more and more areas of human endeavor (the practical, moral, and political projects of everyday life) amenable to measurement and techno-bureaucratic control according to what is invoked as a scientific approach."[11] The critique is not of the rightful place due to techno-cratic knowledge and skills, but of its dominating and colonizing influence, so that the space and ability of learners to exercise critical faculties in deciding the rightness of technical decisions are diminished.[12]

In summary, the discussion of the typification of education and the purpose and success of institutional education in terms of some degree of learning clarifies the first question of what is an adult. By posing the question of learning, at least in the area of human rights (and not a technical or scientific subject), in moral terms, it is preferable to age specifications of the learner. Indeed, radical approaches to adult education seek to liberate learning from the parameters of classification and grades obtained within a formal setting. One cannot make someone grow faster by measuring and testing. Human rights education for adults must be perpetual, self-directed, and justified by promoting moral and social maturity. Adult education is therefore not solely or even predominantly concerned with the transmission of information about law but the achievement of moral adulthood.

Discourse Ethics

Freire's argument about how exclusion from learning is the root of social oppression is similar to Habermas's "discourse ethics." First of all, social problems require moral-political solutions, not scientific-technical ones. The discourse of human rights is part of the rationalization of posited solutions. Through argumentation, debate, and conversation, a number of points of view about appropriate action will be generated. When we opt into communication with others on moral-practical questions, there are a number of presuppositions (rules) of speech itself which the speaker is constrained by for fear of "performative contradiction." In short, each speech act raises validity claims which can only be justified if the view is reciprocally accepted by the hearers. If the view is one that would not be accepted by others, then it is not the best view. The ethical view is one that can be accepted by all. Anything other than argument conducted within this frame of reference is not truly communicative (dialogical).

Habermas proposes a number of argumentative rules that prevent "performative contradiction" and aid moral discourse. He calls these rules conditions of ideal speech, and in a critical conception of adult education, the teacher should be responsible for encouraging an environment that recreates the ideal speech situation.

1. Each subject who is capable of speech and action is allowed to participate in discourses.
2. a) Each is allowed to call into question any proposal.
　b) Each is allowed to introduce any proposal into the discourse.
　c) Each is allowed to express his attitudes, wishes and needs.

3. No speaker ought to be hindered by compulsion—whether arising from inside the discourse or outside of it—from making use of the rights secured under [1 and 2].
A. Whoever engages in argumentation must presuppose the validity of the discourse rules; and
B. that when that argumentation concerns normative claims—that is, ones about alternative orderings for the satisfaction of interests—the participants must, on pain of performative contradiction, admit that universalization is the only rule under which norms will be taken by each to be legitimate.[13]

Following the ideal speech situation, he argues, will provide the most rational basis for democratic moral-practical action. He holds to the view that ethical decisions made by a community in this way ought to be subject to an overarching moral universalism. Habermas is not satisfied with consensus views of what is right, if this view exhibits particularism. This, he would argue, is the result of a discourse distorted by power or rhetoric. The logic of his argument is that there are better and worse ways of determining norms and that faults can be pointed out by recourse to an overriding universalist moral principal in ethical positions.

This is, in a sense, similar to John Rawls's project in his *Theory of Justice*. In order to eliminate power and unfair interests, Rawls made his participants in moral debate argue behind the veil of ignorance. This terrain attempts to eliminate particularist or nonuniversalist reasoning. Decisions made by consensus behind the veil of ignorance must rationally be ones that are reciprocal and generalizable. Habermas, in contradistinction to Rawls, believes that this process of making ethical and moral judgments is inherent in real communication itself.

Habermas uses Lawrence Kohlberg's research on the cognitive development of moral judgment to lend credence to his philosophical position that adopting a generalizable or universalist stance in argumentation can provide a moral Archimedean point of judgment between ethical stances. Although Kohlberg's work is not crucial to Habermas's theory, it lends credence to the view that adulthood entails reciprocal moral reasoning. Fully developed moral reasoning, Kohlberg argues, corresponds to "post conventional" (reciprocal) reasoning: "Stage 6: *The universal ethical principle orientation.* Right is defined by the decision of conscience in accord with self-chosen *ethical principles* appealing to logical comprehensiveness, universality and consistency. These principles are abstract and ethical (the Golden Rule, the categorical imperative); they are not moral rules like the Ten Commandments. At heart, these are universal principles of *justice*, of the *reciprocity* and *equality* of human *rights*, and of respect for the dignity of human beings as *individual persons*."[14]

Discourse ethics, therefore, sets up a procedural framework of rules which, if followed, (it is argued) provide right and generalizable outcomes in moral-practical debate, and (it is further contended) this is a model of mature moral argumentation.

Societal Learning and Critical Citizenship

In *Communication and the Evolution of Society*, Habermas began to adapt Kohlberg's theory of cognitive development to a macro level of societal learning capacities. We reproduce patterns of cultural and social life through communication—communication is foundational to who we are. As people begin to understand the limitations and contradictions of a political system, the necessary motivation to ensure continued reproduction of that system's values is seriously undermined.

The concerns of Habermas's work on moral development are not separable from his more general political project or from his liberal faith in the Enlightenment tradition. His concern with the possibilities of modernity was the subject of his first work, *The Structural Transformation of the Public Sphere*. In documenting the emergence and subsequent decline of an autonomous public sphere in eighteenth-century western Europe, he is essentially analyzing the decline of citizenship.

The relationship between individual moral development and citizenship in combating the rise of instrumental reason in the face of increasing social complexity is an obvious one. A discursive citizenry can be a more morally mature citizenry. Civil society's condition will affect the political culture of the state; an informed citizenry is able to hold political decision makers more accountable. The adequacy of institutions of the public sphere and their capability for reproducing spaces for debate (political will formation) will constitute not only how democratically receptive it is but the quality of social-learning capabilities.

In his critique of Marxism and of political change in eastern Europe, Habermas pinpoints state socialism's failure to reform its elitist technocratic class structure into a more democratic framework. In short, the learning capacity of civil society outstripped the state's ability to satisfy it. A democratic form of decision making in society is a precondition not only of efficiency and rationality, but also of continued viability in the modern world: "The presupposition of rationality is based on the normative meaning of democratic processes, which ought to ensure that all socially relevant questions can be taken up and dealt with thoroughly and imaginatively until solutions have been found that, while respecting the integrity of every form of life, are uniformly in everybody's interest."[15]

Habermas's macro political vision of democratically accountable institutions demands a particular conception of citizenship. One may call it a "maximal"[16] or radical liberal notion where the starting point is the guarantee of civil and political rights. However, the presupposition of an active citizenry involved in political will formation requires a number of substantial commitments. Equal access to the means of contributing to the political process is required, and this would demand a redistribution of financial and cultural capital. One key process in this must be the provision of critical adult education services.

Freire has argued that education is never neutral,[17] and indeed, adult higher education, within this frame of reference, can never be impartial where the background objectives are orientated toward enlightenment and the strengthening of liberal democratic political structures.

Radical Democracy and the Role of Social Movements

Habermas provides insight into actors who could be possible agents of instituting, within their own sphere of action, some conception of radical citizenship. He points in particular to social movements. In the area of adult education, social movements orientated toward social change have been prominent.[18] Historically, the foundations of adult learning have been primarily religious. The teaching practice of the early church missionaries was followed by the Puritan zeal to make the Bible accessible to the people.[19] By the nineteenth century this model was being propagated both at home and in the mission field.

In the nineteenth and early twentieth centuries, the workers movement, trade unions, and related socialist societies were the impetus behind many educational opportunities for working people.[20] In the United States, initiatives like Myles Horton's Highlander Folk School in Tennessee worked with the civil rights movement.[21] The history of adult education in the United Kingdom is therefore witness to the utopian tradition in adult learning. It draws from religious zeal and imagination, liberal ideals fallen short in the establishment of the public sphere, and radical attempts to fashion a different kind of society.[22]

It is arguable, given the changed social composition of the work force and nature of work itself in the late twentieth century, that the unions and related socialist educational initiatives which have done so much to improve adult education will necessarily decline into a more pluralist picture of provision.[23] Increased social complexity and fragmentation of social and class relations, as well as the failure of socialism as a political project, have led theorists of the New Left to abandon the working class as the agent of social transformation. Furthermore, these changes have dented hopes in the project of modernity itself, of which education has always been a central motif: "If modernity has failed, then education has too failed . . . theoretically, conceptually, and institutionally, adult education is still an integral part of this educational project of modernity."[24]

The European Left has turned instead to actors who raise universalistic claims to validity. In terms of communicative action, it is social movements and community groups that generate ideas and sustain forms of life, culture, and values that can be antithetical to the progressive rationalization of modern society. Social movements are, therefore, the yeast that sustains moral practical debate over political choices. It is instructive that the human rights movement is often excluded from discussion of social movements, whereas it is archetypal of a truly universalist communicative community.

Radical Approaches to Adult Education: Learning in a Partnership Between the Human Rights Movement and the University

The idea of integrating teaching and research interests into the life of the surrounding community and the conception of a human rights curriculum in adult education offered in this chapter might not be an immediately palatable one to the majority of academics working in university human rights education. However, I would argue that not only is this a better course of action for the human rights academic but in the long term the best way of preserving a liberal notion of the university.

At the Lindeman Center for Community Empowerment Through Education at Northern Illinois University,[25] the Adult Education Department has attempted to create what might be called a "Communiversity," a radical integration of university and community. The community is no longer the object of study but, instead, a partner in research. The communiversity is perhaps no more than a radical fulfillment of the traditional liberal conception of the university: "The concept of a liberal education is strongly tied not only to the social-corrective role of the university, but also the social-Utopian tradition in Western intellectual thought with its emphasis on a critique of the status quo, and on speculating about what could be and what ought to be."[26] In the same way that Habermas documented the decline of the public sphere which provided a space for critique and association for the bourgeois classes, this notion of liberal education would reconstitute the dialogic community that Habermas seeks.

In the long run this concept may provide the only realistic alternative for most institutions to the "multiversity."[27] As pressures to do applied research and create more vocational or skills-oriented degree programs increase, few universities will survive as "ivory towers" producing research primarily for an academic audience. The "multiversity" idea is certainly of growing importance in the United Kingdom, where the university pragmatically fulfills the vocational needs of the labor market. As there is ostensively no labor market in the human rights field, the communiversity idea, as an expression of the old liberal notion of the university,[28] may well be more attractive in encouraging student, community, and curricular development. Furthermore, the 1980s in the United Kingdom has seen the increased deployment of partnerships between state service providers and the voluntary sector (NGOs) in such areas as residential and community care for people with disabilities and the elderly and in social housing. It would not be a surprise to see further developments in the west, as there have been in developing countries,[29] in this direction in education, for financial rather than ideological reasons.

Therefore, in summary, the human rights movement expressed through NGOs constitutes a new social movement.[30] Human rights education should be part of and complement social movements.[31] Adult education has always been central to old social movements. Human rights educators in higher education must respond to new configurations in political life in which human rights are a central motif. NGOs are working for these aims and require help and reflection which human rights education can provide.[32]

Implications for Radical Adult Education Human Rights Practice

Although I have presented aspects of the theory of communicative action, it is also to some extent a practical or workable theory. Though Habermas has been criticized for divorcing theory and practice, it is abundantly clear that educational strategies will help or hinder individual moral development and hence the individual's ability to play a full part in the public sphere as a citizen. Practical orientations and procedures in teaching adults in human rights flow from an attempt to encourage discourse ethics and postconventional reasoning in the classroom.

Teacher Role

Freire distinguished two forms of learning, "banking education" and "problem posing education." In banking education the role of the teacher is the provider. She or he teaches students something they did not know before and helps them accumulate cultural capital; whereas the "problem posing" model indicates a more facilitating role with no subject-object of education.

Problem posing education is most appropriate for adults because adulthood is typified by the process of becoming independent. Thus the most appropriate form of continuing education, education for life, must mirror the growth process itself with the student gradually becoming less dependent on the teacher and encouraging self-learning on moral-practical concerns. In facilitating self-learning, the teacher is neutral because she or he does not control the outcome of the debate. This model differs from the old "consciousness raising" models which are theoretically untenable. By following discourse ethics, the teacher promotes a framework for moral argumentation. In the truest liberal tradition, the teacher trusts the force of reason.

However, power and hierarchy can destabilize authentic argumentation,[33] which means that the teacher must be responsible for the argumentative environment and dynamic. The teacher is responsible for the process but not the outcome of the debate.

Thus the tutor should promote interpersonal skills. These are not just the three R's—reading, writing, and arithmetic—but include categories of engagement with others where one attempts to understand, empathize, and reach mutually acceptable solutions to differences. This involves listening and questioning skills used with a bona fide intention to understand the other person's point of view. Such skills increase the quality of argument by making the conversation dialogical rather than a series of monological interventions. It is an attempt to transform the learning experience structurally. In short, the dynamic of teaching should attempt to recreate the ideal speech situation.

Therefore, the teacher must be continually reflexive about the content of the course, sifting the excess of information; the teacher must be concerned about conditions of participation within the study group; but most of all, for developing critical thought, the teacher requires imagination.[34] The encouragement of critical skills is not sufficient for the adult educator; there are already many critics of the world's problems. With prevailing conservative cultural and political hegemony, one requires positive and creative thought. Utopian and imaginative thought should be used to supplement discourse ethics, which might be thought to be overly logical and formal:[35] "With imagination we can visualize possibilities for better human relationships and better social arrangements."[36]

Utopian thought is the ultimate expression of a preventative strategy in human rights protection. It encourages contemplation on the possibilities of justice and fairness. A utopianism, however, that is unrealizable and disconnected from practical, foreseeable action is likely to debilitate and demotivate potential learners. What is necessary is a "utopian realism"[37] which can motivate action and reveal taken-for-granted interests and assumptions. One may even argue that John Rawls's *Theory of Justice* is an exercise in one person's utopian imagination. Legal scholarship that admits imagination and subjective experience is gaining more attention, primarily in the United States, and so far appears to be the weapon of the oppressed and marginalized.[38]

Teaching Support

Adult education has, for the most part, been a voluntary or part-time enterprise, but it cannot be assumed that the tutor will bring appropriate skills to the classroom without adequate support services and training. The tutor needs specific organizational and interpersonal skills in order to handle the dynamic of a class that will bring a wealth of personal experience and reflection to the subject matter under discussion.

Self-directed learning does not relieve the teacher of all responsibility for the learning process. Appropriate training is necessary for effective transformative learning forums. Moreover, it cannot be assumed that the tutor will understand how adults learn or, for that matter, what learning support adults may require.[39] This has inevitably created the impetus for a professionalization of adult educators.[40]

The obvious benefits of professional status are subject specialization and a high-quality teaching output. The disadvantages are distancing the subject from the community, the problem of power relations as an expression of status, and the additional danger of a "careerism" in human rights. In structural terms there are analogous fears and opportunities. As a result of professionalization, some adult education programs have moved into universities[41] with the potential benefit of drawing a wider section of the community to the university, whereas the opposite is also true—a risk of taking learning out of the environment of lived experience. The importance of building on familiar learning environments rather than requiring the participants to make a leap out of their own experience cannot be underestimated in encouraging participation, especially among the working classes. Fulfilling learning experiences are more easily facilitated by creating a forum within the context of "a person's totality of involvement with his or her community and society." [42] Therefore, in encouraging moral-practical debate and sustaining a liberal conception of the university, partnership within the community should be encouraged and optimal learning conditions must be the first priority of the program.

Curriculum Content and Legally Defined Rights

Although a radical adult education course on human rights should have a specifically legal aspect, starting with legal texts should be avoided. This may seem strange to the lawyer who always starts from the text as the foundation. However, a critical approach to moral-practical issues which may or may not be codified in law should emphasize options and choices of what is best or even justified and then reduce this to a legal position. Too often we are constrained by the familiar and the accepted—we need to think about what should be before discussing what is. This is consistent with Martti Koskenniemi's conception of the role of the radical lawyer in the postmodern world. His view is that legal discourse in international law reifies and mystifies essentially moral-practical problems facing nation-states and that a radical lawyer ought to pierce through the legal wrapping and expose underlying debates. [43] It may also be the case that the law, as it is, excludes certain voices from its discourse, and therefore to start from this point would be automatically to reproduce existing forms of domination and exclusion. For instance, a typical debate about the limits of the right to freedom of information and the press as opposed to the right to privacy could be settled without hearing a feminist view about the public/private dichotomy.

One might be forgiven for thinking that this proposal is no more than political education "writ large" with no specific human rights component. Certainly, political education and citizenship have been extensively theorized, and the place of human rights teaching and citizenship undertheorized. [44] It is argued that there are a number of practical and pragmatic reasons for human rights education within a political education curriculum. First, human rights is less threatening as a label than political education. There are legitimate fears from all sides of the political spectrum that political education could be hijacked by those with power to mold the curriculum. It is also the case that notions of human rights per se are somewhat indeterminate and abstract, which allows a degree of plasticity in curriculum development. In short, it avoids the politicization of political education while retaining flexibility for the individual educator to develop an appropriate scheme of work.

At a more principled level, one cannot escape the contours of "rights talk." Although some have argued that rights are abstractions and reifications of basic needs, [45] others have persuasively argued that rights are intrinsic and are even the coalescing feature of identity and movements for social change. [46]

Instead, it is probably better to think of rights as imbricated and constitutive of our communicative practices. As such, they are inevitable points of contact with the political domain. Finally also, the notion of human rights can claim certain universal or at least liberal-democratic credentials that transcend national, racial, gender, and cultural boundaries. Though the extent of this claim is obviously contended, it is argued that human rights are more internationalist and cosmopolitan than notions of political education for citizenship, which tends to be restricted to notions of rights and responsibilities within boundaries.

Notes

1. Derick Bell, *The Cultural Contradictions of Capitalism* (New York: Basic Books, 1976).

2. Zygmunt Bauman, *Modernity and Ambivalence* (Cambridge: Polity Press, 1991), 244.

3. David Held, *Political Theory and the Modern State: Essays on State, Power and Democracy* (Stanford, Calif.: Stanford University Press, 1989), 92–93.

4. Bill of Rights for the Adult Learner, *Adults Learning* 3 (1991): 106.

5. Paulo Freire and Donaldo Macedo, *The Politics of Education: Culture, Power and Liberation* (South Hadley, Mass.: Bergin and Garvey, 1985), 10.

6. Charlotte Morgan, "More Than the Three "R's": The Development of Black Adult Education in Manhattan," in *Adult Education in a Multicultural Society*, ed. Beverly Benner Cassara (London: Routledge, 1990), 63–77; Martha Montero-Seiburth, "The Education of Hispanic Adults: Pedagogical Strands and Cultural Meanings," in *Adult Education in a Multicultural Society*, 97–101.

7. Gerri Kirkwood and Colin Kirkwood, *Living Adult Education: Freire in Scotland* (Edinburgh: Scottish Institute of Adult and Continuing Education, and Philadelphia: Open University Press, 1989).

8. Jurgen Habermas, *Theory of Communicative Action: Vol. 2* (Cambridge: Polity Press, 1987); Jurgen Habermas, *Moral Consciousness and Communicative Action* (Cambridge: Polity Press, 1990); Jack Mezirow, *Transformative Dimensions of Adult Learning* (San Francisco: Jossey Bass, 1991); Mechthild Hart, *Working and Educating for Life: Feminist and International Perspectives on Adult Education* (London: Routledge, 1992); Michael Collins, *Adult Education as Vocation* (London: Routledge, 1991).

9. Peter Jarvis, *Adult Education and the State: Towards a Politics of Adult Education* (London: Routledge, 1993), 2–3.

10. American Declaration on Rights and Duties of Man, Article 12, Organization of American States, Resolution XXX, adopted by the Ninth International Conference of American States, Bogotá, March 30–May 2, 1948.

11. Collins, *Adult Education as Vocation*, 2.

12. Ibid., 5.

13. Jurgen Habermas, "Discourse Ethics: Notes on a Program of Philosophical Justification," in *Moral Consciousness and Communicative Action*, 43–115.

14. Lawrence Kohlberg, "From Is to Ought," in *Cognitive Development and Epistemology*, ed. Theodore Mischel (New York: Academic Press, 1971).

15. Jurgen Habermas, "What Does Socialism Mean Today? The Rectifying Revolution and the Need for New Thinking on the Left," *New Left Review* 183 (1991): 16.

16. Terry McLaughlin, "Citizenship, Diversity and Education: A Philosophical Perspective," *Journal of Moral Education* 21, no. 3 (1992): 235–50, at 246.

17. Paulo Freire, *Cultural Action for Freedom* (Harmondsworth: Penguin, 1972).

18. Jarvis, *Adult Education and the State*, 14.

19. Thomas Kelly, *A History of Adult Education in Great Britain* (Liverpool: Liverpool Press, 1970).

20. Paul Armstrong, "The Long Search for the Working Class: Socialism and the Education of Adults 1850–1930," in *Radical Approaches to Adult Education: A Reader*, ed. Tom Lovett (London: Routledge, 1988).

21. John Glen, *Highlander: No Ordinary School, 1932–1962* (Lexington: University Press of Kentucky, 1988); Aimee Horton, *The Highlander Folk School: A History of Its Major Programs, 1932–1961* (Brooklyn, N.Y.: Carlson Publishing, 1989); Miles Horton with Judith Kohl and Herbert Kohl, *The Long Haul: An Autobiography* (New York: Doubleday, 1990).

22. Lovett, ed., *Radical Approaches to Adult Education*, 300.

23. John Field, "Workers' Education and the Crisis of British Trade Unionism," in *Radical Approaches to Adult Education*, 224.

24. Matthias Finger, *Adult Education Quarterly* 40, no. 1 (Fall 1989): 15–22, at 18.

25. Jeff Zacharakis-Jutz, Tom Heaney, and Aimee Horton, "The Lindeman Centre: A Popular Education Centre Bridging Community and University," *Convergence* 24, no. 3 (1991): 24.

26. Hart, *Working and Educating for Life*, 60.

27. Edward Shaffer, "The University in Service to Technocracy," *Educational Theory* 30 (1980): 47–52.

28. Ronald Barnett, *The Idea of Higher Education* (Buckingham: SRHE and Open University Press, 1990); Aharon Aviram, "The Nature of University Education Reconsidered," *Journal of Philosophy of Education* 26, no. 2 (1992): 183.

29. Cesar Picon, "Adult Education and Popular Education in the Context of the State and NGOs," *Convergence* 24, nos. 1–2 (1991): 80.

30. Claus Offe, "New Social Movements: Challenging the Boundaries of Institutional Politics," *Social Research* 52, no. 4 (Winter 1985): 817.

31. Richard Pierre Claude, "Human Rights Education: The Case of the Philippines," *Human Rights Quarterly* 13, no. 4 (1991): 453–524, at 524.

32. Michael Welton, "Social Revolutionary Learning: The New Social Movements as Learning Sites," *Adult Education Quarterly* 43, no. 3 (Spring 1993): 52–164.

33. Matthias Hart, "Critical Theory and Beyond: Further Perspectives on Emancipatory Education," *Adult Education Quarterly* 40, no. 3 (Spring 1990): 125–38.

34. Kieran Egan and Dan Nadaner, eds., *Imagination and Education* (Milton Keynes: Open University Press, 1988); Martti Koskenniemi, *From Apology to Utopia: The Structure of International Legal Argument* (Helsinki: Finnish Lawyers' Publishing Company, 1989), drawing on Unger's reconstructive work in social and legal theory, argues that in relation to international law, "We need to *re-imagine* the game, reconstruct its rules, redistribute the prizes" (p. 501); Richard Rorty, *Contingency, Irony and Solidarity* (Cambridge: Cambridge University Press, 1989), xvi.

35. Nel Noddings, "Conversation as Moral Education," *Journal of Moral Education* 23, no. 2 (1994): 107–18, at 110.

36. Eugene Ineoma, "Vico, Imagination and Education," *Journal of Philosophy of Education* 27, no. 1 (1993): 45–60, at 52.

37. Anthony Giddens, *The Consequences of Modernity* (Cambridge: Polity Press, 1990).

38. Pat Williams, "Alchemical Notes: Reconstructing Ideals from Deconstructed Rights," *Harvard Civil Rights–Civil Liberties Law Review* 22, no. 2 (1987): 401.

39. John Daines, Carolyn Daines, and Brian Graham, *Adult Learning, Adult Teaching* (Department of Adult Education: Nottingham University, 1993); Alan Rogers, *Teaching Adults* (Philadelphia: Open University Press: Milton Keynes, 1989).

40. Alan Chadwick, "Some Current Issues in the Training of Adult Educators," in *Training Adult Educators in Western Europe* (London: Routledge, 1991), 208.

41. Peter Jarvis, "Towards a Theoretical Rationale," in *Training Adult Educators in Western Europe*, 4.

42. Sean Courtney, *Why Adults Learn: Towards a Theory of Participation in Adult Education* (London: Routledge, 1992), xv.

43. Koskenniemi, *From Apology to Utopia*, 490–501.

44. Kenneth Wain, "Human Rights, Political Education and Democratic Values," *Educational Philosophy and Theory* 24, no. 1 (1992): 68.

45. Mark Tushnet, "An Essay on Rights," *Texas Law Review* 62 (1984): 1363.

46. Alan Hunt, "Rights and Social Movements: Counter Hegemonic Strategies," *Journal of Law and Society* 17 (1990): 309; Williams, "Alchemical Notes," 401.

Part III
Specialized Human Rights Training for Professionals

EDITORS' INTRODUCTION

The chapters in Part III focus on specialized human rights training for various professions: law, the military and police, health professionals and public health practitioners, scientists and engineers, as well as journalists. The forms of this training are quite varied, and, by and large, most such professional education is relatively new. Certainly legal training is an exception; it is hardly novel in view of the post–World War II tradition of courses on international human rights and humanitarian law in colleges, universities, and law schools worldwide.

Compared to lawyers and their training, other professions have been slow to integrate human rights materials and issues into their curricula and continuing educational training programs. In 1978 it was quite innovative for the Final Document of the UNESCO International Congress on the Teaching of Human Rights to recommend specialized human rights seminars for the police and directors of penitentiaries.[1] In the case of health workers, professional ethics courses in medical schools have been curricular staples, but when UNESCO addressed this issue in 1978, it was breaking new ground in calling for the teaching of human rights in continuing education for health professionals;[2] no comparable recommendations were made for scientists, engineers, or journalists. By contrast, in 1993 the International Congress on Education for Human Rights and Democracy, meeting in Montreal, took the unequivocal view that: "It is absolutely necessary to promote specialized training for members of professions particularly concerned with human rights, such as judges, doctors, nurses, police officers, journalists, senior personnel in the armed forces, . . . etc., through their national and international organizations."[3] The Montreal statement acknowledged the leading role of legal training, ahead of other professions, but noted, as well, something new among lawyers, that "the education provided through legal counselling by legal aid centers has proved to be very important," especially among the underserved and in deprived areas.[4]

Innovative approaches to legal training, including human rights education for lawyers, owe much to experimentation in the United States during the late 1960s with the setting up of clinical projects. According to one report by recently graduated attorneys in the 1970s, it was the legal clinical programs funded to extend services to the poor by the "Great Society" legislation of the Johnson administration that "brought about the first significant innovation in legal curricula since the hegemony of the case method."[5] Now there are many such programs. In a report to the Montreal Congress on educational innovation in 1993, Heather Gibbs and Magda Seydegart gave an account of clinical programs in Canada and the United States which include human rights training.[6] Among North American programs, some are highly specialized, such as the Harvard Immigration and Refugee Clinic. With two instructor-supervisors and eighteen students per semester, it provides representation to refugees and immigrants in the Boston area. The City University of New York School of Law sponsors the International Women's Human Rights Law Clinic, which has undertaken projects involving violence against women and challenges to rape as a political weapon in the former Yugoslavia and in Haiti. The list of such programs is growing rapidly and includes clinical legal programs at Columbia University, DePaul University, the University of Minnesota, and the Allard Lowenstein International Human Rights Law Clinic of the Yale Law School.[7] Integrated degree programs emphasizing human rights are offered at the Fletcher School of Law and Diplomacy of Tufts University, and the Human Rights Research and Education Centre at the University of Ottawa. The Canadian project links academic, governmental, and advocacy communities in tasks of research, education, training, documentation, and organizational support.

In the first chapter in Part III, Richard J. Wilson of the Washington College of Law, the American University, reports on the program he directs, along with a strong endorsement for participatory experiential learning. He calls it "particularly effective with adult learners." The chapter supplies helpful critical perspectives useful to others inaugurating such programs. For example, Wilson delineates what he calls "ideological or institutional limits," and problems associated with the "service-learning dichotomy." He also identifies suggested areas for evaluation.

Accompanying Wilson's chapter is a sidebar describing the "Law to the Villages" program of the Thongbai Thongpao Foundation (TTF) in Thailand. In one of the most imaginative and bold human rights undertakings of the Asia-Pacific region, the TTF seeks to bring "legal assistance to Thailand's rural people" via comprehensive training "on basic human rights and the law for daily life."

In his chapter on "Human Rights Education for Law Enforcement," Edy Kaufman presents a wide-ranging critical discussion of the challenges associated with infusing military and police training with human rights materials and, where appropriate, with humanitarian law. Drawing examples from experience and from countries all over the world, he summarizes a great deal of empirical and normative literature dealing with law enforcement, and offers useful recommendations. For example, where police and the military are concerned, he insists that evaluation studies of human rights education should be undertaken primarily to assess "if the investment has resulted in attitudinal changes." On this score, he says pointedly that "the reduction of the levels of violations needs to be evaluated in countries with a pattern of human rights violations inflicted through the same institutions that are being trained in HRE" (citing Israel and the Philippines).

In 1990 a Canadian group produced a manual designed to offer syllabi useful for human rights training for various categories of military personnel, officials at prisons and correctional institutions, and the police. Anyone interested in such specialized work should consult the Human Rights Training for Commonwealth Public Officials Manual.[8] Among other things, it sets out a syllabus for the training of military personnel and defense ministry officials. On the same topic, the reader will find considerable detail in the chapter on "Military Training for Human Rights and Democratization" by Commander D. Michael Hinkley. The author was directly involved in the design of the program he describes for the United States Navy Justice School. Historically, human rights training programs linked to U.S. security and development assistance programs have been exposed for ineptness and worse.[9] The result was a legislative reform effort mandating the Expanded International Military Education and Training (EIMET) program. The author's program was developed under this rubric. He takes into account and cites a 1993 Amnesty International critique of U.S. security assistance programs, but he nevertheless argues that "reformed" U.S. programs can become effective when offered to the military of emerging democracies. The author is specific in methodological terms, and supplies an analysis of problems of "measuring success." Nevertheless, given the sharp level of negative criticism that historically has been directed at such programs, a heavy burden falls on those who implement EIMET to show that the program helps and does not hinder respect for human rights.[10]

In his chapter on "Human Rights Education for the Police," Marc DuBois details the program of training called "Human Dignity and the Police," designed by the John Jay College of Criminal Justice in New York. That program, in turn, has been given to several hundred police officers in Latin America and the Caribbean. The author draws on experience with training for law enforcement officers in Zimbabwe and the Philippines to underscore the importance of defining training goals in terms of targeting the factors that foster human rights abuses. Included among them are psychological factors, clarified in the training program by reliance on the "Wolfpack Exercise," a potentially important simulation game designed to help displace destructive competitive behavior with cooperation.

The two chapters that follow focus on health professionals. Among educational approaches for public health professionals, a center at Harvard University is in the forefront of developing courses on human rights for health practitioners and public health officials. The François-Xavier Bagnoud Center for Health and Human Rights has concentrated its work on integrating the promotion of health and the protection of human rights. Jonathan Mann, M.D., the Center's director, and co-authors present some of the methodology to analyze public health issues aiming at optimum effectiveness and also to identify complementary and sometimes competing human rights priorities. Their systematic methodology is groundbreaking because, according to the authors of "Teaching Human Rights to Public Health Practitioners," public health officials heretofore rarely, if ever, methodically and explicitly considered the effects of health policy on human rights or the impact of human rights violations on the health of individuals and populations. The chapter outlines a methodology that can readily be adopted in other schools of public health for purposes of examining reciprocal relationships between health policy and human rights standards.

In a valuable note, Kari Hannibal and Susannah Sirkin of Physicians for Human

Rights focus on the psychiatric, epidemiological, and forensic pathology skills that become critically important to human rights cases and in humanitarian crises. The authors discuss "On-the-Job Human Rights Education for Health Professionals," arguing that if the future brings more conflicts such as those in Somalia, Rwanda, and the former Yugoslavia, then better and more standardized pre-mission training will be necessary for the health professionals called upon for assistance in such volatile countries. Doctors, nurses, and other medical workers need human rights education and training in humanitarian law.

Human rights education sometimes takes place under very difficult circumstances, for example, where the learners are victims seeking ways to improve their situation. This certainly characterizes the situation involved in the case study on "A Cambodian Human Rights Education Program for Health Professionals." Authored by Allen Keller and Gabriel Otterman, both western-trained physicians, and Sin Kim Horn and Sam Sopheap, health professionals in war-torn Phnom Penh, the chapter details the team's work in Cambodia under UN auspices. The curriculum is described in detail, with attention to cultural sensitivities. The analysis of obstacles faced (shortages of practically everything) did not deter the authors from agreeing that the program was enthusiastically received, and they believe that some of its features are suitable for emulation elsewhere.

Rather little has been done on identifying opportunities for connecting science and human rights. Of course, there have been studies of discrimination within the science professions. For example, in 1991, UNESCO published a study on *Women in Science: Token Women or Gender Equality?* [11] and some scholarship has recently focused on human rights and scientific freedom and responsibility. [12] Audrey Chapman, Herbert and Louise Spirer, and Caroline Whitbeck combine to write the first essay available on the possibilities for integrating human rights standards into the teaching of science subjects as well as engineering ethics. Their chapter is clear about the ways that scientists are dependent upon the protection of human rights for their professional work. Further, it details the educational and training work of the American Association for the Advancement of Science and its activities under the rubric of "science in the service of human rights." These activities include the development of a training guidebook on *Data Analysis for Monitoring Human Rights*, a nontechnical primer designed for human rights activists, but found suitable, as well, for enlivening classes in statistics in colleges and in adult education, especially when immigrant students are enrolled. The chapter concludes with an interesting assessment of how human rights issues and values intrude into areas of technology, including decisions made by engineers. The need to sensitize scientists and engineers to the human rights components of professional ethics is argued.

Turning finally to the training of journalists, members of this profession would do well to consult one of UNESCO's specialized publications, *The International Dimensions of Humanitarian Law*, published by the Henry Dunant Institute in Geneva. In the final chapter in Part III, Anita Parlow makes a strong argument that journalists are being shortchanged in their professional education if they do not get some training on the laws of war and international human rights standards. The reasons are that journalists themselves are increasingly asked to undertake risky reporting assignments in areas of conflict and war where humanitarian law applies, and because an ever increasing docket of stories in print and electronic media focus on tragic human rights issues associated with abuses of internationally defined standards of decency. What is more, lest journalists become ensnared in producing an "official story"—as Argentine journalists did in accepting the military government's denial of "disappearances" in the 1970s—they need strong grounding in professional ethics and the obligation to challenge leads provided by self-serving official sources. The extreme case of journalists confessing media manipulation was announced by Chinese news professionals demonstrating in Tiananmen Square with banners reading "We do not believe what we write."

Of course, formal journalism training often includes internships and necessarily demands some experiential learning. As a thematic thread among the chapters here, from that on clinical legal programs to those on training health professionals and journalists, these essays on human rights education for the professions stress the importance of field experience and participation. The practice of teaching human rights experientially is available to training programs outside of legal studies and medical training; indeed, it should also be considered in schools of social work, forensic anthropology, and psychiatry, to note a few examples of professional education not discussed here.

Notes

1. International Congress on Teaching Human Rights, *Final Document* (Paris: UNESCO, 1978); para. 11.

2. Ibid., para. 13.

3. International Congress on Education for Human Rights and Democracy, *Working Document: Achievements and Obstacles in Human Rights Education, from Malta to Montreal (1987–1993)* (Paris: UNESCO, SHS-93/CONF.402/3, 1993), para. 21.

4. Ibid., para. 20.

5. Michael Meltsner and Philip G. Schrag, "Report from a CLEPR [clinical legal education program] Colony," *Columbia Law Review* 76, no. 4 (1976): 581–632, at 582.

6. Heather Gibbs and Magda Seydegart, *Education on Human Rights and Democracy in Canada and the United States* (Paris: UNESCO, SHS-93/CONF.402/INF.9, 1993), 4–8.

7. Victoria Clawson, Elizabeth Detweiler, and Laura Ho, "Litigating as Law Students: An Inside Look at Haitian Centers Council," *Yale Law Journal* 103, no. 8 (1994): 2337–89.

8. Magda Seydegart, Allan McChesney, Iva Caccia, and Douglas Williams, *Human Rights Training for Commonwealth Public Officials Manual* (Montreal: Human Rights Research and Education Centre, University of Ottawa, in conjunction with the Human Rights Unit, Commonwealth Secretariat, 1990).

9. John Samuel Fitch, "Human Rights and the U.S. Military Training Program," *Human Rights Quarterly* 3, no. 4 (1981): 65–80.

10. E.g., Sara Steinmetz, *Democratic Transition and Human Rights: Perspectives on U.S. Foreign Policy* (Albany: State University of New York Press, 1994).

11. UNESCO, *Women in Science: Token Women or Gender Equality?* (Paris: UNESCO/Berg/ISSC, 1991).

12. Richard Pierre Claude, "Scientists and Human Rights: An Historical Partnership," *Netherlands Quarterly on Human Rights* 13, no. 1 (1995): 41–50.

Chapter 16
Clinical Legal Education for Human Rights Advocates

Richard J. Wilson

The International Human Rights Law Clinic (IHRLC) is one of seven clinical programs at the Washington College of Law at the American University in Washington, D.C. It is the newest of the school's clinical programs, founded in 1990 with a grant from the U.S. Department of Education. Clinical legal education, as used at the Washington College of Law, means a course of study combining a classroom experience with representation by students of clients with real cases or projects, under the supervision of a full-time faculty member whose background includes extensive law practice. The clinics charge no legal fees to clients, who normally are unable to obtain representation elsewhere. Clinical courses are open to students in their second or third year of law school.

The IHRLC is unique in the United States in providing students with full case responsibility for human rights litigation, although a number of schools have developed human rights programs in which students are given practical, supervised field experience. In the IHRLC, the primary clientele are of two kinds: applicants for political asylum in the United States and victims of human rights abuses who seek redress in either the U.S. courts or before international human rights enforcement bodies.

A typical asylum case handled in the clinic is a recent trial in Immigration Court in which the U.S. Immigration Service sought to deport a young man from Honduras. Students represented the man in court and proved he was entitled to political asylum here because his left-wing student activism at the largest university in Honduras led him to be targeted by security forces there. He fled the country after he and close family members received death threats and armed soldiers forcibly entered his apartment, held him on the floor at gunpoint, and ransacked his belongings for "subversive materials."

An example of human rights litigation prepared by the clinic for presentation in an international forum is student preparation and filing of a complaint against the government of Colombia before the Inter-American Human Rights Commission, the regional human rights enforcement body of the Organization of American States. The clinic recently filed the action on behalf of an indigenous tribe living in the rain forest near the headwaters of the Amazon River. The government of Colombia, with funds and cooperation from U.S. military forces, placed a radar installation, ostensibly designed to detect airborne drug trafficking, on tribal lands without proper permission from the tribe. The installation caused environmental degradation and polluted the local water supply. The complaint alleges violation of several international human rights treaties, and students will follow the case through the Inter-American human rights system as counsel for the tribe.

Students also work on other human rights projects involving legislative advocacy, such as a recent analysis of the potential legal consequences of U.S. ratification of the International Covenant on Economic, Social and Cultural Rights. Another example of administrative advocacy is the clinic's presentation to an interagency body which makes recommendations to the president regarding trade by the United States with certain countries under the General System of Preferences (GSP). Under the GSP review system, a country can have its favorable trade status removed if it is shown that it systematically violates internationally recognized workers' human rights. In the past two years, students in the clinic have presented petitions seeking review or removal of GSP status for El Salvador and Pakistan. In short, clinic students are given actual opportunities to represent real people in real cases through a carefully structured classroom and courtroom experience.

This chapter is about learning human rights advocacy by doing it. It is also about teaching practical human rights advocacy in the law school context. The methodology of clinical education, however, can be used in other professional training programs as well. Clinical programs present human rights educators with an exciting array of options for effective teaching and learning.

The Strengths of the Clinical Method

Legal education in the United States is a three-year course of study after completion of an undergraduate university degree. The most frequent teaching method used for law school instruction is the Socratic method, a guided teacher-student dialogue, or the lecture. The content of the law is normally taught through the case method; students read and discuss real case decisions by appellate courts. This Socratic-casebook method permeates all three years of law school instruction, but is particularly dominant during the first year, where standard texts and course offerings are remarkably uniform in all U.S. law schools. More than 90 percent of all law schools require first-year students to take courses in contracts, torts, property, criminal law, and civil procedure.[1] On the other hand, once beyond the first year of study, the student is given virtually total discretion in choosing courses. More than 90 percent of all law schools offer between one hundred and four hundred elective credit hours to their students.[2] Among elective courses, those that stress skills training have the highest enrollments.[3] Those courses often are not taught with the casebook method. Instead, the methodologies are more interactive and based in hypothetical fact patterns and real or invented problems. The upper-class law student therefore has a wide array of elective options taught with a focus on law practice.

One of the most frequent criticisms of the case method of teaching is that it is unable to keep students engaged because it is too theoretical, too time-consuming to impart information effectively, and too narrowly focused on the rational formulation of rules for the operation of the legal system.[4] In the human rights area, it might be noted, cases are not used to teach the law. The leading textbooks in the field are organized around discussion of problems.[5] This is in part because resolution of international human rights law issues begins with a study of relevant treaties and international customary practices, and in part because the jurisprudence of international human rights bodies is not yet sufficiently developed to lend itself to the case method of instruction.

Clinical study and other skills courses, on the other hand, permit students to learn experientially in a complex web of issues. Clinical courses offer the possibility of learning and reflection on such wide-ranging areas as legal reasoning, professional judgment, interpersonal and social skills, ethics, oral and written persuasion, and time management. While each of theses skills is used by practicing lawyers throughout the world every day, there is little in conventional legal education that lends itself to their methodical study or to an evaluation of the degree of their presence or absence in a student's work product.

Research shows that participatory, experiential learning contexts such as clinical education are particularly effective with adult learners. Learning patterns of intellectually mature adults are too complex and varied to be susceptible to a single teaching method. Any single approach tends to lead to a leveling of learning which does not accommodate the varied needs of the group. Thus the most successful methods of teaching allow the student to pursue content mastery at an individually determined pace while the contact between student and instructor is kept close to an individual basis.[6] Moreover, research also shows that, like human rights norms, there are universal principles in adult learning. The cross-cultural data indicate that active teaching methods are more effective than rote, formal methods, whatever the cultural context in which the learning takes place.[7] Clinical education is not intended to replace the Socratic-case method of classroom instruction, but participatory, experiential methodologies are reflected in the pedagogy of clinical teaching in law schools and in the specific objectives of the International Human Rights Law Clinic.

There are at least five strengths of the clinical method as a means of training effective human rights advocates. First, the general focus of the method is on students and learning rather than on teachers and teaching. Advocates learn to trust their own experience and judgments and to gain self-sufficiency rather than to rely on the teacher

Figure 16.1. Law students at the University of Western Capetown engage in role-playing as a part of a voter education project. Experiential learning and "learning by doing" are important parts of educational programs designed to promote political participation. (National Institute for Citizen Education in Law [NICEL])

as an "expert" source of all answers to all questions. The teacher still has a role as supervisor and guide, but the two, teacher and student, are in struggle together, not separated by the gulf of alleged special knowledge possessed by the teacher alone. Second, theoretical norms are tested and reflected upon by the student and teacher in their operational context, an issue that is particularly important with the testing of human rights principles in the crucible of real life. Third, the method focuses as much on the process of resolution of disputes as on the content of the rules themselves. This is also an important issue for human rights advocates faced with myriad human rights bodies for determination of human rights claims and their enormously varied and developing methods of fact gathering and factual and legal decision-making functions. Fourth, the clinical method permits the student to use creative, self-determined solutions to problems, as opposed to formal structures imposed from rigid application of rules. This seems particularly important with the evolution of human rights standards in flux as much as they are at the present time. The advocate can, with imagination and persuasive power, contribute to the formulation of effective norms. Fifth, the student develops not only cognitive abilities but affective, emotional responses to the issues involved, and then determines their impact on the effective resolution of issues. This last criterion is particularly important in the practice of human rights advocacy, where theoretical rules cannot be separated from the sometimes brutal reality of human experience in which the law is lived. Powerful emotional responses to human rights violations must be acknowledged, discussed, and reconciled with the sometimes cold and seemingly lifeless legal rules involved in the resolution of real cases.

"Clinical" legal education need not be limited by the definition used at the Washington College of Law. Other law schools use broader definitions of active legal education which might have application in both the legal and nonlegal academic fields. The next section will discuss a more expansive definition of "clinical" education.

What Are the Options for "Clinical" Educational Experiences?

Skills training in legal education is one of the fastest growing areas of law school pedagogy because of the intense desire by students to gain practical experience, and because they are highly motivated by their desire for service to others and the responsibility given to them for real people's lives. Clinical legal education is just one of many methods by which students can gain practical skills experience in human rights advocacy. Other examples of experiential methods of instruction are externships, simulations, role-plays, games, and empirical case studies.

Externships involve the placement of law students in the workplace, usually a nongovernmental organization or law firm, under the supervision of an attorney in that workplace, for law school credit. Externships are used extensively by law schools as a means to provide students interested in the study of human rights with actual experience, either domestic or overseas, where human rights advocacy occurs on a daily basis. Some include a classroom component of instruction, but most require only a formal reporting requirement by the student to an academic dean or a supervising faculty member.

There are several strengths to the use of the externship: immersion of the student in a work ambience in which actual human rights issues are the organizing principle; the possibility of mentorship with an effective, experienced advocate; experience of the time and resource demands placed on a working law firm; and the possibility of future employment for the student. The principal weaknesses of the externship are the often unstructured and menial tasks law students are asked to perform; the possibility of exposure to bad work habits as well as good; and the general lack of intellectual rigor in reviewing the workplace experience from any perspective other than the purely functional examination of the supervisor's work.

Simulations, role-plays, and games are all means by which the teacher can use progressively more complex fact patterns as vehicles for student preparation and performance of particular roles in that controlled context. A simulation can be very complex or very simple. It may be entirely fictional or based in an actual, existing case or fact pattern. An example of a simulation used recently in the IHRLC is a mock trial of a claim under the Alien Tort Claims Act (28 U.S.C. §1350). In the exercise, student lawyer teams represent the alien victim of an alleged violation of the law of nations as well as the defendant charged with those violations. The facts for the exercise come from an actual case in which a judgment was rendered. The professor plays the judge before whom the case is tried. The students play both lawyers and witnesses. Plaintiff's and defendant's counsel make preliminary legal arguments, call two witnesses, offer exhibits, and make opening and closing arguments on the facts and law. The entire exercise takes two weeks of preparation and two class sessions of three hours each for the mock trials.

Role-plays and games are simpler versions of simulations which can generally be carried out in a single class session. Games, as their name implies, are metaphors for actual situations which teach students by example. One of the most effective games used in the IHRLC is the "high jump champion of the world" game, in which the professor announces at the outset of class that he is the current reigning champion of the world in the high jump. Incredulous students are challenged to disprove the assertion by closely questioning the teacher. The entire exercise takes about ten minutes to perform and about twenty minutes to discuss. Students quickly discover that a good liar can make a very credible and presentable witness, and that it is difficult to expose the lie without a confession or by other evidence that exposes the witness as a liar. Questioning to expose lies, the students quickly realize, is an art. Students begin to learn the principles of effective cross-examination and understand that those principles emerge from our common-sense experience and understanding of human behavior.

While not often performed in the law school context, at least in the United States, another experiential learning tool is the empirical research project. Such projects, which usually involve extensive interviewing of subjects in the field, expose students directly to the issues of human rights violations. Human rights missions provide similar learning opportunities and challenges for the human rights advocate.

Designing an Effective Clinical Program in Human Rights: The American University Experience

For those law students who wish to practice in the growing field of human rights advocacy, course offerings in most law schools are still relatively limited. Schools often offer only a single course, taught in traditional classroom style or perhaps as a seminar. Thus there is little experience among teachers in the design and facilitation of courses with more participatory methodologies. We now know the strengths of clinical education and a number of variations on the means by which clinical experience can be gained. This section focuses on the design of an effective clinical program in human rights.

Ideological or Institutional Limits

An inherent limitation on any clinical program will necessarily be the ideological and institutional limits in which it must operate. While clinical programs have always enjoyed a central place in the law school community at American University, other law faculties have been less receptive to clinical legal education, which many see as either a threat to the ideology of the law school classroom experience or simply as too expensive because clinics are so labor-intensive.

Logistical limits may also place constraints on the program. Because clinics operate as law offices, they must be able to provide something akin to a law office in order to be able to conduct their business. For example, there must be private client interview rooms and waiting space in the law school, or there may be problems with client access if the law school or the courts in which it operates are far from clients' homes or difficult to find. The venues in which the clinic operates must be geographically accessible and must permit students to practice before them. In the Washington area, we have the distinct advantage of having a regional asylum office, immigration courts, and the Board of Immigration Appeals, where all appeals from trials in the United States are taken, all in the same city, Arlington, Virginia. All permit supervised law students to appear before them. In the case of some human rights bodies, however, access is nearly impossible. While the clinic would benefit enormously from participation in the annual session of the Human Rights Commission in Geneva, Switzerland, in February and March each year, the venue is simply too far away and too expensive to reach.

The Service-Learning Dichotomy

The broadest goal of any clinical program in human rights is to train students to become effective advocates on behalf of victims of human rights violations. Within that goal, however, there are a number of crucial threshold choices the program must make. Perhaps the most basic involves what might be called the service-learning dichotomy. On the one hand, as with many areas of public interest practice in the law, the potential community to be served far exceeds the resources available. This puts pressure on a clinical program to provide needed services to the community in question. Heavy caseloads thus characterize this model. On the other hand, the clinic also has an obligation to train students in a thoughtful, reflective, and pedagogically sound program that legitimately claims status as an instructional program within the university community. In this model, only relatively few cases are handled, but each case is a reflective paradigm for the student's future lawyering experience. Although many argue that a clinic can effectively serve both objectives, some clinics get caught between these two competing interests, most through the basic question of caseload limits and student-teacher ratios. In the IHRLC, total caseloads for the academic year are generally limited to between twenty-five and thirty-five cases, with about six to eight cases per student team. The student-teacher ratio for all clinics in the law school never exceeds eight-to-one and is often lower.

When the IHRLC began operations in the local immigration courts in 1990, the tension between service to needy immigrants and the clinic's instructional aims became very real. A preliminary decision had been made to provide assistance to individuals seeking political asylum in the United States. These claims raised dramatic and immediate factual and legal issues. The immigrant applicant for asylum must prove a well-founded fear of persecution—that is, broadly, human rights violations—in the applicant's country of origin. Immigration Court judges were delighted to hear that supervised law students would be practicing in their courts, and immediately urged that the clinic's name be included on a list of service agencies available for referrals of the many immigrants who could not afford to hire counsel. The judges noted that the greatest need was for representation of convicted felons from foreign countries who faced deportation for their convictions. Because these persons were not entitled to counsel as a matter of right, lawyers were hard to find for them because few of the immigrants had any assets with which to pay fees; most were incarcerated at the time of their hearings. The clinic declined to undertake this kind of referral or to list itself as a referral agency, both because of a concern that the number of referrals would overwhelm the students and because of a more general concern that these cases were not strictly within the arena of human rights issues, but more within the criminal law field.

Selection of Cases and Projects

In deciding to decline a particular kind of case, the clinic faced another of the difficult threshold issues that any clinic must decide: the types of cases and projects that will be taken. Human rights, as a field, presents a clinical program with a formidable task. It must decide what type of cases it wishes to handle, which may range widely, given the breadth of existing human rights issues and instruments. It may also decide to focus on a particular country or region, or it may wish to raise international issues in its own domestic courts. In the immigration courts, for example, the clinic stood by its original decision to take only political asylum cases, which raise complex issues of international and domestic law, and to take those cases only by referral from local service agencies after a preliminary decision on the merits of the claim. Taking cases by referral from a service agency has the distinct advantage that the agency performs the task of culling out those cases that it will not take or that can be referred to other community service agencies after determining that the individual's case is not one requiring legal intervention. While such experience might be useful for the students, initial client screening consumes enormous time, and much of the work does not require the skills particular to an attorney. In Washington, D.C., the cases involving political asylum tended to come from the Latino community at the time the clinic opened, but as world and hemispheric conditions change, our client base has changed as well. In the past two years, our largest number of asylum clients come from the African countries.

About half of the IHRLC docket is political asylum cases. The other half is a combination of human rights cases and projects such as those described at the beginning of this chapter. Some of these projects are generated from within the clinic and some come to the clinic from outside referral; as the clinic's name and reputation become more widely known, a larger number of case referrals have occurred. One of the most logical places for our work, however, has been with the Inter-American Human Rights Commission, one of the regional enforcement bodies for human rights of the Organization of American States (OAS). The OAS and the Commission both have their headquarters in Washington, thereby making them logical venues in which to conduct a significant portion of the clinic's business.

The Scope of Skills Training in Lawyering

Another threshold question any human rights clinical program must face is the scope of what will constitute "lawyering" for pedagogical purposes. *Lawyering* is the term used to capture those aspects of legal training that involve skills dimensions as distinguished from doctrinal dimensions. In the legal clinics at American University, the traditional focus of the classroom component of the course has been on the teaching of litigation skills, and the cases taken by the clinic focus on advocacy through lawsuits, usually on behalf of individual clients. In the IHRLC, the question of what constitutes "litigation" and who is a "client" are not easily answered.

While cases in the Immigration Courts are adversarial proceedings before a judge, the filing of complaints before human rights bodies presents the legal clinic with dilemmas about the extent to which it is conducting "litigation." Most lawyers picture litigation as taking place in a courtroom, with a judge and jury, with witnesses and evidence offered by both sides as forcefully as each can present their version. In many of the UN human rights mechanisms, however, the process is started with a complaint that may be filed by anyone, not necessarily a lawyer, which delineates the victim's injuries and the alleged violations of human rights. The complaint may then disappear into the system, where it will be resolved by a panel of experts that the lawyer never appears before, and in fact may never see. The case may well be decided in anonymity two, three, or five years later, if at all.

It also may be extremely difficult to ascertain the wishes of the client, or even to determine who is the "client." In the examples given at the outset of this chapter, for example, who is the client when a petition is filed with an interagency body to remove Pakistan from the list of countries to which the United States accords favorable trade under the General System of Preferences? Is the client all abused workers of Pakistan, and if it is, how are their wishes and directions to be ascertained? Is the client the citizens of the United States who passed the law that promotes the use of moral standards in deciding on U.S. trade partners, and will that client wish to pursue this course of action if goods from the country in question are priced higher or taken off the market? Is the client the "issue" of the protection of human rights for workers everywhere, and if so, how is the student to decide how far to push the issue without a concrete client whose real needs are at stake? In the case filed on behalf of the Indian tribe from Colombia, is the client the tribe itself, and if so, how are the collective wishes of the tribe to be determined by their lawyers, working thousands of miles away?

In the end, human rights "lawyering" is made up of a number of components. The student must often operate without knowing a specific client's intent or desires. Because the human rights deliberative bodies are still largely nascent and unsophisticated in the review of complaints, the notion of "litigation" must be understood as advocacy in its broadest sense. Moreover, because the entire field of human rights advocacy is still in the formative stages, litigation cannot be the only arena in which the lawyer-advocate performs. Lawyers working in the human rights field must know and be able to conduct their work through litigation, legislative advocacy, and the media. Thus the most recent syllabus of the course contains class sessions devoted to each of these areas.

Setting Instructional Objectives

Having decided on caseload limits, types of projects to be worked on, and the types of lawyering to be done, there are a number of practical steps that must be taken before the clinic is opened. More than any other single factor, the setting of clear instructional objectives should be the first step in the actual design of any clinical program in human rights advocacy.[8] An objective should be concrete, measurable in both quantity and time, and capable of evaluation at the conclusion of the course. It is not enough to say, for example, that an objective of a clinical program is to "train students to become better writers." There is no way, other than subjective judgment, by which to tell when the student has accomplished the objective of "becoming better" as a writer. Instead, the instructor should be able to anticipate, at the outset of the course, when and if the student has achieved the objective. Thus a good statement of an objective relating to writing would be: "The student will prepare and submit to the Immigration Judge a memorandum of law, after revision of at least three drafts, prior to any court hearing before that judge." Or, if the task is client interviewing, the objective might be as follows: "The student will conduct at least four interviews with clients, each interview to be at least one hour in duration, during the course of the academic year." Writing objectives in this fashion gives both the teacher and the student a clear sense of what is expected and what will be measured at the time course work is evaluated for grading purposes.

Case and Classroom Components

Every good clinical program should include both a casework component and a formal classroom component. Ideally, the teacher in the classroom should also be the student's case supervisor, although many legal clinics function with some variation of this program. When the supervisor is also the classroom teacher, there are much greater possibilities for the integration of the actual lawyering experience into the more theoretical discussions in the classroom. In the IHRLC, the students are enrolled through the entire academic year. Each semester they earn four credits for their work on cases and another two for the classroom component. A rough measure of workload for students is that the student works a total of three to five hours for each hour of credit. Thus the students spend about twelve to twenty hours on cases each week, on average, and about six to ten hours per week preparing for the seminar.

"Case rounds" meetings are the formal bridge between practice and theory in the IHRLC. Every other week through the school year, one student team prepares and leads an hour-long session on a lawyering issue that is ongoing in a specific case. Like their analogue in the medical field, the students diagnose the problem during rounds and offer their proposed "cure." The range of topics is broad, and students may select any topic that meets the approval of the faculty supervisor. Typical topics in rounds include difficult substantive or procedural issues that might benefit from group discussion; difficulties and proposed solutions to researching areas of international law; problems of communication and "nonlegal" questions raised during client interviews and counseling sessions; time management questions; ethical dilemmas presented by clients; and difficulties in collaboration or supervision.

Enhancing Legal Literacy Among Thailand's Rural Poor
by Richard Pierre Claude

The principal law schools and all the major law firms in Thailand are centered in the capital city of Bangkok whose urban sprawl, congested traffic, and air pollution evidence a booming economy in the 1990s. As a consequence of the metropolitan concentration of wealth and power, legal literacy among Thailand's rural poor is very limited. The peasants' lack of knowledge about the law and about their constitutional rights is a key causal factor in the continuing violation of their human rights.

Most internationally defined human rights have been incorporated into modern Thai law and thrive under a democratic regime characterized as a constitutional monarchy. But those largely left behind in Thailand's march toward political stability and prosperity are the rural farming people.

The Thongbai Thongpao Foundation (TTF) brings legal assistance to Thailand's rural people, conducting training on basic human rights and the law for daily life. Participants in the training include teachers, students, and women leaders, as well as poor farmers. Among the peasants and rural folk, a majority of whom are women, TTF directly supplies legal assistance on a free basis to individuals whose problems range from family conflicts to land disputes to human rights violations. The TTF Center set up at the village of Amphur Buayai was organized according to a work plan devised by the people with consulting teachers. Its presence in the community saves peasants with legal problems from expensive and intimidating trips to Bangkok.

Since 1987, Thongbai Thongpao and a team of clinical trainees and lawyers typically leave their Bangkok offices Friday evenings for the village where they have arranged to teach. The lawyers and educators participating in the weekend "Law to the Villages" program take no fee.

Over the course of two full days of education and training, villagers learn about constitutional law, human rights, marriage, loans and mortgages, labor law, and other legal issues that concern them. Lectures and discussion are used, concluding with a dramatized illustration of a court case.

The program is capped by an ingenious idea worthy of emulation and intended to empower peasants. Their troubles are often connected to officials, moneylenders, and developers. Such powerful people usually assume, often correctly, that peasants have no knowledge of the law, have no access to lawyers, and can thus easily be exploited. In the face of this situation, the "Law to the Villages" program concludes each training session by setting up a paralegal committee and giving participants who complete the program a photo identification card with the name and signature of their personal lawyer.

In rural classes when appropriate, Thongbai Thongpao will act as *pra ek* (role model), sharing with country people the history of his own experience, from which he draws two lessons: do not be discouraged by adversity, and use the law to change your lives.

Thongbai Thongpao was born into rural poverty in the village of Maha Sarakham. He managed to pay his Thammasat University tuition for his B.A. in law but "had to drop out of school many times to work for my keep."[1] In 1958, as part of an international exchange program, he was invited to China. On returning, he was arrested at the Dorn Muang International Airport and charged with being a communist, which he denied. He spent the next eight years as a prisoner of conscience in Bangkok's notorious Lard Yao jail. For many this would be enough to lose faith in the law, but Thongbai describes his time in prison as a turning point that led him and other detainees to devote their legal skills to helping political prisoners and the underprivileged.

In 1984, in recognition of his achievements, Thongbai Thongpao received the Magsaysay award, Asia's equivalent of the Nobel Peace Prize. It was given "in recognition of his effective and fair use of his legal skills and pen to defend those who have 'less in life and thus need more in law.'" In 1990 he created the TTF center, which enshrines his ideals and is often compared to other NGOs in the Asia-Pacific area devoted to human rights education and the enhancement of legal literacy such as the José Diokno Foundation in the Philippines and the Legal Aid Institute of Indonesia, founded by Buyung Adnan Nasution.

The challenges to the foundation have not diminished with the expansion of Thai prosperity. Human rights problems are growing, as suggested by the increasing number of cases handled by TTF lawyers and the number of requests for human rights and legal literacy courses in the countryside. Moreover, Thailand's increasing prosperity, quite evident in Bangkok, amplifies old problems and creates new ones for the rural poor. According to Thongbai Thongpao's analysis: "In rural areas, many farmers have become virtual slaves to the moneylenders and to the government's rural credit programs. The farmers are unable to repay their debts and end up losing their land."

Thongbai Thongpao holds government policy responsible for many problems of the rural poor. For example, he point out that "A number of peasants have lost their land to government developments, such as dam construction. They are relocated in areas which are not appropriate for farming." Tragically, these landless farmers often gravitate to the Bangkok slums. He says: "In modern Thailand, the real power of the law and the state resides not with the ordinary people but with the investors and industrialists."

Thongbai Thongpao not only criticizes government policies sharply, but, in

---

1. Interview by the author of Thongbai Thongpao at the TTF office, Bangkok, March 30, 1995.

the spirit of democracy, he also cooperates constructively with government. For example, the TTF works with the Ministry of the Interior to run human rights training programs for government officials who are working in community development projects. It has also developed evening labor law programs and "Law to the Schools" programs for secondary schools.

Summarizing the work of the legal literacy programs in factories and schools, the human rights training programs, and the "Law to the Villages," Thongbai Thongpao denies that his object is to sow the seeds of social unrest. Any such suggestion misunderstands human rights and democracy. He says: "My work is strictly in accordance with the constitution and the law. Indeed, it is our duty to educate people about their rights before the law so that they will be able to be responsible citizens."

Problems Particular to International Human Rights Advocacy

One of the developing practical problems of the IHRLC is that of ongoing cases. Many of the cases or projects in which the clinic provides assistance take more than a single academic year for resolution; some of the cases opened in the first year of the clinic's operation, for example, are still open as of this writing. This type of caseload might be distinguished from that of other clinics such as the Criminal Justice Clinic, where cases are resolved in a matter of weeks due to the entry point in the process and statutory speedy trial rules, or the Law Students in Court Clinic, where high-volume Rent Court practice means adjudication of many cases in a single day. In the IHRLC, about twenty to twenty-five cases will carry over from academic year to year. This means that multiple generations of law students will work with each file and client. This phenomenon has not yet proven too burdensome for the clinic or its students, but may in the future.

Another difficulty in an international human rights clinic is the practical problem of fact gathering, information sharing, client contact, and confidentiality over great distances. In some circumstances, our clients live in another country. The most basic question is how to investigate and document their factual claims without actually traveling to the country. Even without travel funds, additional fiscal resources must be available for the added expense of international phone calling, faxing, and mailing. The clinic often cooperates with local nongovernmental organizations or counsel in gathering facts, but the logistical challenges alone in such situations are formidable. Requests for information often take months to fulfill, and sometimes the information provided barely resembles the request made.

Confidentiality of communications presents another difficulty for the clinic. Ethical obligations of the profession require that all private communications between lawyer and client be protected from revelation by the lawyer. If there is an expectation that the information is provided by the client in confidence, the lawyer must protect that confidentiality under professional rules of law practice. Thus, in every communication with an overseas client, great care must be taken when public means of communication are used, such as telephones or faxes.

Sometimes communication itself may be dangerous or inadvisable for the client. This often happens with asylum applicants who are reluctant to communicate with family members because such communication may request information that cannot be provided without putting the family member at risk, or that may put the family member in danger, if sympathy is suspected by that person with one who is sought as an enemy of the government. It may also happen with a client who is abroad, where contact with a lawyer from another country, if discovered, may put the client's life in danger.

Evaluation of Student Performance

A final concern in human rights clinical work occurs with the evaluation of student performance. Unlike other courses in the law school, where a single test can evaluate the student's ability to remember legal principles and recognize them in factual context, clinic work is experiential and necessarily includes a wide range of skills on which evaluation might be based. Suggested areas of evaluation include legal reasoning, communication skills, professional responsibility, theoretical understanding, clinical judgment, and time management. It is extremely difficult to give a single grade that fairly and adequately summarizes the student's work in the clinic, but such is the task for the law professor.

In the IHRLC, two solutions to this problem are suggested. Although single, separate grades are given each semester for the seminar and casework, students are given a specific sense of their progress and areas in which work is needed at the end of the first semester. Moreover, close supervision and opportunity for self-evaluation and reflection, both before and after the completion of specific tasks, give the students direct and immediate information about their progress in specific areas and suggestions for future improvement.

Conclusion: Teaching Human Rights Experientially in Nonlegal Contexts

This chapter is written from the perspective of the use of clinical education in human rights advocacy in a law school. However, the premises that underlie the use of experiential models for learning, as delineated above, make this style of "learning by doing" available in a much wider spectrum of learning contexts, both within educational institutions and in the field. Moreover, there are a wide range of "clinical" methodologies available to the teacher and trainer which might be incorporated into any human rights education program.

Fact gathering regarding human rights violations by field advocates, for example, might best be taught experientially. Factual documentation of violations usually comes from one of two sources: eyewitnesses who give statements or testimony, or tangible evidence such as documents, physical objects, photographs, or blood-stained clothing. Newspapers and other periodicals sometimes provide accurate accounts of events, but these sources cannot be relied upon to document facts sufficiently for human rights fact-finding bodies, which often operate, sometimes implicitly, with quasi-legal rules of evidence or proof. A lecture on fact gathering might begin to expose the human rights advocate to some of the issues that occur in that context, but arguably the best way to teach the process of fact gathering is to have a student attempt to interview a witness to an occurrence, whether the occurrence is real or invented.

The interview, which may be with an actual client or with another student playing the role of the client, might be conducted one-on-one with the instructor observing or might be conducted publicly in front of a group of student observers. The interviewer can immediately verbalize difficulties in the process, and the student observers can immediately begin to discern principles of effective interviewing which they might apply themselves. The instructor, alert to the issues involved in fact gathering, can begin with the concrete experience of the actual interview and inductively apply that situation to general problems encountered in fact gathering.

Fact gathering is one of several skills used by human rights advocates everywhere, whether they are lawyers or not. Other common skills are interviewing, persuasive written and oral advocacy, speaking to elected representatives, and writing press releases, to name a few that have been discussed here. These tasks are done by human rights advocates from many fields: law, medicine, journalism, anthropology, sociology, criminology, and ethnography are only some. In each of these fields, experiential methods of teaching and learning provide human rights advocates with stimulating and highly motivational contexts in which to develop their skills and knowledge.

Notes

1. William B. Powers, *A Study in Contemporary Law School Curricula* (Cincinnati: Office of the Consultant on Legal Education to the American Bar Association, 1986), 12.

2. Ibid., 18.

3. Ibid., 54.

4. Andrew J. Pirie, "Objectives in Legal Education: The Case for Systematic Instructional Design," *Journal of Legal Education* 37 (1987): 576–97, at 581–82.

5. Richard B. Lillich, *International Human Rights: Problems of Law, Policy, and Practice,* 2d ed. (Boston: Little Brown, 1991); Frank Newman and David Weissbrodt, *International Human Rights: Law, Policy, and Process* (Cincinnati: Anderson Publishing Co., 1990).

6. Frank S. Bloch, "The Andragogical Basis of Clinical Legal Education," *Vanderbilt Law Review* 35 (1982): 321–53.

7. Judith V. Torney, Abraham N. Oppenheim, and Russell F. Farnenet, *Civic Education in Ten Countries: An Empirical Study* (New York: John Wiley, 1975), 151–53. The ten countries were the Federal Republic of Germany, Finland, Iran, Ireland, Israel, Italy, the Netherlands, New Zealand, Sweden, and the United States.

8. See generally, Pirie, "Objectives in Legal Education," 576. Andrew Petter, "A Closet Within the House: Learning Objectives and the Law School Curriculum," in *Essays on Legal Education,* ed. Neil Gold (Toronto: Butterworths, 1982), 77.

Chapter 17
Human Rights Education for Law Enforcement

Edy Kaufman

In the last few years, the issue of teaching human rights to the military and police has become highly controversial.[1] On the one hand, an opportunity emerged when processes of democratization brought to power civilian leaders interested in curbing the past repressive practices of those who monopolized state violence. Both regimes, emerging from bureaucratic-authoritarianism as well as postcommunist societies, have begun to feel a need to retrain their armies and secret services—once instruments for disseminating fear and increasing control—to move toward the respect of individual freedoms. On the other hand, there has been a high degree of skepticism as to the effectiveness and nature of human rights education (HRE) of those who have been responsible for the worst violations. Human rights organizations and educators have been concerned that, given the nature and structure of military institutions, the restrictive conditions for the insertion of this new field into their curricula will provide a fig leaf without significant behavioral impact.[2] From their own perspective, military elites have often perceived human rights to be the weapon used against them by the opposition.[3] Their reluctance to be "reprogrammed" could make such an endeavor futile.[4]

In such a complex world, it is not simple to delineate general priority goals for this kind of instruction. When recognizing the positive nature of HRE as a tool for empowerment and prevention of gross violations, it makes sense to include students from noncivilian institutions in the educating effort undertaken in society at large. Furthermore, since state violence has been conducted through the misuse of such forces, the priority of generating attitudinal change is self-evident. The difficulties involved in the introduction of HRE should not be a deterrent for serious and systematic efforts in its planning and implementation. The point of departure from post-apartheid for the South African police has been to move away from protecting the settlers' interest from the "threats" posed by the indigenous population toward racial equality.[5] In Argentina the armed forces were responsible for the abduction and death of more than twelve thousand "disappearances," and the "dirty war" concept needs to be replaced by a profound respect for the lives of all citizens. The task in many places is formidable. Yet encouraging deference toward the entire range of civil and political rights, which encompasses the acceptance of the legitimately elected government, cannot exclude the socialization of law enforcement agents to guarantee respect for fundamental rights such as the freedom from torture, political imprisonment, or arbitrary killings.[6] Furthermore, in the post–cold war period, with the changing nature of wars from external to domestic, and the replacement of unilateral intervention with multilateral peacekeeping missions, training for a domestic or foreign civilian population becomes an imperative for most armies. Nowadays, the concept of collective security requires a working knowledge of human rights principles in addition to competence in traditional military skills.

In a confidential survey conducted by the University of Utrecht regarding HRE in the military (September 1991), only twelve governments, of the sixty-five countries that responded, provided no human rights education, including a few with some humanitarian law curricula or unclear answers. The remaining fifty-three countries confirmed that HRE consisted of "an introduction to international, regional and national human rights law, and humanitarian law . . . and is compulsory to everyone entering the military service."[7] Most of the states listed were democracies with no significant patterns of gross human rights violations, but the survey also included other countries that, from the author's personal knowledge, do not seem to have a significant program of HRE and demonstrate patterns of serious human abuses. This observation calls for some caution in taking all positive responses by governments to be bona fide. In addition, eight governments, mostly microstates (but also including Costa Rica and Panama), answered that they had no military forces whatsoever—only police. Approximately seventy-two of the nonrespondents do have a military force and in many cases present a pattern of gross human rights violations. But some among them are known to have some degree of HRE. An additional thirty-nine countries, mostly microstates, associated states, islands, and former small trusteeships and colonies without a significant army and no serious record of human rights violations, also failed to respond to the survey.

The status of HRE in this mixed picture has most likely improved in the last three years, and at first glance it reveals a more optimistic picture than would be expected. However, the majority of states may be focusing mostly on humanitarian law—a traditional field in military institutions and related to wartime situations. It is unclear how much space remains for human rights concerns. Focusing primarily on humanitarian law would make more sense for countries where the military is normally not engaged in domestic law enforcement. Furthermore, the mere insertion of human rights issues into instruction is a necessary, but not sufficient, condition. In most cases, the apparently legalistic training does not provide an in-depth analysis of previous and expected behavior of forces that have often engaged in human rights violations in the past decade, and may even continue to do so while exposed to HRE. Many of those who have been through basic training and specialized courses would admit that the reference to humanitarian law, let alone human rights, is conducted in a minimalist and formal manner, with the risk of epitomizing a ritual required by the authorities from above. In some cases, sporadic courses offered to a minority within the military and police institution have been mostly a lip service in response to domestic and foreign pressures. Often the brief references to human rights documents are included in legal courses or in ethics. There are also different cases, such as the Philippines, where it needs to be acknowledged that HRE has been an integral part of an overall systematic effort across military personnel of different levels.[8]

The shortcomings of all new ventures limit this brief study, which attempts to cover in-depth the issue of HRE in law enforcement agencies. Much of the research demanded for such work is yet to be conducted. Only by overcoming both the lack and biases of information, as well as existing suspicions, can involved parties candidly share their attitudes and assessments about the issue. At this stage, what follows should be seen as a preliminary effort, which needs to be followed by a more systematic evaluation as the result of a collaborative venture. The main areas covered are the following: HRE teachers and trainees, HRE and political considerations, the human rights environment and curricula, and HRE and evaluation. At this stage, I have opted to leave out the treatment of the issue of HRE of foreign military and police personnel as provided by regional organizations in Europe and the Americas and bilaterally by the United States. Rich material is already available and merits to be studied and reported more extensively than the limitations of this chapter permit.

Briefly, the Centre for Human Rights of the United Nations has been involved during several years in the area of our concern. Initially, it prepared courses for military, police, and prison officials together. In the last couple of years, through the Programme of Technical Cooperation in the Field of Human Rights and using mostly means at the disposal of the Voluntary Fund, the Centre developed a specific approach for the different law enforcement agencies. Lately the Centre has stressed more exercises designed to "sensitize trainees to their own potential for violative behavior" rather than the simple acquisition of knowledge about human rights standards. When involved in the preparation of a needs assessment of human rights in a given country, the Centre's experts make a point to include the requirements of humanitarian law and HRE for those who are given the monopoly of violence with a view of training them in its legitimate use. Those responsible for teaching are preferably related to the same professional group of the trainees, making a special effort in involving military officers as instructors.

Countries that have been involved in such training include Egypt, Namibia, Ecuador, Georgia, the Russian Federation, the new Palestinian police, as well as Mexico, Chad, Zambia, Nepal, Romania, and Haiti. The Centre's course for law enforcement and prison officials includes the sources, systems, and standards for international human rights law in the administration of criminal justice; the duties and guiding principles of ethical police conduct; the use of force in law enforcement; the crime of torture; effective methods of legal and ethical intervening during arrest and interrogation; the legal status and rights of the accused; standards for search and seizure.

Finally, although this chapter has kept the general format of HRE, the analysis also includes some reference to training. Emphasis on intellectual development and critical thinking skills needs to be accompanied by job-oriented instruction, specifically relating to the limits of legitimate law enforcement tasks of the holders of the instruments of state violence.

The Teachers and Trainees

The issue of the target audiences for HRE varies according to the democratic record of the country concerned and the relative level of stability in the country. According to a defense minister of the Netherlands: "The primary source of my concern with human rights as viewed from my official function is to ensure, both on a purely national and an international level, the compliance with the laws of armed conflict. . . . Increasingly the laws of armed conflict have come to deal with other matters than purely military affairs."[9] Whereas that may be most relevant for some western European countries, in many other parts of the world the military is typically involved in domestic functions, often with actions ranging from the excessive use of force to political killings and massacres. HRE is a priority not only for those normally involved in the policing function, but also for those who exercise legitimate use of violence in their own nations.[10] Hence, as a generalization and in order to play it safe, it may be best to include all branches of the military, the different police forces, and the secret, security, and penitentiary service. New police forces have been organized in several countries, which, from their inception, have included HRE as a salient feature. This includes El Salvador and Ecuador, where the new formations—specifically the Policia Judicial in the latter state—have created tensions with the established military institutions.[11] If not for any other reason, the assumption that the civilian institutions at large are moving toward the introduction of HRE encourages us not to exclude this universal effort.[12] Those who are trained separately should have at least the opportunity to become citizens as conscientious as the rest of the population. Until processes of democratization are completed and the delimitations of the jurisdiction are well understood by both civilian and military personnel, the broader approach should be preferred. Here I deal with the entire range and normally describe them as "law enforcement agencies." Needless to say, the application of the suggested principles requires an adaptation to particular national realities. This may require designing differentiated curricula sensitive to the cultural background, the distinct functions of each force, and the level and age of students in each.

Within such institutions, appropriate curricula should be developed for the different ranks, and as much as possible should be extended to the entire body of members. It may be a point in preselecting those who are going to form the professional and permanent component of the law enforcement agencies in a way in which the personality and values will not be in flagrant contradiction with respect for human rights. Before proceeding to select potential HRE teachers, it is an important consideration that they be selected from among those who have the best chance to be effective and accepted communicators. No less important is to ensure that the personality and motivation of the future trainers should be congruent with humanistic attitudes. Inasmuch as local nongovernmental human rights organizations are well equipped and could be further trained in assuming such a role, it is likely that some law enforcement institutions and their members will perceive their role as an antagonistic ploy, tacitly or overtly resisting it.

That does not mean that one should not aspire to gradually involve nongovernmental organizations (NGOs) as much as possible. In the case of Israel, the Association for Civil Rights and other voluntary organizations carry a significant part of the HRE burden in the police, border guards, and the military; some preliminary evaluations seem to indicate a good level of acceptance by the trainees.[13] In the case of Peru, INIDEN (Instituto de Investigación de la Defensa Nacional), an NGO founded by retired high-ranking military officers, has been sporadically offering a twelve-session course (twenty-four teaching hours).[14] Still, the effect may not be magnified both in terms of its limited scale and in the current informative (rather than formative) curricula. In several cases, the issue of civil-military relations can be represented by training two potential teachers for both sectors, hence making it a subject of common concern and preparation. Whereas some institutions include highly educated, permanent teachers (often with a doctorate) with a military rank, some academies retain only civilians as part of the permanent teaching staff. The military move ahead to continue their career patterns. Even so, their training in HRE may not be an initial loss, but rather a long-term investment since the trainee can carry his pedagogic knowledge to the field units that are often in the areas of conflict. For instance, in Peru the different military zones have a post for a human rights office, and ideally the person in charge also could be trained. In some countries, heads of military academies have later become key figures in the ranks and even have promoted themselves to become military rulers of the country (as in the case of Guatemala's Politecnico).[15] Looking ahead, it would be extremely important to detect those who have the potential to reach the top echelons in the military teaching institutions in order to sensitize them to the advantages of HRE. Ideally, the training of the trainers should strive to involve both the civilian/military staff of the teaching institution as well as NGO personnel committed to professionalizing themselves in the area of HRE.

HRE and Political Considerations

Christian Bay's concept of "political education as a liberating process"[16] can produce different reactions when it relates to the HRE of law enforcement agencies. At the more general level of civil/military relations, it has been argued that the professionalization of such institutions should be meticulously conducted with the purpose of keeping political issues away from their formative training.[17] In an article about the armed forces in Mexico, William Ackroyd insists that as education increases, so does political efficacy that correlates with participation and increases probabilities of military intervention.[18]

Expressing a contrary and widely shared view, a top representative of the Spanish Civil Guard has elaborated the positive experience of his forces in bringing HRE theory closer to praxis by advocating an "active pedagogy" that helps "generate the activity and the habit to work within the respect of the rights and liberties. Generating a moral consciousness that rejects the actions contrary to the respect of the individual's rights, and building an awareness of loyalty towards the community, require a sensibility adequate for perceiving the social demands posed on our public service."[19]

The insertion of HRE within the wider field of social science education reform should be seen as part of the process of acceptance of civil supremacy by law enforcement agencies. It has often been viewed as a renewed politicization of these bodies. This concern is not confined to the cases of transitions from authoritarian rule where the military played a leading role as a corporate body. The introduction of a human rights curriculum could be seen with some preoccupation both in postcommunist as well as postdictatorial regimes. In Poland, for instance, the new National Defense Academy established in 1990 was said to have been "depoliticized," rejecting the previous slogan "every officer is a trained Marxist" and an expert on "political-military matters."[20] The new "educational officer" has to detach himself from such a past. In Mexico, according to Ackroyd, military personnel are less educated than civilians and refrain from participation in politics due to an "inferiority complex." From this the author infers that "Mexico's interaction, therefore, builds an image of superior civilian politicians and diminishes the relative political efficacy of Mexican officers."[21] A contending view stresses that data support the hypothesis that officers with graduate degrees tend to be less absolutist than officers without graduate degrees.[22] While there may be a risk of politicization when dealing with human rights issues—particularly if they are adapted from the universal, abstract level to the concrete problems of a particular country—it only emphasizes the importance of training in a way that avoids development of partisan attitudes and clearly establishes the supremacy of democratically elected ruler as a result of the respect of civil and political rights. In some cases, loyalty to the nation rather than loyalty to the elected ruler has been mentioned as the top priority.[23] In the Philippines, on the other hand, HRE has been seen by Richard P. Claude as a key element in regulating civil/military and police relations, with a comprehensive "top-down" approach.[24]

Among liberal educators, the hierarchical structure and unquestioned discipline of the military have been viewed as potential obstacles in the teaching of human rights. Within a polarized political context, it is understandable that the military establishment views HRE as an effort to "subvert" their ranks from previously held doctrines. Furthermore, there is a sense that such a drive may even internally destabilize the hierarchical order and strict discipline.[25] In the face of such fears, it has been important to make a persuasive case that "respect for human rights enhances discipline in the armed forces."[26]

In Latin America, both civilians and the military have pondered the advantages of the nondeliberative role of the armed forces in nonmilitary matters. However, it is arguable in which direction intense exposure to social sciences actually shapes perceptions of national and international political realities. The attempt to exclude law enforcement agencies from a consensual understanding of the priority values of global human rights, democracy, and the pursuit of world peace is mostly futile and counterproductive.[27] Furthermore, although the evolving technology places demands on sophisticated armies in a constant upgrade of technological knowledge, David Segal predicts that in the long run "the balance will move back toward a recognition of the importance of a liberal education for military professionals."[28] Most likely, in the post–cold war era, such liberal education will increasingly include a dimension of human rights education.

The place of HRE in either secluded military settings or joint civilian establishments should be seen in the overall context of the debate on the advantages and disadvantages of the separateness of law enforcement educational institutions. While not disregarding the technical and specialized nature of military training, the introduction of social science and humanistic curricula within such frameworks can produce different results according to the degree and well-established respect of civilian supremacy and the challenges to the monopoly on the use of force by belligerent groups within the country.

A debate arose in countries such as the German Federal Republic when in 1973 it opened the gates of the first military universities in Hamburg and Munich to officers and cadets of the Bundeswehr.[29] In Israel as well as the United States, holding a B.A. from a university is increasingly an asset for becoming a high-ranking officer. The general trend in the West and in rapidly developing countries such as the Republic of Korea has been toward becoming increasingly dependent on civilian colleges for officer education and toward reflecting the diversity of civilian universities within a military university system.[30] It is difficult to take an overall stand in terms of HRE as to the possible shortcomings of such separateness, but it can be argued that the strengthening of civil-military relations based on clear democratic principles should be seen as an integral part of the educating process.

Inviting selected civilians to be trained at military institutions did not seem to have been sufficiently successful in the acceptance of democratic values and specific respect for fundamental human rights, particularly in the case of Brazil and other developing countries. Since the 1960s, preparation of these countries' militaries in counterinsurgency strategies has resulted in a new professionalism with a role expansion that includes severe control of civilian populations in combat areas, often perceived as the country at large.[31] The answer is not to avoid the political socialization of the law enforcement agents, but rather to make human rights "a constituent part of their being as professionals."[32]

In countries such as Guatemala, the effect of total separation "is to reinforce the 'we-they' distinction setting the officer corps off from the rest of society, and to strengthen a new sense of belonging within the brotherhood of officers that cannot be found outside."[33] Such separation has often resulted in an exaggerated disciplinary supervision, lack of personal responsibility, and blind obedience to illegal commands.

Furthermore, the issue of the rights of the military often arises. From the perspective of the individual soldier, "human rights can play two important roles. In the first place, also soldiers have in principle the right to exercise all kinds of individual rights and freedoms. . . . In the second place, in discharging their duties soldiers have to observe the human rights of the population."[34] In dealing with HRE, the issue is whether or not we want to affect attitudes in both senses or only in the latter. It could be argued that the best way for becoming aware of the rights of the other (civilians) is to be empowered in the demand of their own (law enforcement agencies) rights in a democratic society. However, for some emerging democracies, ideas that may go as far as the right of the military to be unionized may be perceived to be counterproductive, and may damage the possibilities of introducing HRE.

In some countries, particularly in Latin America, the members of the armed forces still do not vote,[35] and in many countries in transition to democratization, particularly in the former Soviet sphere of influence, many have experienced degradation in terms of salary.[36] When casualties of combat in internal violence occur, the lack of adequate compensation for the victim's family is seen as the lack of recognition for the sacrifice that they make for the country's benefit. There is an ambiguity as to the right of law enforcement agencies to discuss and express their views publicly in a matter pertinent to the effectiveness of their work, such as the introduction of capital punishment or conscientious objection and alternative service. To what extent should these issues be part of the HRE curricula? With regard to civilians, I have mentioned Paulo Freire's stress on the empowerment aspect of education.[37] Is this an additional objective for HRE of law enforcement agents? It seems that the "right to know your own rights" is a necessary precondition for the genuine acceptance of the rights of the others. However, one can demand the unconditional observance of fundamental human rights, but the pedagogic question of inner acceptance must also be addressed.

The Human Rights Environment and Curricula Considerations

In addition to the pedagogic advantages and disadvantages of introducing a human rights curriculum as a separate and distinct unit, the above-mentioned political aspects need to be taken into account. In countries where human rights has been perceived as a "subversive" issue, introducing the subject gradually within other broad subjects (often in social sciences, philosophy, or international law courses) may decrease the chances of HRE becoming a meaningless ritual. Hence what would normally be a purely pedagogic consideration in this case also involves the need to legitimize human rights as an integral and salient part of law enforcement agents' process of socialization. The introduction of HRE in law enforcement agencies could be the result of different strategies: (a) a gradual expansion of already existing curricula on "humanitarian law," given that there are many overlapping areas and that many domestic conflicts with a violent opposition are often considered to be belligerent parties; (b) a recognition of the political importance of listing such an item for "public relations" purposes—particularly for increasing the chances of foreign military assistance[38]—a concession that may open up space for potentially good teaching; or (c) as a result of legislation imposed on them by the civilian authorities. For example, in the case of the Philippines, Presidential Memorandum Order Number 20 (dated July 4, 1986) instructs the president as the commander in chief of all armed forces to make sure that the continuance in office of law enforcement officials shall depend on "their successfully completing the course offered under the [human rights education] program."[39] Furthermore, the official Commission on Human Rights has been monitoring compliance and effective implementation.[40]

In western Europe in 1978 the Committee of Ministers of the Council of Europe adopted a resolution requiring member states "to promote the teaching of the safeguard of human rights and the relevant protection machinery in an appropriate manner as part of the training for members of the civil and military services."[41] Rather than confronting the students with HRE as a compulsory subject or a way of "punishment" for past collective crimes, the strategy should be based on reaching an agreement with military academic authorities. Questions may arise when the agreement is a result of dubious considerations. However, the mechanism of institutionalization eventually ensures that we are not left with only cosmetic changes.

Much needs to be said about the importance of the environment for the teaching of human rights. First, we have to acknowledge that in many cases among the ranks HRE may produce some cognitive dissonance with previously accepted values and perhaps concurrent courses that tend to stress aspects of the "national security doctrine"[42] (often antithetical to HRE). Furthermore, it is questionable whether one can deal with the future without acknowledging the importance of past abuses. In an ideal world, it would be best to monitor the entire teaching of the social sciences and nonmilitary subjects with a view to eradicate any negative attitudes toward the respect for civilian supremacy and professional ethics. However, a second-best incremental approach indicates that introduction of human rights as a separate subject is most likely to offer less corporate resistance than the elimination of "negative" existing curricula. Pedagogically speaking, as in all other subjects in the social sciences—which

Figure 17.1. In 1976 a security guard in Johannesburg arrested a peaceful demonstrator for protesting against the apartheid policies then prevailing in South Africa. Apartheid laws, finally repealed in 1990, allowed the ruling minority to segregate and exploit the majority of Africans, Asians, and Coloreds. (UNPHOTO/contact NJ)

often comprehend between 30 to 60 percent of the subjects taught—the best way of learning HRE is interactive, by discussion rather than repetition, and so on. An overall attack on the current teaching techniques may require a transformation that is too demanding for some institutions, albeit necessary. Still, the teaching of human rights can become a little microcosm of the type of effective learning that could be used in other areas, but not necessarily to condition its introduction to the implementation of comprehensive changes throughout the entire school.

On a related issue, Abraham Magendzo[43] and others have pointed out that the institutional environment needs to emphasize the priority of inclusion of human rights issues and positive public reinforcement in the speeches of high-ranking commanders (i.e., "the police are *par definition* the guarantor of human rights"[44]), with specific reference to the pertinent articles of the Universal Declaration of Human Rights (UDHR) or similar national legislation. A "Declaration on the Police" was promulgated by the

Parliamentary Assembly of the Council of Europe in 1979, with strong human rights wording.[45] In the case of the new police force in South Africa, a new code of ethics has been widely circulated,[46] and the Philippine police force has also endorsed the principles of the UDHR. Amnesty International, in its campaigns for the abolition of torture, recommended that the text of the UDHR be posted in all military installations. Views that such recognition is more likely to reduce human rights violations in the same physical premises may be worth exploring. Such dissonance may result in the sharpening of the spirit of the individual person to act according to the established norms, and it may encourage resistance to the principle of "due obedience" to illegal orders.[47]

The celebration of December 10 as a "human rights day" in the world, and in the country of the law enforcement agents, should be an opportunity for joining both the civil and military sectors of society in a joint celebration. In Israel, the Association for Civil Rights in Israel (ACRI) has been instrumental in developing a tradition for the police forces to celebrate December as "human rights month," combining formal and informal educational activities.

In the same vein, it may be important to promote the application of human rights principles in concrete cases by institutionalizing special awards, highlighting successful completion for HRE as a factor for promotion, widely publicizing cases of respect for human rights in difficult circumstances, and so on. Whereas in many countries the issue of impunity for past violations has been raised after the fall of the military from power, less emphasis has been placed on rewarding its observance. This respect for human rights cannot be taken as a given in the short run; it should be stimulated by constructive means and positive arguments.[48] Still, the question of punishing those who committed atrocities in the past remains a highly controversial issue. Notwithstanding that in many places the process of democratization did not provide civilian governments with sufficient political power to implement harsh penalties, the issue of retribution as an effective learning tool is still valid. While discipline within the ranks has emphasized castigation, experts wonder to what extent HRE should relate to such principles.

Some fear has been expressed as to the impact of introducing HRE into the hierarchical structures within the military organization.[49] Whereas automatic and blind obedience can be reduced, it may be argued that a thinking subordinate in the ranks can provide better results in actual combat and control functions over civilian populations. A significant discussion about the functional differences between the civilian and military operational structures can be beneficial, establishing the limits to and need for due obedience in a clearer manner.

The training of teachers for human rights curricula is not to be understood as a one-time affair, but should include tutorial advice, evaluation based on observation in the classroom, and continuous education and further training, up to the point at which the human rights subject becomes integrated and, at the same time, an intrinsically different part of the overall program.

There is wide agreement that the introduction of HRE has first to reflect the understanding of the basic international human rights documents (often referred to as the International Bill of Rights) and the compliance of domestic law to such standards. However, there have often been cases where national legislation and particularly exceptional and emergency clauses seem not to conform to such global principles, creating a dissonance as well as some disbelief about its applicability in a reality test. In many countries, the general erosion of the rule of law has generated, in the eyes of the population at large, a high degree of cynicism where a legitimate gap between the norm and its immediate execution is widely accepted. Furthermore, the need to go beyond the legalistic introduction of the subject has been mentioned by several scholars. We are not only interested in providing the necessary information about humanitarian and human rights law, but essentially interested in affecting people's attitudes in a positive way. Whether behavior can also be affected positively has been debated by some American defenders of the current International Military Education and Training Program.[50] In any case, approaching the subject matter solely on the theoretical level without insisting on discussing its application to reality, may be, to say the least, a noneffective method of teaching. It may even result in the previously mentioned "fig leaf" of serious violators with a human rights certificate. The use of audiovisual material about other countries and their own society may be a powerful mean for generating in-depth discussions. Educational material in the human rights field is available. It may be important to use proactive learning and experiential techniques such as role-playing, facilitating discussions, and so on, to make HRE not only an informative but also a formative experience.

Evaluation

The controversial nature of this field requires, above all, confidence-building strategies and a genuine effort to assess the advance in the implementation of such a new and controversial field. Such evaluation should be undertaken not only on terms of financial cost-benefit, but primarily in assessing if the investment has resulted in attitudinal changes. More specifically, the reduction of the levels of violations needs to be evaluated in countries with a pattern of human rights violations inflicted through the same institutions that are being trained in HRE. Such has been the claim of the Human Rights Commission in the Philippines[51] and in some of the comments of the NGO involved in the HRE of the Israeli Border Police. Sometimes superficial evaluation efforts are only a response to civilian institutional demands, and the answers are bluntly manipulative or shallow.[52] In most cases, the absence of evaluation altogether or its incipient use justifies the development of evaluative tools and their systematic use to conduct many case studies across the globe, with a view of learning both from shortcomings and potential successes.

From the little that has already taken place in the field, it becomes imperative that the evaluation task be conducted by independent and competent experts selected from the field of human rights, education, and the military. In the case of the training of foreign military personnel by the Department of Defense, such possibilities have been initially restricted by the lack of interest of those involved in the running of such programs. Perhaps it may be worth considering having the military and police personnel joining such teams in order to facilitate the introduction of future adjustments to their current HRE programs. In all cases, given the premature stage of this field, an open-ended planning process that takes into account the feedback of evaluation results is required in order to satisfy the internal institutional and external oversight function of government, regional, and international organizations.

The evaluation process will not be revised if the selection and organization of goals and contents have been respected. It will check to see if existing prejudices and stereotypes have diminished, as well as if the attachment to human rights values has been evolving as planned.

Conclusion

The introduction and improvement of HRE for law enforcement agents is an important element for the consolidation of democracy and should be conducted from within and above the institutions. Specific constitutional references to HRE could be a public indication of the country's preference, and active participation of the military and police authorities in translating such principles into practical guidelines can bring about the necessary internal legitimacy to make such HRE a meaningful addition to the existing curricula. In these cases, the far-reaching approach to HRE should include the following objectives:

1. To understand that the universality of human rights and the monitoring of their respect by governments is a worldwide policy, without ideological restrictions of right and left.
2. To define human rights as indivisible (civil-political and socioeconomic-cultural) as represented by the totality of those listed in the UDHR. From this entire list, the law enforcement agents are directly responsible for the respect of an important number (mostly the rights of the integrity of the person) but a limited number, as the civilian government is responsible for the overall maintenance of the entire list.
3. To regard HRE as an effort toward society at large, which requires attention to be paid to the abuses of human rights by armed opposition against civilian and military targets, including every single citizen in the learning process of conflict resolution through nonviolent means.
4. To acknowledge the separate and often shared responsibility of civil and military authorities in instigating, endorsing, ignoring, or condoning human rights violations and acting effectively if such situations arise.

5. To guarantee the rights of the members of law enforcement agencies by the civil authorities as well as the protection of their own and families' well-being, education, standards of living, voting rights, and so on.

6. To ensure the soldiers' and officers' right to know their own rights within their institutions, to include the issue of "due obedience" to illegal orders and the hierarchy's responsibility for human rights violations by subordinates. At the same time, it may be reasonable to discuss societal demands on military institutions, such as equal access to the armed forces and police by all citizens without any discrimination, including gender and sexual orientation.

Undoubtedly, this list may be seen as too ambitious for countries that have timidly undertaken the process of democratization, and where the political culture has blocked many such subjects from the educational institutions of law enforcement agencies. Its gradual introduction may be more suitable for most cases, but the consolidation of democracy implies the acknowledgment of the entire list as an ultimate goal.

A step closer to Utopia? We will not know until HRE is tried in a rigorous and systematic manner, involving academic experts to design and train in laboratory conditions the prospects of the field. Let the subject of human rights come to the military academies through the front door and not the back. No lofty expectations should be built on the immediate impact of HRE. In the words of a human rights commissioner in the Philippines: "The matter of human rights is now being taken seriously. At least, it is being discussed in earnest. . . . I am not talking here of a sudden conversion as in a religious experience, but a dawning that opens with the entry of new knowledge, a realization, and, we hope, an internalization, of the primacy and universality of human rights. . . . For all these efforts, the military responded, initially defensively, strongly insisting on its position. But inevitably, they see the light and changes are made."[53]

Notes

1. For helping me address this difficult topic I express my gratitude to Kristina M. Maccubbin, a talented student at the University of Maryland at College Park, who aided me with the research and editing, and Dr. Richard P. Claude and Abraham Magendzo who provided valuable comments on an earlier draft.

2. The Chilean expert Abraham Magendzo begins his paper by pointing out that he is approaching the subject of human rights education (HRE) for the military with "great caution" as well as "mistrust and a high level of doubts": *Algunas reflexiones en torno a la capacitación en derechos humanos para miembros de las FF.AA. y de la Policia* (Santiago: Programa Interdisciplinario de Investigaciones en Educación [PIIE], August 1993), 1.

3. In a conversation with a high-ranking Latin American officer responsible for a regional defense teaching institution, he opposed introducing lectures on human rights within the curriculum on grounds that it will be seen as a "red banner," and then clarified that he referred both to the communist flavor as well as the bullfighter attitude toward the color.

4. Commissioner Sicam stressed the hostility within military circles in the Philippines to

human rights and the bias they perceived among human rights advocates for the "enemy": Paulynn P. Sicam, "Reaction Paper," International Conference on the Military in Democratic Transition, Ternate, Cavite, June 29–30, 1991, 1.

5. Etienne Marais and Janine Rauch, *Policing South Africa: Reforms and Prospects* (Policing Research Project, Psychology Department, University of the Witwatersrand, ca. December 1992), 7.

6. "In order to attain such an objective, it becomes indispensable to train members of the armed forces and police in the norms and fundamental principles of human rights, both at the national and international level, as well as the nature of the relationship between democracy and fundamental rights, with the aim of achieving the adjustment of the performance of the armed forces in the fulfillment of their tasks and the respect of human rights" (quoted from document *Presentation of Program*, Programa de Capacitación de Derechos Humanos para Fuerzas Armadas y Policia, Instituto Interamericano de Derechos Humanos, p. 3).

7. The quoted sentences appear in statements of most countries that confirmed the existence of HRE training in the military. See R. A. Tieman and J. C. Hammelburg, *Draft Report on Human Rights Education in the Military* (UNESCO, International Humanist and Ethical Union [IHEU], University of Utrecht) (confidential manuscript, October 1991). Names of countries withheld.

8. Already in 1991, a few years after the introduction of HRE as an instructional subject within all state institutions, two thousand military personnel were taking specific courses in the subject.

9. *Draft Report of the UNESCO/IHEU Seminar on Human Rights and the Military* (Zeist, Netherlands, September 4–6, 1989), 1.

10. For further references see John Cottingham Alderson, *Human Rights and the Police*, 2d ed. (Strasbourg: Council of Europe Publishing and Documentation Service, 1992); and Armand Reynaud, *Human Rights in Prison* (Strasbourg: Council of Europe, Publication Section, 1986).

11. An outstanding illustration of this gap between HRE for the new Judiciary Police and the absence of such reference from the agenda of the military in Ecuador is a book published paradoxically under the auspices of the Latin American Association for Human Rights by Colonel Alberto Molina Flores, *Las Fuerzas Armadas Ecuatorianas: Paz y desarrollo* (Quito: Asociación Latinoamericana por la Defensa de los Derechos Humanos, 1993). Although it covers a large variety of topics, there is hardly any specific reference to human rights.

12. "Although there is a tendency to emphasize human rights education in the formal setting of the school, it must be made clear that human rights education and awareness must reach all corners of society": Charles Henry, "Human Rights Education for a New World Order," in *Human Rights for the 21st Century: Foundation for Responsible Hope*, ed. Peter Juviler et al. (New York: M. E. Sharpe, 1993), 241.

13. Observations based on an interview with Orna Shem-tov, at the Association for Civil Rights in Israel (ACRI) offices, Tel Aviv, January 1993.

14. The Instituto de Investigación de la Defensa Nacional (INIDEN) trains officers in "basic knowledge of human rights exploring the philosophic, legal, political and international perspectives" under the authorization of the ministers of Defense and Interior, both of whom are generals (see outline of *Curso de derechos humanos*, p. 1). The learning of human rights focuses on Peruvian realities.

15. Franklin Patterson, "The Guatemalan Military and the Escuela Politecnica," *Armed Forces and Society* 14, no. 3 (Spring 1988): 359–90.

16. Christian Bay's concept and Paulo Freire's arguments for conscientization in relation to HRE are discussed more in-depth in Richard Pierre Claude and Edy Kaufman, "Reflections on Human Rights Pedagogy: A Draft Concept Paper," document prepared for a consultative meeting that took place at the Law School, Yale University, May 1992.

17. The two classic approaches that developed in the field were represented by Huntington's advocacy of autonomous and politically neutral military institutions (Samuel P. Huntigton, *The*

Soldier and the State [Cambridge, Mass.: Harvard University Press, 1957]) and Janowitz's advocacy of a politically sensitive professional military concerned with the degree of force needed in the fulfillment of its international role (Morris Janowitz, *The Professional Soldier: A Social and Political Portrait* [Glencoe, Ill.: Free Press, 1960].

18. William S. Ackroyd, "Military Professionalism, Education, and Political Behavior in Mexico," *Armed Forces and Society* 18, no. 1 (Fall 1991): 91.

19. Paper prepared by Eduardo Romero Quintanilla, general of the Spanish Civil Guard and professor at the Center of International Humanitarian Law of the Spanish Red Cross, submitted to the Workshop of Experts for the Preparation of a Human Rights Enhancement Program for the Armed Forces and the Police in Central America and the Andean Countries, International Institute of Human Rights (IIDH), San José, Costa Rica, May 1993.

20. A maxim of General Wojciech Jaruzelski, mentioned in an article on Poland by Major Peter J. Podbielski, "Military Education Reforms," *Military Review* (December 1990): 72–73. By April 1994, however, the academy had already hosted a conference on human rights, showing that the subject had become accepted as a universal rather than a partisan issue.

21. Ackroyd, "Military Professionalism," 91.

22. Raoul Alcala, "A System for Educating Military Officers in the United States," *International Studies*, Occasional Paper 9, ed. Lawrence J. Korb (Pittsburg: International Studies Association, 1976), 135.

23. In relation to Poland, see Podbielski, "Military Education Reforms," 72.

24. The functional components of this "top-down" strategy include emphasis on environment (institutional history and public opinion); command functions (leadership and functions); program acceptance (legitimacy); resources (program development, funding, and staff); and operational activities (systematic implementation and evaluation). See Richard P. Claude, "Human Rights Education in the Philippines," *Human Rights Quarterly* 13, no. 4 (1991): 501.

25. For a discussion of the importance of liberal education, see William E. Simons, *Liberal Eduction in the Service Academies* (New York: Bureau of Publications, Teachers College, Columbia University, 1965), 19–30.

26. Title of a paper by Maria Concepción Bautista, Chairperson of the Commission of Human Rights of the Philippines (*Human Rights Seminar Kit*, Commission of Human Rights, 1991).

27. See discussion of HRE in the wider context in Edy Kaufman, *The Relevance of the International Protection of Human Rights to Democratization and Peace* (Notre Dame, Ind.: University of Notre Dame Occasional Papers, June 1994), 45–47.

28. David R. Segal, "Military Education: Technical Versus Liberal Perspectives," revision of a paper presented at the International Research Seminar on Euro-Atlantic Security on "The Role of Military Education in the Restructuring of the Armed Forces," held at the NATO Defense College, Rome, December 3–5, 1992, 14.

29. Wayne C. Thompson and Marc D. Peltier, "The Education of Military Officers in the Federal Republic of Germany," *Armed Forces and Society* 16, no. 4 (Summer 1990): 587–606. The authors strongly emphasize the trainees as an "army of democrats" and "citizens-in-uniform."

30. Segal, "Military Education," 11.

31. For further references, see Alfred Stepan, *Rethinking Military Politics: Brazil and the Southern Cone* (Princeton, N.J.: Princeton University Press, 1988), particularly the last chapter, "Democratic Empowerment and the Military: The Tasks of Civil Society, Political Society and the State," 128–46.

32. Magendzo, *Algunas reflexiones*, 5.

33. Patterson, "The Guatemalan Military," 381.

34. Summary of the intervention of Dr. Herman Von Hebel (Netherlands Institute of Human Rights, University of Utrecht), in *Draft Report of the UNESCO/IHEU Seminar on Human Rights and the Military* (1989).

35. At the beginning of the century in the Netherlands, soldiers were not allowed to exercise their right to vote, and "until very recently" some soldiers were not allowed to marry without the permission of their superior: *Draft Report of the UNESCO/IEHU Seminar* (1989).

36. According to Jan Oberman, the low social prestige of the military in Czechoslovakia is related to a large extent to poor living conditions and meager wages: Jan Oberman, "Military Reform in the Czech Republic," *RFE/RL Research Report* 2, no. 41 (October 15, 1993): 38. See also Jan Oberman, "The Czechoslovak Armed Forces: The Reform Continues," *RFE/RL Research Report* 1, no. 6 (February 7, 1992): 48–54.

37. Paulo Freire, *Education for Critical Consciousness* (New York: Seabury Press, 1975).

38. In the case of the Peruvian armed forces, it is interesting that a colorful brochure on the "Decalogue of Human Rights" was published in both Spanish and English, the second language probably to show off in Washington and other western capitals the increased dedication of the military in this Latin American country to the pursuit of human rights. The cost of the printing was apparently covered by the Agency of International Development office in Lima.

39. Claude, "Human Rights Education in the Philippines," 510. The effective implementation of such an outstanding principle has been questioned by human rights NGOs in the Philippines.

40. A letter from the Commissioner in Charge of Public Information and Education of the Philippines includes a list of programs for HRE of the police, military, and law enforcement agencies: eight-day programs for regional trainers to cover the entire country (for police, military, jail officers, trainers, and some NGO representatives), three-day advocacy courses/seminar workshops linked with regular police and military courses, seminar kits for course work, and sporadic courses by the Commission on Human Rights open to all sectors (letter of March 15, 1994, from Paulynn Paredes Sicam, Komisyon ng Karapatang Pantao [Commission on Human Rights], Manila).

41. Resolution (78) 41 of the Committee of Ministers of the Council of Europe, in Alderson, *Human Rights and the Police*, app. 7, 181–85.

42. See Roberto Calvo, *La doctrina militar de seguridad nacional* (Caracas: Universidad Catolica Andres Bello, 1979).

43. Magendzo, *Algunas reflexiones*, 3.

44. Or the statement "the safe-guarding of human rights is an important task for the police," making this area a shared concept for the institution rather than the possession of "the other." See the intervention of T. Soukan, "Aspects on Policing/Police Training and Human Rights: General Issues and Recent Developments in Sweden," in Committee of Experts for the Promotion of Education and Information in the Field of Human Rights (DH-EH), *Proceedings of the Meeting of Directors and of Representatives from Police Academies and Police Training Institutions* (Strasbourg: Council of Europe, November 26–28, 1990), 119.

45. See Resolution 690, in Alderson, *Human Rights and the Police*, 14.

46. See Marais and Rauch, *Policing South Africa*, 1–21; and Clifford D. Shearing and Mzwai Mzamane, "Community Voices on Policing in Transition," *Occasional Paper* (Belleville, South Africa: Community Law Center, University of the Western Cape, June 1992).

47. The fragility of independent judgment in the observance of human rights principles was shown most dramatically in Argentina, when civilian President Raul Alfonsin agreed to promote and pass legislation on "due obedience" releasing the subordinates in law enforcement agencies for serious crimes committed during the years of the previous military dictatorship. See the Americas Watch Report, *Truth and Partial Justice in Argentina* (New York: Americas Watch Committee, 1987).

48. For instance, "to describe the police function in its positive form is to endow it with explicable qualities . . . to describe the enforcement and upholding of laws as a means of enabling the quality of life for all to improve": comments by John Cottingham Alderson, formerly chief constable in the United Kingdom, from the Police Studies Center, University of Exeter, in Committee of Experts, (see note 44), 99.

49. And the other side of the coin: some HRE experts have questioned the real possibility of educating the armed forces and police in this field, given their "hierarchical and authoritarian nature": see Magendzo, *Algunas reflexiones*, 3.

50. For several references to the inability to evaluate behavioral change and assessing that the effects can only be the results of "incidental exposure," see Jennifer Morrison Taw and William H. McCoy, Jr., *International Military Student Training: Beyond Tactics* (Santa Monica, Calif.: Rand Corporation, N-3634-USDP, 1993).

51. See letter to the author from the Commission on Human Right of the Philippines (note 40 above).

52. The Department of Defense produced a document on the U.S. Congress's demand for an evaluation of the Expanded IMET program that was met with severe criticism. See, for instance, Washington Office on Latin America (WOLA), "Human Rights Education and Training in U.S. Policy Toward Latin America," *Issues in Human Rights*, WOLA Paper 3 (1994).

53. Sicam, "Reaction Paper," 2, 7.

Chapter 18
Military Training for Human Rights and Democratization

D. Michael Hinkley

This chapter addresses the initiatives in human rights training undertaken by the U.S. Navy's Naval Justice School (NJS) on behalf of the Department of Defense (and, in particular, the Defense Security Assistance Agency [DSAA]) under the U.S. government's Expanded International Military Education and Training (EIMET) program. The opinions and analyses contained herein are those of the author and do not necessarily reflect the official views of the U.S. Navy, the U.S. Department of Defense, or the U.S. government.

The purpose of this chapter is to provide the reader with two basic analyses: (1) an examination of this recent (and highly successful) development in the U.S. government's approach to providing human rights training to emerging democracies under the auspices of the Department of Defense's Security Assistance program; and (2) a suggested methodology for providing this training in various nations worldwide, notwithstanding the major differences in, for example, cultures, history, political climate, ethnic tensions, and economic stability from country to country. My perspective stems from my responsibilities and experiences both as a supervisor of the school's International Training Program from its inception and as a human rights/international law instructor for the program in several African nations. Considering the growing pains experienced by many newly emerging democracies as they wrestle with how to establish a new government freed from the shackles of dictatorships, military juntas, or communism, it is not enough for the U.S. military to say "Follow me" or "Do as we do." Rather, the school had to devise a method of instruction that took into account the political sensitivities, open disagreements between opposing forces, and, in many cases, historical partisan enmity in a given nation before any effective training could take place. What follows, both in methods employed and "lessons learned," will provide the reader with some ideas for constructing or designing effective human rights educational programs in similar situations.

The Background of the Naval Justice School's EIMET Program

In 1990 the provision of the Foreign Assistance Act of 1961 dealing with International Military Education and Training was amended in two ways that gave rise to the involvement of the Naval Justice School in the EIMET program. The first was that the act authorized spending U.S. security assistance dollars to train not only military personnel but also civilian officials who work with foreign defense establishments (thus "expanded" IMET). The second, and more significant, was to earmark no less than $1 million of appropriated funds to provide training in human rights, civilian control of the military in a democratic society, military justice systems, and defense resource management.[1]

The Navy immediately expressed an interest in developing a curriculum that would meet this new requirement. The Navy took the lead on this project, and directed the Naval Justice School in Newport, Rhode Island, to develop various curricula to meet this need. The Naval Justice School was particularly well suited for this task: with a faculty of more than thirty instructors and an accompanying civilian support staff, NJS had the physical facilities and the experience not only to develop the program but also to teach it. While its original mission centered on the training of military personnel as paralegals and attorneys for the Navy, Marine Corps, and the U.S. Coast Guard, several staff members volunteered to take on the task of expanding the school's training role to include this international human rights training program. The volunteers included active-duty military attorney instructors, Reserve attorneys recalled to active duty for this endeavor, and enlisted paralegal instructors resident at the school.[2] By augmenting the original cadre of volunteers with both attorneys and other military officers from all branches of the armed forces, NJS was able to form multiservice teaching teams of four to five instructors each to meet the rapidly growing demands of the new program. The school currently administers the EIMET teaching program through its International Training Detachment, co-located with the school in Newport, Rhode Island.

Course Content

The basic course centers on most of the main subjects identified for the EIMET program: civilian control of the military, effective military justice systems, and human rights. The school learned early on that, contrary to initial perceptions, the teaching of any human rights course to emerging democracies could *not* be an off-the-shelf production. In other words, while the school could easily create a one-size-fits-all version of a course on generally accepted "basic" human rights (founded primarily on the Universal Declaration of Human Rights and, perhaps, commonly accepted principles regarding the "law of war" contained in, for example, the relevant Geneva Conventions),[3] its ease of creation would be inversely proportional to its effectiveness as a teaching tool. Dealing with the key players and power brokers in emerging democracies would not be like teaching either the uneducated or children: in most cases, the challenges to the instructor team included the fact that the new nation was "new" in name only—its culture or civilization had often been in existence for a substantial period of time, and frequently longer than the United States (a fact most international students were never reluctant to point out). Additional (and sometimes related) challenges include:

a strong sense of student patriotism and national pride, giving rise to a reluctance to listen to "outsiders" or "foreigners" (or, worse yet, neocolonialists) trying to tell them what's right or wrong;

divisive internal political tensions, especially in newly formed democracies trying to feel their way forward in the democratization process without alienating either the general populace (who demand solutions to oppressive situations, and quickly) or the former power brokers (who may be reluctantly giving up power in the face of overwhelming popular clamor but still control enough economic, military, or paramilitary forces to derail the democratization process if they feel the result of the process either will not protect them or, even worse, will seek retribution against them);

a highly educated group of heterogeneous military and civilian students who, in many instances, had more personal involvement in human rights movements or international programs than did the majority of the instructors;

experienced military students who generally had very recent experiences in internal armed conflict situations, and had either seen evidence of or been affected by human rights abuses such as torture, rape, looting, or attacks on civilians in wartime; and

the language barrier, in most cases. While we in the United States often have (and rely on) the luxury that much of the rest of the world speaks at least some English, it became clear that our instructors' sometimes strained ability to order lunch in a foreign eatery was woefully inadequate when, using the interactive teaching methodology the school devised to teach human rights effectively, it came time to discuss the subtleties of due process of law, the concepts of necessary and proportional use of armed force, and the system of shared powers inherent in the basic democratic process. Reliance on professional simultaneous or consecutive translation services became essential to the program.

In the face of these challenges, the Naval Justice School in 1991 began building a library of course modules to support the centerpiece of its international human rights training, the five-day executive seminar on human rights, civilian control of the military, and effective military justice systems. The modules focus on specific subtopics of either human rights, civilian control of the military, or effective military justice systems and generally contain subject matter that can be covered in fifty minutes, leaving either time for a logically consistent break before proceeding to a related sub-topic (e.g., starting with a presentation on "The Rights of a Military Accused Facing a Court-Martial," breaking, then reconvening for a fifty-minute block on "Court-Martial Procedures") or covering the topic sufficiently to prepare the students for follow-on discussions. These modules are continually updated and the library augmented as necessary to reflect changes in both international and U.S. law, and to add new topics such as analyses of UN "peacekeeping"[4] operations or permissible uses of the military for civic action "public works" projects. While this may appear to some to make the school's program at least partially "off-the-shelf," the reader should not be deceived or misled by such an interpretation: as explained in the next section, these modules merely serve as starting points or basic reference materials which each team of instructors must examine and then tailor to the particular concerns of the nation in which the training will take place. For example, in 1993 and 1994, both Madagascar and Rwanda had requested that the Naval Justice School's EIMET programs for their nations cover "UN Peacekeeping Operations." However, the Malagasy concern was centered on the legality and mechanisms for the potential involvement of their armed forces in future UN peacekeeping operations, while the Rwandese (having only recently signed a peace accord, in August 1993, between the government forces and the Rwandese Patriotic Front [RPF] forces) were interested in the role and authority of UNAMIR (United Nations Assistance Mission in Rwanda) forces stationed in Rwanda to monitor the peace accord. Accordingly, the team of U.S. Navy and U.S. Army instructors had to design separate modules of instruction (in French as well as English) for both nations and create separate discussion problems for each nation's seminars.

Teaching Methodology

As mentioned earlier, the centerpiece of the EIMET program has been the development of a three-phase executive seminar on human rights, civilian control of the military, and effective military justice systems. This seminar was presented for the first time in September 1992 in both Sri Lanka and Papua New Guinea, and has since been successfully taught in Senegal, Madagascar, Guatemala, the Republic of the Philippines, Rwanda, and several other emerging democracies throughout the world. The unique features of this course are its multiphased development, the use of small discussion groups, and the ability of the instructors to make the course host country-specific.

When the Naval Justice School realized that something much more than an off-the-shelf course was not only desired by the "client" nations but also required for an effective human rights training program, the instructors examined various teaching methodologies in an effort to find the most effective instruction techniques for teaching a heterogeneous group of up to sixty adults at one time, with a spectrum of student educational experience ranging (in some cases) from secondary school credentials to graduate or doctorate degrees. The student mix also included military

officers, members of the legislature and judiciary, and other government officials—
factions of government which, in places such as Sri Lanka, had at best only infre-
quently sat down together for meetings before, often due to mutual distrust or bad
personal experiences involving past military abuses or government corruption. Perhaps the extreme example of potential for mistrust and suspicion within the student
group was during the January 1994 training in Rwanda, where, for the first time since
the signing of the peace accords in August 1993, the opposing military forces which
had recently been firing at each other in that country's civil war had actually come
together to begin planning for follow-on integration of the new Rwandese military
forces. The tension of this meeting was evident by the requirement that UNAMIR
forces escort the (former) rebel representatives to the seminar site and provide security throughout the course; thankfully (both for the peace process and for the security
of the instructor team), the seminars concluded successfully and without incident.[5]

After much thoughtful analysis, the school decided that participative learning—
emphasizing role-playing, problem solving, and small group discussions—would be
the most effective way to teach the specific blocks of instruction to the anticipated
adult audience, combining sessions of interaction/small group problem solving with
relevant lectures to the student body as a whole to help identify, and possibly resolve,
specific issues and problems highlighted in the lectures. This was an experimental
approach that, to the best of the school's knowledge, had not been tested before in
any such foreign training programs; this method had, however, been extremely successful at the Naval Justice School in training more homogeneous groups of adults
(e.g., newly commissioned military judge advocates and paralegals), and we believed
it could be applied to the EIMET program. It was apparent that U.S. efforts to provide
human rights training under the auspices of security assistance in the past had been,
in many respects, less than effective in their final results. In fact, a May 1993 report by
Amnesty International sharply criticized what it perceived to be a failure of the U.S.
government to enforce, in twenty nations, section 508B of the Foreign Assistance Act,
which essentially prohibited spending security assistance dollars for nations demonstrating a "consistent pattern of gross human rights violations."[6] Similar arguments
for the ineffectiveness of prior training efforts could be made based on evidence of
human rights abuses found in the recent (1990s) State Department Country Reports
to Congress regarding human rights practices worldwide.[7] Given these data, the Naval
Justice School decided it was time to shift paradigms from traditional military training methods (e.g., lectures, rote repetition, one-way communication of information)
and break new ground.

The Executive Seminar

The executive seminar generally works in three phases. In Phase I a survey team visits
the host country to meet with military, governmental, and nongovernmental personnel and organizations (including, when available, "opposition" representatives) in

order to assess logistical support capability and the present status of the country in the areas of human rights, civilian control of the military, and the military justice system currently in place. These visits are coordinated through the local U.S. embassies, the State Department, and the U.S. military commanders-in-chief (CINCs) who have area responsibility for the nation in which the seminar will take place.

This survey is followed by Phase II, a visit of four to six representatives of the host country to either the Naval Justice School or another stateside military command where members of the teaching team are assigned, where they are given the opportunity to see the U.S. system of both military and civilian jurisprudence, as well as our protection of basic human rights, both being taught and in action (at the Naval Education and Training Center [NETC], Newport, or elsewhere). This includes tours of military training sites, calls on civilian law enforcement and judicial officials, and observation of military and civilian criminal courts in action. Significantly, in addition to the standard familiarity visit of foreign personnel to the United States, the curriculum for that nation, as developed based on the survey, is fully discussed and refined during this phase so that it is host country-specific and is "owned" by that country. While the host country representatives must have a high level of English language proficiency, neither the U.S. government nor the Naval Justice School instructors choose them. This is the prerogative of the host country and has two advantages: it preserves their concern for "independence" and "sovereignty"; and it strengthens the fact that the host country is now responsible for the content and, in many respects, the quality of the seminar conducted during Phase III.

In Phase III of the EIMET seminar process, the teaching is conducted over a period of five days, during which the students are in class approximately six and a half to seven hours a day. Each day of the program is a combination of lectures and small seminar groups; generally, there will be one or two one-hour lectures to the plenary group for each half day, followed by dividing the class into small (eight-to-ten-person) discussion groups that proceed to separate classrooms and discuss, among themselves, a fact pattern specifically designed to foster discussion regarding the main themes of the preceding lecture. The fact patterns are custom-designed to address the concerns of the country in which the training is being held (and as had been identified by that country's representatives during Phase II of the program). Each nation's scenarios are written by the members of the U.S. instructor team who serve as both lecturers and seminar group facilitators. The seminar leaders are those students who were chosen to represent the foreign nation during the Phase II visit to the United States. Each of the leaders takes charge of a different discussion group and remains with that group (as do the facilitators) throughout the week. These leaders become, in effect, both sponsors of the training (and its methodology) and validators of the learning process. The role of the U.S. instructors is primarily to ensure that the discussion groups fully address the teaching objectives of the main lecture and, in a nonjudgmental way, explore the rationale behind the groups' conclusions with regard to the seminar scenarios.

The U.S. instructors' neutrality is crucial to the success of this training program:

instructors must overcome the (perhaps natural) tendency either to assert their expertise in a given field or to give the impression that they possess the "right" answers to the problem that the group is working on. If this were to happen, it would be disastrous to the week-long learning process in that it would, at a minimum, promote defensive reactions by some students and could easily chill further valuable discussion. With this in mind, the program assiduously avoids "preaching" either U.S. democracy or the "American way": the theme of the program emphasizes that the United States, as a nation, struggled with many of the same issues these newly emerging democracies are now facing. In mentioning past successes *and* mistakes in U.S. history, the program emphasizes that U.S. "trial-and-error" development is something that other nations may wish (but are not required) to examine as they decide on what system of government works best for them—both for a sovereign nation in the international community and for its people—and how their military forces will best fit into that government. To be sure, our instructors can (and are frequently called upon to) give examples of U.S. practices or of personal experiences with such issues as protection of "due process" rights in the military court-martial system, treatment of prisoners during Operations Desert Shield and Desert Storm, the aerial bombing of Libya, and so on. Their ability to discuss, for example, concrete instances of how bombing decisions were made, what targeting alternatives were not chosen, or how a defense counsel guards his client from government overreaching is invaluable to the students and generally appreciated. However, the teaching team must be careful not to overstep its bounds as facilitators, or the progress being made could easily disappear.

The instructors also learn by experience not to get trapped into taking sides. For example, the initial stages of the first of two seminars conducted in Rwanda contained what appeared to be a lot of posturing by representatives of both the Rwandese government and the RPF (rebel) forces regarding their political positions on the future Rwanda government. A popular RPF theme was to liken the situation in Rwanda to the colonial United States in 1775, intimating that perhaps "armed rebellion" was a legitimate recourse, or at least that the U.S. instructors should endorse its legitimacy because of its historical role in the democratization of the United States. We instructors scrambled a bit but realized that, although no answer would be satisfactory to all, we could certainly facilitate the class discussion on the *legitimacy* of the issue and let the class, in discussion groups, come to its own conclusions.[8] This turned out to be not only good politics but also good sense. The EIMET instructors are not involved in this program either to provide U.S. government policy decisions or to speak on behalf of the U.S. government. In fact, the instructors stress a "nonattribution" policy regarding statements made or opinions rendered during the seminar in order to promote full and frank discussion.

While, during the course of any given one-week seminar, the general topics of military justice systems, civilian control of the military, human rights, and the law of armed conflict are covered, the central thread of respect for and protection of human rights is woven into each block of instruction. This is done in a proactive way that emphasizes not only how respect for "the rule of law" will protect human rights, but also how it will do so in a way that does not interfere with either mission accomplishment or the effective and expeditious administration of justice. This type of analysis appeals to the self-interest of the military students and often assuages some fears of the civilian attendees. This appeal to self-interest is another important factor leading to the success of the program. While the Naval Justice School's human rights training and subsequent programs have been favorably received both worldwide and by the U.S. government,[9] certain "buttons" had to be pushed to minimize the natural reluctance to accept "outside" trainers and to bolster the credibility of the individual instructors, especially at the beginning of the seminar. Several means were used to overcome this resistance.

Appeal to Self-Interest (the "Greed Factor")

It is not enough to lecture adults; they must see how what you are telling them will benefit them or how they can use your information to their advantage. This is crucial to the audience's accepting and internalizing basic human rights principles so that the lessons learned in the seminar will be applied by the students in the future. In this regard, the school's program is essentially preventive, not corrective, in nature: it is geared toward progress and development, rather than focusing on any sins of the past. A theme emphasized during the "Law of Armed Conflict" presentations and discussions, for example, is that following "the law" in protecting against human rights abuses is not only easy (and, of course, right), but also makes good common sense: why, as a military leader of troops, would you waste time, money, and effort destroying civilian structures, pursuing or harassing noncombatants, and allowing your troops to plunder villages, when all these activities use up valuable time, squander supplies or ammunition, cause hate and entrenchment in the civilian populace, heap international scorn on your activities, and lead to a breakdown in unit discipline as your soldiers become more interested in lining their pockets with loot than in your mission accomplishment? When phrased in such terms, heads begin to nod in agreement: to the military commander, this makes sense, and helps him.

Use of Military Instructors

This may be a double-edged sword, given a potential civilian student distrust for *any* military figure, but our experience showed that in our seminars the military attendees make up at least 50 percent of the students—and instructors in uniform command a certain "instant credibility": the military students may harbor initial resistance and may strongly disagree with some of the concepts discussed in class, but they invariably give more weight even to opposing positions if presented by a "comrade in arms," someone who knows military life and has experienced its positive and negative sides as well as its unique characteristics and needs for good order and discipline. Our experience is that the potentially negative side of the sword, "civilian mistrust," has not been a problem: this is probably because our teaching teams are generally at least 50 to 75 percent military attorneys and because of the generally higher reputation for professionalism that the U.S. military enjoys worldwide, relative to other nations' forces.

Instructor Experience and Expertise

Human rights cannot be taught in a vacuum. We found that quoting excerpts from either the Geneva Conventions or the Universal Declaration of Human Rights was relatively meaningless if the instructors did not have real-life examples of the principles generally espoused in such documents to illustrate how the rights could be protected in reality. With this in mind, one key to the selection of members for our instructor teams was personal experience. We chose military attorneys from all five branches of our armed services (Navy, Marine Corps, Army, Air Force, Coast Guard) who had extensive experience and expertise either as military judges, law of armed conflict advisors, or as policymakers. Similarly, the line officers chosen were thoroughly familiar with not only how "the law" worked but, more important, how they could apply the law, conform their actions to it, and still maintain good order and discipline within the ranks while pursuing mission accomplishment.

The Concept of Team Teaching

One key to the seminar's success lies in the teaching team's ability to adapt the discussion problems and individual blocks of instruction to the needs of the host nation and the students, and to keep the debate ongoing and lively. Another key is that each instructor must be present for and knowledgeable in the other instructors' areas of expertise so that, as the week progresses, each teacher can use the points emphasized in an earlier presentation to point out their interrelationship with the present module. The scenarios used involve frequent role-playing and often force the students to take both military and civilian perspectives into account in reaching a solution. Additionally, the scenarios are designed to remain "hypothetical" (thus nonthreatening) and involve fictitious incidents and nations while simultaneously weaving into the problem the exact concerns raised by the host nation during Phases I and II of the program. Instructors sometimes draw parallels to the hypothetical problem from the U.S. experience in establishing its own democratic form of government over its two hundred-plus years, but again this specifically avoids preaching U.S. values or conveying the impression that the U.S. experience is the answer for all nations and all times. The instructors emphasize U.S. "trial and error" in working toward democratization and protection of basic rights, leaving the final answer (as it must be) up to the group to decide.

During the actual seminar, the class (designed for forty to fifty students, although we have taught up to sixty) is divided into heterogeneous discussion groups that are tasked to solve hypothetical problems founded on present legal and military situations. These discussion problems, which are assigned following blocks of informational lecture, give all participants the opportunity to relate the concepts taught to actual "real-time" situations and to participate in the problem solution. Each group then presents its solution for general group discussion when the class is reunited for a general wrap-up discussion of the scenario. An amazingly popular initial seminar scenario successfully used in several nations involves putting each discussion group shipwrecked on a desert island with no hope of rescue in the immediate future, and tasks them with forming not only a system of government but also a system of group security. The identification of the basic needs (e.g., food, shelter, order) for the group, then figuring out how to protect those needs, quickly focuses on the fundamental balances between individual rights and group (or societal) needs inherent in the basic democratic society. As the group starts identifying the basic needs, the instructor (or facilitator) draws parallels to basic human rights themes, weaving in the principles underlying generally accepted notions of basic human rights[10] and letting the students conclude how the respect for such rights becomes essential to the success of their "democratic" island society.

As a general rule, the hypothetical problems given to the class are quickly put by the students into the context of their own country's present military situation. Each problem assigned builds on information derived from previous (Phase I or II) preparation but, more important, is refined to reflect what the students are saying in the discussion groups. The purpose of the seminar is both to expose the class to the fundamental legal principles that govern these areas of international and military law, and to let the students work out the solution to *their* nation's challenges, using their military or legal framework and their own experience. Again, the Naval Justice School's program provides a forum and parameters for discussions: the students work diligently to come up with solutions within those parameters. In many cases (Rwanda and Papua New Guinea, for example), the seminar serves as a starting point from which the nation can continue its progress toward democracy and protection of human rights.

Pitfalls in the Process

There are several factors that instructors need to be cognizant of when attempting this school's type of human rights training in foreign nations. First, many "client" nations are not used to participative learning. In fact, for students who had been previously trained by instructors from the former Soviet Union, our Socratic or interactive approach to problem resolution was initially a shock. In several cases it took at least the first day, and sometimes the second or third day, for the students to feel comfortable enough with both the instructors and the other students to be able to speak out.

Given the tight time schedule of a five-day seminar, this reticence was a major hurdle for the instructors. However, this problem was reduced by two factors: in our heterogeneous student group, it was often easier (after any initial reluctance to "outsiders" was overcome) for the students to talk with the "outside professional" than with students from a different political or ethnic group; and the instructors spend numerous hours before and after class, during breaks, and at meals or other social events trying to break down any perceived social barriers. If an instructor in this program thinks he or she can merely do a fifty-minute block of instruction and then retreat to a hotel room, that instructor is sorely mistaken! The success of the program requires constant social interaction to promote the trust required for full and open discussions. Also, there is always the fear that the client nation is only accepting what we pejoratively call the human rights "vaccination": accepting the training not for its intrinsic value but as part of a public relations effort to get more U.S. financial aid. Thankfully, we have not seen much evidence of this, but the concern still exists. In addition, the U.S. government's human rights training program has not been as firmly established as other foreign aid programs, giving rise to differing interpretations of policy, overlapping programs, and questions of control or direction.[11] As the school's continued successes grow, however, the program's foundation solidifies. Finally, the program retains no control over either the initial selection of students or any follow-on training. While we may have certain ideas, based on Phases I and II, of who should be represented in the seminar's student body, actual attendance is the decision of the host nation. It has been indicative, however, of the extremely favorable acceptance of the school's program and its reputation that attendees regularly include deputy ministers, cabinet-level personnel, legislators, trial judges, and flag officers. Illustrative is the fact that, in Papua New Guinea, Sri Lanka, and the Republic of the Philippines, senior officers were recalled from the front lines of combat with rebel forces to attend the seminar.

Measuring Success

If there is a drawback to the Naval Justice School's human rights training program, it may be the difficulty in measuring success. As a general rule, government auditors need to be able to measure success (or failure) in order to ensure that public funds are properly spent. Counting numbers of students trained is deceptive because the numbers are minuscule when compared to a nation's total population. Similarly, documenting subsequent changes in the number of reported human rights abuse cases in a nation is misleading because this does not measure the quality (or effective reception) of the training, but only assesses the frequency of reports and can fluctuate depending on local definitions, reporting procedures, and administrative control over the reports process itself. Somewhat paradoxically, increased reporting of human rights abuses may well signal not *ineffective* but *successful* training in that, with growing awareness of human rights, previously unreported cases are now being brought forward.

There is no easy answer to measuring success in this area. While we feel that current praise for the program, requests for follow-on training (for example, the school has "trained the trainers" in Sri Lanka, setting up a program [Phases IV and V] wherein the nation could train its own personnel using similar modules of instruction and methodology, and is planning similar phases elsewhere), and ongoing U.S. relations with the client nations are several ways to measure success, we still need something better. The U.S. General Accounting Office (GAO), in a September 1992 report to Congress, also came to this conclusion and recommended that the Department of Defense direct the DSAA to complete the implementation of a means to evaluate the effectiveness of this expanded IMET program.[12] Perhaps the real answer is "wait and see": after all, the United States has been working on, and fine-tuning, its own version of democracy for more than two hundred years. Perhaps it is too early to say with any accuracy how effective the Naval Justice School's EIMET program is. While I am not suggesting that the GAO should wait two hundred years, there appears to be no quick means of measuring success: whether the present conflict in Rwanda is an aberration or merely a detour on the road to democracy remains to be seen, and it may take several years before we know whether or not the program succeeded.

Conclusion

The experiment with a nonjudgmental, participative learning approach to human rights training under the EIMET program has worked, and worked exceedingly well. Shifting from traditional military training methods has created a much more instructor-intense program than originally envisioned, but, by using the proper mix of experienced military instructors committed to putting in the extra effort required by this methodology, the school has produced a training program that has received U.S. government as well as worldwide acclaim. By avoiding ramming "the American way" down the students' throats, by breaking away from traditional military training, and by letting the students themselves logically work through nonoffensive hypothetical problem scenarios and apply generally accepted principles of basic human rights, we have crafted a proactive and preventive strategy both for human rights education and for the fight to prevent human rights abuses. In accordance with this strategy, the students see more than human rights principles. They see, in a practical setting, how respect for human rights is: common sense, relatively cost-free, internationally expected of civilized nations, and conducive to public support for the government in a democratic society. This realization comes from the students themselves as they struggle with the discussion problems, and not from the "outsiders" (instructors). This proactive approach gets directly to the senior decision makers in the nation, and sets the stage for both follow-on training and further independent national analysis. How far the students in any given nation will take what they have learned remains unclear; no nation has rejected the course, and several have asked that different phases of the program be brought back for further training. The Naval Justice School has every ex-pectation that this method of providing "military" human rights training to emerging democracies will continue to be a model for success.

Notes

1. Foreign Appropriations, Export Financing, and Related Programs Appropriations Act of 1991, Pub. L. No. 101–513. Title III, Military Assistance, 1991 U.S.C.C.A.N. (104 Stat.) 1979, at 1997, specifically requires IMET funds be spent for

> developing, initiating, conducting and evaluating courses and other programs for training foreign civilian and military officials in managing and administering foreign military estab-lishments and budgets, and for training foreign military and civilian officials in creating and maintaining effective military judicial systems and military codes of conduct, including ob-servance of internationally recognized human rights . . . [civilian personnel] shall include foreign government personnel of ministries other than ministries of defense if the military education and training would (i) contribute to responsible defense resource management, (ii) foster greater respect for and understanding of the principle of civilian control of the military, or (iii) improve military justice systems and procedures in accordance with interna-tionally recognized human rights.

2. The initial success of the Expanded International Military Education and Training (EIMET) program at the Naval Justice School was due in large part to the Reserve component of the Navy's Judge Advocate General's Corps and the groundbreaking work done by Captain Norm Miller, JAGC, USNR, and Captain (select) Robert Kasper, JAGC, USNR. Both these at-torneys were recalled to active duty for the creation of this program, and their efforts, with the active-duty assistance of Commander Hal Dronberger, JAGC, USN, and Commander John Crowley, USCG, were crucial in establishing curriculum proposals, staffing requirements, and the commitment of the Naval Justice School to the viability of this untested project.

3. For a fine compilation of the Geneva Conventions and other relevant treaties, see W. Michael Reisman and Chris T. Antoniou, eds., *The Laws of War* (New York, Vintage Books, 1994).

4. The term "peacekeeping" is used here as a generic term to describe all UN-sponsored uses of military forces under the authority of either Chapter VI or Chapter VII of the UN Charter. It covers operations that have frequently been referred to in other contexts by such terms as peacekeeping, peacemaking, or peace enforcement operations. It would, for example, include the coalition operations conducted during the 1991–92 Arabian Gulf crisis, the UN presence in Somalia, and UN-sponsored efforts in the former Yugoslavia.

5. A memorable example of propaganda, perhaps designed to spread distrust during the con-flict, surfaced in Kigali, the Rwandan capital, and around the conference site. Many schoolchil-dren gathered around the seminar students during the lunch breaks and, after a few moments of shyness, asked why they weren't able to see the rebel force personnel's "tails." Apparently, they had been told that the rebel forces were somewhat less than human!

6. Brian Best, *Human Rights and U.S. Security Assistance* (Washington, D.C.: Amnesty Interna-tional, USA, May 1993).

7. See, e.g., *Country Reports on Human Rights Practices for 1990*, submitted to the Senate Com-mittee on Foreign Relations and the House Committee on Foreign Affairs, 102d Cong., 1st Sess. (Committee Print 1991), and similar reports documenting human rights abuses worldwide.

8. While during the January 1993 seminars both sides of the Rwandan struggle seemed to accept that, in today's world, there are several preferred alternatives to armed conflict as a way

to achieve democracy, this concept unfortunately had no time to take root beyond the seminar attendees. The untimely (and highly suspicious) deaths of the presidents of both Rwanda and Burundi in the skies over Kigali, Rwanda, on April 6, 1994, were enough of a spark to re-ignite an age-old ethnic conflict and once again plunge Rwanda into a devastating civil war. These hostilities are chillingly reminiscent of situations described by Dr. Vamik D. Volkan in his psychological studies of ethnic tension. See in particular his book *The Need to Have Enemies and Allies* (Northvale, N.J.: Jason Aronson, 1988), which examines the tremendous psychological hurdles that need to be conquered before resolving deep-seated ethnic hostilities. In the face of such obstacles, human rights training in areas such as Rwanda is indeed a long road.

9. *Report of the Committee on Appropriations to Accompany H.R. 5368, Foreign Operations, Export Financing, and Related Programs Appropriations Bill, 1994*, S. Rep. No. 419, 102d Cong., 2d Sess. (September 23, 1992).

10. The basic principles also include "human rights" as defined by section 116(a) of the Foreign Assistance Act. These rights include freedom from torture or other cruel, inhuman, or degrading treatment or punishment; prolonged detention without charges; disappearance due to abduction or clandestine detention; and other flagrant denials of the rights to life, liberty, and the security of the person.

11. In this regard, Captain Guy R. Abbate, JAGC, USN, has been the lead advocate, mentor, and stalwart guardian of the Naval Justice School's International Training program. He has served as the "point man" for all dealings with and through the State and Defense departments, effectively taking the concept initiated by his predecessors and making it both a reality and a worldwide success. As director of the program for the past two years, Captain Abbate is truly its "founding father," sorting out political, financial, and interagency concerns in a way that has made the program work for all parties.

12. General Accounting Office Final Report GAO/NSIAD-92–248, *Security Assistance: Observations on Post-Cold War Program Changes*, September 30, 1992 (GAO Code 465397), OSD Case 8962-A.

Chapter 19
Human Rights Education for the Police

Marc DuBois

Human rights organizations vary greatly, but their ultimate goals are fairly similar. The "watchdog" objective so common to the work of human rights organizations consists of holding leadership accountable, of using public opinion to force officials to sanction or control abusers and to dismantle structural supports for the violation of human rights. As is evidenced by this book, there is also a growing emphasis upon legal rights education. Essentially, the aim of education is to transform the ignorance and powerlessness upon which violators feed into awareness and resistance. This education, in turn, creates an internal, localized focus upon the behavior of the leadership which complements "watchdog" activities.

To a surprising extent, however, the battle against human rights violations has focused almost exclusively on these two targets, the political elite and the masses, while ignoring the actors, the men and women[1] comprising the police, army, or security forces of a country. These are the performers in this tragic political drama, the ones who execute suspected insurgency sympathizers, beat the soles of detainees' feet, break into houses to seize activists' files, or simply impose "tolls" upon peasants carrying their produce to the market. Government officials must share final responsibility, but the policeman's baton and warrantless search are the points where inequitable power relations intersect victims of abuse.

The subject of this chapter is human rights education (HRE) for police and other law enforcement agents (LEAs).[2] Its purpose is to give shape to the possible roles of nongovernmental organizations (NGOs) in this educational process. The chapter first examines two (of the few) existing examples of HRE aimed at LEAs. It then shifts to a discussion of some of the factors causing human rights violations by the police, so that those developing new training courses will be better able to define their educational objectives. The final sections identify the pedagogical and political issues surrounding NGO involvement in such training and explore various options in terms of format and content options.

Before continuing, though, it is necessary to address the boundaries of this chapter. First, while HRE is a young and developing field, the study and implementation of human rights training for LEAs is at an even earlier stage, with few tested methods and little academic scrutiny. This chapter, therefore, is unable to resolve some questions or proffer a tested formula. However, insofar as it is necessary to contextualize any training program for LEAs, this chapter examines possibilities and highlights issues that must be addressed at the local level. Second, the focus of this chapter is upon those problems specific to HRE for LEAs. Readers should consult other sections of this book for guidance with respect to educational concerns such as planning or evaluation. Third, generalizations are unavoidable, even though there is great variation among the security forces or human rights organizations of even one country. Although this paper concludes that NGOs can successfully cooperate with governments in the human rights training of LEAs, it certainly does not imply that this is universally possible. Finally, HRE for security forces has its limits. It is unreasonable to expect education to extinguish violations within an environment rife with systemic abuse or to cure violators who revel in the perverse pleasure of inflicting pain or exercising physical power over life.

Two Examples of Human Rights Training Programs for the Police

When compared to most governments, the expertise of NGOs in the area of human rights (and, perhaps, education) makes their participation a vital component of effective training. It is with that in mind that I turn to a brief examination of two existing programs. The first is a course called "Human Dignity and the Police," developed by the John Jay College of Criminal Justice (New York). The second is a program of LEA education seminars given by the Legal Resources Foundation of Zimbabwe. These two programs were selected because the contrast in approaches and content illustrates the broad range of options and highlights many of the important issues. Other examples of human rights training for LEAs might just as well have been chosen, such as in the Philippines or in the Commonwealth, but descriptions of such programs are available in other publications.[3]

Course Outline for Human Dignity and the Police[1]

Day 1

1. Orientation and introduction.
2. Survey of issues. Participants complete short survey concerning public perception of police and the participants' thoughts concerning violations of human dignity.
3. Discussion of survey responses, with emphasis upon the diversity of opinion. Breakdown into subgroups assigned to explain divergent answers to particular questions.
4. Discussion to develop a working definition of human dignity.
5. Discussion of the history of human dignity.

Day 2

1. Evaluation and summary of Day 1.
2. Examination of personal experiences where dignity was violated. Participants, in groups of two, relate a childhood experience in which an authority figure violated their dignity.
3. Violations of dignity in contacts with the police. Participants are asked to describe a time when their or a friend's dignity was violated by the police.
4. Recollection and discussion of ways in which participants or other police officers have had their dignity violated by the police organization.

Day 3

1. Evaluation and cumulative summary of the course.
2. Group identification and the power of peer groups. "Wolfpack" exercise: participants engage in a group exercise that fosters group feelings such as identity, aggressiveness, conformity, and so on.
3. Vulnerability: an examination of society's response to deviants and outcasts. Participants are asked to develop strategies to protect these groups.
4. Personal responsibility and behavior. Participants analyze the forces that impact negatively on a police officer in hypothetical situations and develop plans to address the problems faced by that officer.

---

1. This outline has been distilled from both the participant's guide and the "Instructor's Notes" to the course "Human Dignity and the Police." Both the documents were provided to the author by the Special Programs office at John Jay College (and remain on file with the author).

Day 4

1. Evaluation and cumulative summary of the course.
2. Participants develop a workable police code of conduct.
3. Police/citizen communication: participants identify ways to improve communication (with emphasis on ability to know what the community wants).

Day 5

1. Course summary, assessment, and application of learning, written evaluation of course.

A Course in Human Dignity

Commenced in 1992, the John Jay course has been given to more than 330 police officers in Latin America, South America, and the Caribbean basin as part of the U.S. government's International Criminal Investigations Training Assistance Program (ICITAP).[4] The five-day course on human dignity is not offered in conjunction with ICITAP training courses designed to improve the technical competence of foreign police but is a self-contained unit. Part of its success lies in the diversity of those responsible for designing and implementing the course. In addition to LEAs and educators, the staff also includes a sociologist specializing in family therapy, experts in ethics, interpersonal communications and criminal justice systems, and a drama therapist. While such a medley might be difficult to duplicate, it provides an idea of the way in which one course incorporated input from various disciplines.

The foundation of the course is a belief that human dignity precedes human rights; that after learning to respect human dignity, LEAs will (re)conceptualize human rights as possessing innate value rather than as impeding the rule of law and order. The course involves a variety of exercises and discussions intended to: (1) establish participants' intellectual understanding of human dignity; (2) have participants recall a violation of their dignity by authority figures both in the past and by the police organization; (3) increase participant awareness of the vulnerability of marginalized sectors of society; (4) increase their understanding of the effects of peer pressure and personal responsibility; and (5) generate potential solutions and codes of conduct from the participants themselves. The course employs a "nontraditional" method of teaching which draws upon the participants' own experiences with loss of dignity: "Teaching police to understand how it feels to have their dignity taken away is the exact nature of this course."[5]

There are several features that distinguish "Human Dignity" from other courses. First, the course seeks to impact directly on human rights through a change in attitudes, but without confronting the trainees as if they were all potential or actual abusers.[6] Avoiding antagonism is crucial to the success of the course (see also below, "Pedagogical Issues: Effectiveness"). To begin with, the participants, rather than the outside world, develop the working definition of the word *dignity* to be used in the course. This precludes them from later denying its validity in their reality. Ensuing exercises ask participants to present a historical figure who championed human dignity, to reexperience an incident in their childhood when an authority figure violated their dignity, and to do the same for a recent occasion when the police organization violated it. Participants realize that violations of dignity cause permanent scars, and instructors lead the analysis so as to nullify rationalizations (e.g., being abused is good for a person because it toughens him or her). These early exercises aim to break down the "we-they" mentality that permeates security forces by situating LEAs in the position of victim and establishing a kinship with those injured by abusive authority.

These exercises also ease suspicions about the course and demonstrate that the instructors care about the participants.

A second virtue of the course is the way in which it strikes at the group processes and normative systems underpinning violations of human dignity by LEAs. In the opening exercise, participants complete a brief survey that asks, for instance, whether they have witnessed an abusive use of force by the police or whether such violations can have profound, lifelong impact. The subsequent discussion of responses establishes the diversity of opinion and validity of a range of perceptions within a group of respected peers. In this way, individuals realize that their understanding of what is necessary and true (e.g., justifications for abusive behavior) is not the only "true" understanding. In the "Wolfpack" exercise, lauded by "Human Dignity" staff members as having a stunning impact upon the participants, they experience the way in which acting within a group or unit alters one's behavior, stifles dissent, fosters aggressiveness, and thereby jeopardizes human dignity.

The Wolfpack Exercise
"Human Dignity" Group Communication and Achievement Exercise

The course participants are divided into two teams of about a dozen each. You get selected for the Blues, along with a few of your friends from the course, and the others are on the Green team. The Greens are taken off to another building. The instructor explains that the object of the exercise is to earn as many points for your team as possible. She then explains the rules:

Members of the Blue group can send two messages (an X or a Y) to the Green group.

Members of the Green group can send two messages (an A or a B) to the Blue group.

The result of the exchange of messages is as follows:

If	the Blues send	and	the Greens send		
	X		B	$\longrightarrow$	Blues gain 15 points Greens gain 0 points
	Y		A	$\longrightarrow$	Blues gain 0 points Greens gain 15 points
	Y		B	$\longrightarrow$	Blues gain 5 points Greens gain 5 points
	X		A	$\longrightarrow$	Blues gain 0 points Greens gain 0 points

The groups will meet separately and communicate with each other only through the letter messages A, B, X, Y, as described above and transmitted by the authorized emissaries (the trainers). This portion of the exercise will take one to two hours.

Your team discusses strategy for a while, but the answer is obvious—send an X. The Greens send an A. Zero to zero. After a half hour and seven passes it is still zero to zero. You are furious with the "Green dogs." You begin to suspect that the emissary is somehow working for them. Somebody to your left says that the group should try sending a Y, but a few of you shout at him that he must be crazy. And a good thing too, the Greens send an A. If you had sent a Y, it would have been 15–0, their favor. This is no time for wavering. The group is angry but convinced that the Greens will crack first. After nearly an hour you get your break—you send an X and they send a B. The fools! Everybody does "high fives." The Blues congratulate each other on having been the stronger. Joseph was right—the Greens were stupid. On the very next turn the Greens send another B. 30–0! You can't believe your luck.

Somebody suggests that the Greens are trying to send a message. The whole team scoffs at his naivete. All you have to do now is send X's for the rest of the game and a win is guaranteed.

Victory for the Blues? Or did both teams fail? *The instructions say nothing about trying to earn more points than the other team.* To maximize points earned, the Blues and the Greens should cooperate to earn five points each per exchange, meaning that far more than thirty points could have been earned.

The illustration above is typical—at least one team attempts to "win" by trying for 15 points or insuring zero for the other team. The beauty of the "wolfpack" exercise is that it requires nothing more than the division of a group. Once separated and anonymous, human nature and group dynamics take over. As the name insinuates, participants under these conditions become predatory, projecting negative characteristics—they're sneaky, they're weaker, they're going to fall for our trap—onto fellow course participants with whom they have been cooperating in other exercises. As one participant commented, "This was the most incredible exercise in my life. I never knew what group behavior was about."

Trainers should record group dialogue for later analysis in the debriefing session and remind people of their own words. *It is important to circumvent denial and have participants look honestly at their behavior. Condemnation should be avoided by stressing that everybody acts about the same way.* ("Human Dignity" *trainers commented that human rights advocates participating in the exercise were indistinguishable from police participants.*) "Human Dignity" faculty members add that even a team taking the "moral high road" (e.g., a Blue team sending Y to a Green team which continues to respond with A) might be competing, not for points but for some other reward, and self-righteousness can be just as powerful a force as competitive greed.

Several exercises are designed to develop a sense of personal responsibility for one's actions. Participants are asked to: (1) help a close friend understand his son, once a thoughtful and caring person, who, after joining the police force, is becoming cynical, distrustful, and judgmental; (2) in a variation of no. 1, to help the friend understand the son who is cynical and depressed (suicidal) as a result of receiving dangerous assignments and being shunned by other officers following his testimony against fellow officers; and (3) to develop a plan of action in response to a letter from a mother whose twelve-year-old son suffered brain damage from a beating (in a case of mistaken identity) by the police. All three of these exercises demand that participants examine the various forces influencing police behavior (such as peer groups and authority) and reflect upon what can be done to combat their negative effects. The final exercises of the course direct earlier learning to practical problems, such as designing a workable police code of conduct and a plan for improving police relations with the public.

Educational Seminars for Law Enforcement Agents

A network of paralegals and volunteers created by the Legal Resources Foundation (LRF) disseminates legal advice and offers legal rights education throughout Zimbabwe.[7] In conjunction with this work, the LRF has conducted week-long seminars for police officers, community relations liaison officers (CRLO, a branch of the police), and, most surprisingly, Central Intelligence Office (CIO) agents. There is also an attempt to train police instructors so that they are then able to incorporate relevant information in regular police training programs.[8]

The LRF's LEA education program does not focus directly on human rights but on legal competence. The program is based on the perception that, after years of emergency regulations, LEA personnel do not know or understand current law.[9] The assumption underlying the approach of the program, then, is that by teaching the relevant law in areas where abuses occur—arrest; detention; entry, search, and seizure; confessions, statements, and admissions; bail—violations of rights will be decreased. The course also aims to sensitize LEA personnel as to the role of LEAs, lawyers, judges, and the public. Lessons are comprised mainly of lecture and discussion, and the subject matter is predominantly legal: relevant legislation and definitions, powers conferred on the police, and the nature of infringements on rights as delineated by court decisions or human rights articles. Furthermore, there is an effort to strike a balance between a theoretical and practical understanding of the laws. In the end, recommendations are made and suggested police procedure is outlined.[10]

Upon completion of the seminar, trainees are asked to fill out an evaluation form. Responses highlight several issues pertinent to this chapter.[11] General comments indicate that most trainees valued learning the law and felt that it would enable them to perform their jobs better. One remark that appeared on a great number of evaluations was the belief of the participants that their superiors needed to attend the same seminar. Otherwise, it was felt, the chain of command (along with political interference) inhibited their ability to do their work correctly. While many perceived the repeal of emergency legislation as a positive step, there were also a substantial number of participants who believed that in their line of work they needed extensive powers to deal with certain individuals. These latter two comments underscore the importance of education designed to change notions of personal responsibility or the relationship of rights to law and order, for while some participants might better understand and comply with the law, underlying norms conducive to abuse rest unaltered.

Understanding the Objectives of HRE for the Police

Human Rights Education LEAs: An Underdeveloped Approach

The concept of human rights training for LEAs appears neither novel nor problematic. Although the possibility that human rights NGOs might perform this training is somewhat trickier, this does not explain the near absence of trials, research, and resources devoted to such a project. While NGOs may not be able to repeal laws permitting arbitrary detention, NGOs *are* in a position to develop and implement training programs for police.

Why this neglect? On the one hand, the hostility of some governments toward human rights prevents cooperation. On the other hand, though, it is perhaps difficult for the human rights community to see the importance of human rights education aimed at the rank-and-file abuser. There is a sort of paradigmatic blind spot: it is difficult to conceive of violations as resulting not from malevolence but from psychological processes or a lack of understanding. Or perhaps NGOs are not aware that research establishes the existence of popular support for training. A survey in the Philippines shows that 45.6 percent of Filipinos believe that the lack of education for officials regarding the law on human rights is the reason that human rights violations are a serious problem (as opposed to a lack of popular human rights literacy).[12] Finally, it is difficult for NGOs to evaluate the impact of training or to show funding agencies quantifiable results.

To assess fully the need for training aimed at LEAs, the conceptualization of *significant* human rights violations must be expanded so as to include the mundane as well as the dramatic. It makes no sense to state that one person tortured can be equated to X number of persons being harassed less violently. It does make sense, however, to comprehend human rights violations as encompassing the multiple daily assaults upon the physical and psychological well-being of individuals. "An act of force, whether it be torture or simply a policeman's demands that a panhandler 'move along,' begs for legitimation"[13] and entails abuse where illegitimate. These "lesser" violations depend more on the attitude of the perpetrator than on, say, the lack of an independent judiciary or laws permitting indefinite detention. Therefore, training programs for LEAs should target these everyday abuses of power, and evaluations of such training should be certain to "count" them.

Defining Objectives: Targeting the Factors That Foster Abuse

The first step in planning a training program for LEAs is to identify the major institutional and individual factors that contribute to abuse. Once identified, diminishing the impact of these factors becomes the educational objective that determines the content of the course. Note, however, that even within a country, these factors may vary according to rank, service, or geographic region. The second step is to design a course that takes into account the fact that HRE for security personnel differs from other education because the subject itself antagonizes the students, creating a formidable barrier to learning.

In and of itself, human rights education for LEAs will be unsuccessful without a certain level of structural support, meaning that watchdog activities must continue. However, the remedial capacity of structural change is also limited. The luster of its desirability regularly outshines its effectiveness in transforming or even ameliorating the lives of the oppressed. This is partly because police forces both inherit and develop their own standards, operating procedures, and autonomy. Eliminating legal and political structures that allow human rights violations to take place is of crucial importance, but such efforts must be accompanied by an attack upon the *normative systems* within security forces which evolved along with those structures.

New governments and laws do not automatically lead to an improvement in the human rights climate of a given country because of hangover effects—the ways of the past flourish in the present via individual policemen. Their experience from an era of violation—their ignorance, rationalizations, and power relationships—survives. In the context of human rights there are several hangovers that mitigate the positive effects of structural changes, each of which might be addressed in training: colonial, state-of-emergency, and impunity hangovers.

The legacy of colonization is that foreigners introduced police forces not to preserve law and order for the benefit of the citizenry but to perpetuate inequity and injustice for their benefit. This original structure has not disappeared; it continues to shape organizational patterns and perceptions long after decolonization. To counteract this effect, both police and the public need to reconceptualize their relationship. An effective exercise might explore the negative connotations associated with colonialism and then ask trainees to compare the present police force with its predecessor. A state-of-emergency hangover stems from the sheer number of internal security forces (ISF) personnel who were trained or who served while the nation was under a state of emergency (or other similar phenomena such as martial law). The problem is that emergency restrictions tend "to become perpetual or to effect far-reaching authoritarian changes in the *ordinary legal norms*."[14] Even where there is no absence of de jure protection, some security forces operate in an atmosphere of impunity, able to violate the law with no fear of retribution. As a consequence of these three phenomena, LEAs incorporate abuse into modes of operation and create values capable of enduring new legislation or elections.[15]

As the preceding discussion makes apparent, the treatment for these hangovers must include both a dose of new structure and a regimen of perceptual modification. This is because abuses such as the use of torture or arbitrary detention do not evolve in a vacuum—policemen have been taught that their actions are justified. In short, LEAs do not measure the ethical component of their actions against the backdrop of international human rights law. Instead, normative subsystems within the force, unit, or peer group justify many violations.

To a large extent, justifying abusive behavior involves discrediting human rights law. Security forces conceptualize human rights as contradicting their primary objective—preserving law and order. Research by the Centre for the Victims of Torture (Nepal) indicates that torturers are "trained to believe that what they are doing is right . . . and [those concerned] have to understand that they think that torture is the right thing to do."[16] This conceptualization of human rights galvanizes the "we-they" mentality pervading security forces: "we" need to arrest criminals, "they" speak to us of procedural rights; "we" understand what is reality, "they" speak of utopian aspirations; "we" risk our lives in the line of duty, "they" endanger the country; "we" need to stick together against "them." Moreover, this "we-they" dichotomy is fueled by the "inequity" of human rights law itself, insofar as it applies to actions by LEAs but not to actions of criminals or (sometimes) rebels.

There are two processes common to virtually any law enforcement agency which should be dealt with in HRE for the police because they interplay with all of the above factors. The first is the way in which chain of command structure dislocates the individual officer, extinguishing his sense of responsibility for his actions. The excuse that one is following orders enables the individual officer to ignore both the law and his own sense of right and wrong. The second is the way in which being part of a group, in this case a peer group composed of other LEAs, affects behavior. The group dynamics in which much of police work takes place or is judged pressures LEAs to maintain a certain image (e.g., one cannot afford to appear to others as being soft) and allows a policeman to justify behavior by the fact that it comports with the behavior of others (each of whom is performing the same externally focused justification).

There are other reasons for abuse which can be addressed by HRE and which do not involve such complex psychological phenomena. In some countries, the elements of a law or the boundaries it places on the exercise of police discretion are incomprehensible. In particular, this ambiguity characterizes new decrees, the terms of which have not yet been defined by the courts or senior officials (as in the case of a return to constitutional rule following a state of emergency). A typical law might state that in order to make an arrest "[t]he (detaining authority) must *first* be *satisfied* that a person: a) is *concerned* in *acts* prejudicial to *public* order, or b) has been recently *concerned* in *acts* prejudicial to public order."[17] There is nothing in this law which delineates permissible actions or guides a decision regarding the arrest or questioning of a person. What is an act "prejudicial to public order?" What does "satisfied" mean? Changes in written law restoring constitutional protections to the people do not by themselves alter, say, the policeman's sense of how much suspicion (if any) is needed to arrest and question an individual. The Legal Resources Foundation's LEA education project articulates the need for its training program as follows: "A majority, if not all, of Zimbabwe's law enforcement agents were trained during the existence of the state of emergency in terms of which extraordinarily wide and extensive powers were given to them. With the removal of the state of emergency, these powers have been drastically curtailed, the result being that a vacuum has been left because law enforcement agents have never had to operate and effectively perform their duties under what may be regarded as peace-time conditions."[18] In other cases, ignorance rather than ambiguity is the problem. In discussing UN human rights training courses for more than three thousand administrators of justice, government officials, LEAs, and others, Jan Martenson (former UN under-secretary-general for human rights) stated: "The result was invariably the same, the people said: We didn't know, we didn't know that these standards existed, that our country had ratified them, and particularly we didn't know that we had to apply them also in our daily activities."[19]

In the end, a host of tangled factors cause violations of human rights.[20] Since it is neither politically nor financially possible to replace the rank-and-file personnel of these forces in most countries, retraining and reeducation are imperative. To reiterate, effective human rights training for LEAs can reduce violations by: (1) educating LEAs as to the limits placed by substantive law upon the behavior of security personnel; (2) breaking down the normative system in which LEAs operate, allowing policemen to evaluate their own actions from a different perspective; (3) aiding security personnel to understand and respond to the pressures placed upon the individual by either authority or the professional peer group. The mere possibility of successful training, however, must be tempered by the dictates of reality, such as the human and material resources of an organization, the receptiveness of the police to "outside" ideas, and the political climate of a country.

Pedagogical Issues in Human Rights Education for the Police

Effectiveness

Although much remains to be learned, some lessons can be drawn from the foregoing discussion. Generally speaking, perhaps the most important factor in human rights education for LEAs is to create an atmosphere that is nonthreatening. For instance, research by the Washington Office on Latin America (WOLA) shows that the mere

Figure 19.1. Police students in Kinshasa are examined on methods of citizen identification consistent with judicial requirements and standards of human rights. Increasing', democratic countries are requiring their police to learn and apply human rights norms. Such training is constitutionally mandated by the Constitution of the Republic of the Philippines (Art. 3, sect. 17) and by the Constitution of Peru (Art. 14). (UNPHOTO I/PAS)

mention of the term human rights "makes Latin American officers bristle; it's accompanied in their minds by the word 'violation,' and so . . . is perceived as accusatory."[21] Furthermore, demonstrating a sensitivity to human rights or dignity issues invites the label of "soft" and jeopardizes the standing of a policeman in his professional peer group. Finally, as has been pointed out by Dean James T. Curran of John Jay College, for police officers in many parts of the world the only alternative to being an LEA is abject poverty, meaning that they fear disturbing the status quo because it places their livelihoods at risk.[22]

In addition to the examples of programs discussed above, successful programs must combine two approaches to overcome the antagonism or skepticism of participants. First, they should not focus expressly on human rights but upon human dignity, professionalism, or other "disguised" subjects (see below). As one academic has stated along these lines, "[h]uman rights is something wimps do, and 'human rights training' is perceived as an oxymoron. You've got to find an expanded vocabulary."[23] Second, whether using role-play, group projects, or questions based on hypothetical situations, it is important to remain practical, to build upon the experiences and assignments of the participants. A survey of actual or potential trainees would be one way to develop a course grounded in their reality. Another way would be to involve police officers or experts capable of speaking to the police culture in the planning and implementation stages of the course. With regard to this problem, an official in the Philippines, where government human rights training for police and military is part of a nationwide, constitutionally mandated HRE campaign, proposes ten ways to increase acceptance of human rights education by Philippine military and police.[24]

1. Arrange for clear command structure endorsements, meaning that commanding officers should be physically present at the education in order to send a clear signal of its importance.
2. Avoid legalese and emphasize the Filipino context so as to ensure understanding.
3. Use some trainers who are members of LEAs in addition to outside specialists.
4. Appeal to professional ethics and codes of conduct.
5. Standards must be fair, meaning that violations shall include abuse by criminals or insurgents.
6. Underscore the point that respecting human rights is in each officer's best interests.
7. Emphasize basic human needs by using carrots (promotions) rather than sticks (threats of investigations and sanctions) in such a way that the satisfaction of the trainee's human needs (e.g., food for the family, education for the children) is tied to respecting the human needs of others.
8. Establish a reward system for trainees.
9. Establish a reward system for trainers.
10. Make use of external and internal assistance and resources.

Once these initial obstacles have been cleared (or minimized), it is the interplay between course format, instructor identity, and course content that will determine the effectiveness of the course.

Course Format: Reality Check

Perhaps the most important thing about format is simply that it must accommodate both the content and the participants. Delivering a lecture would not be conducive to changing the way LEAs experience dignity, nor would group debate work well in a class of several hundred. As is discussed elsewhere in this book, the use of participatory schemes, group exercises, role-plays, audiovisual input, and *practical* hypotheticals enhances educational effectiveness and should be encouraged. In particular, lectures become increasingly productive as one moves away from straightforward presentation of laws or rights (e.g., recitation of the Universal Declaration of Human Rights) toward methods that lead to greater internalization of the message. While large audiences may not be able to participate in group exercises or discussions, films or skits could be used to *show*, rather than simply say, how human rights laws affect the police. There is probably no pedagogical limit to the number of people who can be struck by a film. If, on the other hand, an organization has the resources to conduct a course based on group-level learning exercises and dialogue, the faculty of "Human Dignity" has found that approximately thirty participants per session works well for its course. More than thirty becomes unmanageable and inhibits group exercises, while less than thirty is not conducive to discussion or diversity of experience.[25]

There are also questions surrounding the composition of the participants. The faculty of "Human Dignity" has drawn several conclusions from its experience which suggest more general rules. In terms of impact, cadets or LEAs on the force a relatively short time are generally the most receptive to the course. The reason is that they have only partially adopted the normative values and perceptions of more veteran officers. Additionally, their distrust of outsiders and sense of "we-they" is less acute. Another point is that while valuable interchanges take place when participants come from disparate ranks, these sessions are more difficult to manage effectively. A particular problem surfacing in mixed-rank sessions stems from the educational and social gap between high-ranking officers and lower-level LEAs. There is a tendency for the latter group to be intimidated (less than forthcoming about problems) and for the higher officers to dominate the discussions and presentations. One way to counteract this is to place all the ranking officers in the same group, so that other voices can be heard. Finally, the John Jay faculty recommends against sessions drawing participants from a mixture of agencies or branches (e.g., prosecutors, police, military) in a course similar to "Human Dignity."

Instructors: The Need for Credibility and Expertise

Human rights education for LEAs resembles any other form of education in that the teachers must be both credible and competent. Several factors make it particularly problematic to combine these two traits in training for policemen: (a) chain-of-command structure; (b) deep-rooted skepticism on the part of the students toward the subject matter; and (c) historical antagonism between LEAs and human rights organizations.[26]

Credibility is perhaps the more troublesome obstacle, because it involves not just the trainer but the message as well. The primary concern about the role of the human rights community in ISF training is "whether efforts by human rights activists would be so poorly received by military personnel that they would simply be a waste of time."[27] At the School of the Americas (SOA), for instance, U.S. training policy (of foreign military personnel) is formulated around a belief that "using trainers with commensurate rank and experience to the trainees, [is] understood as crucial to the credibility of the trainer."[28] Using military officers as instructors, however, is equally criticized as a solution. Military or police officers typically lack the requisite expertise or commitment in the fields of human rights and education or training to enable them to conduct an effective course. A related problem is presented when foreigners—officers or human rights experts—are brought in to teach. According to a former instructor at SOA (where instructors are U.S. officers), "students quickly realize that it's a gringo course, so 'when they get back to their countries they can forget it.' "[29] In short, there is the risk that the message will appear alien or will be resented as paternalistic. As for governments teaching their own personnel, many simply lack the authority to teach human rights, given other policies that contradict those teachings. This "do as I say, not as I do" attitude sends a mixed signal, thereby neutralizing educational effects. In a chain-of-command structure, mixed signals "can fatally undermine educational efforts," a situation that has been found to subvert program legitimacy in the Philippines.[30]

One possible solution to the problem of selecting credible and competent instructors is to do both at the same time. In other words, to employ multidisciplinary teams of instructors, some of whom are human rights experts and others of whom are LEAs. According to the staff of "Human Dignity," a key factor in the program's legitimacy is the presence of instructors who are current or former police officers. Similarly, the LRF's program employs outside resource persons from the government, such as judges and prosecutors, in addition to its own staff attorneys. According to evaluations, this measure increases the practicality and authority of its LEA training.

Content: A Wealth of Untested Options

Still at its inception, HRE for security forces is in need of time-consuming essay and evaluation across a broad spectrum of contexts. It is up to academics, human rights organizations, and governments to create and experiment with new ideas in this field. Aside from what has been discussed above, there are other potentially fruitful curricula. For instance, teachings from religion might be used to help convince LEAs of the need to respect the rights or dignity of others. Similarly, specialized content could deal with issues such as sensitizing LEAs to the rights of women or the needs of female sexual assault victims. To reiterate, for programs to be effective, they must change attitudes in both individuals and forces (dismantle normative frameworks that justify abuse) and eliminate deficiencies of knowledge or skill that give rise to abuse.

They must also relate to the participants, meaning that HRE should focus on those laws (from that country's constitution or UN documents) that directly define the behavior of LEAs, rather than model documents that are not operative locally (in other words, there is probably little value in teaching Latin American LEAs about the U.S. Constitution). In the end, there can be no rules governing content because nothing will work everywhere. The context—the instructors' capabilities, the composition of the participants, the state of human rights protections and violations in the country and so on—must determine the content.

One approach to human rights training has been a focus on professional conduct. In defense of the now-defunct International Police Academy program, the U.S. Agency for International Development (USAID) stated that its training resulted in improved professional attitudes toward the use of firearms, especially in crowd or riot control. They also cited some impact on police behavior in arrests, detentions, and interrogations.[31] The basic idea is to encourage respect for human rights as a matter of honor and institutional dignity rather than to focus directly on human rights. The strength of this approach is that by building on these existing values it is not necessary to deconstruct the normative system. Such training would work well with an emphasis on potential situations, using hypotheticals to develop participants' sense of correct behavior (e.g., a suspect surrenders after fighting with officers or an unarmed person accidentally approaches a roadblock in a high-security zone). The major drawback to professionalism training is that following orders or refusing to testify against a fellow officer are also matters of honor, ones that push policemen to act contrary to human rights law. Therefore, if professionalism training is to work, it must be accompanied by training directed toward changing LEA perception of honor and duty where they conflict with human rights.

Hypothetical problems such as those mentioned above could also be used to enliven human rights lectures. Instructors might develop tests or games of competition that depend on the ability of a group to resolve correctly the dilemma facing the officer in the problem or identify the governing law. Where drama or film is used, many possibilities exist. In order to teach about rights, "good cop" versus "bad cop" scenarios could be used in situations such as interrogating a suspect or searching a house. Or the suffering caused by or injustice of human rights violations could be depicted to underscore the importance of respecting the dignity of fellow humans. The message is more powerful if the trainees identify with the victim (e.g., an African civil servant being beaten by a colonial master or the wife of a policeman being raped by a soldier).

Where lectures or seminars are not possible, NGOs might produce materials for distribution to LEAs. Stories told in comic book style, simplified versions of the civil rights held by citizens of that country, or a picture book could be used to explain the law. An example of the latter which could be used as a model is the pamphlet "Rules for Behavior in Combat" produced by the International Committee of the Red Cross.

Finally, in one of the final exercises of "Human Dignity," the participants are asked to design their own code of police conduct and develop a strategy to implement it. This exercise should prove extremely fertile for human rights activists. It is difficult for outsiders to understand the inner dynamics of a particular police unit or force. Given the great perceptual gap between LEAs and activists, a key to effective structural changes and developing appropriate (and therefore successful) training curricula could lie in these expert suggestions. The fox knows best how to protect the hens. It is simply that we would not entrust it to do so.

NGO Participation Problems in HRE for the Police

An NGO must address a series of political and strategic considerations in making the decision to participate in HRE for the police. The solutions to these issues will be very different for an international NGO advising a government on training methods than they will for a small torture-monitoring NGO asked to lecture for a day about human rights at boot camp for new police recruits.

The central issue is whether or not involvement in such a program compromises the integrity or image of the organization. First, developing a relationship with the police (or military) might endanger the trust placed in the organization by the public. Losing this trust will hamper the ability of the organization to perform its other activities (e.g., popular legal education, interviewing victims of abuse). Furthermore, revelations of abuse committed by security personnel involved in training by an NGO could embarrass or discredit that organization. Second, it is always the possibility that an NGO's participation will be used by a government to improve public relations or legitimize training programs (and foreign assistance) involving more than just human rights.

The flip side of this issue is equally problematic: does the human rights community want governments to be responsible for teaching human rights? The moral fiber of governments aside, it is the expertise in both the subject matter and educational technique that make NGO participation crucial to the success of a program. Speaking generally of human rights education, Richard P. Claude surmises that "there may be no more important predictor of successful program development and implementation than the prevalence of strong, independent, and critical NGOs and educational institutions."[32] In the end, perhaps NGO cooperation provides an opportunity for NGOs to be watchdogs from the inside.

Even if willing to cooperate, there are a variety of reasons why it might be difficult for one organization to play both the role of watchdog and educator. In Zimbabwe, for instance, the activities of the LRF (and LRF staff) include opposing certain government policies and supporting torture victims. Such activities do not pass unnoticed by the government: the Central Intelligence Organization discontinued its participation in the LRF workshops in retaliation to criticism of certain CIO actions (and for the political activities of certain LRF personnel), and other police commanders have

Figure 19.2. In a provision bearing on police training, the African Charter on Human and Peoples' Rights says that signatory states "shall have the duty to promote and ensure through teaching, education, and publication, the respect for the rights and freedoms contained in the present Charter and to *see to it that these freedoms and rights as well as corresponding obligations and duties are understood*" (Art. 25, emphasis added).

occasionally become wary of participation. One solution to this dilemma might be patterned upon the corporate world's separation of function. In other words, perhaps NGOs specifically designed to conduct human rights education for LEAs (or just HRE) need to be developed (or subdivisions within large NGOs). To begin with, such an organization would not have to oppose the government actively to develop the trust necessary to perform its function. Along these same lines, trainees would not be overly suspicious or skeptical of the organization providing the education. Second, developing an effective training program would be facilitated by the expertise that accompanies specialization. Most important, specialization eliminates the inevitable frictions that develop where an NGO is both monitoring and assisting the government. Finally, specialization might also increase the ability of the organization to obtain funding because its mandate is more clearly defined.[33]

A potential drawback to the specialization approach is that the organization's existence (hence jobs) would depend on the relationship with the government. It would be extremely difficult for a specialized educational NGO to withdraw should such a measure be warranted by continued government disdain for human rights, thereby ending its own existence. There are also problems caused by duplication within an environment of scarce resources (i.e., for how many computers can human rights organizations in a certain country receive funding?)

For many of these reasons, special attention should be given to the potential role of universities in HRE for LEAs. In the first place, expertise in both education and human rights exists at most universities, as does the ability to experiment. In the second place, universities possess the international contacts and resource capacity necessary to follow developments in this relatively rapidly evolving endeavor. In the third place, most universities are government institutions, meaning that they are less likely to frighten the security establishment and more likely to be able to initiate cooperation than typical human rights NGOs (of course, circumstances vary from country to country). At the same time, the university must be independent enough to resist subjugation in order to implement a credible course. In the fourth place, universities do not usually engage in human rights monitoring, meaning that collaboration is less likely to cause conflict with the government or interfere with the university's other functions.

Conclusion

For any sort of LEA education to take place, government cooperation is necessary: venues must be set and LEAs must be made available. In the case of "Human Dignity and the Police," the sponsorship of the U.S. government elicited the cooperation of foreign police forces. Such cases will be rare. In the case of the LRF's educational seminars, contacts between LRF directors and government leaders resulted in cooperation. The program was marketed as a way for security forces to improve their relationship to the public and for the government to prosecute criminals more successfully (the judiciary regularly dismissed cases where the police abused suspects or obtained evidence illegally). Realistically speaking, governments will establish human rights training for security forces when it is in their interest to do so. Some of this political will develops when leadership realizes (is taught) that abuse of power by LEAs destabilizes society and weakens the legitimacy of the regime. It also means that pro-human rights organizations and governments must pressure recalcitrant leaders to establish HRE for LEAs.

Human rights education for LEAs should be a vital component of the movement to rid global society of human rights violations. As the international human rights community focuses more attention on human rights education, it must recognize the potential benefits of directing such education at the large population of everyday violators. It is therefore the responsibility of human rights organizations to attack the actors as ardently as they criticize oppressive leadership and the structural underpinnings of abuse.

At this early stage, it is perhaps large international NGOs, UN agencies, or universities that must make human rights training for LEAs a priority, using their resources to develop model curricula, training exercises, and teaching materials and to encourage local self-sufficiency through training of trainer courses. There is also a need for a comprehensive analysis of existing programs around the world and a similarly extensive assessment of their impact. It is then the work of local NGOs to adopt these models to fit the local context, taking into consideration the factors contributing to abuse at that level. At the same time, local NGOs must begin to approach the complicated question of how best to communicate with local LEAs.

Unfortunately, the existence of government forces with guns is an ineluctable part of modern life. Mutual distrust between security forces and the public—those with and those without guns—frustrates nation building and obstructs the path toward stability. Pro–human rights government, de facto accountability, and hours of lectures may curtail important violations by the police, but without striking at the decades of learned behavior and normatively reinforced attitudes, spectacular violations will only be as far away as the next structural loophole, and mundane violations will continue to afflict the daily lives of the people.

Notes

1. In the case of human rights abuse by internal security forces, the author is uncomfortable implying some sort of gender equality, and will hereafter use masculine terminology.

2. Note, however, that certain points made in this chapter stem from studies of training programs for military personnel, and much of the analysis would be applicable to the training of soldiers, prison guards, customs officials, and other security personnel.

3. See Richard Pierre Claude, *Human Rights Education in the Philippines* (Manila: Kalikasan Press 1991); Richard Pierre Claude, "Human Rights Education: The Case of the Philippines," *Human Rights Quarterly* 13, no. 4 (1991): 453; Human Rights Research and Education Centre, *Human Rights Training for Commonwealth Public Officials Manual* (Ottawa: Human Rights Unit, Commonwealth Secretariat), 1990.

4. Much of information about "Human Dignity" comes from conversations with and materials provided by the staff members of the course. Conversations took place between October 1993 and April 1994. Materials on file with the author include the participant handbook, *Human Dignity and the Police* (1993) and the "Instructor's Notes" for the course (1993). The author greatly appreciates the assistance of Dean James Curran, Raymond Pitt, Julio Hernandez-Miyares, Carmen Rodriguez, Cheryl Fiandaca, and Officer Robert Donato.

5. *John Jay Quarterly* 2, no. 4 (1993) (John Jay College; on file with author) (statement of Dean of Special Programs James T. Curran).

6. Washington Office on Latin America (WOLA), "Human Rights Education and Training in U.S. Policy Toward Latin America," background paper for a June 1992 seminar, 19.

7. As a Columbia Law School human rights intern, the author worked at the Legal Resources Foundation (LRF) during the summer of 1992. The author greatly appreciates the assistance provided by LRF staff members.

8. Legal Resources Foundation [LRF] (Zimbabwe), "Proposal Summary for Law Enforcement Agent Education Programme" (on file with author).

9. "Following the repeal of the Emergency Powers Regulations after 27 years, law enforcement agents have needed virtually to be re-educated on how to perform their duties in peacetime conditions." LRF, *Seventh Annual Report of the Legal Resources Foundation*, year ending June 30, 1991, p. 32.

10. Lesson plans from LEA education program (on file with author).

11. Capsule summaries of the evaluations from several seminars are on file with the author.

12. Claude, "Human Rights Education," 506.

13. Candace McCoy, "The Cop's World: Modern Policing and the Difficulty of Legitimizing the Use of Force," *Human Rights Quarterly* 8, no. 2 (1986): 270.

14. International Commission of Jurists, *States of Emergency: Their Impact on Human Rights* (Geneva: I.C.J., 1983), 415 (emphasis added). The reporter on Uruguay noted that people there "have become accustomed to the emergency regime to the point that it has become the 'normal' machinery of government" (ibid., 358). Is it not reasonable to assume that the internal security forces (ISFs) have grown just as accustomed? See also John Hatchard, "The Implementation of Safeguards on the Use of Emergency Powers: A Zimbabwean Perspective," *Oxford Journal of Legal Studies* 9 (1989): 116.

15. Although the subject of this chapter is training designed to change the attitudes of law enforcement agencies (LEAs), it will also be necessary to sensitize the public to the proper role of the police. It is very likely that an oppressed public will distrust and fear both LEAs and the government. Furthermore, years of abuse condition the public to expect certain behavior: a relationship between the police and the people has been constructed and must be dismantled from both sides. For example, in India, very often "the people themselves expect the police to beat up goondas and when this is not done charges of bribery and corruption are hurled." Shailendra Misra, *Police Brutality: An Analysis of Police Behavior* (New Delhi: Vikas, 1986), 52.

16. Centre for the Victims of Torture, Nepal, *Voice Against Organised Violence* 5 (1993): 15.

17. Armed Forces and Police (Special Powers) Decree No. 24 of 1967 [Nigeria], cited in Olisa Agbakoba and Tunde Fagbohunlu, "Nigeria's State Security (Detention of Persons) Decree No. 2 of 1984: Exploding the Myth of Judicial Impotence," *Journal of Human Rights Law and Practice* 1 (1991): 45–61 (emphasis in original).

18. LRF, *Proposal Summary*.

19. "Interview," *Human Rights Newsletter* (Geneva: UN Centre for Human Rights) 4, no. 3 (July 1991): 5.

20. Not mentioned are those violations resulting from technical incompetence (e.g., confessions are forced from suspects in part because LEAs have not been taught or lack the resources to investigate crimes in any more scientific way). Technical training in areas such as investigatory or crowd control techniques can, therefore, render LEAs less abusive. There is a danger, though, that technical training will simply render more efficient the oppression and abuse caused by a particular force or unit. This chapter, however, is concerned with human rights training.

21. WOLA, "Human Rights Education," 31 (citing "an academic").

22. Conversation with James T. Curran, March 18, 1994.

23. WOLA, "Human Rights Education," 31.

24. Claude, "Human Rights Education," 514–15 (citing his interview with Amancio Donato, director of the Commission on Human Rights Public Information and Education Office).

25. "Instructor's Notes" (note 4 above).

26. Claude, "Human Rights Education," 512–14. Claude found that in the Philippines many

trainees "thought human rights teaching involved externally imposed standards 'just to make Westerners and United Nations types feel good'" (ibid., citing interview with Professor Raphael Lotilla). Another human rights instructor stated that "red labeling" of human rights NGOs poses a problem (ibid., citing interview with Rodolfo Felicio).

27. WOLA, "Human Rights Education," 29.

28. Ibid., 18.

29. *Newsweek* (International Edition) August 9, 1993, 37.

30. Claude, "Human Rights Education," 513.

31. Lawyers Committee for Human Rights [LCHR], *U.S. Assistance to Foreign Police Forces* (New York: LCHR, 1992), 130. Critics of the very political International Police Academy counter that such limited improvements do not warrant training programs that help abusive ISFs improve their efficiency and contribute to solidifying esprit de corps. See, e.g., Martha Dogget (Lawyers Committee for Human Rights), *Underwriting Injustice* (New York: LCHR, 1989), 11.

32. Claude, "Human Rights Education," 524.

33. Sufficient funding poses a serious obstacle. The LRF notes that "we have battled to obtain funding for the programme which is somewhat ironic [given that it] . . . has had a marked impact": *Sixth Annual Report of the Legal Resources Foundation,* year ending June 30, 1990, p. 22. It is perhaps a problem that education produces uncertain and long-term effects, while funding institutions frequently favor more quantifiable results.

Chapter 20
Teaching Human Rights to Public Health Practitioners

Jonathan Mann, Zita Lazzarini, Lawrence Gostin, and Sofia Gruskin

Education about human rights, including its relationship to health policy and programs, has been generally absent from academic programs in public health and medicine. Consequently it is not surprising that the vast majority of public health professionals, untrained in the fundamentals of human rights thinking and practice, rarely consider explicitly the effects of health policy, programs, or practices on human rights, nor do they focus on the impact of human rights violations on the health of individuals and populations. In turn, this lack of knowledge reduces the potential for constructive dialogue and interaction between health and human rights professionals and organizations. The Harvard School of Public Health is developing a coordinated program to educate public health students on the fundamental concepts of human rights and their practical application in the public health context. To symbolize this commitment, the school has distributed a copy of the Universal Declaration of Human Rights to each graduating student at commencement ceremonies since 1990. In 1991 the major course on the subject was instituted, "Human Rights for Public Health Practitioners," with support from the John D. and Catherine T. MacArthur Foundation. Additional educational activities have been developed within the context of the François-Xavier Bagnoud Center on Health and Human Rights, established in January 1993. These include a Health and Human Rights seminar series, a course on child rights and child health, a short course (part of the school's continuing education program), a project to help physicians identify human rights violations and identify their health implications, and a manual for community-based health and human rights organizations focusing on AIDS, health, and human rights (developed in collaboration with the International Federation of Red Cross/Red Crescent Societies, the Danish Center for Human Rights, the McGill Center on Ethics, Law and Medicine, the International Commission of Jurists, and the Society of Women against AIDS in Africa).

This chapter focuses on the pedagogical approach to educating public health students about human rights. The overall goal is to link a conceptual understanding of human rights with an appreciation for the pragmatic implications of the complex health-human rights relationship, in the specific context of public health.

Course Objectives

The first course objective is to provide basic literacy about human rights. "Literacy" is defined as familiarity with the basic history, core concepts, documents, institutions, and practices of modern human rights. Human rights thinking and practice is presented as a set of concepts and a language. (This approach is consistent with educational goals involving such core public health fields as epidemiology, biostatistics, management, and environmental health, as taught in schools of public health and through continuing education programs.) The goal of basic literacy includes fostering a capacity for further self-learning, collaboration with experts in the field, and integration of concepts into relevant professional activities. By analogy with other first-level courses, such as in epidemiology (the core science of public health), the course is not intended to render students capable of sophisticated practice in human rights. Rather, the course ensures that each student knows the basic concepts of human rights thinking and methodology, so as to be capable of critical analysis of research and writing on human rights, to engage in meaningful dialogue with persons working in human rights (including an awareness of critical and inherent limitations), and to know how to use human rights analysis to help identify and resolve public health problems. In this manner, literacy about human rights is the essential foundation for linking human rights with public health practice.

The second objective is to introduce and explore a three-part framework for thinking about important interactions between health and human rights. The first relationship involves the impacts (positive and negative) of health policies, programs, and practices on human rights. The second relationship considers the individual and public health impacts of severe violations of human rights, both during conflict and in peacetime. The third relationship explores a deeper, fundamental interdependence between promotion and protection of human rights and promotion and protection of health. Familiarity with this framework and the methodologies involved with each element builds upon and strengthens "literacy" about human rights by linking rights with specific public health roles, details of practice, and professional responsibilities.

The third course objective is to stimulate participants to identify and collaborate with human rights experts and organizations in their professional setting. The strengthening of confidence and skills for interdisciplinary collaboration is extremely important. It is only through meaningful cooperation between experts in human rights and in public health that truly effective action can be achieved. Human rights workers may not have the proficiency to identify and quantify the effects of human

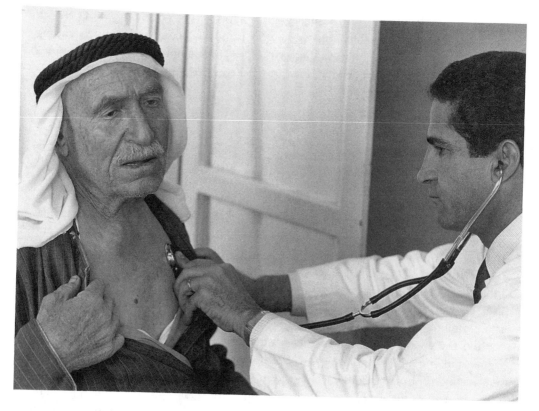

Figure 20.1. A Palestinian refugee receives health care in a Jordanian camp. The International Covenant on Economic, Social and Cultural Rights recognizes "the right of everyone to the enjoyment of the highest attainable standard of physical and mental health." (UNRWA photo 85386/ M. Nasr)

rights violations on the health of populations. Nor do public health practitioners have the skill necessary to analyze the human rights violations and seek remedies in national or international settings. Only through learning the fundamental concepts of human rights can public health practitioners exercise leadership in disseminating information about health and human rights, both within their traditional professional environment and with the community of people working on human rights. Together, human rights and public health workers can achieve a synergy of effort and purpose that would not be possible within the confines of a single discipline or approach.

The Context: Human Rights for Public Health Practitioners

The pedagogical approach must also consider who we are teaching. Public health practitioners have several relevant and important general characteristics. First, their public health work complements and builds on a high degree of professional expertise in a specific field, such as medicine, nursing, social work, or management. A second, related feature is the extraordinary diversity of backgrounds, reflecting both a variety of disciplines and the many tasks of public health, ranging from political officials to fieldworkers. Third, public health workers generally have little or no experience with law, legal language, or human rights. Finally, the student's age, level of training, and extent of "real world" experience mandate an adult learning approach to human rights.

The specific skills to be taught, and methods to be used, derive from these characteristics of the public health audience. The pedagogical approach focuses on the ability to understand and identify substantive human rights issues, with less emphasis on the mechanisms for reporting human rights violations or the details of the international human rights machinery. In addition, students are helped to analyze familiar situations involving health policy and programs from a new perspective of human rights. To be successful, the approach must use and build on public health traditions, values, and methods. The health worker must be able to see how his or her skills can connect directly with human rights, such as applying epidemiological skills to document health effects of human rights abuses, or using a "two-by-two" table to illustrate and then consider the human rights impacts of health policies. Finally, a genuine connection between health and human rights has both professional and personal dimensions for the public health practitioner. Accordingly, we encourage discussions about professional roles and responsibilities, as well as urging personal reflection to explore concepts such as the relevance of dignity to health.

Curriculum

The curriculum is divided into five sections. The first section, entitled "Introduction to Modern Human Rights," starts with a history of major trends and developments in human rights with an emphasis on the post–World War II era. The documents comprising the International Bill of Human Rights are presented as a basic foundation for the course. Finally, the differences and similarities between civil/political and economic, social, and cultural rights are discussed. The capacity of nonlawyers to read and understand the basic human rights documents is stressed.

Core principles of human rights thinking are described, such as inalienability, universalism, indivisibility, and the differences between derogable and nonderogable rights. Two vital issues are also introduced at this point: the potential for restriction of rights on public health grounds; and the debate about whether human rights have universal application to all cultures and societies or whether they are culturally specific. It is important to present these two issues as early as possible in the curriculum, to encourage critical thinking about these complex problems as students learn about human rights. In addition, delaying discussion of these issues may lead to a disconnection between learning about human rights concepts and practitioners' assumptions about public health and their personal experience with cultural diversity.

Finally, selected rights are described, using illustrations with particular relevance to health. For example, "security of person" is discussed with reference to the concept of informed consent; similarly, nondiscrimination is introduced in the context of access to health services.

The institutions and practices relevant to monitoring, promoting, and enforcing human rights are then presented, with particular attention to the United Nations and related institutions, and to the vital role of nongovernmental organizations. Emphasis is given to the principles, rather than the procedural details of human rights practice. At this stage, students may experience difficulty in understanding the nature, limits, and evolving quality of human rights enforcement; students' reactions often reflect the extremes of overconfidence in law as an instrument for influencing behavior and underconfidence in laws (international or national) that cannot be readily and effectively enforced.

Next, the course develops and explores the three dimensions of the conceptual framework for the relationship between health and human rights described above. The three basic relationships are outlined; the straightforward nature of the first two (impact of health policies, programs, and practices on rights; health impacts of rights violations) is emphasized, while the third (fundamental interdependence of promoting and protecting both health and human rights) is presented as a central hypothesis.

The second section of the course discusses the positive and negative impact of health policies, programs, and practices on human rights. Students are first reminded of the central mission and core activities of public health: assessment of health problems, policy development, and assurance of relevant services.[1] Then, using three case studies involving well-known public health problems (childhood immunizations, HIV infection among commercial sex workers, and injury control), students examine how public health policies and programs may create burdens on human rights.

At this stage, rather than attempt to impose an externally derived set of criteria to mediate this conflict (e.g., the Siracusa Principles),[2] a systematic and pragmatic approach has been developed to identify, describe, and negotiate conflicts between public health goals and human rights norms. This "public health/human rights impact assessment" instrument seeks to maximize attainment of public health goals while minimizing human rights burdens. Students work through a process of "mapping" the public health quality and the human rights quality of a particular policy or program. This leads to an assessment of specific ways in which human rights burdens may be reduced or eliminated without sacrificing public health goals. When apparent conflicts emerge, a thoughtful balance of public health and human rights dimensions is encouraged. Constant reference to the international human rights documents helps to structure a systematic approach to considering the restriction of rights in the context of public health.

This process, which emphasizes the potential for a "win-win" situation (good public health/supportive of human rights), challenges the assumption that public health, as articulated through specific policies and programs, is always an unalloyed public good that subsumes human rights norms. Concerns that the course attempts to place human rights above public health goals must be addressed. Accordingly, it is important to help students recognize how explicit negotiation between public health and human rights goals can result (almost always) in improved quality of health policies and programs without abdication of health leadership by public health authorities. This approach leads to acceptance of the concepts that "public health policies and programs must be considered as potentially burdensome on human rights until proven otherwise" and that "by limiting the burdens on human rights, the public health benefits can actually be enhanced." The implications of these maxims include a need for those who make health policy and design health programs to speak with individuals and groups potentially affected by a particular policy or program to discover whether, and in which specific ways, discrimination or other burdens on human rights may be occurring.

The third section of the course focuses on the impact of human rights violations on health, both in situations of violent conflict and in peacetime. The basic assumption of this section is that systematic violations of most, if not all, human rights have impacts on health, which are often unrecognized and unmeasured. In this section, the World Health Organization's definition of health as physical, mental, and social well-being is invoked, ensuring a broad approach to identifying health impacts of rights violations.

Starting with reports from conflict situations such as Bosnia or Iraq, the application of traditional public health methodologies, and particularly epidemiological analysis, to documenting health impacts is presented. Then the particular methodological and practical issues involved in documenting the long-term health effects of torture and imprisonment under inhumane conditions are explored, using the example of Vietnamese and other southeast Asian refugees. Special considerations relevant to research in multicultural settings are also emphasized. These first examples, involving clear and readily understood health effects as a result of rape or torture, help students realize the importance and power of applying health methods for documentation and analysis.[3]

This awareness sets the stage for considering the health effects of human rights violations in peacetime. Critical methodological issues include: documenting a systematic violation of rights; identifying and assessing the health outcomes; and establishing a causal, or at least plausible, relationship between the violation of rights and specific health outcomes. These issues are explored using the example of women's educational attainment (violations of rights to education and nondiscrimination) in the context of the World Bank's statement that increasing educational attainment of women is one of the most important interventions for improving health in developing countries.[4] The example of access to reproductive health information is also used as a specific example for this powerful discussion.

The general principle that human rights violations have health impacts, and that these impacts are largely unrecognized and undocumented, must be linked to the public health professional's broad responsibility for safeguarding the health of populations. The course proposes that public health workers have a positive responsibility to work with human rights organizations to identify and document such health impacts, thereby contributing to societal dialogue about human rights.

The fourth section of the course presents and explores a central hypothesis: the promotion and protection of human rights and the promotion and protection of health are fundamentally and inextricably linked. As this is a hypothesis, this section emphasizes creative analysis and identification of approaches for constructive exploration and research. To discuss this hypothesis, four subjects are considered: the relationship between enjoyment of human rights and vulnerability to HIV infection; the possible impacts of violations of dignity on health; the special features of children's rights in relation to children's health; and the right to health. This section suggests the possibility that promoting and protecting human rights may justifiably be considered an integral part of public health work, explores some of the practical consequences of this approach, and identifies research priorities for further evaluation of this hypothesis.

Finally, the fifth section returns to how human rights thinking can become part of the work of public health. In addition to analytic processes, specific studies that could be undertaken, and research priorities to be explored, additional practical suggestions include building a personal library of human rights documents, establishing connections with local, national, or international human rights organizations, networking, and dissemination of information about health and human rights.

Readings

It is essential for public health practitioners to read and become familiar with the core human rights documents (e.g., the Universal Declaration of Human Rights, the International Covenant on Civil and Political Rights, and the International Covenant on Economic, Social and Cultural Rights). While exploration of the human rights literature is strongly encouraged, a genuine sense of comfort with and understanding of the core documents and concepts is critical.

In addition to case studies and journal articles on specific topics, we have developed the "public health/human rights impact assessment" instrument in two forms. A narrative has been prepared which presents a structured approach to negotiating apparent conflicts between health and human rights goals. In addition, we provide a "two-by-two" table analytic approach. This involves locating a particular health policy or program within a grid containing two dimensions: its public health quality and its human rights quality. Together, these tools help to reframe the problem as one of seeking a "win-win" (good for public health and good for human rights) solution to an apparent conflict of goals. Finally, we encourage active searching of daily newspapers and magazines for current and emerging issues relevant to human rights and health.

On-the-Job Human Rights Education for Health Professionals
Kari E. Hannibal and Susannah Sirkin

The health care community has begun to provide human rights education to medical and nursing students and to professionals in practice. These pioneering programs, although few in number, generally offer education about human rights in the following areas:

1. classroom instruction and curriculum on ethical standards and the responsibility of the health professional facing situations involving possible violations of international human rights and medical ethics;[1]
2. instruction and experiential learning on the medical documentation of violations of international human rights and humanitarian law, and the design of appropriate responses to those violations;[2] and
3. training in the medical and psychological treatment of survivors of torture and other traumatic human rights violations.[3]

To give one example, Physicians for Human Rights (PHR) has developed an innovative pedagogy involving learning by doing, principally involving fact-finding activities. In this relatively new field of study, health professionals are trained in the skills of documenting and reporting human rights abuses.

Since its founding in 1986, PHR has sent more than forty teams of health professionals and scientists to more than thirty-five countries and territories to investigate violations of international human rights and humanitarian law. To conduct these investigations, many of which have produced irrefutable medical evidence of human rights abuses, the organization has, of necessity, recruited some medical or scientific specialists with little or no training in human rights. The process of conducting field investigations and preparing human rights reports and professional journal articles in a rigorous manner

---

1. Examples of such academic programs are: (1) the Center for the Study of Society and Medicine, Columbia University, 630 West 168th Street, New York, NY 10032, FAX (+91) (212) 305–6416; (2) the François Xavier-Bagnoud Center for Health and Human Rights, Harvard Medical School, 8 Story Street, 5th floor, Cambridge, MA 02138, FAX (+91) (617) 496–4380.

2. For information on this kind of training, contact: (1) Physicians for Human Rights, 100 Boylston Street, Suite 702, Boston, MA 02166, FAX (+91) (617) 695–0307; (2) Johannes Wier Foundation, P.O. Box 1551, 3800 BN Amersfoort, The Netherlands, FAX (+31) (33) 726–811; (3) the Medical Action Group, 150 K-6th Street, Kamias, Quezon City, the Philippines, FAX (+63) (2) 921–8702.

3. Consult these groups: (1) Rehabilitation and Research Centre for Torture Victims (RCT), P.O. Box 2107, DK-1014 Copenhagen K, Denmark, FAX (+45) (31) 33760500; (2) Center for Victims of Torture, 717 East River Road, Minneapolis, MN 55455, FAX (+91) (612) 626–2465; and (3) Instituto Latinamericano de Salud Mental y Derechos Humanos, Casilla 119, Correo 29, Santiago, Chile, FAX (+56) (2) 223–2473.

has resulted in the on-the-job education of dozens of medical human rights specialists.

Epidemiologists trained in survey methodology have worked to adapt questionnaires to specific refugee populations and to analyze their findings in light of human rights law. Specialists in emergency medicine and primary care have used the Geneva Conventions to assess violations of the right to access to care for the sick and wounded in war. Forensic pathologists skilled in performing autopsies on crime victims within a familiar legal framework have transferred their skills to obtain forensic evidence of mass executions for an international tribunal or human rights commission. Prison health experts have studied international minimum standards and worked to adapt evaluation instruments to countries with vastly different resources. All have learned the critical importance of political impartiality in human rights fact finding and have become versed in the translation of information into advocacy.

These doctors, nurses, and other health professionals have learned their human rights lessons on the job. They now represent a cadre of committed professionals who have returned to lecture at medical school courses, speak at association meetings, and, in turn, train the next generation of medical human rights investigators.

Experience

Based on several iterations of the course, a fairly reproducible sequence of students' response over time can be described. At first, the rapid acquisition of new knowledge about human rights (replacing the vague concept of human rights with information about documents, core principles, and institutions) evokes an excitement for learning more about the subject.

The second phase arises several weeks later, as the complexities of applying human rights thinking and practice within a public health context become evident. Any unspoken expectations vanish that human rights thinking or practice will immediately resolve or even contribute immediately toward solution of difficult health issues. At this point, increasing frustration and skepticism about the value of human rights results—sometimes expressed as anger or dismissal of human rights as "just talk" and "utopian"—should be anticipated.

Gradually, this nadir of confidence yields to a more reflective synthesis of human rights concepts with realities of public health experience and practice. The potentially positive contributions of rights perspectives to public health are reinforced, while the fears of having to abdicate judgment and influence over public health to lawyers and other human rights professionals diminishes. In addition, the seemingly overwhelming set of responsibilities for public health practitioners (the need to evaluate all policies and programs for rights burdens; the responsibility to measure and respond to health impacts of rights violations; and the need to promote rights actively as an integral part of public health practice) yields gradually to understanding that specific, concrete steps are possible and are within the influence and scope of public health practice. At this stage, the real potential for collaboration between health and human rights emerges.

Conclusions

The relationship between health and human rights is an evolving field. Resulting complications for teaching public health practitioners about human rights include the limited literature linking the two fields (exceptions include HIV/AIDS and women's reproductive health). However, health and human rights is an exciting new area for research, education, and advocacy. Every public health student exposed to human rights thinking significantly increases the body of health professionals who have formal human rights training. From the educator's viewpoint, the highest reward is to contribute to kindling the genuine excitement of public health professionals about human rights and to promote their commitment to and practical engagement in them.

Notes

1. Institute of Medicine, *The Future of Public Health* (Washington D.C.: National Academy Press), 1988.

2. UN Economic and Social Council, "Siracusa Principles," the Status of the International Covenant on Civil and Political Rights, UN Doc. E/CN.4/1985/4/28, September 1984.

3. H. Jack Geiger and Robert M. Cook-Deegan, "The Role of Physicians in Conflicts and Humanitarian Crises: Case Studies from the Field Missions of Physicians for Human Rights, 1988–1993," *Journal of the American Medical Association* 270 (1993): 616–20. R. F. Mollica and Y. Caspi-Yavin, "Measuring Torture and Torture-Related Syndromes," *Psychological Assessment* 3, no. 4 (1991): 1–7.

4. International Bank for Reconstruction and Development, *World Development Report 1993: Investing in Health* (New York: Oxford University Press), 1993.

Chapter 21
A Cambodian Human Rights Education Program for Health Professionals

Allen S. Keller, Sin Kim Horn, Sam Sopheap, and Gabriel Otterman

An integral part of the peacemaking efforts and reconstruction of Cambodia is the promotion of human rights. In a country where complete disregard for human rights has been a hallmark of much of recent history, education is an essential tool for ensuring human rights for all Cambodians. As part of its recent mission in Cambodia, the United Nations initiated a broadly based human rights education program. Local and international nongovernmental organizations also developed and implemented many projects to disseminate information and education concerning human rights throughout Cambodia to all facets of society.

In April 1993, at the invitation of the Human Rights Component of the United Nations Transitional Authority in Cambodia (UNTAC), Cambodian and international staff of the American Refugee Committee (ARC), a nongovernmental organization, began developing an unprecedented and innovative human rights education program for Cambodian health professionals. This program was developed in cooperation with the international human rights organization Physicians for Human Rights (PHR). Health professionals are an important group to focus attention on for human rights education as they have a unique role to play in promoting human rights. In particular, health professionals are responsible for providing health care to all in a respectful and ethical manner and for medically evaluating, documenting, and treating victims of human rights violations. Given their expertise, health professionals also have an important role to play in advocating and educating about human rights.

In implementing this program, project coordinators Allen Keller and Sin Kim Horn recruited a team of Cambodians and international staff with diverse backgrounds in health and human rights. The team developed a twenty-hour curriculum and an accompanying one hundred-page syllabus[1] in both Cambodian and English providing an overview of human rights with attention to the special role of health professionals in protecting human rights. More than three thousand Cambodian health professionals, including medical and nursing students, as well as practicing doctors, nurses, medical assistants, and midwives, have received human rights training through this program since its inception. This human rights education program for health professionals is the first of its kind in any developing country, and can serve as a model to be used in other countries.[2]

Cambodia's Health Care System

From 1975 to 1979 the Khmer Rouge ruled in Cambodia under a reign of terror. The entire populations of the capital and provincial towns were forcibly marched out into the countryside to work as slave labor. Countless individuals were tortured and executed. Hundreds of thousands more died of mistreatment, malnourishment, and disease. In the less than four years that the Khmer Rouge ruled, more than one million people died as a result of the government's brutal policies.[3]

Cambodia's health care infrastructure was entirely destroyed by the Khmer Rouge. Hospitals and health centers were burned or left in disrepair. Most of Cambodia's doctors and other health professionals were either killed or fled the country.[4] When the Vietnamese ousted the Khmer Rouge in 1979, Cambodia had one of the world's most neglected health care systems. Subsequently the Phnom Penh government began rebuilding the system and increased the number of practicing Cambodian physicians. The quality of training, however, was poor. The twelve-year civil war that followed continued the cycle of violence and destruction.

In October 1991 the warring Cambodian factions signed a peace agreement, the Paris Peace Accords, which included plans for UN-supervised elections. There followed a large influx of international aid and development efforts into Cambodia. Following the UN-supervised elections held in May 1993, the first free elections in Cambodia in twenty-five years, the different Cambodian factions, with the exception of the Khmer Rouge, formed a new coalition government.

In the midst of this rebuilding, Cambodia's health care system continues to face the demands of a population plagued by disease and years of war. Health indicators in Cambodia are among the poorest in the world.[5] One in five Cambodian children dies before the age of five, and maternal mortality ranks among the highest in the world. Epidemic diseases such as malaria, tuberculosis, diarrhea, and dengue fever are extremely prevalent. Because of the widespread indiscriminate use of land mines in recent years,[6] Cambodia has the world's highest percentage of mine amputees. One in every 236 Cambodians has lost a limb from a land mine injury.

An abysmal human rights record has also left physical and emotional scars on the country.[7] Most Cambodian families suffered tremendous losses under the Khmer Rouge rule and subsequent civil war. Torture was routinely practiced by the Khmer Rouge and continued under the subsequent regime. For years there was no system of due process under the law. Arbitrary arrests were common. The legal system is only beginning to function again. Prison conditions remain poor. Crimes against women, including rape and domestic violence, still often go unpunished.

Before 1990 only a handful of voluntary organizations worked in Cambodia. Presently more than fifty international organizations are providing assistance in health-related fields. With this support, several of Cambodia's hospitals are better equipped now than they were during the war. Health conditions are beginning to improve. However, lack of basic medical services in many areas of the country remains common. Cambodian health professionals face additional difficulties including shortages of necessary medicines and medical supplies. Salaries for health staff are often very low. The health care needs of the population are great.

Curriculum Development

The project team developed a curriculum for Cambodian health professionals which provides fundamental human rights information and is relevant and applicable to the human rights issues Cambodian health professionals encounter. This includes providing health care for all individuals regardless of ethnic or political background; caring for victims of human rights abuses including torture, police beatings, rape, and domestic violence; caring for land mine injury victims; and monitoring and improving prison conditions. Emphasis is also placed on the role of health professionals in promoting human rights through advocacy and education. The curriculum incorporates core cultural values, such as the relationship between Buddhism and human rights.[8]

The human rights project team included Cambodian doctors, medical assistants, nurses, midwives, and a Cambodian law student. Several of the Cambodian staff were returning refugees who received health training while living in refugee camps on the Thai-Cambodian border. Others were teachers at the Faculty of Medicine and School of Nursing in Cambodia. Two of the staff brought with them the painful experience of being victims of torture during the Khmer Rouge rule. International staff included an American physician with experience in human rights work and in evaluating victims of torture, a French nurse who was involved with children's rights issues, and a British lawyer who previously worked with Amnesty International.

The team spent approximately two months developing the curriculum. Discussions took place about what are human rights and what is the role of health professionals in protecting and promoting human rights. Project staff with particular expertise shared their knowledge with the rest of the group. Human rights material translated into Cambodian was provided by the UNTAC Human Rights Component.[9] PHR served as an important resource in providing curriculum material and guidance. A project library with relevant human rights books and articles was organized.

Project coordinators identified several other individuals with backgrounds in human rights who participated in staff training and curriculum development. This included Cambodian staff working for the UNTAC Human Rights Component, a

Buddhist monk, and a Cambodian with an extensive background in mental health. Representatives of local and international human rights groups also discussed their work with project staff.

The curriculum was developed at a time when a great deal of human rights education was going on in Cambodia. The Paris Peace Accords[10] specifically stated that human rights education was part of the mandate of the UN mission in Cambodia. The Human Rights Education Project for Health Professionals in Cambodia was developed in cooperation with the Ministry of Health and the Faculty of Medicine in Phnom Penh, with good working relations established. Their support greatly facilitated implementation of this project.

During the period immediately before the elections in May 1993, there was a great deal of tension and unrest in Cambodia. The Khmer Rouge chose not to participate in the elections and threatened to disrupt them. Episodic violence and intimidation by both the Khmer Rouge and government forces occurred with alarming frequency. Rumors abounded that a full-scale civil war would break out. Several nongovernmental organizations markedly curtailed their activities during this period. Human rights project staff, however, continued working, with the conviction that their work was a reaffirmation of the peace process.

The curriculum developed consists of ten two-hour sessions and the accompanying one hundred-page syllabus in Cambodian and English mentioned above.[11] Project staff practiced teaching lectures to one another and critiqued each other's teaching styles. After each of the initial classes at the Faculty of Medicine and School of Nursing in Phnom Penh, staff evaluated whether the lectures were effective and then made appropriate revisions based on this experience. Similar discussions continue to take place each time the course is taught. Furthermore, course participants are asked to provide feedback about the course.

Curriculum Sessions

1. What Are Human Rights? Why Is It Important for Health Professionals to Learn About Them?

In this introductory session, human rights are defined.[12] Teaching staff discuss the relationship between Buddhism and human rights. Course participants are introduced to the special role of health professionals in protecting human rights through evaluating and treating victims and medically documenting human rights abuses.

2. The Universal Declaration of Human Rights and Its Significance for Health Professionals

This section provides the historical background for the Universal Declaration of Human Rights and reviews basic freedoms, including civil and political rights, as well

Figure 21.1. Sin Kim Horn, a medic and coordinator of the Health and Human Rights Project of the American Refugee Committee, teaches a course on human rights to nurses in Phnom Penh. The curriculum for the course was developed by a team working with Dr. Allen Keller of Physicians for Human Rights. (Physicians for Human Rights)

as cultural, economic, and social rights.[13] Fundamental principles outlined in the Universal Declaration of Human Rights, including equality, the right to life, and the right to freedom from torture, are discussed. The role of health professionals in protecting these rights are evaluated.

3. The Right to Health Care

Course participants review the right to health care, regardless of age, sex, and political, social, ethnic, or economic background. Teaching staff lead discussions regarding case examples particularly relevant to Cambodia, such as caring for ethnic Vietnamese or members of the Khmer Rouge. The right to health care of prisoners[14] and simple strategies for improving health conditions for prisoners are also discussed.

4. Professional Responsibilities

Teaching staff provide an introduction to medical ethics and professional responsibility.[15] This includes a discussion regarding the health professional's duties to weigh the benefits and risks of any treatment and to use medications appropriately in the face of severe shortages. Course participants learn about the relationship between Buddhism and medical ethics, as well as codes of medical ethics such as the Declaration of Geneva, a modern version of the Hippocratic Oath.

5. Communication Skills for Health Professionals

The course provides an overview of effective communication skills and their therapeutic value.[16] Teaching staff emphasize the importance of communication skills, particularly with victims of human rights abuses who may be frightened, embarrassed, distrustful, and reluctant to talk about what happened to them. Course participants also discuss issues of privacy and confidentiality.

6. The Medical Evaluation of the Victim of Human Rights Abuse

Course participants learn about specific medical and social information important to obtain in performing a detailed evaluation of a victim of human rights abuse. This includes methods for effectively and respectfully obtaining a thorough medical history and performing a complete physical examination. Teaching staff also review the proper format for writing a detailed medical report concerning a human rights victim.[17]

7. Human Rights and Health Care for Women and Children

The course reviews human rights issues and documents focusing on the rights of women and children.[18] Emphasis is placed on the role of health professionals in promoting children's right to health through providing preventive care such as vaccines, curative care, and education such as effective rehydration methods. Course participants are encouraged to consider the role health professionals can play in treating and protecting children from child abuse, sexual abuse, homelessness, child prostitution, and war-related injuries such as land mines.

Health and human rights issues discussed relating to women include rape and sexual assault, domestic violence, and forced prostitution. Domestic violence is argued to be a human rights abuse, as it is widespread and there are no effective legal barriers in Cambodia for preventing and then punishing the offenders, and thus in effect is state-sanctioned.[19]

8. Torture and the Responsibilities of Health Professionals

The course provides an overview of the physical and psychological aftereffects of torture and the role of health professionals in examining and caring for survivors of torture.[20] Materials, including excerpts from a Khmer Rouge interrogator's manual, are cited, exposing the mind-set of those performing torture.[21] Emphasis is placed on the role of health professionals in documenting, reporting, and advocating against torture.

9. Land Mines and the Responsibilities of Health Professionals

Teaching staff emphasize the responsibility for providing care to victims of land mines, including providing prosthetics, rehabilitation, and emotional support, and the importance of documenting mine injuries and advocating against their use.[22] Land mines are offered as an example of a human rights issue in Cambodia around which health professionals can organize and play an essential role in increasing public awareness.

10. Human Rights and Mental Health

Course participants learn about the relationship between human rights and mental health.[23] They learn about mental illnesses that may be seen in victims of human rights abuses, including depression and post-traumatic stress disorder. Trainers emphasize that empathic listening skills are important in caring for human rights abuse victims.

Teaching Methods

Case studies are incorporated into the curriculum in order to emphasize the relation between health and human rights. The case studies focus on the role of health professionals in evaluation, treatment, documentation, and advocacy for victims of human rights abuses. In addition to examples from Cambodia, case studies from other countries, including the United States, are cited in order to demonstrate that human rights are important concerns for health professionals worldwide.

Class discussion and participation is an integral part of the educational process. Students are called upon and asked to comment on what they would do in a particular situation. Others are encouraged to share their opinions. Although there is often initial reluctance about participating, enthusiastic discussion inevitably follows.

Case Studies

Case 1: The Right to Health Care Regardless of Race or Nationality

A twenty-five-year-old Vietnamese woman living in Cambodia is brought to the hospital after suffering a gunshot wound when her village was attacked by a group of armed men, who went through the village shooting everyone they saw and yelling "Kill the Vietnamese." Ten other people are dead, including four children.

During the period before the elections, there was a great deal of racial violence directed against ethnic Vietnamese living inside Cambodia. In reviewing this case, discussion focuses on the basic human rights principles violated, including the right to life and the right to protection against racial discrimination. The responsibility of health professionals to provide medical care regardless of race, nationality, or ethnicity is emphasized.

Case 2: Professional Responsibility

A nineteen-year-old man comes to a doctor complaining of fatigue and headaches. He generally appears to be in good health. Physical examination is normal. The doctor gives him an injection of Vitamin C in his left buttock. One week later, he returns complaining of pain. The doctor examines him and finds a large, infected area at the injection site. Did the doctor act correctly by giving the injection of Vitamin C?

Unnecessary injections, under less than sterile conditions, are common in Cambodia. In presenting this case, the class is divided in half with one half suggesting possible benefits of such injections and the other half suggesting possible risks. Possible benefits frequently mentioned include providing vitamins and psychological and emotional benefit. Risks include unnecessary treatment, expense, possible allergic reaction or infection, and possible blood-borne infections including hepatitis and AIDS. This case is intended to demonstrate the need for health professionals to weigh the benefits and risks of any procedure or treatment and to inform patients of these. In this particular case, course participants are taught that the risks far outweigh the possible benefits.

Case 3: Health Professionals and Torture

A thirty-five-year-old male is arrested. He has a history of high blood pressure. Before he is interrogated, the prison doctor (who is willingly working in the prison) checks the prisoner's blood pressure, which is found to be normal. The doctor tells the guards that the prisoner can withstand the interrogation.

The prison guards subsequently begin to question and beat the prisoner, hitting him in the stomach and back, yelling that he should confess. The doctor is standing in the corner of the room watching. The prisoner then receives several electrical shocks from a device that one of the prison guards is holding.

After approximately twenty minutes, the doctor checks the prisoner's blood pressure again and finds that it is now elevated. The doctor instructs the guards to allow the prisoner to rest for a few minutes. Ten minutes later, the patient's blood pressure is still elevated. The doctor gives the patient some medicine, and twenty minutes later the patient's blood pressure is normal. The doctor informs the prison guards that they may resume their interrogation.

This particular case emphasizes the principle that health professionals must not participate in torture, as either torturer or attendant. The health professional's responsibility to try to stop torture and report violators is emphasized. The history of health professionals who risk personal safety to protest human rights violations is reviewed, while risks of taking such a position are discussed.

Case 4: Caring for the Victim of Domestic Violence

A twenty-year-old woman, who is five months pregnant, is admitted to the hospital after being severely beaten by her husband following an argument. He reportedly tied her arms behind her back, hit her in the face, and kicked her in the stomach. He cut her hair with a knife and threatened to kill her.

When you go to speak with the patient, the husband is sitting next to her and says that he is sorry. The patient, who is looking down at the ground, says she forgives him.

This case is used to discuss domestic violence, a health and human rights issue worldwide. Initially, course participants frequently comment that domestic violence is a private, family matter in which health professionals should perhaps not get involved. This leads to discussion about professional responsibility. Initial interventions, such as separating the woman from her husband, are discussed.

Case 5: Post-Traumatic Stress Disorder

A thirty-year-old taxi driver is brought to see you by his wife, complaining of headaches, nervousness, and insomnia. His symptoms started one month ago, after witnessing a friend being beaten by a group of police. At the time, his hands became shaky and he sweated profusely. He could not continue his work that day as a taxi driver because he thought that he could not control himself in traffic. Since then he reports sweating and becoming very nervous whenever he sees police. He also has frequent nightmares of being beaten. His wife reports that he often awakens in the middle of the night screaming "Please don't beat me." He then cannot fall back to sleep.

His wife tells you that her husband is much more irritable than before and they are arguing a great deal. Last week they had a fight over financial matters and for the first time he hit her.

On further history, you learn that he was admitted to the hospital last year because of being unconscious after he was beaten up by a group of bandits while traveling.

Human rights violations can result in or contribute to mental illness, including depression or in this case post-traumatic stress. Identifying such problems and using empathic "active" listening skills are emphasized. This case demonstrates that victims of human rights abuses who do not receive appropriate supportive care may in turn violate the rights of others. For example, in this case the man has started hitting his wife.

In addition to case discussions, the course uses a variety of other innovative teaching methods. For example, in reviewing the Universal Declaration of Human Rights, the class is divided into small groups. Each group discusses a specific article of the Declaration and how it relates to the rights and responsibilities of health professionals, and then makes a presentation to the entire class. Course participants review and discuss videotapes of human rights abuses, including an infamous case in Los Angeles, California, where police officers were caught on videotape beating a suspect.[24] Examples of human rights problems in many different countries are provided to illustrate that human rights concerns exist worldwide. In teaching communication skills, role-playing of effective and poor communication skills is done with great success.

Project Results

More than three thousand Cambodian health professionals have received human rights education through this program since it began in April 1993. Participants receive a certificate at the end of the course. The course is taught to students in their last year at the Faculty of Medicine and the School of Nursing in Phnom Penh, as well as at provincial nursing schools. All courses are taught in the Cambodian language, Khmer, and the syllabus concerning health and human rights was developed in both Khmer and English.

Intensive one-week courses are also taught to practicing health professionals, including doctors, nurses, village medics, and traditional birth attendants in Phnom Penh and many of the provinces. These courses are held in a variety of locations including provincial and district hospitals, Buddhist temples, and headquarters of local human rights groups. These courses are more challenging given logistics as well as the fact that individuals attending the course are more experienced, often including prominent local health officials. Project staff were initially concerned about discussing delicate issues, but with experience have gained great poise and confidence.

Response to the course has been very enthusiastic. In one class at the School of Nursing in Phnom Penh, following a heavy rain, students went so far as to wade through three feet of water to attend. Participants have frequently commented at the completion of the course that they gained a much better understanding of what are human rights and the role of health professionals in protecting these rights. Many have also noted that they learned important skills, particularly communication skills, for the evaluation and treatment of human rights abuse victims that they can integrate into their daily practice. There are numerous requests for additional training to be conducted in Phnom Penh and the provinces.

The Human Rights Education Project for Health Professionals in Cambodia's curriculum was recently approved to become a permanent part of the medical curriculum at the Faculty of Medicine and the School of Nursing in Phnom Penh. Thus, in the future, all health professionals in Cambodia will receive human rights training. The curriculum has also been adapted for use in other countries including Zaire.[25]

Future Project Objectives

With the continuation of this project, Cambodian staff have assumed responsibility for the program's management. Efforts are focusing on developing sustainable means for continuing human rights education for health professionals in Cambodia. This includes intensive faculty training and development at the medical and nursing schools to allow for a successful integration of the human rights curriculum at these institutions.

The human rights education program has also led to other health-related human rights projects. For example, in March 1994, ARC project staff began collaborating with PHR, the UN Center for Human Rights in Cambodia, and Columbia University College of Physicians and Surgeons on a program to monitor and improve Cambodian prison conditions.[26] This included coordinating with local health practitioners who work in the prisons and training them in providing optimal medical care and maintaining public health practice in prisons. Furthermore, technical expertise is being provided to government agencies responsible for the health of prisoners. Mechanisms are being established for continued assessment of progress in prison conditions.

In an effort to develop sustainable means for continuing human rights programs for Cambodian health professionals, ARC is helping to establish a local nongovernmental organization, the Cambodian Health and Human Rights Alliance (CHHRA). This organization's mandate includes continued human rights education for health professionals as well as advocacy, investigation, and provision of health services for victims of health-related human rights abuses.

Conclusion

Human rights education is an important part of medical education. Clearly the situation in Cambodia, with the tragic opportunity to redevelop an entire country following its previous total destruction, is unusual. The level of UN support is also unprecedented. Nevertheless, the Human Rights Education Project for Health Professionals in Cambodia is evidence that such projects can be implemented successfully in a variety of settings. Curricula must be clinically relevant and applicable to the situation of the country in which they are taught. In order to offer an appropriate and sustainable program, it is essential that local staff assume a leadership role in the development, implementation, and management of the program.

In his book *Step by Step* the Cambodian Buddhist monk, the Venerable Maha Ghosananda, writes: "The suffering of Cambodia has been deep. From this suffering comes great compassion." Cambodian health professionals have endured years of hardship while continuing to deliver care in difficult circumstances. It is our hope that the Human Rights Education Project for Health Professionals in Cambodia will make a contribution to strengthening Cambodia's health care system, and will serve as a model for similar programs in other countries throughout the world.

We are indebted to Stephen Marks, former chief of education and training for UNTAC Human Rights for his vision and encouragement. Eric Stover of Physicians for Human Rights provided invaluable guidance and support. We are also grateful to Brian Heidel, Graham Adutt, Khou Somatheavy, Karen Johnson Elshazly, Tony Kozlowski, Anne Goldfeld, Arlys Herem, and Leslie Wilson of the American Refugee Committee, and Kari Hannibal, Barbara Ayotte, and Susannah Sirkin of Physicians for Human Rights for their encouragement and support. Members of the original human rights project team who developed the curriculum, including Chan Savan, Sor Sontheary, Phaly Hor, Marie Cammal, and Kathryn English, showed an extraordinary degree of dedication. Several gifted individuals, including Kassie Neou, The Venerable Yos Hut Khemacaro, Meas Nee, Kek Galabru, Suzanne Groisser, Heng Bun Sieth, Bob Maat, Lori Dostal, and Sophie Biacabe, served as invaluable resources in the development of this program. Dr. Otterman participated in the prison assessment project through the Clinical Fellowship Program in Human Rights and Medicine, Center for the Study of Society and Medicine, Columbia University College of Physicians and Surgeons.

Notes

1. Allen S. Keller and Sin Kim Horn, eds. *Human Rights Education for Health Professionals in Cambodia* (Phnom Penh: United Nations and the American Refugee Committee, 1993).

2. Allen S. Keller, Sin Kim Horn, Sam Sopheap, and Gabriel Otterman, "Human Rights Education for Cambodian Health Professionals," *Health and Human Rights* 1, no. 3 (1995): 256–71.

3. David P. Chandler, *The Tragedy of Cambodian History* (New Haven: Yale University Press, 1991).

4. Eva Mysliwiec, *Punishing the Poor: The International Isolation of Kampuchea* (Oxford: Oxfam, 1988).

5. *Cambodia: The Situation of Children and Women* (Phnom Penh: United Nations Children's Fund, Office of the Special Representative, 1990); see also Holly Myers and Anne Goldfeld, M.D., *Cambodia Can't Wait* (New York: Women's Commission for Refugee Women and Children, February 1993).

6. Eric Stover and Rae McGrath, *Land Mines in Cambodia: The Coward's War* (New York: Physicians for Human Rights and Asia Watch, 1991); also Eric Stover, Allen Keller, James Cobey,

and Sam Sopheap, "Letter from Phnom Penh: The Medical and Social Consequences of Land Mines in Cambodia," *Journal of the American Medical Association* 272 (1994): 331–36; *Landmines: A Deadly Legacy* (New York: Human Rights Watch and Physicians for Human Rights, 1993).

7. See Amnesty International, *Cambodia: Human Rights Concerns, July to December 1992* (London: Amnesty International, February 1993); Amnesty International, *Kampuchea, Political Imprisonment and Torture* (London: Amnesty International, 1987); Asia Watch, *Cambodia: Human Rights Before and After the Elections* (New York: Asia Watch, May 1993); Asia Watch, *Political Control, Human Rights, and the UN Mission in Cambodia* (New York: Asia Watch, September 1992); Lawyers Committee for Human Rights [LCHR], *Cambodia: The Justice System and Violations of Human Rights* (New York: LCHR, May 1992).

8. See Maha Ghosananda, *Step by Step* (Berkeley, Calif.: Parallax Press, 1992); see also Bob Maat, *Newsletter of the Coalition for Peace and Reconciliation* (P.O. Box 144, Phnom Penh, Cambodia, 1993).

9. Cindy Burns, Anne Campbell, and the Venerable Yos Hut Khemacaro, eds., *A Human Rights Teaching Curriculum for Cambodians* (Phnom Penh: United Nations Transitional Authority in Cambodia [UNTAC], 1992); and United Nations, *Human Rights: A Compilation of International Instruments* (New York: United Nations, 1988; Cambodian trans., Phnom Penh: UNTAC, 1993).

10. United Nations, *Agreements on a Comprehensive Political Settlement of the Cambodia Conflict* (Paris: United Nations, October 23, 1991).

11. Keller and Horn, eds., *Human Rights Education for Health Professionals in Cambodia.*

12. Richard Pierre Claude and Burns H. Weston, *Human Rights in the World Community: Issues and Action*, 2d ed. (Philadelphia: University of Pennsylvania Press, 1992); David McQuoid-Mason, Edward L. O'Brien, and Eleanor Green, *Human Rights for All* (Pretoria: Lawyers for Human Rights, South Africa, National Institute for Citizen Education in the Law, USA, 1991); James Nickel, *Making Sense of Human Rights* (Berkeley, Calif.: University of California Press, 1987); United Nations, *The ABC's of Teaching Human Rights* (New York: United Nations, 1989); United Nations, *Human Rights: Questions and Answers* (New York: United Nations, 1987).

13. Amnesty International, *The Universal Declaration of Human Rights* (London: Amnesty International, British Section, 1983).

14. United Nations, *Standard Minimum Rules for the Treatment of Prisoners* (New York: United Nations, 1955).

15. Thomas Beauchamp and James Childress, *Principles of Biomedical Ethics* (New York: Oxford University Press, 1989); Edie Roderick, *Medic Training Manual* (Minneapolis: American Refugee Committee, 1991); Amnesty International, *Ethical Codes and Declarations Relevant to the Health Professions* (London: Amnesty International, 1985).

16. Mack Lipkin, Jr., M.D., Samuel Putnam, M.D., and Aaron Lazare, M.D., eds., *The Medical Interview* (New York: Springer-Verlag, 1994): The portions of the syllabus on communication skills, the history and physical examination of victims of human rights abuses, and the evaluation and treatment of victims of rape and domestic violence used materials developed by Cambodian and international staff of the American Refugee Committee (ARC) for the ARC health training program in Thailand.

17. Physicians for Human Rights, *Medical Testimony on Victims of Torture: A Physician's Guide to Political Asylum Cases* (Boston: Physicians for Human Rights, 1990); Physicians for Human Rights, *Human Rights and Medicine: The Uses of Medical Skills in Documenting Abuses and Treating Victims* (Boston: Physicians for Human Rights, 1992).

18. *Cambodia: The Situation of Children and Women*; and Meyers and Goldfeld, *Cambodia Can't Wait* (both in note 5 above); Amnesty International, *Women in the Front Line* (London: Amnesty International, March 1991); Judy Ledgerwood, *Analysis of the Situation of Women in Cambodia* (Phnom Penh, Cambodia: UNICEF, 1992); and C. Zimmerman, *Plates in a Basket Will Rattle: Domestic Violence in Cambodia* (Phnom Penh: Asia Foundation, December 1994).

19. Zimmerman, *Plates in a Basket Will Rattle.*

20. Amnesty International Medical Commission, *Doctors and Torture: Collaboration or Resistance?* (London: Bellow Publishing Co., 1989); Andrew Clare, *Medicine Betrayed* (London: British Medical Association, 1992); Anne Goldfeld, M.D., Richard Mollica, M.D., RF, B. H. Pesavento, and S. V. Faraone, "The Physical and Psychological Sequelae of Torture," *Journal of the American Medical Association* 259 (1988): 2725–29; David Hawk, ed., *Khmer Rouge Prison Documents from the S-21 (Tuol Sleng) Extermination Center in Phnom Penh* (New York: Cambodia Documentation Commission, 1984); Eric Stover and Elena O. Nightingale, M.D., *The Breaking of Bodies and Minds: Torture, Psychiatric Abuse, and the Health Professions* (New York: W. H. Freeman and Company, 1985); Ole Vedel Rasmussen, "Medical Aspects of Torture," *Danish Medical Bulletin* 37, supp. 1 (January 1990): 1–88; Principles of Medical Ethics Relevant to the Role of Health Personnel, Particularly Physicians, in the Protection of Prisoners and Detainees Against Torture and Other Cruel, Inhuman or Degrading Treatment or Punishment, adopted by the UN General Assembly, Resolution 37/192, December 18, 1992.

21. Hawk, *Khmer Rouge Prison Documents*.

22. Stover and McGrath, *Land Mines in Cambodia*; Stover et al., "Letter From Phnom Penh"; *Landmines: A Deadly Legacy*.

23. The portion of the curriculum on mental health was written by Mea Nee, former director of the COERR Mental Health and Traditional Healing program, Site 2 refugee camp, Thailand. Nee is currently working in community development with Overseas Service Bureau, Australia, in Battambang; see J. David Kinzie, R. B. Fredrickson, Jenelle Fleck, and W. Karls, "Post-Traumatic Stress Disorder Among Survivors of Cambodian Concentration Camps," *American Journal of Psychiatry* 141 (1984): 649–50; Richard Mollica and James Lavelle, "Southeast Asian Refugees," in *Clinical Guidelines in Cross-Cultural Mental Health* (New York: John Wiley and Sons, 1988), 262–303; Richard Mollica, "The Trauma Story: The Psychiatric Care of Refugee Survivors of Violence and Torture," Frank Ochberg, ed., *Post-Traumatic Therapy and Victims of Violence* (New York: Brunner/Mazel Publishers, 1988), 295–314; Richard Mollica et al., "Assessing Symptom Change in Southeast Asian Refugee Survivors of Mass Violence and Torture," in *American Journal of Psychiatry* 147, no. 1 (1990): 83–88; Richard Mollica, *The Harvard Trauma Questionnaire* (Boston: Harvard Program in Refugee Trauma, Department of Health Policy and Management, Harvard School of Public Health, 1991); Richard Mollica et al., "Indochinese Versions of the Hopkins Symptom Checklist-25: A Screening Instrument for the Psychiatric Care of Refugees," *American Journal of Psychiatry* 144 (1987): 1567–72; Norihiko Shinfuku, *Mission Report for the World Health Organization on Mental Health Programme in Cambodia* (Geneva: World Health Organization, December 1992); UN General Assembly, *The Protection of Persons with Mental Illness and the Improvement of Mental Health Care* (New York: UN General Assembly, February 18, 1992).

24. *U.S. v. Koons*, 833 F. Supp, 769 (C.D. Cal. 1993). In this case, Los Angeles, California, police officers were convicted in U.S. Federal District Court of violating the civil rights of Rodney King during his arrest.

25. Scott Campbell, *Les droits de l'homme pour les professionnels de santé au Zaire* (Kinshasa, Zaire: Association Zairoise de Défense des Droits de l'Homme, 1994).

26. Gabriel Otterman and Eric Stover, *Health Conditions in Cambodia's Prisons* (Boston: Physicians for Human Rights, 1995).

Chapter 22
Science, Scientists, and
Human Rights Education

Audrey Chapman, Herbert Spirer, Louise Spirer,
and Caroline Whitbeck

On a superficial level, science and human rights would seem to have little in common, but the two are related in a number of fundamental ways.

1. Human rights is a fundamental basis for scientific investigation. Far from being unrelated, many of the rights and freedoms set out in the Universal Declaration of Human Rights and the major international human rights instruments are essential to the conduct of science.[1] These include freedom of expression and opinion; the right to seek, receive, and impart information and ideas; freedom of movement; the right to education and training; the right to work and choice of work; and freedom of association and assembly. Freedom of thought, communication, and travel are particularly central to the advancement of science. Scientific inquiry—the search for and certification of knowledge, which may lead to the discovery of universally applicable concepts and laws—depends on openness. Scientific research requires the free flow of information and ideas between scientists, regardless of national borders, political ideologies of their respective governments, or the backgrounds of the scientists involved. As an international enterprise, science requires freedom of movement. Because unbiased and objective examination of data, confirmation of observations, and independent retesting of hypotheses are essential for scientific discovery, scientific research and advancement are dependent on an atmosphere conducive to critical and open debate on the part of scientists and laypersons.

2. Scientists, with some frequency, have a predisposition to come into conflict with repressive governments that engage in human rights violations. This tendency may reflect the fact that scientists have a professional ethic that inclines them to be objective and questioning. Trained to share their discoveries and views and to maintain a professional allegiance that is international rather than national in scope, scientists also are vulnerable because they are viewed as posing a threat to authoritarian regimes. Scientists may suffer because the very nature of their work is viewed as political by authori-

ties or because they have become involved, either professionally or as private citizens, in the struggle for human rights—rights that are a sine qua non for the performance of responsible research. The risks incurred by scientists as dissenters, whether expressing views in opposition to official thinking on science or technology, the denial of human rights, or the government itself, are essentially the same whether the political system is of the right or left. Those who question official policies may lose their jobs, have their degrees revoked, be refused the right to publish or travel, be jailed, or even lose their lives. The "honor roll" of prominent scientists whose persecution has inspired an international response is but the tip of the iceberg. For every scientist suffering human rights abuses who is as well known as Anatoly Koryagin, Andrei Sacharov, or Fang Lizhi, there are hundreds of less well-known scientists who have suffered similar or worse fates. The *1994 Directory of Persecuted Scientists, Engineers, and Health Professionals,*[2] published by the American Association for the Advancement of Science (AAAS), documents 468 active cases representing a wide range of professionals and specializations, with medical professionals and engineers the two largest groups.

3. Because scientific knowledge may be used for destructive as well as constructive purposes, it is important that scientists be familiar with human rights standards and guard against potential abuses of science that may result in human rights violations. Issue areas involving the misuse of science to carry out human rights abuses that are listed in the AAAS *1994 Directory* include the misuse of psychiatric treatment for political purposes in China, the damming of rivers and estuaries by the Iraqi government to cause the forced migration and death of thousands of Marsh Arabs, the alleged use of prohibited chemical weapons against the Kurds in Iraq and Turkey, and the forced involvement of scientists in the infliction of torture and other forms of cruel and unusual physical punishment by Israel, Malaysia, and Singapore. The abuse of psychiatry for political purposes is perhaps the best-known example of the misuse of science. Human rights groups and other practitioners have documented the abuse of psychiatric procedures, techniques, knowledge, and hospitals to detain compulsorily and "treat" individuals for their political, social, or religious views rather than for genuine medical reasons in a number of countries including the former Soviet Union, Chile, Argentina, China, Somalia, Romania, and South Africa. While it is not as well known, the collusion of health professionals in torture and its concealment has been an even more serious issue. Health professionals' involvement in the administration of the death penalty and participation in corporal punishment, such as the amputation of hands, feet, and fingers as punishment, also contradict the most fundamental precept of medical ethics: "above all, do no harm."[3]

4. Scientific methods have important human rights applications. Recognizing that science can make a singular contribution to protect and promote human rights, the AAAS Science and Human Rights Program expanded its focus within a few years of its establishment to developing scientific methods for monitoring implementation of human rights, and promoting a greater understanding of and support for international human rights within the scientific community. The program has assisted human

rights groups and organizations by providing scientific expertise related to human rights in the forensic sciences, genetics, statistics, computers and information management, medicine, the prevention of torture, and the treatment of torture survivors. To expand the availability of these services, the program recently established a human rights consulting service to match requests for scientific assistance from U.S. and overseas human rights groups with scientists interested in using their skills on behalf of human rights.

These linkages between science and human rights have implications for human rights education. Typically the education of scientists does not include human rights, and scientists are therefore unaware of the relevance of human rights standards for their profession or the potential contributions they can make to promoting human rights. There is a need to incorporate intentional training about human rights in the education of scientists, engineers, and health professionals so that scientists can better understand the intimate connection between science and human rights. Scientists' solidarity in decrying violations of the rights of colleagues has proven useful in obtaining the release of fellow scientists or an improvement in their situation. Membership in professional societies, whose achievements and prominence are well known, give scientists even greater opportunities to attract government attention to human rights problems and possibly influence policy, but for them to do so requires sensitivity to the potential for human rights abuses and awareness of particular cases. It is also important to sensitize scientists, engineers, and health professionals to relevant international human rights standards so that they will respect these principles when conducting their work. While the rapid evolution of science, engineering, and medicine creates opportunities to improve human welfare, it also introduces practices that pose risks to the integrity and dignity of the individual. Human rights education as part of a professional curriculum can assist individual scientists, engineers, and health professionals in applying human rights principles to their research, clinical trials, and daily work. Human rights advocates can make use of scientific expertise and methodologies only if they have some understanding of their relevance to human rights research and documentation.

This chapter reports on the initiatives of the AAAS and other organizations to develop human rights awareness, training courses, resources, and academic programs that link science and human rights. Sections will deal with the role of the AAAS and other professional societies, data analysis training in human rights education, incorporating human rights issues into scientific education for statisticians and other quantitative disciplines, and human rights education for engineering and science students.

The Role of Professional Societies in Human Rights Education

In 1976 the American Association for the Advancement of Science established a program to bring effective aid to foreign scientists, health professionals, and engineers who have experienced violations of their internationally recognized human rights or their academic freedom. The AAAS Science and Human Rights Program later expanded its focus to include advancing the use of scientific methods and procedures in the documentation and prevention of human rights violations and promoting greater understanding of and support for human rights within the scientific community. The program's work is based on the premise that scientific societies should encourage international respect for the human rights standard embodied in the Universal Declaration of Human Rights and other international treaties as a matter of scientific freedom and responsibility. Because the AAAS is an umbrella organization with nearly three hundred affiliated scientific, medical, and academic societies, the program is able to draw on scientists and scientific societies from a multiplicity of disciplines. In addition, the AAAS has been able to serve as a catalyst for the establishment of human rights committees in many of its affiliates and for the formation of independent groups of scientists and physicians concerned about human rights. The Science and Human Rights Program currently works with a network of seventy-five scientific organizations.

The AAAS seeks to promote commitment to human rights within the scientific community in a variety of ways. To raise awareness of human rights violations experienced by scientists, the program publishes an annual directory compiling current cases. Since November 1993, the program also has been operating an electronic network, called the AAAS Human Rights Action Network (AAASHRAN), to circulate current information on human rights violations to individuals throughout the scientific communities. Alerts are sent via electronic mail to AAASHRAN subscribers, along with copies of letters of inquiry or appeal that the AAAS has submitted on the case to relevant foreign governments.

The AAAS, as well as other scientific societies, sponsors seminars, conferences, and consultations on science and human rights themes. Since the AAAS is a multidisciplinary scientific organization with 146,000 members, its annual meetings provide an important venue for these events. The AAAS also co-sponsors or participates in symposia, committees, and forums at the annual meeting of other scientific societies on human rights themes. Working consultations on specific themes, for example, promoting compliance with human rights standards in the life and health sciences, can both promote awareness of human rights and develop programs and resources.

The Science and Human Rights Program also prepares a variety of publications intended to educate scientists about human rights and the potential contributions of science. For example, *Taking Up the Challenge: The Promotion of Human Rights*[4] describes the activities of scientists in the documentation of human rights violations. It also challenges scientists to examine how they can get involved in promoting human rights internationally. Chapters deal with the forensic sciences, the medical profession, measuring economic, social, and cultural rights, genetics, human rights, and the environment, and the use of statistics in human rights reporting. Similarly, promotional materials for the new AAAS human rights consulting service are attempting to educate both potential users and scientific volunteers about the relevance of certain types of

Figure 22.1. Dr. Clyde C. Snow trains a team of archaeologists and anthropologists as they exhume a grave in Guatemala to identify victims and search for evidence of responsibility for past human rights violations. (Physicians for Human Rights)

scientific expertise to human rights. The AAAS Science and Human Rights Program also publishes a semiannual newsletter, *The Report on Science and Human Rights.*

The AAAS has also organized a number of training programs to develop specific scientific expertise applicable to the field of human rights. In several cases, the AAAS pioneered human rights applications of scientific methods and then conducted training programs overseas to facilitate use. For example, following a symposium at an AAAS Annual Meeting that identified the relevance of the forensic sciences to human rights investigations, the AAAS was invited to send a team to Argentina to begin the exhumation of mass graves and identification of the victims by the newly installed democratic government. After sending a group of experts to Argentina, the AAAS also initiated a training program for students of medicine and anthropology in 1984 to establish the foundations for forensic anthropology teams. The training programs imparted methods to enable the team members to undertake exhumations of mass graves, determine the cause and manner of death of the victims, and identify the remains of the "disappeared." Eight years later the program undertook a similar training program to establish a forensic anthropology team in Guatemala (1992–94). In 1993 the AAAS co-sponsored a one-week intensive training seminar with the University of Colombia in Bogotá to acquaint faculty members and students in the Department of Physical Anthropology with the application of the forensic sciences to human rights. The AAAS also sponsored a fellowship program to bring physicians and forensic scientists from developing countries to the United States for forensic science training applicable to human rights investigations.

Recognizing that scientific methods can contribute to the work of grassroots human rights organizations, the AAAS Science and Human Rights Program is also attempting to disseminate scientific skills more broadly. A "bottom-up" approach has many advantages because the use of scientific methodologies from the beginning can make human rights investigations far more accurate, reliable, and credible. Scientific data analysis can also provide quantitative measurements of the scale of human rights violations and the degree of association with other societal factors. This can provide valuable evidence of the causes of human rights abuses and the patterns of distribution in space or time. To be able to disseminate scientific methods to grassroots groups with little background in science or mathematics, however, is very demanding and requires innovative teaching methods and resources.

The AAAS has held workshops on the application of the forensic sciences to human rights investigations in the Philippines, Costa Rica, and Guatemala for lawyers, judges, physicians, and human rights advocates. The objective was to enable them to understand the relevance and limitations of forensic science methodologies rather than to develop sufficient expertise to use these methods. The workshops in Central America also focused on relevant UN standards set forth in the *Manual on the Effective Prevention and Investigation of Extra-Legal, Arbitrary, and Summary Executions.*[5] While these training workshops have been useful in laying a foundation, the lack of appropriate written and video resources reduced their effectiveness.

Realizing the importance of developing resources geared to nonscientists, the AAAS attempted to establish a better foundation for its work on statistics and information management applied to human rights. The AAAS's initial publication on this subject, *Human Rights and Statistics: Getting the Record Straight,*[6] is largely nonmathematical and the examples provide broad coverage of a variety of topics on the collection and use of statistical data on human rights violations. However, the treatment is still geared more to academics and professionals than to grassroots human rights advocates. Before conducting training workshops with HURIDOCS (Human Rights Information and Documentation Systems International), with whom the Science and Human Rights Program has a collaborative relationship, the AAAS decided to commission the drafting of a handbook. The next section describes this unique resource written by Herbert and Louise Spirer. Designed to give human rights advocates the methods for analyzing and presenting data concerning human rights violations, *Data Analysis for Monitoring Human Rights* features practical methods that use as little mathematics as possible. The language, while not compromising statistical principles, is accessible to all readers, including those with English as a second language. Translations into French, Spanish, and Arabic are planned for the future. The volume emphasizes practical human rights fieldwork, legal advocacy, and the presentation of evidence. The methods have been chosen for their compatibility with the specific requirements of human rights workers. As such, this handbook provides a model for the way in which scientific methods can be incorporated into human rights education.

Data Analysis Training in Human Rights Education

Pedagogical Strategies

By and large, human rights workers rarely have more background in scientific or mathematical methods than one introductory statistics course. They frequently have little mathematical education, often identify themselves as innumerate, and in many cases are either frightened or overtly hostile to statistical or numerical approaches. Many of these same human rights workers, however, have expressed a desire to acquire some scientific approaches they could put to use. As one human rights advocate wrote when appealing to the American Statistical Association (ASA) for assistance, "To get around the brick wall which only permits statistical or econometric or other 'hard data' to enter the walled city of official institutions . . . , it is necessary to use the tools of formal quantitative research."[7]

An appropriate strategy for training this intelligent and committed adult student body is to formulate tools that can be used in their work, based on the development of synthetic as well as analytic skills. While the emphasis on analytic reasoning in tracing the logical progression of deduced relationships is still common in science education, the approach that achieves mastery of synthetic as well as analytic skills through the study of examples and cases has a long history in legal and business education and is now being rediscovered in science and engineering education. (Massachusetts Institute of Technology and the other six schools of the Engineering Coalition of Schools for Excellence in Education and Leadership [ECSEL] Coalition currently receive $3 million a year from the National Science Foundation to reform engineering education by putting design at the core of the curriculum.) The first approach can be described as "deductive" or as teaching "analytic" skills, whereas the second should be described as teaching problem-solving and "synthetic" skills (putting it all together), not just as inductive, since induction (in philosophy of science and scientific method) implies mere generalization. There is a vast body of literature on this approach which has yet to find its deserved place in education and training in data analysis and statistics.[8]

The most effective strategy thus far is based on presenting various cases and then demonstrating how statistical tools were used in collecting, analyzing, and presenting the results. This method develops the student's desire to master those statistical tools that can be used to solve the problems raised. In its synthetic nature, this approach closely mirrors the daily routines of scientists conducting field research.

Pedagogical Methodology

A sound guide to education and training in these areas can be based on the pedagogical approach of the Chinese proverb, "I hear and I forget, I see and I remember, I do and I understand." The focus of the training is the use of real-world examples that involve the participants in critical thinking, problem solving, and discussion. The pedagogical tactics involve having the participants ask questions and solve problems, rather than having them listen and repeat methods of analysis that they have been shown but that they have not made their own.

A key requirement of this approach is to have a suitable "handbook" that provides the data analytical methods, the examples and cases, and suitable exercises for this pedagogical method. Responding to this need, the AAAS initiated a project using the expert resources of the American Statistical Association Committee on Human Rights, which resulted in Herbert and Louise Spirer preparing *Data Analysis for Monitoring Human Rights*[9] for publication by the AAAS.

The pedagogical approach used in this handbook illustrates principles through the use of examples and through having the participants play an active role in discussing the examples. Since all the examples are based on actual situations in which there are problems of human rights violations, the participants can immediately relate to the problems. Participants then form groups for exercises related to the preceding discussions. The purpose of a participant discussion group is not to develop a group consensus as to the best solution, but to help each member of the group develop skills to analyze and address similar problems. After the small groups have worked together, they then return to the class and discuss their positions (reporting as individuals). This is the classic case method applied to data analysis for human rights. Several groups of international human rights advocates served as subjects for the development of this handbook in a "pedagogical laboratory." Annually, the Center for the Study of Human Rights at Columbia University in New York runs a Human Rights Advocates Training Program whose "aim . . . is to facilitate training and development of 10–12 human rights advocates from Africa, Asia, Eastern Europe, and the Middle East."[10] In addition, in both 1993 and 1994, training sessions were conducted on this model using these materials for voluntary participants who are graduate human rights majors in Columbia University's Schools of Law and International and Public Affairs. There is no scientific evidence to prove conclusively that the approach worked on these international advocates and graduate students. However, those who participated have strongly recommended that other human rights advocates and monitors participate in the next training sessions offered, and some are making arrangements to establish similar courses in their own countries.

Incorporating Human Rights Issues into Scientific Education for Statisticians and Other Quantitative Disciplines

Pedagogical Strategies

The strategic approach for students in statistical, economic, and other quantitative disciplines in the AAAS handbook is based on the recognition that quantitative human rights applications have the same essential structure as applications in other fields. Sampling surveys conducted to determine the scope of human rights violations of populations have the same essential elements as do sampling surveys conducted to determine household attributes.[11] Detection of outliers in time series of human rights variables uses the same statistical analyses as are used in, for example, economics and in industrial quality control. Even concepts of experimentation can be shown to have applicability in comparable human rights situations.[12] Examples of applications of tools of quantitative analysis to human rights are thus as reasonable a candidate for such use as are the business, scientific, sports, or any other examples commonly used in illustrating statistical tools.

Pedagogical Methodology

Certainly one of the first methodological steps in contributing to the training of professionals and educators in the area of human rights statistical and data analysis is to include examples of the application of these tools to human rights cases. There are more than sixty examples of statistical tools applied to human rights cases and dozens of such exercises in *Data Analysis for Monitoring Human Rights*, with new possibilities for different applications occurring regularly. Readers may use the cases in *Data Analysis* or build on them with examples they find in the media or in publications of human rights organizations.

Mary Gray, professor of mathematics and statistics at the American University, suggests that the use of a text that focuses on human rights may have a special advantage in the teaching of statistics. "Those of us who have to teach the subject of statistics to students who don't necessarily want to learn may find the book [*Data Analysis*] useful."[13] The Salem (Massachusetts) State College provides a unique example of this added value of framing statistics in a human rights format. This college has an interdisciplinary program for students who have English as a second language, most of whom are recent immigrants to the United States. For these students, the usual examples, assignment topics, and educational context have limited meaning and interest. However, the staff of the program found that almost all had firsthand experience with human rights violations and that there was a high level of interest in the subject. Previously the faculty oriented its work toward human rights issues in, for example, English and literature. Statistics was a special problem, however, as it is well known that students who have English as a second language have difficulty in mathematical subjects. By integrating statistics with human rights in a human rights-based statistical textbook (using *Data Analysis*), they have gained the interest of their students.

The synthetic approach as illustrated in *Data Analysis* can thus serve a dual purpose—as a tool for the training of human rights advocates and monitors, and as a supplementary text and guide to the integration of human rights into scientific education.

Human Rights Education for Engineering and Science Students

Pedagogical Strategy

There are two distinct contexts for teaching human rights material to engineering and science students, and each of these requires a distinct strategy. The first context is that of a course on technical subjects, such as genetics, statistics, or biomedical engineering. Here illustrations of the application of technical knowledge to problems of human rights can be offered. These illustrations both introduce students to human rights concerns and help them recognize the larger social context of science and engineering. Even when very brief, perhaps confined to one section meeting, such introductions are very important because they broaden the perspective of students who are unlikely to think much about ethics unless it has first been shown to be relevant to their technical studies.

The second context is a course that is at least in part about ethics (courses on professionalism in engineering that address questions of professional ethics or courses on research methods and research ethics are examples). When professional ethics or research ethics are taught without any discussion of broader ethical norms, including human rights, students often get the impression of ad hoc professional rules and standards. This impression leads to cynicism about these standards. On the other hand, when ethics is approached in a very general way, engineering and science students see it as a topic to debate rather than as a subject that informs action.

Discussion of human rights specifically supports a further goal of giving students exposure to the areas of cross-cultural agreement on moral requirements (although perhaps not necessarily on the formulation of those requirements) notwithstanding cultural diversity. Although many factors contribute to the harsh exchanges among students about bigotry and intolerance on the one side and political correctness on the other, one major factor is the struggle to find or establish some area of moral agreement and the real difficulty in doing so. The notion of human rights provides an important way of expressing norms that have broad cross-cultural support without taking sides on more contested issues of ethics.

Pedagogical Methodology

Engineering and science students pride themselves on being problem solvers, and so a problem-oriented approach to ethics teaching is a natural one for engineering and science students and teaches by engaging students in learning by doing. Examples of human rights applications of science and engineering introduced into technical courses should, of course, fit the subject matter of that course. For instance, examples of application of molecular biology to the forensic sciences and of medicine to the care of survivors of torture can be found in *Taking Up the Challenge*. When health is understood as a human right, it is important to recognize that engineering work in the provision of clean water and sanitation systems is at least as important as medical care. Many examples are available of dramatic improvements in health status due to civil engineering projects.

Engineering and science students often bring to the study of practical ethics a variety of experiences and backgrounds. They also bring widely differing experience and competence in discussing questions of ethics. When confronted with a broad diversity of views from their classmates, some students question whether in ethics everything is a matter of preference or opinion. Others may despair of being able to discuss with fellow students any deeply held ethical concerns without appearing dogmatic. This is readily apparent in technical subjects that have an ethics component, but also true in subjects on research methods and research ethics or on professionalism and professional ethics.

Students also need a way of understanding the deliberations about how best to respond to a situation that does justice to the synthetic character of those deliberations, and hence a way of understanding how there often can be a range of good responses to a moral problem without moral reasoning being merely subjective preference. The analogy between ethical problems and design problems (problems of engineering design or problems of research design) draws on their common experience as engineering or science students to show that there may be a multiplicity of good responses to a moral problem, as there often are to a single design problem, without the distinction degenerating into a mere matter of taste. Even those moral problems that actually are conflicts between opposing sides or principles are often most constructively addressed as problems in which there are multiple (moral) constraints that may or may not turn out to be simultaneously satisfiable.

Questions of the priority of one side or one type of consideration do not necessarily lead to disagreement even then, since if anyone can find a response that does a better job of achieving all of the goals in question, the question of which goal one would choose over another does not arise. To put the matter another way: before asking how to make some trade-off, it is worth inquiring whether or to what extent a win-lose or trade-off situation can be transformed by an elegant solution into a win-win situation.

The method that best simulates facing an actual moral problem is that of respond-ing to an open-ended scenario. In order to simulate reality closely, it is important not to present the student with a choice of alternative responses. Ethical problems do not come with candidate choices formulated; they are not multiple-choice problems.

It is also an advantage if the scenario presents a situation that is in some ways ambiguous, and if students are challenged to respond in a way that will be fair to everyone, however things turn out. It is important to allow the students to interro-gate the case and ask specific questions about the context in which it arises, and to consider what alternative situations could arise from various different answers to their questions. It is a mistake to demand that the student just respond to the problem as stated. In real life the responsible person will try to understand the situation before responding.

Historical (actual) cases can also be useful for learning moral lessons, or, if the case is typical of many others, about the complications that commonly occur. Cases that have been recently in the news often peak student interest, but it is important to have backup materials to check the accuracy of newspaper accounts.

The Place of Human Rights in Methods for Teaching Ethics

Using the analogy with design problems, human rights appear in ethical problems as general ethical constraints. These often go unstated, much as do background as-sumptions in engineering design problems, such as the assumption that the device or experiment should operate in a range of conditions close to standard temperature and pressure.

Human rights also come to explicit attention in three ways in professional and re-search ethics. First, as was discussed above, the work of some scientists and engineers includes detection and investigation of human rights abuses or care for those who have been abused. Second, scientists and engineers are among those whose human rights are threatened. The cases that fit most easily within courses in professional ethics are those in which the persecution of scientists and engineers occurs while fulfilling professional obligations and ideals regarding patient care, public safety, or worker safety. There are many such illustrations in the annual AAAS *Directory of Perse-cuted Scientists, Engineers, and Health Professionals.* "Caught in the Crossfire,"[14] a recent AAAS mission study, describes the plight of physicians in Peru who are being sub-jected to long terms of incarceration for having provided medical treatment to mem-bers of insurgent groups. A detailed example of an engineer so persecuted may be found in Loren Graham's book[15] about Peter Ioakimovich Palchinskii, a multifaceted and extremely talented engineer in the U.S.S.R. during the Stalinist era. Palchinskii frequently criticized government policy for such things as inattention to the health and safety of workers as well as for short-sighted planning. He was charged with trea-son and executed, although his criticisms were those of a responsible engineer and not of a political nature. Another is Benjamin Linder, a mechanical engineer who was dedicated to making appropriate technology available. He was killed by the Contras in Nicaragua in April 1987 as he was working on a dam for a small hydroelectric plant. Such examples focus attention on what Stephen Unger aptly describes as the "right of an engineer to be ethical,"[16] that is, it focuses on ethical aspirations of engineers, scientists, and physicians, rather than on the moral rules that they are expected by others to obey.

A third context in which the subject of human rights arises in the context of professional ethics is in discussion of the requirement of informed consent as a condition for the use of human subjects in research. Many engineers, as well as physicians and scientists, conduct experiments involving human subjects. The history of human rights abuses in the Nazi experiments and in the Tuskegee syphilis study provides vivid and compelling evidence for the importance of ethical constraints on research. The Tuskegee syphilis study illustrates the way in which a project that begins reasonably (in this case, monitoring of patients with syphilis for whom treatment was not available) may evolve into one that grossly violates human rights and to which many people close their eyes.

The question of the use of experimental subjects, human and nonhuman, or even the use of corpses provides an opening to the subject of moral standing, that is, who counts, from a moral point of view. The issue of moral standing is the question of whether the well-being of such entities is important in itself and not just as a means to human well-being. The question of moral standing also arises naturally in connection with the question of engineers' or scientists' responsibility for the environmental effects of their work. Either way, the question of moral standing bears on the question of whether various types of individuals have the same moral standing, and hence the question of the nature and basis of human rights.

It is important to be clear that the claim to existence of human rights is more than the special pleading of the human species—or speciesism—analogous to racism and sexism. For the claim of human rights to have ethical validity, those rights must be on the basis of some characteristics that people typically possess rather than membership in a privileged species.

One basis for the claim that people have a special moral standing that includes human rights is that people are themselves moral agents, that is, beings whose actions can be morally evaluated. (We may say that the storm was responsible for three deaths and heavy property damage, meaning that the storm caused these outcomes. Although the storm was the agent of destruction, the actions of the storm are not subject to moral evaluation. The storm is not guilty of murder or even manslaughter because it is not a moral agent.) According to this argument, human rights are moral claims to the freedom or opportunity to act in a morally responsible way. If one uses some argument such as this to provide a warrant for human rights, it is clear that if some nonhuman species, such as porpoises or extraterrestrial beings, were to turn out to be able to act for moral reasons, then their human rights ought to be recognized. In particular, it would then be morally obligatory to obtain their informed consent for research performed on them. Whatever one thinks of the moral justification of using lower animals in experimental research, it makes no sense to require their consent, if they are not the sort of beings who can give consent.

Conclusion

The topic science and human rights education encompasses several different types of training. There is a need for education about human rights for scientists, engineers, and health professionals to promote observance of human rights standards and greater awareness of and response to human rights violations. In order to realize better the contributions of scientific methods to human rights, both scientists and human rights advocates require further education and training. While the dissemination of scientific methods to grassroots groups holds considerable promise, it also raises many fundamental pedagogical issues. The innovative and pioneering programs and resources described in this chapter are but a beginning.

Notes

1. For a study of the observance and violations of the human rights of scientists in the participating states of the Helsinki Accords, see John Simon, Paul Sieghart, and John Humphrey, *The World of Science and the Rule of Law* (Oxford: Oxford University Press, 1986).

2. Science and Human Rights Program, *1994 Directory of Persecuted Scientists, Engineers, and Health Professionals* (Washington, D.C.: American Association for the Advancement of Science [AAAS], 1994).

3. See, for example, British Medical Association, *Medicine Betrayed: The Participation of Doctors in Human Rights Abuses* (London: Zed Books, 1992).

4. Kari Hannibal, *Taking Up the Challenge: The Promotion of Human Rights* (Washington, D.C.: AAAS, 1992).

5. United Nations, *Manual on the Effective Prevention and Investigation of Extra-Legal, Arbitrary and Summary Executions* (New York: Centre for Social Development and Humanitarian Affairs, 1991).

6. Thomas B. Jabine and Richard P. Claude, eds., *Human Rights and Statistics: Getting the Record Straight* (Philadelphia: University of Pennsylvania Press, 1992).

7. Pamela Sparr, To Be Jericho to the Wall: Protecting Theory-Based Policy from Reality-Based Data (attachment to letter from the Center of Concern, January 1991).

8. See, for example, HBS Case Services, Harvard Business School, *The Use of Cases in Management Education* 376–240 (Boston: Harvard Business School, 1976). For a fuller discussion, see Philip Cottel and Bette Millis, *Cooperative Learning and Accounting* (Cincinnati: South-Western Publishing, 1994).

9. Herbert F. Spirer and Louise Spirer, *Data Analysis for Monitoring Human Rights* (Washington, D.C.: AAAS, 1994).

10. Center for the Study of Human Rights, *Human Rights Advocates Training Program Action Plan* (New York: Columbia University, 1994).

11. In fact, this analogy was the basis of a proposal to study gross human rights violations during the repression called Anfal 1988 in Kurdistan by the Iraqi government.

12. Thomas B. Jabine, "The Emerging Field of Human Rights Statistics," in *Statistics and Public Policy*, ed. Bruce D. Spencer (New York: Oxford University Press, in press).

13. D. L. Wheeler, "Professor Turns Statistics into a Weapon in the Battle for Human Rights," *Chronicle of Higher Education*, March 16, 1994, A41.

14. Daniel Salcedo, "Caught in the Crossfire: A Mission Report on the Plight of the Peruvian Medical Profession," AAAS, November 1993.

15. Loren Graham, *The Ghost of the Executed Engineer: Technology and the Fall of the Soviet Union* (Cambridge, Mass.: Harvard University Press, 1993).

16. Stephen H. Unger, *Controlling Technology: Ethics and the Responsible Engineer* (New York: John Wiley, 1994), 43–48. See also Mark Frankel, ed., *Science, Engineering and Ethics: State of the Art and Future Directions* (Washington, D.C.: AAAS, 1988).

Chapter 23
Beyond the "Official Story": What Journalists Need to Know

Anita Parlow

The Emperor, however, showing more perspicacity than his police, understood that sadness can drive one to thinking, dissapointment, waffling, and shuffling, so he ordered distractions, merriment, festivities, and masquerades for the whole Empire. His Noble Majesty himself had the Palace illuminated, threw banquets for the poor, and incited people to gaiety. When they had guzzled and gamboled, they gave praise to their King. This went on for years, and the distractions so filled people's heads, so corked them up, that they could talk of nothing but having fun. Our feet are bare but we're debonair, hey ho! Only the thinkers, who saw everything getting grey, shrunken, mud-splashed, and moldy, skipped the jokes and the merriment. They became a nuisance. The unthinking ones were wiser; they didn't let themselves get taken in, and when the students started holding rallies and talking, the nonthinkers stuffed their ears and made themselves scarce. What's the use of knowing when it's better not to know? Why do it the hard way, when it can be easy?

Ryszard Kapuscinski *The Emperor*[1]

On April 14, 1995, Frederick J. Cuny, an engineer, journalist, and relief worker, was executed in Chechnya by rebel force leaders who had abducted Cuny, a Russian interpreter, and two Russian doctors affiliated with the International Committee of the Red Cross. Just prior to what would be his last trip, Cuny had published an article on the Russian-Chechen civil war for the *New York Review of Books*.

The previous year, on May 1, 1994, the United Nations reported that two journalists from the United States had been killed and another injured when their car ran over a mine near the south Bosnian city of Mostar. The dead were identified as Francis W. Tomasic, accredited to the music-culture magazine *Spin*, and Brian Brenton, a photographer accredited to *Magnolia News*, a Seattle weekly. *Magnolia News* officials said Brenton had been affiliated with the newspaper for only one week, after he offered to provide photographs in return for press credentials. A UN spokesman said the incident occurred as the journalists tried to skirt a frontline road that was marked as being mined.

In the same month, the New York-based Committee to Protect Journalists (CPJ) reported that 126 journalists were held in prison for their reporting, jailed under no charges, or charged with "separatist propaganda," "treason," "counterrevolutionary activity," or "undermining national security." The crime that these journalists committed was to have written something that their governments disliked.[2] Additionally, CPJ reported that of all noncombatant professions, journalism sustains more casualties in the line of duty than any other.

Cuny's execution, the Mostar deaths, the accidental deaths of more than thirty others killed since the Balkan war broke out in 1991, and scores murdered worldwide reflect the necessity that journalists be better prepared to report on complex situations in adverse terrains.

CPJ also reports that more local reporters and opinion writers are assassinated around the globe for their journalistic activity than are killed in war-related incidents. In 1993, CPJ documented fifty-six murders of journalists who covered local stories and fourteen others that appear to be politically motivated.[3]

Conceptualizing Human Rights and Humanitarian Stories

Heightened personal risks and interpretive challenges facing journalists also challenge journalism schools to produce professionals equipped to negotiate this terrain. But with few exceptions, schools are more concerned with concerns of "craft" rather than content.[4] For working journalists, the literature is developing. In a 1993 report, "Reporting on War and Surviving in Yugoslavia," CPJ discusses how to prepare for war conditions and what to look out for. Cable News Network (CNN) reporter Peter Arnett provided useful advice in his recent book, *Live from the Battlefield*,[5] in which he describes the contents of a still relevant twenty-four-page pamphlet written by the Associated Press (AP) bureau chief in Vietnam to prepare reporters for combat conditions.

In addition to preparation for war conditions, the sheer mass of media requires more analytic treatment of realities behind the chaos that engulfs the post–cold war world.[6] A steady supply of human rights information by nongovernmental organizations (NGOs) and the press that was unthinkable only a decade ago has intensified the relationship between journalism, public opinion, diplomacy, and justice.[7] For example, as journalists feed back stories from even the most remote parts of the globe, NGOs involved in humanitarian assistance beg for more analysis of the complexities that give rise to epic stories of human suffering.

As recent cases of Rwanda, Somalia, Bosnia, and Haiti have shown, politicians could not avoid world opinion formed by nightly news broadcasts even as they shaped policy. With television and other communications media bringing instantaneous eyewitness capability into more and more homes throughout our "global village," NGOs are increasing their demands for more analytical coverage to offer better responses to the large- and small-scale disasters that have moved from the periphery to center stage. As the world's citizens are asked to shoulder the responsibility of knowing

about atrocities even as they occur, demands for more analysis and informed reporting to undergird the public's clamor to "do something" has meaning when coverage
operates from an informed base.

This convergence of technology and a need to understand the chaos that is en-
gulfing the post–cold war world makes it necessary for journalists to understand the
dynamics of human rights and humanitarian intervention. Beyond reportorial skills,
human rights and humanitarian coverage demands critical thinking that illuminates
the underlying issues that have given rise to the growing number of humanitarian
crises.

Such coverage presents an evolving interdisciplinary challenge in our "new information order," requiring journalists to draw from and remain conscious of the links
between human rights, the laws of war, democratization, empowerment, enforcement
options, and the degree to which the sovereign prerogative is used to shield gross inequities that give life to human rights and humanitarian disasters.

Human rights and humanitarian reporting frequently focuses on actions that
governments want to suppress, therefore requiring specific investigative and analytical preparation for coverage. On a practical level, promotion of human rights and
humanitarian obligations bolsters possibilities for democratic, pluralistic, and just
societies, or, minimally, for an international order of states committed to governments
that are responsive to their citizenry. These responsibilities require the journalist to
take more personal and intellectual risks.

Ideally, journalism schools would incorporate more human rights and humanitarian specialties to apprise students of the complexities of human rights and humanitarian law, international relations, relevant human rights and humanitarian institutions, the meaning of cross-cultural sensibilities, and the ability to report better on
how democratic institutions are both destroyed and constructed. Without such depth,
media personalities are left to banter about "who has the upper hand."

On humanitarian intervention, for example, covering interfaces between regional
and UN efforts and between humanitarian and military operations, to interpret more
ably and reflect upon U.S. policy has become a specialty that requires more understanding of the interplay between military and humanitarian regimes.

Familiarity with the evolution of the worldwide human rights and humanitarian
movements includes how a state's obligation to its citizenry is measured and experienced. Contentious debate is evolving a conceptual framework to define how human
rights might be monitored in war zones or what standards might be developed to
determine when to intervene or what endgame is envisioned. At this writing, the primary categories of abuse reported by human rights monitoring organizations such as
Amnesty International and Human Rights Watch offer factual bases for many under-
reported stories. The most serious absence of information is precisely in those segments of the population that are the most vulnerable to human right abuses, such as
ethnic minorities, women, and children.[8] While human rights information gathered

by NGOs offers insights into stories that might otherwise remain ignored, official stories of NGO human rights and relief groups, which do offer access to primary sources in the humanitarian universe, must equally be probed for veracity.[9]

Despite the universality of some operative legal principles and some common objectives regarding human rights as codified in the Universal Declaration of Human Rights, human rights coverage is increasingly reflecting nuances of culture, the degree of political space, and economic conditions. In the Bangkok Declaration adopted at the World Conference Regional Preparatory Meeting in April 1993, the participating Asian states "recognize that while human rights are universal in nature, they must be considered in the context of a dynamic and evolving process of international norm-setting, bearing in mind the significance of national and regional particularities and various historical, cultural and religious backgrounds."[10] The Vienna sessions also reflected a shift in global attention from ongoing violations to the individual—such as torture, slavery, and genocide—to the current debate regarding the degree to which states are obligated to correct economic deficiencies or follow humanitarian norms. Although diversity of culture, politics, and economic realities offers appropriate bases to challenge the application of a single, distinctive, and coherent international human rights regime,[11] the 1993 Vienna Declaration (para. 1) moved forward the cause of human rights by its reinforcement of the universal nature of the UN Charter and other instruments relevant to internationally accepted principles of law.

Journalists are more frequently required to reflect upon assumptions regarding what human rights and humanitarian standards are universally applicable, and how tradition and culture define both discourse and action.[12] The UN Population Conference in Cairo, which has pitted the pope, Islamic groups, and Christian evangelicals against what they view as western materialism, is a case in point. Of equal interest are tensions between official stories based on cultural relativism and reflection on the degree to which these stories serve to protect abusive state action.

Getting Beyond the Official Story: A Free Press and Government Sources

The exodus from Rwanda and continued fighting in Bosnia have been, in part, attributed to government-controlled radio broadcasts that encourage these actions for political gain. Along with the increasing numbers of journalists murdered for their reporting, press freedom has declined worldwide, despite a peak in open presses immediately following the demise of the centralized control of media in the former Soviet Union.[13]

Beyond issues of government or corporate control lies the responsibility of the journalist to maintain personal standards of political and intellectual independence. To do so requires reflection on assumptions as well as an obligation to challenge any lead provided by government sources.

The American journalist James Reston once wrote that the press requires not mere compliance but "a relentless barrage of facts and criticism, as noisy but also as accurate as artillery fire."[14] He also acknowledged enormous pressure to render citizens passive and promote conformity of belief. The birth of the *New York Times* op-ed page more than twenty years ago was accompanied by stated reverence for the truths of dissenting opinions, the free exchange of ideas, and open public debate. Political philosopher Herbert Marcuse acknowledged that substantial debate does exist in the United States, but warned that liberal constitutional governments also appear to require a pretense of discussion to maintain their continued legitimation.[15]

The Committee to Protect Journalists has reported that the American media demonstrated some complicity with U.S. foreign policy objectives during the cold war, raising the question of whether U.S. strategic interests define the degree of scrutiny of human rights or humanitarian stories. In 1989 Freedom and Accuracy in Reporting (FAIR) pointed out that twenty-two of the twenty-seven programs broadcast by *Nightline* between January 1985 and April 1988 dealt principally with problems or conflicts in Nicaragua; not one focused on Honduras, Guatemala, or El Salvador. FAIR's study prompted Ted Koppel to concede that *Nightline* had been covering Central America too narrowly, with not as many programs on state terrorism commensurate to the practices of the government of El Salvador. More recently, CPJ reported that a pattern of selective reporting on the Universal Declaration of Human Rights evident in thirty-two U.S. news stories and editorials published on the Declaration's fortieth anniversary reflects an "unconscious constraint" affecting reporters and editors alike. Only five newspapers referred explicitly to economic and social rights, two reprinted the Universal Declaration in its entirety, and only one daily, the *Boston Globe*, noted that the U.S. government had yet to ratify either the Civil and Political Covenant or the Socio-Economic Covenant which had already been adopted by eighty-seven and ninety-two states, respectively.[16]

Review of coverage, including reflections on "pack" mentality, is useful to probe why a story is or is not covered. Not until two American journalists were trapped in military crossfires did the U.S. mainstream press report on the brutality of Indonesia's occupation of East Timor. Human rights journals point out that, during the thirteen days of occupation by a U.S.-financed government, the few reports on the ensuing massacre escaped public attention in either the United States or Europe. When the *New York Times* and *Newsweek* did report on the Indonesian invasion, *Human Rights Quarterly* asserted that press coverage distorted what actually occurred because of its "reliance upon official Indonesian accounts."[17]

In 1970s Vietnam and 1980s El Salvador, successive U.S. administrations, motivated by a desire for ideological victories, impugned the credibility of journalists and their newspapers. Peter Arnett, who endured accusations of treason by some government officials for his reporting from Baghdad during the Gulf War, wrote of his early days in Vietnam that Saigon embassy and domestic-side officials viewed the press corps's assessments as undermining Washington's official optimistic pronouncements.

Journalists were again at loggerheads with American political authority when Alma Guillermoprieto for the *Washington Post* and Ray Bonner for the *New York Times*[18] reported news of a U.S.-trained Atlcatl Battalion engaged in a massacre at the small hamlet of El Mozote in the war-torn Department of Morazan, El Salvador, in December 1981, when the U.S. Congress was debating whether to increase its aid to the Salvadoran government or stop payment because of human rights abuses. Central to that debate were public perceptions of how the war was being prosecuted by an army leadership trained, in part, by the United States. After interviews with survivors, the reporters wrote that more than seven hundred defenseless civilians had been massacred by government troops in a noncombat zone. The U.S. embassy, the State Department, and President Ronald Reagan questioned both the numbers killed and the accusation that they were killed by the army. Again, the credibility of the reporters as well as their patriotism were placed in question.[19] Such scenarios test journalistic ethics regarding the protection of a source, demonstrate the politics of truth, distinguish advocacy and coverage, and invite discussion regarding implicit or explicit assumptions of both journalists and editors.

In other contexts, where the state is a consistent human rights violator, simply being a journalist may be viewed as a sufficient threat to draw the state's repressive apparatus.[20] The fact that the world community does not view free speech and a free press as nonderogable rights indicates the extent of the global dilemma. However, just as the presence of torture rehabilitation programs helps expand political space in countries that widely practice torture so, too, do programs of human rights and journalism contain the potential to enhance democratization.[21]

Familiarity with International Human Rights Law, Humanitarian Norms, the Laws of War, and the Human Rights Machinery

Democratic possibility appears somewhat elusive as an estimated thirty internal wars are currently under way around the globe. From the Rwanda genocide to Bosnia or Sudan, with war crimes seemingly on the rise, the international community is attempting to use treaties, customs, and international law to bring war criminals to justice. If one purpose of an open and free press is to enlarge democratic possibility and inform a global citizenry of the realities that effect their lives, it is imperative that journalists be more aware of principles of international law that underlie humanitarian interventions, war crimes tribunals, and other actions taken by states or the United Nations. The reason is to join together moral and legal principles with political and operational realities.[22]

Both the UN Charter and the Universal Declaration of Human Rights (adopted without dissent by the UN General Assembly on December 10, 1948), affirm that a government's behavior toward its citizens is a legitimate matter of concern to the international community. Following the adoption of the Declaration, the United Nations Commission on Human Rights drafted the remainder of an International Bill of Human Rights: a Covenant on Economic, Social and Cultural Rights; the Covenant on Civil and Political Rights; and Optional Protocols to the Civil and Political Covenant.[23] Additionally, the United Nations has drafted, adopted, and promoted scores of multilateral treaties, covenants, and other instruments dealing with such issues as genocide, racial discrimination, torture, and the rights of the child.

Coverage that includes mention of these documents and how to gain access to them is useful, as is coverage regarding government resistance to efforts to extend rights to categories such as land rights accorded to indigenous peoples, prohibition of use of land mines, or protections accorded to women. Additionally, reflection on choices of coverage, such as the suppression of writers by Muslim fundamentalist groups rather than the more ignored murder of reporters and writers in non-Muslim states, might provide a basis for examining assumptions and biases endemic to all societies.

Journalists increasingly see a need for a working knowledge of the expanding network of domestic laws, international treaties, governmental agencies, private advocacy groups, and international norms designed to protect human rights.[24] Equally useful is familiarity with UN bureaucracies[25] or, in the United States, legislation that limits financial assistance to human rights and humanitarian violators, as well as the proliferation of human rights-monitoring NGOs such as Amnesty International and Human Rights Watch. As attention to NGOs that have increased the effectiveness of citizen diplomacy worldwide and have held States Parties to agreed-upon standards grows, nonstate actors that are reshaping the international system are more in focus, particularly as parties transform transnational norms. As international NGOs effectively lobby for the placement of initiatives on international agendas that states often suppress, the rights of civilians, despite any sovereignty barriers, have increasingly become part of the world's collective conscience. However, more coverage is warranted regarding states' efforts to minimize, exclude, or repress opposition forces or domestic NGOs from participating in local or international debate.[26]

Familiarity with universally accepted principles concerning civilian populations in war zones who are legally protected under the terms of the Geneva Conventions, its additional protocols,[27] and the Hague Conventions is essential to reporting the interplay between international law and politics regarding decisions to intervene. Along with the post-Iraq intervention in Kurdistan is a growing corpus of international human rights law that has sought to legitimate intervention in internal wars, primarily if a state is in collapse, or alleviate large-scale human suffering. The spectrum of activities that the international community is entitled to undertake includes nonintrusive instruments for state compliance, that is, fact-finding missions, reports, allegations of abuses that can be presented at appropriate UN agencies, and some resolutions. However, these instruments are noncoercive, the result of reportorial arrangements, and do not legitimize the use of force. At the other end of the spectrum fall genocidal types of massacres. As a result of the 1948 Genocide Convention, the international community is legally empowered to respond to genocidal activity, although the relevant legal provisions have never been activated to stop genocide in progress. However, key provisions of the Convention have been incorporated into the statutes of the International Tribunals for both the former Yugoslavia and Rwanda.[28]

The legal literature discusses under what conditions noncoercive intervention is legally protected and in what circumstances coercive intervention is legally obligated to alleviate mass suffering. None of the instruments relating to the laws of war, in particular those that govern how victims of conflict must be treated by belligerents, contains provisions that codify circumstances that would trigger the use of force to protect civilian populations (although any use of force raises the question of in what circumstances force is justified). Short of containing genocide, the legal basis for legitimating the use of force to mount a relief operation is shaky, at best, with the exception of situations where the Security Council perceives a threat to international peace and security. Here legal considerations meet operational and political ones, including the will of the international community to engage in the challenging task of postconflict peace building. If the political will exists to engage, legal developments follow. Coverage is an active part of the equation.

As the United Nations Secretary General attempts to create a rapid reaction force to meet modest crises when international security interests are not directly at stake, thus placing the question of state sovereignty at issue, the press is obligated to engage these debates in a responsible manner.

The Changing Character of the Media Business

Given the global reach of the mass media, the extended ability of ordinary citizens to communicate via fax and cyberspace, and a shift in relationships between information providers and information consumers, it is harder today for a society to engage in unnoticed acts of repression. Such relative transparency poses added responsibilities for journalists to probe for examples of governmental abuse and cover stories about those who dissent or otherwise seek to empower themselves. The global network creates an obligation to move outside of "pack journalism" and use human rights and humanitarianism as a lens to raise fresh questions that anticipate the kinds of global sea changes that are defining the post–cold war world.

With CNN and other networks reporting live from the front lines of world tension, television has become an agent of history as its satellite-transmitted images influence government policies and public opinion, appearing to shape events themselves. Although how influential the images are in terms of long-term public opinion and policy is unclear, live broadcasts, with their ability to be everywhere at once, contain the capacity to convey the most immediate images and to probe better the dialogues of dissent.

With the growth of a small but influential audience made up of people, transnational corporate executives, NGOs, and even wealthy pleasure travelers whose lives stretch across geographical boundaries, the inclination of the increasingly concentrated media worldview is to perceive itself as speaking exclusively to this emerging family of international citizens.[29] The challenge is not only to facilitate their movement but to challenge conformity of thought by presenting realities that probe their assumptions.[30] The electronic media obligate all other forms of journalism to give meaning to the democratizing capability of global television.[31]

In coverage of humanitarian intervention, "compassion fatigue" is often identified as a reason for a restricted U.S. role. Calling "compassion fatigue" a rationalization for not engaging in or rethinking policy, NGOs point out that humanitarian aid has been used as a "fig leaf" for foreign policy. Both the phrase and the policy dilemmas must be explored if problems that are confronting us into the twenty-first century are to be meaningfully covered.

Two competing models of communications are typically advanced in discussions regarding content for the exploding numbers of band widths: Ted Turner's English-language internationalism which supplies a global elite with a common news base of information that parallels the interests of an interconnected global economy; and the mass of viewers, listeners, or readers whose interests and vision is primarily local, and who want cultural, linguistic, and national reporting that serves more specialized interests.

Despite the concentration of ownership of the mass media, the combination of cyberspace, the fax machine, American talk shows, and the ability to travel virtually across time via inexpensive travel has increased the variety of opportunities available for people to bypass journalists altogether. Despite wide telebroadcasts of the Tiananmen Square massacre in 1989, for example, the Chinese government severely restricted the information that reached its own public. Press coverage is frequently suppresed by the world's governments, requiring creative approaches to convey information. In some cases, government leaders have spoken to the international community while suppressing the same information at home. The French newspaper *Actuel* coordinated a global "fax-in" to help Chinese citizens learn about the violations of their fellow citizens' human rights in June 1989. The French editors simulated an issue of the official Chinese Communist Party organ, *People's Daily*, with Chinese reporters describing the ongoing repression following the government crackdown. The material was printed in thirteen publications in Europe and North and South America, along with instructions about how to fax it to China, relying on a published list of fax numbers in Chinese universities, bureaucracies, trade associations, and workplaces. Perhaps the most enduring legacy of the shootings at Tiananmen Square is the China News Digest, a web server and mailing list that routinely figures among the top ten most popular lists.[32] Such devices defy national frontiers, requiring today's journalists to probe far more deeply than newsbytes, faxed messages, or CNN-style images of suffering.[33] The point is to reconnect information with knowledge, if not wisdom.

Human Rights and Empowerment

Human rights and humanitarian coverage raises a distinct set of questions regarding the empowerment of people. Stories of how people extricate themselves from repressive regimes, build democratic institutions, or test government accountability during times of crisis are news to those who seek to undo repression.

In 1972 Brazilian scholar Paulo Freire developed a pedagogy based on local resistance to repressive regimes. Freire's model emphasized community participation in the identification of community wants, collective action to promote social transformation, and the use of information to support community-articulated goals and objectives by those disempowered or marginalized.[34] For journalists, systematic collection of information and reporting on community efforts raises the viability of empowerment efforts. Such coverage also identifies global trends, as responses of the world's most impoverished or marginalized make visible the root causes of conflict.

Our world televises poverty, disempowerment, and mass killing. Today's responsible journalism takes reporting out of the victim class, offering a depth of coverage that invites understanding and therefore the potential for durable resolution of human rights and humanitarian disasters. Through our new communications order, a presentation of human rights and humanitarian experience might offer more of the world's peoples access to tools that allow qualitative improvements in their daily lives.

This chapter is part of a series of human rights and humanitarian stories supported by the Uniterra Fund, the Public Welfare Foundation, Reebok International, the William Penn Foundation, and Mrs. Keith Montgomery.

Notes

1. Ryszard Kapuscinski, *The Emperor* (New York: Vintage, 1983), 99.

2. Committee to Protect Journalists [CPJ], *Attacks on the Press in 1993: A Worldwide Survey* (New York: CPJ, March 1994), 16.

3. The CPJ also reported in 1993 twelve to fifteen cases of deliberate political assassinations of war correspondents. See also the New York-based PEN and the London-based Article 19 for additional statistics. PEN is the international organization of literary writers and editors whose most significant work is protecting free speech and press, often in environments of gross human rights abuse.

4. The Columbia School of Journalism, American University School of Journalism, UCLA, and Neiman Fellows Program at Harvard University have taken the lead in incorporating human rights and humanitarian issues in curricula. Projects such as the Humanitarianism and War Project at the Brown University Watson School of Internatonal Affairs, the Freedom Forum, and others have conducted seminars for working journalists to encourage discussion of humanitarian coverage.

5. Peter Arnett, *Live from the Battlefield: From Vietnam to Baghdad* (New York: Simon and Schuster, 1995), 83, 87.

6. Interview with Larry Minear, August 28, 1994.

7. Lewis A. Friedland, *Covering the World* (New York: A Twentieth Century Fund Paper, 1992).

8. David Forsythe, *The Internationalization of Human Rights* (Lincoln: University of Nebraska Press, 1991), 47.

9. Nongovernmental organizations (NGOs), financed by governments or responsible to private funding constituencies, sometimes offer stories that might be enlarged to serve other interests, no matter how commendable.

10. "Issues at the UN World Conference on Human Rights," doc. IOR 41/WU/02/93, March 29, 1993.

11. Bilahari Kausikan, "Asia's Different Standard," *Foreign Policy* 92 (Fall 1993): 24; See also Abdullahi Ahmed An-Na'im and Francis M. Deng, eds., *Human Rights in Africa: Cross Cultural Perspectives* (Washington, D.C.: Brookings, 1990).

12. Philip Alston, "The U.N.'s Human Rights Record: From San Francisco and Vienna and Beyond," *Human Rights Quarterly* 16 (May 1994): 383.

13. Leonard R. Sussman, *Good News and Bad: Press Freedom Worldwide* (New York: Freedom House, 1994), examined journalists and press in 186 countries.

14. James Reston, *The Artillery of the Press: Its Influence on American Foreign Policy* (New York: Harper and Row, 1966).

15. Herbert Marcuse, *An Essay on Liberation* (Boston: Beacon, 1969); his comments on "Repressive Tolerance" offer a conceptual framework for readers to challenge their own assumptions.

16. Martin A. Lee, "Human Rights and the Media: An Overview," *Committee to Protect Journalists Newsletter* (Summer 1989). While the Civil and Political Covenant has subsequently been ratified, the Covenant on Social and Economic Rights remains unratified and politically contentious.

17. Carlo Filice, "On the Obligation to Keep Informed About Distant Atrocities," *Human Rights Quarterly* 12, no. 3 (August 1990): 397.

18. Ray Bonner's coverage of the Rwanda genocide and its aftermath for the *New York Times* was as solid as was his coverage in El Salvador.

19. The United Nations Truth Commission corroborated the reporter's accounts, as did an exhumation conducted by Argentine forensic anthropologists. See Mark Danner, *The Massacre at El Mozote* (New York: Vintage, 1993).

20. Sussman, *Good News and Bad.* The report concluded that sixty-eight countries (36.6 percent) were judged to have free media. In sixty-four countries (34.4 percent) the press is called "partly free," and fifty-four (29 percent) "not free." The criteria used to rate the countries included the influence of laws and administrative rules affecting media content, political pressures on the media, economic influences from government or private entrepreneurs, and overt repressive actions against journalists or their institutions.

21. Erik Holzt, *Torture* (Copenhagen: International Rehabilitation Council for Torture Victims, 1993).

22. In this context, the primacy of the state is subordinate to its citizenry; universally accepted principles demonstrate the obligation of the state and the international community to the world's peoples, who are entitled to be informed of political actions that impact their lives.

23. Frank Newman and David Weissbrodt, *International Human Rights* (Cincinnati, Oh.: Anderson Publishing, 1990).

24. Donna Gomien, ed., *Broadening the Frontiers of Human Rights* (Oslo: Scandinavian University Press, 1993). Article 19 of the Universal Declaration of Human Rights applies in theory to all member states. Although it has been treated as the most derogable of those rights ennumerated in the Universal Declaration, it states: "Everyone has the right to freedom of opinion and expression; this right includes freedom to hold opinions without interference and to seek, receive and impart information and ideas through any media and regardless of frontier." Despite the high number of incidences of murder and harrassment of reporters, few cases have been successfully prosecuted.

25. Edwin S. Maynard, "The Bureaucracy and Implementation of US Human Rights Policy,"

Human Rights Quarterly 11 (May 1989): 177; Howard B. Tolley, Jr., *The International Commission of Jurists: Global Advocates for Human Rights* (Philadelphia: University of Pennsylvania Press, 1994), 110–11. The International Federation of Editors in Chief asked the ICJ to prepare an instrument that would protect journalists on dangerous missions, claiming that the 1949 Geneva Conventions provides inadequate protection. The government representatives at the UN Commission on Human Rights weakened the provisions and agreed to provide support to the international press corps only to the extent that they offered protection to their domestic journalists, which given the global climate regarding journalists, the ICJ viewed as a pretext for restricting rather than protecting rights. See also Maynard, "The Bureaucracy and Implementation of US Human Rights Policy,"

26. Laurie Wesiberg, "Human Rights Nongovernmental Organizations," *Human Rights in the World Community: Issues and Action,* 2d ed., Richard Pierre Claude and Burns H. Weston, ed. (Philadelphia: University of Pennsylvania Press, 1992), 372–82, at 373. Discusses the highly political nature of NGOs that attempt to hold governments accountable for their behavior, thereby requiring scrupulous attention to the credibility of their evidentiary bases regarding charges of state-sanctioned abuses.

27. By June 15, 1993, the Geneva Conventions of 1949 were binding for 181 states and their Additional Protocols widely accepted, with 125 States Parties to Protocol 1 and 116 States Parties to Protocol 11. In addition, 36 states were bound by the 1980 Convention on Restrictions on the Use of Certain Conventional Weapons. The core of the Law of the Hague consists of the treaties adopted by the two Hague conferences. The tsar of Russia convened the first Hague Peace Conference in 1899 as a step toward international disarmament. Although the conference failed to achieve this grand aim, it did result in three conventions: for the peaceful adjustment of international differences; regarding the laws and customs of war on land; and for the adaptation to maritime warfare of the 1864 Geneva Convention. Also included in the Law of the Hague are restraints regarding civilian deaths and the 1925 Geneva Protocol for the Prohibition of the Use in War of Asphyxiating, Poisonous or Other Gases, and of Bacteriological Methods of Warfare. See Keith Suter, *An International Law of Guerilla Warfare: The Global Politics of Law-Making* (New York: St. Martin's Press, 1984).

28. Some of these observations are drawn from conversations with George Andreopoulos and Richard Claude, whom the author thanks for their clarity of vision. See generally Michael Howard, George J. Andreopoulos, and Mark R. Shulman, *The Laws of War: Constraints on Warfare in the Western World* (New Haven, Conn.: Yale University Press, 1994).
    Article 8: Any contracting party may call upon competent organizations of the United Nations to take such action to prevent and suppress acts of genocide or acts punishable under the Genocide Convention. This includes the Security Council which can authorize force. Also, Chapter 7 of the UN Charter, which addresses peace or acts of aggression, is broad enough to justify enforcement measures to deal with genocidal measures. The problem is typically a matter of political will and is grist for in-depth coverage.

29. Lee W. Huebner, *Brown Journal of Foreign Affairs* (Winter 1993–94): 190.

30. Anthony Smith, *The Age of Behemoths: The Globalization of Mass Media Firms* (New York: A Twentieth Century Fund Paper, 1991).

31. Robert J. Donovan and Ray Scherer, *Unsilent Revolution: Television News and American Public Life* (Cambridge: Cambridge University Press, 1992).

32. The Digest was started by a group of Canadian and American expatriate Chinese students to spread news about Tiananmen Square. Six years later, tens of thousands of subscribers receive a daily synopsis of news stories about China published in newspapers and magazines throughout the world.

33. Bill Dedman, *Power Reporting: A Complete Guide to Computer Assisted Reporting,* A Project of the Freedom Forum (New York, 1993).

34. Paulo Freire, *Pedagogy of the Oppressed* (New York: Continuum, 1983). On October 16, 1995, at Louis Farrakhan's "Million Man March," he counseled his virtually all-male, all-black audience that "there is no way we can integrate into white supremacy and hold onto our dignity as human beings." Television commentators spoke with a degree of surprise at the number of attendees. Full coverage of black America would reduce the assumptions of supremacist attitudes and perhaps dissolve the demogogic approaches Farrakhan has found useful.

Part IV
Community-Based and Nonformal Human Rights Education

EDITORS' INTRODUCTION

The chapters presented here describe and analyze critical efforts by nongovernmental organizations (NGOs) to undertake social change and to promote human rights education programs in societies in transition. In all these cases, the events of the *annus mirabilis* 1989 constituted a watershed. The end of the cold war has made a difference, and not only among diplomats. The demise of the bipolar system shifted the focus from the preoccupation with externally induced challenges to national security, to an internally induced problematic in which any articulation of security concerns has to be viewed as inextricably linked to human welfare. UN Secretary-General Boutros Boutros-Ghali has said as much. In an early assessment of the *Agenda for Peace* document, he used the term "human security" to describe this new challenge facing states and societies in the post–cold war period. If, however, what now looks like "groping into the unknown" is to result in a paradigmatic shift, human rights education must play a central role. Few would argue with this proposition since one of the major tenets of human rights education is the exploration and articulation of the transformative capacities of knowledge, capacities firmly grounded in a commitment to the development of moral reasoning.

"Human security" is the common concern of these chapters, whose contributors share a set of assumptions, especially the following three.First is *the importance of nongovernmental organizations in promoting and sustaining concerns for human rights education.* For example, Richard Pierre Claude's chapter emphasizes the role of NGOs as catalytic prompters of governmental action, sponsors of nonformal human rights education, and major agents of social change. His analysis offers wide-ranging examples of NGO activities in terms of three educational functions: planning, implementing, and evaluating. The author links his review of ever-increasing NGO activity to "global society perspectives" on world affairs. In this view, by virtue of their fact-finding, lobbying, and educational activities, NGOs have become major actors on the international landscape.

The key to improving the efficacy of NGOs is well-planned and well-implemented training for their staff members and constituents. For example, "Diplomacy Training for NGOs," a program in New South Wales, Australia, is designed exclusively to serve Asian- and Pacific-based human rights activists and members of nongovernmental organizations. The objectives of the program take into account the global maldistribution of NGOs, which puts such groups in the South at a disadvantage; it is in response to this situation that the diplomacy training program seeks a remedy. Training sessions promote NGO familiarity and competence in using the UN human rights system. Relying on small group exercises, role-playing, rigorous coaching, and presentation/discussions, Asian and Pacific NGO members can develop expertise and confidence in using UN procedures and standards without undertaking expensive travel to Geneva forums.

Second is *the importance of a participatory approach to human rights education.* As Edward L. O'Brien notes in his chapter, "Community Education for Law, Democracy, and Human Rights," years of experience in organizing "street law" programs for youth in inner city areas of the United States convinced him that participatory approaches, even for troubled teenagers, resulted in increased knowledge of the legal system, but also produced "a change in attitudes and a corresponding reduction of the factors commonly associated with delinquency." He cites studies from various countries supporting the view that participatory educational programs enhance prospects for successful education, whether directed at prison inmates, refugee camp residents, or magistrates and judges being introduced to new legal concepts. Convinced that "participatory methodology is a necessary and required ingredient for effective human rights education," the National Institute for Citizen Education in Law (NICEL) produced a textbook emphasizing participation. NICEL's book, *Human Rights for All,* first states legal standards and then calls on participants to debate controversial issues relating to the human rights issues described. O'Brien argues forcefully on behalf of the efficacy of case studies, questions for discussion, small group decision making, scripted dramas, and so on. In one such exercise developed for South Africa, a conflictive and violent family scenario was cited and designed for acting out in Zulu. In a case focusing on wife beating and reported from Durban, South Africa, role-play generated a debate over the cultural tradition that accepted such action. O'Brien reports that the chief stepped in, saying "we have to begin to change some of our traditional ways of doing things."

A major stumbling block to changing traditional ways is the selective use of both traditional culture and the "lessons" of history by elite and competing interest groups as rationalizations for the continuation of oppressive institutions and discriminatory policies. As J. Paul Martin, Cosmas Gitta, and Tokunbo Ige argue in their chapter on the prospects for a new consciousness respectful of human rights in sub-Saharan Africa, human rights education must emphasize the "cultural adaptation of international norms." But in order to achieve that, the official version of certain oppressive cultural practices needs to be challenged on the grounds of both its accuracy and its representative character within the cultural discourse in question. In the meantime, human rights education must promote those interpretations of contested cultural practices which are consistent with international human rights norms.

In a case study on legal literacy from Botswana, Unity Dow and co-authors illustrate the resistance faced by women as they attempted to mobilize and use legal reform on behalf of standards of equality. They clearly show how, for such a perspective to gain acceptance, the legacy of patriarchy must be rebutted both for its overt sexism and for its unrepresentative character among the population. They also show clearly the importance of securing evidence, in the form of the chief's blessing, for the legitimacy and credibility of their program of litigation and education.

Third is *the importance of strong civil society lending credibility to NGO-sponsored non-formal education.* Although most authors recognize the importance of governmental support for human rights education, in particular because of the government's influence, its control of formal education, and—most critically—its ability to create through its commitment to the rule of law a framework receptive to human rights values, the record indicates at best the government's questionable commitment to these matters. The assessment varies in accordance with the level of the development of civil society and prior experience (or lack thereof) in democratic governance.

In the case of sub-Saharan Africa, the legacy of democratic values found at the village level has yet to materialize at the national level. The absence of democratic institutions and structures at that level makes the task of any human rights education program all the more formidable since, according to Martin and Gitta, "without government support, it is impossible for human rights education to reach more than small segments of the population." On the other hand, the case of the Botswana women's campaign for legal literacy and education in human rights shows the capacity inherent in energetic community organizing, especially when the targeted social sector (women) is ready for mobilization. In Chile, according to Abraham K. Magendzo, the years of the Pinochet military government have chilled institutions of civil society and inhibited the development of human rights education, even after the more recent inauguration of democratic elections. Years of repression have created resistance on the part of teachers in formal educational institutions to undertake human rights education, viewing it as "too political." Those engaged in curriculum planning for human rights education are too easily given to avoidance behavior when faced with the challenge of fostering and promoting critical analytical skills by students within the framework of human rights education. Program legitimacy is fragile and develops slowly against a historical background of military dictatorship.

Likewise in Argentina, according to E. Débora Benchoam and George C. Rogers, the reconstruction of democratic discourse was undermined by the inability of both the Alfonsín and Menem governments to deal decisively with the legacy of gross human rights violations during the seven-year military rule. In their brief note, however, Benchoam and Rogers show what a difference NGOs can make. Even during the period of military rule, elements of civil society survived, including several indigenous human rights NGOs. With the return to electoral democracy, NGOs took the lead in designing programs of human rights education, partly drawing strength and legitimacy from a heroic past, as in the case of Servicio Paz y Justicia América Latina (Peace and Justice Service in Latin America [SERPAJ]), founded by Nobel laureate Adolfo Pérez Esquivel.

In his chapter on Germany, Alexander von Cube reports on initiatives taken by trade unions with particular reference to issues relating to foreign labor. He shows how some unions have promoted human rights education, and he demonstrates that their enhanced credibility on this score stems from their "historical role as champions of the social underdog" as well as from their own experience under Nazi rule.

The unions' honorable tradition of taking a firm stand on social issues, including their efforts to combat prejudice against foreigners, stands in marked contrast to facile generalizations about sweeping xenophobia among Germans. Von Cube connects German labor union educational programs to relevant norms promoted by the International Labour Organization, a component of the United Nations.

Human rights education developments in Central and Eastern Europe are reviewed in the chapter by Theodore S. Orlin and co-authors. They argue that in the case of Romania the rapid politicization of human rights discourse has led school authorities to conclude that it was primarily an opposition weapon geared toward a critique of government policies, hence an issue that did not belong in the classroom. What compounded this negative impression was a growing belief that all the social problems associated with Romania's transition to postcommunist rule (high crime rates, unemployment, and general uncertainty about the future) were caused "by the commitment to democracy" rather than viewed as the product of the unfortunate legacy of the Ceauşescu regime.

In such a context, the role of NGOs becomes even more important as they have to sustain their commitment to human rights education programs in the face of government indifference or, at times, outright hostility. The opposite of such hostility, however, is also illustrated here in chapters that describe exceptional cases of government support for human rights education, such as the positive role of the Human Rights Subsecretariat of the Argentine Ministry of the Interior and the German labor unions which function within a social milieu receptive to the rule of law.

These chapters describe and analyze the work of numerous NGOs, including Al-Haq and B'Tselem, respectively Arab and Jewish human rights NGOs, which worked together to plan HRE curricula; the Women in Law and Development in Africa (WILDAF) and the International Federation of Women Lawyers (FIDA), which deal with the legal rights of women in Africa; the Zairian Human Rights Group (AZADHO) and the Legal Resources Foundation in Zimbabwe, which educate Zairian and Zimbabwe citizens about their rights vis-à-vis their governments through the use of published materials; the Metlhaetsile Women's Information Centre in Botswana under the leadership of attorney Unity Dow; the challenges facing SERPAJ and Citizens' Power (Poder Ciudadano), both grassroots organizations committed to citizens' empowerment in Argentina; the uphill struggle of the Romanian Independent Society for Human Rights (SIRDO) to initiate human rights educational programs in schools and offer teacher training courses; the promising collaboration between the Bratislava branch of Amnesty International (AI/B) and the Milan Šimecka Foundation to inaugurate the "Human Rights in the (Slovak) Schools" project, whose main aim is "to convey to teachers basic human rights information and methods to effectively teach their students"; the creative critical support provided by the Dutch, Norwegian, and Finnish Helsinki Committees in conjunction with UNESCO, for the launching of a national project in Albania whose aim is "to familiarize teachers with human rights norms and the principles of democratic education and bring these lessons to the classrooms"; and the creative use of the Robert Jungk method and the related Human Rights Education kit by the German labor unions to combat violence and hostility against foreigners.

Finally, on the question of assessing the effectiveness of these programs, there is a widespread feeling that the jury is still out. This stems not only from the realization that most of these programs are very recent, and hence their transformative impact will not be felt for a long time, but especially because in most cases they operate in an uncertain milieu. As societies embark on the challenging task of postauthoritarian and postcommunist reconstruction, there is a temptation to view the growing list of social and economic problems as the product of the currently unfolding democratic process rather than as the legacy bequeathed by an authoritarian/totalitarian past. To overcome such debilitating perceptions may well prove to be the greatest task confronting the human rights community.

Chapter 24
Global Human Rights Education: The Challenges for Nongovernmental Organizations

Richard Pierre Claude

The promotion of human rights depends upon promises made and promises kept. Endorsements for human rights education have been proclaimed in various global and regional legal instruments ever since 1945 when the Charter of the United Nations announced as one of its purposes cooperation "in promoting and encouraging respect for human rights and fundamental freedoms" (Article 1, Sec. 3). The Charter's references to "promoting and encouraging" create state responsibilities for educating and teaching. Despite international endorsements and promises, the goal of human rights education, which includes teaching people their rights, has just begun and has not yet been widely or well implemented. Indeed, with some exceptions, there remains a discernible lack of commitment on the part of many governments to keep their promises to promote human rights through education.

Despite governmental inertia in teaching people their rights, there is progress to report. As pedagogies for empowerment become more widespread, as civil societies reemerge in Central Europe, as voluntary associations proliferate in less developed countries, vitality and initiative are evident among nongovernmental groups concerned with human rights and human rights education. Nongovernmental organizations (NGOs), both on their own and as catalytic prompters of governmental actions, have begun to undertake primary tasks in human rights education (HRE). In the post–cold war era, as we grope toward the twenty-first century, NGOs may be expected to increase their educational work, viewed as a preventive strategy to diminish human rights violations, as a way of ensuring participation in promoting economic development, and as a foundation for democracy.

This chapter examines some of the challenges faced by human rights NGOs alone and with governmental agencies as they increasingly become involved with various educational endeavors. These include producing educational materials, participating in teacher training, networking with collaborating institutions, undertaking technical assistance, and attending to the important task of educational evaluation. These activities are aggregated in the analysis presented below under the functional categories of planning, implementing, and evaluating.

Strengthening and Expanding Partnerships

Human rights NGOs have made their most visible contributions in the field of nonformal education. But examples abound of NGO achievements in the development of human rights formal, nonformal, and informal education. Some definitions are in order. *Formal education* refers to the normally tripartite structure of primary, secondary, and tertiary education for which governments generally have the principal responsibility. *Nonformal education* is any organized, systematic educational activity carried on outside the formal system to offer selected types of learning to particular subgroups in the population, adults as well as children. *Informal education* may or may not be organized, and is usually unsystematic education, having its impact on the lifelong processes by which every person acquires and accumulates knowledge, skills, attitudes, and insights from daily experiences and exposure such as through radio, television, and the print media. NGOs have performed numerous roles in furthering the cause of human rights learning in all of these formats.

In some countries where human rights education takes place, such as Costa Rica and the Czech Republic, government and educational officials undertake activities to promote human rights as the framers of the UN Charter anticipated in the sense that they expected state officials to be the burden-carriers for membership duties. For example, in Peru, which by 1995 had weathered serious human rights and constitutional challenges, the constitution was amended to require human rights education. Article 14 says: "Drawing from the constitution and human rights, an ethical and civic foundation are necessary for the entire program of civilian and military educational processes."

In a few states, governmental officials have taken the lead in seeing to it that formal education and nonformal education conspicuously promote respect for human rights, for example, in Sweden, the Netherlands, and the Philippines. But even in cases of enlightened governments possessed of the political will to initiate HRE, when their education bureaucracies find themselves strapped for funding, expertise, and experience, they sometimes look to external support. Thus the pattern of interaction and potential partnerships between human rights NGOs and education officials has become more visible; it is quite variable in form. NGOs have shown they can help in many settings and ways.

In 1990–91 this writer undertook a comprehensive implementation study of those provisions of the new Philippine Constitution which mandate the teaching of human rights at all levels and in all fields of study for the populace as well as for military and police personnel. The resulting findings, scanning human rights educational ventures

Figure 24.1. An NGO delegation of Native Americans attends a meeting of the United Nations Human Rights Commission. The UN Centre for Human Rights works with NGOs in the development and distribution of human rights educational materials. (UNPHOTO 163 204)

since 1987, revealed three different patterns of operational activities and administration: bottom-to-top, mixed, and top-to-bottom.[1] HRE programs, especially involving NGOs in the democratic atmosphere of civil society in which they thrive in the Philippines, are conceived as bottom-up operations emanating from grassroots organizational activities. Their work is addressed to informal, nonformal, and sometimes formal education as well, illustrated by the case of the José Diokno Foundation, a human rights NGO, which designed HRE study modules adopted by the Department of Education, Culture and Sports for use in public primary and secondary schools.

International organizations concerned with the promotion and encouragement of human rights and fundamental freedoms have been slow to recognize or acknowledge the potential creativity and "spark-plugging" capabilities of NGOs in the field of human rights teaching. Given that the United Nations is a creature of state governments, it is not surprising that until recently most UN-sponsored concern with HRE has focused on state responsibilities, rather gently urging governments to take on the promotion of human rights through formal and nonformal education.

In 1978 the United Nations Educational, Scientific, and Cultural Organization (UNESCO) sponsored an International Congress on the Teaching of Human Rights held in Vienna.[2] It generated multiple guidelines on the preferred content of human rights education and reflected widespread assumptions that government officials would initiate such programs. Very little was said about NGOs.

A sharp contrast is evident in comparable meetings in more recent years. For example, in 1990 a World Conference on Education for All met in Jomtien, Thailand and produced a ten-article declaration. Article 7 calls for "an expanded vision" at the heart of which should be "strengthened partnerships" by governments with NGOs to contribute to "the planning, implementation and evaluation of basic educational programmes."[3] Such new partnerships should ally educational authorities with private sector groups including nongovernmental organizations. In the same spirit, at the World Congress on Human Rights meeting in New Delhi in 1991, Hans Thoolen called for "new modes of cooperation between intergovernmental organizations and NGOs in the processing of human rights information and education."[4]

The Jomtien conference was dominated by practical concerns. The resulting World Declaration on Education for All, issued in 1990, lamented the many increasing constraints facing teachers in meeting basic learning needs, constraints said to be imposed by rapid population growth, economic stagnation, civil strife, preventable deaths of children, and widespread environmental degradation. In the face of these serious problems leading to setbacks in basic education, the Jomtien conference said that educators must reach out to new sources of support, prominently noting the need for strengthened partnerships with NGOs. Article 7 of the Declaration, as previously noted, says that "genuine partnerships" contribute to the planning, implementing, and evaluating of basic educational programs.[5]

Under these categories, the balance of this chapter offers examples of NGOs in "genuine partnership" and comments on the challenges involved in such arrangements.

Planning

Professional educators who are concerned with the development of teaching materials and the preparation of curricular innovation stress that the first step in such program planning requires the sorting out of ends and means. Educators should specify the goals and objectives sought by any given project. In *Teaching for International Understanding, Peace and Human Rights*, Judith V. Torney-Purta reminds us that "within education it is important to articulate the objectives of programs and activities rather than simply to provide the raw material."[6] An example of such "raw material" in HRE would be the Universal Declaration of Human Rights (UDHR), which may, to some readers, seem daunting and unfathomable without accompanying explanation. Thus the mere posting of the UDHR in police stations, as recommended by Amnesty International, is a mindless exercise in the absence of carefully planned instruction and exposition. The challenge in using this foundational document is to identify the target group undergoing education, specify the goal to be met for their education, and present the document in the context of the chosen objective. Different target groups (women, law students, police, illiterate street children) call for different plans. Groups concerned with HRE may pursue many different objectives: attitude changes; value clarification; cognitive skills in matters of law, government, and society; and the development of solidarity behavior and attitudes, among others.

An instructive example of educational planning involves a project in Israel designed for Arab and Jewish students. "The Rules of the Game" is called by its designers a "bottom-up" curriculum. This term draws attention to the fact that, from its inception, the project was developed with the full participation of an equal number of Arab and Jewish teachers. The objective of the group of twenty educators was to cooperate in developing a curriculum to foster the understanding of democratic principles including both majority rule and minority rights. The planning phase encompassed a year of debate and discussion with intensive workshops drawing materials from Al-Haq and B'Tselem, respectively Arab and Jewish human rights NGOs. "Rules of the Game" is supposed to build and reinforce attitudes of tolerance, mutual respect, and individual freedom, but it is primarily a curriculum emphasizing a cognitive approach aimed at helping students distinguish empirical findings from value judgments, eyewitness evidence from hearsay, and a logical argument from an emotional one. The teacher-planners of the project expressed the hope that "a 'grass roots' curriculum, introduced by the very same teachers by whom it was developed, might secure good will and cooperation that are so direly needed in order to overcome negative attitudes and resistance to change."[7]

The Middle East example of interactive planning involves teaching to achieve social change. According to research findings in social psychology, change agents encounter more difficulties in introducing innovation into groups by reliance on outsiders to the exclusion of in-group participation.[8] By contrast, "Rules of the Game" enlisted teachers and students in planning operations from the beginning, thereby enhancing the likelihood of acceptance of change favoring the realization of human rights.[9]

Where the development of human rights teaching materials and curricula is concerned, interactive strategies might not always seem practical. Teachers and others intent upon initiating human rights education often face many different difficulties. These may include elementary problems of not knowing where to begin, being unsure of the content and scope of human rights standards, or feeling intimidated by the reliance of the field on unfamiliar legal terminology. Of course, there is also occasionally the more serious problem of facing risks in a hostile domestic political atmosphere.

When that problem is combined with the circumstance of not having access to potentially helpful domestic human rights NGOs, then contacts with international NGOs may be critically important. Under any of these circumstances, but especially when complicated by a history of authoritarian politics, those planning HRE projects may well benefit by consultation with overseas international NGOs. Thus this choice may entail sacrificing the benefits of interactive participation which such relatively open civil societies such as Israel make possible.

Examples of constructive external consultation in planning HRE projects may be cited from Latin America. In 1989 the Uruguayan Council of Education and Science and the Provincial Government of Andalucia entered into an agreement with Amnesty International resulting in the publication of a "how-to" manual on teaching human rights. The 307-page book supplies a wide-ranging educators' guide on methods for infusing human rights lessons into various conventional disciplines common to primary and secondary schools in Uruguay.[10] As a reference and a guide, the manual is both theoretical and pedagogical, even supplying model lectures and lessons on human rights topics for the classroom. The full title of the book reveals its objectives: *Derechos humanos: Propuesta de educación para la paz basada en los derechos humanos y del niño* (Peace-Centered Education for Human Rights and the Rights of the Child). José Tuvilla Rayo, the editor, explains that the book is necessary to help teachers creatively inject peace and human rights lessons into their teaching, a task made more challenging and more necessary by virtue of Uruguay's history in the 1970s and 1980s of military rule marked by patterns of gross violations of human rights. As Uruguay now restores its historical respect for democracy, it becomes important to do so by relying on the Universal Declaration of Human Rights to identify foundational values for democracy.

Democracy, peace, and human rights are values promoted throughout the Americas by the institutions established under the American Convention on Human Rights. The Department of Education of the Inter-American Institute of Human Rights has published a series of study booklets on human rights which provide materials adaptable to formal and nonformal education. To ensure that human rights standards are clarified in recognizable cultural settings, the teaching materials of the institute rely heavily on real case studies, often drawn from NGO reports. For example, one paperback booklet recounts various cases, episodes, and experiences that teachers may find useful to draw upon to introduce human rights information from real-life events. These vignettes—"raw materials" in Torney-Purta's terms—could be used in classes in history, social science, civics, and international affairs, among others. A typical selection in *Experiencias* focuses on the social importance of new communications technologies, for example, computers, modem linkages, and fax communications.[11]

The experiential presentation recounts events associated with the fall of Paraguay's dictator Alfredo Stroessner. Radio transmission is credited with bringing the news speedily to the Movement for Justice and Peace, a Latin American human rights NGO, which notified Paraguayan refugees scattered throughout the western hemisphere. Circumstances are described surrounding the work of a refugee Paraguayan solidarity group in Brazil. It was able to fax information from its base in Porto Alegre, Brazil, to San José, to the office of the Inter-American Human Rights Institute. The Brazilian group's information, sent to Costa Rica, led to the identification of mass grave locations outside of Asunción used for opponents of the fallen Stroessner regime. The "experience" carries many lessons. It shows that high technology communications can be "human rights friendly," that NGOs can be effective actors in the protection of human rights, that the truth about the cruelty of the dictator's arbitrary rule can eventually be told, and that the most difficult human rights problems should not be cause for despair.

The examples of educational planning sketched above illustrate the importance of enlisting NGOs in preparatory phases of education or at least relying on NGO-generated information and cases to bring the topic of human rights into the realm of historical and cultural reality. The "Rules of the Game" illustrates teachers investing time in serious deliberations and debates among themselves to clarify their objectives for curriculum development regarding emotionally charged topics—topics that, if not dealt with sensitively in the classroom, might well be dealt with only in the streets. *Experiencias* supplies teachers with a wide range of carefully developed realistic scenarios on which to draw in planning their own classes, programs, and curriculum, and into which they may wish to infuse some human rights issues.

Implementation

By contrast with the preparatory nature of planning, implementation involves putting a plan into action through systematically organized programs of dissemination, training, management, resource sharing, and networking. Illustrations of these activities bear consideration with special attention to NGO participation in the implementation of human rights education.

In the 1990s Amnesty International has moved from the planning to the implementation phase of human rights education for the young in India, the Philippines, Nigeria, Senegal, Tunisia, Brazil, Chile, and Mexico. In these and many other countries, projects are targeted to the poorer and most needy sectors of society. Dissemination of appropriate educational materials is the program priority for the regional resource centers that have opened or that will be opened in coming years. Such centers are accessible to anyone who wishes to use them. They will offer inexpensive materials such as videos, booklets, information packets, and teachers' guides, as well as advisory services. Charles P. Henry reports that these centers also "will organize the translation of particularly successful materials into new languages and encourage the exchange of experiences and ideas."[12]

Amnesty International's implementation of a network of centers is complemented by an independent and ambitious plan by another nongovernmental group also concerned about the implementation of human rights on a global scale. The People's Decade of Human Rights Education (PDHRE) seeks to energize educators and interested community groups in effective networking worldwide. The PDHRE (initially called "The Organizing Committee for the Decade of Human Rights Education") has a New York headquarters. Founded by Shulamith Koenig, the objective of the Decade is to endorse, enhance, and facilitate the development of formal, informal, and nonformal HRE in all sectors of society throughout the world. The strategic vision of the PDHRE is to involve grassroots organizations in HRE, drawing from those concerned with and working on issues of women, children, food and shelter, refugees, indigenous peoples, racism, minorities, health education, development, labor, religion, environmental protection, and peace. The objective of the Decade is to facilitate the efforts of such groups to promote an integrated approach to human rights. The hope is to move toward regional and finally subregional centers for human rights education in every nation of the world by the early years of the twenty-first century. Such centers would join in an international network to share information, materials, methodologies, and experiences, so as to make human rights education a popular creative activity everywhere by the year 2005.

Of course, internationally organized religious denominations often constitute existing "international networks," and many are significant transnational organizations. Church groups are among the many organizations developing plans consistent with the objectives of the United Nations Decade of Human Rights Education. One example is the Philippine National Council of Churches (Protestant), which publishes sermon outlines and liturgy and worship guides with human rights themes, including biblical readings in conjunction with relevant articles from the Universal Declaration of Human Rights. Another example involves the Catholic clergy in the United States. In 1994 the principal Catholic institutes or "religious orders," including the Jesuits, the Franciscans, and the Dominicans, agreed to celebrate the fiftieth anniversary (1998) of the Universal Declaration of Human Rights by planning and implementing a program of human rights education. According to the Conference of Major Superiors of Men (CMSM), the plan will be implemented through the institutions, ministries, and personnel of all the religious congregations combining to educate their many audiences about human rights, including economic, cultural, and social rights. The CMSM's stated objective is to effect direct social change on a specific topic of international justice and peace, training teachers to demonstrate the role of human rights in bringing about an international system of justice and peace.

Human rights education has evolved in the 1990s to the stage that widespread recognition exists for the need for systematic programs of teacher training. Such efforts are under way with the sponsorship of UNESCO (Associated Schools Project for International Cooperation and Peace), the Council of Europe (Teacher Bursary Scheme), the International Institute of Human Rights (Strasbourg training sessions), the World Association for the School as an Instrument of Peace (Geneva, training for high school teachers), and the Inter-American Institute of Human Rights (Departamento de Educación). Columbia University in New York has organized a four-month "Human Rights Advocates Training Program," and other North American colleges and universities are beginning to establish academic human rights programs as well. Such programs often seek to organize internships for students to have the valuable experience of working with NGOs.[13] Such an interdisciplinary program, planned for implementation in 1997 by the Townsend Institute for the Humanities of the University of California, Berkeley, affords students of public health and others the opportunity to accompany NGO fact-finding missions.

Those who lead, facilitate, and teach human rights need specialized training, and they can benefit by interaction with NGOs. The argument favoring a high priority on teacher training was strongly advanced by Peter Leuprecht, director of Human Rights of the Council of Europe. In language deserving extended quotation, he said:

Human rights education is not just an addition to the school curriculum; it should underlay the teaching of all school subjects and permeate every aspect of school life. If such education is to be successful at all levels, it will be necessary to train teachers and provide them with proper facilities. Much remains to be done in this regard, and improving the situation should be the aim of the efforts not only of the Council of Europe but also of the national authorities, non-governmental organizations and institutions, groups and individuals participating in this noble task. The challenge is a considerable one: it involves laying the foundations of tomorrow's society, a society which we hope will be democratic and imbued with respect for the dignity and inalienable rights of all people.[14]

Among regional institutions, the Council of Europe has blazed a pioneering trail. Its work in promoting and implementing human rights education is managed by a Council for Cultural Cooperation which operates the most successfully implemented large-scale program of human rights education anywhere. The Council's success illustrates the benefits of being close to the activities it seeks to support and the problems to which it seeks to respond. As an intergovernmental organization, its links to NGOs are multiple. The Council's education program covers schools, higher and adult education, and higher educational research and documentation. By maintaining communication links to human rights NGOs, the Cultural Cooperation Council can move swiftly in the development and dissemination of materials and the sharing of resources bearing on current issues as they arise: the growth of anti-Semitism and intolerance of minority groups such as gypsies; the rise of anti-refugee sentiment; and impunity of new fascist gangs and xenophobic groups.

The Council seeks a common core of human rights education for European schools. In building a human rights culture, Europeans promote increasingly close ties among themselves and advance the cause of continental integration. By virtue of serving multiple countries, the Cultural Commission has achieved economies of scale in its implementation of HRE. At the same time, to ensure both independent sources of information and adaptability to changing issues facing European countries, the

Council is straightforward in recommending teachers' reliance on materials prepared by NGOs.

In planning sessions directed toward the goal of preparing a comprehensive program of human rights education in Europe, the Council sponsored numerous conferences and international meetings of experts, teachers, and NGOs between 1978 and 1985. Their work led to a set of recommendations on implementing European HRE. The proposals were presented to and accepted by the Committee of Ministers to the Council of Europe member states: "On Teaching and Learning About Human Rights in Schools," Recommendation R(85)7.[15] It gives specific goals and objectives regarding curriculum, skills and knowledge to be acquired, the climate of the schools, and teacher training.

Recommendation 4.2 from the European Committee of Ministers deserves attention in the context of this chapter insomuch as it calls on schools "to work with non-governmental organizations which can provide information, case-studies and first-hand experience of successful campaigns for human rights dignity." Of course, from the point of view of the NGOs so relied upon, it must be recognized that new expectations coming from governmental and intergovernmental groups are bound to place added pressures on the already strained and slim resources of such European human rights organizations as the Minority Rights Group, Survival International, the International Lelio Basso Foundation for the Rights and Liberation of Peoples, and Justice et Paix.

The HRE program of the Council of Europe is a sophisticated model for the management and implementation of promoting human rights through education. It employs a mixed strategy of centralized planning and decentralized provision for services. The incorporation of NGO participation in planning and information sharing appears to avoid problems of co-optation and manipulation of NGOs inherently possible in such relations insofar as human rights organizations often criticize governments. But even assuming goodwill and constructive patterns of cooperation, such relations do tend to draw down NGO resources; thus NGOs must be mindful of possible imbalances in their relationships with governments and intergovernmental organizations. For example, it bears notice that the encouragement of teachers to use NGO materials should not substitute for Council of Europe responsibilities to find ways efficiently to share educational materials and resources. NGOs, typically short on financial resources, need to rely on the most cost-effective strategies possible.

Confronting Prejudice and Discrimination: Excerpt from an NGO Trainer's Guide from Ethiopia[1]

Overview: An understanding of prejudice, discrimination, racism, sexism, and ethnocentrism is an important part of human rights education. These forms of moral exclusion are fundamentally manifestations of the central problem of the denial of human dignity that makes possible various types of discrimination. Groups suffering from discrimination include ethnic and language minorities, refugees and displaced persons, and religious and other minorities. Women constitute the largest social group suffering from systematic discrimination and the failure to understand that women's rights are human rights, that is, rights to which women are entitled simply because they are human. This might seem obvious, but many people fail to place women's demands for equality in the context of human rights. It is prejudice and ignorance that promotes the dehumanization of women and minorities and which in turn fosters and supports many forms of discrimination.

Objectives: Participants should:

- reflect on the meaning and nature of prejudice
- reflect on the process and characteristics of discrimination and its origins in prejudice
- be able to identify groups of people who are the victims of prejudice and discrimination
- examine discrimination from the point of view of national and international human rights standards

Procedures: The facilitator must use creativity to explain the distinction between prejudice and discrimination and to ensure the participants understand the connections involved. As this can be a very sensitive topic for many; it will be important to allow adequate time for diverse views to be expressed. The facilitator should not try to "correct" views that sound prejudiced, but allow others to comment on them. Step 4 is rather complex, so the facilitator should plan to "float" among various groups to ensure that they understand their tasks.

Materials: Universal Declaration of Human Rights, Constitution of the Ethiopian Federal Democratic Republic.

---

1. This exercise is excerpted from *The Bells of Freedom: A Trainer's Guide with Resource Materials for Facilitators of Non-Formal Education and 24 Human Rights Echo Sessions* (Addis Ababa, Ethiopia: Action Professionals' Association for the People [APAP], 1996), 57–59.

Sequence: **Step 1.** Facilitator input: Explain that prejudice and discrimination are closely related.

Prejudice involves beliefs, feelings and attitudes. Feelings of prejudice stem from the belief and attitude that certain people are inferior and should be treated in an undignified way or even with contempt. Prejudice is the fertile ground in which custom, habit and attitudes take root and grow into systematic oppression. Prejudice and ill-feeling are often directed at women, as well as other groups in society: refugees and displaced persons, members of various religions, ethnic groups and language groups, etc. Prejudice tends to be strongest in persons and societies where reasoned judgment is weak and where ignorance explains prejudicial processes of moral exclusion of others and the process of denial of the right to equal and fair treatment. It is ignorance that says that exclusion and denial are "natural."

Discrimination involves action, often based on unfair rules. Acts of discrimination are based on the prejudice that one group, considering itself better than others, deserves to deny the other group basic human rights and access to the benefits of society. Thus discrimination is a denial of human dignity and equal rights for those discriminated against. The actions involved deny human equality and impose a life of problems and struggles upon some, while endowing others with privileges and benefits. Just as prejudice gives birth to discrimination, so discrimination gives birth to exploitation and oppression, and when exploitation and oppression are reinforced by custom and tradition, they are difficult but not impossible to uproot and change. The subservience of women involves both exploitation and oppression, and in the Ethiopian context, it is reinforced by custom and tradition.

Ask the participants if they understand these distinctions and ideas and urge them to ask questions.

Step 2. Ask participants to share their feelings about various groups, and whether such feelings may be based on prejudice: people with a different language accent? street vendors? people who beg on the streets and scavenge for garbage? Do they feel these people are crazy? Sub-human? Inferior?

Step 3. Ask the participants if they think social prejudices are also generally directed against women? What explains prejudice that makes life more difficult for women than for men?

Step 4. Divide the participants into small groups. Each group should have (1) a chairperson. In addition, each group should have: (2) a reporter who reports on problems of *prejudice* and attitudes that people have about the category of people discussed; and (3) a reporter to report on problems of *discrimination* or acts of exclusion, exploitation and oppression, directed against the category of people being discussed. The two reporters present the discussion and conclusions of the group to the plenary sessions. There should be one group on each of five categories, and each such group should consider certain questions:

- (1) *women*: should they be given equal opportunities in the family, villages, community gatherings, administrative responsibilities in the *kebele/woreda (community meeting)*?
- (2) *refugees and displaced persons*: should they be kept out of the community and separated into tent cities, and otherwise excluded from the community?
- (3) *people with a different language accent*: should they be sent back where they came from? Are some people less civilized based on their language, dialect or accent?
- (4) *street vendors*: Should they be allowed to sell cigarettes, candy, chewing gum, newspapers undisturbed? Do the police have positive attitudes toward them, or do they seem to harbor prejudice?
- (5) *people who beg on the streets and scavenge for garbage*: Are they mentally unstable and volatile persons? vagabonds? unethical? criminal?

Step 5. Ask the participants to reconvene in groups to examine the situation of the five groups from the point of view of the equality and non-discrimination provisions of the Universal Declaration of Human Rights and the Constitution of the Ethiopian Federal Democratic Republic [EFDR]. In light of these laws, how should the people discussed be treated?

Appendix for Exercise 15. *UDHR (1948); Constitution of the EFDR (1994)*
Universal Declaration of Human Rights.
Article 1. All human beings are born free and equal in dignity and rights. They are endowed with reason and conscience and should act towards one another in a spirit of brotherhood.
Article 2. Everyone is entitled to all the rights and freedoms set forth in the Declaration, without distinction of any kind, such as race, color, sex, language, religion, political or other opinion, national or social origin, property, birth or other status.
Article 7. All are equal before the law and are entitled without any discrimination to equal protection of the law.
Article 13. Everyone has the right to freedom of movement and residence within the borders of each State.
Article 14. Everyone has the right to seek and to enjoy in other countries asylum from persecution.
Article 21. Everyone has the right to equal access to public service in his [her] country.

Constitution of the Ethiopian Federal Democratic Republic
Article 25. All persons are equal before the law and are entitled without any discrimination to the equal protection of the law. The law shall guarantee to all persons equal and effective protection without discrimination on grounds of race, colour, sex, language, religion, political or other opinion, national or social origin, wealth, birth or other status.

The worldwide computer-based Internet has begun to demonstrate enormous cost-saving advantages in supplying on-line human rights educational materials. Those who say that electronic mail and the telephonic Internet are "first world toys," of no significance for the poorest of the poor in less developed countries, are often ill informed and in need of updated information. Consider, for example, the ninety-page human rights education trainer's guide entitled *The Bells of Freedom*, from Ethiopia. It is freely accessible on-line from the University of Minnesota Human Rights Library website. This manual, with twenty-four exercises and resource materials for African facilitators of nonformal education, was designed by an NGO in Addis Ababa, Action Professionals' Association for the People (APAP). The guide is deliberately not copyrighted so as to facilitate maximum cheap and easy distribution. It is designed for the training of illiterate participants, including street children, the homeless, prostitutes, garbage scavengers, and the rural poor, with special attention to women and children.[16] One of the more complex of the twenty-four lessons is set out as a sample in the accompanying sidebar.

International use of electronic mail and the communications Internet hold great promise to perform the clearinghouse function of sharing information and even educational materials. In 1995 the Civitas Conference in Prague brought together people interested in teaching about human rights and democracy. With the assistance of the United States Agency for International Development, those attending organized CIVNET, an electronic mail service that facilitates the international sharing of teaching materials on human rights and democracy. For example, using CIVNET one can access on-line the text for *Teaching Democratic Citizenship: An International Guide*. It was developed by the American Federation of Teachers, an NGO.[17]

Despite the CIVNET services and Strasbourg activities to put European teachers in touch with NGO materials, problems remain in poorer countries with meager and expensive but outmoded and underdeveloped communications infrastructures. The challenges to NGOs concerned with human rights education are most acute in least developed countries with the least resources. J. Paul Martin of the Columbia University Center for the Study of Human Rights pinpoints the needs involved in these terms: "Conversations with human rights activists and educators from poorer countries reflect their desperate need for materials. It is quickly apparent that even a small local resource center with materials originating in other countries and organizations could provide some of the resources teachers need to be able to teach a well organized course, especially if the availability of the literature were complemented by expert advice."[18] As Martin's comments suggest, once a program of implementation has commenced, those responsible should expect constructive criticism and suggestions for improvement. Program users must have opportunities to express their needs and to participate in program planning and implementation.

Evaluation

The construction of a program of education should always be open to comment and criticism. The process of formalizing feedback so as to improve a program is called "developmental evaluation" by professional educators. No serious program of educational innovation is well designed without careful attention to undertaking evaluation.

Educational programs that include evaluation activities of various kinds are more likely to succeed in gaining support and in meeting their objectives than unevaluated programs. At the most pragmatic level of concern to NGOs, who are often dependent on private funding sources, their prospects for externally secured grants are enhanced by building evaluation procedures into their projects. In the absence of such careful, data-based evaluation, HRE will continue—as is too frequently the case—to be dismissed by funding agencies as the human rights "soft option," compared to the "hard option" of monitoring human rights violations, a task that received the lion's share of private funding during the 1970s and 1980s. Funders should consider as a high priority support for NGOs' access to the computer Internet and electronic mail, which now carry otherwise cost-free educational materials.

Human rights education in the 1990s bears the burden, as yet unmet, of demonstrating that it has practical value and is capable of achieving its goals and objectives. Because by its very nature human rights education is designed, broadly speaking, to promote change, we can say that evaluation of HRE involves the inspection and assessment of available information concerning the student, the teachers, and the program, often with special attention to ascertaining the degree of change in students. It is also used to form valid judgments about effective teaching methods and to come to a critical understanding of the effectiveness of the program.

The need for education evaluation in various formats has long been recognized by organizations devoted to teacher training and curriculum development. They are concerned with several feedback processes. For example, *formative evaluation* involves judgments about an ongoing program and is used to provide information for product or program review, identification of strengths and weaknesses of the instruction process, and the assessment of the teaching process. By contrast, *summative evaluation* is a terminal judgment process that seeks to provide a general assessment of the degree to which the objectives of the course or program have been obtained for all or part of them. It is used to discern whether or not the learner has achieved the objectives for instruction that were set up in advance. Whether formative or summative, evaluation of human rights education, like educational evaluation in general, is not an end in itself. It should be used as a means for identifying alternative options and thereby reaching decisions aimed at improving the program and its methods. In fact, evaluation of human rights education may have many purposes:

1. assessing the consistency between announced program goals (such as attitudes reflecting empowerment and political efficacy, or the achievement of cognitive

knowledge, such as learning the range and scope of internationally defined human rights and the relationships among them) and making suggestions to reduce inconsistency;

2. encouraging shared critical reflections in the spirit of human rights values, emphasizing cooperation, tolerance, and respect for diverse views;

3. improving program elements by clarifying their relation to each other, (e.g., lectures on theory and simulation exercises involving student participation);

4. suggesting where resources such as new materials and advisory services are needed (e.g., seeking mechanisms for the exchange of teaching materials, and identifying human rights activists and NGO personnel who might serve as classroom speakers or participants in nonformal education);

5. assessing the relative effectiveness of specific strategies used to achieve program goals (such as the posting of the Universal Declaration of Human Rights in all school buildings as is done in Chile, and suggesting alternatives, e.g., organizing student art contests to illustrate provisions of the Declaration);

6. providing information about the nature and effectiveness of HRE as a foundation for democracy and peace in order to enhance discussion about them in the wider community and promote informed judgments about their value and legitimacy consistent with the objectives of the UN Charter; and

7. supplying a system of accountability to funding and sponsoring agencies to elicit continuing support of the program and dissemination of tested models.[19]

Because the evaluation of human rights education includes a varied array of goals, as suggested by the listing above, it requires diverse methodological approaches. They may be both quantitative and qualitative. They may include measurements[20] based on student test results, scored judgments by a panel of teachers, administrators, or observers and experts, as well as an amalgam of subjective impressions, critical observations, and other kinds of evidence.[21] In any event, HRE programs should always have built-in plans for evaluation. Viewed as an imperative, this injunction is a challenge for NGO personnel involved in human rights education because they may not have professional educational training that would alert them to the need for and advantages of educational evaluation.

Evaluation Instrument

From "Personal Knowledge and Attitude Questionnaire," Human Rights Unit, *Human Rights Training for Public Officials, Manual* (Ottawa: Commonwealth Secretariat, 1990). This form is for course organizers only. No other person will see your questionnaire. This questionnaire will later help you to assess how much you have learned through this course. It will be returned to you at the conclusion of the session.

Please indicate (X) whether you agree or disagree with the following:

1. Human rights should be as crucial an element of national policy as economic development and national security. Yes ___ No ___

2. The role of women should be a priority consideration in every development programme. Yes ___ No ___

3. The only **fundamental** human rights are democratic, political and legal rights. Yes ___ No ___

4. The United Nations human rights system fails to provide anything other than debate, platitudes, and stacks of repetitive documents. Yes ___ No ___

5. The attention paid to human rights in our national policy satisfies a domestic and external constituency but is not of real importance for the conduct of domestic and international affairs. Yes ___ No ___

6. The use of torture by police should be permissible under international law if it were the only way to learn the location of a time bomb threatening civilian lives. Yes ___ No ___

7. The enjoyment of human rights is not possible in the absence of a climate of democracy. Yes ___ No ___

8. The following should be recognized as economic or social rights:

a. right to receive or to grow food. Yes ___ No ___

b. right to adult literacy. Yes ___ No ___

c. right to economic development. Yes ___ No ___

d. right to a safe environment. Yes ___ No ___

e. right to adequate health services. Yes ___ No ___

f. right to an adequate standard of living. Yes ___ No ___

g. right of workers to bargain collectively. Yes ___ No ___

9. Policy makers and administrators dealing with immigration and refugee policies should be vigilant to ensure that:

a. we avoid the transfer of inter-religious conflicts from other countries. Yes ___ No ___

b. we deny false refugee claims made by "economic migrants" from other countries. Yes ___ No ___

10. The human rights record of a country should be a major factor in whether and how aid is given to it. Yes ⎯ No ⎯

11. The knowledge of human rights abuses elsewhere helps us to appreciate our own human rights record. Yes ⎯ No ⎯

Either quantitative or qualitative evaluation, or both, may be addressed to various student outcomes of their HRE programs, in terms of the acquisition of knowledge,[22] aptitudes,[23] skills,[24] and behaviors.[25] The professional literature on the methodologies of education evaluation is very extensive, and those interested would do well to consult *Evaluating Global Education: Sample Instruments for Assessing Programs, Materials and Learning*, a looseleaf service published by Global Perspectives in Education, Inc.[26]

An example of a pretested attitude measure has been developed in Canada to evaluate the teaching of government officials. It is recommended by the Human Rights Unit of the Commonwealth Secretariat (Ottawa). It is an instrument for students' self-evaluation in HRE programs designed for public officials, including police and military personnel. The "Personal Knowledge and Attitude Questionnaire" is used in the Commonwealth human rights training manual as a "technique to ensure the engagement of the learner." It allows students to measure their growth during the course. At the beginning of the course, each participant checks off "yes" or "no" options on a short list of questions and then puts the questionnaire in a sealed envelope to be seen only by that individual at the end of the course. Then the same questionnaire is administered at the conclusion of the course and the answers are compared by the individual student. The instrument is shown here to afford the reader the opportunity, unusual for many, to self-evaluate.

Conclusion

The participation of NGOs in global efforts to plan, implement, and evaluate human rights education is a relatively new phenomenon. It parallels efforts generated by peace and development educators and anti-sexist, anti-racist movements in education. It is consistent with "global society" perspectives on world affairs in the late twentieth century when states are no longer the only actors on the stage of international relations.[27]

Can NGOs become significant actors on the stage of world affairs? They are summoned to do so by the Universal Declaration of Human Rights. As they become more involved in HRE, their efforts help to breathe life into those provisions of the Universal Declaration that call for the promotion and encouragement of human rights based on "national efforts and international cooperation" (Article 22). Such cooperation bolsters expectations that human rights education is an essential part of preparation, both for life in democratic, pluralistic, and just societies and for a world order of peaceful states in the world community. More and more, NGO participation in human rights educational activities gives concrete meaning to that otherwise most abstract provision of the Universal Declaration of Human Rights: "Everyone is entitled to a social and international order in which the rights and freedoms set forth in this Declaration can be fully realized" (Article 28). This injunction was written in 1947 and adopted by the UN General Assembly in 1948 at a time when the thinking of diplomats and students of international relations was dominated by "realists" who conceived of states as the primary actors in world affairs. By contrast, more recently, individuals and groups other than states have forced themselves on the attention of international society, and the international law of human rights has been both the response to this and the handle for further progress.

The late R. J. Vincent, a British international relations political theorist, concluded his study of *Human Rights and International Relations* in 1986 with the view that "'realists' may be missing a transformation from international relations to world politics as significant as that which established the society of states and for which the idea of human rights is a kind of midwife."[28] The new phenomenon to which Vincent refers is the advent of NGOs as participants in world affairs through their activities involving fact finding, lobbying, and education. In this light we may venture the expectation that human rights education constitutes an essential element in moving beyond the gestation of the international law of human rights and toward a new global community more nearly consistent with the vision of Article 28 of the Universal Declaration of Human Rights.

Notes

1. Richard Pierre Claude, "Human Rights Education: The Case of the Philippines," *Human Rights Quarterly* 13 (1991): 501, 523–24.

2. UNESCO, Proceedings of the International Congress on Teaching of Human Rights, Vienna, 1978. Of the ten guidelines, seventeen program recommendations, twelve teaching materials proposals, fifteen methods recommendations, and twelve structure proposals, only one method referred to NGOs, calling for their inclusion in a "series of workshops on the practical methodology of human rights education" (C. Methods 7).

3. UNESCO, *World Declaration on Education for All* (Jomtien, Thailand, 1990).

4. UNESCO, *World Congress on Human Rights*, Conclusions and Recommendations by Committee 9, "Human Rights Information, Teaching and Research" (New Delhi, 1991).

5. UNESCO, *World Declaration.*

6. Judith Torney-Purta, "Human Rights," in *Teaching for International Understanding, Peace and Human Rights*, ed. Norman J. Graves, O. James Dunlop, and Judith V. Torney-Purta (Paris: UNESCO, 1984), 63.

7. Ilana Felsenthal and Israelit Rubinstein, "Democracy, School, and Curriculum Reform: The 'Rules of the Game' in Israel," *Education for Democratic Citizenship: A Challenge for Multi-Ethnic Societies*, ed. Roberta S. Sigel and Marilyn Hoskin, (Hillsdale, N.J.: Erlbaum, 1991), 87–102, at 95.

8. E. Katz and P. H. Lazarsfeld, *Personal Influence* (Glencoe, Ill.: Free Press, 1955).

9. J. H. Young, "Participation in Curriculum Development: An Inquiry into the Response of Teachers," *Curriculum Inquiry* 15 (1985): 387–413.

10. José Tuvilla Rayo, ed., *Derechos humanos: Propuesta de educación para la paz basada en los derechos humanos y del niño* (Junta de Andalucia, 1990).

11. "Telefoneando tambien se llega a Roma," *Experiencias* (San José: Instituto Interamericano de Derechos Humanos, Departamento de Educación, cuadernos de estudio 2, 1990): 115–18.

12. Charles P. Henry, "Educating for Human Rights," *Human Rights Quarterly* 13 (1991): 420–23, at 422. Global Education Associates (New York) is an international society of teachers whose annual meetings and publications stress the importance of dissemination of information and

materials helpful to teachers concerned with international issues. For secondary school teachers they published *Breakthrough: Human Rights*, ed. Patricia M. Mische and Melissa Merkling, 10 (1989): 2–3. Also appropriate for high school use is Marvin E. Frankel and Ellen Saideman, *Out of the Shadows of Night: The Struggle for International Human Rights* (New York: Delacorte Press, 1989).

13. For a college course and curriculum guide, see *Peace and World Order Studies*, 6th ed. (Boulder, Colo.: Westview Press, 1994). See also Ingemar Fagerlind, "Developing Graduate Programs in International Education: The Institute of International Education, Stockholm," in T. Neville Postlethwaite, ed., *International Educational Research: Papers in Honor of Torsten Husen* (Oxford: Pergamon Press, 1986).

14. Peter Leuprecht, "The Case for Human Rights Education," *Forum* (Strasbourg: Council of Europe) 2 (1986): 4.

15. Committee of Ministers, "Recommendation No. R (85) 7 of the Committee of Ministers to Member States on Teaching and Learning About Human Rights in Schools" (Strasbourg: Council of Europe, May 14, 1985).

16. *The Bells of Freedom, with Resource Materials for Facilitators of Non-Formal Education and 24 Human Rights Echo Sessions* (Addis Ababa, Ethiopia: Action Professionals Association for the People, 1996). On-line access with downloading capacity is available from the Minnesota Human Rights Library: http://www.umn.edu/humanrts/education/materials.htm.

17. For CIVNET information and papers from the Civitas Conference and for information about *The International Guide*, contact Steven Fleischman, American Federation of Teachers, by fax: 001 202 879 4502; or by E-mail: sfleisch@aftemail.attmail.com.

18. J. Paul Martin, "International Human Rights: The Educational Imperative," unpublished memorandum of July 24, 1991, Center for the Study of Human Rights of the Columbia University of the City of New York.

19. Some features of the above analysis rely on Judith Torney-Purta, "Evaluation: A Critical Step in Program Development," unpublished paper for the Meeting of the American Forum on Educational and Global Competence, St. Louis, Missouri, May 1988.

20. Charles D. Hopkins and Richard L. Antes, *Classroom Measurement and Evaluation*, 2d ed (Itasca, Ill.: F. E. Peacock Publishers, 1985).

21. Richard Pierre Claude, "Evaluating Human Rights Education in the Philippines," *Human Rights Education Newsletter (Human Rights Education Network*, Westminster College, Oxford) 11 (Summer 1995): 1–2. See also Patricia Ramsey, *Teaching and Learning in a Diverse World* (New York: Teachers College Press of the Columbia University of the City of New York, 1987).

22. Lorna Z. Segovia, *The Development of a Human Rights Awareness Scale* (Manila: Philippines Normal College, 1987).

23. Lorin W. Anderson, *Assessing Affective Characteristics in the Schools* (Boston: Allyn and Bacon, 1981).

24. "Evaluation," in "Human Rights Information Handling in Developing Countries, Manila, 1988," *HURIDOCS News* 7, Special Issue (April 1989).

25. Robert M. Hunger, "Law-Related Educational Practice and Delinquency Theory," *International Journal of Social Education* 2, no. 2 (Autumn 1987): 52–64.

26. Judith Torney-Purta, ed., *Evaluating Global Education: Sample Instruments for Assessing Programs, Materials and Learning* (New York: Global Perspectives in Education, 1986–87).

27. Richard Pierre Claude and David R. Davis, "The Global Society Perspective on International Human Rights," in *International Rights and Responsibilities for the Future*, ed. Timothy Mack and Kenneth Hunter (Westport, Conn.: Greenwood Publishing Group, 1996).

28. R. J. Vincent, *Human Rights and International Relations* (Cambridge: Cambridge University Press, 1986), 124.

Chapter 25
Community Education for Law, Democracy, and Human Rights

Edward L. O'Brien

Without law there can be no human rights; without human rights there can be no just laws; without human rights there can be no democracy; and without democracy there can be no human rights nor just laws. I draw these conclusions from my work over the past twenty-six years in citizen education in law, human rights, and democracy in the United States, Latin America, Eastern Europe, and, most of all, in South Africa. Between 1986 and 1994, in South Africa, I have seen the teaching of law, human rights, and democracy come together. My American-based organization, the National Institute for Citizen Education in the Law (NICEL),[1] has been operating law-related education programs in the United States since 1972; I began teaching law to high school students in 1968. It was only by examining what was done in South Africa, however, that I have learned the necessary connections among these three separate but invariably linked substantive areas.

Why I learned so much from leaving the United States and then returning could be the subject of another article. Suffice it to say here that my work for the past ten years in South Africa led me to conclude that those interested in human rights and human rights education in the United States can learn a great deal from South Africa. This includes lessons in program and curriculum design, methodology of delivering human rights education, and, most significantly, how human rights education helps create a culture of human rights, justice, and democracy. It was in South Africa that I met lawyers, educators, and human rights activists who possessed the vision, commitment, and energy needed to work under the most difficult circumstances. It was in South Africa, despite hideous violence and enormous racial and ethnic problems, that I found many people with considerable optimism, hope, and a genuine desire to move on.

I discovered this in the first black South African I ever met: (now Archbishop) Desmond Tutu. In 1985 I met him at the gift shop in the Nairobi airport, where he greeted me casually yet warmly. He said "your work is very important; I think it is greatly needed in our country, and I believe it can be done. I wish you the best of luck on your mission." Since then, I have found this same attitude among the vast majority of the hundreds of black and white South Africans with whom I have had the good fortune to work. I also perceive this same optimism when I hear or read the words of that most remarkable South African, President Nelson Mandela, who after twenty-seven years of being unjustly jailed, preaches the politics of reconciliation, nonracialism, and hope. He constantly promotes the need for justice, human rights, and democracy.

This chapter makes the case for combining education about the law with education about human rights and democracy. It is only through this combination that we, as human rights educators, can achieve our vision of a world that protects human rights for all. Human rights education is based on the same optimism that Archbishop Tutu and Nelson Mandela possess, not the negativism and despair of many others. This is true even in countries where the most egregious human rights violations occur. Those who succeed with this type of education do so because they believe things can and will get better: that human rights education can contribute to improvement of their society and the lives of their citizens.

In this chapter I share NICEL's experiences in the United States, South Africa, Latin America, and Eastern Europe and give examples of how this educational method can be delivered in classrooms, community settings, and through other educational media including television, radio, pamphlets, posters, cartoons, murals, and drama. I illustrate how educational programs have been designed to address the needs of urban and rural people, readers and nonreaders, men and women, who play special roles in society (e.g., police officers, prison inmates, correctional personnel, medical personnel, and political leaders).

To be effective, human rights education must be practical. For this chapter to be useful to readers, it too must be practical. Thus concrete, interactive teaching exercises are included that illustrate the use of methods such as case study, role-playing, and small group discussion. All these are taken from curriculum materials that NICEL developed in law, human rights, and democracy.[2] These exercises are provided for two reasons. First, they clearly demonstrate the way practical exercises can be used to illustrate the connections between law, democracy, and human rights. Second, I include them with the hope that practitioners will adapt them to meet the educational needs of citizens in their own countries, and then use them in their human rights education programs. I also hope readers will send comments on how these exercises do or do not work in their countries.[3] These comments, based on your experience, are vital to our learning and the positive progression of the field of human rights education.

Street Law and Law-Related Education

NICEL's work in the field of law-related education began in 1972. Three Georgetown law students and I ventured into two inner city high schools and initiated a class called

"Street Law." Our goal was to create a practical law course that provided information on how to avoid legal problems and what to do when such problems arose. Areas of the law covered were criminal, consumer, family, housing, and individual rights law. The practical situations we explored included what to do if: (1) the police stopped you; (2) you bought a bicycle and a month later it didn't work; (3) your parents were getting a divorce; or (4) your apartment had no heat in the winter. The class was well received; it appeared that the students, who had initially been very negative toward the law, changed their attitudes dramatically as they came to understand that law was not just punitive, but also could be protective.

This program expanded the next year into a course at Georgetown's law school where law students were awarded academic credit for teaching every week in a high school and for attending a seminar where they received training both in the law and in the methodology of teaching. This law school model has since expanded to more than thirty-eight law schools in the United States and nearly twenty law schools in other countries.[4] The program brings about considerable learning on the part of the law students in the law they teach, in how to convey the law in a simplified manner to nonlawyers, and in the legal problems of people who usually come from socioeconomic backgrounds very different from their own. As it usually becomes institutionalized (i.e., the funding and administration are picked up, over time, by a university or other local entity), the program is an especially important model for human rights educators to consider.[5]

The materials the law students developed initially for this program evolved into a set of curriculum materials first published in 1975 under the title *Street Law: A Course in Practical Law*. This book (now in its fifth edition)[6] has become the most popular high school law text in the United States. It is taught in all fifty states, the District of Columbia, and Guam, in schools as well as other settings including prisons, community colleges, and adult education centers.

The following is an example of a teaching exercise from the *Street Law* text that utilizes the case study approach. This is the most common method of instruction in both the *Street Law* text and other law-related materials. This approach is also incorporated into all of NICEL's other law, human rights, and democracy curricula.

The Case of Gerald Gault

Gerald Gault, age fifteen, was taken into custody and accused of making an obscene phone call to a neighbor. At the time Gerald was taken into custody, his parents were at work, and the police did not notify them of what had happened to their son. Gerald was placed in a detention center. When his parents finally learned that he was in custody, they were told there would be a hearing the next day, but they were not told the nature of the complaint against him.

Mrs. Cook, the woman who complained about the phone call, did not show up at the hearing. Instead, a police officer testified to what Mrs. Cook told him. Gerald blamed the call on a friend and denied making the obscene remarks. No lawyers were present, and no record was made of what was said at the hearing.

Since juries were not allowed in juvenile court, the hearing was held before a judge, who found by a preponderance of the evidence that Gerald was delinquent and ordered him sent to a state reform school until age twenty-one. An adult found guilty of the same crime could have been sent to county jail for no longer than sixty days. Exercises:

> a. Make a list of anything that happened to Gerald Gault that you consider unfair. Explain your reasoning for each item on the list.
> b. How would you change any of the things you thought were unfair?

Like most of NICEL's case studies, this one has been taken from an actual case[7] where the U.S. Supreme Court delineated the rights of juveniles when they are arrested, during a trial, and when they appeal. By using an intriguing fact situation and then placing the students in the position of decision makers, this method perks students' interest and develops close reading and analytical skills. It also promotes hope for the future by asking students how they would change the things they found to be unfair. Though we did not realize it when this exercise was designed, it is human rights education, since it addresses what human rights a juvenile has when accused of a crime. These are the same rights addressed by many human rights documents, including the Covenant on Civil and Political Rights (Articles 9, 10, 14), the Convention on the Rights of the Child (Article 40), and the U.S. Bill of Rights as interpreted by the U.S. Supreme Court in a number of cases.

Only through my work in recent years in South Africa, and subsequently in co-authoring the *Human Rights for All* text, did I begin to see that *Street Law* is in fact human rights education: not only does it address the rights of juveniles accused of crimes, but it also addresses human rights issues such as the right to education, housing, property, freedom of expression, and participation. This curriculum is also democracy education: its goals are promoting an understanding of the law and the legal system, improving the administration of justice, and promoting the participation of citizens in a democratic system. Most important, it educates people about how to work to improve the system—a very democratic idea.

Through this international work, I discovered a different language is used in much of the world. Americans speak in terms of civil rights and not human rights, and even though we see ourselves as the champions of human rights in other countries, we often neglect to examine our own society critically in relation to these same human rights.

To most Americans the term "human rights violation" refers to torture and atrocities in other countries, and not to homelessness, the death penalty, the lack of adequate education, or the lack of health care that exists in this country. Though it refers to them as legal issues, the Street Law program and text address all these human rights and democratic issues. This insight has made clear to me the connection between *Street Law*, the field of law-related education in the United States, and what the rest of the world refers to as human rights education.

The Participatory Methodology Most Effective in Teaching Street Law, Human Rights, and Democracy

At the very beginning of the Street Law program, it became a guiding principle that if high school students, prison inmates, or citizens were to experience a new type of education, they could not be bored as so many of us had been in our own high school civics classes. An interesting methodology of instruction was needed. From the beginning, it was evident that the content should be practical. When I asked a class of high school students, "Does anyone know what your rights are when you are stopped by the police?" the students' faces lit up with interest and their hands shot up with questions. The fact that I was asking them practical questions and not just lecturing them in a monotone voice made a difference, and it soon became apparent that one of the hallmarks of Street Law was active participation by students.

Street Law was not the first program and NICEL was not the first organization to make participation the core of good instruction. Over the years we have found that effective education programs exist not only in the United States but also in Africa, Latin America, and Asia.[8] They all use a similar approach.

Unfortunately NICEL has also found that most educators worldwide think the more information they can cram into a fifty-minute class period, the more students will learn. This, we believe, is very wrong, as these "speed lectures," by their very nature, diminish student interest and reduce their motivation to learn. Lecturing also emphasizes rote learning and memorization, which retard the development of important critical thinking and problem-solving skills citizens need if they are to participate actively in their societies.

In the early 1980s the U.S. Justice Department commissioned an evaluation of law-related education's impact on students. It was not surprising to learn that researchers found participatory methodology an essential ingredient for making this type of education successful. This success included not only high student interest but also increased legal knowledge, a change in attitudes, and a corresponding reduction of the factors commonly associated with delinquency.[9]

The participatory methodology that NICEL has employed over the past twenty years involves not only questions, answers, and discussions centered around cases, as illustrated above, but also considerable use of students' natural interest in acting. This interest is drawn on through the use of role-plays, both spontaneous and scripted, and other simulations such as mock trials, moot courts, legislative hearings, and floor debates.

In the South Africa Street Law program, an annual "Space Colony" simulation is conducted in which high school students of all races gather together at a university campus for several days. There they take on fictitious roles of people from different countries and cultures who are negotiating and writing a constitution and bill of rights for a colony in outer space.[10] These kinds of activities consistently succeed, whether they are being tried with prison inmates in Santiago, Chile,[11] high school students in the High Court of Lesotho,[12] Southeast Asian immigrants in a refugee camp in the Philippines,[13] or with magistrates and judges interested in learning both English and U.S. law in Romania.[14] I could give hundreds of examples that affirm the success of teaching law, human rights, and democracy through participatory methodology. Experience has led educators at NICEL and many others worldwide to conclude that participatory methodology is a necessary and required ingredient for effective human rights education.

Human Rights Education

In South Africa, many progressive people and organizations have a strong desire to create a human rights culture for a new South Africa, and it was there that I began to learn what the field of human rights education was all about. As I began my work in South Africa, I also learned there was a whole cadre of experienced human rights educators in the United States and in many other countries. Many grew from the work of Amnesty International,[15] which clearly has been the pioneer in the field, and through the work of human rights education promoters such as the Decade of Human Rights Education,[16] the United Nations Human Rights Centre, the Helsinki Committees, the Council of Europe, and now the North America Partnership for Human Rights Education. I also found, and continue to find every day, that there are dedicated human rights educators all over the world conducting classes in places as diverse as rural Mali, the jungles of Guinea, and the hillsides of Qua Zulu in South Africa.

After researching what had been achieved in human rights education, NICEL joined with two leading progressive groups in South Africa: Lawyers for Human Rights (LHR)[17] and South African Street Law.[18] With the help of an experienced U.S. educator who had considerable experience with Holocaust education,[19] we produced a text called *Human Rights for All*. This text filled a gap in available materials; it took the International Declaration of Human Rights and applied established methods of curriculum design and methodologies used in *Street Law* and other law-related education materials to teach the basic principles of human rights in an interesting, practical, and participatory way.

Human Rights for All differs from much of the available human rights education material in that it does not focus principally on issues such as torture, the death penalty, or political and civil rights. Instead, it tries to teach about all the major political, civil, social, and economic rights, and even ventures into the so-called third tier of rights which includes environmental rights and the right to development.

The text employs an approach that NICEL has used in all its educational materials: it first states what the law is (in this case what the international community has agreed upon in international treaties and other documents), and then asks participants to debate controversial issues relating to the specific human rights involved. This is done to the chagrin of some human rights activists, who argue that if a certain right exists, no debate is needed. An example comes to mind from the piloting of the *Human Rights for All* text in South Africa with a group of paralegals from a human rights organization that took the position that the death penalty was immoral and a violation of human rights. This group became disturbed when the materials suggested a debate should take place on whether the death penalty was per se a human rights violation. In response, I pointed out that the international community was still quite divided on this topic, and though I personally was against the death penalty, I emphasized a strong belief that students studying human rights should have the right to decide such questions for themselves.

I believe the role of the teacher is not to advocate a strong position one way or another. If we are to espouse democracy and human rights, we must also give people all the information available and allow them to make their own free choices on the issues. Indeed, this is the very essence of critical thinking. Support for this point of view can be found in 1980s research in U.S. schools that found it essential to present high school students with both sides of an issue; otherwise the students are likely to be indoctrinated into a specific point of view.[20]

The methodology employed by NICEL in *Street Law* and its other law-related educational materials has proved successful in *Human Rights for All.* Case studies, questions for discussion, small groups, continuums, and scripted dramatizations all work very well with a wide variety of participants. Most effective may be spontaneous role-plays based on real-life fact situations. An example of the use of the role-play technique follows. This exercise is taken from a chapter in *Human Rights for All* entitled "The Political Rights in a Democracy."[21]

The Case of the School Boycott

In one country, schools for one ethnic group are much worse than those for all the others. Their schools have no libraries, laboratories, gymnasiums, or playgrounds, while schools for the other ethnic groups have all these things. They have no school buses, so even the youngest children usually have to walk as much as several kilometers. Old textbooks are shared among children sitting on wooden benches. Class sizes are as big as fifty pupils and more. Teachers may teach five or six classes in a single subject and have time only to read and correct one composition a month from each student.

Because of these conditions, students of the less privileged ethnic group decide to boycott their schools. They believe boycotts are the only way to get what they want.

There are some students of the same ethnic group, however, whose parents do not agree with the boycott. They demand that their children continue to attend school. Many see education as the ladder to a higher standard of living and as the freedom road itself. Therefore, some of these students choose not to participate in the boycott.

1. Assume some students in each group wished to convince others to agree with them. Role-play a discussion between the students.
2. Why did some students want to boycott their schools?
3. Why did some students oppose this boycott? Is their refusal to participate a violation of the rights of the students who wish to boycott?
4. Was the method used to convince the students to boycott a violation of their human rights? If so, are there any methods you think would have been better to use? Describe them.
5. If a small number of children are not allowed to participate in the school boycott, should the government protect them and their parents against threats and the use of force? Why or why not? Explain your thinking.
6. Assume students who are against the boycott wish to convince other students not to boycott. If the boycotting students do not allow them to speak to others, have their human rights been violated? If yes, how?

This problem is taken from actual events that occurred many times in South Africa. It illustrates such rights as freedom of speech and freedom of education; it shows how both sides on the boycott question may have some legitimate claim to thinking their method is the best way to exercise these rights, and it helps students explore whether the use (or threat) of violence is ever justified. This exercise can also lead to discussion of the right to revolution.

I conducted this exercise many times with South African youths and adults, Americans, and human rights educators and activists from around the world. Participants consistently enjoy the role-play, finding considerable humor in an otherwise very serious situation. They always concur that the role-play technique is a very useful way to teach important principles of human rights.

The school boycott role-play also embodies the connections between law, human rights, and democracy education. One cannot adequately debrief this role-play and conduct a thorough discussion without examining which of a country's laws created such a disparity in education as well as what the human right to education means. Nor can one discuss the issues of free expression without looking at the laws of the country and whether the country is truly a democracy that allows open political dialogue and participation by all its citizens.

In South Africa a cooperative effort to spread the teaching of human rights has been undertaken by LHR and South African Street Law. This is unusual, as I have found that public interest organizations, even those working in the field of human rights education, often compete more than cooperate—a situation probably caused to some extent by the often tight competition among NGOs for funding. The South African partnership has resulted in Lawyers for Human Rights jointly publishing not only *Human Rights for All* but also some excellent pamphlets as part of a series called "Know Your Rights," as well as posters and a unique and very exciting Human Rights Day mural project.[22]

The mural idea began in Durban, South Africa, where the founder of the South African Street Law program, who has also served as a regional leader of LHR, convinced the South African prison authorities and the local mayor to allow local artists to paint a mural on the walls of the Old Durban Jail to celebrate International Human Rights Day on December 10, 1992. Many artists turned out and created beautiful wall murals depicting many of the provisions of the Universal Declaration of Human Rights. This became a permanent human rights education art exhibit. This exhibit is on one of Durban's main streets, and the murals are on one of the most significant symbols of human rights violations in South Africa: the jail.

Lawyers for Human Rights and the Street Law program also made December 10th an important day during each of the last four years by conducting conferences for youth that featured human rights speakers, workshops, and mock trials involving human rights issues. They have also sponsored an annual "electronic dialogue," in which a group of South African students in locations including Soweto, Durban, Port Elizabeth, Pretoria, and Cape Town discussed human rights problems with Street Law students in Washington, D.C. Most poignant have been discussions comparing South African police brutality to the beating of Rodney King by white police officers in Los Angeles, and the students' views of crime and violence in their countries as human rights violations.

This electronic dialogue takes place annually with aid of the United States Information Agency and always includes students in both countries of various races, ethnic, social, and economic backgrounds. In 1992 students in the United States stayed an hour and a half after the transcontinental conversation ended to carry on a discussion of whether students felt the education they were receiving in the public schools of Washington, D.C. violated their "right to an adequate education." They did. Another year, the dialogue between the American students resulted in plans to follow up and conduct joint activities between students at the public and private schools they attended. I believe this shows that human rights education is an excellent tool for bringing diverse people together and for promoting dialogue and understanding between them. It also illustrates again that South Africa has much to teach the United States.

The inventiveness and energy of the LHR education efforts resulted in excerpts from *Human Rights for All* being published in three leading newspapers in South Africa. Each of these newspapers has readerships from various racial and ethnic groups. In South Africa, Street Law, human rights, and democracy education has truly been offered "for all," as efforts have been made to include members of all of South Africa's various ethnic groups.

Lawyers for Human Rights has made it a priority to conduct human rights education sessions in the community for adults drawn from women's organizations, youth groups, church organizations, service organizations, civic associations, political parties, and trade unions. Though this work is most important, LHR candidly admits it is also the most difficult of its efforts. This is because one must recruit the adult audience and then retain their interest enough to get them to return for a series of workshops. Their return is vital: participants with only limited exposure will commonly have a correspondingly low level of attitude change. Studies of the impact of law-related education in the United States verify this.[23]

LHR states that participants often drop out after one or two workshops. Consequently it is considering having residency workshops, perhaps including overnight accommodations. Though the cost would clearly be higher, the benefits to participants and the program should be worth it. South Africa has demonstrated the use of residence programs before in the "Space Colony" project mentioned above and the newer "Green Street Law." The latter provides a fascinating opportunity for urban youth of all races to come together in a game reserve or other natural setting and learn about human rights. Classes are hands-on, held around the campfire at night and on various sites on the reserve, where students work on cooperative environmental projects.

Another difficulty LHR has experienced is meeting rural people's need for adequate human rights instruction. LHR has an excellent network of regional offices throughout the country; it conducts national trainer of training programs to give paralegals and others in legal service professions the skills needed to use their human rights materials. The long distances human rights trainers must travel to conduct rural workshops, as well as literacy problems, language and cultural differences, and the inadequacy of the *Human Rights for All* text in meeting the needs of rural South Africans make this type of education difficult. A possible solution LHR is considering is an adaptation of *Human Rights for All* to meet the needs of rural people.

NICEL has worked with another South African organization, the Community Law Centre (CLC), which has done an outstanding job in addressing this problem. Based in Durban, the CLC created a model human rights education program for rural people. This model is community-specific and includes extensive meetings with rural communities to assess their human rights problems and needs, followed by the implementation of a democratic process in which a paralegal committee is elected to conduct each program. The paralegal committee hires one of its own community members to be trained by the CLC and to act as liaison with the CLC central offices in Durban.[24] Because the paralegal conducting the education is from the area, local citizens relate well to this trainer. CLC's rural education programs include both human rights education and legal assistance for people in each area.

When the CLC began its formal human rights education efforts, I had the good fortune of assisting them both in helping edit their materials and in trying out techniques to meet the needs of rural people. For example, with the aid of their Zulu-speaking staff members, I conducted a human rights education session on a hillside

Figure 25.1. South African farm workers are pictured at the conclusion of a human rights workshop conducted by co-director Edward O'Brien and educator Elly Greene. (National Institute for Citizen Education in Law [NICEL])

outside a tribal courthouse in May 1990. This was a wonderful experience because more than three hundred rural people attended, a large number walking many kilometers on foot, then waited three hours or more for the workshop leaders to arrive. Once there, after a general discussion of what "human rights" were (unfortunately there was no equivalent word in Zulu), we had volunteer participants act out scripted dramatizations (written out beforehand in Zulu). These role-plays were designed and written in Zulu with the aid of members of the community who helped me and CLC staff learn the current human rights problems the community faced.

Examples of current human rights problems included theft of cows (the right to property and legal redress), corrupt pension officials, and the beating of women by their husbands for failure to perform "wifely duties." This last issue generated a major debate. A young, better-educated woman took on an older man who claimed that established cultural traditions gave him the right to discipline his wife for failure to perform her "wifely duties." A good result of the discussion was that the chief stepped in and said "our country's laws now forbid such actions, and we have to begin to change some of our traditional ways of doing things." Again the interconnection between law, human rights, and democracy came up in this very successful workshop.

Following the workshop the CLC embarked on the writing of a human rights education book entitled *Human Rights (Amalungelo Oluntu)*, which is one of the best rural human rights educational resources I have seen to date. This book uses large cartoons to illustrate each article of the Universal Declaration of Human Rights and on facing pages contains a simplified description of the right in both English and Zulu. I helped draft the questions the rural paralegals verbally ask participants about the human right depicted in the illustration. The illustrations have been done by the same outstanding illustrator of all the Street Law materials and much of LHR's human rights educational materials as well.[25] These illustrations have been particularly effective because they are action-oriented and show the emotion of the people involved in each practical situation. Moreover, they require participants to analyze the content of the drawings in the context of their own lives.

Democracy Education

Our work in South Africa between 1985 and 1994 paralleled the growth of democracy in that country. When we began, we were told that any teaching of human rights was impossible and might result in teachers and others being arrested. All education had to be limited at first under the rubric of "law," though it was possible to teach "criminal law" and, under that heading, such topics as the "rights of people under the security laws." In 1990 after the release of Nelson Mandela, it became possible to teach "human rights," and, as the negotiations progressed, this led to the idea of "democracy education."

Following the release of Nelson Mandela, the unbanning of the African National Congress, and the progress of the negotiations, the emergence of a democratic South Africa became more and more possible. Along with this came the realization of the human right to participate in one's government (a right that is articulated in Article 21 of the Universal Declaration of Human Rights and in many other human rights documents). When we conducted an exercise from the *Human Rights for All* curriculum which asked participants to pretend they were starting a new society and had to decide what were the most important human rights they wished to have, time and again participants listed "the right to vote" or "the right to participate in government." This differed from the responses the same exercise engendered in the United States or in Latin America, where voting was usually not listed as the most important human right. It appears that many U.S. and Latin American citizens often take this right for granted or feel it has very little meaning in their everyday lives. South Africans, after being deprived of a real democracy for so long, clearly thirsted for the right to vote and viewed democracy as an essential human right.

As dates for the first free elections were set, massive voter education projects were designed and funded. These involved many South African organizations, including the Center for Development Studies, the Institute for Democracy in South Africa (IDASA), the Institute for Multi-Party Democracy, the Street Law program, Lawyers for Human Rights, and the Community Law Centre. Also participating in "human rights education and voter education" programs were many well respected U.S. organizations including the National Democratic Institute, the National Republican Institute, and the Joint Center for Political Studies. The outreach and ultimate success of these voter education efforts were amazing, especially considering the short time frame and other obstacles including escalating violence and political intolerance.

Though we at NICEL played a relatively minor role in South African "voter education," we used the year before the election productively to launch a longer-term democracy education project involving the development of a new text entitled *Democracy for All.* This text, published in South Africa by JUTA one month before the election, attempts to form the basis of a broader education program, to develop, in the words of South Africans, a much-needed "culture of democracy and human rights."[26]

Developed as a joint project between NICEL, the South Africa Street Law program, and Lawyers for Human Rights, the "Democracy for All" program and text drew on the expertise of many nongovernmental organizations in South Africa that had been active in voter education, anti-apartheid activities, and other human rights work. It was co-authored by a multiethnic and multiracial team of five people.[27] This team brought different perspectives, and researched the available literature on what the term *democracy* was thought to mean to people all over the world.

The result is a text that applies the participatory methodology that had proven so successful in NICEL's law-related and human rights education materials to teaching the basics of democracy. The resulting user-friendly book may be best illustrated by looking at an exercise entitled "The Road to Democracy" from the text's first chapter: "What Is Democracy?" This exercise, which follows, incorporates a number of participatory methodologies including the use of art, brainstorming, and small groups.

On the Road to Democracy

Assume you are traveling on a road to a country where the perfect democracy exists. The road has many wrong turns, bumps, and dangers which make it difficult to reach the perfect democracy. However, there are signposts along the way which guide you in the right direction. The signposts name the basic principles that people in a democracy support. You are determined to find that perfect democratic country.
Divide into groups and:

1. Draw a map of the "Road to Democracy." On your map, give your "perfect democracy" a name.
2. List the basic principles of democracy on a separate sheet. Now create the

signposts along the road which give information about the basic principles of democracy. These signposts should name basic essentials that must exist in order to have the perfect democracy.

3. List the factors that prevent you from reaching your perfect democracy. Now create the signs for wrong turns, obstacles, and dangers along the road. These signs indicate difficulties in achieving democracy.

4. At the end of the road is your perfect democracy. List the benefits people will have in your perfect democracy.

5. Compare your group's map with that of the other groups. Did you name the same signposts, obstacles, dangers, and benefits as the others?

The drawings the groups in South Africa create when taking part in this exercise have been interesting from an artistic point of view, but, more significantly, they illustrate how average citizens understand the basics of democracy. The signposts, or principles of democracy that people list, closely mirror what the authors found through their research and have identified as the principles of an effective democracy. These include the following elements.

Citizen Participation. One of the most basic signposts of a democracy is citizen participation in government. Participation is the key role of citizens in a democracy. It is not only their right, but it is their duty. Citizen participation may take many forms including running for election, voting in elections, becoming informed, debating issues, attending community and civic meetings, being members of private voluntary organizations, paying taxes, and even protesting. Participation builds a better democracy.

Equality. Democratic societies emphasize the principle that all people are equal. Equality means that all individuals are valued equally, have equal opportunities, and may not be discriminated against because of their race, religion, ethnic group, gender, or sexual orientation. In a democracy, individuals and groups still maintain their right to have different cultures, personalities, languages, and beliefs.

Political Tolerance. Democratic societies are politically tolerant. This means that while the majority of the people rule in a democracy, the rights of the minority must be protected. People who are not in power must be allowed to organize and speak out. Minorities are sometimes referred to as "the opposition" because they may have ideas that are different from those of the majority. Individual citizens must also learn to be tolerant of each other. A democratic society is often composed of people from different cultures, racial, religious, and ethnic groups who have viewpoints different from the majority of the population. A democratic society is enriched by diversity. If the majority deny rights to and destroy their opposition, then they may also destroy democracy. One goal of democracy is to make the best possible decision for the society. To achieve this, respect for all people and their points of view is needed. Decisions are more likely to be accepted, even by those who oppose them, if all citizens have been allowed to discuss, debate, and question them.

Accountability. In a democracy, elected and appointed officials have to be accountable to the people. They are responsible for their actions. Officials must make decisions and perform their duties according to the will and wishes of the people, not for themselves.

Transparency. For government to be accountable, the people must be aware of what is happening in the country. This is referred to as transparency in government. A transparent government holds public meetings and allows citizens to attend. In a democracy, the press and the people are able to get information about what decisions are being made, by whom, and why.

Regular, Free, and Fair Elections. One way citizens of the country express their will is by electing officials to represent them in the government. Democracy insists that these elected officials are chosen and peacefully removed from the office in a free and fair manner. Intimidation, corruption, and threats to citizens during or before an election are against the principles of democracy. In a democracy, elections are held regularly every so many years. Participation in elections should not be based on a citizen's wealth. For free and fair elections to occur, most adult citizens should have the right to run for government office. Additionally, obstacles should not exist which make it difficult for people to vote.

Economic Freedom. People in a democracy must have some form of economic freedom. This means that the government allows some private ownership of property and business, and that the people are allowed to choose their own work and labor unions. The role the government should play in the economy is open to debate, but it is generally accepted that free markets should exist in a democracy and the state should not totally control the economy. Some argue that the state should play a stronger role in countries where great inequality of wealth exists due to past discrimination or other unfair practices.

Control of the Abuse of Power. Democratic societies try to prevent any elected official or group of people from misusing or abusing their power. One of the most common abuses of power is corruption. Corruption occurs when government officials use public funds for their own benefit or exercise power in an illegal manner. Various methods have been used in different countries to protect against these abuses. Frequently the government is structured to limit the powers of the branches of government, to have independent courts and agencies with power to act against any illegal action by an elected official or branch of government, to allow for citizen participation and elections, and to check police abuse of power.

Bills of Rights. Many democratic countries also choose to have a bill of rights to protect the people against abuse of power. A bill of rights is a list of rights and freedoms guaranteed to all people in the country. When a bill of rights becomes part of a country's constitution, the courts have the power to enforce these rights. A bill of rights limits the power of government and may also impose duties on individuals and organizations.

Accepting the Results of Elections. In democratic elections, there are winners and losers. Often the losers in an election believe so strongly that their party or candidate is the best one that they refuse to accept the results of the election. This is against democratic principles. The consequences of not accepting the results of an election may be a government that is ineffective and cannot make decisions. It may even result in violence which is also against democracy.

Human Rights. All democracies strive to respect and protect the human rights of citizens. Human rights means those values that reflect respect for human life and human dignity. Democracy emphasizes the value of every human being. Examples of human rights include freedom of expression, freedom of association, freedom of assembly, the right to equality, and the right to education.

Multiparty System. In order to have a multiparty system, more than one political party must participate in elections and play a role in government. A multiparty system allows for opposition to the party that wins the election. This helps provide the government with different viewpoints on issues. Additionally, a multiparty system provides voters with a choice of candidates, parties, and policies to vote for. Historically, when a country has only one party, the result has been dictatorship.

The Rule of Law. In a democracy no one is above the law, not even a king or an elected president. This is called the rule of law. It means that everyone must obey the law and be held accountable if they violate it. Democracy also insists that the law be equally, fairly, and consistently enforced.

Exercise: Is Democratia on the Road to Democracy?

Look at the following situations and decide whether each is a sign that Democratia is on the road to democracy. Give reasons for your answers.

Identify one or more of the signposts described above which relate to each situation.

1. The legislature passes a law requiring all youth between the ages of four and sixteen to attend school. Government schools are provided.
2. Members of one of the local churches held a political forum and allowed representatives from only one political party to attend.
3. The parliament had a gallery built in their assembly room so that visitors could watch the proceedings.
4. The constitution requires a presidential election every five years.
5. Teachers in the schools of Democratia do not like their working conditions and decide to go on strike.
6. The police stop and shoot a known criminal. The criminal was not resisting arrest but had killed other people.
7. The constitution says that only people over the age of eighteen who have lived in the country for more than one year may vote.

8. A law requires all working citizens to belong to a union.

9. The constitution requires all working adults to pay a small amount of money when they vote in order to help finance the expense of the election.

10. No convicted prisoner may be a candidate in an election.

11. A political party that loses the election demands that another election be held immediately.

12. The president is required to give a report to the people every year explaining what he or she has done and the plans for the upcoming year.

13. The government determines what are "fair prices" for all food sold in the country.

A close look at these signposts leads to the conclusion that most of these signposts are also either themselves internationally accepted human rights or closely linked to such principles as freedom of expression, free and fair elections, the rule of law, and human rights. Once again the connection between law, human rights, and democracy becomes clear; this reinforces the need to teach these three separate but interconnected areas together.

I encourage human rights education practitioners to use this exercise or to adapt it to fit the needs of your audiences. In using this exercise, you will see the advantage of the method of brainstorming, where you ask participants to list as many ideas for signposts to democracy as they can, without allowing others in the small groups to criticize their choices. The small group discussions that follow also usually involve close to 100 percent of the participants, and this models democracy in action. This can be pointed out to participants beforehand to set the stage for learning, or, better yet, mention it afterwards as part of a debriefing discussion on why the exercise was done the way it was. The *Democracy for All* text has many exercises like this which use attention-getting participatory techniques to spark interest and involve as many participants as possible.[28]

Conclusion

This chapter has, I hope, illustrated and perhaps even convinced readers that law, human rights, and democracy education are inextricably linked and should be taught together. I believe that such education can succeed because I have seen it foster citizen participation and critical thinking in many countries, especially the not-so-easy country of South Africa.

Today governments, including the United States and South Africa, and organizations such as the United Nations are linking democracy, human rights, and the rule of law.[29] Some are beginning to realize that human rights education may be the world's best hope to tackle problems such as racial and ethnic conflict, violence, crime, and the lack of social and economic rights that exist to some degree in every country, including the United States.

If these problems are to be addressed, funders, governments, and NGOs must make human rights education a priority. In March 1994 I conducted democracy education workshops in South Africa one month before the historic elections. At one such workshop at New Orleans High School in a town in the Western Cape called Paarl, I asked for the definition of democracy. A girl of about fifteen raised her hand and said, "I think it's people working together for something." This is an excellent definition, perhaps better than the ones I have seen in dictionaries and political science literature. It is also the message we must all take to heart if we are to succeed with our human rights education programs and attain cultures of democracy and human rights throughout the world.

Notes

1. NICEL is a not-for-profit nongovernmental organization (NGO) that grew out of the Street Law Project at Georgetown University Law Center, where law students receive academic credit for teaching law to high school students and prisoners. NICEL operates many programs for youth and adults in Washington, D.C., across the United States, and in other countries. It also hosts visitors from around the world. For information on any of NICEL's programs and materials, contact NICEL, 711 G Street, S.E., Washington, DC 20003 (tel. 202-546-6644; fax 202-546-6649).

2. NICEL developed law-related educational books and materials, including *Street Law*, which is mentioned in this chapter; *Teens, Crime and Community*, a curriculum for youth that teaches about crime and what they can do to help prevent it; *We Can Work It Out*, a curriculum for teachers on how to teach conflict resolution skills; *Great Trials in American History*, a book of short stories and follow-up questions pertaining to famous U.S. court cases.

In addition, NICEL conducts juvenile justice education programs for youth who have been in trouble with the law, prisoners, correctional personnel, and people with disabilities or special eduction needs. NICEL is also interested in human rights training for police officers and legislators.

3. Comments can be sent by mail or fax to the address in note 1 above.

4. Information and a list of law schools can be obtained from NICEL. These law schools include: Yale, Columbia, Georgetown, University of Tennessee, Notre Dame, University of San Francisco, Seattle College of Law, Cleveland State, Detroit Mercy College of Law, University of Connecticut, University of Natal (South Africa), universities in Chile, Ecuador, Bolivia, and Panama, the University of Ettos Lorrand in Budapest, and Almaty University in Kazakhstan.

5. It has been NICEL's experience in the United States and other countries that projects which are university-based, or closely aligned with a university where law students receive academic credit do not end when outside funding terminates. The administrators, faculty, and students (law, high school, and so on) usually support the program so strongly that they find a way to keep it going. Consequently Georgetown's program has continued for twenty-three years. The University of Tennessee, University of San Francisco, and Cleveland State University programs are all nineteen years old. Notre Dame's has existed for more than fifteen years, and the University of Natal in South Africa has an eight-year-old program.

6. West Publishing Company (St. Paul, Minnesota) deserves great credit for taking a risk and publishing the first edition of *Street Law* in 1975 and, since then, many other NICEL books. These succeeding works include *Human Rights for All*, the first major U.S. high school textbook in the field of human rights. Requests for examination copies of these texts can be made to West Publishing Company, 610 Opperman Drive, P.O. Box 64526, St. Paul, MN 55164-0526 (tel. 800-328-2209).

7. *In re Gault*, 387 U.S. 1 (1967).

8. For an overview of human rights education efforts in the Philippines, for example, see Richard Pierre Claude, "Human Rights Education: The Case of the Philippines," *Human Rights Quarterly* 13 (1991): 453–524.

9. Robert M. Hunter, "Law-Related Educational Practice and Delinquency Theory," *International Journal of Social Education* 2 (1987): 52–64.

10. Information on the Space Colony program as well as all the Street Law materials developed in South Africa can be obtained from: Street Law Program, Centre for Socio-Legal Studies, Education and Innovation Centre, University of Natal, Francois Road, Durban 4001, South Africa (tel. 031-260-1291; fax 031-260-1540).

11. Information on the project in Chile can be obtained from Maria Therese Muñoz, Matias Cousino 82, Os. 1302, Santiago, Chile (tel. and fax 562-695-2294).

12. Information on the program in Lesotho can be obtained from Margaret Fisher, University of Puget Sound, 950 Broadway Plaza, Tacoma, WA 98402-4470 (tel. 206-591-2215; fax 206-591-6313).

13. Information on the program in the Philippines for Southeast Asian immigrants can be obtained from Peter Lacey, U.S. Embassy in Tokyo, who designed and taught this program, or from Dean Eduardo de los Angeles, Ateneo De Manila University, Office of the Dean, College of Law, P.O. Box 154, 130 H.V. do la Costa S.J. St., Salcedo Village, Makati, Metro Manila, 3116 (tel. 00-63-2-8153172).

14. Information on this program can be obtained from Gabriella Varzaru, National Institute for Magistrates, Ministry of Justice, Blvd. M. Kogalniceanu 33, et. 6, Bucharest, Romania (tel. 401-643-2230; fax 401-312-1154). This program was sponsored by the "Rule of Law" program of the United States Information Services (USIS).

15. Great credit is due Nancy Flowers, Bill Ferendes, David Shiman, Elizabeth Dreyfuss, and others who have worked to make human rights education a priority at Amnesty International. This has resulted in many workshops and educational materials being available from Amnesty, including a good newsletter, *Human Rights Education: The Fourth R.* Amnesty also has a good bibliography of human rights education materials: International Secretariat, 1 Easton St., London WC1X8DJ U.K.

16. The Decade of Human Rights Education was founded and is led by its dynamic and indomitably spirited director, Shulamith Koenig, who has done more to promote human rights education in the United States and worldwide than anyone I know. My involvement in many aspects of this field, including the writing of this chapter, is largely due to her inspiration, unmatchable energy, and many phone calls.

17. The Lawyers for Human Rights, led by its director, Brian Currin, its committed former deputy director, Peter Mothle, and their education director, Cecille Van Riet, have led South Africa in human rights education. They can be contacted at 713 Van Erkom Building, Pretorius St., Pretorius 002, South Africa (tel. 12-21-2135; fax 12-325-6318).

18. The South African Street Law Program's address and facsimile number are listed in note 10 above.

19. Eleanor Greene co-authored *Human Rights for All* with David McQuoid-Mason (the founder of Street Law in South Africa) and myself. She is a former social studies teacher in Fairfax County, Virginia, and Massachusetts. Currently, she is completing a master's degree in conflict resolution at George Mason University in Virginia.

20. See note 9 above. This study found that when teachers taught only one side of a controversy, students became more negative toward the law (e.g., when students were taught police were brutal toward citizens, most students adopted this attitude). Therefore, the evaluators and NICEL recommend a balanced approach to teaching controversial issues, airing both sides of an issue.

21. *Human Rights for All* (JUTA Publications, Capetown, South Africa). For copies contact JUTA Freepost, No. CBO622 7790 Kenwyn, South Africa (tel. 011-27-21-797-5101; fax 011-27-21-762-7424). Copies of the South African Street Law books *Introduction to Law, Criminal Law, Consumer Law, Family Law, Welfare and Housing Law, Employment Law, Human Rights for All,* and *Democracy for All* can also be obtained from JUTA at the above address.

22. See note 17 above for Lawyers for Human Rights. Contact them to obtain further information on their human rights education projects and materials.

23. See notes 9 and 19 above.

24. For information on all the Community Law Centre's programs and materials, including *Human Rights (Amalungelo Olumntu)* and their democracy texts, annual reports, and newsletters, contact the CLC at Berea Centre, Seventh Floor, 249 Berea Road, Durban 4001, South Africa (tel. 031-202-7190; fax 031-210140).

25. The illustrator is Andy Mason, who directs Artworks. He can be contacted about all the Street Law, human rights, and democracy education materials at 113 Brand Road, Glenwood 4001, P.O. Box 5138, Durban 4000, South Africa (tel. 011-27-31-216084; fax 011-27-31-218113).

26. *Democracy for All* is available from JUTA, a South African publisher; see note 21 above.

27. In addition to myself, the other authors are Mary Curd Larkin of NICEL, Professor Mandla Mchunu, National Street Law program director in South Africa, Dean David McQuoid-Mason, and Professor Karthi Govender of the University of Natal Law Faculty (Durban, South Africa).

28. See notes 25 and 21 above for information on how to obtain this text.

29. Speech by Warren Christopher, U.S. Secretary of State, UN Conference on Human Rights, Vienna, Austria, June 1993.

Chapter 26
Promoting Human Rights Education in a Marginalized Africa

J. Paul Martin, Cosmas Gitta, and Tokunbo Ige

> Open societies that value human rights, respect the rule of law, encourage popular participation and have an accountable system of governance provide a better and more enabling environment for sustainable economic development.
>   Layashi Yaker, executive secretary, UN Economic Commission for Africa

> More should be done not only in terms of convincing our countries to integrate the African Charter into national legislation, but also in popularizing human rights studies in schools and colleges.
>   Salim Ahmed Salim, secretary-general, Organization of African Unity

These comments, made at the fourteenth annual session of the African Human Rights Commission held in Addis Ababa in 1993, mark the new significance of human rights in Africa. Over the last few years, the number of nongovernmental organizations (NGOs) has expanded exponentially, notably in the form of self-help development groups, women's organizations, and human rights organizations.[1] African NGO development was strengthened significantly at the 1993 UN Human Rights Conference in Vienna. Many of the African groups were able to meet there for the first time and soon discovered the importance and effectiveness, albeit with limitations, of collaboration, and the influence they could exert on both international agendas and the priorities of their own governments. Such developments reflect a new consciousness of self-reliance and the recognition that, although essential, international agents can go only so far in promoting human rights in Africa. Much, therefore, must depend on responses within each country, on the part of both the government and the citizenry. Activists are now calling for greater popular participation and for local mechanisms of human rights enforcement that do not depend on a country occupying the international spotlight. This recognition that democracy must be a bottom-up process and that the promotion of human rights is based on principles of self-reliance and expanded popular participation necessitates new strategies on all sides.

Across the continent the human rights NGOs, women's organizations, and development groups are emphasizing popular education in the belief that the survival and consolidation of their mostly embryonic movements depend on increased grassroots support. Greater popular awareness, it is hoped, will lead to new demands to respect human rights and to a more democratic, peaceable social order now seen by them as the prime condition for economic development.

Based on interviews with leaders of some of the human rights and women's groups from different regions of sub-Saharan Africa, this chapter examines the human rights educational goals and activities that reflect and encourage this new consciousness in sub-Saharan Africa, a region largely marginalized both politically and economically. The findings are based on interviews conducted since the Vienna Conference by the authors with more than sixty African human rights leaders and educators from East, Southern, and West Africa.[2] The interviews were guided by a simple open-ended questionnaire designed (a) to elicit organizational goals and the leaders' ideas and priorities, rather than replies to specific questions, and (b) to help them describe their current programs on human rights education and training.

The Growth of Human Rights Consciousness in Africa

In the first years of decolonization, during the late 1950s and the 1960s, most Africans welcomed the achievement of political independence and the new political orders that replaced the old colonial regimes. In the course of events the international human rights movement began to bring to the world's attention the patterns of human rights violations in Idi Amin's and Milton Obote's Uganda, Sergeant Doe's Liberia, and the National Party's South Africa. The resulting consciousness coupled with the realization on the part of many Africans that their countries still lacked effective and equitable state structures, motivated more members of those societies to organize and to work toward the elimination of human rights violations and the creation of new social orders. African exiles in Europe and the United States began to form pressure groups to expose the repressive regimes they had been forced to flee. As these expatriate and international human rights voices were echoed in their home countries, new internal response patterns evolved. Both with and without external support, Africans within certain key professions, such as law and the media, began to form local human rights groups, often benefiting from the help of labor unions and church organizations. Led by, or at least learning and profiting from the lessons of, the anti-apartheid movement, the new groups worked with the European and American nongovernmental and human rights organizations as well as with the United Nations and other international agencies. African governments also responded with the promulgation in 1982 of the African Charter of Human and People's Rights, which created the African Human Rights Commission, the first continentwide organ of its kind. The Geneva-based International Commission of Jurists then used its annual meetings to bring together some of the new human rights groups for training in advocacy.

For Africa as well as other parts of the world, the year 1989 was the watershed that opened up a new era. The end of Marxist-Leninist governments in Europe, the radical changes in South Africa, and the increasing attention to human rights violations in parts of Africa other than South Africa encouraged Africans all over the continent to call for more democratic and equitable social structures.[3] Not all the 1989 changes were beneficial. External aid resources once allocated to Africa began to be diverted to the new Eastern Europe. Nevertheless, major changes in political attitude took place and a continentwide trend toward democracy was evident.

Calls for political change were reinforced by the economic failures of most postcolonial administrations in Africa. Among the most telling indicators of Africa's economic plight is the fact that between 1983 and 1990 debt servicing consumed 30 percent of the continent's export earnings. The annual interest on past loans paid by most African countries now exceeds the level of new loans received, eviscerating local reinvestment potential.[4] Increasingly, Africa's small professional and business classes have recognized their continent's marginalization and are urging internal political and economic reform. They have also realized that, despite any validity in blaming their fate on external forces, it will accomplish little. Accepting the structural adjustment programs imposed by the International Monetary Fund and the World Bank is therefore seen as a necessary evil, even though many critics believe that popular resentment and human rights violations in their countries have increased on account of the program. The debate on appropriate economic policies, however, continues, fueled by occasional reports such as one in 1994 that the economies of fifteen African countries have begun to respond positively to structural adjustment policies.[5]

Within this change-oriented environment of the last six years, local human rights activities in Africa have increased in number and diversity, reinforced by a similar explosion of women's organizations and development groups.[6] One of the most common reasons given by the leaders we interviewed for the recent changes is the popular desire for effective democracy and economic development which can only happen, they argued, within an orderly and peaceable society. In most African countries, NGOs now form a small but evolving civil society, seeking to respond to specific social needs and to participate more effectively in national economic and political decision making. This includes demanding greater accountability and transparency on the part of their governments. As interest in the promotion of human rights has grown, NGOs have responded with new programs ranging from paralegal training and legal clinics, to seminars and workshops on penal reform and capital punishment. Many of them reexamine the relationship between their own government practices and universal human rights theory and practice. The increased use of electoral process and the presence of external election observers have provided further opportunities for education and training. Moreover, external aid organizations, disillusioned with supporting corrupt and inefficient governments, have been more ready to redirect aid to the private sector. These changes have benefited human rights NGOs, whose primary source of financial support is now foreign governments. Although their numbers are still modest, given the enormous size of the continent and its population and the absence of statewide political parties, African NGOs are forces to be reckoned with in the eyes of African governments.

Led by women's groups especially, intra-Africa networking is growing. With its headquarters in Harare, Zimbabwe, Women in Law and Development in Africa (WILDAF) has officers assigned to Francophone, South African, and East African subregions and plans to open offices soon in Zambia, Mozambique, and Botswana. WILDAF gives priority to providing legal rights education for women, offers technical assistance to new NGOs, and has on call a cadre of trainers ready to run training workshops as the need arises. Another continentwide women's network is FIDA (Féderation Internationale des Avocates [International Federation of Women Lawyers]), which has branches in a number of African countries. In West Africa, l'Union Interafricaine des Droits de l'Homme (Inter-African Union for Human Rights), based in Ouagadougou, spearheads another networking initiative linking groups in eighteen countries. In East Africa, a regional center for human rights and development is being formed in the newly independent Eritrea. Annual regional human rights training programs have begun in Senegal, Uganda, and Zimbabwe. Inspired by the experiences and some of the resolutions developed at the Vienna Human Rights Conference, interest in other forms of regional collaboration is increasing.

External assistance has been crucial throughout the process. The United States, Canada, and most Western European governments have provided aid in the form of cash and equipment, consultants, and overseas travel, as well as study programs for the leaders of the new groups. Links with governmental, intergovernmental, and nongovernmental external organizations have provided protection in moments of conflict with governments, but also have led to problems when the recipients were labeled unpatriotic because of the external contact. As in Eastern Europe, human rights leaders from some African countries, such as South Africa, Mali, and Chad, emerged from the recent democratic revolutions as national political leaders to replace the authoritarian figures who inherited power from the colonists. Some African NGO leaders have received major international awards for their achievements, while others now head such international human rights organizations as Amnesty International and the International Commission of Jurists.

These successes, however, are often more visible from abroad than they are in daily life for ordinary citizens in both rural and urban Africa.[7] For the vast majority of Africa's millions, little has changed for the better. Continentwide, human rights violations permeate the daily lives of millions of African women and children. They include economic and social discrimination, domestic violence and gender-biased inheritance laws. The absence of health care and education, inadequate diets, and lives disrupted by civil violence have adversely affected millions of African children. With notable exceptions, such as in Zambia, the continent's prisons and criminal justice systems remain abysmal. Famines due in no small part to human failures and corruption continue; labor remains poorly paid; social services and government accountability are minimal. More localized violations include the effects of civil wars, coerced internal and crossborder migrations and family separations, the deprivation of basic political and economic emancipation, and serious levels of ethnically defined discrimination and conflict. The whole spectrum of violations is further complicated (especially in those that concern women) by arguments seeking to explain ostensibly discriminatory and offensive practices on the basis of traditional culture and religion. Equally complex are the causes and thus the rectification of these multiple violations.

Political changes that have improved Africa's rating on some democracy charts and brought new leaders and new constitutions with enhanced provisions for human rights have yet to change village life. They have, however, heightened professional and popular awareness of the gap between the ideal and practice. Expectations are rising. More people are motivated to seek change rather than live with injustices as if they are unavoidable. The most obvious evidence of these forces is the formation and recent rapid expansion of the NGOs, and the new commitment to electoral processes and multiparty democracy. Within this movement, human rights education is gaining in appeal.

The Definition of Human Rights in Africa

Human rights and international human rights in particular are evolving concepts in the sense that their meaning is continually being refined. The core of all human rights activism remains legal, namely, the definition of common norms and the creation and use of the national and international institutions necessary to enforce the norms. The modern international human rights movement has its roots in the anti-slavery movement of the early nineteenth century and in the attempts to protect minorities in Eastern Europe after World War I. The substantive issues have been defined successively through the responses to the evils of Nazi Germany, to the elimination of nineteenth-century colonization, and, again most recently, in replacing the totalitarian regimes of the last part of this century and in responding to humanitarian crises. The consensus on the comprehensive definition of human rights is growing. It is articulated primarily in the International Bill of Rights, notably the Universal Declaration of Human Rights, the fifty-three articles of the International Covenant on Civil and Political Rights, and the thirty-one articles of the International Covenant on Economic, Social and Cultural Rights. The African Charter of Human and Peoples' Rights, which entered into force in 1986, has gained stature and efficacy but slowly. In practice, if one takes these standards and applies them across Africa, violations are quickly manifest in terms of those afflicted and the variety of infringements. The worldwide human rights movement, impelled by its NGO component, once symbolized by Amnesty International and its concern for political prisoners, has, like Amnesty itself, expanded and diversified to incorporate a wider range of objectives and strategies.

Figure 26.1. African women and men singing a song with lyrics that stress the importance of participation in political decision making. (UNPHOTO/TW 1b)

In Africa the first local human rights NGOs were composed primarily of lawyers and focused on legal advocacy, notably through the use of courts to seek redress. The limitations of the legal process in most countries, however, coupled with a low level of popular consciousness and the real range of violations have compelled the activists to adopt a more inclusive strategy and to use international forums. The future promotion of human rights is now seen to depend on a broader popular base and a commitment to the rule of law and democratic process within each country. No longer only a question of legal and paralegal training, the promotion of human rights is seen to require organizational and educational work focused on the promotion of democracy, political participation, and conflict resolution. Included in the African NGOs' agenda is the search for new political cultures, drawing on traditional values, to overcome the problems created by regimes based on the coercive power of military rule or distorted by ethnic conflict. Constitutions are now proposed as the necessary "mother of all laws" to guide the political process, not just as a step to decolonization. In Africa, political activism is increasingly defined by the growth in numbers and political influence of women's groups, with their decidedly local agenda of economic betterment starting in the home, and the reduction of gender discrimination.[8] As indicated above, women's groups have created new national networks that reach out into villages and across state lines, and their cooperative style benefits and expands the agenda of the more traditional human rights NGOs. Increasingly, NGOs in Africa are creating national organizations with chapters across the country.

These developments are accompanied by a search for new African conceptualizations of human rights. Tanzanian law professor and theorist Issa Shivji sees the basic rights as group rather than individual rights.[9] For him the basic rights are those to self-determination and to freedom of association, provided these rights take root in truly democratic and participatory social units. Only once these group rights are assured can individual rights be protected.[10] The leaders interviewed for this study argued that people who are free to act and participate in the decisions that affect their lives make for a better economy. These sentiments also underpin the words of Layashi Yaker quoted above, and they are increasingly the basis for thinking about human rights in Africa.

Our informants frequently emphasized that African human rights ideology is more solidaristic than the European version.[11] They also expressed the conviction that rights processes ought to avoid win/lose dichotomies at variance with traditional African patterns of consensual justice.[12] They saw this conceptualization as a necessary means to promote a society where each person sees him or herself as the keeper of the other's rights. Rather than being inimical to human rights, African scholars like Shivji portray traditional African societies as protectors of rights. Rights are viewed by them not as a fence to protect the individual from the community, but rather as rules for living together in community. In more ambiguous terms, African political leaders also appeal to traditional societies, and seek to portray their own governments as the protector of rights. Outside major upheavals, modern African states have been less constrained than their European counterparts by popular voices or the forces of civil society because the latter is so small. Moreover, as African professionals and intellectuals are often the employees of the state, African human rights advocates, including scholars, can be reluctant to oppose state action. Together, these ideological and practical forces have defined differently from those of European countries the relationship between the state and the individual citizen.

Equally more characteristic of African than European thinking is the view that poverty and economic marginalization are as great a threat to human dignity as violations of civil rights, and therefore must be at the core of the human rights agenda. Thus, in other than specifically legal processes, in Africa it is difficult to separate out a human rights agenda from broader social justice concerns. When mediating conflicting claims and working out solutions, traditional judicial process in Africa was based on the assumption that the litigants would remain corporate members of the same community. This meant that reconciliation and corrective justice were primary considerations. As indicated above, rights were viewed as necessary not to protect the individual from the community, but rather as rules and values for living together.[13] These differing points of emphasis were reflected in the interviews with the NGO leaders. They also expressed a vision of a new African society which goes beyond a legal civil rights agenda, one that would require building new political cultures that incorporate traditional cultures but are adapted to new state and economic structures.

Human Rights Education to Promote Self-Reliance and Preventive Action

The message that former Tanzanian president Nyerere preached on self-reliance in the 1960s is now being rediscovered at the grass roots. Awareness of the limitations of the international human rights movement, both with regard to its predilection for civil and political rather than economic and social rights and to what is perceived as limited interest in Africa as compared with the former socialist countries in Europe, has forced African human rights activists to examine how they can better help themselves. Rather than acting simply as collaborators in collecting information for reports to international organizations on human rights violations in their countries, human rights advocates in Africa want to focus on their countries directly and in the best way possible. Amnesty International, for example, offers them a useful international network, but few Africans want to devote their energies to working on human rights violations in countries other than their own as required by the traditional Amnesty International mandate. They want to address the complexity, immensity, and structural nature of the forces that cause violations of human rights to vast segments of African peoples. The protection of human rights is now seen by them as part of the formula to prevent political violence and to create an equitable social order that can lead to peace and economic progress. The function of human rights standards is to create order and stability and is thus closely related with the promotion of the rule of law.

The goals of African human rights educators are still tentative, and their projects even more so. They see the general need to correct the negative impact of colonialism and its continuation through economic inequities and ineffective political structures. They advocate an education that fosters the attitudes and skills that encourage self-reliance and responsible citizens and leaders. Now that the limited ability of governments to provide needed social services is evident, the freedom to organize independently is seen as a prerequisite to real social and economic betterment. The net result of this consciousness is the understanding that the promotion of human rights depends on the expansion of popular consciousness, which depends in turn on educational programs that reach wider segments of the population than are presently accessible to the human rights NGO community. The persistent necessity for external resources and other forms of external support that can defend them from excessive government control imposes on them a continuing but undesired mode of dependency.

Existing Programs in Human Rights Education

The initial core human rights work in Africa has revolved around public interest and legal work. The evolution adding education to the agenda is most visible in the work of women's groups in both urban and rural areas in Africa. Given the limited number of qualified lawyers available for this outreach work, the demand on the part of women for legal services (stemming, for example, from violations of their rights with regard to inheritance, divorce, and other proceedings) necessitated the training of paralegals to identify and document violations and to provide basic legal assistance. To respond to these and other needs, human rights education is expanding at all levels. Universities are creating human rights programs, private primary and secondary schools are developing human rights materials and curricula, and NGOs are organizing educational programs in villages. These embryonic endeavors are worth examining in greater detail than is possible here, at least as a means to share their experiences with others.

Higher Education

African universities occupy an uneasy position. Whether or not a western model of the liberal spirit is alive and well, professors and students are viewed by most governments as the most likely groups to agitate against them. Students and faculty are therefore often under constant surveillance and subject to quick government reprisals. This situation, coupled with the de facto financial government control of the universities, has contributed to the exclusion of human rights education from the curriculum of most universities in Africa. Until recently human rights was thus often little more than a theoretical segment in an international law course for law students. It was rarely related to the domestic economy or to political problems in the way suggested by Layashi Yaker's quotation above.

Substantial changes are now taking place. At many universities, interest in establishing human rights education, training, and resource programs is visible. In Uganda, for example, at the University of Makerere, there is now a three-year-old Center for Peace and Human Rights based at the law school which has recently received major funding for its own building. From a tiny room next to the dean's office, the center publishes a journal, promotes curriculum development at the university and in secondary schools, organizes programs on campus, and encourages Makerere students to work with human rights NGOs. The university at Addis Ababa now offers courses in human rights and supports a Center for Democracy and Human Rights. The new University of Namibia has provision for a human rights center in its charter. At the University of Nairobi, however, the law faculty still does not offer a course on human rights, although members of the department are active with human rights NGOs. At the University of Dar es Salaam, law students receive instruction on human rights as an aspect of international law, administrative law, constitutional law, and jurisprudence. The university has recently set up a Human Rights Resources Unit to collect data, provide services to faculty and students, and to develop courses and programs at the university on human rights. At the University of Zimbabwe, professors from the law school have been visible defenders of human rights through local NGOs and in the courts, and there is now an interest in creating a master's program and a regional resource center to serve Zimbabwe's neighbors. In Liberia, for the last two years, an independent Center for Law and Human Rights Education has worked with a severely depleted and often closed university and with local NGOs, seeking to respond to the immediate consequences of the civil war and preparations for peace. Liberia joins a number of other university programs in Africa that have recently incorporated legal clinics through which faculty and students provide legal services to the indigent. This is a significant step away from the exclusively academic courses that have so far characterized legal education in Africa. It follows the example of law students in the present-day Philippines, which now has up to more than ten years experience in grassroots and community service and has substantially influenced the character of the legal profession there.[14] In South Africa a revived University of Fort Hare has a chair in human rights, and the United Nations is advising on its development into a center with a regional focus.

The most concentrated level of human rights activity in Africa outside of South Africa is undoubtedly in Lagos where lawyers have founded diverse public interest and legal aid groups, Amnesty International has a national section, and the Nigerian Bar Association—with approximately 25,000 members—has human rights committees in all its national sections.[15] Human rights education in Nigeria, however, is still limited to small segments in some law courses at scattered universities. Elsewhere in West Africa, the faculty of law and political science at the University of Yaounde II recently introduced a course on human rights, covering the problems of minorities (notably the English-speaking), the problems of censorship and the media, multiparty politics, and the implementation of the new constitution.

Research at these universities on human rights is still minimal and is mostly focused on women's rights, notably the right to inherit and own land, and on custody and family laws. African contributions in the field of human rights in local and overseas journals have been diverse but not prolific. Research, for example, by the Nigerian scholar Samuel Folorunso Ogundare on the "Human Rights Orientation of Prospective Social Studies Teachers" in Nigeria[16] examined African students' understanding of human rights concepts. His work showed that comprehension of the meaning of rights varies from one right to another and from region to region; on the other hand, there was little difference between male and female students. Most existing research has come from scholars in exile or from scholars in Africa with access to external sponsorship. This pattern reflects the more general problems of academia in Africa.

Central though they are to national development, Africa's institutions of higher education, with few exceptions, remain distressingly weak. In most African countries, affluent and influential parents prefer to send their children overseas for higher—if not also secondary—education, leaving the national universities without the interest and commitment of the government officials, business leaders, and more successful professionals in the best position to help them. This neglect, along with deteriorating library facilities and limited research resources, inadequate faculty salaries and run-down facilities, has made African universities less than competitive.[17] Government fear of student activism which has kept the police, if not also the military, hovering close to campus, still circumscribes academic freedom and creativity. Human rights activities and teaching have been especially suspect. External organizations support-ing human rights activities have also shied away from African universities because of their poor overall financial circumstances and the sense that, susceptible as they are to government manipulation, they do not offer a stable base for progress. Prospective human rights teachers in such a negative political environment have thus found it dif-ficult to obtain research and institutional support, including the materials necessary for their courses and their libraries.

Primary and Secondary Education

Secondary and primary institutions in Africa already face major financing and staff-ing inadequacies. Enrollment is increasing while budgets are shrinking. Some even talk of an impending breakdown of the public systems in such countries as Zaire. In-adequate funding has long undermined government planning for universal primary education, seen by many as an essential condition for a working democracy and a suc-cessful economy. Improving primary and secondary education is closely linked with the more general process of democratization in each country. More countries are be-ginning to review their primary education programs in the light of the new demands of nation-building as well as the more traditional ones of job training. Civic education has already been introduced into some national curricula. In practice it is often little more than simplified history or, as in the case of Zaire, a form of political socializa-tion designed to legitimize the ruling party. The growing commitment to democratic processes has not yet been complemented by curricula that introduce students to the meaning of such concepts as the rule of law, human rights, popular participation, and accountable government in terms meaningful to their country and their village. Few curricula as yet address deliberative skills, civic virtues, nonviolent conflict reso-lution, and the like. African human rights activists generally believe that these human rights concepts need to be introduced into official primary and secondary curricula in ways that incorporate traditional African concepts of responsibilities and obliga-tions toward the community and its constituent members.

Among the initiatives to introduce human rights education in primary and sec-ondary schools is that of the Inter-African Union for Human Rights, which is working with secondary schools in member countries, notably Togo, Benin, Mali, Guinea-Bissau, Niger, and Gabon. In Zaire there is a small movement among public school teachers, aided by the Catholic Church, to develop and integrate curricular units on human rights and democracy into existing civic education programs. The content includes topics such as the UN Universal Declaration of Human Rights, the promotion of tolerance, nonviolence, and the avoidance of ethnic discrimination and violence, as well as discussions on the electoral process. In Cameroon about three thousand primary and secondary schools have human rights education programs designed by NGOs. Pedagogical approaches vary. Participatory learning, role-playing, and theatrical presentations are being introduced. Information on the preparation of primary and secondary teachers for the teaching of civic or human rights education remains sketchy.

In some countries, small private programs are being set up to promote human rights education and civic education in secondary and primary curricula. One such program is the proposed Center for the Promotion of Civic Education and Democracy in Kampala, Uganda. Its curricular goals are to include more history of Uganda and its cultures and societies, and the study of democratic values. The stated goal is to prepare students to participate in the national political process. Civic education is seen as the means to empower citizens and help them realize the importance of constitutional governance, the rule of law, and the respect for such human rights and fundamental freedoms as the protection of life and property, freedom of conscience, expression, assembly, and association. Recognizing a general lack of awareness among young people in particular, the center proposes to focus on developing curricula and education materials and on the training of human rights educators to use them. Overall, human rights NGO leaders see the need for human rights education in primary and secondary schools, but few groups have been successful in incorporating human rights content into the curricula of schools run by the state or into the curricula of teacher-training colleges.

Professional and Other Education

Human rights education directed toward key professions is also increasing in Africa. Among the professions now offering special courses in one or more countries are the legal professions (practicing lawyers, magistrates, and judges), the police, the military, and prison officials. These activities have been made possible largely by external funding. About a third of the 1992 projects supported by the U.S. government's Africa Human Rights Fund Project ($484,000) fell under the rubric of legal assistance. Another source of human rights training for government officials in countries that comprise the British Commonwealth has been the Commonwealth Secretariat. This intergovernmental agency works with governments rather than NGOs. Governments are becoming more open to such training. In Zimbabwe, for instance, after being forced by the courts to pay high compensation to some victims of police violence, the government saw it to be in its own interest to train their police officers better in the principles of due process and detention procedures, requesting a local NGO, the Legal Resources Foundation, to carry out the training. In Côte d'Ivoire, the main national NGO has also been called upon by the government to provide training for police officers. The need for these special initiatives highlights the fact that adequate professional training is not being provided by the governments themselves. These single initiatives, however, only reach a small segment, and cannot replace full government involvement in human rights training of its officers.

Increasing numbers of African NGOs, largely with external financing, have begun to supplement human rights teaching and training with published human rights materials. The Zairian Human Rights group AZADHO (Association Zairoise de Défense des Droits de l'Homme) publishes a range of materials delineating the rights of Zairian citizens vis-à-vis the government. Materials prepared by the Legal Resources Foundation in Zimbabwe educate people on their rights with regard to arrest procedures, making wills, civil freedoms, and a wide range of other legal issues that affect people's daily lives.

Informal human rights education characterizes many NGO meetings and activities. An example of NGOs organizing more structured rural education programs is Zaire's AZADHO, which sends out, in a borrowed Land Rover, a mobile unit comprised of a doctor, a journalist, and a lawyer to spend three or four days in a village providing health care, legal aid, and human rights education. Other NGOs are developing human rights resource centers for teachers and the general public, often aided by shipments of materials from external organizations. Admirable though all these initiatives are, the outside observer cannot but be struck by the contrast between these hard-won gains and the size of the task ahead.

Growth of Civil Society

After thirty plus years of independence, civil society in African states is now beginning to diversify. Poets and writers like Wole Soyinka, Ngugi wa Thiongo, and Chinua Achebe have become international figures, and their governments must take into account their opinions on national affairs. National associations of lawyers have grown in influence. Although varying from state to state, the local press, virtually nonexistent at independence, plays an uneven but important role in creating space within the new states for political debate. Radio stations, once the exclusive prerogative of government, have become more open to materials generated by local artists, and some African countries, such as Mali and Uganda, now permit private radio stations. The latter also permits private television stations. In some countries, filmmaking, which has brought international renown to Africa, has opened new local avenues of communication and reflection. Theater, both traditional and modern, plays a significant role in many West African societies and is now being tested as an educational tool elsewhere in Africa, notably in Uganda. Among those who do not speak English or French, indigenous "intellectuals," many of whom are musicians and balladeers, use vernacular languages as a medium of social criticism.

Long one of the few nationwide organizations other than government, the churches in Africa have displayed a wide range of responses to social issues and to the work of the secular human rights NGOs in particular. Institutions like the Roman Catholic Commissions on Justice and Peace in Zimbabwe and Liberia, as well as the Interfaith Council in Kenya, have been closely allied with more typical human rights groups in opposing government corruption and human rights violations. In Mozambique, the National Council of Churches played an important role as an independent observer of the violence by both guerilla and government forces, and the Catholic Church assisted initially in the peace negotiations. In Malawi, Catholic bishops led the call for political reform through a pastoral letter that was read throughout the country in 1992, setting off a wave of democratic demands that resulted in a new constitutional order. In Nigeria, embroiled in competition with Islam, the Christian churches have remained distant from the secular human rights groups. In Zaire, churches have played a significant role in promoting human rights in a society where until recently human rights organizations have been active only in the capital. In Uganda, the late Emmanuel Cardinal Nsubuga was one of the few open critics of Idi Amin's and Milton Obote's repressive regimes from within the country, but today there are no strong patterns of collaboration between the religious and human rights communities in Uganda.

The contribution of Africa's labor unions to human rights education has yet to be evaluated. Union membership and networks are much smaller than those of the churches, and they have tended to focus on economic rather than wider social issues. Nevertheless, the unions produced some of the leaders in recent social and political reform. The current president of Zambia, for example, comes from the labor movement. Labor has yet to find its identity in a post-structural adjustment Africa. The movement as a whole has stagnated in recent years. Outside South Africa, there have been limited but no significant alliances with the human rights movement, even where, for example in Sudan, unions have been a major target of government oppression.

The net result of these various activities, educational and otherwise, is the internal diversification of African societies through the creation of new and independent organizations and the weakening of the organizational prerogatives and coercive powers that governments inherited from the colonial order. Their overall impact on long-standing ethnic lines and problems of nation-building is varied and yet to be fully evaluated. The very existence of more independent groups, however, even without predominant human rights goals, makes them political actors able to engage both the government and people in debate.

External Support

The role of external organizations and funding remains central to human rights activities in Africa. External support, which in Africa means primarily that of western governments rather than the private sector, plays a major role indirectly through voter education and election-monitoring programs. The African Governance Program of the Carter Center in Atlanta, Georgia, for example, provides technical assistance and educational inputs through election-monitoring projects, workshops on developing economies and new democracies, and training government officials and leaders in community development. The Carter Center collaborates with other U.S. and European groups such as the National Democratic Institute for International Affairs (NDI) and the International Foundation for Electoral Systems. NDI itself, often in collaboration with its sister organization, the International Republican Institute, conducts training in party politics. The Canadian government, through the semi-independent Center for Human Rights and Democracy, provides funding and technical assistance for a wide range of human rights programs in Africa. The in-country libraries, communication, and education services maintained by the cultural services of foreign embassies are another useful external resource. The British Council, the United States Information Services, and the French government, among others, support libraries and information services in a number of African countries and channel African nationals to educational opportunities abroad.

The funding and other services provided to African NGOs directly or indirectly by foreign governments from Europe and North America far exceeds their other sources of income. The negative aspect of access to funds from foreign governments is that it makes recipient African NGOs vulnerable to the dangerous criticism that they are beholden to the priorities of foreign interests. On the other hand, the level of this financial dependency makes it difficult to imagine they can develop locally the level of support they would need to survive without external funding.

External NGO support for African human rights NGOs is far more modest. The Geneva-based International Commission of Jurists schedules regular training programs prior to meetings of the African Human Rights Commission to help NGOs improve the professional training of their personnel. The International Commission of Jurists' activities have not only provided training but have also built contacts among human rights and legal advocacy groups, and enabled them to participate in and, to some degree, build up the importance of the commission meetings. Other North American and European NGOs and some universities are active throughout Africa, developing a range of collaborative training and educational ventures. The American Association for the Advancement of Science monitors the freedoms of scientists and the acquisition of scholastic journals. Materials inspired by the street law materials developed at the National Institute for Citizenship Education at Georgetown University, and modified in South Africa, are being used in various parts of Africa. In this work, many if not most of the American organizations rely on the support of the United States, typically through the U.S. Agency for International Development.

External support remains essential to the African NGOs and to the development of human rights education in particular. Although the variety of potential sources of aid assures a degree of NGO independence, the feeling persists among them that they are beholden to "Northern" agendas and models. There are as yet no mechanisms that permit sustained analysis of aid priorities between donors and representatives of groups of potential recipients. In spite of a common rhetoric of collaboration, awards continue to be made on a one-on-one basis, where one is the donor and the other the needy.

New Opportunities

The core challenge as seen by the leaders of many African NGOs is acquiring what they call substantive democracy, that is, a day-to-day practice where leadership at all levels is fully responsible and accountable to its constituency and where the latter actively participates in the decision-making process. While welcoming programs in election-monitoring and voter education and the help of external organizations, the NGO leaders have not lost sight of this larger goal. They view using elections as a litmus test for democracy and the legitimacy of governments as inadequate. The leaders want a more comprehensive view of democratic society.

The expansion of communications technology in its various forms—satellite TV news channels, fax machines, CD-ROM, and E-mail—means that a small investment of little more than $1,000 in a laptop computer, a modem, and a telephone line has put some groups in contact with the world's data and communications systems. While Africa obviously lacks the resources of the industrialized world, modern electronic communication networks exist in Africa, at least at some of its university libraries and medical schools. A modest investment in training and hardware in this area could improve exponentially the resources available to human rights work in Africa. The creation of national human rights resource centers proposed by many NGOs in Africa offers a cost-effective way to assure a minimum level of local access to education and research materials and a depository that international donors could use for documentary materials and communications technology.

Most of those interviewed agreed that a new era in human rights education was essential, one that encompasses more than the mere knowledge of one's legal rights. It should include understanding principles of democracy, the organization of government and elections that are capable of promoting rights, economic development and human rights, and the promotion of behaviors that are respectful of others. African human rights advocates emphasized the need to impart principles of justice, tolerance, equality, freedom, solidarity, dignity, rights, and civic duties and responsibilities. A necessary precondition is the preparation of teachers and classroom-ready materials that can bring this learning to the African masses. This requires cultural adaptation of international norms and even of national legal systems. This education must also respond to the objective need to reduce injustices and sufferings and to improve the daily life of Africa's populations.

Increasing the exchanges of information and human rights materials within Africa is critical and was the goal of an all-Africa conference on human rights education held in South Africa in September 1994. English-language materials developed in one part of Africa have been found useful in others, thus saving time and expense. This could be expanded. Africa's slowly evolving common markets are establishing new patterns of collaboration, common political interests, the need for shared standards, and economic stability. The creation of the South African Development Coordination Conference (SADCC), the Preferential Trade Area (PTA), the Economic Community of West African States (ECOWAS), and other intergovernmental regional bodies established to address common political and humanitarian problems indicates the importance of human rights groups creating parallel networks to ensure their concerns are addressed and that human rights standards are observed and taught in the various peacekeeping and peacemaking processes.

Given the size of Africa and the dearth of resources likely to be available, national government support is crucial. Unlike legal advocacy, human rights educational strategies require working with government officials to achieve common goals rather than taking them to court. Governments have yet to be convinced of the importance of human rights to the political and economic development of their countries. A new era of government-NGO relations is called for, one in which governments find ways to encourage the civic values, rule of law, and economic entrepreneurship envisioned in the words of Layashi Yaker. Without government support, it is impossible for human rights education to reach more than small segments of the population. With government support, human rights educators could help elaborate new curricula and teaching materials, these materials could be circulated, and secondary and primary teachers trained. This degree of government cooperation is rare.

Despite the many changes taking place, research to study and record current developments is minimal. Little is being written in Africa about its recent history or analyzing and bringing to public debate the complex questions concerning the causes of recent human rights problems and ways to avoid them in the future. Africans complain that funds go to researchers from overseas to prepare papers and hold conferences in and on Africa, but that little reaches them. For the promotion of human rights, a commitment to "never again"—that is, a sense of horrors to be avoided at all costs—is a critical step toward making the sacrifices and concessions necessary to develop a society that responds to the interests of all its members. Without the research and debates that bring recent history alive, both popular and governmental commitment to reform will diminish. The idea of democracy, which certainly has its roots in most villages, has yet to find national structures adapted to modern urban and rural

Africa. The challenge to devise these structures is not being addressed in an institutional way by Africa's universities, but only by a few individual activists, artists, and scholars.

Looking to the Future

The pervasive constraints are economic. The quality and spread of human rights education in Africa are radically determined by access to resources both human—where African countries are not lacking—and material, where hard priority choices have to be made and where external aid remains crucial. Time is of the essence. The general, worldwide move toward democratic structures has created a window of opportunity in Africa of uncertain duration. Actions today might not be possible tomorrow. Human rights education, popular and professional, is the preventive measure for building political cultures that will discourage human rights violations in the future. This extensive task focuses on the need to train different categories of people for human rights education and training.

From their interviews with African NGOs, the authors identified the following priorities for human rights education in Africa:

1. the promotion of increased communication and exchanges among local NGO and other human rights education initiatives
2. the organization of training and human resource development programs that (a) use and strengthen local resources and (b) make existing services available to a wider range of groups
3. making available the resources of African law schools and universities for human rights and civic education
4. the preparation of classroom-ready materials for secondary school teaching and for adult and professional education
5. training focused on capacity building for NGOs as key elements in civil society
6. programs to expand and improve NGO-government relations
7. training to help local NGOs use new technologies and media such as radio, popular theater, dance, and song

The expanding numbers of NGOs in Africa offer a window of opportunity to develop institutions for human resource training and to build a more substantial civil society. Giving priority to education helps African societies become more self-reliant and capable of developing the necessary skills and resources. The challenge lies in choosing the most effective educational strategies.

Notes

1. The most comprehensive listing is available in the "Master List: A Listing of Organizations Concerned with Human Rights and Social Justice Worldwide," *Human Rights Internet Reporter,* supplement to vol. 15 (1994).

2. The authors visited groups and interviewed their leaders in Côte d'Ivoire, Ethiopia, Eritrea, Kenya, Liberia, Nigeria, Uganda, Upper Volta, Senegal, South Africa, Togo, Tanzania, and Zimbabwe in 1993–94. They also met with leaders from other countries at sessions of the African Human Rights Commission, as well as in New York. No statistical methodology was attempted, primarily because the field of human rights education has been little studied. This chapter implicitly recognizes a standard breakdown of the educational process: (a) objectives and goals (cognitive, attitudinal, and behavioral); (b) institutions and personnel; (c) means, strategies, and methodologies; and (d) evaluation processes, outcomes, and benefits.

3. Dwayne Woods, "Civil Society in Europe and Africa: Limiting State Power Through a Public Sphere," *African Studies Review* 35, no. 2 (September 1992): 77–100.

4. Salim Lone, "Africa Moves Towards Radical Reconstructuring of Political Framework," *Africa Recovery* 5, no. 1 (June 1991): 1.

5. *New York Times,* March 13, 1994.

6. Roy Laishley, "Faster Growth But No Economic Turnaround," *Africa Recovery* 8, no. 2 (April–September 1994): 11.

7. For an extended discussion of democratic reforms in Africa, see Richard Joseph, "Africa: The Rebirth of Political Freedom," *Journal of Democracy* 2, no. 4 (Fall 1991): 11–24.

8. Mairi Aili Tripp, "Gender, Political Participation and the Transformation of Associational Life in Uganda and Tanzania," *African Studies Review* 37 (April 1994): 111 ff.

9. Issa Shivji, *The Concept of Human Rights in Africa* (Dar es Salaam: CODESRIA Books, 1989).

10. Ibid., 69–89.

11. Osita C. Ize, *Human Rights in Africa* (Lagos: Nigerian Institute of International Affairs, incorporated with Macmillan Nigeria Publishers, 1984), 12–14.

12. Francis Ssekandi and Cosmas Gitta, "Protection of Fundamental Rights in the Uganda Constitution," *Columbia Human Rights Law Review* 26 (Fall 1994): 210–13.

13. See Legesse Asmaron, "Human Rights in African Political Culture," in *The Moral Imperatives of Human Rights: A World Survey,* ed. Kenneth W. Thompson (Washington, D.C.: University Press of America, 1980).

14. See Richard Pierre Claude, *Human Rights Education in the Philippines* (Manila: Kalikasan Press, 1991), 44–56.

15. For a detailed early analysis of human rights education in Nigeria, see L. Adele Jinadu and U. M. O. Ivowi, eds., *Human Rights Education in Nigeria* (Lagos: Nigeria National Commission for UNESCO, 1982).

16. *The Social Studies* (November–December 1993): 267–70.

17. William Saint, *Universities in Africa* (Washington, D.C.: World Bank, 1992).

Chapter 27
Looking at Women's Empowerment Initiatives from a Grassroots Level

Unity Dow, Sheryl Stumbras, and Sue Tatten

Metlhaetsile, "the time has come" for the union between development initiatives and human rights educational efforts focused on rural women.[1] With "democratization" the catch phrase for newly emerging nation-states around the globe, greater emphasis and attention have been directed at targeting historically marginalized segments of evolving societies to gather them into the democratic fold. Women, especially hard hit by inequities in all spheres of public and private life, have been identified as a priority for educational programs to improve their opportunities for increased participation in the civil and political realm as well as the economic, social, and cultural arenas of their respective nations.

Metlhaetsile, a woman's information and education center in the country of Botswana, provides an example of one such initiative. Although the project is barely two years old, it provides an interesting glimpse at the process of designing a program that derives not from a paradigm borrowed from a development consultant's training manual, but from the efforts of village women. These women, from all segments of the society, recognized the need for a program that would fill a void left by the metamorphosis caused by a rapidly developing civil society and an eroding agrarian community desperately seeking to maintain its cultural identity.

The Metlhaetsile Centre has successfully wed two schools of seemingly incongruous development thought into a workable village-based legal aid and education scheme. One school suggests that development will reach rural villages through a "trickle down" approach emanating from centralized programs of economic and structural development. Government policies and programs that concentrate on such an approach will be seen to eventually reach the rural poor, who will thus be the beneficiaries of the anticipated increases in revenue. An alternative development approach suggests that sustainable development can be achieved only by working with people at the grassroots level. Central to this philosophy is the necessity for initiatives focusing on participatory schemes that include community input in planning, implementation, and evaluation of development projects.

The Metlhaetsile staff have combined both approaches and applied it to their legal education strategies, hoping that through increased knowledge of their role as citizens and members of a greater community, women will have the tools to improve their development potential. Metlhaetsile staff realize that to empower women to function effectively in Tswana society, they must understand both worlds in which they live—the civil, centrally based realm as well as locally based mechanisms influenced largely by the tribal hierarchy.

Furthermore, the Metlhaetsile staff have added an additional strategy to their overall objectives by providing human rights and international law in its training programs. The human rights framework, too often viewed as an academic and intellectual maze for the urban-centered elite, has been transported from its cloistered Geneva home to the village of Mochudi. Village members who are knowledgeable about human rights law conduct training courses on international mechanisms to widen the knowledge base of village women and to provide additional options for addressing women's rights issues. Thus the human rights framework is made applicable to the lives of rural women who can see beyond their village and country. They can then view themselves as members of a wider world community of women faced with similar problems and striving for common goals. This is ultimately what must happen for a world human rights movement to be truly global and responsive.

The Metlhaetsile project is one that uniquely addresses the macro as well as the micro levels of development and empowerment efforts. As the following pages attest, Metlhaetsile planners have carefully configured the complexities of the women's rights dilemma from a number of different angles and analyses. An analysis of the macro level from an international perspective will be made, gradually focusing on the grassroots, or micro-level view of the issues that Metlhaetsile planners faced when developing their project.

The Macro Level: Women's Rights and the International Community

Although equality between the sexes is ostensibly guaranteed by many international law instruments and a growing number of constitutions, in reality these provisions are devoid of substantive protections for women. Traditional customs and practices dominate the lives of women, tending to exclude them from positions of power, thereby preserving basic legal inequities. Such practices often perpetuate violent and degrading treatment of women and the mentality that will relegate them to a subservient status indefinitely. Thus, despite legal reforms that have been made to improve women's status, their effect has yet to be felt by many.

While women the world over are forced to bear the burdens of providing sustenance for their families and communities, in too many cases their active participation in democratic institutions and processes remains absent.[2] The 1985 Nairobi Conference on the United Nations Decade for Women recognized the slow progress of women's overall advancement and attributed much of it to the lack of female partici-pation at all levels of society. Again and again, the meetings showed that, in many countries, women's voices were muted in the political, legal, economic, social, and cul-tural arenas at both the national and local levels. Unlike men, women did not have the same choices in educational attainment or economic opportunities, and, most criti-cally, in marriage and personal family decisions. In addition, the Nairobi participants postulated that development initiatives would continue to enjoy minimal success as long as women were excluded from public and private decision-making processes. Without input from the majority of the world's population, poverty, disease, famine, and other social and environmental ills would assuredly persist unchecked.

After much discussion and deliberation, the Nairobi Conference recognized that the slow pace of advancement for women was due in large part to the lack of mecha-nisms to promote gender equality and equal access to the legal system. As such, the conference highlighted the need for a concerted program of legal reform and edu-cation to bring about an improvement in women's status. As a result of the Nairobi findings, a number of women's organizations throughout the world reevaluated their development strategies either to include a legal component in their planning or to establish new organizations directed at issues of women's equality and access to the law. Over the years, some of the programs came to focus exclusively on impact litiga-tion and legislative efforts at egalitarian reform, while others have concentrated on educational programs stressing knowledge of women's legal rights.

Alternative Strategies

While there has been some success in achieving gender equality through legal chan-nels, evaluations of women's efforts of the past decade point to the need for these programs to look beyond the law as the sole solution to the gender dilemma. Country-specific gender ideologies regularly diminish the impact of legislative attempts to equalize gender disparities. Customary practice is often articulated as the "natural order." It is overwhelmingly patriarchal in philosophy, invariably underpinning and influencing the legal system of certain societies.[3] Women are exhorted to eradicate "ignorance, poverty, and disease" in the name of "natural order" and national devel-opment; yet when attempting to effect changes in their own lives, they are accused of threatening economic development or cultural tradition.[4] These traditional notions of gender roles that view women as inferior have proven very difficult to supplant de-spite legislative reforms.

Consequently groups are now reworking their program objectives to include re-form measures that are more holistic in outlook and reflect all aspects of women's lives including customary practices. Educational programs that take into consideration women's economic, educational, social, and cultural as well as legal realities are now taking root in the discourse on efforts at women's equality. Equally important is the inclusion of a needs analysis component for target communities before adopting educational strategies that are either irrelevant or inappropriate to the population served.

In addition to a needs analysis, a number of groups have recognized the critical importance of consulting with all women, particularly those whose voices have not been heard because of poverty, inaccessibility to urban areas (where most of the decisions on development take place), fear of reprisal from family and community members, lack of time due to familial responsibilities, and so on. As a result, groups are designing nonformal, participatory approaches in their education and empowerment training. By adopting such a strategy, women's groups can tailor their programming efforts to meet the unique needs of females within a particular community.

Thus a multilevel strategy for fostering women's advancement must be adopted to ensure that women's equality is achieved in the legal realm as well as in the practical reality of the female experience. While women's full civil rights as citizens of their nations should be enshrined in law, there must also be an equivalent commitment to equality in economic, social, and cultural arenas. The overall status of women will be enhanced only if social and economic support structures exist, legal discrimination is eliminated, and negative stereotypes are banished. This strategy must be pursued from the grassroots level throughout all sectors of society. Most important, the "beneficiaries" of development and educational programs should be included in the planning, designing, and implementation of such initiatives to ensure their long-term success.

An African Perspective

While the western world appears enthralled at the genesis of democratization efforts in many African nations, the status of women remains relatively unchanged and often is not calculated into the "democracy" equation. As such, women in Africa must still overcome obstacles from all sectors of society to become active, fully participating members of their nations. With cultural biases favoring male superiority over the personal as well as public realm of African life, patriarchal institutions and attitudes thrive despite the rhetoric proclaiming the victory of democracy over colonialism and authoritarianism in the Africa of the late twentieth century. Although some success has been achieved in bringing the argument of African feminists to bear on legal obligations assumed by nation-states, women's challenges to inequality are stubbornly resisted by governments which base their opposition on the premise that gender equality will destroy the remnants of African culture and tradition. In countries where the government has played a paternalistic role in preserving culture and tradition against further neocolonialist degradation, African people are far less likely to criticize government policies. Especially where African men may feel threatened with losing their superior position within the home and community, resistance is steadfast against women's attempts to gain a foothold in the future development of their nations.

Women's Development Efforts in Botswana

"Mosadi ke thari ya sechaba" ("Woman is the carrier of the nation"). This saying has been part of the Tswana culture for time immemorial and reflects the reality of Batswana women's lives.[5] From the nineteenth-century missionary influence of Robert Livingston and others of his genre, to the colonial protectorate paternalism and imposition of the hut tax on Tswana families that caused an outflux of Batswana men to the gold mines in South Africa, women's lives have changed dramatically, creating demands that tradition had not previously imposed on them. Had it not been for the strength and resiliency of Batswana women, it is unlikely that Botswana would have achieved what it has today.

Botswana is frequently epitomized as the shining example of democracy in Africa because of its multiparty parliamentary system of government, unfettered respect for freedom of speech and association, an independent judiciary, and regard for human rights principles. That lustrous veneer begins to tarnish, however, when exposed to critical inspection, particularly with regard to gender equality. Laws and practices that discriminate against women are outmoded in a democracy such as that in Botswana; yet they remain on the statute books and in the minds of a large segment of the population.

Botswana Law

Like a number of African countries that possess colonial legacies, Botswana has a hybrid legal system given the convergence of colonial, customary, and statutory law. This refers to the application of both general law on the one hand and customary law on the other. General law refers to both the received law, derived from British and Roman-Dutch law, and statutory law enacted by the Botswana Parliament. General law is interpreted by the Magistrate's Court, High Court, and Court of Appeals. These institutions are predominantly male-controlled. Moreover, these judicial officers are educated in both formal institutions of higher learning and the more powerful realm of custom and socialization perpetuating the gender-biased social, political, and legal systems.

Customary law is made by husbands, fathers, uncles, headmen, chiefs, and the House of Chiefs. Women seldom are actively involved in its development, although they are expected to uphold customs and traditions in their roles as wives, daughters, and mothers. Only where certain family issues are involved might women have a say in the outcome of a dispute; otherwise the customary law decision-making structures continue to be the headman and chief.

Botswana law as a whole, whether it be general law or customary law, is overwhelmingly patriarchal in nature, upholding the supremacy and leadership of the male gender. For example, vestiges of both English and Roman-Dutch legal influences are retained through the marriage laws of Botswana. General law continues to view the husband as possessing the marital power over his wife, while customary law presumes that the male is the head of a family. Women who marry are still treated as wards of their husbands and fall subject to the "marital power" which prohibits a wife from having independent contract rights. Upon divorce, many women and their children are made homeless and divested of property they themselves may have purchased or improved with their own funds during the marriage.

The judicial system is often unresponsive to the particular legal problems that Tswana females face. Women must fight fervently for maintenance payments for their children and are often met with disdain by court officials when they resort to the legal system for relief. Domestic violence and sexual assault are only grudgingly prosecuted, often with little chance of conviction or minimal sentences conferred when a conviction is obtained. All these practices indicate the perpetuation of an ideology of male dominance over women rather than a luminous example of democratic principles.

Recent Legal Developments in Botswana

This dominance is further evidenced by women's status as less than full citizens, despite the recent ruling of Botswana's highest court in the case of *Attorney General v. Unity Dow*. In *Dow* the Court of Appeals held that gender discriminatory legislation is unconstitutional.[6] Moreover, until the *Dow* case, the responsiveness of the Botswana government toward the role of women during the country's rapid development had been slight, especially in terms of reforming discriminatory legislation and enforcing existing laws that adversely affect women.

The *Dow* judgment sent the government reeling and nudged it out of its complacent attitude that Batswana women have no reason to complain of inequitable treatment in one of Africa's "most highly regarded democracies." This decision is a landmark not only in Botswana but for evolving nations in Africa and other parts of the world because it recognizes that contemporary society dictates that women assume their rightful place in partnership with their male counterparts in the development of their societies.

While women's rights activists have won the battle in the courtroom, the war still rages throughout the country. Nearly two years after the Court of Appeals handed down the judgment, the Botswana government refuses to enforce the decision. Unofficial accounts indicate that the government planned to hold a referendum to amend the constitution of Botswana in order to legalize sex discrimination. Further, the government has refused to issue passports to children who would, according to the *Dow* decision, be eligible for Botswana citizenship. Rumors and misunderstandings about the ramifications of the citizenship decision abound, mainly phrased in terms of the judgment signaling the demise of Tswana culture and tradition and wholesale adoption of western values and practices. Phrased in these terms, the average Botswana citizen would likely vote in favor of the referendum.

Does Democracy Include Women in Botswana?

In addition, public consciousness is relatively unaffected by the debate on the principles of rights, democracy, or justice.[7] These predominantly western-influenced concepts appear foreign to the average Motswana who lives, in large part, according to custom and tradition. Upholding custom and tradition are compelling arguments for a society that has been subjected to colonial dominance and imperialist interests for more than a century. The constitutional rhetoric of the urban-centered elite may serve powerful interests in giving the system "an appearance of liberal economic and social order."[8] While appeasing the international community with a facade of democracy, however, the Botswana government appeals to its citizenry with promises to maintain customary practices and halt further deterioration of the traditional order—all to the detriment of women's advancement.

Complex arguments for preservation of culture and freedom from the colonial grasp leave women in a disadvantaged position in relation to the modern nation-state and traditional beliefs.[9] Arguments propose that women, as bearers and preservers of African culture, should be protected. Control over women serves as a means of dealing with the lack of ability of some developing nations to achieve self-determination. If the primary colonial and neocolonial forces that keep Africa in a state of subjection continue to exist, it is viewed that at least women can be kept pure for the sake of African authenticity. The weight of moral pressure, often backed by law, is exerted on women in order to reverse or hinder possible changes in the power and authority relationships between the sexes.[10]

Women's Efforts at Countering Botswana Government Propaganda

Recognizing the enormous influence of the government over its citizenry, especially in light of the arguments made to disregard the *Dow* decision, feminist activists in Botswana are attempting to counteract the government's message and educate the public about the effects of discriminatory laws on women. Until recently, the women's rights movement in Botswana had been predominantly confined to the capital city of Gaborone within educated circles of enlightened women and men. Advocacy groups have recognized their top-heavy urban, intellectual focus and, through their own institutional growth process, are now responding to the necessity of outreach activities into the rural areas, where the majority of Botswana's population lives.

The Micro Level: Metlhaetsile Women's Information Centre

One such outgrowth of the rural expansion is the Metlhaetsile Women's Information Centre, a grassroots project conceived of and run by women in the village of Mochudi. Located 40 kilometers from the capital city of Gaborone, Mochudi is the capital of the Bakgatla tribe and is a rural community with the majority of its 25,000 people involved in cattle and arable farming scattered throughout small river villages.

At the core of the Metlhaetsile Centre's philosophy is the recognition of the importance of a democratic, participatory approach to women's development and human rights. Included in this philosophy is the necessity of developing a program in light of local custom and tradition with the understanding and support of the average citizen. Hence the center's programming and objectives are generated by women who are in close contact with the intended beneficiaries of the project's services and who can monitor the center's responsiveness to the needs of the community.

The ultimate goal of the center is to empower local women through education to build better lives for themselves by participating more fully in the development process in Botswana. This is being accomplished through ongoing educational workshops in key areas of interest as identified by local women themselves. It is hoped that over time more and more local women will receive training from the center, will go on to become trainers of these workshops, and will take an active role in the center's outreach efforts. The center also provides the first rural-based legal aid service of its kind to poor women who would otherwise have no access to the legal system.

History of the Metlhaetsile Centre

The Metlhaetsile project underwent several stages in its evolution as an education and information center. Rather than impose a prefabricated model of legal aid and legal education borrowed from another program, Metlhaetsile's planners envisioned a careful analysis of the specialized needs and concrete realities of a proposed legal aid and education scheme within the Mochudi context. A nonformal, participatory approach devised by women and integrating the historical, legal, economic, cultural, political, and social aspects of women's lives in Mochudi, and in Botswana, was a prerequisite to success of the proposal.

In March 1991, women students participating in the Mochudi Brigade (a vocational training program), a teacher from the brigade, and a Mochudi-based attorney held a series of impromptu meetings to discuss issues affecting village women's progress. Based on the group's desire for greater input into a potential village-based project, a Motswana researcher then interviewed approximately twenty-five women to determine the main areas of concern for them and to gauge their interest in a local information and education center for women. Major topics identified by the research included the law and how it affects women and their families, employment issues (including sexual harassment), constitutional law, women in politics, and women's health issues (including family planning and AIDS prevention).

Based on the results of their needs assessment, the core working group decided that a series of pilot workshops would be held on certain target issues as specified by the research participants. The group convened a total of fourteen workshops over the following six-month period, involving ten to fifteen women per session. From these workshops and further discussions with local women from various backgrounds, the issues of major concern were further scrutinized and the idea of a village-based women's education and information center evolved.

Center Location and Staffing

The planners believed the location of the center to be crucial to its success and strategically placed the office in the middle of the village, next to the local bank and post office, where it was easily accessible and highly visible to the community. In addition, center personnel are within walking distance to all community offices including the police station, hospital, District Commissioner, Magistrate's Court, and the traditional court. Transport and logistical problems common in a rural village like Mochudi are then minimized. Furthermore, the center has become a part of the village network, and women can be comfortable in knowing there is an alternative avenue for them to utilize if necessary. Thus the mere presence of the center in the village is empowering in itself and sends a message to rural women that their needs are important and will be addressed. Operating with a volunteer staff and board, on November 4, 1991, the Metlhaetsile Centre, opened its doors as the first women's information center in Botswana. Local Batswana women volunteered their time to staff the center, ensuring that it would keep its doors open and enhance visibility of the center's efforts. Once the center had established itself and began providing services to the community, donor agencies supplied additional funding for its expansion.

Eventually, the board hired full-time personnel consisting of a director, social worker, legal aid officer, and an administrator/paralegal. All of the full-time staff members are Botswana women who reside in Mochudi. Each worker has undergone specialized training of trainers courses to complement her respective skills. They deliver workshops and seminars in their fields of emphasis for the benefit of grassroots women and local agencies such as clinics, schools, and civic organizations. In this way, they can broaden their outreach activities by training other community workers and interested individuals to share their learning with village women unable to attend the workshops due to familial, employment, or other responsibilities. Using the "train the trainers" model will assist local women in taking over the responsibility for their own learning and will ensure that as many women as possible have access to the workshops. As a result, a local network of informed women who live throughout the village can be available to offer sensitive and confidential advice to neighbors, friends, and family members.

Support of the Village Chief

Metlhaetsile staff realized that community acceptance of the center was critically important in ensuring its success. With this in mind, the staff sought formal approval from the village chief, Kgosi Linchwe II. When rumors started to spread throughout

the village regarding Metlhaetsile's purpose within the community, the staff held preliminary talks with the chief. He proved to be extremely supportive of the Metlhaetsile
endeavor.

To demonstrate his support for the center, the chief called a *kgotla* meeting to
bring community members together and to introduce Metlhaetsile and its staff.[11] In
early February 1992 the chief held a *kgotla* meeting with more than five hundred villagers in attendance. After a two-hour discussion, the village members voted their
unanimous support of the center. In this way, people became aware of the center's
true purpose while also providing strong public support through the approval of the
chief. The use of traditional methods of communication and dissemination of information within the community facilitated local acceptance of the new institution.

This point cannot be stressed enough. Without the approval of the chief as required by Tswana custom, Metlhaetsile would not have been so readily accepted within
the village and may have been looked upon as a pariah. Without the chief's blessing,
it would have been increasingly difficult to communicate its objectives in providing
legal assistance and education. The use of the *kgotla* also provided village members
with a familiar forum in which to ask questions and hear from the center staff. Moreover, the chief's welcoming of the center as a village institution hastened its credibility
as an acceptable avenue for the resolution of issues.

Center Activities

With the acceptance of the community, Metlhaetsile's staff diligently began working
toward establishing a resource, counseling, and advice center, conducting workshops
and publishing educational materials with the purpose of introducing gender inequality into the country's consciousness. The Resource Centre has been established
and is open to the public. The center's collection of books, magazines, newspaper
articles, and other women's material continues to grow and expand.

In addition to written materials, the center also shows videos on a monthly basis.
Video topics have varied from women's rights, AIDS, child bearing and rearing to
rape and wife battering. Demand has been so overwhelming that the center has been
forced to limit the audience to women and girls. Also, the staff has found that an
all-female group tends to create a more comfortable and uninhibited environment in
which women can share their opinions in discussion groups held after the video presentation.

The family counseling and legal advice components are also rapidly growing.
The counseling services have successfully extended beyond the individual women to
counsel the family as a whole. The family is considered so integral to the resolution
of problems within Tswana society that the center staff urge clients to bring family
members to the counseling sessions. In fact, in most divorce cases, Metlhaetsile staff
will not initiate proceedings unless the family is involved in consultations. The staff
realizes that their client ultimately must return to her village surroundings where she

will need the support of family members throughout her life. By encouraging women to rely on family involvement in solving difficult issues, the staff can avoid alienating family members who traditionally would be involved in such negotiations.

The unit assists an average of seven new clients a day and provides a wide range of services from staff members acting as "escort" officers for women too intimidated by local courts to seek maintenance to staff members acting as legal counsel in cases appearing before the High Court. The vast majority of cases relate to child maintenance, violence against women, and unfair employment dismissal.

Both the counseling and legal aid staff have been instrumental in providing options for women to solve their grievances, using the legal system as a last resort. Women know they can rely on the center as an avenue to assist them in problem solving without resort to a complex and impersonal court system. In turn, resolution of legal problems outside the courtroom lessens the burden on the justice system and fills the void where traditional structures previously existed and may not be functioning properly.

Workshops and Public Meetings

Educational workshops and a series of local public meetings have also been conducted. Workshop topics have included women and the law, women and politics, and women and health. These forums are very popular and an effective means for disseminating information. Additionally, they provide a unique opportunity for women to discuss their problems in an innocuous environment. The public meetings, on the other hand, concentrate on informing the public about the activities of the center. This is an intrinsic element of the center's success since it continues to strengthen the community's bond with the center.

The goal of producing educational materials is also coming to fruition. Although the center has only been in operation for a short time, it is currently working on creating a manual on the UN Convention on the Elimination of All Forms of Discrimination Against Women (CEDAW) for use in developing human rights training programs. A brochure, published in both Setswana and English, describing the center and its activities is also approaching completion and will be widely distributed.

Collaboration with Other Women's Organizations

As the center strives to bring issues of gender inequality into the mainstream, it has recognized the benefit and necessity of working in association with other local, national, and international nongovernmental organizations (NGOs) with similar goals. The center is a member of the Botswana Women's NGO Network as well as the NGO Forum, which was the planning body for Botswana's participation in the 1995 Women's World Conference in Beijing.

The center is nurturing its relationships with Botswana women's groups through several activities. First, the center has held several consultative seminars to introduce it to possible partners and confer on ways in which the organizations can be most effective. Additionally, the center's staff function as a resource at workshops hosted by other NGOs. These staff members also participate in training workshops for their own development.

Second, the center is actively supporting the creation of local NGOs working toward equal rights for women focused in rural areas. Metlhaetsile has been indispensable in assisting with the requisite legal formalities for formation of these entities and continues to support their growth. Third, the center has organized public meetings to celebrate women's development issues. Last March the center organized a public meeting to celebrate International Women's Day in Mochudi. The occasion attracted more than 800 women and men from Mochudi as well as other villages in Botswana. One purpose of the celebration was to familiarize the public with the center and focus public attention on women's issues. Educational activities at the celebration included a poetry and art competition held at the local secondary schools, dramatic presentations on women's themes, and songs and dances performed by primary school children and women's groups. The center staff and village members concluded that the celebration was a great success, and plans are in place to hold similar annual events.

In addition, future community meetings will focus on engaging the government in dialogue addressing women's equality. This dialogue should also strengthen links with national NGOs and ultimately intensify women's lobbying power to pressure for change in gender bias laws. Metlhaetsile's experience has forced the staff to recognize that, without unifying the community and national and international NGOs, it cannot alone persuade the government even to reflect on its gender bias laws. A concerted effort from all levels, therefore, must be harnessed to achieve reform.

The center has adopted the following activities for this purpose:

1. The publication of the official documents from the *Attorney General v. Dow* judgment. The center's position is that it is up to women to acknowledge the *Dow* judgment as a turning point in Botswana women's legal history.
2. Mobilizing the enforcement of the *Dow* judgment. On International Women's Day of 1994, a number of Batswana women came together to file passport applications for their children affected by the *Dow* ruling. To this day, the government has refused to issue the passports. The center is planning a direct challenge to the government's refusal through a mandamus action to enforce the Court of Appeals decision. The center believes that unless women stand up to claim their rights, even gains that they have made will become meaningless.
3. Researching on the extent of the citizenship problems and how women's lives are affected in Botswana border villages. Indications are that the situation is much more serious than the general public seems to think and that the problem is by no means limited to the urban areas.
4. Lobbying and mobilizing for the ratification of the Women's Convention. Cen-

ter staff feel that very little work has been done in this area and that the political climate may be right for lobbying ratification.

Metlhaetsile Assessment

Working for change always attracts both negative and positive reactions. The efforts of Metlhaetsile have been welcomed by many women and viewed with mistrust by some men (and some women). Generally the center is viewed as an effective village-based strategy to address complex and frustrating dilemmas for many women and their families. While ideal solutions are not always readily available, the center provides women with options to which they otherwise would not have been exposed. Women are encouraged to decide for themselves which choice is best for them and to be actively involved in carrying out their decision. By developing the confidence and problem-solving abilities of the women it serves, Metlhaetsile paves the way for sustainable and positive change that can benefit the entire community.

Conclusion

There is a great need for more programs of the type modeled by the Metlhaetsile Centre. The center, however, should not be duplicated in other areas without adequately evaluating the needs and expectations of the community within which it will be placed. The necessity to evaluate such an endeavor properly cannot be stressed enough. While the Metlhaetsile Centre can serve as an example for groups attempting to develop a similar project, the realities and individualized needs of a particular culture and society must be considered. Donor-driven philosophies of mass-marketed quick solutions to the issue of women's access to development are unworkable and unprofitable. That is where the Metlhaetsile Centre can provide the most illumination—the need to work with local structures and institutions, but most of all with the intended beneficiaries of the project through their own worldview.

Postscript

In August 1995 the Botswana Parliament enacted legislation, compatible with the *Dow* decision, that provides for the conferral of citizenship in a gender neutral manner. This legislative initiative represents an unprecedented victory for the women's movement in Botswana and paves the way for reform of all gender discriminatory laws presently on the books in the country. The unrelenting determination of women activists to create avenues for social change in Botswana supplies a remarkable example of nonformal human rights education in the "learn by doing" mode and serves as a model for advocacy efforts in countries around the world attempting to achieve gender equality in law and practice.

Notes

1. *Metlhaetsile* is the Setswana word for "the time has come."

2. Davidson Nicol and Margaret Croke, eds., *United Nations and Decisionmaking: The Role of Women*, Conference Proceedings of United Nations Institute for Training and Research (UNITAR) Colloquium on Women and Decisionmaking in the United Nations, 1977 (New York: UNITAR, 1978), xiii.

3. Diane Bell, "Considering Gender: Are Human Rights for Women too? An Australian Case," in *Human Rights in Cross-Cultural Perspectives: A Quest for Consensus*, ed. Abdullahi Ahmed An-Na'im (Philadelphia: University of Pennsylvania Press, 1992), 346.

4. Christine Obbo, *African Women: Their Struggle for Economic Independence* (London: Zed Press, 1980), 144.

5. *Tswana* is the root form for this ethnic group. *Batswana* is the plural for a person from Botswana, and *Motswana* is the singular version. Setswana is the language spoken by the Tswana people.

6. *In re Attorney General v. Dow*, Court of Appeals No. 4/91 (Ct. App. 1992) (Bots.) (3–2 decision). Specifically, the Botswana Court of Appeals upheld a High Court opinion which found certain provisions of a gender discriminatory citizenship act unconstitutional. The 1984 Citizenship Act provided that male Botswana citizens who married noncitizens would automatically pass Botswana citizenship to their children and allow for naturalization of their wives. Female Botswana citizens who married noncitizens were prohibited from passing citizenship to their children or naturalization privileges to their spouses. See *In the Matter Between Unity Dow vs. Attorney General*, In the High Court of Botswana Held at Lobatse, Misca. 124/80, June 1991, pp. 22–23.

7. Yash Ghai, "The Role of Law in the Transition of Societies: The African Experience," *Journal of African Law* 35, nos. 1–2 (1991): 8, 13.

8. Peter Slinn, "A Fresh Start for Africa? New African Constitutional Perspectives for the 1990s," *Journal of African Law* 35, nos. 1–2 (1991): 1, 5.

9. Chandra Talpade Mohandy, Ann Russo, and Lourdes Torres, eds., *Third World Women and the Politics of Feminism* (Bloomington: Indiana University Press, 1991).

10. Obbo, *African Women*, 15.

11. *Kgotla* is the Setswana word for the community court, which also serves as a gathering place for the dissemination of information to members of the tribe.

Chapter 28
Problems in Planning Human Rights Education for Reemerging Latin American Democracies

Abraham K. Magendzo

In the reemerging democracies of Latin America, many tensions and problems are felt among those who are engaged in the important tasks of planning human rights education (HRE). This chapter discusses the most prominent such challenges found in the relationship between education and human rights, particularly in the postdictatorial countries of Latin America. Problems with human rights education are many and varied. Whether those problems arise in human rights theory, pedagogy, or the organization of human rights institutions, solutions must be developed and applied.

The value and significance of human rights education is enormous for countries trying to outgrow an authoritarian past. Human rights education is important because it can penetrate and affect three sensitive levels of society.[1] On a values level, human rights orient the axiological conscience of a people. On the political level, human rights defend the interests of the disadvantaged within society. Finally, human rights become an ideological-cultural spark that empowers people.[2] Such empowerment leads to greater democracy and concrete actions, resulting in greater opportunities for those empowered individuals and society at large. In short, it is potentially very important but not always recognized as such in the process of implementation.[3]

A simple anecdote illustrates one of the many problems faced in the implementation of HRE. The Chilean (governmental) Center for Training, Experimentation, and Pedagogical Research asked our private institute, PIIE (Programa Interdisciplinario de Investigaciones en Educación [Program for Interdisciplinary Research on Education]), to discuss human rights issues with the supervisors of the Chilean educational system. We were allotted a single morning to approach the topic, a short time indeed. When asked what the day's agenda would be, we were told that work on the topics of gender and environment was to be done as well as human rights. We were surprised to find these topics dealt with separately and independently from one another.

In countries such as Chile, Argentina, Paraguay, and Brazil, there is widespread discussion about how to overcome the vestiges of dictatorial rule and move toward democracy with a human rights culture. Conversations and debates on such topics are widespread. I will make it my task to report on some of these conversations and debates, supplying my own perspectives as well. For example, a typically wide-ranging debate reflects a tendency in Latin America to deal with topics such as women's issues, environment, ethnic minorities, and others separately. Such boundary lines oversimplify real problems. At PIIE, we believe that all of these topics find a framework for action through human rights. Why, then, should they not be dealt with together under the rubric of human rights?

Some argue that human rights education advocates attempt too much; they try to cover everything and lose salience in the process because the standards of human rights are too general and comprise a movement with no domain of its own but with a tendency to invade the domain of other topics. To me, such thinking is wrongheaded. It simply fails to understand fully one of the axioms of human rights analysis, that the very meaning of human rights, indeed the strength of the human rights movement, is based on the interdependent relationships among all types of discrimination, other violations of human dignity, and ultimately the consequences of such abuses in the form of threats to peace and justice.[4]

Based on my experience with PIIE in Chile and with the Interamerican Institute of Human Rights in Costa Rica, I have gained some perspective on several problems in the field of education in human rights with special attention to Latin America. Specifically, I will try here to illuminate four key problems with human rights education as I have encountered them in debates and implementation planning sessions with others. These problems, which are especially sensitive in Latin America, are fraught with tension because of our historical and authoritarian past and repeatedly impinge on discussion of plans for implementing initiatives in human rights education. They can be grouped into four areas: (1) conceptual problems, (2) problems relating to participants in the debate and the persons affected, (3) problems of pedagogy and course content, and (4) muted or silenced problems—those topics about which there is almost no public debate due to their highly political nature. Of course, this is not meant to be an exhaustive grouping.

Conceptual Problems

The fundamental challenge in planning HRE in emerging democracies is also elementary; it is the problem of defining human rights. The goal of human rights is to build a world respectful of human dignity. The integral conception of human rights focuses on the importance of civil and political rights, but at the same time demands respect for economic, social, and cultural rights; moreover, it supports the consolidation of the people's rights.

While this problem may be stated as if it were elementary and therefore simple, the need arises in grappling with it to create a paradigm of rationality different from the instrumental rationality common to conventional education, and by contrast to traditional methods, to unveil the contradictions underlying the latter. This approach to the definition of human rights and HRE implies giving up models of a dichotomous, Cartesian, absolutist, universalist character. It favors an integrating, experiential, and organizing kind of learning where there is interaction between subjective and objective views, between order and disorder, and where there is room for particular and universal, social and individual, rational and irrational ideas.[5]

A fundamental problem arises when attempting to determine the issues that should be discussed in teaching human rights. For some, education in human rights should include topics such as education and gender, education for peace and nonviolence, education and native populations, education and racism, education and multicultural societies, education and environment, and so on. Others, however, restrict the area of education in human rights to its normative, historical, and value aspects, and state that the topics mentioned above should not be directly included in the concept of education in human rights. The second approach restricts education in human rights as a discipline with its own substance and thereby denies HRE its quality of education for change at odds with the status quo.

As Latin American democracies embark upon policies of industrial privatization and governmental decentralization, another problem involving HRE arises, having to do with the respective roles that governments and nongovernmental organizations (NGOs) are playing and should be playing in HRE. Modern states have restricted themselves to a facilitating, regulating, and subsidiary role. In this spirit, any given governments may eschew responsibility for HRE, decentralizing its role (and therefore responsibility) in HRE, making room for intermediary institutions. All this seems consistent with allowing market laws to prevail together with privatization and the reduction of the state. But under these circumstances, a natural concern arises about who is responsible for the ethical orientation of society as a whole. On certain occasions and for political reasons or compromises in the search for consensus, the state lets the NGOs take the initiative. NGOs must then jump financial and resource hurdles to develop HRE programs with an experiential nature. These programs invariably do not reach the whole of the population as the education in human rights demands.

In the context of some emerging democracies, especially those with histories marred by coups d'état and where fear of the military remains palpable, where violence and human rights violations are a constitutive part of culture, the question is whether HRE is possible at all. The most pessimistic will say that it is simply impossible to educate people about human rights in a reality saturated with inherent contradictions and tensions. Others, I think with better authority, believe that it is precisely among contradictions and tensions of societies beset by such fear and concerns where the best programs for HRE can be developed. For example, in Paraguay, with no prior twentieth-century experience with democracy, human rights education is now being undertaken seriously in the schools.

Of course, where fear prevails, prudence is important. During one of our summer courses on human rights education, a teacher asked vehemently, "Why did the Chilean Ministry for Education and the media not start a quick and comprehensive campaign to educate people in human rights?" He asked with a tone of urgency: "why, after a democratic regime came into power, did we proceed so slowly?" Indeed, HRE has gone very slowly in Chile and in too many other reemerging Latin American democracies. If we take human rights education seriously, we must understand that such education bears mostly long-term fruits, but this is no excuse for delay. We must begin promptly lest a whole generation be passed over while we wait. Who will be held responsible for such a delay?

Some believe moderation will prevail and there is no need to hurry. My own view, growing out of experience in Chile and Costa Rica, is that while impatience is understandable and often justified, those of us concerned with program implementation must also recognize that educational planning is very sensitive and, whether we like it or not, change generally comes slowly. Ideological struggles within education have occasionally led to intense social explosions, especially when such struggle is politically divisive. Thus the pace of HRE must be gradual.

Some argue, I think incorrectly, that human rights education is politically destructive. Afraid of the repercussions of using the term *human rights*, they say that we have to talk of education for love, peace, for peaceful coexistence. These people hold that, by all means, we should avoid any language that may introduce conflicts, contradictions, tensions, and disagreements in education. Education, they say, should offer a consensual, objective, neutral, and dispassionate kind of language. In planning for HRE, we must stand up to this view, knowing that all education is value-laden and not value-neutral. Therefore, the term *human rights* along with its value system must be incorporated into education, lest we teach something other than human rights.

When debate along these lines descends from the level of philosophical abstraction to the concrete, I often hear teachers acknowledge that, without any doubt, the topic of human rights must be dealt with in school. But there is no need to refer to recent times because "this can be interpreted as politics." The relationship between politics (a term in many Latin American countries often discouraged, if not prohibited, in education) and human rights is seen as problematic. A teacher says "every time I mention human rights, administrators and even parents sometimes tell me I am introducing politics in school. They tell me the school is not ready for this yet." In such revelations and discussions, deeply rooted fears come to the surface. Those of us who advocate HRE are then led to wonder whether it is possible to educate at all while denying our own history. How will a whole generation of teachers be judged who were not able to face their own truth, however difficult, dramatic, and contradictory this may have been? We must face up to our history, and as educators we must face up to this issue, as we engage in human rights education planning.

Another strong and structurally rooted tension arises in the implementation of

Figure 28.1. In September 1984, Chilean police employed excessive force against demonstrators in the Plaza of the Americas. Article 20 of the Universal Declaration of Human Rights proclaims that: "Everyone has the right to peaceful freedom of assembly and association." In the reemerging democracies of the Southern Cone countries of Latin America, human rights education must take the history of political repression into account. (Science and Human Rights Program of the American Association for the Advancement of Science)

HRE. The tension derives from change-averse educational institutions. Experience has shown that the introduction of human rights into education brings a critical and questioning attitude that traditionalists, conservatives, and others with a stake in the old system will attempt to reject.

Strategies of radical and quick implementation of HRE usually arouse defense mechanisms either openly or concealed. People feel insecure and disturbed. Negotiation is necessary between guardians of the status quo and those who promote change, between tradition and innovation. If human rights are likely to question everything, complete rejection is risked.

The tension between reformers and traditionalists may be exacerbated by human rights idealism. To suggestions of gradual implementation of HRE and gradual change, the human rights idealist demands: "Can human rights really be negotiated? Doesn't compromise undermine progress? What is the point of an education in human rights that simply serves the status quo?" In my judgment, at least at the initial stage of program implementation, negotiators should be willing to say, "let us make room for human rights in the open curriculum." With that important initial victory, we will have time enough to make further progress. In short, the process of beginning HRE is partly a political process. These questions and tensions must play themselves out in any attempt to implement HRE.

The Participants

One of the central problems with the implementation of widespread HRE is the training of human rights educators. Who should assume responsibility for this training? The government will usually default on this task, leaving it to the NGOs. The NGOs are unable to train thousands of teachers, due to lack of resources. Furthermore, there are only a few teacher-training institutions in Latin America which have introduced human rights training into their curricula. Problems arise as to the scope of HRE programs, for example, where they should take place. Some believe HRE should be present at all levels of education, both formal and nonformal.[6] The belief is that HRE must be incorporated into adult education, into literacy programs and more informal educational programs, as well as into the formal structures of primary school through university study. Whatever the level of governmental activity on behalf of HRE, NGOs should not hesitate to undertake responsibility for such education. For human rights groups to be ahead of the state in such matters may serve a pathbreaking function in planning activities and may generate pressure for governmental responsibility.

In arguing for NGO activity in the area of human rights education, I have learned that an important problem must be faced: defining the prerequisites for human rights educators, determining the level of knowledge, skills, attitudes, and values those educators must have. Education in human rights can neither be the exclusive responsibility of professional educators, nor can it be left in the hands of activists or professionals alone who, out of sheer engagement or spontaneous enthusiasm, set themselves to teaching without any kind of pedagogical training.

There is agreement that some kind of specialization is needed, together with the acquisition of certain skills. Most problems deal with the definition of these skills. Some say that the training of educators in human rights should concentrate mainly on the knowledge of normative and legal instruments, whereas others think that the topic of values and attitudes is more relevant. There are, of course, still others who believe in a kind of integral training.

The problem of defining who is an educator in human rights, and which skills he or she must have, leads to questions about ways of training these educators. There are different perspectives and positions in this respect, especially because it is not possible to consider only one kind of generic educator. It is certainly different to train an educator in human rights who works in formal education from one who works with people in a nonformal situation, or one who carries out his or her educational activities in a primary school from one who works at a university. Differentiation must occur even at the highest levels; HRE at a law school will be different from that at a medical school.

Despite differences in approach to HRE, common ground remains. General principles and tendencies regarding methods of training educators in human rights have surfaced. Holistic, integral approaches that are experiential and concerned with personal development, and approaches that foster participation are more popular, and in my view, more promising than the more academic approaches.

Recently, in Chile, HRE has been implemented through popular education, including nonformal education associated with social movements. Indeed, since popular education is defined as an educational model that attempts to break with vertical, authoritarian models and to offer an alternative relationship between education and society, HRE becomes the articulating paradigm of such popular education. It is within this level of popular education where the most intense and meaningful HRE has taken place, since it is precisely the social groups involved who suffer the most dramatic violations of their human rights.

Even as popular education makes progress, those of us involved in HRE planning and research remain worried about the topic of education and human rights and whether its implementation is being undertaken with efficiency, seriousness, and depth. Because HRE is seen by some as controversial, and because its implementation involves a huge and all-embracing task, the need has arisen to legitimize the teaching and knowledge of human rights. Accordingly, teachers must be properly trained, materials must be adequate, and proper research should guarantee the pedagogical tasks. But the fact is that teachers in Latin America are not properly trained, materials have not been prepared, and research is scarce. The InterAmerican Institute for Human Rights has tried to rise to this challenge, for example, by preparing teachers' guides for human rights curriculum development.

Human Rights Education Among NGOs in Argentina
by E. Débora Benchoam and George C. Rogers

In 1983 Argentina returned to democracy after fifty years of alternating civilian and military government and seven brutally repressive years of military government beginning in 1976. Now Argentina confronts a complex dilemma: how to install a democratic human rights-based value system within a culture impregnated with authoritarian values, paternalistic relationships, and dismantled citizen participation. For years, generalized repression, or fear of it, cast a pall of silence over the discussion of issues of daily life among students, workers, political groups, and others. Still lingering in people's memory is the authoritarian model of education distorted by political indoctrination rather than knowledge or critical thinking skills. With human rights guarantees constituting only a very thin legal layer of protection today, education is the principal and most efficient means by which people can form ethical values protective of their human rights.

The protection of human rights cannot be constructed on the basis of simply teaching a list of human rights values. Required is a multifaceted approach that is predominantly experiential. It is necessary to build an awareness of basic rights as well as appreciation for the effects of their violations on individuals and on society. To this end, various public and private organizations in Argentina have engaged in formal and nonformal educational programs to broaden the understanding of human rights standards, to analyze their applications in particular situations, and to promote sustainable respect for basic human rights.

The Ecumenical Movement for Human Rights (MEDH), a religious-based umbrella organization, has supported one of the largest and most diverse human rights education programs in the country, generally focused on formal public education, particularly at the primary school level. MEDH's objective is to instill habits of reflection and analysis in young people so as to nurture their potential as active agents of change and to increase national consciousness. In 1989 the group produced a handbook for primary school teachers entitled *Aprender con los chicos: Propuesta para una tarea docente fundada en los derechos humanos,* by Daniel Lopez, Rosa Klainer, and Virginia Piera. Coordinating with the teachers union, MEDH conducts ongoing workshops for teachers in outlying provinces, and since 1993 has sponsored a correspondence course on education and human rights for teachers where workshops are not feasible.

In two provinces, the projects noted above are supplemented by a participatory program in which more than a hundred school directors attend programs to support initiatives in human rights education. In the Province of Santa Fe, high school students also hold an annual "Children's Right to be

Heard Congress" to experience working in democratic institutions. The congress is composed of one elected participant from each public school in the province charged with presenting her or his views at the different sessions.

The Center for Legal and Social Studies (CELS) maintains an important popular legal assistance program in three poor neighborhoods in the capital district of Buenos Aires. The goal is to stimulate alternative conflict resolution mechanisms primarily using mediation and conciliation techniques.

Headed by Nobel Laureate Adolfo Pérez Esquivel, the Peace and Justice Service (SERPAJ) has tried to promote grassroots consciousness raising focused on human rights and moral responsibility. These programs are carried out in different regions of Argentina among poorer neighborhoods or "Christian base communities," and they focus on daily problems such as police violence, unemployment, land rights, and health care. The working methodology used by SERPAJ is to develop and train representatives who are among the natural leaders of the neighborhoods in which they work and participate, empowering them to become capable representatives of their communities. Such activities, when well implemented, may generate new leaders, promote patterns of cooperation, and enhance the functioning of democracy. SERPAJ has also successfully raised interest in human rights among university students by bringing them together from different provinces in Argentina for seminars to discuss basic rights problems affecting their respective communities.

Citizens' Power (Poder Ciudadano) seeks to empower citizens to be active participants in democratic government through a number of programs that aim at controlling or putting an end to corruption. For example, "Reflection Groups" of about five people involved in cooperative learning have been used to discuss issues of governmental corruption, brainstorming to define corruption, examine its causes and the persons whom it benefits and harms, and to design strategies for citizens' action to combat corruption. In addition, the group tries to build respect for an independent and properly functioning judiciary and to promote understanding of how to participate in government policymaking. These and other group learning devices are useful in building a long-term, broad-based consciousness of what constitutes ethical conduct among public officials, what the limits of government action ought to be, as well as the rights and responsibilities of the individual.

The Human Rights Subsecretariat (a department of the Ministry of the Interior) has adopted programs directed at broadening the base of persons informed about human rights values and their place in modern Argentina. One of their central programs informs government officials of the basic rights of all persons and the channels through which complaints about violations should proceed. Because of the historical involvement by security forces in gross violations of human rights during the repressive military rule, this program aims to reach the police and prison systems, judges and judicial clerks, prosecutors, officials from the Ministries of Justice and the Interior, and other public officials. For its teaching and leadership staff, the program draws upon academics, lawyers, and human rights professionals as well as experts from the United Nations, local NGOs, and officials within the Argentine Foreign Ministry. While this government program reflects new and welcome commitments, the human rights education program of the Subsecretariat is limited by the assumption that expounding on the existence of international human rights norms will automatically produce behavioral results.

Human rights education programs in Argentina are quite diverse. Some are more effective than others, and the most effective recognize that the reconstruction of Argentina's ethical and democratic values will not develop fully if it is focused only on formal education and cognitive abilities. What we need is a combination of programs promoting cognitive abilities and empowering people with critical skills, new attitudes, and behaviors as well as a combination of formal human rights education and nonformal educational strategies. Such efforts are critical to the effective restoration of a pluralistic, society-based respect for human rights and to the successful reweaving of the foundational components of the country's damaged social fabric.

Materials must be prepared for all ages and contexts, research must be undertaken, and the task must be accomplished with optimal quality. If this is done, HRE will gain credibility and legitimacy. But to achieve this end, more is needed. I am convinced that HRE must gain the attention of the media in order to be totally successful. Versatile public service media-based teaching methodologies, with great appeal and scope, must contribute to informal human rights education and must predominate in order to convey the message and knowledge of human rights. At the same time, such knowledge should not be commercialized or in any way trivialized by the media.

Although the mass media are a powerful tool capable of reaching almost everyone, a complete human rights education requires a real, not simply a technologically devised, social setting. It requires the group, the clash of ideas, the collective life experience rather than only the electronic one. Nevertheless, we must reach as many as possible, and as such there is a dilemma to be grappled with in disseminating the knowledge of human rights.

Contents

Questions regarding the selection of the proper curriculum, or contents and objectives to be reached within the teaching of human rights, are many. A distinction has been made between the open and the hidden curriculum. The former refers to the kind of knowledge, skills, values, and attitudes that students should develop and internalize in an intentional and deliberate manner. The hidden curriculum refers to the learning produced as a result of the interaction with the daily culture of the educational institution and its disciplinary rules, organization, and routine. In both learning environments there are implicit messages related to human rights.

Some support the position that human rights should be included directly as a differentiated teaching subject. Others consider it essential to found school curricula as a whole upon the ethical principles of human rights.

Another position, though a minority point of view, favors stress on the hidden curriculum against the inclusion of the topic of human rights in the open curriculum, making a point of the danger of institutionalizing the topic. Similarly, some stress the decisive importance of interpersonal relations and personal development for any serious program of human rights education, although they do not reject the inclusion of this topic in the open curriculum.

Recognizing that many school curricula are insufficient or faulty when it comes to human rights, I believe, nevertheless, that what is needed to give validity to the content of HRE is a full immersion in human rights. Under such circumstances, human rights are felt everywhere, experienced in all subjects, both inside and outside the classroom. Human rights must become both a formal subject within the school curriculum and an educational experience without formality. Let me explain in terms of a few distinctive issues.

Teaching Methodologies

A pedagogical process that includes HRE will have a characteristic integrating approach. This means that human rights education permeates the entire educational experience. In this manner, human rights become integrated within the process of development of intellectual skills. This should be done through a learning dynamic between teacher and student that is experiential in nature.

Here is an extended example based on several elements: (1) a problematic situation, (2) the specification of the human rights involved, and (3) a classroom activity to prompt reflection. Consider this situation. In many Latin American countries, it is common for poor families living in the country to send their children to live with relatives in the city so they can study. In these homes, they have many jobs as well as going to school. But domestic tasks and school are often competing responsibilities. Applicable here are rights of children to free and compulsory primary education as well as the right not to be permitted to work in ways that will harm their health or education. Thus children might potentially seek their right to education by exposing themselves to maltreatment. Based on this not uncommon situation, the teacher might organize an exercise for students to deepen their understanding by putting themselves in the place of others. As an activity, the teacher tells students this story.

Ana came from the country to live with her uncle and his family in Asunción. Ana helps her uncle by doing housework, and he sends her to school. Sometimes her uncle treats her badly and, in addition, she is not paid. He only gives her a room, food, and old clothes that belong to her cousin; sometimes the family even treats her in a demeaning way which they do not even do with their domestic help. Ana doesn't really know who she is: a relative or a hired worker. Perhaps even her uncle doesn't know.

The teacher then forms groups to act out the narrated situation, the objective being for students to put themselves in the other's position. For this it is necessary to describe in detail each of the characters: Ana, the aunt, uncle, the household employee, a cousin, and Ana's mother and father in the rural area. After the presentations, new groups are formed so that students play different roles. This can be followed by discussion about such questions as: How did you feel in playing a given role? Why does the character act as he or she does? How could the situation be changed?[7]

Using teaching techniques of this sort, special emphasis is placed on the experiential dimensions and the integrating approaches inherent within HRE. Reality must be the main reference of any system of HRE. The students' real-life situations, the environment they live in, should be the reference point for human rights discussions. A related goal of the implementation of HRE and a by-product thereof should be personal development. A methodology of HRE which has a two-pronged strategy of human rights education and personal development will be the most successful.

When this HRE implementation strategy is adopted, an atmosphere of democratic cohabitation both within and outside the classroom should develop. The democratization of school activities should be sought to foster this goal. A methodology of participation makes the joint solution of problems possible. It motivates the members of a community to self-management of their own development, and for many it allows self-identification with the group. Consequently, participation in HRE becomes a socializing process that will sow the seeds for a human rights culture.

Any HRE implementation strategy, however, will have to find its way into the curriculum first to be effective. Thus the salient question again becomes: How is the knowledge of human rights legitimized as a teaching subject, and who will accomplish this goal? The answer to this question entails the method of teaching, broadly conceived.

I believe that parents, teachers, professionals, and others should bear the burden of teaching human rights and in that respect of participating in the legitimization of human rights education. In other words, the human rights movement and everyone involved in it should help to legitimize the teaching of human rights. The legitimizing of the human rights movement is a process of valuation, persuasion, dialogue, and understanding the role education should play in the task of forming generations respectful of human rights.

The problem in legitimizing HRE is one of demonstrating the value of human rights education. Sciences are valued because of the palpable benefits they bring to society in technology and enhanced knowledge of our surroundings. How does human rights fit into the cost-benefit analysis society will make?

The methodology of human rights education must incorporate techniques for understanding and responding to social tensions. Comprehending human rights comes with the realization of the contradictions present within a society where silence exists regarding human rights issues and yet human rights violations beg for attention. To understand these contradictions within a society, to understand the underlying ideology of these contradictions, and to offer possible solutions thereto are all central tasks to be put forward by HRE.

Preventing students from facing these contradictions and other problematic situations has been a typical feature of traditionally based Latin American education. There has been an attempt, either implicitly or explicitly, to keep students from facing these problems. Hence an aseptic, innocuous, or "neutral" ambience is fostered.

Society is constantly faced with continuing human rights issues. The political process or the courts must decide whether freedom of expression or national security shall prevail. The public interest must be weighed against the private. Even mature democratic societies—especially mature democratic societies—maintain a continuing debate on human rights issues.

Despite this fertile dynamic within society, human rights dialogue has customarily been kept out of the schools because of the tension with the traditional school curriculum. The lack of curricular momentum due to a mind-set in the service of the status quo and conventional thinking within the administrative bureaucracy forms an obstacle to human rights educators. Supported by an empirical-objective world, the curriculum tacitly denies the evident conflict between the normative and the intellectual. In his book, *Ideology and Curriculum*, Michael Apple points out that instead of regarding conflict and contradiction as the basic "driving forces" of society, the elementary assumption too often prevails that conflict between groups of people is fundamentally and essentially wrong, and as such should not be taught.[8] We must recognize that when the knowledge of human rights in introduced into the school curriculum, it will inevitably provoke tensions. Only as long as we are aware of this fact shall we be able to offer solutions and approach the difficulties with objectivity and without personal prejudices. To adopt a naive attitude and think that introducing human rights into the curriculum is similar to incorporating a new theorem, a new chapter in history, means not to know the real nature of human rights. Those who wish to ignore the tensional character of this topic say: "Well, after all, in education we have always taught human rights, we have always worked for them." This is a very explicit and evasive expression of "no tension tension."

While keeping our eye on our educational objectives, which are challenging and transformative, we must also attend to details. For example, we must prepare educational materials that do not ignore the human rights dynamics played out within society. Many questions regarding materials are basic. Should they be given to educators or students? Should textbooks or audiovisual materials be used? Is more methodology and pedagogy needed, or is historical and legal material more necessary? Finally, should the production and diffusion of materials be in the hands of NGOs or the state?

A review of the currently available materials shows that they are rather scarce and oriented to educators more than students. Materials often include group activities and creative games that approach the topic in a lively fashion, with participants taking an active role. NGOs have clearly taken the lead in the production and dissemination of the existing materials. These materials need careful evaluation.

Determining whether HRE is effective may be gleaned from the evaluation of specific teaching programs and the materials used. There is general agreement that evaluation is essential for the process of teaching human rights to grow deep roots. However, such evaluation should not be performed with conventional tools such as examinations. Instead, class discussions, student behavior, and written assignments should be evaluated.

If we take the challenges of HRE seriously, we must evaluate our innovative teaching methodologies. Evaluation must raise critical questions about what our programs are and are not doing, and in this respect we should especially concern ourselves about what is not being done and what is not being said.

Silenced or Muted Problems

My experience has been that within the general population, and among the citizenry of most Latin American and many Caribbean countries, there is a startling lack of dialogue about human rights topics.[9] Certainly such a lack prevails on such important topics as military and police impunity in postdictatorial countries; amnesty policies for public officials and enforcement authorities in countries such as Uruguay, Paraguay, and El Salvador; the "end of discussion policy" in Chile; and the historical record of past human rights violations and lack of compensation to victims throughout much of the Central and South American republics. I have noticed a collective self-censorship, a kind of "forget it" attitude. These topics are definitely not discussed in school.

What is not noticed is that this attitude of omission, censorship, and avoidance reflects a very penetrating and formative implicit educational message. The situation faced will become more critical since future generations will blame us for our compliance, our silence, and our fear of the history that shapes our culture.

We are not talking sufficiently about the seemingly taboo subjects that are so characteristic of democracies emerging from dictatorships—impunity and responsibility. Thus we have a responsibility to answer the question, "what must we say?" We are obliged to say that past human rights violations must be discussed. We must talk about the current political questions regarding human rights in an open fashion. Silence in this respect will only encourage a repeat performance of the heinous crimes perpetrated against humanity. Silence means no accountability. Lack of accountability breeds arrogance and defiance. Silence equals acceptance.

Notes

1. Jorge Osorio, "La educación en derechos humanos: Propuesta de proyeccion programatica," Documento de Trabajo, Concertación de Partidos por la Democracia (Santiago: Comision de Justicia y Derechos Humanos, 1989).

2. Gonzalo Elizondo, "Educación en derechos humanos," *El Proyecto de Educación del IIDH* (San José, Costa Rica: Instituto Interamericano de Derechos Humanos [IIDH], 1989).

3. Migual Soler, "Derechos humanos y educación," *Cuadernos de pedagogia* 164 (Barcelona: Editorial Fontalaba, 1988).

4. Esther Zavaleta, *Aportes para una pedagogia de la paz* (Santiago: UNESCO, 1986).

5. Pablo Salvat, "Hacia una nueva Racionalidad: La latea de construir un paradigma basado en los derechos humanos," in Abraham K. Magendzo, ed., *Superando la racionalidad instrumental* (Santiago: Programa Interdisciplinario de Investigaciones en Educación [PIIE], 1991).

6. Ibid.

7. This exercise is presented in more detail as "Un Ejemplo," in Abraham K. Magendzo, Mirtha N. Abraham, and Claudia S. Dueñas, *Manual para profesores, Curriculum y derechos humanos* (Santiago: IIDH, 1993), 82–84.

8. Michael Apple, *Ideología y curriculum* (Madrid: Akal, 1986).

9. CEALL (Latin American Adult Education Commission), *Crisis y desarrollo: Presente y futuro de America Latina y el Caribe* (Santiago: CEALL, 1985).

Chapter 29
Implementing Human Rights Education in Three Transitional Democracies: Romania, Slovakia, and Albania

Ligia Neacsu-Hendry, Ivan Turek, Jana Kviečinska, Kozara Kati, and Theodore S. Orlin

> Human beings make their own history even if, as Marx reminded us, they do so under circumstances influenced by the past.
> Paul Kennedy, *Preparing for the Twenty-First Century* (1993)

The traumatic events that altered the form of government of these three Central European states, despite some differences, epitomize the transition toward democracy that was, and hopefully continues to be, endemic throughout Europe. The fall of the Berlin Wall and the end of the cold war did not just mean the end of totalitarianism, but brought with it new and troublesome difficulties associated with transitions. For the former European Marxist-Leninist states, who by their own rhetoric and international commitments are now openly committed to pluralism, human rights, and democracy,[1] the events and problems associated with this transition mean more than changes in governmental structure and political processes. The communist regimes wanted to ensure that their children would be enthusiastic supporters (or at least not be a threat to the continued existence) of their system. Accordingly their educational programs were geared to inculcate their ideology via the curriculum and the pedagogical process. The challenge for the transitional regime is simultaneously to change the governmental system with a constituency educated in an anti-democratic climate and to prepare future generations for a society that will be committed to human rights. If these societies are to change in a way consistent with human rights norms, it is essential that the political culture begins to reflect democratic values.[2] Certainly the education process is the primary means to accomplish this end.

The processes described in this chapter are attempts on the part of nongovernmental organizations (NGOs) and educators not only to bring about changes in what children are taught but to create an educational environment that encourages the skills and talents necessary for developing a social and political culture consistent with human rights. The obstacles to establish a human rights education program in countries emerging from more than four decades of totalitarianism are considerable. In each of the examples here, a large number of the educational bureaucracy was trained and promoted by the totalitarian regimes and continues to be resistant to change due to either their disdain toward democratic change or their continued commitment to policies allegedly discarded by the transitional governments. In many instances a desire to hold on to influence and salaries gained during the communist regimes is the primary motivation to resist change.[3]

Further, in each of these examples the transition from a command market system to a free market imposes considerable burdens on resources and provides yet another barrier or excuse to delay or deter the implementation of change. Nonetheless, an attempt to change is being led by determined and dedicated human rights activists. They continue to press for human rights programs in the schools, despite these obstacles, in the hope that their effort will alter the educational system and bring with it a brighter, more democratic future.

On the positive side, each of these states has made commitments to its citizens through constitutional laws and to the international community to adhere to and promote human rights. Hence the NGOs can and do remind their governments of these legal, political, and moral commitments to ensure human rights education as a primary means to "promote human rights." All three of these States Members of the United Nations and ratifiers of the international covenants have an international legal obligation to promote "universal respect for . . . human rights and fundamental freedoms" (Article 55 of the UN Charter; similar phrasing exists in the Preamble of the International Covenant on Civil and Political Rights and in the Preamble and Article 13 of the International Covenant on Economic, Social and Cultural Rights).[4]

Romania and Slovakia, as members of the Council of Europe are also ratifiers of the European Convention for the Protection of Human Rights, which imposes on these states a duty to "secure to everyone within their jurisdiction the rights and freedoms defined" in the Convention and its accompanying protocols (including Protocol 1, Article 2, which protects the right to education). Accordingly human rights education is an important element in meeting this commitment in order to ensure that there will be a broad understanding of the Convention, the European enforcement machinery, and the ratifier's obligation to abide by its provisions. Romanian and Slovakian NGOs have as part of their work the task to promulgate the Convention and the remedies it secures for individuals claiming that their rights are violated, especially for the school-age generation who will be the participants in a new Europe dedicated to human rights and democracy.

Albania has recently become a member of the Council of Europe. Although it has not ratified the European Convention, it is a participating state in the Organization for Security and Cooperation in Europe (OSCE). The accords of that process provide NGOs with additional support in their efforts to propagate human rights education. The Charter of Paris for a New Europe (Nov. 21, 1990) states that "Human rights and fundamental freedoms are the birthright of all human beings, are inalienable and are guaranteed by law. Their protection and *promotion* is the first responsibility of government" (*Human Rights, Democracy and Rule of Law*; emphasis added). In addition, the Charter sees an important role for NGOs in facilitating the implementation of OSCE commitments: "These organizations, groups and individuals must be involved in an appropriate way in the activities and new structures of the OSCE in order to fulfill their important tasks" (*Non-Governmental Organizations*).

Given these international documents and the agreement of these three transitional democracies to their provisions, it is clear that the legal commitments to human rights have been made. What remains is implementation and protection. A primary step, as the Charter of Paris notes, is "promotion." Undoubtedly a major component in promoting human rights is education. NGOs, as this chapter documents, have an important role to play in working toward the establishment of a human rights culture and a commitment to democracy.

What follows are three commentaries by educators and human rights advocates concerning the legacy of the communist past, the present conditions of human rights education in their schools, their efforts to bring change to their systems, and the obstacles they encounter and must overcome to make human rights education a reality.

Romania: Ceauşescu's Legacy and the Prospects for Human Rights Education

The Communist Past and the Postrevolutionary Change

Nicolae Ceauşescu's control over Romania was almost absolute. Adding to the country's isolation was that all of its neighbors were also Marxist-Leninist states, so that Romanians did not have the ability to access the West via radio and TV. With the exception of Radio Free Europe, Romanians were so isolated from western traditions and thought that speaking to a foreigner was an offense—failure to report conversations with non-Romanians to the police could have serious repercussions. Unlike other European states, Romanians were left only to consider the teachings and propaganda of the state's communist party.

Consistent with the teachings of communism and Ceauşescu's totalitarianism, ideological propaganda was integrated throughout the curriculum and in almost every school activity. In music classes, children were taught songs praising the party and its leadership. Literature was relegated to the recital of poems in praise of the general secretary. Faculty meetings were devoted to discussions of the party's published successes for the proletariat. History became a vehicle to extol the virtues of communism and to warn of the dangers of capitalism and the evil of monarchy.[5]

The rhetoric of Marxism was ever prevalent, with children inculcated with communist dogma. Central to the teaching message was the equality of peoples guided by the working class via the party. The lessons were directed to stress the value of work as a revolutionary duty with the reminder that the failure to work after finishing school was an offense that could result, for repeat offenders, in imprisonment.

Accordingly, the curriculum was designed to diminish the values of individualism, stressing that Romanians should be working for the strengthening of the party. The reward for conscientious Romanian students was the eventual attainment of party membership. Only "exemplary" citizens became "members"; honor students could begin to strive for party membership by participating at school age in the Young Pioneers and later by becoming Utecists (members of the Young Communist Union). The ladder of success was made clear. Only party membership could ensure professional success. Commitment to the system began and could easily end in the Romanian schools. Learning as an endeavor was a secondary pursuit and became primarily a means to gain acceptance within the system. The schools were a training ground for future party membership and a place where students were tested by the state for their loyalty and commitment to Romanian communism. In this system, the place of religion and personal belief was abolished. Children were taught that God is a myth created by the rich to exploit the workers. The promise of an afterlife, the former state institutions taught, is a device to coerce the poor to work for the advantage of the rich.

Not only were individualism and personal beliefs frowned upon, but they were seen as a threat to the political monopoly that the communist party imposed on society. Pluralism, a central theme of a human rights culture, was not an ideal to be pursued, but rather the antithesis of the communist promise and an unpatriotic challenge to the homogeneity that the Romanian regime hoped to achieve.

Every school was forced to teach standardized, party-approved propaganda. The school bureaucracy was politicized, and students perceived their teachers as agents of the state. Individual teacher initiative was rare. Variations in the state line resulted in suppression and sanction. Teacher promotions were often based on whether or not the file was "good," and grading often depended on the influence of the student's parents. Uniforms were compulsory, reflecting that even outer appearances must strive for homogeneity. The curriculum was compulsory, and sports, as well as academic contests, were made part of the great socialist effort to transform Romania into a communist nirvana.

It was inevitable that students would begin to appreciate the contradictions between the proclaimed goals and the actual realities that became increasingly apparent. While outwardly students followed the party line, inwardly they knew the truth about the ideology they were forced to espouse. The lessons that described free elections were made empty when students turning eighteen learned they had only one choice at the polls and that Ceaușescu's reelection would go unchallenged. The stringent law was applied in less than equitable fashion, with the growth in corruption in full view in every field of activity including the schools. The chasm between ideology and reality grew, coming apart with the 1989 revolution.[6]

The air was filled with freedom and the chance for change, and the effervescence of postrevolutionary life affected all Romanian institutions. Students sensing this opportunity made modest demands, asking for the removal of uniforms, modification of the curriculum, and the removal of undemocratic rules. They hoped the rigid attitudes of the school administration and the teachers would change with Romania's political upheaval, but were quick to learn that their "communist mentality" would be difficult to alter.

This new and open political environment saw the reemergence of political diversity, not seen since the beginning of the Marxist-Leninist regime. Outside the schools, discussion was rampant, reflecting the pluralism of political thinking common to open societies. Nonetheless, despite active debates in homes and in communities, students were forbidden to engage in political activity in their schools.

An essential part of the political debate was the rhetoric of human rights. In their campaigns, parties and candidates claimed support for democracy and protection of human rights. The terms quickly became "wooden" and began to lose their actual meanings. These principles were not explained or properly understood. To school officials, human rights were merely another part of the political debate and therefore forbidden as part of the prohibition to discuss politics in the schools. To further complicate matters, the elected party now ruling Romania was accused by its opposition of violating human rights. School authorities came to view any discussion and distribution of human rights literature as a partisan political act.

The result of this climate was that an objective understanding of human rights was not being provided by the educational establishment. Further, the problems associated with transitions—increased crime rates, unemployment, social unrest, and uncertainty for the future—were attributed to the turn toward democracy and the espoused commitment to civil and political rights. Society's problems were seen as caused by the commitment to democracy. On the other hand, the economic, social, and cultural rights found in the covenants were often seen as too similar to communist propaganda and were not taken seriously by Romanians who hoped that the future would be different from the past.

These new conditions left the public confused about the real meaning of human rights and the schools unwilling and unable to alter the pervasive misconceptions. Teachers who were sympathetic to change often identified human rights as just another form of unrealistic political propaganda or were fearful that their jobs would be threatened if they included these topics in their classrooms. Other teachers, recalling their own educational experience, were concerned that the espousal of a rights theory would discourage students from accepting responsibility and encourage anarchy in the school.

The prevailing attitude was that the protection of human rights was a concern for other state institutions and did not belong in the classroom. There was little understanding that individuals have an obligation to adhere to human rights norms in their everyday relations or that a civil society must be the impetus to ensure that the state respects its human rights commitments. Nor was it understood that the schools have an obligation to deliver that message to their students.

The Present Status of Human Rights Education in Romania

The four years since the revolution have seen some promise for change in the schools, but by no means is human rights education a truly integral part of the curriculum. A new subject has been introduced by the administration, "Civic and Moral Education." This required course, taught one hour per week for the seventh and eight grades, includes lessons on democracy and human rights. Included also are discussions of the United Nations, international human rights treaties, and other topics relevant to a civic culture. The topics are presented either superficially or too theoretically, and there are no activities designed to make these lessons come alive or demonstrate their relevance to everyday life.

Generally the teachers who present this material are not selected because of skill or interest, but often they are retired teachers who once taught social studies during the old regime. Significantly, those teaching this course often do not reflect the new values consistent with the subject they are teaching. There are a few teachers who are enthusiastic for this topic, but they are the exception rather than the rule. It should also be noted that these teachers have not attended training courses, since the school system rarely provided teachers with pedagogical training in this field.

Public opinion has not yet objected to this state of affairs. The public's interest is still primarily directed at the poor state of the economy; if the public has an attitude about changes to the system, it is more one of frustration and rejection of the political change that seems to blame for the economic calamity the country faces. The public must now deal with the problems often encountered during transitions: high crime rates, failure of social services, and a decreasing standard of living. For many, the "hope" of the revolution has now become disillusionment. They see government as powerless.

Given this situation, the call for human rights education is weak. Because of this pessimistic public attitude there is fear among many democrats that the rights guaranteed by the new Romanian Constitution could be lost by those who call for a return to old methods to restore the economy and order in the society. Ironically, given these social and economic conditions, the need for human rights education is immense while its support is low.

Further complicating the situation is the relative lack of human rights information available nationally. Few textbooks on democracy or human rights are available in Romanian. One of the first Romanian human rights textbooks was printed in May

1993.[7] These books were distributed free (but on a rather limited basis by two NGOs with external financial support. SIRDO (Societatea Independentá Româná a Drepturilor Omului [the Romanian Independent Society for Human Rights]) prepared and published *The ABC of Human Rights*.[8] This guidebook, compiled especially for Romanian teachers and including Amnesty International texts with additional UN material, has been distributed by SIRDO in coordination with its work.

Another NGO, LADO (Liga Apararii Drepturilor Omului [the League for the Defense of Human Rights]), translated Jean-Louis Decamp's book, *Human Rights Told to Children*. This, too, has a limited distribution.

Despite this effort, it is clear that the human rights message rarely reaches the masses. No newspaper has made an initiative to provide articles describing the human rights theory or informing the public of Romania's international commitments. What is even more disturbing is that the concrete cases of human rights abuses, known to the NGOs, are rarely reported. Romania's population of more than 23 million people remains either misinformed or uninformed about human rights and how it relates to a pluralistic democracy.

Strategy for Change

The Romanian NGOs realize that a long-term strategy to ensure that a pluralistic democracy prevails requires the creation of a political culture committed to human rights values. The methods for accomplishing this end remain to be developed, although some efforts are being made to create conditions conducive to the protection of human rights.

Family life remains the primary social development opportunity. To inculcate families with human rights values requires that other institutions be used to bring the democratic message home. Although the role of the mass media cannot be dismissed, the schools remain the best institution to alter these values. While a mass media campaign that describes the human rights theory and provides the international documents of protection would certainly be useful in establishing a human rights culture in Romania, ultimately the daily contact children and parents have with the educational system seems to be of greater importance. Yet it would certainly ease the process of change in the schools if the mass media supported a human rights culture and paved the way for acceptance of change in the schools. If the media began to reflect this attitude, they would deliver the message to the educational establishment that change is in order and that human rights is not political rhetoric, but rather a system of values that should govern a pluralistic society. NGOs continue to try to make use of the media, but must act to institute educational change with or without the media's assistance. To date, newspapers have been less than interested, often reporting more sensational items. Nonetheless, every effort should be made to encourage newspapers, radio, and TV to cover issues that help to develop a human rights culture.

The goal should be to introduce human rights lessons, both formally and informally, through the curriculum and school activities. The school should also teach by example. The process by which schools are governed should reflect democratic values and be a school for democratic decision making. Rules and regulations should reflect the values found in the Convention on the Rights of the Child, the international covenants, and the Universal Declaration of Human Rights.

Students are quick to pick up when lessons and actions differ. If students hear one lesson but see that the administration does not comply with its own teachings, they will see the hypocrisy, and the effort will not only be meaningless but destructive. Faculty must be made aware that adherence to democratic values does not necessarily mean anarchy in the schools. There are a variety of provisions within the international documents that provide ample room for democratic control and the protection of an order conducive to good teaching.[9] Teachers and administrators need to be made aware of the difference between democracy and anarchy.

The entire educational effort should be directed toward encouraging both the understanding and acceptance of human rights. For this reason, human rights should not be relegated to merely a separate social studies topic or course. It should be integrated across the curriculum and made part of a variety of courses including but not limited to history, civic education, philosophy, literature, and art.

The classroom should be a democratic model where the freedom of expression is protected and students are not only respected for their different views, but encouraged to debate the merits of their position. In short, the schools must be altered from what they were—a training ground for the homogeneity that the communists espoused—to a place to learn where a forum of ideas is encouraged. If the schools develop in this fashion, it is hoped that the lessons will go beyond their gates and be brought home to the family and the greater society.

SIRDO's Human Rights Education Program

SIRDO, a human rights NGO with a variety of programs, has made one of its highest priorities the creation of an education program as a primary means to promote and protect human rights. The aim is to ultimately reach every region of the country and to bring the human rights message beyond Bucharest where it maintains its offices. The plan, partly operational in spring 1993, is to maintain a human rights educational center in Bucharest, Romania's largest city with more than 2 million inhabitants, and then to create regional branches. The centers will house resources useful to teachers and schools as well as others who wish to learn about human rights.

Before 1993, SIRDO's efforts, due to lack of finances, were on a smaller scale. The focus had been mostly directed to the schools. Yet a recent commitment of support from the Dutch Foreign Affairs Ministry has allowed for some expansion of its efforts, including the opening of a new branch in Tirgoviste and Iasi.

Despite its small budget, SIRDO's experience with the schools has been considerable. The aim to date is to encourage teachers not to wait for formal programs from the establishment, but immediately to begin informal efforts to teach human rights across the curriculum. In its contacts with teachers, SIRDO also attempts to facilitate the growth of new attitudes toward students. The human rights education program consists of seven areas.

1. Teacher Union Support and Endorsement

One of the first steps was to make contact with the teachers' trade unions in the hope that their endorsement and support would give SIRDO access to and legitimacy with the teachers as well as the schools. Agreements were made with the more important unions: FPR—Fratia, FSIPR, FSAIP, and CNSRL. Their support made it possible to visit the schools and provided encouragement for the teachers to take the human rights message seriously. The school administrators are less likely to deny the request for access if the invitation comes directly from the teachers and their bargaining unit. This technique has proved successful and has given SIRDO the image of not wanting to threaten the orderly operation of the school.

2. Preparing Human Rights Resource Materials

Central to SIRDO's program is preparing translations of human rights books into Romanian and publishing new material. The intent is to provide students with interesting classroom material and teachers with guides to assist them in their presentation of human rights topics.

As already mentioned, SIRDO's first publication was a teacher's manual, *The ABC of Human Rights*, now used in coordination with its presentations. This book included the translation and republication of the UN booklet *Human Rights—Questions and Answers*. More than eight thousand copies have been distributed throughout Romania and six hundred to the Republic of Moldova. Another book translated and distributed to Romanian teachers was *Human Rights for Children—A Curriculum for Teaching Human Rights, Ages 3–12*.[10] This book, prepared by the Human Rights for Children Committee, has been used at SIRDO training sessions.

Using existing materials has allowed for the testing of the suitability and effectiveness for Romania of human rights material prepared for the world market. At the same time SIRDO quickly realized the need to prepare material especially for Romanian society. Most recently it designed and wrote a small coloring book prepared for Romania's primary school children, *O poveste pentru copii despre . . . Declaratia Universala a Drepturilor Omului (A Story for Children About . . . The Universal Declaration of Human Rights)*.[11] The theme of the book is the Universal Declaration of Human Rights. Several of the rights were selected and presented in such a fashion that it would be relevant and attractive to children. The illustrations were done by a talented Romanian artist. Response to this project seems to be enthusiastic, and SIRDO is hopeful that this device will bring the human rights message to students early in their school career to encourage the shaping of values at an early stage.

3. School Visits and Teacher-Training Courses

SIRDO makes frequent visits to Romanian schools. In addition to holding discussions and doing programs for the students, the staff meets with teachers and discusses with them the use of human rights educational materials as well as useful pedagogical techniques. It also attempts to encourage parents to join the process and tries to get the teachers to initiate projects that could involve parents.

In addition to school visitations, SIRDO has organized two teacher-training conferences for human rights. On March 30 and April 4, 1994, two three-day conferences were held in Bucharest and Iasi, respectively. The SIRDO trainers were assisted by two Amnesty International educators, Nancy Flowers and Ellen Moore. Active learning was employed in the training, and the trainers encouraged teachers to change their attitude toward students and alter their classroom approaches. The content emphasized was the basic human rights documents including the International Bill of Rights.

In attendance were 130 teachers from a variety of Romanian cities. These courses were financed by the Dutch Ministry of Foreign Affairs and the United States Information Agency. This was the first time that such an endeavor was attempted in Romania by a human rights NGO. The response from participants was enthusiastic, and as a result SIRDO has received requests by teachers from other regions to attend future conferences.

SIRDO is convinced that, although these efforts are received enthusiastically, there remains a need for further training. The attitudinal problems of the old system are so entrenched that one session may not be sufficient to bring about the results SIRDO desires. SIRDO faces the question of whether future courses should be directed at new teachers or at those who have already attended one training session. One thought is that future sessions will be attended by some who completed the training session and others who did not. The hope is that the more experienced human rights teacher may positively influence the novice. This experiment will be tried within the year.

4. Organizing Human Rights Clubs and Other Extracurricular Activities

SIRDO's strategy is to establish human rights clubs within the schools. The intent is to encourage change in social attitudes to facilitate the growth of a human rights culture. Despite some resistance, as some see this as a recreation of communist youth activity, the goal is to encourage students to appreciate human rights values in their everyday activities.

SIRDO is very excited about the prospects of dramatic arts groups that began

(May 1994) in one pilot school. The scripts are prepared by the students and have human rights messages. The hope, if this experiment is successful, is that the idea will be used elsewhere.

5. Establishing Human Rights Educational Centers and Media Material

As of spring 1994 there are two SIRDO Educational Centers, Bucharest and Tir-govíste. The centers house and lend human rights material to schools and teachers, including audiovisual material as well as written material. The hope is that each of Romania's counties will have such a resource center. SIRDO will continue to seek funding for this project, although it realizes that it must move incrementally to meet this ambitious goal.

An important part of this effort is the preparation of audiovisual material. SIRDO has enlisted the assistance of writers, artists, and media experts to produce human rights material.

6. Participating in Media Discussions

SIRDO realizes that the human rights message must go beyond the schools and reach a broader audience. Every opportunity to reach the public is taken, including participating in roundtables and other public forums where the press is invited.

From October 1993 to March 1994 a SIRDO representative has appeared once a week for six minutes on a Romanian radio show. Each session has been devoted to the discussion of a particular right and its relevancy to a Romanian context. The first shows were devoted to a discussion of general human rights theory and explanation of the International Bill of Human Rights. From there, time was given to an explanation of the meaning of "democracy," including the importance of the freedom of expression and the right to receive information.

From the general, the show moved to the specific with emphasis on human rights issues that have contemporary relevance for Romanians. For example, in a discussion of the right to life, considerable attention was given to the death penalty, a very controversial issue in light of the rising Romanian crime rate. The intention was to provide the general public with arguments against its reintroduction and thereby improve the quality of the debate that is presently ripe in the Romanian press.

Another topic that proved to generate some controversy was "the right to freedom of movement." Many Romanians, who were once forbidden to receive a passport or permission to travel abroad, now feel considerable frustration in not being able to get travel visas or permission to emigrate to another country from the more economically developed states. This show addressed the true criteria for political asylum and the distinction of being an economic refugee. In addition, the position of the western countries and their fears of being inundated with Romanian refugees were discussed within a human rights context. As with the other discussions, the hope was that an honest and accurate discussion of this human right would elevate the understanding and improve the quality of the public debate of these issues.

7. Organizing Topical Roundtables

SIRDO visits different Romanian population centers where it organizes open discussions with the public, focusing on contemporary topics, for example, sexual minority discrimination and refugee problems. Invited to these sessions are representatives of the different political parties, members of other NGOs, and spokespersons of linguistic and racial minorities. The human rights implications of these policy areas are presented at these meetings. SIRDO often goes to rural areas where the opportunities to discuss these matters are limited.

In a program funded by the German Marshall Fund of the United States, SIRDO concentrated on the issues surrounding the very sensitive Romanian minority problem. The attempt was to elevate the discussion by providing accurate information on the meaning of "minorities and their rights" and to move the debate away from the intense feeling toward ethnic minorities. Described in the meeting was that "minorities" means not only ethnic minorities but religious groups, sexual minorities, refugees, and others. The message was that human rights education is a powerful tool for altering feelings of intolerance toward minority groups. Sessions were held in areas where the tensions are or may be considerable: Iasi, Constanta, Tirgu Mures, and Deva.

Some Obstacles to Overcome and Conclusions

Perhaps the greatest practical difficulty in implementing SIRDO's program is convincing the educational establishment that human rights education is not political and therefore is suitable for inclusion in the schools' programs. Although some progress has been made in this respect, as described earlier, much more effort needs to be done. It is hoped that, with experience and with the schools' witnessing SIRDO's efforts, the authorities will be ultimately convinced that human rights is not necessarily political, but rather reflects Romania's proclaimed legal commitment to respect and implement human rights. Further, SIRDO hopes that with each encounter with SIRDO volunteers and staff, school administrators and teachers will begin to believe that an NGO can be committed to change without necessarily espousing or supporting one political cause over another. Accordingly, all SIRDO presenters are aware that their human rights message should be as objective as possible without reflecting any one political party or agenda. Our only agenda is the principles found within the Universal Declaration of Human Rights and other international instruments. Since the Romanian Constitution proclaims adherence to these principles, our position becomes credible for dubious school authorities.

In addition to this problem, SIRDO has experienced other practical difficulties in implementing its program. An often expressed concern on the part of teachers is that there is just not room in the already overcrowded curriculum. They claim there is not ample time to teach all the required subjects, let alone human rights. For this reason SIRDO attempts to encourage the integration of human rights education into existing subjects. The strategy is to include, where possible, human rights lessons within substantive lessons. Certainly history and social studies classes lend themselves to this, but human rights can also be included in art and literature classes as well as other subjects.

SIRDO is also aware of resistance on the part of parents toward the human rights message. Although it has not yet devised an effective strategy to address this problem, SIRDO attempts to encourage parental involvement in schools and tries to break down the resistance of an older population that has suffered during the Romanian totalitarian experience and is reluctant to accept human rights values.

As described, the lack of human rights school materials remains a considerable problem despite SIRDO's efforts. Much more must be done in this area, but with the government facing economic difficulties in this transition, the prospects of overcoming this problem in the near future are not promising. State institutions nonetheless must be encouraged to address this problem and to commit even limited resources to altering this situation.

Finally, SIRDO views the general lack of motivation and initiative that is pervasive among Romania's population as a major impediment for the development of human rights education programs. It attributes this attitude to a generally held view that the inertia of the past and the confusion of the present political situation have the public waiting for some central authority to set Romania on a new path. This may be understandable, given the history of centralized planning and charismatic leadership that dominated public institutions for so long, but it is unacceptable for building a human rights culture. In its programs SIRDO attempts to encourage a change in this attitude by convincing all those concerned that change will only come via the initiative of those directly involved in the schools. While it is also firmly convinced that attempts to improve general awareness by working through the mass media must be pursued simultaneously, schools remain the major target for change.

It is for this reason that SIRDO places so much of its efforts working alongside teachers and school administrators. Its strategy is to convince them so that they may deliver the message in the classroom and students can relay the message to their families and neighbors.

Overall SIRDO's conclusion is that since no political leader or party has fully embraced the necessity to teach human rights laws and values, the attempt by an NGO to bring the human rights message to Romania's future, its students, is a difficult one. The lesson that needs to be taught, which at present has only just begun, is that the individual must be protected not just from state abuse but from his fellow citizen. Students must learn that their values and behavior are important in creating a human right culture. SIRDO remains genuinely committed to this end, but realizes much must be done before its goals can begin to be achieved.

Slovakia: The Reemergence of Nationalism and the Call for Pluralistic Education with Respect for Minorities—The Impact and Prospects for Human Rights Education

Czechoslovakia's Past and the Birth of the Slovak Republic

Unlike the Romanian example, Slovakia must not only face the transition from a communist past, but also the challenges of the division of Czechoslovakia. This is especially troublesome as its emergence as an independent republic was largely motivated by desires to create a Slovak national state. With its independence the challenge of implementing the commitment to human rights became all the more complicated.

Czechoslovakia after the "velvet revolution", consistent with the Charter 77 movement, took active steps toward integration into Europe and positive action toward the respect of human rights. As a full member of the Council of Europe, it had ratified the European Convention for the Protection of Human Rights, opening the possibilities for its citizens to appeal to the European Commission and Court in Strasbourg after the exhaustion of domestic remedies. Furthermore, its participation and hopes for increased participation in the European system became an incentive to move toward the development of a pluralistic democracy committed to human rights.

In January 1993, after the election of the Meciar government and independence, Slovakia's pace and direction toward full protection of human rights were altered. Increasing concern for minority protection, in the wake of the realization of a nationalistic agenda, has caused considerable anxiety among the human rights community. The question many pose is: will these new developments thwart the progress gained as a result of the 1989 turn to democracy? Adding to the discomfort is the call by many in government for the official, exclusive, and compulsory use of the Slovak language, including in education, even among minority communities.

This separation even complicated the status of human rights treaties for the new republic. Many of these international agreements had been ratified by the former Czechoslovak state. Their applicability to Slovakia was questioned until very recently. A positive indicator is that since 1993 the Slovak Republic has ratified most of the major human rights treaties.[12] These treaty obligations provide impetus for state efforts to promote human rights and ammunition for NGOs to insist on the educational promotion of human rights norms.[13]

*Efforts for the Inclusion of Human Rights in the Schools Since
the Velvet Revolution and Their Assessment*

In addition to recent events, like the other former eastern bloc countries, there is much in Slovakia's communist past that continues to impede the full implementation of human rights education in its school system. The impact of attitudes resulting from the educational practice of decades cannot be overturned even by revolutions, whether violent or velvet, or simply by a desire to change. The present situation must be understood in the context of the past.

In the Socialist Republic's curriculum, "civics," taught at both the primary and secondary levels, was directed toward shaping the Marxist-Leninist worldview of students so as to be consistent with the policy of the Communist Party. Stressed in the lessons were the principles of class character, political consciousness, and ideological awareness. Any notion of a "rights theory" reflected communist dogma. Moreover, instructions addressed to teachers also reflected the communist view of human rights and class divisions.

Absent from texts and the curriculum was an explanation of classical human rights theory, discussions of the Universal Declaration of Human Rights, the UN system, or the other aspects essential for understanding the role of human rights law in protecting individuals from state abuse. Access to documents, let alone an understanding of human rights treaties, was rare.

With the November 1989 revolution the school situation began to reflect societal changes. Consciously, in a desire that the Czechoslovak state would not retreat back to totalitarianism, the intent was that there would be included in the educational process the teaching of human rights. Beginning in 1990/91, "civics" was altered to convey the human rights message. For the third year of secondary school, eighteen lessons on the theme "Man as a Citizen of a Democratic State" were mandated. Included among the subjects presented and discussed are democratic principles of government, the role of rights and the rule of law in a democratic regime, international human rights documents such as the covenants, the Convention on the Rights of the Child, and the Helsinki Accords.

Similarly the curricula were altered for different levels and forms of the educational system. In the two- and three-year vocational schools, high schools, and gymnasiums, human rights education was incorporated in ways consistent with their missions.

By the 1992/93 school year, research was completed by the Methodic Center in Prešov. It assessed these efforts to teach human rights at the secondary school level. The sample survey included 250 teachers, headmasters, and their assistants, selected at random from vocational schools, secondary schools, and professional high schools from eastern Slovakia. The questionnaire was supplemented with interviews.

The results confirmed the original hypothesis of its preparers, that the Slovakian efforts were less than satisfactory and were not meeting the aims they were intended to accomplish. Only about a third of those responding considered human rights education as an important component for the school's educational mission. Nearly a half of the sample never participated in any preparatory training or lecture on human rights teaching. Further, 80 percent of the secondary schools never had any organized extracurricular events dealing with human rights issues.

As for an understanding of basic human rights theory and knowledge among the survey responders, only 41.9 percent claimed to have read the Universal Declaration of Human Rights, 34.2 percent the Convention on the Rights of the Child, 13.5 percent the International Covenant on Civil and Political Rights, and 7.1 percent the European Convention for the Protection of Human Rights and Fundamental Freedoms.

More dramatically, more than half the respondents admitted to not having dealt with human rights issues in their classes during the 1992/93 school year. Only 6.1 percent of the headmasters admitted to creating a human rights program in their schools. The survey indicated that only 2 percent of teachers had an excellent understanding of human rights issues, with 15.2 percent believed to have a "good understanding" of human rights.

On a scale of 1 to 5 (1 being excellent and 5 insufficient), the respondents self-evaluated the quality of human rights education in their own schools. The average was between 3 and 4, attributing their lack of success to insufficient skills and methods to teach human rights, poor motivation ("no one compels such education"), and lack of teaching materials and aids.

The conclusion drawn by the survey preparers is that, four years after the 1989 revolution, human rights education is not satisfactory. While some human rights issues are included in secondary school civic classes, and while some schools have discussed this problem at their administrative planning sessions, generally the efforts being made to inculcate Slovakia's school students with human rights values is less than successful. The knowledge level of Slovakian teachers of basic human rights concepts is low. The literature available to them is limited, with few textbooks and other study devices in the Slovak language published.

It is the opinion of the researchers, based on their findings, that basic human rights documents—for example, the International Bill of Human Rights, the European Convention, and the Constitution of the Slovak Republic—must be made available to students and teachers alike. More fundamentally, it is essential that the educational process be restructured to reflect principles of humanity, democracy, and the respect of human rights and fundamental freedoms. In the same light, it is equally important that the process begin to teach students, early in their school careers, the importance of the rule of law and the basic concepts underlying the legal system.

Accordingly, the discussion of contemporary human rights issues should be integrated throughout the curriculum in addition to civics instruction. The lessons should reflect the reality of the problem, but at the same time the importance of seeking nonviolent solutions to the problems.

The conclusions of the survey and experience suggest the need for the creation of didactic classroom games to convey the human rights message in a creative manner. Such devices as role-plays, psychodramas, and oral history projects need to be developed and encouraged so that human rights lessons will have more impact with school children.

In order to motivate teachers and administrators there is a clear need for training workshops and conferences. The hope is that a concerted effort to encourage more enthusiasm will translate into better and increased attention to human rights education in Slovakian schools. Undoubtedly, with increased human rights teaching, there will be a need for pedagogical research to test and reformulate techniques and material based on classroom successes and failures. In order to accomplish these ends, attention must be given to persuade and encourage the Ministry of Education and Science, as well as other government authorities, to commit its resources to human rights education.

The Response of NGOs to the Need for Human Rights Education in Slovakia

In response to this apparent need to address the lack of quality of human rights education in Slovak schools, the Bratislava branch of Amnesty International (AI/B) began a project in primary and secondary schools. The group, made up primarily of teachers and psychologists, understood firsthand the need for such a program and made it part of its agenda. Since AI/B was a newly founded group, not yet registered as an official entity, without funds, it approached the Milan Šimecka Foundation to sponsor the program. This small but active foundation, whose agenda, in some sense, is similar to Amnesty International,[14] agreed to this arrangement in May 1992. AI/B and the Šimecka Foundation sought and received assistance in its efforts from the Department of Education Human Rights Section of Comenius University, Bratislava, the Slovak Center for Conflict Prevention and Resolution of Comenius University (SCCPR), and the Partners for Democratic Change (PDC-Slovakia). It also received financial and methodological support from a number of international organizations, including the Open Society Fund, the National Endowment for Democracy, the Human Rights Advocacy Project (HRAP), the German Marshall Fund, and the Council of Europe.[15]

This project, known as "Human Rights in the (Slovakian) Schools," set as its working objective to convey to teachers basic human rights information and methods to teach their students effectively. The ultimate goal is to inculcate attitudinal changes so that "autonomous thinking" will prevail, contrary to the methods that were used during the communist regime. The primary vehicle used by the project is a series of workshops for teachers. While there is some attempt to introduce human rights theory and documents to teachers, the strategy is focused on motivating teachers and changing their attitudes toward human rights. Many Slovakians, given the recent past, have feelings of inferiority, including many teachers, as though their country does not measure up to the international standards. The workshops are used to encourage teachers to break out of the apathy that appears to prevail and to inculcate them with positive attitudes toward democracy and human rights principles.

The workshops, often held outside of Slovakia's capital city, in regional centers, are led by a team, made up of AI/B members, some of whom are experienced teachers, one or two psychologists from the SCCPR and PDC-Slovakia, and Slovak and foreign human rights experts. Although the inclusion of foreign guests can become expensive, experience confirms that their participation is beneficial for a successful workshop. The presence of a foreign expert not only provides confirmation to Slovak teachers as to the importance of this effort, but encourages them to think about human rights from a different perspective. A presentation from a non-Slovak lends a sense of importance for the teaching of human rights in the schools and allows Slovak teachers to question the state of education abroad. It permits them to compare their own experience with others and to test whether or not other models can be an acceptable alternative to their own.

Further, the inclusion of foreign experts may provide some incentive for government cooperation. The first two workshops, one for basic education and the other for secondary school education, which had participation from Amnesty International trainers from the United States, the Netherlands, and Austria, received the support of the Ministry of Education.

The workshop experience, given a training team size of three to five, suggests that the maximum number of participants should not exceed forty and they should be divided into two groups.

The intent of these workshops is not only to encourage attitudinal changes but to demonstrate creative approaches for classroom teaching of human rights. Often used are a variety of role-plays and games, demonstrating to the participants that teaching human rights can be not only informative but entertaining.

The program is generally divided into three main themes: (1) a "Psychological Section"; (2) a "Methodological Section"; and (3) the "Theoretical Background of Human Rights". The group, approximately forty teachers, is divided at the beginning of the course into two equal groups. The arrangement requires that directors and teachers from the same school must not participate in the same group. An attempt is made to place inexperienced teachers with experienced ones. Both groups participate in all three sections that are in one and half-section blocks. The lectures provide the same material to both groups but are flexible enough to allow for change if the circumstances require. The longer programs also allow for the groups to separate and discuss such topics as the value orientation of secondary school students.

The "Psychological Section" focuses on teachers' attitudes toward contemporary human rights issues with an emphasis on introducing nonviolent methods of conflict resolution and increasing opportunities to facilitate open dialogue. Participants suggest examples of conflict situations that are prevalent in their schools, and the psychologists help the teachers develop skills to bring about resolutions. The training includes techniques to evaluate behavior and attitudes, and the effective use of vocabulary and nonverbal communication. Role-playing is used to demonstrate methodological approaches to deal with common problems found in Slovakian school settings.

In Slovakia a major theme often discussed is the rights of linguistic and other minorities in the schools. The psychologists who conduct these sessions use techniques to elicit underlying feelings of prejudice held by Slovakian teachers toward minority students. Hence very often attitudes toward the Hungarian and gypsy (Roma) minorities make for interesting and at times volatile discussions. The emphasis on the part of the workshop leader, in a nonthreatening manner, is to engage the participants in exercises that attempt to sensitize teachers to the problem and to resolve conflicts within the schools. Taught by examples are communicative techniques that will assist teachers in the classroom to deal with often difficult and intense problems.

The workshop trainers are aware of the importance of answering the concrete questions and concerns of participating teachers. They attempt to assist teachers by dealing with such issues as how to increase class participation, how to encourage students to express their true feelings, and how to deal effectively with aggressive behavior.

The "Methodological Section" is practical training introducing cooperative pedagogical methods that stress the underlying principle that "the greatest learning is achieved by active participation in the learning process." Discussed, demonstrated, and practiced are topics such as teaching human rights issues, overcoming prejudice and the elimination of stereotypes among students and staff, the interrelation of curriculum with human rights issues, evaluation techniques, the integration of human rights values in everyday life and behavior, dealing with the balance between order and liberty, and students' rights and teachers' rights. The workshop trainers are prepared and encouraged to modify their program to meet the specific needs of teachers and often deviate from the prepared program to deal with issues that are revealed through the workshop process.

The third part of this workshop, the "Theoretical Background of Human Rights," is often presented by a Slovak professor of human rights, Miroslav Kusý, chairman of the Human Rights Department, Comenius University. Professor Kusý, a former political prisoner and Charter 77 spokesperson, provides a formal lecture on human rights theory and leads a discussion. When the course is dedicated to minority problems, he provides a lecture on "Minority Rights and Standards".

Another topic dealt with is the appropriateness of the death penalty for a democratic Slovakia. This controversial topic has often been presented by an American lawyer living in Slovakia, John A. Young. Before the discussion he presents them with a questionnaire revealing their attitudes to the death penalty, and then he responds to their answers, demonstrating that there are other approaches to this controversial issue. Also included is a discussion of the way NGOs work, describing the various methods NGOs use to protect human rights. Amnesty International is often used as an example to demonstrate how individuals working through groups can assist in protecting human rights.

Presented to the participants and used during these discussions are a number of publications including the UN International Bill of Rights, the *ABC of Teaching Human Rights* (see the section on Romania, above, for a description), Amnesty International U.S.A. Section's *Human Rights for Children*, the Council of Europe's *Short Guide to the European Convention on Human Rights* as well as their pamphlets, and Jean Imbert's *La peine de mort*.

The teaching of techniques is often led by foreign experts, but the Amnesty International participants lead discussions on the importance of accentuating autonomous thinking in the classroom and new approaches to education. This is often accomplished by asking the teachers to participate in games and role-plays. The fact that the Amnesty International trainers are classroom teachers lends credibility to their remarks and gives the participants an opportunity to discuss practical problems in implementing human rights education in Slovak schools. At the workshop's conclusion the trainers spend time reinforcing the lessons that were learned by repeating the generalized principles of the sessions and encouraging the use of this experience in their schools and life experience.

Feedback from these sessions, confirmed by formal evaluations, has been positive. Teachers often comment that they have never before experienced sessions where there was such an emphasis on participation. The inclusion of role-play and games is a new experience for many, and not only does it reflect a difference of pedagogical approach, but effectively engages the teachers in dealing with human rights problems in a realistic and meaningful manner.

The success and interest in the project is confirmed by a response to a letter seeking cooperation from regional authorities in future workshops. Twelve regional administrations are seeking to conduct such workshops and have agreed to pay for the costs out of their budgets. In planning for the future, though, the project coordinators are less than certain that this commitment can be met, given the precarious nature of the Slovakian education budget. Nonetheless, this cooperative effort of Amnesty International/Bratislava and the Šimecka Foundation, along with the other organizations, plans for the continuation and expansion of this program.

Albania: Insular Communism and the Need for Education Conducive to an Open Society

Albania's Separatist Socialist Past and Its Impact on Education

Of the three examples discussed in this chapter, Albania's communist past was significantly different and the most isolated. Although Ceauşescu's Romania created a distinct Marxist political system, divorcing itself from Moscow's influence and establishing close ties with the People's Republic of China and western democracies, Albania's independent course was unique for a Marxist-Leninist state. First a close ally of Tito's Yugoslavia, then moving toward Stalin's Soviet Union, then becoming China's sole ally in Europe and ultimately separating itself from its influence, Albania's communist past was marked by an isolation unlike any other country in Europe.[16] Enver Hoxha's absolute power coupled with his "purist" Marxist ideology impacted education in a peculiarly separatist fashion.[17] Since 1990 this small and poorest of European countries is now openly committed to democracy and the values pronounced in the OSCE Accords and has an overwhelming need to reform its educational system. Its past has marked the problems it must now confront.

Just as Hoxha built literally thousands of bunkers to keep foreigners from intruding into Albania,[18] the regime built ideological walls about its schools. For the forty-five years of communist rule, the educational system was intentionally designed to serve the communist regime and its altering policies and to be a tool for maintaining the party's power. The totalitarianism of the party-state exerted authoritative methods in pedagogy at every level of the educational system. Albania's communist methodology preached isolation and extreme xenophobia. Authorities denounced as dangerous any kind of ideology, practice, or method different from the official one. Certainly the principles of democracy, pluralism, and human rights were alien to Albania's communist education system. The primary theme of the educational system was the inculcation of the importance of the "class struggle." Teaching of all substantive subjects was colored by the party's desire to influence the masses and varied as the party changed its ideological bent.

Like other communist educational systems, schools and educational advancement became a process of selecting a cadre of dedicated communists to serve the state. High school became a privilege for those who were considered to have a good and reliable past and a future in the Marxist ruling system. It remained an unfulfilled dream for those who did not conform to the state's political demands.

Teachers and students and their interaction were affected by the requirements of the importance of class struggle. Beyond question the independence and personality of the teacher were affected. Diversity of ideas and opinions was not accepted, and in the rare instances where they were demonstrated, severe repercussions resulted. Punishment was not only directed against the teacher, but would often be imposed on family members.

Paradoxically the management of the school system was weak, with mediocre administrators who gained employment and promotion not based on talent or hard work but rather on their commitment to the party. Their work was not governed by good pedagogical theory but by orders from the top. Quality was affected by the myopic agenda of the communist system. Teacher education, even before the creation of the State University of Albania in 1957, was minimal, with few two-year teacher preparatory schools.[19] After World War II the large majority of teachers began to work in the school system without any teacher education.

While the creation of the university did improve this situation somewhat, most teachers remained poorly prepared and badly armed with educational materials that either came from the Soviet Union or were prepared by the Albanian communist administration.

After achieving power in 1944, the communists altered the prewar educational system to conform to the eastern model. Prior to this time, the Albanian school system, although admittedly limited in that it reached very few rural Albanians, was nonetheless influenced by western European systems.[20] The eastern influence, largely the Russian one, was very powerful and was adopted for the Albanian schools.[21] Russian pedagogical methods were in use until 1961, when Albania broke its diplomatic relations with the Soviet Union.

With Albania turning to China as its principal protector and model, from 1961 until the end of the 1970s, the good relations with the People's Republic of China were clearly reflected in the educational system.[22] The so-called reform of the schools was to be consistent with revolutionary principles.

The most essential priority for improving the schools—the improvement of teachers and their methods—was the lowest priority for Hoxha's Albania. The "Chinese period of reform," while altering the system consistent with the change of ideology, altered the schools to a degree, but they still relied heavily on the Russian model and brought no real positive change to the educational system. The Chinese Cultural Revolution did, however, have a great influence in Albanian life and significantly intruded into the educational system. Class struggle became even more evident and cruel. Teachers in the classroom could be criticized openly by their pupils. The infamous *dacibaos* (*dacibao*, in Chinese, was a handwritten poster that was used openly to criticize enemies of the people), called in Albanian *flete-rrufe* (a paper that is lightning), were used as weapons against particular teachers, administrators, and others who appeared to be disloyal to the party line. Thus, with these derogatory devices, the teachers' authority was diminished and the quality of instruction was further damaged. The textbooks at all levels were regularly contaminated by the political line.

The Marxist-Leninist education of teachers was an important state goal. Once a week, every Friday, all teachers, as all the rest of the intellectual class, were required to attend afternoon educational classes. This was a perpetual process that was directed at all elements of administration and intellectual life. Regularly the party would insist that those who went through this process had to be active in discussions and to study and be prepared to show their commitment to the party line. Via this process, called "political forms," opportunities to question the value of the system were thwarted, not only by repeating the party line, but by not allowing time and energy to explore other options.

Military training was made one of the most important components in school life. Modeled after the Chinese experience, everyone, teachers and pupils alike, had to attend military training conducted by military officers. The Albanian state pressured the public consistently to train to be able and prepared to defend the country against "inner enemies" and attack from "outside aggressors." Physical training was mandatory, conducted at a precise time every morning at all work places including the schools.[23]

Consistent with the themes of the cultural revolution and the revolutionary triangle, one month a year all middle-level school pupils, accompanied by their teachers, were obligated to work without compensation on the construction of roads, railways, and other public works. In fact, almost all the existing railways in Albania were constructed by students and their teachers. In almost all large construction projects, the contribution of the unpaid work of students and their teachers was enormous. At the time of the harvest, teachers and students were sent to the fields as a "great revolutionary action" to assist peasants with their seasonal work without compensation. The popular slogan describing the intent of this action was "gju me gju me popullin" ("knee to knee with the peasants").

In Albania, human rights education as a school subject was not known to exist, and not until the fall of the communist regime in 1990 could it be considered. The most important subjects were the history of the Albanian communist party, Marxist theory, and dialectic and historic materialism. Pupils were required to pay much attention to these topics, and to have good grades in these subjects was a demonstration of their devotion to the party. The grades one received in these subjects would be an important factor in the decision as to whether one would be permitted to attend high school.

Politics and the party line intruded into every subject taught in the schools, with the exception of the new mathematics, which was introduced late in the communist regime. The first page of a reading primer showed a large color photo of Hoxha followed by other pictures with political messages. Illustrations of children holding guns, enemies, partisan wars, agricultural cooperatives and production, and pioneers loyal to the party were the first images presented to children as early as their first year of elementary school. Students were required to learn verses about the party and their beloved leader by rote. The message was clear: the happy life of Albania was a direct result of the great concern that Hoxha and his party had for the people. Families taught their children at home to be obedient to the party and to applaud appropriately during public occasions in preparation for their attending kindergarten, knowing full well that a political mistake at school would not be appreciated by the authorities and could have bad results.

A demonstration of how the party line intruded into the curriculum can be found in a 1990 edition of the mathematics book still used for third grade: "In one of the bookshops in Tirana, 123 copies of *The History of the Albanian Party of Labor* were sold in the morning, while the number of copies of the same book sold in the afternoon was three times larger. How many books were sold in the afternoon?" The problem clearly is not just designed to teach mathematics. Its message to the student is that the number of books sold in the afternoon was three times larger than those sold in the morning.

Another subject taught in the secondary schools then and now is health education and home economics. The 1990 edition for the third year of secondary school demonstrated that the concern was not for the individual but for the collective and began with a saying often recited by Enver Hoxha: "The building of socialism and the defense of the motherland requires healthy and physically strong people" (*Health Education and Home Economics*, p. 5).

In the 1990 edition of the literature textbook for the second year of secondary school, the number of selections from foreign authors is only seven out of sixty-nine. The foreign authors included were those who were considered politically correct: Maksim Gorky and Vladimir Mayakovski (Russian revolutionary authors), Victor Hugo, A. Nesin (a Turkish humorist), Jules Verne, and so on. These writers were either well-known socialist realist writers or those who reflected socialist ideals such as the Americans Theodore Dreiser and Jack London. Not all their work was published, but only carefully selected examples that reflected socialist ideals considered politically correct. Often the portions with artistic value were not included.

These authors, together with many Albanian writers, who praised and moralized the successful building of socialism through "positive heroes," demonstrated that the only way to happiness is the socialist society and that everyone has to defend it with all their abilities, strength, and a willingness to sacrifice their lives. The socialist realist school of literature was the only one considered acceptable, and the positive hero would serve as an inspiration and model for the young.

This process went so far that even dictionaries gave the explanation of many words and expressions using a political example. Foreign language textbook glossaries went even further in giving explanations of political treatises used throughout the material.

Despite these conditions of political intrusion into the educational system, there were a number of Albanian teachers who made great efforts to obtain more knowledge about the methods of teaching in western countries. Attempts to break out of the socialist frame of teaching were quite difficult and sometimes even dangerous. Inspectors from the pedagogical institutions often observed classes, and teachers had to be concerned to stay within the tightly constructed curriculum. Deviation from the determined practices or curriculum would result in punishment or other sanctions such as being labeled as a "nonrevolutionary teacher," which would be included in one's file.

The fall of communism brought new problems to the educational system. Between December 1990 and March 1992, the crisis of removing the communist system and replacing it with democracy resulted in considerable upheaval. Fifty-two schools were burned, 514 were occupied by force with people using them for housing, and 997 were heavily damaged, including the destruction of books and materials.[24] While the government, with the assistance of foreign aid, made efforts to repair the damage, much remains to be done.

Bringing About Changes in the Albanian Educational System

In order to alter the shortcomings inherited from the previous socialist educational system and to provide much-needed in-service training for Albanian teachers, a national project was prepared and is now being implemented. This project was initiated in 1992 by the Ministry of Education and was given to the Instituti i Studimeve Pedagogjike (Institute of Pedagogical Research, Tirana) to design and administer. The project is partially funded by PHARE (Democracy Programme of the European Union), with the cooperation of the Dutch, Norwegian, and Finnish Helsinki Committees and UNESCO, as well as other NGOs and international organizations. The initiative for the project began with informational seminars on human rights education, and the institute has divided the labor among the various groups. ANA (Aid Norway Albania) took the responsibility to prepare and publish teacher and student human rights manuals in cooperation with the Ministry of Education, which is responsible for teacher training.

The aim of this project is primarily to familiarize teachers with human rights norms and the principles of democratic education and to bring these lessons to the classroom. For this purpose a group of specialists and qualified teachers from Albania and other western countries are working together within Albania.

The project aims:

1. to make Albanian teachers and educators conscious of the necessity to change, to instill in them the necessity to carry out changes during this difficult transition period;
2. to acquaint them with the philosophies, politics, principles, and legislation that is the basis of a democratic state and to ensure that the educational system reflects such values;
3. to introduce teachers and educators to the educational systems and methods of other western democracies and concomitantly to point out the national moral values that have to be considered in light of the Albanian experience;
4. to replace the totalitarian, bureaucratic, inefficient, insular supervision and inspection system of the old regime with an open democratic educational administration and management;
5. to change the teaching methods in the classroom and to encourage among students the development of democratic values and the respect for human rights; and
6. to prepare pedagogical material and tools for Albanian educators consistent with these goals.

In order to accomplish these ends the initial task of the Albanian/international working group was to prepare a basic human rights teachers manual. This was completed in the fall of 1994. The intent was that they share their experiences and skills in compiling and producing human rights and democracy education materials for teachers and pupils at all educational levels. The subject matter includes the texts of the International Conventions on Human Rights and related documents, along with an explanation of the rights and obligations persons have toward themselves and society.

Pedagogical methods and practical classroom exercises are included in this manual. It has been designed to encourage and prepare teachers to implement human rights education in the curriculum. The methods suggested will aim to bring the human rights message into the classroom by preparing the teacher with the necessary tools to make human rights interesting and relevant to the student. The book includes short stories, historical accounts, illustrations, and photographs. Its content draws on the Albanian experience and international topics of interest relevant to Albanian needs. The book is meant to serve as a pedagogical tool for teacher training. The teachers manual will ultimately be presented in three different versions adapted to the various school levels.

This manual will be followed by children's activities textbooks, designed to be smaller and less costly, for the use of pupils in the different grades. These textbooks, prepared for eight different educational levels, from primary to secondary schools, are in the process of completion and will be ready for distribution soon. Assisting the Albanian working groups are experts from the Netherlands Helsinki Committee, the Danish Centre for Human Rights, and Amnesty International. The resources used for these books are numerous and come from a variety of countries with experience in human rights education, but are shaped and altered to meet the Albanian mentality and experience.[25] The intent is for the first editions to act as a pilot to be tested in the classrooms and then changed to meet the needs that were learned from the classroom experience. This project was partially completed in 1994.

This national project will be responsible for training teachers and educators at a variety of levels:

1. preschool education (from three to six years): 2,784 institutions; 81,117 children; 5,643 educators (January 1994: 4,541);
2. compulsory education (from the first to the eighth grade and, starting in 1995, the twelfth grade): 1,779 institutions; 525,892 students; 29,553 teachers (January 1994: 35,734);
3. general middle education (middle school): 9,599 teachers (January 1994: 6,627);[26]
4. state and private middle schools;
5. technical subject teachers in agricultural and mechanical schools;
6. pedagogical training in middle schools dealing with psychology, pedagogy, didactics, and so on;
7. art teachers in middle and secondary schools.

The plan includes the preparation of teacher trainers who will receive training abroad in pedagogical techniques including textbook preparation, classroom methodologies, and test preparation. Those selected will come from a variety of academic disciplines. This select group will prepare local trainers who will actually work with Albanian teachers. In 1994–95 a series of teacher-training seminars was held for three days, in Tirana, Škodra, Korca, and Peškopia. Six hundred teachers at all educational levels participated in this effort from all over Albania. This was for many their first contact with these pedagogical methods. From later communications with this group it became apparent that they quickly incorporated many of the techniques demonstrated at the seminar into their classrooms. From their school publications it was learned that many of these teachers began to train their colleagues in these methods.

In addition, there were a number of programs held in the primary schools where techniques could be tested. Trainers and teachers went back to their schools where the ABCs of human rights were explained and discussed. In some instances, contests among pupils were held, first in their classrooms, later competing with other classes and then other schools. Winners were awarded prizes.

In spring 1995, the Convention on the Rights of the Child was translated and published in Albanian and is being distributed to teachers. The children's version of this convention, especially prepared by the Institute of Pedagogical Research for students below fourteen, will be included in the children's activity textbook to be made available to all schoolchildren.

An important aspect of this project is the eventual creation of a National Center of Documentation, Training, and Information for Education. The center will supply documents and other necessary materials for the qualification of specialized teachers as well as all the other categories that are not included in the project.

Some Additional Obstacles to Overcome and Conclusions

A considerable concern in achieving the aims of this project is the size of the student population. Albania, with a population of just over 3 million people, has 650,000 school students, approximately a little less than 20 percent of the population. In addition there are more than 45,000 active teachers distributed throughout the country. The Albanian infrastructure (roads, railways, and so on) is in very poor condition, making it difficult to travel and communicate easily. This is especially true in winter, during the school year, when communications with the north are a problem. Given the mountainous terrain, lack of travel funds, and large numbers involved, it is extremely difficult to hold national or regional training sessions and seminars. This is one of the rationales for relying on local trainers to bring change to the schools in their regions.

Unlike other Central European countries, Albania does have an advantage in implementing this project in that there is one common language. With the exception of a Greek minority in the south,[27] all Albanians now use, unlike in an earlier time, their own language in the schools, which is grammatically uniform and has no distinct dialects.

While the long road to change has begun, the realities of an entrenched totalitarian culture combined with poverty and social upheaval require that concerted efforts be made to change the educational system. Despite these considerable obstacles, the staff of the Pedagogical Institute and the others working on this project are not only competent, but are eager to formulate actions that will bring change. Their optimism in light of a bleak situation provides impetus for others to change. The draft project is well designed and has reasonable expectations, using resources at its disposal and dividing tasks in a realistic fashion. It is designed in an incremental fashion, involving the appropriate NGOs at the various stages of the work. Ultimately it is planned that more than one thousand qualified teachers, presently working part-time, will be directly involved in this project. While there is presently sufficient support to begin this effort, more resources must be found to make it a nationwide program. The hope is that the initial success of this program will attract additional support to complete its worthy aims.

Conclusion

The common threads of these three country commentaries are the difficulties that must be overcome in order to alter educational systems that had been designed to perpetuate totalitarian regimes and at the same time to initiate long-term change in the political culture. While there are differences in the intensity and character of the Romanian, Slovakian, and Albanian totalitarian experiences, each of these states now has a considerable challenge to realize the promise made to its own citizens and to the international community to secure human rights and fundamental freedoms. Nearly half a century of communist rule is not an easy condition to alter and cannot be achieved easily or instantaneously, especially for the educational establishment.

Central to these states' efforts to conform to the commitments to the covenants and the OSCE Accords is the need to make fundamental changes as to how new generations will be educated. Yet, as was documented in this chapter, the existing inertia and pressures against change are considerable. Governments, now responsive to the democratic will and the demands of the international community, must also take into account the pressures and influence of those still in control of the educational bureaucracies, who have vested interests in not changing, as well as a population unfamiliar and perhaps apathetic to democratic values practiced in the schools.

In addition, overhauling an entire educational system not only takes considerable resources in economies already strained in their conversion from a command system to a free market, but takes energy and trained talent. This talent is often rare or undiscovered in emerging democracies. While foreign experts can play a positive role in the transition, ultimately indigenous actors, teachers, and administrators, must be the primary agents of change. They must be convinced and trained to become human rights advocates to convert the schools into places where human rights are taught and respected. This will take time, effort, and creativity.

The energy is often absent as well. Given the volatile political climates of these states, educators, still suffering from the scars of the earlier regimes, are reluctant to be too enthusiastic in support of democratic change, fearing that the political wind will change again and their futures will suffer from having chosen the wrong tack. In addition, in states where prosperity is still a dream, economic reality often makes change difficult, as teachers are often more concerned with keeping their job and pleasing their superiors than with teaching human rights.

Pressure to change continues to come from outside. Certainly international organizations, advisors, and foreign governments can and ought to continue to assert influence to ensure that Romania, Slovakia, and Albania comply with their international commitments to "promote" human rights. Their badly needed aid and advice should be used to create educational systems that are consistent with human rights norms. Yet, despite the power of aid, ultimately change must be wrought by citizens insisting that human rights be the norm and not the exception and that the schools become the vehicles to teach future voters the value of democratic ideas and respect for human rights.

Given these realities, NGOs have an important role to play. As this chapter witnesses, local groups dedicated to altering former totalitarian societies to democratic ones can be important catalysts that facilitate the establishment of educational systems conducive to a human rights culture. Yet there is no one clear path or method. A perfect and successful transition from communism to pluralistic democracy is still not known. The present experience is not complete, and each former communist state must deal with its own peculiarities of the past and present. As these commentaries point out, each of these groups is struggling to find the cure to rid the present of its past, so its future will reflect the values it now espouses. These groups can and do receive some help, financial and otherwise, from the outside (arguably too little of the first and perhaps too much of the second), but "the change" is their responsibility and the outcome will be primarily theirs to live with.

Notes

1. All three states are UN members and are bound by the Charter. Romania ratified the two international covenants (the Covenant on Economic, Social and Cultural Rights, 1976; the Covenant on Civil and Political Rights, and the Optional Protocol, 1993), along with the Convention on the Rights of the Child (1990). It also ratified the European Convention on Human Rights in spring 1993, accepting the right of individual petition and the jurisdiction of the Court. Slovakia has ratified the covenants and the Optional Protocol as well as the Convention on the Rights of the Child (1993) and the European Convention (see note 9 below). Albania ratified the international covenants (1993) but not the Optional Protocol. Since it has not yet been admitted to the Council of Europe, it has not ratified the European Convention

on Human Rights. All three states are participating states in the Organization for Security and Cooperation in Europe (OSCE) and have agreed to the OSCE Accords.

2. See Paul M. Kennedy, *Preparing for the Twenty-First Century* (New York: Random House, 1993), 16 note 18: "In fact, the most important influence on a nation's responsiveness to change probably is its social attitudes, religious beliefs, and culture."

3. Ibid., 17: "Cultural obstacles to change are common to all societies, for the obvious reason that an impending transformation threatens existing habits, ways of life, beliefs, and social prejudices. They are as likely to occur in advanced societies as in underdeveloped ones. . . . To respond to change might mean altering one's own social priorities, *educational system*, patterns of consumption and saving, *even basic beliefs about the relationship between the individual and society*" (emphasis added).

4. United Nations Centre for Human Rights, Geneva, *Human Rights: A Compilation of International Instruments* (New York: United Nations, 1993). Article 13, para. 1 of the International Covenant on Economic, Social and Cultural Rights: "The States Parties to the present Covenant recognize the right of everyone to education. *They agree that education shall be directed to the full development of the human personality and the sense of its dignity, and shall strengthen the respect for human rights and fundamental freedoms.* They further agree that eduction shall enable all persons to participate effectively in a free society, promote understanding, tolerance and friendship among all nations and all racial, ethnic or religious groups" (emphasis added).

5. From 1866 until 1947 Romania was a monarchy. Romania's King Michael fled the country and was perceived as a threat to the communist regime. His influence in Romanian politics continues to remain considerable. His visit to Romania in 1992 drew thousands into the streets, with many of his supporters calling for his return to Romania. Since then he has not returned to the country. See Robert D. Kaplan, *Balkan Ghosts: A Journey Through History* (New York: St. Martin's Press, 1993). In 1940 Michael, at age eighteen, assumed the throne in the wake of a revolution that toppled his father, King Carol. Initially he was a figurehead to General Ion Antonescu, a controversial fascistic leader, but later conspired against Antonescu and engineered his overthrow. He left for Switzerland, not returning until 1992, as he was seen as a threat to the communists as he is now a threat to the present government (ibid., 96, 130).

6. Andreé Codrescu, *The Hole in the Flag* (New York: William Morrow and Company, 1991), 88. He cites the December 29, 1989 edition of *Adevárul* (*The Truth*, a Bucharest newspaper), which, at the height of the revolution, called for "the restructuring of the educational system along student demands."

7. At the end of 1992, IRDO (Institutul Roman Pentru Drepturile Omului [Romanian Institute for Human Rights]), a parliamentary-sponsored institute, published *Drepturile Omului: Religie a sfirsitului de secol (Human Rights: Religion of the End of the Century)*, written by Adrian Nastase, at the time minister of external affairs and since 1993 president of the Chamber of Deputies, the lower house of the Romanian Parliament, and leader of the majority party, PDSR (Patidul Democratiei Socialiste din Romania). The book was written for legal specialists and is not intended for use in the school system.

8. *The ABC of Human Rights* should not be confused with *ABC Teaching Human Rights: Practical Activities for Primary and Secondary Schools*, mentioned in the discussions of Slovakia and Albania.

9. Articles of the Convention on the Rights of the Child can provide a guide for a democratic school regime. For example, Article 28 (2): "States Parties shall take all appropriate measures to ensure that school discipline is administered in a manner consistent with the child's human dignity and in conformity with the present Convention." Article 29 (1): "States Parties agree that the education of the child be directed to: (a) the development of the child's personality, talents and mental and physical abilities to their fullest potential; (b) the development of *respect for human rights and fundamental freedoms,* and for principles enshrined in the Charter of the United Nations; (c) the development of respect for the child's parents, his or her own cultural identity, language and values of the country in which the child is living, the country from which

he or she may originate, and for civilizations different from his or her own; (d) the preparation of the child for responsible life in a free society" (emphasis added).

10. V. Hatch et al., *Human Rights for Children* (Alameda, Calif.: Hunter House-Amnesty International, 1992).

11. L. Neacsu, with C. Turcu, illustrator, *O poveste pentru copii despre . . . Declaratia Universala a Drepturilor Omului (A Story for Children about . . . the Universal Declaration of Human Rights* (Bucharest: SIRDO, 1994).

12. Milan Kollár, director, International Law Department, the Republic of Slovakia, explained in an interview with HRAP (Human Rights Advocacy Project) co-director Theodore S. Orlin in January 1992 the secession problem of human rights treaties. On December 6, 1992, before Slovak independence, the upper house of the Czechoslovakian Parliament made a commitment that Slovakia would honor all the Czechoslovakian international commitments. This, according to Kollár, had legal effect, as the Chamber of Nations within the Czechoslovakia system represented the Slovak Republic.

Kollár also made clear that there would be no new reservations to the agreement and they would also include the protocols; hence the Optional Protocol allowing for individual complaint regarding the international covenant was binding on Slovakia before it officially reratified it. This status was published in the *U.N. Journal.* The *Council of Europe Information Sheet* 32 (January–June 1993): 1 reports: "The Czech and Slovak Federal Republic was a Contracting Party from 18 March 1992 to 31 December 1992. Following declarations made by the Czech Republic and Slovakia of their intention to succeed the Czech and Slovak Federal Republic and to consider themselves bound by the European Convention on Human Rights as of 1 January 1993, the Committee of Ministers decided on 30 June 1993 that these States are to be regarded as Parties to the convention with effect from 1 January 1993." They are also bound by Article 25, the Right of Personal Petition, and Article 46, acceptance of compulsory jurisdiction of the European Court of Human Rights (ibid., 3).

13. According to the UN Centre for Human Rights (March 1, 1994), the treaties ratified by the Slovak Republic are: the International Covenant on Economic, Social and Cultural Rights, the International Covenant on Civil and Political Rights, the First Optional Protocol, the International Covenant on the Elimination of All Forms of Racial Discrimination, the International Covenant on the Suppression and Punishment of the Crime of Apartheid, the Convention on the Elimination of All Forms of Discrimination Against Women, and the Convention on the Rights of the Child.

14. The Milan Šimecka Foundation, with an office in Bratislava, active in the Czech Republic (working along with Czech groups) and in the Slovak Republic, has as its mission the support and initiation of activities aimed at the development of democracy, the enhancement of culture, and the cultivation of intellectually aware citizens able to function in this new political environment.

15. The National Endowment for Democracy (NED) provided $26,900, and the Open Society fund gave $7,500 for the project. Before the breakup of the republics, the Czechoslovak Federal government supported this project with funds that were used to publish documents and training materials disseminated through the workshops.

16. See Nicholas C. Pano, *The People's Republic of Albania* (Baltimore: Johns Hopkins University Press, 1968) for a detailed account of Albania's relationship with the communist world.

17. Pano states that "the period from 1949 to 1953 also witnessed improvement in the Albanian educational system, the objectives of which were the propagation of communist ideology and providing the academic and technical training necessary for the construction of a socialist state and society" (ibid.). He notes that by 1950 the illiteracy rate fell from 60 percent (1946) to 31 percent (Pano, *Albania*, 103).

18. The official estimate is that 300,000 bunkers were constructed throughout the country to

protect a population of 3 million. It is often cited that each bunker cost $10,000 to construct. These monuments to Albania's xenophobic past remain, as no program has yet been devised to destroy these fortifications. They are found everywhere from the beaches to urban settings and have become an integral part of the Albanian landscape.

19. Pano, *Albania*, 103: "the government established five institutions on the secondary level to train teachers for service in the primary and seven-year schools and a two year teachers' college to provide faculty for the secondary schools [reference to Stavro Skendi, ed., *Albania* (New York: F. A. Praeger, 1956), 278–79 note 31]. . . . By 1950, the number of schools, pupils, and teachers had doubled in comparison with the total for each of these categories in 1945."

20. See Anton Logoreci, *The Albanians: Europe's Forgotten Survivors* (London: Victor Gollancz, 1977), for details of Albania's prewar educational system. He notes that in 1938 there were 650 primary schools and only 20 secondary schools, with only 36 percent of Albanian children receiving education of any kind. The number of university graduates was ninety. Nonetheless, he cites the operation of schools by American foundations, Jesuits, and Franciscans (p. 62). He also notes that there was an Austrian influence. The Austrians opened a primary school in Škodër in 1855 and later established several others. Italians, as well, opened schools in Catholic areas. These schools did not teach in Albanian, nor did the schools established by the Ottoman authorities (1840s), who taught in Turkish and stressed Islamic religious training. The same was true for the Greek Orthodox-sponsored schools where Greek was the language of study. Hence the call for teaching in Albanian became a nationalistic patriotic cause (ibid., 37–39).

21. From 1948 "Albania adopted the Soviet system of education lock stock and barrel, and became dependent on Moscow for the training of most of its professional people and specialists. There was an acute shortage of teachers of every type. To overcome this, several colleges were set up for training primary and secondary school teachers. A number of vocational schools were also established to meet the increasing demand for skilled or semi skilled workers. . . . Russia contributed to this educational advance by providing Albanian schools and colleges with specialists and technical equipment" (Logoreci, *The Albanians*, 112 and 169). See Paul Lendvai, *Eagles in Cobwebs* (Garden City, N.Y.: Doubleday, 1969), who notes (p. 230) that during the early stages of the communist regime, Yugoslavia had considerable influence in the Albanian educational system, with 1,500 Albanians going to study in Yugoslavia and Serbo-Croatian being made a compulsory subject in the schools.

22. "In 1967 educational reform became part of the cultural revolution when Hoxha announced the broad principles of future development. He admitted that the uncritical adoption of the Soviet system had been a mistake in view of the great disparities between the two countries" (Logoreci, *The Albanians*, 170).

23. Logorici describes the 1970 reform (ibid., 170–71): "Boys and girls from six to eighteen attending eight-grade schools, secondary or vocational schools, devote six and half months to academic study, two and half months to productive work, one month to military training and the remaining two months to holidays. Military training based on the theory and practice of partisan or guerrilla warfare takes place within the school itself and later in conjunction with units of the armed forces. The system gives pride of place to China's so-called "half work half study " schools."

24. *Intensive Retraining of Teachers and Educators of Albania in the Years 1993–1995* (Tirana, Albania: Pedagogical Studies Institute, Oct. 1992–Jan. 1993).

25. Among the sources used were: the Australian Human Rights Commission, Education Series, *Teaching for Human Rights: Grades 1–4 and 5–10*: Betty Reardon, *Educating for Human Dignity: Learning About Rights and Responsibilities: A K–12 Teaching Resource* (Philadelphia: University of Pennsylvania Press, 1995); Gary Smith and George Otero, *Teaching About Cultural Awareness* (Denver: Center for Teaching International Relations, University of Denver, 1989); William J. Kreidler, *Creative Conflict Resolution* (Glenview, Ill.: Scott, Foresman and Co., 1984).

26. Ibid. These figures were updated from information provided by the Albanian Ministry of Education, summer 1995.

27. See M. van der Stoel, "Recomendations by the CSCE High Commissioner on National Minorities upon His Visits to Romania and Albania," *Human Rights Law Journal* 14, nos. 11–12 (1993): 435, where he notes: "7. The Government's statistics shows that there are a total of 81 schools with 4,545 pupils from the Greek minority. Legislation, which would allow parents from the Greek minority to start private schools anywhere in Albania, is under preparation. 8. The State will open two Greek secondary schools, one in the district of Gjirokastra and one in the district of Saranda, provided that the necessary contingent of pupils is guaranteed. . . . Furthermore the printing house in Gjirokastra has undertaken to print nine textbooks for instruction in the Greek language." At this stage in the development of the human rights education project, there have been no steps taken to accommodate the needs of the Greek minority.

Chapter 30
Labor Union Human Rights Education on Foreign Labor Issues in Germany

Alexander von Cube

This chapter discusses human rights education (HRE) of German labor unions principally for foreign wage earners. In educational programs, it is wise to consider who educates, to what end, where, whom, and how, in order to understand the strengths, limitations, and biases. This holds true for the program described below, which may have very limited applicability elsewhere. It is well known that transferability is not appropriate in all contexts or at least not without modifications. Failures of technological, cultural, and political transfer are only too familiar and bring to mind images of goodwill but incompetence. Competence in human rights is especially important because the victims of incompetence are always persons.

Migration: The Source of Germany's Recent Human Rights Problems

Human rights issues in Germany in the mid-1990s are governed by three developments: European unification, German unification, and the breakup of the former Soviet empire. These events, each in its own way, are triggering new human rights issues for Germany. European unification is working toward a single market without borders in which the free movement of goods and persons is guaranteed. Along with this development the role of the individual needs to be newly evaluated, new rights need be anchored, and old ones strengthened. Since the collapse of the former East German regime in 1989, there has been an influx of population from the so-called new German states to the former Federal Republic of Germany (FRG) of almost 1.5 million people. German reunification brought major social and economic instability, dislocation, and uncertainty as well as sacrifice in an extended process aimed at achieving equal living conditions in the united Germany. The breakup of the former Soviet empire resulted most directly in significant migration of ethnic Germans to Germany. The political changes in Eastern Europe have contributed to a hitherto unknown freedom of travel and movement among the people of that region, who are

TABLE 1. Asylum Seekers, Germany, Selected Years 1970 Through June 1994

Year/Month	Persons	Year/Month	Persons
1970	8,645	1991	256,112
1975	9,627	1992	438,191
1980	107,818	1993	322,599
1985	73,832	1994 January	13,154
1986	99,650	1994 February	10,487
1987	53,379	1994 March	12,181
1988	103,076	1994 April	8,789
1989	121,316	1994 May	9,287
1990	193,063	1994 June	8,104

Source: Federal Statistical Office, Wiesbaden, Germany, 1994

eager to participate in the affluence of those countries whose population is economically better situated. This has activated the migration potential of the Eastern European reform states. Thus it is primarily from the issue of migration that Germany's current human rights problems emanate.

Human rights problems in Germany are placed in context of the major migration flows of the past several years. While the migration pressure on Western Europe generally has increased in recent history, Germany has carried by far the major burden accompanying significant immigration. The trigger of this migration has been the breakup of the former Soviet empire. Some of the contributing circumstances are unique to Germany, such as Germany's geographic proximity to Eastern Europe; its lenient asylum law compared to other European countries (prior to July 1, 1993); the return of ethnic Germans from Eastern Europe, particularly from the former Soviet Union, Poland, and Central Asia, especially Kazakhstan; and other factors of immigration including population pressures in developing countries and widespread poverty throughout Africa.

Statistical Evidence of Migration

The following presents the most recent migration events in a demographic statistical context and then provides some statistical evidence of human rights violations.

The German asylum law in force through June 30, 1993 required that a thorough examination regarding factual circumstances and legal facts be conducted for every asylum seeker who claimed political persecution. This was a lengthy administrative and legal process during which the asylum applicant as a rule was permitted to remain in Germany. As Table 1 indicates, the number of asylum seekers steadily climbed until the most recent past. In 1982 there were 37,000 applicants, but only ten years later, in 1992, the annual figure had reached twelve times that number. During that time, "Germany was the destination for a total of more than 1.65 million asylum seekers . . .

TABLE 2. Total Foreign Population, Germany (up to and including 1990 old FRG only; thereafter united Germany), Selected Years

Year	Number of Foreigners	Year	Number of Foreigners
1961	686,160 (Census)	1990	5,342,532
1970	2,438,600 (Census)	1991	5,882,267
1987	4,145,575 (Census)	1992	6,495,792
1988	4,240,532	1993	6,878,117
1989	4,845,882		

Source: Federal Statistical Office, Wiesbaden, Germany, 1994

TABLE 3. Immigration of Ethnic Germans to Germany, 1980 through June 1994

Year/Month	Persons	Year/Month	Persons
1980	52,071	1991	221,995
1981	69,455	1992	230,565
1982	48,170	1993	218,888
1983	37,925	1994 January	18,827
1984	36,459	1994 February	13,932
1985	38,958	1994 March	16,495
1986	42,788	1994 April	15,980
1987	78,523	1994 May	14,714
1988	202,673	1994 June	17,695
1989	377,055	Total	2,150,241
1990	397,073		

Source: Federal Statistical Office, Wiesbaden, Germany, 1994

far more than half of all asylum seekers in the European Union."[1] At the end of 1993 there were 2 million refugees in Germany, up from 610,000 in 1985. This number included those with and without refugee status according to the Geneva Convention, including 400,000 civil war refugees for 1993, largely from the former Yugoslavia. Thus the total foreign population for Germany at the end of 1993 had increased tenfold to 6,878,117 since the 1961 Census when it stood at 686,160 (see Table 2).

In addition, and not included among the foreign population, Germany since 1980 accepted approximately 2.1 million ethnic Germans from the states of Southeast and Eastern Europe, the former Soviet Union and its successor states, the bulk of which arrived since 1988. Table 3 indicates the inflow of ethnic Germans from Eastern Europe since 1980.

Human Rights Violations

This minimal demographic profile provides the background and context against which human rights violations in Germany must be viewed. Rising unemployment and the prevailing shortage of housing were contributing factors which increasingly jeopardized integration of foreigners into German society purportedly due to the annually mounting numbers of immigrants. There are mechanisms for facilitating integration of foreigners, such as the Aliens Act of January 1991 and a generally cooperative network among federal, state, and local governments, churches, unions, employers, and welfare organizations. However, the public perception is that integration can no longer be warranted unless immigration is controlled. There is widespread fear among the German population that standards of living are being eroded by the influx of foreigners: "A high percentage (approximately two-thirds) are reserved towards immigrants, blame them for burning social problems and concede them only minor rights."[2]

In this milieu the most atrocious human rights violations are being committed in Germany against foreigners, seen as the scapegoats, by largely young, often unemployed youth. But the human rights violations include not only those of the most dramatic nature, such as firebombings of homes of foreign residents, but also a broad sprectrum of other violations which are not necessarily captured in statistics and which will be addressed later in this chapter. Relevant, too, is that the sudden increase of personal attacks on foreigners does not necessarily reflect a widespread anti-foreign attitude on the part of Germans, if one believes survey data.

According to the German Bundeskriminalamt tracking *fremdenfeindliche Straftaten* (criminal acts against foreign citizens), there was a sudden increase in criminal acts committed against foreigners in 1991 for a total of 2,426 cases, while the recorded cases between 1987 and 1990 averaged around 250. About three-fourths of the anti-foreign acts included distribution of propaganda material, disturbing the public peace, and property damage without violence. Nonetheless, the serious violent attacks also increased; for example, in 1991 there were 239 cases of attacks against persons, including 336 cases of setting fire to residences occupied by foreigners. This trend continued in 1992, 1993, and the first half of 1994, as is evident from Table 4, when the total incidents on foreigners averaged around 6,000 cases.

Ultimately the question must be asked to what degree HRE is addressing itself to the most severe excesses of human rights violations. Before discussing this point further, that is, how well HRE is responding to the greatest needs, a profile of the offenders beyond the mere statistical acts of violence is provided here, as seen by the authors of one study that evaluated police records.

Helmut Willems and co-authors, in a 1993 study on violence against foreigners, went beyond pursuing a single case history of violence to determine who the suspects were and what the genesis of these violent acts was.[3] The study evaluated nearly 1,400 police records from nine states and 53 judicial records that refer to 148 offenders, and assembled a profile of these persons committing the criminal acts. They determined that more than 70 percent of the offenders were between fifteen and twenty years of age, with only 5 percent over age thirty and 96 percent being males. The great majoriy

TABLE 4. Monthly* Distribution of Anti-Foreign Crimes,** Germany, 1991 through June 1994

	1991	1992	1993	1994
January	40	276	614	299
February	47	274	530	205
March	43	257	463	219
April	68	274	373	245
May	64	206	508	244
June	71	201	1,479	179
July	70	220	495	
August	104	461	380	
September		314	1,163	296
October	961	816	267	
November		420	1,158	276
December		224	1,030	1,040
Total	2,426	6,336	6,721	1,391

*These figures include murders, attempted murders, aggravated assaults, explosives violations, arson, attempted arson, crimes of property, disturbing the peace, and miscellaneous anti-foreign crimes.
**In defining the phenomenon of anti-foreign crimes, the police use the following definition: anti-foreign crimes are criminal acts aimed at persons whom the perpetrators deny the right of temporary or permanent residence in the area or anywhere in the Federal Republic on the basis of their actual or supposed nationality, ethnicity, race or color, religion, philosophy, origin, or on the basis of their outward appearance.
Source: Bundeskriminalamt, Bonn, Germany, 1994

of the offenders had a low to medium formal educational level and came, disproportionately to the rest of the age group, from the ranks of the unemployed. Almost 50 percent of the suspects were already known to the police, and 25 percent had prior criminal records. Membership in groups on the political Right was another frequently observed characteristic. Among the small percentage of older offenders, high unemployment, repeated criminal behavior, and membership in rightist organizations were characteristic.

The authors noted that acts of violence against foreigners in the former German Democratic Republic (GDR) were committed as part of mass violence 64 percent of the time, in contrast to the old German states where that pattern occurred only 21 percent of the time and where the share of individual actors of groups of ten and fewer was more frequent. Nevertheless, more than 90 percent of the acts were committed by groups categorized by the police as "skinheads 38%, rightist groups 25%, anti-foreign 19%, other 10%." More than 79 percent of the offenders came from the same geographic areas as the victims, 20 percent even from the same neighborhood. These acts of violence are rarely preplanned but occur spontaneously where anti-foreign motives and action-oriented violence requirements play a major role. Although not necessarily preplanned, the act of violence itself is executed according to a planned procedure.

According to the Willems study, the offenders can be characterized as being guided by "diffuse feelings and ideas of a general threat and sense of disadvantage of Germans vis-à-vis 'the foreigners,' especially vis-à-vis the asylum seekers." The authors of the study further noted that "with the mounting number of asylum seekers, the corresponding local conflicts, and the public debate of these issues, anti-foreign groups no longer felt marginalized and stigmatized but supposedly considered themselves as the avant-garde of a broader movement."

What has been the reaction of the German public to human rights violations? There is widespread public outrage regarding hatred of foreigners; this expresses itself in public opinion polls, in candlelight parades in 1993, in letters to the editor, in political comments, in work on the community level by local groups, and in work by churches. Another segment of German society, the labor unions, have also dedicated themselves to attacking human rights violations on foreigners.

Human rights violations in Germany are hostile acts against foreign citizens. The more general condition of this state of affairs is called *Fremdenfeindlichkeit*. This chapter presents selective aspects of HRE without claiming to be a country study, and it does not attempt to formulate a theory of human rights education. It is simply a case study offering some principles of human rights education through the example of the work of labor unions in Germany.

German Labor Unions and HRE

Practitioners of human rights education generally acknowledge the need to move from covenants, conventions, and declarations to the applied level of "how to." Strategies of jurisprudence, that is, the legal anchoring of rights of individuals to fair treatment and freedom from violence in constitutions, must now be followed by strategies of implementation. HRE is an antidote to violence; it "is a preventive influence in the curbing of abuses."[4]

Labor unions in Germany have recognized the need for HRE. The tradition of labor unions speaking out on social issues, including prejudice against foreigners, goes back to before World War II. Human rights education has up till now neither advanced to a level that is desirable or necessary. Yet this transition from legal human rights to strategies of implementation and teaching of human rights is well on the way among German labor unions. Even if the term HRE in the traditional sense of the word *education* might not be warranted, the unions' efforts are a positive beginning.[5] Members of the Deutsche Gewerkschaftsbund (DGB) to whom I spoke, and who themselves did some human rights education, were the first to exercise self-criticism and admitted that to speak of widespread HRE in German unions might be misleading. Focusing on the HRE of unions is, nevertheless, justified for two reasons: first, important HRE by union officials is being done, although not in all unions; and second, the DGB, as the umbrella organization of unions, is encouraging this work and is thus providing leadership for HRE.

At the beginning of 1994 there were sixteen autonomous labor unions in Germany with a total membership of 10.3 million. These included 800,000 organized dues-paying members with foreign citizenship, refugees and labor migrants among them. German unions, as well as the DGB, have made many pronouncements and recommendations, and lay claim to be not solely interested representatives of organized labor (*Arbeitnehmerschaft*) but also to constitute a social movement. The DGB understands its policy toward labor force participants of foreign citizenship as a contribution toward the integration of foreign workers and their families. As a social institution in the center of society, the influence that labor unions exert is far-reaching.

Whether HRE is being done in a union hinges on a number of factors including personal initiative of officials in the respective union and the demographic, ethnic, and social makeup of the labor force. Without conducting a survey on HRE of each individual union, there is no way to determine the extent of this work. It is clear that many unions are doing nothing beyond meeting equal tariff and wage obligations for all members. The examples of HRE cited here stem from the Frankfurt am Main area.

HRE Program Examples from the Frankfurt am Main Area

HRE examples are taken from the Frankfurt am Main area as more such programs exist there than anywhere else because of the city's large share of foreigners. In fact, Frankfurt holds a special position within Germany because it has the largest foreign population in the country. At the end of 1993 the foreign population of the city was 191,600, up from the previous year's total of 185,480; this represents approximately 30 percent of the total population of the city of Frankfurt.

The resident population of the city of Frankfurt can be characterized as bipolar; on the one hand, the native population is demographically aging as a substantial share of the younger native professionals have moved to the suburbs. On the other hand, there is a foreign population that is largely young. In addition to the demographic difference there is a "foreign-native" divide along socioeconomic lines, not solely along lines of nationality. The foreign population is employed primarily in restaurants and in low-skill, low-paying service sector jobs. They come predominantly from Southern, Central, and Eastern Europe. They are in part those nationals who were hired before 1973 under the so-called Gastarbeiter program when German companies recruited either directly in the countries of origin or at the German border until such recruitment stopped in 1973. Although according to the German government, Germany does not consider itself an immigration country, there are those who claim that after the recruitment freeze Germany effectively became a country of immigration, with the first major contingent of immigrants being those who decided not to return to their own country when the German government offered to provide travel and other incentives for their return. As a result, 65 percent of all children under twenty years of age in Frankfurt today are of foreign citizenship. This sociodemographic profile leads to what Germans call *Überfremdungsängste* with the native population, that is, the fear of being absorbed by foreigners.

What union programs exist? Programs against extremism on the right, racism, and intolerance are integrated into the general educational work of the unions. Union officials and interested members are potential attendees of weekend seminars, or members are given special education leave of one or two weeks.

First-level responses by unions to public violence against foreigners are written recommendations, upheld and promulgated by union officials to their own membership, and designed to counter such violence. These recommendations are being disseminated to the membership via union publications, information bulletins, company newspapers, and through general educational work. As union membership represents a cross section of German middle-class society, there are a considerable number of union members who also hold hostile positions toward foreigners and who would be willing to demonstrate their attitudes, for example, in their voting behavior. Some of the hostility stems from the practice of employers hiring non-union foreign labor below scale. Some unions have been conducting campaigns against illegal work and against temporary special contracts for female workers from Eastern European countries. These are cases where union interests collide with the interest of maintaining jobs in tariff contractual arrangements. HRE by unions focuses primarily on problems of integrating foreigners into the workplace, that is, on persons who have come to Germany to work. The examples that follow reflect this objective.

The Bald Project

In the realization that integration issues and rectifying human rights violations involve bringing both parties—German natives and foreigners—together, BALD (*Bildungsprojekt mit Deutschen und Ausländern* [Educational Project with Germans and Foreigners]) was initiated and designed by the Social Academy at Dortmund under a grant from a German labor union foundation, under the umbrella of the DGB educational branch. The object of this project, which began in 1985, was to acquaint German and foreign families with each other, to determine the commonalities between them. It was the first time that pedagogy was brought into the unions. This project selected themes, provided guidelines, and set as its objective the removal of prejudices through familiarization and getting-acquainted sessions.

Methodology was initially rather crude. One might more appropriately speak about guidelines on which to focus, including the reduction of fears. Problems were understood in terms of building blocks to be analyzed and broken down into small components. Union members were organized into seminars they attended on a voluntary basis, where topics of discrimination were being dealt with. Union members were made aware that, regardless of nationality, members shared the same concerns. Only language and citizenship separated them. Weekend seminars were organized where families became acquainted with each other, German and foreign. These seminars were not intended to be *Bildungsseminars*, that is, not designed to pass on "information and knowledge" in a strict time schedule per se but simply for purposes of discussion and getting acquainted and reducing stereotypes of "fundamentalists with headcloths." The first women seminars were organized under the BALD program. Bus trips for thirty to forty women and children were arranged with activities planned for children including child care. It was stressed that, although women might have come here for work, that "we are not here for work only." The idea was to get away from a strictly instrumentarian viewpoint about the foreign female labor force. The organized activities brought the various nationalities together, not just Germans and foreigners, but also foreigners among each other, for example, Spaniards and Turks. Conflicts regarding integration originate not just from confrontations between foreigners and Germans but are present between foreign groups as well, that is, older foreign groups that are competing against newly arrived foreigners with a similar claim: "give us the rights first."

Educational Resources from the International Labour Organization on Integration and Nondiscrimination Issues
by Richard Pierre Claude

The International Labour Organization (ILO) is a specialized agency of the United Nations with 171 members. Its numerous publications include many that are designed to be helpful to educators and trainers concerned with labor issues. For example, *Training for Change: New Approach to Instruction and Learning in Working Life* by Yrjö Engeström is useful for anyone interested in turning workplaces into learning organizations.

The ILO deals with internationally defined labor standards and workers rights; thus an important ILO project objective is to reduce discrimination by informing policymakers, employers, workers, and trainers engaged in anti-discrimination training on how legislative measures and training activities can be rendered more effective. Such project activities are under way in Belgium, Canada, France, Germany, the Netherlands, Spain, the United Kingdom, and the United States; larger participation is being sought. An ILO publication, *Gender Inequality in the Labor Market: A Manual on Methodology*, by Janet Siltanen, Jennifer Jaraman, and Robert M. Blackburn, is a user-friendly manual that can serve as a self-learning guide or as a teaching tool to analyze occupational data.

The ILO is a norm-setting international organization. For example, ILO Recommendation Number 99 specifies guidelines and standards for the development of services for the disabled: *Basic Principles of Vocational Rehabilitation of the Disabled* (Geneva, 1983). It applies to all handicapped persons, whatever the origin or nature of their disability, and covers the essential features and scope of vocational rehabilitation, and the basic principles and methods of vocational guidance, training, and placement of the disabled. On the crucial question of job opportunities, the recommendation underscores the need to emphasize the aptitudes and working capacity of the disabled worker, on the theory that the disabled deserve to be judged on their abilities rather than their handicaps.

Another ILO aim is to provide support to migrant-sending and migrant-receiving countries to improve the protection of migrant workers and members of their families. On this topic, the ILO has published *The Work of Strangers: A Survey of International Labor Migration*, by Peter Stalker.

The ILO is involved internationally in many activities and efforts to improve working conditions. Of interest to educators and trainers may be the following.

The ILO advocates the principle of equality of treatment for migrant workers and the elimination of discrimination against them. After the "Gulf

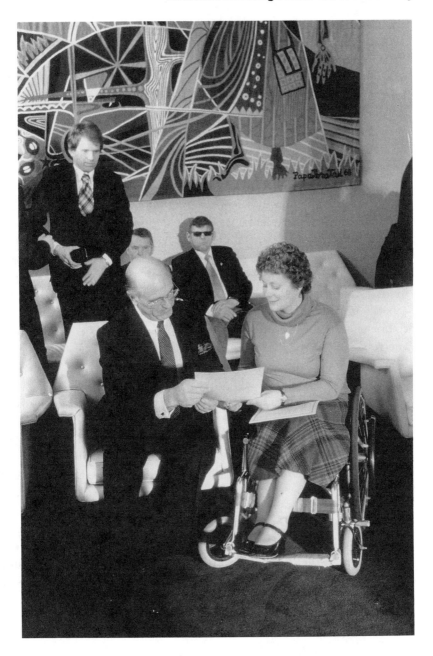

Figure 30.1. The Charter for Citizens with Disabilities is presented by Sharon Limpert to Ambassador Rüdiger von Wechmar, president of the UN General Assembly, to mark the conclusion in 1992 of the United Nations Decade of Disabled Persons. In closing the Decade, the International Labour Organization's projections for the future noted that those especially disadvantaged in the job market would likely be disabled women, disabled migrant workers, and disabled refugees, all of whom consititute a silent minority without effective pressure groups. (UNPHOTO 145 588 by John Isaac [PK])

crisis" in 1991 had revealed the precarious status of migrant workers, the 11th Asian Regional Conference (Bangkok, 1991) and the 70th (1992) Session of the International Labor Conference adopted resolutions calling on the ILO to strengthen its activities with respect to the protection and promotion of migrant workers' rights.

The ILO has introduced interregional projects to combat discrimination against migrant workers and ethnic minorities in the world of work with focus on industrialized migrant-receiving countries to fight widespread persistent de facto discrimination. An ILO manual is being prepared aimed at southern European trade unionists to inform them better about current inflows into their countries and how to defend migrant workers' rights.

The ILO Interdepartmental Project on Migrant Workers covers twenty-two migrant-sending and receiving countries in Africa, the Americas, Asia and the Pacific, and Europe. The objective of this work is to promote the progressive application of international labor standards concerning migrant workers in these countries. Its immediate aims therefore are: (1) to reinforce national capacity in the countries concerned to establish the institutional structures, competence, and techniques required to manage the movement of incoming and returning migrant workers; and (2) to provide support to the countries concerned with a view to achieving broader acceptance and application of international labor standards

The ILO has organized a database of international labor standards called ILOLEX. Organized on CD-ROM, ILOLEX is a full-text database of documents pertaining to international labor standards adopted by the ILO. The multilingual (English, French, and Spanish) software and retrieval system provides access to more than 56,000 full-text documents. Users can query in any of three languages and can do so by subject, document type, country, convention, or by doing a free text search. Information about the ILO and its publications may be obtained from the International Labor Office, Suite 801, 1828 L Street N.W., Washington, DC 20036. To order ILO publications and ILOLEX, write: ILO Publications Center, 49 Sheridan Ave., Albany, NY 12210 (fax 518–436–7433). To order ILO publications in languages other than English, write: ILO Office, 4, route des Morillons, CH-1211 Geneva 22, Switzerland (fax 011 41 22 798 8685).

The BALD project had as one of its objectives to fill information deficits related to foreigners, dealing with a variety of topics in the form of "teaching kits." These contained components such as a background article to satisfy an informational deficit within unions and was tailored to specific groups. On the basis of this background paper, a series of theses or discussion points would emerge. For example, one thesis is entitled: "No Inclination for Double Burden—Foreign and German Women Between Work and Family." This discussion revolves around women in the labor force within Germany, discussing women's labor force participation in various sectors as well as work conditions, the wage situation, qualifications and job training, and the woman at work and in the family. The paper also stresses various relevant factors such as sexual identification and finally elaborates the following points.

Men identify themselves primarily via their profession and also obtain their sense of security and feeling of self-worth from it, while women still identify themselves primarily through the family.

Women's double role in the family and at work helps explain the attitude of men regarding their own wives' participation in the labor force and how it is being rationalized: "it is not necessary that their wives work."

Working women point out that they are exposed to discrimination in two ways: with the pressure of the "back to the kitchen" as well as the *Ausländer raus* ("foreigners, go home") slogans.

Poor working conditions and the multiple burden of foreign women contribute to a relatively higher incidence of psychological and physiological illness.

Women are at a disadvantage in regard to unemployment; foreign women are disproportionately affected by this condition as they also are regarding legal status and its interpretation concerning their rights. For example, the threat of losing their residency permit as a result of divorce. In terms of family rights, for example, in cases of divorce, the legal status of the husband's home country is decisive in matters of the woman's status, which generally places her at a disadvantage.

In logical sequence of the discussion points above, a summary of suggested demands on behalf of women follows.

more intensive informational work regarding the rights of women
the right to work
shortening work hours
controls for the enforcement of the principle of equality in tariff policy and in the framework of co-determination
dealing with the issue of wage discrimination (equal wages for equal work)
raising the wage scale for the bottom wage groups
opening up other professions to women beyond the dominating service sector and office and secretarial professions

raising the share of training positions for young women

expanding social measures to improve compatibility between profession and family for both men and women

strengthening representation of women in all decision-making bodies in the organization

including foreign colleagues in the cultural work of unions

protecting foreign citizens against forced return to their country of origin as a result of receiving unemployment or social benefits

facilitating residency permits for partners and children of employees.

The Robert Jungk Method

Beginning in 1990 a methodology was applied in HRE which Robert Jungk called the "future shop."[6] This social problem-solving method operates as a group process with the objective of answering questions. It demands no expert knowledge and is based on participatory action rather than passive, idle absorption of knowledge. The Robert Jungk method as applied in labor union HRE consists of three steps: first, the realist phase; second, the utopian phase; and third, the implementation phase. All three phases require role-play and small groups.

The first or realist phase might be considered an inventory directed at answering the question "What do I want." This is done by pooling all negative experiences, accumulated frustrations, critical analyses, and implied difficulties, by a step-by-step extraction of the most important concerns of the group, and finally by shaping these into a consensus. This method is based on incrementalism, on small steps, and recognizes the idea that change is difficult to bring about. HRE applications might be the collecting of signatures to submit petitions or dealing with unwieldy, resistant bureaucracies. This method is beneficially applied against the backdrop of reality, where there might prevail an environment of contradictions such as having a residency permit but not being allowed to work, of having been born in the country but being unable to vote.

A set of posted guiding rules for participants can help both the moderator and the group enhance the success of the final outcome: no discussion and explanations in the plenum; critical points should be briefly formulated (keywords); aim for examples (away from generalities); maintain topical relevance; and visualize all expressions.

The second phase is the utopian phase, which requires abstracting: If this is my goal, how do I get there, where do I apply leverage? It allows for no power above you. The ground rules for this phase (in addition to no discussion, use of keywords, and visualizing) are: reference to topic (but do not force issues); positive thinking (do not excessively criticize the presented material); free expression of thoughts (everything is valid and possible); openness toward everything; take proposals of others and develop them further; and have the small groups write down utopias.

The third phase is the implementation or praxis-related phase. Implementation does not necessarily mean taking a ready product home. Instead, however sketchy, tentative, and incomplete the product might be, the "future shop" itself should only be the initial spark for the actual work after the workshop. The main rules for this phase are: maintain thematic reference; clarify practical orientation of this phase; allocate and coordinate available time to intended result; propose realistic implementation steps; and specify follow-up activities or meetings.

The Kit Prepared by the Gewerkschaft Handel, Banken and Versicherungen (HBV)

In 1993 the HBV (Union for Trade, Banking, and Insurance) initiated a program that provides extensive materials, called "basic service," in the form of kits including hints and prepared letters for local union councils in various companies. These kits provide concrete help and suggestions in their daily work for creating programs, give background information, and provide arguments for subjects to be dealt with, such as "racism and intolerance against foreigners."

The prepared HRE material includes advice for conducting a company union meeting on the subject of "Racism and Intolerance in Companies and Society." Reference is made to the events of 1993 in Hoyerswerda, Rostock, and Solingen, where violent attacks on foreigners resulted in fatalities and the burning of asylum seekers' quarters. The material formulates suggested anti-discrimination statements, designates confidence persons in companies, and makes suggestions for resolutions to be passed against any kind of violence and intolerance against foreigners, including joint statements between union and company. The implementation guidelines state that even negative examples, such as cases of anti-foreign graffiti, are to be cited if they occur, in order to state clearly that such acts of discrimination would have labor-law consequences. While prejudice cannot be overcome in this way, it must be made plain that the human dignity of all members of the company is of concern to the union council. Other prepared material might revolve around topics such as "what is the meaning of 'another culture'?" or "images of friend and foe."

Prejudice Against Foreigners, a Unit for a Teach-In

Learning Objectives

Participants receive a brief overview of the relevance of the topic of hate and prejudice against foreigners and how it relates to society in general and unions in particular. A brief introductory presentation of the topic could be coupled with a video; key here is that both foreigners and locals must be addressed in such a video; if the content focuses only on one group, the discussion might be blocked.

1. The terms racism and prejudice should be applied sparingly; differences in terms should be brought out clearly, for example, between "reservations,"

"prejudices," "hatred of foreigers," and "racism." Also in need of clarification are the conditions in which prejudices turn into hatred of foreigners and racism.

2. Recognize that many actions are anti-foreign without being racially motivated because they discriminate against foreigners.

3. Federal policy against foreigners is a form of institutionalized discrimination against foreigners because it refuses fundamental rights and characterizes foreigners as a "problem" and thus does not sufficiently distinguish itself from demands of the far right of "foreigners, go home."

4. Recognize that expressions of hatred of foreigners have specific causes and fulfill specific functions.

5. Develop and recognize strategies to counter anti-foreign sentiments.

Methodology

The subject "prejudice against foreigners" is not just a subject of concern to unions and society in general, but is also a particularly sensitive subject which can quickly arouse emotions. So it is important to observe some elementary rules or general guidelines.

1. Leave sufficient time for debate to allow all interpretations to be presented.

2. The instructors should make certain that participants with prejudices against foreigners are not immediately branded as such, otherwise free exchange of views is impeded and prejudices might, in fact, intensify rather than decrease.

3. Union experience with integrated audiences has shown that a key first step is to establish a climate where Germans and foreigners alike are willing to discuss their attitudes openly.

Content and Goals

1. Group members present, learn to recognize, and judge experiences, cases, extent, and form of hatred of foreigners in companies, federal and local agencies, housing, and simple everday occurrences.

2. The participants should discuss and analyze anti-foreign expressions, practices, and prejudices and the differences between reservations and prejudices, hatred of foreigners, and racism.

DGB Debate Aids on Prejudicial Statements

Over the signature of a board member of the DGB, a publication was issued intended to assist members of the employees' union councils to counter statements of prejudice by providing arguments for the most frequently voiced prejudicial statements against foreigners. Partial arguments are provided here to illustrate the approach taken. Examples include the following.

Statement: *Foreigners take away our jobs.*

Response: Only rarely do foreigners and natives compete for a position. More than two-thirds of all employed foreigners are in positions that Germans have left in favor of better ones. The jobs foreigners have taken are often dirty, monotonous, loud, dangerous, unhealthy, physically taxing, and poorly paid.

Statement: *Foreigners take away our housing.*

Response: The current housing shortage applies equally to low-income Germans and to foreigners. Key here is that the shortage was not caused by ethnic Germans or foreigners, asylum seekers, and so on, but rather that it is a failure of the government not to respond to the shortage. There is a growing demand in the face of a shrinking supply; according to one housing organization, there is a shortage of 2.5 million units, 1.5 million of these in the old Federal Republic. In order to meet the rising demand, Germany needs to build 600,000 new housing units annually during the next ten years.

Statement: *Foreigners are aggressive and criminal.*

Response: This prejudice rests on misinterpretation of crime statistics which include offenses committed by tourists, foreign military personnel, and administrative offenses against the asylum law, immigration, and so on (that is, offenses that cannot be committed by Germans). The age structure of the foreign population is disproportionately larger in the young male age groups where most crimes are being committed. Education is also a factor that influences propensity to crime, and education is generally lower among the foreign population than among the general German population. Disproportionately more foreigners (than natives) are being accused of criminal offenses without actually being guilty of the crimes.

Statement: *Foreigners are taking over.*

Response: Foreigners were invited into the country in the 1960s by industry because of a labor shortage. Due to the prevailing law in the European Union (EU), all citizens of member states are entitled to reside in Germany. In 1992, 8 percent of the total population was foreign, which cannot be considered excessive. In Germany the foreign population increases by approximately 80,000 annually solely on the basis of births, as children born to foreigners are not considered German citizens, contrary, for example, to the case in France. Expressions such as a "flood of foreigners" merely serve to make foreigners responsible as scapegoats for the general problems of society.

Statement: *Foreigners are taking advantage of our social system.*

Response: In Germany almost 4 million persons depend on social welfare because income is insufficient. The main cause for receiving public assistance is unemployment. Foreigners can obtain a right to residence only if they have been employed in the country for eight years. The German economic recovery after the war would have been unthinkable without foreign labor. In 1989 foreigners paid 7.8 percent of the contribution to the pension system. Ethnic Germans receive unemployment and a support payment while learning their language for a period of ten months. Ending the prohibition to work for asylum seekers has reduced the dependence of foreigners on social welfare.

Statement: *Foreigners do not want to integrate.*

Response: The fact is that foreigners, especially of the second and third generation, show great willingness to integrate. These foreigners were hired in the 1950s and 1960s by industry and may have had as their goal to work for a while in a foreign country and then return home again. Foreigners of the second or third generation know the country of their parents only from vacation trips back home. Sixty-one of every one hundred foreigners have lived in Germany for more than ten years. Almost every fourth foreigner has left his home country more than two decades ago. Many Germans misinterpret integration as one-sided conformity. Most foreigners, especially of the first generation, have strong ties to their home country and maintain their traditions and religious customs. According to a study of a German foundation, 67 percent of foreign labor did not consider themselves part of German society. Integration requires the willingness of the foreign as well as the German population to want to live together. German immigration policy so far has ignored the fact that Germany has long been a country of immigration. In considering the time of residence of foreigners in Germany, one notices that the center of their lives is within Germany but the status of their residence is not in proportion to it.

Statement: *Foreign children lower the standards in school.*

Response: Currently there are approximately 1.5 million foreign children or adolescents residing in Germany. The situation in schools and professional training reflects the fact that foreign children are at a disadvantage. The educational training of foreigners is not on an equal footing with that of Germans. For example, only 9.8 percent versus the German population's 22.8 percent attend high school. The reason is poor personnel staffing, especially the poor preparation of teachers for multicultural classroom teaching. The support for foreign children is insufficient.

This instructional publication also provides information regarding the obligation of union councils in relation to the foreign employee, such as assuring the integration of the employee within the company. It then lists the various paragraphs of the legal provisions promoting integration. Especially when it comes to professional educational opportunities, foreign workers ought to be included.

Historical Materials and Exhibits

Historical materials, for example, Hitler's takeover sixty years ago and the Reichstag fire, provide a backdrop against which to organize exhibits on radical extremism and minutes of silence for recent victims of violence and firebombings. If applicable, such as in the German case, historical references can serve to drive home relevant HRE objectives, if parallels to the present can be made clear. The DGB provides drafts of speeches for union council representatives which remind audiences of the suppression of unions during the Hitler regime and discuss the suppression of minorities and foreigners as a threat to democratic stability. The remarks are designed to sensitize the union membership against half-truths—asylum seekers turn into an "asylum flood," the occasional drug offender becomes "all foreigners are drug dealers"—and it provides the speaker with quotations such as Einstein's "It is harder to split prejudice than atoms." The kit includes helpful hints on preparing overhead projections on the historical context of aggression against foreigners, linked to the Nazi era, and also shows mass candlelight demonstrations as the glimmer of hope against such violent acts.

Support from Union Members and Company Executives

Peer involvement in HRE can provide inspiration for union council meetings and might include the union council president of a bank welcoming the foreign nationals of the bank in their native language; the union council president and the company treasurer personally removing anti-foreign graffiti from restrooms and hallways; a group of union members organizing a graffiti removal campaign; or members of a steel company agreeing on a telephone help line for the protection of their foreign peers. All are exemplary demonstrations of support for foreigners. Other peer support measures are groups of workers taking over "sponsorship" of asylum seekers' quarters, company headquarters being made available as a meeting place for joint participation in demonstrations to prevent anti-foreign discrimination, or an insurance company inviting the government representative as guest speaker to discuss the affairs of foreign citizens.

Another prepared text for a possible local union council speech against anti-foreign discrimination discusses the exchangeable images of the scapegoat which the extreme political right is conjuring up, the misconceived, self-declared "proud German" as they term themselves. The text emphasizes the need for sending clear signals in companies and in our everyday private and professional lives. It urges the union membership to stand firm against those who insult foreigners in public places or on public transportation because of their clothing or appearance. Other overhead projections might show a prepared statement of the local union council in the company, and the management, and finally there might be encouragement to sign a petition, participate in a demonstration, or join in a company call for a minute of silence. Similarly, flyers might be prepared on what it means and does not mean to be a "proud German."

Language, Ads, Communications

The prepared material for flyers suggests the incorporation of individually tailored language, for example, for banks: "Do tolerance and humanity in Germany still have credit?" or "Bullish on the course of humanist values." Prepared material for trading companies might point out that they deal with products from around the world and sell to persons of all nationalities, and how particularly inappropriate it is to subscribe to violence and anti-foreign sentiments in such a context. This flyer might conclude: "Our best-sellers are tolerance and humanity."

Another prepared text aims at a local company newsletter and papers in the trade field with the text couched in the form of a nightmare in which all the goods produced in foreign countries have suddenly disappeared. This scenario appeals to our every-day consumption patterns and demonstrates the absurdity of anti-foreign behavior in this logical realist perspective. Another suggestion for a house organ to counter anti-foreign sentiments suggests the title "What did you do at the time?" The prepared text suggests that hate and violence are directed against all of us and our living together, and reminds us of the consequences of inaction. Even customers can be politely reminded that anti-foreign expressions are not welcome in this company. An article on the term *asylum seeker* and its abuse in the German language describes how it no longer elicits sympathy for the politically persecuted or wrongfully imprisoned, but that it often connotes the scapegoat for all evil. This article includes the admonition: "You, behind the counter at Karstadt, Aldi and Tengelman (various firms), you at the German Bank, at the computer at Allianz, in the boardroom or with the union, you the student, entrepreneur, or employee in a leadership position, you men and women, it is your turn—all of us. Silent rejection of violence and discrimination is not enough—it is our country, and we cannot leave it to the hateful and the instigators of violence."

Another proposal is to formulate ads against violence and hostility against foreigners and to have these jointly financed by staff and company. Also included in the background material is factual information meant to equip discussants to counter prejudicial statements against foreigners. Examples are statistical information on the number of foreigners living in Germany, comparisons to other European countries, and other relevant factual information that informs the debate about foreign citizens in Germany. This includes the fact that Germany's foreign population increases with each birth of a child to a foreign mother, thus artificially inflating the number of foreigners vis-à-vis other countries where children born of foreign parents are considered citizens of the country of birth. Other stereotypical statements made against foreigners include misinformation, for example, regarding public assistance, so prepared material must communicate data on the amount of public assistance an asylum seeker actually gets and data on costs for housing asylum seekers. Information on foreigners as criminals should point out that the criminal acts committed by foreigners often get inflated because of the offenses against the foreigner act.

Conclusions

The results of HRE by German labor unions in the form of seminars or dissemination of prepared materials to their membership and councils have been generally positive.

Participants have reduced their so-called touching fears. Some of the participants register in repeat seminars on different topics. According to union officials, the discussion topics among members are broad and range, for example, from the imminent situation of establishing a Muslim burial site in Frankfurt, to problems of lack of service care personnel with foreign language skills in old age institutions and the real possibility of wrong medical diagnosis due to inadequate language communication.

Initially, in the 1950s, mostly foreign men were being hired by German Industry. Awareness that women and children eventually joined them emerged only later. The presence of families was not planned, and the receiving country was not prepared for it. There was a lack of infrastructure such as housing and kindergartens, as well as pedagogical concepts. Today, three generations later, the children of foreign workers still have a difficult time, less success in the educational system, inadequate job training, and comparatively greater risks of job loss. Recently arrived refugees and asylum seekers have also generally come as family units. In a society ill-equipped for absorption of foreign citizens, integration issues and ethnosocial problems are certain to continue.

To Whom Should Human Rights Education Be Addressed?

Against this background and the burdens it has produced in cities and communities, labor unions saw a need for HRE to deal with the accommodation of immigrants, with an often emotionally charged public, and with a number of deaths as a result of acts of violence against foreigners. HRE is also needed to prepare the way for a change in German constitutional law regarding asylum, so that truly politically persecuted individuals may still find asylum while the number of economically motivated asylum seekers is reduced. No matter how the immigration debate in Germany is viewed, there is agreement that integration efforts must be promoted and HRE intensified so that foreigners currently living in the country will not be further marginalized and so that their human rights will be guaranteed.

A special problem with human rights implications concerns foreign children and youth. In many cases parents are overextended regarding the eduction of their children, and the lack of proper education ultimately exacerbates integration issues for young foreign men and women. Many foreign groups have come here with very little education themselves, and local unions are appealing to parents. On the initiative of job training centers, the DGB has asked those responsible for help. There is a fear that the children of some ethnic groups will be worse off than their parents because the young people are left out of the educational loop. For example, some daughters of Muslim parents are still expected not to enter a profession even if they complete high school. The children are thus often caught in a conflict over values, for example, Moroccan and Turkish youths are torn between German society and their own ethnic groups in which the parents worry that their children are drifting away from their culture. At the same time the children are unable to integrate fully into German culture or to compete successfully in education and job training programs. The unemployment situation for foreign youth in the Frankfurt area is 18 percent due to a large proportion with inadequate training. Local unions in cooperation with each other have initiated outreach job training programs.

A legitimate human rights issue emerges from the status of children of foreigners who are born in Germany but are not granted equal status with other Germans, that is, German citizenship. The result for these youths is status conflict, by virtue of not being fully recognized German citizens, and at the same time cultural alienation within their own groups. The consequence is that some youths drift into crime, lethargy, and little motivation to participate in professional training. For others there is a process of withdrawal, reinforced by a lack of programs and guidance on how to structure their status and integration into society.

Labor unions are among the social institutions in Germany that have initiated human rights education, first through their umbrella organization, the DGB, and also selectively via local labor unions. Individual efforts have been described above. It is clear that HRE cannot be reduced exclusively to a utililitarian dimension, although labor unions, unlike churches, for example, can argue from a realist-utilitarian perspective, rather than a moral perspective, that harmonious internal labor relations are good business for unions. Additionally, the unions have not forgotten their historical role as champions of the social underdog and their own experience in Nazi Germany when they were outlawed and became victims of persecution themselves.

While there is little doubt about the beneficial impact of HRE conducted by labor unions, the question must be asked if HRE is addressing itself in each case to the proper demographic, social, and ethnic groups. For example, if the most atrocious crimes on foreigners are being committed by young men—perhaps not even within the labor force—then the questions that need to be pursued are what is the sociodemographic profile of those most likely to commit acts of violence on foreigners and how can that group be reached? Perhaps it is precisely in this context that labor unions might be persuaded to make another contribution to HRE with projects aimed at those unemployed young men most likely to be the potential violators of human rights among Germany's foreign population. The immigration into Germany of migrants, including ethnic Germans, is expected to continue, although asylum seekers are arriving in somewhat diminished numbers compared to recent statistics. Thus it is anticipated that human rights education in Germany will remain an important issue.

Notes

1. Bundesministerium des Innern, Bundesrepublik Deutschland, *Bericht der Regierung der Bundesrepublik Deutschland für die Internationale Konferenz für Bevölkerung und Entwicklung 1994* (Bonn: 1994).

2. Klaus F. Geiger, "Attitudes Towards Multicultural Society: Results of Representative Inquiries in the Federal Republic of Germany," *Migration* (September 1991): 12.

3. Helmut Willems et al., *Fremdenfeindliche Gewalt: Eine Analyse von Täterstrukturen und Eskalationsprozessen*, Forschungsbericht, vorgelegt dem Bundesministerium für Frauen und Jugend und der Deutschen Forschungsgemeinschaft (Bonn: 1993).

4. Richard Pierre Claude, "Inventing New Educational Ideas," in *Human Rights in the New Europe: Problems and Progress*, ed. David P. Forsythe (Lincoln: University of Nebraska Press, 1994), 233.

5. The author is indebted especially to Sebastian Wertmüller, union organizer, DGB, Wiesbaden; Bernd Kuske-Schmittinger, DGB, Ausländerberatungsstelle, Frankfurt am Main; and Leo Monz, national board, DGB, Düsseldorf, for sharing their experiences regarding HRE of unions in Germany.

6. Robert Jungk and Norbert R. Müllert, *Zukunftswerkstätten: Mit Phantasie gegen Routine und Resignation* (Munich: Heyne, 1989).

Part V
Resources and Funding

EDITORS' INTRODUCTION

The chapters presented here are concerned with various kinds of resources essential to the development of human rights education (HRE). Such resources are of three types: institutional, technological, and financial. While institutional resources have been referenced throughout this volume, detailed analysis is presented below regarding technological and financial resources, too often least understood by human rights educators.

Institutional Resources. The United Nations constitutes an institutional resource with which every human rights educator should become familiar. From its inception, the United Nations has gained considerable experience in human rights public information and education. For example, on December 10, 1948, the same day the Universal Declaration of Human Rights was adopted, the UN General Assembly adopted Resolution 217 D (III) calling on Member States to publicize the text of the new Declaration, to disseminate, display, read, and expound it, principally in schools and other educational institutions.

Today the UN Centre for Human Rights provides for the translation into many local languages of basic human rights documents as well as the production of popularized versions of the Universal Declaration in audio form in local languages for widespread distribution. The center also supplies expert help in building institutions of human rights, through elections, the drafting of constitutions and laws, and through the training of judges, lawyers, police, army officials, and public administrators in human rights.

Fortunately for human rights educators with computer-equipped libraries, the full range of UN materials on human rights is now available in the form of *Human Rights on CD-ROM.*[1] This valuable, user-friendly compact disc contains 12,000 bibliographic references giving educators access in English, French, and Spanish to UN documentary resources. Moreover, anyone may review the historical record of the United Nations via the "UN50 Secretariat," which marks a half century of activities on behalf of peace and human rights and draws from an information bank accessible through the computer Internet.[2]

Over the years, the United Nations Educational, Scientific and Cultural Organization (UNESCO) has taken particular responsibility to promote human rights education.[3] For example, UNESCO has produced numerous studies and guides for teachers, especially at the primary and secondary levels. The Associated Schools Project and its participants can count on UNESCO's suggestions relating to human rights published in the biannual *International Understanding at School.* In the 1970s, UNESCO consolidated its human rights research and promotion into a new Division of Human Rights and Peace, which was responsible for several international conferences on HRE, the first being the International Congress on the Teaching of Human Rights, held in Vienna in 1978. It led to a seven-year plan for the development of the teaching of human rights; the creation of a Voluntary Fund for the development of knowledge of human rights through teaching and information; a UNESCO Prize for the Teaching of Human Rights; and an occasional bulletin, *Teaching of Human Rights*.

Nongovernmental organizations (NGOs) have taken major initiatives in developing human rights educational resources. The Human Rights Internet in Canada, associated with the International Centre for Human Rights and Democratic Development (Montreal), promotes human rights education, stimulates research, and encourages the sharing of information. One of their successful publications is *Teaching About Genocide*, a guide for teaching at the university level.[4]

Among NGOs, the International Committee of the Red Cross (ICRC), the Watch Committees, and Amnesty International have begun to supplement their primary task of monitoring political repression with more recent efforts to advance knowledge about humanitarian law (ICRC) and to organize human rights training (Amnesty International) as well as informal human rights education through the sponsorship of human rights film festivals (Watch Committee).

Amnesty International has taken a leading role in promoting human rights education. It defines human rights education as the range of activities specifically designed to transmit awareness and knowledge of human rights, to foster values and attitudes that uphold the same rights for all, and to encourage action in defense of these rights. Its work in this field takes place through formal channels such as schools and training institutes, and through informal methods such as street theater or community workshops. For example, in 1991 Amnesty International-Philippines launched a program aimed at training youth leaders and educators on human rights issues and training methodologies so that they themselves could go out and train others. As a result of their efforts, they produced a creative paperbound volume, *Shopping List of Techniques in Teaching Human Rights*.[5]

Amnesty International has made a commitment to support a network of regional resource centers for HRE. The effort grew out of a Norwegian fund-raising initiative by high school students "to contribute to the establishment of an international environment of respect for human rights." The plan gives life to the vision of a global village as Norwegian workers and young people contribute a day's work and financial contributions to a London-based NGO to inaugurate educational programs in Thailand, Senegal, and Central America.

Technological Resources. This theme of an emerging "global village" is further amplified by Lloyd S. Etheredge's chapter, "Human Rights Education and the New Telecommunications Technology." Today we can look forward to a twenty-first-century world of instant communication served by satellite dishes, super-range radio, computer networking, electronic mail, cheap worldwide fax service, and improved jet age travel. Meanwhile, we see apparently limitless expansion of the computer Internet, a loose collection of thousands of computer networks available to millions of people around the world. Indeed, there is now a realistic prospect that the resources of the world's research libraries will be brought to the desktop.

Of special interest to human rights educators is the formation of a consortium of law librarians, university-based human rights centers, and NGOs cooperating on a project that combines the evolving "information superhighway" and the needs of human rights advocates, educators, and researchers around the world for timely, authoritative literature in their field of interest. The project, entitled DIANA (Direct Information Access Network Association), is expanding to include all major human rights treaties, judicial decisions, and a "brief bank" consisting of legal briefs from some of the most significant human rights cases. DIANA is one of the many resources identified in the sidebar accompanying Etheredge's chapter and by Judith Dueck in her appendix listing of materials and organizations which may be useful to human rights educators. Dueck's chapter, "Setting Up a Human Rights Education Resource Center," reflects the planning advice of a professional librarian and educator; she supplies readers with very practical advice regarding the identification of goals, human resources, and collection development suitable to serve diverse educational needs. While Etheredge's chapter surveys the information superhighway, supplying the reader with various cautionary notes, Dueck empowers the reader with the planning and organizing advice necessary to set human rights educators on the powerful information track.

Financial Resources. While some new technologies such as electronic mail and Internet service are very inexpensive, nevertheless, the process of planning and implementing a program of human rights education is inevitably costly. Magda J. Seydegart and Edward T. Jackson provide a constructive chapter likely to be of considerable interest to human rights educators who lack government support or who suffer from insufficient government funding. In "Fund-Raising for Human Rights Education: Enduring Principles, Emerging Techniques," the authors set out specific strategies, give useful examples, and present instructive case studies. It is most helpful, as well, in referring readers to more thorough guides about funding projects involving human rights education. For many persons instrumental in initiating HRE programs, much of the advice given here will be fresh, for example, the importance of "targeted approaches," "alliance-based relationships," and "social investment" plans. Also, few readers are likely to be familiar with the UN International Endowment Fund for Human Rights Education. Finally, the notion of "fund-raising as an educational activity" will be novel to many. The chapter is realistic and practical throughout, and has the potential to empower interested parties in the crucial financial aspects of human rights work.

If human rights educators can make good use of institutional, technological, and financial resources to meet their objectives, then we shall have moved at least one step forward, however small, toward a new model of world affairs. It is one involving a globe webbed by networks of interconnected and interconnecting state and nonstate

546   Part V: Editors' Introduction

actors who see politics on the surface of the earth as an increasingly integrated process operating in a single community. If, as human rights educators, we use our resources wisely, we may ask the question raised by Václav Havel in *The Power of the Powerless*: is the "brighter future" really always so distant? "What if, on the contrary, it has been here for a long time already, and only our own blindness and weakness have prevented us from seeing it around us and within us, and kept us from developing it?"[6]

Notes

1. *Human Rights on CD-ROM: Bibliographic Database for United Nations Documents and Publications* (New York: United Nations E.GV.94–100677–5, 1993).

2. Internet access can be used for Mosiac (a Web viewer) connecting to URL: HTTP://WWW. undp.org. For Gopher, connect to: gopher.undp.org. For Telnet, type: open fatty.law.cornell. edu; at log-in, type: gopher; at main menu, select: Other gopher and Information Services; at next menu, select: International Organization; at submenu, select: United Nations. For E-mail access only, send a message to gopher@undp.org for step-by-step instructions.

3. See United Nations, *United Nations Action in the Field of Human Rights* (New York: United Nations, 1988), paras. 147–69.

4. Joyce Freedman-Apsel and Helen Fein, eds., *Teaching About Genocide* (Ottawa: Human Rights Internet, 1992).

5. Human Rights Education Project of Amnesty International—Philippine Section, *Shopping List of Techniques in Teaching Human Rights* (Quezon City, Philippines: Zamora Press and Publications, 1994).

6. Václav Havel et al., *The Power of the Powerless* (Armonk, N.Y.: M. E. Sharpe, 1990), 96.

Chapter 31
Human Rights Education and the New Telecommunications Technology
Lloyd S. Etheredge

Any major change of technology alters the context for human rights and civil liberty. In the 1990s the world has begun to encounter an accelerating, logarithmic rate of change in telecommunications technology that will be more rapid than any other period of history. The trends suggest the possibility of both new threats and opportunities for human rights and civil liberty.

For example, previously, communication across large distances, and to many people, was relatively expensive, accessible only to a few actors, and used technologies that could be readily regulated by governments. Soon the technical and economic barriers—although perhaps not all the political and regulatory barriers—will be mitigated. Text communication will become available and affordable at most sites worldwide, using both traditional (wired) networks and the new generations of low-earth-orbit cellular networks. By early 1994 Internet Radio was multicasting to 100,000 people worldwide; by the year 2000, it will become as easy and inexpensive to broadcast video to many global sites as it was to make a single long-distance telephone call at the beginning of the decade.[1]

The effects may be revolutionary in world history—not simply in the political effects of altering, to a degree, the five hundred-year drama of nation-state personae squaring off against each other and supplanting it by normal, workaday relationships across old national boundaries, but also by empowering a new generation of transnational actors, including educational institutions and advocacy groups. This revolution will also allow, to a greater degree, the presentation of human rights education and claims directly, without the intervening images of a more controlled news media that may shape sensibilities to be more acceptable to political regulatory bodies.

This chapter explores the implications of these new technological changes for a human rights curriculum (based upon social science) that prepares students to anticipate and deal with their effects; opportunities for the strategic use of new technologies to support human rights education in formal educational settings; and opportunities for the strategic use of new technologies for human rights education of wider publics.

Forecasting the Human Rights Effects of New Communication Technology

This chapter takes the viewpoint of the policy science tradition in jurisprudence, an approach to the analysis of law and society based upon social science. The policy science approach specifies goals, analyzes past trends and causes, forecasts likely futures, and proposes new practices that will produce improved results.

In the policy science tradition the assessment of effects on human rights is a task of measuring "who gets what, when, and how," and the achievement of a world commonwealth of human dignity. In turn, this goal is measured directly by outcomes—the level and distribution of eight basic values—to everyone.

The eight basic values are power, wealth, enlightenment, respect, well-being (physical and mental), skill, affection, and rectitude (or morality). Just as increased wealth can be reinvested (in processes analyzed by macroeconomics) to produce greater wealth, so any change in the level and distribution of this wider list of values to individuals and institutions, in turn, can be used to promote further change.[2]

The accomplishment of human rights will be shaped by global social, political, and economic processes, all of which may be affected, directly and indirectly, by new telecommunications technology. Limitations of space preclude a comprehensive inventory of the many causal pathways that may link changes in telecommunications technology to changes in human rights. However, the following example will illustrate possible interactions between broader processes and the specific details of the new telecommunications revolution. Any new technology secures greater power for a new class of specialists who are knowledgeable and skillful in its use. Specialists in the new telecommunications technologies (e.g., from the American youth counterculture of the 1960s; hacker/Internet culture; and university-based research scientists) share such values as open access, freedom, democracy, and scientific progress. If their power grows along with the adoption of the new technology they create (e.g., the Internet; the global satellite; and cellular networks underwritten by pioneers in the computer industry), these causal pathways may add strong support for these values that are central to human rights.

Technological Forecasts

The basic forecast—rapid technological change—reflects new freedoms and political and economic forces, alongside solely scientific and engineering accomplishments. Major corporate and political players and governments perceive extraordinary opportunities for national and global telecommunication empires, worth hundreds of billions of dollars in annual revenue and with major benefits to their societies.[3] Traditionally, the world's common-carrier telecommunications systems (postal systems, television, radio, telegraph, telephone) have been state-owned or state-regulated monopolies and oligopolies. By the early 1990s, deregulation had become the trend in the telecommunication sector within almost every industrialized country.[4] By the mid-1990s, a second global stage of transnational competition had begun, although (primarily) via global alliances among existing national companies and (still) a minimum of direct foreign invasions of one another's traditional home territories. Three networks—CNN, BBC, and MTV—currently offer, or plan to offer, global public television channels (the U.S. Information Agency's WorldNet is a fourth, available only outside the United States), but the capacity for hundreds of global channels is being planned.

The Range of Possible Outcomes

There is an instinct—which may be right—to see the new telecommunication revolution as an extraordinary and unmixed contribution to human welfare and freedom. However, both stark alarms and messianic enthusiasms can each be stated with a degree of plausibility. Two classic, and very different, scenarios produced by western culture are: (1) the global village hypothesis, promoted by Marshal McLuhan and others, which sees an exciting cosmopolitan, mature, richly diverse, and creative global utopia just ahead;[5] and (2) darker scenarios, exemplified by George Orwell's *1984*. This scenario already has proved itself an empirical possibility via Hitler's committed political use of modern propaganda and the new technologies of mass media (print and film). Such experience is a thoughtful reminder of the deep skepticism of mass democracy, and mankind's alleged susceptibility to demagoguery and skillful propaganda, which began with Greek observations of their own experience. By this scenario, ahead is the use of mass communications and electronic technology to create a "media politics" of superficiality, image, and misdirected priorities and perhaps—depending upon who is drawn to use the new technologies—newly retribalized, readily monitored, totalitarian societies.[6]

Self-Reflective Education

In limited space, this chapter will focus on aspects of the second scenario since the role of social science-based education and forethought may be especially valuable to identify inimical trends. To begin—with a skeptical look at pro-technology enthusiasm—it is valuable to clarify for Americans, and American students, that their popular expectations are, to a degree, an artifact of unique circumstances and can lead to erroneous and hasty expectations that fail to appreciate other variables that affected the unique character of earlier American experience.

(1) The American baseline interpretation is that forces within American culture—and perhaps (given its Enlightenment-based self-understanding) human nature and history—favor constructive instincts and progress, including progress in human rights. The benefits of science are part of the broad story of progress.

(2) Since it was introduced, American television has seemed benign and has

grown without the state control, including demagogic manipulation and mind-numbing boredom, of government television in totalitarian societies. The political benefits of American television have been achieved by the interaction of technology with opportunities for profit-maximizing firms to compete for mass markets. At first, partly because of limitation of the broadcast spectrum, broadcast television was limited to three channels in each urban area. These broadcast channels were available by government license and subject to review. They also became, in many markets, highly profitable oligopolies.

Quickly, the three stations in each area aligned themselves with other stations to produce three competing national networks (ABC, NBC, CBS) that organized substantial flows of national advertising for their affiliates. These new national channels also provided higher quality entertainment, news, and sports than single stations with limited budgets could afford. To maximize advertising revenue, the three national networks sought mass audiences (and the largest market share in each time slot). There was a "wasteland" of inoffensive and generally benign, common-denominator entertainment: incentives for profit produced program menus that resembled one another, just as competing mass market, fast food restaurants (Wendy's, Hardees, McDonald's) locate near one another with menus that resemble one another. The new medium—with its national revenue bases—also shaped a national culture and sensibility. (The dialect of American English was standardized by selecting Salt Lake City as the norm.)

(3) In America, television news became relatively responsible, objective, and more trustworthy than the statements of government leaders or other news media. The American newspaper profession contributed uniquely high professional standards to the early days of television. The high standards were encouraged and maintained by expectations of elite national publics influential in the government licensing process. Oligopoly profits also could underwrite the more high-minded standards for television journalism as a civic tax paid for the licenses.

However, the new interactions of technology, economics, and regulation may give different—and less benign—results on the road ahead. For example:

(1) Vastly expanded technical capabilities will produce larger numbers of new channels that compete for niche (rather than mass) markets and thereby empower social and political effects by groups that were previously unorganized, marginalized, and ignored in mass markets. For example, as the new technology of cable television grew, so did the television evangelists, with organized political followings and cash incomes provided by the new technology.

Thus a homogenized, cosmopolitan, and tolerant culture is not an inevitable consequence of new telecommunications technology. Human rights education may be needed to an even greater degree than in the recent past. Soon, if people decide they really do not like one another and the homogenizing option of a mass culture, they can begin to retribalize and live within separate and fragmented realities and neighborhoods surrounded by electronic walls: black channels, Jewish channels, Hispanic channels, Chinese American channels, youth channels (MTV), regional channels, and so on. The new tribes of 1984 may, to a greater degree than Orwell predicted, have an electronic (rather than geographic) organization. Political power may become more readily available to charismatic, demagogic personalities skilled in the use of television, now with ready access to channels unconstrained by licensing review.

(2) Deregulation and increased competition will again ignite the earlier debates that produced the initial regulations of the common-carrier (postal, telephone) systems within each nation-state. Battles will again be fought to secure rights to universal access, for common standards and interoperability, for rate structures that act as de facto taxation and redistribution mechanisms to subsidize service for certain groups and institutions, and for other such causes.

Similarly, the decline of regulatory review may increase the incentives of new carriers to intrude upon privacy, especially in securing data (e.g., spending habits) that can be resold to other for-profit companies.

(3) With more freedom, as the trend to deregulation and competition grows, the average standards of truth, journalistic integrity, and taste of broadcast media will decline and begin to mirror more fully the diversity of the print media. There will be analogs to the *National Enquirer*. Opportunities for audience share and profit at the boundaries of respectability (e.g., pornography; sensationalist charges; violence, potential scandal, and disaster; gambling) will be more candidly exploited.

(4) Competitive pressures will increase the number of low-budget (and, in part, low-quality) shows. In-depth reporting of news and public affairs will tend to disappear on most mass market networks.

(5) The rapid expansion of the ability to communicate across national boundaries (and at low cost) may reignite issues of the preservation of national sovereignty and cultural identity. This might occur even in America as the first Japanese global channels begin to broadcast across American national boundaries without American government control, and draw advertising revenues and audiences from traditional American-owned channels.

Beneficent outcomes, then, cannot be taken for granted. If previous telecommunications technology has encouraged a national and civic culture, and cosmopolitan sensibility, and thereby has contributed implicitly to human rights education, it has done so because political and economic incentives have, in interaction with specific details of the new technology, produced such favorable results. The same political and economic context may not apply as automatically in the years ahead; and the attention to this context will itself be a desirable part of any education for strategic planning to advance human rights.

Against this background, it is perhaps a useful guide to draw an analogy to the formal rules and incentives of political election and their effect for the mediation of ethnic conflict. (If politicians must be elected by majority voting in competitive, multiethnic districts, they have an incentive to promote equity and respect for all groups.)

Similarly, new communications technology will affect human rights via its introduction in a context of the formal rules and incentives of competitive, profit-maximizing firms. If there is an international legal and economic regime that allows major profit-maximizing suppliers to compete globally for pluralist audiences, the new technology may play a key role in the evolution of a cooperative, progressive world order.

The Prediction of Counter-Learning

An additional historical caution: since the invention of movable type, there has been an early enthusiasm that new communications technology will free citizens and society from traditional authority and thereby provide a fundamental revolution in the claims of human rights. These initial claims are typically overoptimistic and ignore the (dialectical) phenomenon of counter-learning. Once a new technology begins to prove successful, a countermovement is set in motion: groups with opposing interests learn to adapt and organize to regain control and neutralize adversarial advantages. After a period of initial freedom and enthusiasm, a period of greater regulation follows; and this in turn produces lengthy historical battles to regain the rights that appeared, in the earliest days, to be secure.[7]

For example, Gutenberg invented movable type and the printing press in 1451, and in its early decades the technology was used relatively freely, often to publish Bibles and other established and respectable texts for those who could afford them. But as printing became more widely used as a tool for political change, restrictions followed, although with a lag: in Germany, censorship of books was introduced in 1529; the legal restriction on the right to publish was introduced in England in 1557; in 1559 the Catholic Church introduced the *Index Expurgatorius*.

Similarly, radio was invented in 1895 and (at first) was used freely. By the 1920s, after the U.S. Navy began to experience interference with its activities, the case for government regulation steadily grew. More recently, the hypothesis that television news coverage of the Vietnam War would inhibit future American military action has proven erroneous. The Bush and Reagan administrations learned from the earlier experience and curtailed the new influence of the news media in covering the invasions of Grenada, Panama, and the Persian Gulf War.

Telecommunications Technology and Human Rights Education in Academic Settings

Legal Education

In academic settings the renewed debates about the effects of new telecommunications technology on human rights can be understood, using a social science framework, as the competition among three layers of (very different) legal regimes. These have evolved in different historical periods to govern older communication technologies, and each has different technical characteristics and potential political and economic effects:[8] (1) the laws of speech and press, which enjoy the fullest protection of freedom (e.g., no licensing or taxes, no prior restraint, no laws or other regulations) in democratic countries; (2) the law of common carriers (telephone systems, telegraph, postal services) that are partially regulated (usually to assure full access and connectivity), taxed, and subject to controls of price; and (3) the newest legal doctrines developed for the electronic age of radio and television broadcasting to mass audiences—the highly controlled technologies—with government allocation of portions of the broadcast spectrum to specific uses and users; licenses issued only to suitable operators; and legitimate government review of content (e.g., for political fairness or equal time; regulation of advertising; review of pornographic or violent content, and so on).

A newspaper that begins to broadcast electronically via satellite or cable directly to television screens at millions of sites, rather than being hand-delivered in print by local delivery boys, will illustrate the issues. It is unclear whether the First Amendment guarantees, so explicitly honored for print and speech, will continue to protect electronic speech and print.

The question will be critical for this reason: by the late 1990s all major modes of communication will begin to converge to the new digital forms of the electronic age, and operate across the wires, cables, and frequencies of the broadcast spectrum of the more regulated (mass) mediums. Thus the older legal doctrines that govern speech and press—the most protected, with the greatest assurance of freedom—will not automatically govern the future. Instead, they may protect only a diminishing proportion of social and political communication in a society and world that become, in this respect, less free.

Ironically, the spread of new technology, even while it increases individual freedom, also may reduce individual power. Before the extraordinary invention of mass communication systems, freedom of individual speech always was (and was understood to be) a consequential grant of potential political power. Individual freedom to speak assured the possibility of genuine political influence in the towns and public halls of the eighteenth century.

Yet the traditional freedom of individual speech may no longer be enough to assure the de facto presentation of political claims, especially in an era when many other voices have competitive access to mass public channels. (Indeed, freedom of individual speech may thereby be easy for governments to grant.) Thus among the more interesting developments will be the emergence of a broader claim of a *right to communicate* that (like public financing of political campaigns) seeks to assure access to minimal effective routes of political influence.[9]

New Resources and Opportunities

The discussion of legal doctrines aside, there also will be new opportunities to use new technologies to achieve a more efficient and effective use of national and global resources for human rights education. For example, beginning in the mid-1990s it will be possible, for the first time in history, to create global virtual libraries of all relevant text-based material. Videoconference and videobroadcast channels can share educational resources more efficiently: each university can take x amount of dollars of its speakers budget, videotape its own colloquia, and contribute program material, receiving many times this value from a global channel. Similarly, nongeographic research colloquia and seminars for creative discussion can begin to meet on a continuing basis, without the current limitations of money and distance.

If institutions and groups work together, new curricula can also develop and be available widely at low cost. Courses on human rights, conflict resolution, the Holocaust, ethnic disputes, and many other problems are often marginal to traditional curricula and educational budgets. But soon entire courses by leading teachers and specialists can be universally available. Research materials (including videotaped oral history interviews with participants, now available only in very specialized settings requiring physical travel to reach) can be available to students and scholars worldwide. These national and global archives and channels for human rights can begin with a low cost, low bandwidth system that uses the Internet and the legal freedom from government review of content that has (so far) been widely enjoyed by telephone and other common carriers in most countries.

Cruising on the Information Highway
by Richard Pierre Claude

Humankind has come a long way since the design of the printing press. When Johannes Gutenberg invented a device that expanded the mind without the need for travel, English Levellers in the seventeenth century turned political pamphleteering into a cottage industry. Historians tell us that the result was an innovation in communications which materially contributed to the "Glorious Revolution" and the adoption of the English Bill of Rights of 1689. Today we can look forward to a globe-belting electronic network capable of supplying rapid information exchange and bringing the promise of the Universal Declaration of Human Rights to every quadrant of the globe.

For example, today a human rights curriculum-design specialist at the Philippine Normal University (Manila) can enhance a lesson on rule of law by accessing the latest opinion from the InterAmerican Court of Human Rights by Internet computer transmission and electronic mail from Minneapolis, Minnesota. From the same source, a Canadian funder reviewing plans for a rural development project in Nepal can quickly find out whether that country has ratified the Convention on the Elimination of all Forms of Discrimination Against Women (with its requirement in Article 11 that women "participate in and benefit from rural development"). An attorney in San Salvador can draw on a lawyer's "brief bank" in Cincinnati, Ohio. Such information sharing is being seriously planned, and much is now available by the global system of sharing information through electronic mail.

People all over the world benefit from the new information technologies. Attorneys and human rights activists, no less than students and teachers and others engaged in planning programs of human rights education can gain access to current information and authoritative documents, securing current research results of interest and accurate information about the legal standards undergirding the entire field of international human rights. All persons involved in promoting human rights causes and in related programs of education can now satisfy these needs quickly through electronic delivery of documentation to scores of countries worldwide via the "information superhighway," thanks to the Internet.

The computer Internet, initiated in the 1970s, is a loose collection of thousands of computer networks available to millions of people around the world. Using the Internet, human rights activists, policymakers, educators, and students can bring to their desktops an entire library of human rights treaties, texts, judicial decisions, legal briefs, journals, and myriad research materials.

For example, the University of Minnesota Human Rights Center at the College of Law has organized its substantial collection of documents on line. The

Minnesota Human Rights Library supplies users the text of all human rights treaties and rulings as well as reports of the InterAmerican Human Rights Court and Commission. They are accessible from the University of Minnesota Human Rights Library at its Internet address: http://www.umn.edu/humanrts/index.html.

The Science and Human Rights Program of the American Association for the Advancement of Science (AAAS) periodically publishes in hard copy a booklet entitled "Human Rights Information Sources on the Internet." It supplies current addresses for sources on such topics as the human rights of women, children, and refugees, and human rights with a national focus, for example, Russia, China, Pakistan, Iran, as well as sites with an organizational focus, such as the Arab Organization for Human Rights. The directory is freely available on request from the AAAS. [1]

Of course, access to the Internet favors those with the communications facilities necessary to use it. In a speech at Princeton University in June 1996, President Clinton said that his advisers estimate that by 1999, 100 million people will have access to the Internet.

Increasingly its services are accessible in developing countries, if only through academic institutions and governmental and nongovernmental offices. To those who say the Internet is a "first world toy" of no significance for the poorest of the poor in less developed countries, take a look at the ninety-page human rights education trainer's guide entitled *The Bells of Freedom* from Ethiopia, also accessible on the University of Minnesota Human Rights Library Web site at http://www.umn.edu/humanrts/education/materials.htm. This manual was designed for the training of illiterate participants, including street children, the homeless, prostitutes, garbage scavengers, and the rural poor, with special attention to women and children.

Another very ambitious resource, partly in place and undergoing development in the late 1990s, is called DIANA (Direct Information Access Network Association). As resources permit, the collection will diversify and increase; eventually the information resources of many of the world's major human rights collections will be added to the database.

The creation of DIANA—a central electronic depository for human rights materials—is the project of a consortium of collaborating law librarians, human rights centers, and nongovernmental organizations. They have constructed a database named after the late Diana Vincent-Davies, a Yale Law

---

1. The Science and Human Rights Program, AAAS, 1200 New York Avenue N. W., Washington, DC 20005. For further information, contact Steven Hansen, at 202–326–6796; E-mail: shansen@aaas.org. Visit the AAAS science and human rights Web site at: http://www.aaas.org/spp/dspp/shr/shr.htm.

School librarian and deputy director of the Orville H. Schell, Jr., Center for International Human Rights at Yale Law School.[2]

The staff members of the DIANA project are institutionally scattered. They are centered at the University of Cincinnati College of Law Library's Center for Electronic Text in the Law, the Urban Morgan Institute for Human Rights, and the Orville Schell Center in New Haven. DIANA staff plan to expand the archive of human rights information over time and to make it "user friendly." For example, information from Peacenet, Econet, and the Global Democracy Network should eventually be available in full-text search form on DIANA. Data files will be organized so as to facilitate access using indexed keywords or a string of words. Thus difficulties associated with conventional research methods are minimized because the user need not be familiar with precise documentary titles or citations in order to conduct productive research.

Materials on human rights published by various international organizations are voluminous. Nevertheless, the DIANA staff will minimize complexities facing users by selecting, scanning, and organizing such documentation in a fashion that enhances its value for the researcher. Included in the documents collections will be materials published by the Council of Europe: the Organization of American States, the Organization of African Unity; the United Nations Committee on the Elimination of Racial Discrimination; the UN Human Rights Committee; the UN Committee on Economic, Social and Cultural Rights; the Committee on the Elimination of Discrimination Against Women; the Committee Against Torture; and the Committee on the Rights of the Child. Moreover, relevant information will be included from UN agencies such as the International Labour Organization, the World Health Organization, the Food and Agricultural Organization, and the UN Education, Scientific and Cultural Organization.

Among organizations around the world offering human rights information, a division of labor is developing and specialized sources of information are evolving. For example, the Queens University of Belfast has organized a Web site containing legislative texts and other relevant information on states of emergency in countries with sensitive human rights situations around the world.[3]

---

2. Nicholas D. Finke, Taylor Fitchett, Harold Koh, and Ronald Slye, "DIANA: A Human Rights Database," *Human Rights Quarterly* 16, no. 4 (1994): 753–56. See also Adam C. Bouloukos and Dennis C. Benamati, *A User's Guide to Selected Online Human Rights Information Sources*. Order from: Human Rights Internet, 8 York St., Suite 202, Ottawa, Ontario K1N 5S6, Canada. Fax: 1–613–789–7414. In this useful reference, basic methods of accessing and retrieving sources are described. Users should have basic computer knowledge and experience with electronic retrieval systems.

3. For more information, contact the Project Manager, States of Emergency Database Centre, Faculty of Law, Queens University of Belfast, Belfast BT7 1NN, Northern Ireland, UK. Visit the Belfast Web site at: http://www.law.qub.ac.uk/qub_law/preface.htm.

Scholars and policymakers are just beginning to speculate about the impact of the Internet on world affairs. Just as the new technology of the printing press served seventeenth-century pamphleteers circulating new ideas about natural rights, so today's new communications technologies prompt a broader social consciousness regarding issues of rights and responsibilities of governments, groups, and individuals. Indeed, we appear to be moving toward a new model of world affairs in which human rights become salient on the plane of international relations. While governments dally with "quiet diplomacy," NGOs turn up the volume on complaints to mobilize shame and to enlist world public opinion regarding egregious rights violations. By framing complaints in the *lingua franca* of human rights terms, domestic groups can realistically hope to enlist the concern of receptive groups overseas. As this process becomes increasingly easy because of innovations in communications, we are moving toward a new model of international relations. It is one involving a globe webbed by networks of interconnected and interconnecting state and nonstate actors who see politics on the surface of the earth as an increasingly integrated process operating in a single community. In this process, states constitute an important subsystem in the global social community, but by no means the only or even the principal actors. Nonstate actors, such as human rights NGOs, become significant actors on the international scene, particularly as they rely on improved capabilities in rapid international communication. The result is that people throughout the world are participating in international relations.

These first global channels can build on the proven technology of Internet Radio, which now multicasts to 100,000 people worldwide. A modest improvement adds a clear picture or slide, every one to two minutes, to the audio signal: it can be a speaker's slides or images sampled from a videotape. The effect will be similar to listening to a speaker and watching his or her slides in a darkened auditorium. It is a system that can run on a desktop PC or provide files to view on fast-forward. It can be transmitted by a smart hub-and-spoke system, called multicasting, which knows to send only one copy of a message to Paris, then create 17 clones of itself, and so forth. The system can be run centrally or (perhaps better) as a decentralized cottage industry with each university contributing two to three hours per week. At least for the next several years—and perhaps longer, with good strategic planning by the human rights community—almost anyone in the world can become (by using the Internet) a television broadcaster on a local, national, or global scale without requiring licensing.

Telecommunications and Human Rights Education in Mass Publics

The world has not been lacking in authoritative prescriptions that, if adopted, would improve human rights. The Golden Rule and the Ten Commandments are relevant examples. Even God has had implementation problems. Is there hope for more rapid improvement than achieved by the Christian model, which derived (in a more religious age) the authority of the Golden Rule from a Supreme God and the rewards of Heaven and the punishments of Hell?

New approaches to human rights education may be the answer. In his recent Presidential Address to the American Economic Association, the economic historian Charles Kindleberger suggested: "Man in his elemental state is a peasant with a possessive love of his own turf; a mercantilist who favors exports over imports; a Populist who distrusts banks, especially foreign banks; a monopolist who abhors competition; a xenophobe who feels threatened by strangers and foreigners . . . [it has been the task of social science education] to extirpate these primitive instincts."[10]

Similarly, the pursuit of human rights for all peoples probably requires education (and maturity) to a much greater degree than most other political agendas. The denial of human rights to others often (but not always) is a primitive effort to secure denied or threatened rights for oneself and one's group: security, economic opportunity, respect, or power. The strong case for human rights may, as Kindleberger suggests, depend upon education: a wider empathy and a developed capacity for abstraction that recognize that the legitimate agendas of all groups might be met more effectively by a strong human rights regime for all.[11]

Codifying Lessons

The use of telecommunications technology to promote human rights education is an intriguing possibility. Established techniques sell soap, breakfast cereals, automobiles, and political candidates. Can they be adapted, and married with new telecommunications technologies, to produce similar effects for human rights education in mass publics? The commitment to promote human rights education in mass publics is a long-term venture. Previous experience, thoughtfully evaluated and refined by a study of other cases, could be used to increase professional expertise. One useful and constructive project might be to interview practitioners and systematically codify their operating ideas and practices. Next, these ideas can be refined by further investigation and perhaps new ideas and techniques can be invented.

For example, modern activist organizations employ a wide range of media to promote human rights. They use public or private telecommunications media to transmit reports of abuses, notify members of requested actions, and promote the strengthening of human rights norms. Economic boycotts have been promoted by newspaper ads. Global television shows have been mounted by entertainers to motivate action to end hunger.[12] Environmental groups have become increasingly professional in selecting animal species (whales, dolphins) that exemplify their cause and appeal to young children, and in selecting photographs (based on test marketing) that convey intended messages vividly and memorably.

Earlier cases, too, could be studied. Georges Sorel's astute analysis of the general strike, and his other *Reflections on Violence*, emphasized that the power to capture public imaginations was a critical psychological and political ingredient in revolutionary and progressive politics. *Uncle Tom's Cabin* helped to crystallize Northern support for the liberation of slaves in America. Gandhi's battle was not won solely in India, but in England in the pages of the *London Times*. Martin Luther King's battle was not won only in Selma, but in the broad sympathies and support won through the news reports and vivid dramatizations of the struggle he led.

An especially fruitful set of lessons might be drawn from both the national liberation movements and decolonialism after World War II. Political interests on all sides used the new technologies of mass communication and ideological symbols to advance their causes. New communication technologies helped to empower mass politics, alter the universe of imaginative possibilities, and empower millions of people to fight, against the traditional circumstances and history imposed upon them, and even to die, for a better, freer, and more self-determined future.[13]

However, among recent cases, the end of the cold war, and the dramatic restructuring of the former Soviet Union and its former empire in Eastern Europe, may be unusually informative for the design of future international campaigns to promote human rights and democratic evolution.

Learning from History: A Recent and Special Case

Western cold war telecommunications strategy invites analysis because several social scientists, experienced with the analysis of propaganda from World War II, helped to devise plans for the effective use of new communications technology (especially the programs of Radio Free Europe/Radio Liberty [RFE/RL] and the Voice of America) to support human rights and political evolution in communist bloc countries. By the late 1960s, for example, Ithiel de Sola Pool at Massachusetts Institute of Technology (MIT) was directing a rigorous and extensive project to use the new capacities of mainframe computers, and data from emigrés and other sources, to model short-wave audiences, develop theories of influence and political development, and refine programming.[14] Researchers at RFE/RL studied at MIT and adopted and expanded these computer models for their own subsequent research.

Thus an unusually rich body of theory and data—and the lessons (still unverified) practitioners thought they were learning—can be mined. The evaluation of the RFE/RL experiment can provide insight in its own right, and an intellectual structure to study the broader process that used new telecommunications capabilities to support fundamental improvement in human rights.[15] The case is especially valuable to study because traditional policies (such as nuclear deterrence) could explain only the continuation of a cold war. Something more—for example, changed images of the West—may have been involved to explain the rapid end of all hostility, the rapid shift to internal democracy, the open invitation to western (capitalist) investors, and the quick dismantling of the Warsaw Pact.

The case suggests several hypotheses that might guide further research, and experiments, in the promotion of human rights education in future international campaigns.

(1) Overt hostility and advocacy of violent revolution (techniques used before the Hungarian revolution of 1956) were less effective than a more benevolent image combined with support for indigenous groups promoting human rights nonviolently, for example, recognizing their struggles, reading suppressed indigenous works at transcription speed (techniques used after 1968).

(2) New, wider, and more cosmopolitan identities—for example, as creative artists or scientists—proved attractive options that strengthened the appeal of human rights needed to pursue them. For key groups, these wider identities proved more engaging than potential future lifetimes spent as Marxist ideologues or traditional ethnic identities and roles.

(3) The detailed knowledge of freedom and human rights in other countries was a powerful incentive to change: the knowledge that western societies offered greater freedoms (for travel, reading, association) raised standards for evaluating one's own government.

(4) Young people proved especially open to identities based upon freedom, idealism, and critical rejection of hierarchical controls of established authority. In Eastern Europe and the former Soviet Union, for example, the cumulative impacts of appeals to youth and the nature of several types of persuasive political pedagogy apparently were underestimated by the original planners. Rock-and-roll, jazz, and blue jeans were

a powerful political argument about human rights and freedom. Across several generations of young people, these de facto arguments (especially in comparison with the limited self-expression and boring rigidities of communist regimes) may have been more directly persuasive than many "political" programs and arguments.[16]

(5) One lesson from many struggles—whether anticolonialism, the success of the Vietcong, or the undermining of the Soviet empire in Eastern Europe—is that ethnic and nationalist identities have proven a vital and sustaining admixture in the battle to promote human rights. For example, communist planners sought to use their state-controlled media to promote new, collective, and more universal Marxist identities (and they did, in fact, promote greater rights for women). On the opposite side, western planners fought, more successfully, to strengthen ethnic and nationalist identities (with, at times, a special enthusiasm to stir Islamic fundamentalism) to promote the assertion of human rights and foster the breakup of the Soviet Union and communist bloc.

The Radio Free Europe/ Radio Liberty case is especially intriguing because it contrasts sharply with other cases in which communications-based strategies were not successful. (For example, efforts beamed at Cuba and mainland China have not yet shown similar success.)[17]

The policy science tradition emphasizes the possibility of learning by the sensitive use of social science. Thus, after codification of current theories, and an examination of relevant historical cases, further analysis may be productive. Looking forward, a wide range of new experiments can be undertaken and evaluated. As changes unfold, ongoing study groups, combining the skills of social science and the sensibilities of practitioners, can clarify the lessons of experience, invent alternatives, and improve the use of new telecommunications technology for human rights education in mass publics.[18]

Notes

1. For a broad overview, see Ithiel de Sola Pool, *Technologies Without Boundaries: On Telecommunications in a Global Age*, ed. Eli Noam (Cambridge, Mass.: Harvard University Press, 1990).

2. A comprehensive overview is Harold D. Lasswell and Myres S. McDougal, *Jurisprudence for a Free Society: Studies in Law, Science and Policy* (New Haven, Conn.: New Haven Press, 1992), 2 vols. Sales and distribution by Kluwer Academic Publishers.

3. The end of the cold war and the allure of new markets in the former Soviet Union, Eastern Europe, and China have encouraged the abandoning of formerly secure niche (national) markets in favor of free competition.

4. For an overview, see Harvey Sapolsky et al., eds., *The Telecommunications Revolution: Past, Present, and Future* (New York: Routledge, 1992).

5. E.g., Marshall McLuhan, *The Global Village: Transformations in World Life and Media in the 21st Century* (New York: Oxford University Press, 1989).

6. For a comprehensive historical overview, see the four-volume series edited by Harold D. Lasswell, Daniel Lerner, Hans Speier, et al., *The Symbolic Instrument in Early Times* (vol. 1); *Emer-*

gence of Public Opinion in the West (vol. 2); *A Pluralizing World in Formation* (vol. 3); *Propaganda and Communication in World History* (vol. 4) (Honolulu: University of Hawaii Press, 1979–80).

7. Similarly, when the language of human rights comes to define progressive politics, all groups will be drawn to recast their claims into such language. With only modest casuistry, the claims of both group integration *and* group separatism can promote themselves for inclusion in human rights education.

The claims for respect of traditional cultures and native peoples will be a special challenge: various myths of national or tribal virtue notwithstanding, traditional practices have— almost universally—been partially egregious; worldwide, discrimination remains ubiquitous.

8. This section draws heavily on the pioneering work of Ithiel de Sola Pool in *Technologies of Freedom* (Cambridge, Mass.: Harvard University Press, 1983).

9. E.g., Desmond Fisher and L. S. Harms, eds., *The Right to Communicate* (Dublin: Boole Press, 1983); George Gerbner and Marsha Siefert, eds., *World Communications: A Handbook* (New York: Longman, 1984), passim for earlier discussions of the UNESCO controversy concerning the New World Information Order and other issues; International Telecommunications Union and UNESCO, "The Right to Communicate—At What Price?" (World Telecommunications Development Conference, March 21–29, 1994), draft.

10. Charles Kindleberger, "International Public Goods Without International Government," *American Economic Review* 76, no. 1 (March 1986): 1–13, at 4.

11. Global communication—even the global search for disasters to secure audience share on news programs—may encourage this wider empathy, especially so if the global competitive opportunities (discussed above) become available.

An informative study of the causal pathways by which liberal arts education may increase support for human rights and civil liberties is David Winter, David McClelland, and Abigail Stewart, *A New Case for the Liberal Arts* (San Francisco: Jossey-Bass, 1981).

12. For a memoir by one of the creators of rock concerts to raise money and consciousness to end hunger, see Bob Geldof, *Is That It?* (New York: Wiedenfeld and Nicolson, 1987).

13. The extensive modern literature begins with the study of revolutionary symbols in the 1930s: see the four summary volumes edited by Lasswell, Lerner, and Speier (above, note 6) and references therein.

14. Ithiel de Sola Pool, "Communication in Totalitarian Societies," in *Handbook of Communication*, ed. Ithiel de Sola Pool et al., (Chicago: Rand McNally, 1973), 462–511. For a brief summary, see Ithiel de Sola Pool, "The Changing Soviet Union: The Mass Media as Catalyst," *Current* (January 1966): 12–17. William Griffith, a senior colleague of Pool's at MIT, served as political adviser to Radio Free Europe beginning in the 1950s.

15. The CIA distributed, covertly, tens of thousands of short-wave receivers during the 1950s as part of the communications strategy.

Broad overviews include Robert T. Holt, *Radio Free Europe* (Minneapolis: University of Minnesota Press, 1958); James L. Tyson, *U.S. International Broadcasting and National Security* (New York: Ramapo Press, 1983); Sig Mickelson, *America's Other Voice: The Story of Radio Free Europe and Radio Liberty* (New York: Praeger, 1983); Henry Rositzke, *The CIA's Secret Operations* (New York: Readers Digest, 1977), 166–74; Burton Paulu, *Radio and Television Broadcasting in Eastern Europe* (Minneapolis: University of Minnesota Press, 1974).

An overview of issues of causal inference and program evaluation (i.e., viewing the work of RFE/RL as an experiment) is provided by the work of Donald Campbell, e.g., "Reforms as Experiments" and "Qualitative Knowing in Action Research," reprinted in E. Samuel Overman, ed., *Methodology and Epistemology for Social Science: Selected Papers, Donald T. Campbell* (Chicago: University of Chicago Press, 1988), 261–89, 360–76.

For example, in December 1989 a Romanian newspaper wrote, "Radio Free Europe has done more for the cause of Romanian independence than the entire NATO arsenal"; quoted in Scripps Howard Editorial, "Radio Necessary for New Democracies," *Durham Morning Herald*, January 1, 1990. Extended and appreciative discussions have also appeared in the Soviet press.

A relevant model is Robert A. LeVine and Donald T. Campbell, *Ethnocentrism: Theories of Conflict, Ethnic Attitudes, and Group Behavior* (New York: John Wiley, 1972).

16. Václav Havel gained earlier prominence defending a rock-and-roll group, the Plastic People. (The Rolling Stones have been guests of state in Czechoslovakia.) A broad discussion is Timothy W. Ryback, *Rock Around the Bloc: A History of Rock Music in Eastern Europe and the Soviet Union, 1954–1988* (New York: Oxford University Press, 1990).

17. Paulu, *Broadcasting*, 148–52, discusses several earlier comparisons.

18. See, for example, Lasswell and McDougal, *Jurisprudence*, 1106–18, concerning decision seminars.

Chapter 32
Setting Up a Human Rights Education Resource Center

Judith Dueck

A resource center is an access point to information an organization needs in order to carry out its functions. Information is useful only if it is accessible; information that cannot be accessed is obviously of no use. This chapter examines some of the fundamental principles involved in setting up a resource center to serve a human rights education (HRE) program effectively. The focus is on resource centers in nongovernmental organizations, although the principles hold for the creation of larger, more comprehensive libraries.

What is a resource center? A resource center could be a volunteer worker with modem connections to needed information; a large library with professional, technical, and clerical staff; a documentalist with filing cabinets of cases; a sysop managing an on-line or off-line database; a small collection of books, magazines, or pamphlets with a reference assistant; an audiovisual collection, viewing room, and technical assistant; or any other organized collection of materials with staff to assist users to access the information.

One can reasonably argue that any human rights resource center is a form of human rights education since it provides information needed by the organization and its clients. However, specific human rights education programs do have specific needs in terms of resources depending, of course, on the program's specific mission, goals, and objectives. Usually resource centers supporting specific human rights education programs direct users to effective teaching methodologies, curricula, and instructional support materials in addition to resources in the organization's key subject areas.

This chapter considers the following aspects of setting up a human rights education resource center: mission, goals, and objectives; human resources; collection development; collection organization; facilities; and resource center program. Source materials that may be useful for organizations setting up HRE resource centers are listed in the notes and in the Appendix. Readers may find the following publications particularly useful since they include further discussions of the principles presented below: *Information for Human Rights: A HURIDOCS Reader for Information Workers,*[1] *ILO Manual for Labour Information Centres,*[2] and *A Guide to Establishing a Human Rights Documentation Centre.*[3]

Mission, Goals, and Objectives

It may seem obvious that any organization or program must set out its mission, goals, and objectives clearly. Yet many organizations do not do this and as a result are unable to define, as an organization, what they do, why they do it, how they do it, and, perhaps most important, what progress they have made. Their resource centers are often an ad hoc collection of materials that may or may not relate to the mandate of the organization.

However, a resource center should exist to support an ongoing program or organization. Its mission, goals, and objectives must reflect those of the larger body it serves. So the process of determining these directions must be done for the organization as a whole and also for the specific resource center.

A mission statement indicates the long-term core purpose of the organization, program, or resource center. What are the characteristics of a mission statement? It should be expressed in broad general terms; it should be less than seventy-five words; it should include broad statements related to philosophy, target, or client group and perhaps future direction; and it should reflect the image of the organization.

Goals, on the other hand, give short-term or long-term shape to the mission statement. In general terms, what is the organization or program going to do in order to carry out the mission statement? Goal statements are more specific than mission statements. They are broad aspirations, subject to review, which more clearly define the user or target group, time frames, partnerships, and general methodology. An organization has one mission statement and may have a number of general goals that support the mission statement.

Objectives are short-term, very specific statements that describe the details of who will do what to meet the goals. Objectives must be measurable: how will progress be measured? They must indicate the end point: what demonstrates that an objective has actually been fulfilled? They must be realistic: can this really be achieved? They must be acceptable: do the people in the organization actually want to do this? They must logically tie to specific goals: will success assist in meeting the goal?

For example, the mission statement of Organization X might be to increase public awareness in City Y about the human rights situation in Country Z. Some of the goals of Organization X might relate to the school system, university student groups, cultural events, or the media. The objectives for a goal concerning the school system might involve strategies for influencing teacher-training institutions in universities, school boards, school administration, teachers, and students themselves. The objectives of Organization X resource center in reference to teacher training in universities might involve collecting relevant materials and increasing the awareness of effective teaching methodologies, curriculum, materials (lesson plans, audiovisual materials, books, magazines), bibliographies, speakers, and electronic sources of information.

If a human rights education program sets out its mission, goals, and objectives clearly and precisely, the resource center that provides the information foundation can then follow by building its mission, goals, and objectives around the needs of the program. Without this, it is impossible to make wise decisions about how to spend funds, which items to obtain, how to design facilities, and how to use human resources. Creating mission statements, goals, and objectives all involve identifying clients, outlining services, specifying human resource needs, assessing the financial base, and determining the relationship of the organization to the larger general and human rights community.

Human Resources

The identification of appropriate personnel to carry out the objectives of the resource center relate directly to the effectiveness of the resource center. Information in today's world is complex, technical, and immense. Reports, academic literature, conference proceedings, journal articles, and statistical information are available at unprecedented levels. Print resources, however, are not necessarily the first form of communication. Technology allows for mass media communication via television, video, and E-mail. On-line searching of worldwide computer databases and electronic networks with specialized human rights conferences are not something of the future. Technical expertise in managing these resources and, perhaps more important, in helping clients use electronic resources effectively is crucial.

According to Laurie S. Wiseberg,[4] the number of human rights organizations that have developed computerized and manual documentation centers continues to grow. In addition, she notes that where there has been a shift from an authoritarian government to a democratic style of government, there has been a corresponding shift in priority to education, research, and teaching. Information collected at the grassroots level for the protection of individuals is used for quite different purposes in educational settings. Human rights education workers often need more assistance than is provided with choosing, processing, and using the vast quantity of information available. A cooperative approach between an information specialist and teachers in a human rights education program creates a team that can creatively and effectively develop educational strategies, locate needed information, design learning activities, and implement the program. Trained library personnel at various levels are crucial in handling information complexities, in organizing information in a usable manner, in training staff and clients in information use, as well as in generally increasing the accessibility of available information from inside and outside the organization.

Organizations need to consider both the number of staff required as well as the qualifications. Professional, technical, and clerical staff may all be required to meet the goals and objectives set by an organization. Regardless of the background and training of personnel, steps must be taken to provide ongoing professional development. The areas of human rights and technology can both change quite dramatically within short periods of time. HURIDOCS (Human Rights Information and Documentation Systems, International) offers training courses designed specifically for personnel in human rights organizations wishing to establish human rights documentation or resource centers.[5]

Collection Development

What will be housed in the collection? The many options include periodicals, reference books, legal documents, newspaper clippings, teaching materials, videos and other audiovisual resources, information stored in microfilm format, database access via modem or CD-ROM, E-mail and Internet access, materials at easy reading levels, highly academic materials, primary firsthand information such as testimonies, interviews, and photographs, directories, and general references such as almanacs, atlases, and foreign-language dictionaries.

Decisions regarding not only the medium of the resources but also the subject matter of the collection must be made. Will the scope of the collection be limited to materials about particular countries, issues, programs, specific types of cases, rights, age groups, organizations, or time periods?

The amount of information that can be accumulated is immense. Resource centers do not have the financial or human resources to obtain and organize all available human rights materials. So decisions must be made about what is important to the organization and what is possible to handle. Even donated or free materials cost money in terms of staff time.

Organizations producing publications may wish to establish exchange agreements with other organizations publishing materials of interest. While this is often an excellent idea, staff time, space, and relevance should be considered before such agreements are made. In making acquisition decisions, the following criteria should be considered.

Materials should be consistent with the mission statement, goals, and objectives of the organization.

Needs of the users and the organization itself must be identified and considered.

Factors such as durability, safety, ease of storage, and ease of use should be considered.

Factors such as language, reading level, accuracy, relevance, quality, date, cost, and priority in the organization's development are important.

Availability of material elsewhere is an increasingly important factor, especially with decreasing budgets and increasing technological capabilities to share information.

There is a plethora of human rights material available, as is obvious even from the very limited listing in the Appendix to this chapter. Many human rights resources are very expensive. Reviews in books and journals, annotated collection lists, personal recommendations, previews, sample copies, photocopied contents, and sample pages are all helpful in making decisions about how to spend the limited funds of a resource center. Publishers' catalogues are generally designed to sell the material, and while they may point to possibilities, more detailed critical information about the material is usually necessary.

Is there a basic HRE bibliography that could be used as a starter collection? While this would be convenient and easy, organizations will not find that their collections suit their needs at all if they simply rely on "retrospective" listings of available and good materials. The Appendix identifies a variety of types of materials with some examples which may be useful as organizations choose the focus of the collection that will support their HRE program.

Collection Organization

Once the materials have been acquired, the next step is to organize them in some way that provides easy access to them. This is not a simple task, but it is a crucial one. Information is useless if it cannot be located when it is needed. Procedures and routines on both selection and organization should be clearly outlined.

Classification

Physical materials must be stored in a physical place and labeled so that they can be located. Libraries in the past have used a variety of methods to organize materials physically. Physical size, date of purchase, access level, the type of material, and topical classifications have all been criteria used by different libraries for placement of materials. The most common method at present is the arrangement of materials by medium (e.g., chart, video, periodical, book) and then by general topic or classification. This type of classification provides users with direct, first access to the documents held in the center. Of course, systematic searching in the collection requires good indexing, possibly with a computer and the assistance of documentalist or librarian.

The generally accepted classification systems used today for bibliographic materials are the Dewey Decimal Classification and Relative Index[6] in smaller libraries and the Library of Congress *Classification*[7] in larger libraries such as those in universities. Although these systems have the advantage of being ready-made, universal, and somewhat adaptable, neither is particularly suited to human rights materials. Nor has there been a broadly used classification system developed specifically for human rights resource centers.

However, unless an organization decides to adapt a widely recognized system, it is faced with the task of designing a system that will work specifically for its needs—

a highly complex task that should not be undertaken without a full exploration of classification methodology. It also involves going back to the mission, goals, and objectives of the organization. The general principle to use is: how will users most easily find the material? If users search by country, then organization of materials by country may be the most useful. Country codes have been developed by HURIDOCS and could be used to order materials on the shelf.[8] If users search by topic, then a list of topics will have to be made specific to the organization. Materials will have to be identified with one of these topics. Because the material can be in only one place, sometimes problems develop when a resource covers more than one area. Such problems can be rectified with good indexing.

Indexing

Determining subject headings for materials is again a very complex task. Yet it is crucial if users are to have adequate access to the materials. Good indexing leads the user to relevant material regardless of where it is physically housed. It identifies the key subject areas of the materials. Standard library tools such as Sears List of Subject Headings[9] or the Library of Congress Subject Headings[10] will likely be too general to use for in-depth human rights materials. A number of specialized human rights-related subject heading lists and thesauri have been developed to meet specific needs.[11] Although subject classification and indexing is complex and time-consuming, it is essential that this be done thoroughly and carefully to provide maximum access to the collection.

Cataloguing

Subject indexing is part of a larger process that involves cataloguing or describing the material. This cataloguing includes identifying the author, the title, the date of publication, the length of the material, the subject headings, and so on. HURIDOCS has used the well-developed area of library cataloguing techniques and standards to adapt a simplified system particularly useful for smaller human rights organizations without access to professional library staff.[12] This system is increasingly used by many human rights organizations throughout the world.

Organizations using primary documents such as affidavits, police records, land deeds, personal descriptions, photographs, and court proceedings related to particular cases or victims may find *Standard Formats: A Tool for Documenting Human Rights Violations* useful for organizing their records in either a manual or computerized system.[13] An accompanying computer program entitled EVSYS may prove useful for organizations with access to computers.[14]

Records

Traditionally records for materials are kept in a card catalogue. Any given item will have catalogue cards for the author(s), the title(s), and the subject or index terms. Users can locate the materials by looking up the author, title, or the subject of interest. The classification or location is noted on the card, and the item can then be located on the shelf.

In modern times, this is often done on a computer. HURIDOCS has designed a program based on CDS-ISIS called MODEL.[15] This program uses the HURIDOCS bibliographic formats as the starting point and will be helpful to organizations using computers. These formats leave organizations free to choose their own hardware and software while enabling the exchange of information. Computers can greatly increase access points to materials if there are enough computers to meet user needs. In addition, using standard formats for records of bibliographic or primary information tremendously increases the potential for electronic communication as well for sharing records and information between organizations.

Facilities

What type of space is needed to carry out the activities of the resource center? Usually organizations are limited by constraints of existing space or finance. Available space should be maximized to accommodate the type of activities that will occur. A consideration of facility design includes analyzing the need for study tables or individual carrels; a comfortable reading area; group meeting area(s); a computer/CD-ROM area with appropriate electrical wiring; a modem with phone lines; audiovisual viewing and storage area(s); shelving for reference materials, periodicals, circulating books, and so on; preservation of materials; storage for newspaper clippings, cases, and other files; work area(s) for staff where material is not available to users; classroom or conference room; and the entrance or reception area. Again the mission statement, goals, and objectives must be considered in making facility design decisions.

Resource Center Program

Activities

The activities of the resource center program are based on the mission statements, goals, and objectives of the organization and the resource center itself. Activities might include reference service to clients inside or outside the organization, audiovisual presentation or material preparations, instruction in information technology, publishing projects, preparation of bibliographies, information searches, research assistance, participation in other projects, as well as cooperative planning with others.

Even in small organizations, it is crucial that the librarian, information specialist, or person in charge of the resource center communicate effectively with other staff in the organization. Often people do not know what is available in a resource center, what the information specialist can locate, what the mission, goals, and objectives of the resource center are, or how the resource center can assist their particular projects or interests. This type of communication is essential if the resource center is to serve its organization well. It is not enough to "house" the material. The material must be used, the services of the resource center must be advertised, the expertise of resource staff must be tapped, and the direction of the resource center within the overall plan of the organization must be fully understood by all staff, including administration, colleagues, and support staff.

Connections to Outside Organizations

Given the limited resources in the human rights community, cooperation and networking are essential. The issues are too important for organizations or people to be egocentric and isolated. Networking takes time but is well worth the effort. Sharing the workload is invigorating. More work gets done; what is done is used by more people; inspiration for further projects is enhanced; more ideas are generated; and the strength of the human rights movement grows.

For example, it may be more effective for small organizations to encourage larger organizations such as university, public, or other libraries to carry the kind of resources they need. Or a group of organizations may wish to organize a resource center cooperatively to meet their needs. Or organizations may choose to put funds into jointly developing the technical capabilities and expertise to access information electronically instead of duplicating what other organizations already have. On the other hand, a financially limited resource center can often develop a small in-depth collection in a highly specialized area. This kind of unique collection could be a valuable reference point for larger cooperating agencies.

Human rights education is based on the fundamental principle of sharing information. There are a number of human rights directories that can be of assistance in identifying other organizations with related mandates.[16] Certainly encouraging human rights information specialists to share ideas, publications, projects, problems, and other matters will benefit all concerned. Interactions designed to meet this purpose will enhance the work of all.

Information Technology and Networking

With the advent of electronic communication, the potential for networking is greatly enhanced. The potential for electronic sharing of full-text resources, computerized catalogues, and general information is immense and may be feasible for many organizations at relatively low communication costs. Decisions must be made regarding which documents to make public, how to standardize entry of information, who will have access to the documents, as well as how the documents will be organized and subsequently accessed. The use of modems for on-line searching or E-mail, CD-ROM technology, or ordinary disks for sharing information are all options. All of these decisions, however, are very complex and should not be made without very careful thought and wide consultation within the broader human rights community.

Conclusion

The world today seems to be moving toward a greater awareness of human rights principles. Human rights units are taught in many school systems. Human rights programs have been developed at university levels. Grassroots organizations have developed local human rights programs designed to educate the local population in many practical ways. The very publication and contents of this book point to the importance of human rights education. The Commission on Human Rights at its fiftieth session adopted resolution 1994/51 of March 4, 1994, entitled "Proclamation of a decade for human rights education." The role of HRE programs could be increasingly important in preventing the continuation of violations that destroy the dignity and sometimes the very life of individual people. The role of the resource centers that support these programs will prove crucial in supplying the necessary access to required information and materials about human rights cases, situations, and principles.

The author wishes to thank the following people for their input into this chapter: Lucy Bernier, Human Rights Internet; Gerald Brown, library consultant; Debra Guzman, HRNet; Aida Maria Noval, human rights documentation consultant; Herbert F. Spirer, University of Connecticut; and Berth Verstappen, HURIDOCS.

Bibliographic Appendix

The following list identifies materials and organizations that may be useful in the process of collection development. The list is clearly not comprehensive and has been selected on a rather ad hoc basis with a focus on recently published North American materials on general human rights topics. Clearly the information needs of every organization will vary. Specific and in-depth resources will be needed on particular topics of interest to each organization. The following information sources are intended to provide an idea of the wide range of materials that could be considered in developing a human rights education collection. Print indexes, abstracting services, and microfilm resources are not covered below due to lack of space. Directories, library tools, and other materials covered in the notes are also not listed here.

Compilations of Legal and Human Rights Instruments as Well as
General Reference Works

Blaustein, Albert P., Roger S. Clark, and Jay A. Sigler, eds. *Human Rights Sourcebook.* New York: Paragon Institute Books, 1988.
Brownlie, Ian, ed. *Basic Documents on Human Rights.* Oxford: Clarendon Press, 1992. *Canadian Human Rights Yearbook.* Human Rights Research and Education Centre, annual, 1983–.
DIANA: Direct Information Access Network Association. New Haven, Conn.: Schell Center for International Human Rights, Yale Law School. An ongoing, on-line resource initiated in 1993.
Human Rights: A Compilation of International Instruments. New York: United Nations, 1988.
Lawson, Edward, ed. *Encyclopedia of Human Rights.* New York: Taylor and Francis, 1991. A revised version is in preparation for 1994–95.
Osmanczyk, Edmund Jan. *The Encyclopedia of the United Nations and International Agreements.* Philadelphia: Taylor and Francis, 1985.
States of Emergency Database. Belfast: Queen's University of Belfast. An on-line resource available on the Internet since 1994.
Westerveen, Gert, ed. *International Instruments of Human Rights (20 Years Covenants).* Paris: UNESCO, 1986. French edition, 1988.

Human Rights Information on Countries

Standard reference materials such as atlases and almanacs will likely be needed. Specific human rights reference works providing information on countries may also be needed. The United Nations Commission on Human Rights, Amnesty International, Human Rights Watch, and many other organizations produce a wide range of specific country publications. Examples of general reference works include the following.

Annual Report. London: Amnesty International, 1962–.
Country Reports on Human Rights. Washington, D.C.: U.S. State Department, annual.
Country Reports on Human Rights Practices. New York: Gordon Press, 1994. 3 vols.
Critique: Review of the Department of State's Country Reports on Human Rights Practices. New York: Lawyer's Committee for Human Rights, annual, 1983–.
Human Rights in Developing Countries: Yearbook. Oslo: Scandinavian University Press, annual, 1986–.
Humana, Charles. *World Human Rights Guide.* Toronto: Oxford University Press, 1992.
Sottas, Eric. *Development and Human Rights.* Geneva: World Organization Against Torture, 1990.
Weinberg, Meyer. *World Racism and Related Inhumanities: A Country-by-Country Bibliography.* New York: Greenwood, 1992.
World Report. New York: Human Rights Watch, annual, 1992–.

Instructional Aids and Audiovisual Materials

An education resource center often includes videos, films, filmstrips, tapes, transparencies, charts, large maps, posters, and other materials that are useful in making presentations and teaching groups or individuals. *WorldViews* (*see under* "Selection Assistance" below) presents a listing of available audiovisual materials by topic and region. There are a variety of producers, distributors, and organizations that sell or loan human rights-related audiovisual and instructional materials. A sample of these organizations is listed below.

American Friends Service Committee, 1501 Cherry Street, Philadelphia, PA 19102
Amnesty International (international, national, and regional divisions)
California Newsreel, 149 9th Street, # 420, San Francisco, CA 94103
Cambridge Documentary Films, P.O. Box 385, Cambridge, MA 02139
First Run/Icarus Films, 153 Waverly Place, 6th Floor, New York, NY 10014
Franciscan Communications, 1229 South Santee Street, Los Angeles, CA 90015
Full Frame, 394 Euclid Avenue, Toronto Ontario, M6G 2S9
International Development Educational Resource Association (IDERA Film and Video), 200–2678 W. Broadway Ave., Vancouver, BC V6K 2G3
Maryknoll World Productions, P.O. Box 308, Maryknoll, NY 10545
Mennonite Central Committee, 21 South Street, Akron, PA 17501 (also regional offices)
Social Studies School Service, 10200 Jefferson Boulevard, Box 82, Culver City, CA 90232–0802
World Council of Churches, 475 Riverside Drive, New York, NY 10115

Curricula, Teacher's Guides, and Specifically Education-Related Materials

Fein, Helen and Joyce Freedman-Apsel, eds. *Teaching About Genocide*. Ottawa: Human Rights Internet, 1992.
Human Rights Training for Public Officials: Manual. London: Commonwealth Secretariat, 1990.
An Inventory of Human Rights Teaching Materials. Winnipeg: Manitoba Human Rights Commission, 1989.
Lynch, James, Delia Modgil, and Sohan Modgil, eds. *Human Rights, Education and Global Responsibilities*. New York: Taylor and Francis, 1992.
Shiman, David. *Teaching Human Rights*. Denver: University of Denver International Relations Publications, 1993.
Starkey, Hugh, ed. *The Challenge of Human Rights Education*. New York: Cassell, 1992.
Tarrow, Horma Bernstein, ed. *Human Rights and Education*. New York: Pergamon, 1987.

Universities with human rights education programs often have course outlines, texts, and other teaching resources.

CD-ROM Resources and Other Computerized Databases

The following list is a sample of organizations that have computerized databases for internal use and varying degrees of public access. Space here does not permit identifying the types of databases and other details of the holdings. Some organizations have some of their materials on-line, some are in the process of going on-line, some have or are moving toward CD-ROM production, and some are available only internally. More information can be obtained from the specific organizations or from *Access to Human Rights Documentation* (see "Selection Assistance" below).

Academia Mexicana de Derechos Humanos, Mexico City, Mexico
American Civil Liberties Union's Political Asylum Project and the Centre for National Security Studies, Washington, D.C., USA

Amnesty International, London, UK
Associación Pro Derechos Humanos (APRODEH), Lima, Peru
Associación Pro Derechos Humanos de Espana, Madrid, Spain
Bijeen Third World Information, Den Bosch, The Netherlands
Boltzmann Institute of Human Rights, Vienna, Austria
Canadian Centre for Victims of Torture, Toronto, Canada
Canadian Immigration and Refugee Board, Ottawa, Canada
Central American Documentation Exchange, Austin, Texas, USA
Centre for Documentation on Refugees (CDR), UNHCR, Geneva, Switzerland
Centro de Estudios Legales y Sociales (CELS), Buenos Aires, Argentina
Comisión Ecumónica de Derechos Humanos, Quito, Ecuador
Commission for the Defence of Human Rights in Central America (CODEHUCA), San José,
    Costa Rica
Council of Europe, Strasbourg, France
Danish Center of Human Rights, Copenhagen, Denmark
Ecumenical Documentation and Information Centre for Eastern and Southern Africa (EDI-
    CESA), Harare, Zimbabwe
Henry Dunant Institute, Geneva, Switzerland
Hong Kong University Database Project, Hong Kong
Human Rights Information Centre, Council of Europe, Strasbourg, France
Human Rights Internet (HRI), Ottawa, Ontario, Canada
Inter-American Institute of Human Rights, San José, Cost Rica. On the legal dimension of
    human rights
International Committee of the Red Cross (ICRC), Geneva, Switzerland
International Institute of Human Rights, Strasbourg, France
International Labour Organization (ILO), Geneva, Switzerland. Information available on CD-
    ROM, in French, English, and Spanish
International Network for Development Information Exchange (INDIX), International Devel-
    opment Research Council (IDRC), Ottawa, Canada. DAI CD-ROM and IDRC on-line re-
    sources
International Rehabilitation and Research Centre for Torture Victims (RCT), Copenhagen,
    Denmark
Minority Rights Group, London, UK
Netherlands Institute of Human Rights (SIM), Utrecht, Netherlands
Norwegian Institute of Human Rights, Oslo, Norway
OECD, Paris, France. Numerous CD-ROM databases
Third World Resources, Oakland, California, USA
United Nations Bibliographic Information System (UNBIS) data bank, the United Nations
    libraries in New York and Geneva. Also available on CD-ROM
United Nations Department for Economic and Social Information and Policy Analysis, Statisti-
    cal Division, New York, USA. Numerous machine-readable databases
United Nations Educational, Scientific and Cultural Organization (UNESCO), Paris, France.
    Directory available on CD-ROM
United Nations High Commissioner for Refugees, NGO Liaison Unit, Geneva, Switzerland
United Nations Publications, New York
Zentrale Dokumentationsstelle der Freien Wohlfahrtspflege für Flüchtlinge (ZDWF), Bonn,
    Germany

Public Access On-Line Resources

The American Association for the Advancement of Science (AAAS) keeps an excellent updated listing of human rights sites on the Internet. Further information is
available at shansen@aaas.org or http://www.aaas.org/spp/dspp/shr/shr.htm. This

listing includes sites with general human rights information and also references sites with specific information on women, children, refugees, scientists, organizations, regions, and political prisoners. Both World Wide Web URIs are included as well as E-mail addresses and gopher sites.

The Amnesty International Database is available on the Manchester host, which is part of the GEONET System. Documents include annual reports, research papers, newsletters, press releases, reports, and urgent actions. Amnesty publications are also available on microfilm from Inter-Documentation Company, Leiden. In addition, Georgia Tech's frequently updated "The Human Rights Source" (http://www.gatech.edu/amnesty/source.html) is an excellent link to Amnesty International chapters and resources.

The Association for Progressive Communications (APC) is a worldwide partnership of member networks dedicated to providing low-cost computer communications services for individuals and nongovernmental organizations working on environmental, human rights, social, economic, and justice issues. Member networks pool resources to further the global spread of progressive communications. APC offices are located all over the world. Contact: apcadmin@apc.org

DIALOG Information Services (Palo Alto, Calif.) allows users to dial-in search in many of the more general indexes including *AV online, Historical Abstracts, Legal Resource Index, PAIS International, Religion Index*, and others.

Direct Information Access Network Association (DIANA) is an international human rights computerized database with a core set of universal human rights documents. Contact: slye@mail.law.yale.edu

Human Rights Net (HRNet) is a human rights information service comprised of multilingual information on many aspects of human rights at an international level. By soliciting information from a carefully maintained network of NGOs, individuals, UN, and other international bodies, HRNet distributes bulletins, reports, urgent actions, appeals for help, petitions, news items, book reviews, press releases, and organizational information to a wide variety of recipients around the world. HRNet can be accessed via ComLink, Web, EUnet, Internet (POP Hamburg), and other systems. Contact: debra@oln.comlink.apc.org

Human Rights Resource Page (http://www.traveller.com/~hrweb/resource.html) by Catherine Hampton is a thorough and frequently updated set of links to human rights information on the Internet.

PeaceNet is the U.S. member of APC and part of the Institute for Global Communications (PeaceNet, EcoNet, ConflictNet, and LaborNet). PeaceNet contains news, alerts, reports, analysis, and opinion from thousands of news services, organizations, publications, and other sources. Contact: ggundrey@igc.apc.org

States of Emergency Database at Queen's University of Belfast is a legal database containing legislative texts and other relevant information on states of emergency in more than nine countries. Contact Chris Martin at FLG0004@qub.ac.uk

WEB is the Canadian member of APC. Materials are available from human rights organizations such as Amnesty International, Survival International, Anti-Apartheid Network, Die Grünen, European Green Movement, European Parliament, Green Alliance, Labour Party (UK), Parliamentarians Global Action, and others. Contact: support@web.apc.org

WILSONLINE and WILSEARCH (Bronx, N.Y.) provide a number of on-line general databases that may be of interest to human rights workers. These include Education Index, Humanities Index, Index to Legal Periodicals, Social Sciences Index, Vertical File Index, and Readers' Guide to Periodical Literature. Many of these indexes are also available on CD-ROM or in print format.

Yahoo! is useful for finding a variety of home pages with human rights information. The most useful section of Yahoo to contact is http://www.yahoo.com/Society_and_Culture/Human_Rights

Many university libraries now have on-line access to large legal databases. These tend to be expensive and affordable only by large institutions. *Westlaw* (West Publishing, St. Paul, Minn.) has about fifty years of U.S. legal documents and information including *Human Rights*, American Bar Association, Chicago. *Quick Law*, QL Systems, Kingston, Ontario, has about ten years of Canadian legal documents and information. *LEXIS/NEXIS*, Mead Data Central, Dayton, Ohio, has U.S. and international legal information as well as newspaper and journal articles.

Periodicals

A sample of human rights, library, and education periodicals includes the following.

ABC Human Rights Teaching. UNESCO, irreg., 1980. Also available in French and Russian.
Breakthrough. Global Education Associates, bimonthly, 1986–.
Development Education. Development Education, 3/yr., 1980–.
Human Rights Education: The Fourth R. Human Rights Internet and Amnesty International USA, semiannual.
Human Rights Internet Reporter. Human Rights Internet, quarterly, 1976–.
Human Rights Quarterly, Johns Hopkins University Press, 1979–.
Human Rights Resources. Human Rights Resource Center, bimonthly, 1985–.
Human Rights Watch. Human Rights Watch, quarterly, 1988–.
HURIDOCS News. HURIDOCS, quarterly.
IAEWP Circulation Newsletter. International Association of Educators for World Peace, bimonthly, 1969–. Includes summaries in Arabic, French, and Spanish.
Netherlands Quarterly of Human Rights. Netherlands Institute of Human Rights, 1982–.
Nordic Journal on Human Rights. Norwegian Institute of Human Rights, quarterly, 1983–.
Peace Progress: IAEWP Journal of Education. International Association of Educators for World Peace, annual, 1974–.
Social Education. National Council for the Social Studies, 7/yr., 1937–.
Third World Resources. Third World Resources, quarterly.

Selection Assistance

With the plethora of information available, it is highly important to make good selection decisions. The following sources might be useful in making decisions on what to buy, how to cooperate, and what to share.

Bibliographies and Other Information Sources

Access to Human Rights Documentation: Documentation, Databases and Bibliographies on Human Rights. Paris: UNESCO, 1991.

Andrews, J. A., and W. D. Hines. *Keyguide to Information Sources on the International Protection of Human Rights.* New York: Facts on File, 1987.

Bernier, Lucy. "An Adaptation of *Suggestions for Building a Core Collection of Human Rights Documentation* by Laurie Wiseberg" (1988). Ottawa: HRI, 1994. Unpublished.

Bouloukos, Adam C. and Dennis C. Benamati. *Selected Online Human Rights Information Sources.* Ottawa: HRI, 1994.

Directory of United Nations Databases and Information Services. New York: United Nations, 1990.

Fenton, Thomas P. and M. J. Heffron, eds. *Human Rights: A Directory of Resources.* Maryknoll, N.Y.: Orbis Books, 1989.

Franco, Beatriz. "Human Rights and Related Topics in Canadian Education: An Index of Literature, 1987–1990." *Multiculturalism* 13, no. 3 (1991):

Gelman, Anne, and Milos Stehik. *Human Rights Film Guide.* Chicago: Facets Multimedia, 1985.

Ginger, Ann Fagan, Beverly Wilson, and Linton Hale, eds. *Human Rights Organizations and Periodicals Directory 1993.* 7th ed. Berkeley, Calif.: Meiklejohn Civil Liberties Institute, 1993.

Haddon, Tom, Colm Campbell, and K. S. Venkateswaran. *A Database on States of Emergency: A Report of a Feasibility Study.* Belfast: Queens University, 1992.

Hall, Katherine C. *International Human Rights Law: A Resource Guide.* Queenstown, Md.: Aspen Institute, 1993.

Human Rights Bibliography: United Nations Documents and Publications 1980–1990. 5 vols. New York: United Nations, 1993.

Human Rights Resources: A Directory of Organizations in Canada That Promote Human Rights and a Catalogue of Their Publications, Audio-Visual Presentations and Promotional Items. Ottawa: Canadian Rights and Liberties Federation, 1989.

Kerschow, Mette. "Who's Got It?" Oslo: Norwegian Institute of Human Rights and HURIDOCS, 1992. Unpublished.

Stanek, Edward. *A Bibliography of Selected Human Rights Bibliographies, Documentary Compilations, Periodicals, Reports and Reference Books Essential for the Study of International and Comparative Law of Human Rights.* Monticello, Ill.: Vance Bibliographies, 1987.

Tobin, Jack, and Jennifer Green. *Guide to Human Rights Research.* Cambridge, Mass.: Harvard Law School Human Rights Program, 1994.

Vazquez, Lourdes. *Human Rights Electronic Resources,* Preliminary List, New York: WomanSource Documentation Centre/International Women's Tribune Centre, 1995.

Wiseberg, Laurie. *Human Rights Documents: Cumulative Guide: 1980–1988.* Leiden: Inter Documentation Co., 1990. Actual documents are available on microform.

Whalen, Lucille. *Human Rights: A Reference Handbook.* Oxford: ABC-Clio, 1989.

WorldViews: An Annotated Guide to Print and Audiovisual Resources from and About Africa, Asia, Latin America, Middle East. Maryknoll, N.Y.: Orbis Books, 1994.

Universities with Human Rights Programs and Human Rights
Collections in University Libraries

The following list is a sample of such programs. The professors and librarians in such institutions can be invaluable in helping organizations locate materials and work through many of the issues in developing a resource center.

Center for the Study of Human Rights, Columbia University, New York, N.Y., USA
Human Rights Program, Harvard Law School, Cambridge, Mass., USA
Human Rights Research and Education Centre, University of Ottawa, Ottawa, Ontario, Canada
International Human Rights Program, Faculty of Law, University of Toronto, Toronto, Ontario, Canada
Schell Center for International Human Rights, Yale Law School, New Haven, Conn., USA
Urban Morgan Institute for Human Rights, University of Cincinnati College of Law, Cincinnati, Ohio, USA

Information Departments of International, Intergovernmental,
and Nongovernmental Organizations

Any of the organizations noted above may be useful. Others can be identified by examining the directories listed in note 16.

Notes

1. *Information for Human Rights: A HURIDOCS Reader for Information Workers*, ed. Agneta Pallinder (Oslo: HURIDOCS, 1993).

2. Laura Alpern, *ILO Manual for Labour Information Centres* (Geneva: International Labour Office, 1991).

3. *A Guide to Establishing a Human Rights Documentation Centre* (Ottawa: Human Rights Internet, 1988).

4. Laurie S. Wiseberg, *Access to Information and Documentation on Human Rights and Democracy* (Paris: UNESCO, 1993).

5. HURIDOCS can be contacted at 2, rue Jean-Jaquet, CH-1201 Geneva, Switzerland (tel. 41 22 741 1767; fax 41 22 741 1768; E-mail: HURIDOCS@oln.comlink.apc.org).

6. *Abridged Dewey Decimal Classification and Relative Index*, devised by Melvil Dewey (New York: Forest Press, 1990). Unabridged editions are also available.

7. Library of Congress Office for Subject Cataloguing Policy, *Classification* (Washington, D.C.: Library of Congress). Volumes on specific subjects published at different times are available.

8. *HURIDOCS Standard Formats: Supporting Documents*, compiled by Judith Dueck, Aida Maria Noval, and HURIDOCS Task Force members (Oslo: HURIDOCS, 1993).

9. *Sears List of Subject Headings*, ed. Martha T. Mooney (New York: H. W. Wilson, 1991).

10. *Library of Congress Subject Headings*, prepared by the Office for Subject Cataloguing Policy (Washington, D.C.: Library of Congress, 1992).

11. Jean Aitchison, *International Thesaurus of Refugee Terminology* (also available in French), published under the auspices of the International Refugee Documentation Network (Dordrecht: Martinus Nijhoff, 1989). Iva Caccia, *Human Rights Thesaurus* (available in French and English) (Ottawa: Human Rights Internet, 1993). Graciela Carbonetto and Ricardo Cifuentes, *Tesauro*

Centroamericano sobre Derechos Humanos (bilingual Spanish/English) (San José: Programa de Defensa de la Autonomia y Solidaridad con las Universidades Centroamericanas: Confederacion Universitaria Centroamericana—CSUCS, 1987). *Macrothesaurus for Information Processing in the Field of Economic and Social Development* (available in English, French, and Spanish) (Paris: United Nations Organisation for Economic Co-operation and Development, 1991). Bjorn Stormorken and Leo Zwaak, *Human Rights Terminology in International Law: A Thesaurus*, published under the auspices of Human Rights Documentation Centre, Council of Europe (Dordrecht: Martinus Nijhoff, 1988); *HURIDOCS Standard Formats: Supporting Documents* (above, note 8).

12. Aida Maria Noval et al., *HURIDOCS Standard Formats for the Recording and Exchange of Bibliographic Information Concerning Human Rights* (Geneva: HURIDOCS, 1993).

13. Judith Dueck et al., *Standard Formats: A Tool for Documenting Human Rights Violations* (Oslo: HURIDOCS, 1993).

14. Ricardo Cifuentes, *EVSYS: A Computer Program for Handling Information About Human Rights Violations* (Geneva: HURIDOCS, 1994).

15. Jeannine Thomas, *Bibliographic Data Base "Model" Using HURIDOCS Standard Formats Based on CDS-ISIS Version 3.06*, updated and revised by Kirsti Sparrevohn et. al., with user manual (Geneva: HURIDOCS, 1994).

16. *A Directory of Human Rights Organizations in Asia and the Pacific: 1991–1992* (Taipei: Initiative for an Asia Pacific Human Rights Database, 1992); *Encyclopedia of Associations: International Organizations* (Detroit: Gale Research, annual, 1989–); *Liste des organisations non-gouvernementales accordées le statut d'observateur auprès de la Commission Africaine des Droits de l'Homme et des Peuples* (Banjul: Commission Africain des Droits de l'Homme et des Peuples, 1993); Thomas P. Fenton and Mary J. Heffronds, *Third World Resource Directory, 1994–1995: A Guide to Print, Audiovisual and Organizational Resources on Africa, Asia and Pacific, Latin America and Caribbean, and the Middle East* (Maryknoll, N.Y.: Orbis Books, 1994); Hugo Fruhling, Gloria Alberti, and Felipe Portales, *Organizaciones de derechos humanos de America del Sur* (San José: Instituto Interamericano de Derechos Humanos, 1989); *Funding Human Rights* (Ottawa: Human Rights Internet, 1993); *Guíia de ONG de derechos humanos* (San José: Instituto Interamericano de Derechos Humanos, 1991); *Human Rights, Refugees, Migrants and Development: Directory of NGOs in OECD Countries Compiled by OECD Development Centre, UNHCR and HURIDOCS* (Paris: Development Centre of the Organisation for Economic Co-operation and Development, 1993); *List of Non-Governmental Organizations in Consultative Status with the Economic and Social Council* (Geneva: United Nations, 1991); Répertoire des instituts des droits de l'homme des Etats membres du conseil de l'Europe (Strasbourg: Centre d'Information sur les Droits de l'Homme, Conseil de l'Europe, 1994); *The Status of Human Rights Organizations in Sub-Saharan Africa* (Stockholm and Washington, D.C.: International Human Rights Internship Program, Swedish NGO Foundation for Human Rights, 1994); *World Directory of Human Rights Research and Training Institutions* (Paris: UNESCO, 1992), trilingual: English, Spanish, French (also available on CD-ROM and microfiche; 2d ed. in preparation); *Yearbook of International Organizations* (Brussels: Union of International Organizations, annual, 1967–); Human Rights Internet, based in Ottawa, Canada, produces and updates various regional human rights directories. Their annual publication, *Master List of Human Rights Organizations and Serial Publications*, is a comprehensive list of worldwide human rights organizations. Further information concerning ongoing projects in the compilation of directories can be obtained from HURIDOCS.

Chapter 33
Fund-Raising for Human Rights Education: Enduring Principles, Emerging Techniques

Magda J. Seydegart and Edward T. Jackson

There is no magic to raising money for human rights education at the onset of the twenty-first century. The keys to success are, as they always have been, the relevance, integrity, and quality of programs and projects, and the people who run them. While good ideas and good people can never guarantee successful fund-raising, they are by far the most important requirements for success. Yet much can—and must—be done beyond getting fundamentals right. This chapter makes the case that successful fund-raising for human rights education (HRE) in the 1990s and beyond must be based on a combination of the enduring principles of effective fund-raising that have been employed in the past together with a range of new and exciting emerging techniques.

Of course, above all, fund-raising is plain hard work. It takes energy, commitment, a willingness to face adversity, and, quite simply, *endurance*. Strength of character, physical well-being, and a permanent sense of personal and professional empowerment are also prerequisites for becoming a successful fund-raiser. So is a sense of humor, which can help practitioners through the most difficult of times. Finally, there is group solidarity and organizational support; setbacks are more easily managed, and success more joyfully shared, when fund-raisers are members of a group or organization in which they have abiding faith.

Human rights education in the context of fund-raising is understood to include any educational initiative that promotes the values embodied in the International Bill of Human Rights and for which special funds are required. This includes programming in formal education systems (pre-primary to post-secondary), nonformal education, and informal education. It spans national, regional, and international strategies, as well as village and schoolyard projects, immigrant resettlement initiatives, efforts in war zones and refugee camps, and any other human rights educational activities for young people and adults, in any part of the world.

The World Plan of Action on Education for Human Rights and Democracy, adopted at the UNESCO World Congress on Education for Human Rights and

Democracy in Montreal, 1993, describes the range of activities, the players in the global movement, and the reasons for concerted action. No one fund-raising strategy is applicable to this myriad of scenarios. Each educational effort must be thoroughly conceived, background research needs to be done on potential sources of funding, and a detailed plan of action must be established.

The Uniqueness of the Current Context

At the macro level, literally at the *global* level, it must be said that the character of the world in which we live now is significantly different from earlier periods in the history of HRE fund-raising. These conditions give rise to the necessity and, at the same time, the *possibility* of new techniques.

What are these unique conditions? First, governments are broke. Consequently, access to public money for human rights education is more restricted than was the case at any other time since World War II. Second, competition for all types of funding has heated to a fever pitch, through direct-mail campaigns, telethons, donor nurturance, and other aggressive approaches. A growing array of causes are competing for charitable attention, including more "recent" environmental issues as well as those campaigns dealing with the human and material damage inflicted by savage regional wars and so-called natural disasters.

Furthermore, individual and institutional donors—whose disposable incomes have been constrained and often, even, in real terms, reduced as a result of the recent dramatic economic restructuring of the industrial economies—have hit a wall of "donor fatigue." Not only have donors reached their limits in terms of the numbers of groups approaching them for funds; they also demand to see more results, more value, for their "investments." And they have every right to do so. Finally, until very recently, education for the promotion of human rights has been seen as the softest side of the already "soft" human rights portfolio. Most donors have gravitated toward human rights projects that involve immediate strategies for dealing with gross violations and their aftermath, rather than long-term preventative strategies.[1]

Paradoxically, at the same time, there are some important factors that *promote* rather than constrain fund-raising potential in human rights education. The first of these is the globalization of the world economy. Integrated capital markets and strategic corporate relationships, and globalized information flows more generally, enable HRE fund-raisers to identify and approach funders from around the world more rapidly than ever before. A second factor is the widespread and growing interest, among peoples and governments, in good governance, democracy, and human rights, in the North, the South, and the East. Third, there is a growing interest among governments and citizens in global education, including development education, multicultural education, peace and conflict-resolution education, and anti-racist education.[2] Finally, long-term funders of human rights work, and others who are new to the field or may be persuaded to join in, are increasingly looking to support strategies for change and transformation, strategies that will prevent drastic or pervasive abuses, and that will build generational values of the inherent dignity of all human beings. All of these factors impel public and private donors to seek out opportunities to support HRE.

This is the challenging context of fund-raising for HRE in the late 1990s. It is a context facing human rights educators in North America, Western Europe, and elsewhere in the industrialized world. Of course, human rights educators based in Africa, the Middle East, Central and South America, Asia, and Eastern Europe face even greater obstacles to finding resources for their work. In still too many cases around the world, human rights educators must find strategies not only for raising money but also for staying out of jail—or simply staying alive.

This chapter is not a "how-to" manual. Several such manuals do exist, and they provide excellent guidance for practitioners and scholars alike.[3] Here, instead, we set out the proven principles and emerging techniques in successful HRE fund-raising. Blending these approaches in new and creative ways will generate new funds for HRE.

Enduring Principles for Human Rights Education Fund-raising

The basic principles upon which effective fund-raising strategies can be developed for present and future HRE are not so different from those of previous years. These principles may be summarized as follows.

Comprehensive Strategies

Fund-raising strategies must seek funds from both public and private *sources*, institutional as well as individual donors, at all levels: local, national, and international. By private sources we refer particularly to charitable foundations, corporate giving programs, and private members of the public. Government agencies typically include state or provincial authorities, national ministries and commissions, and multilateral bodies such as the United Nations, UNESCO, and the International Labour Office (ILO). Maintaining a diversified portfolio of funders is essential so that sudden shifts in one funder's priorities do not irrevocably destroy good work.[4]

Moreover, *techniques* for fund-raising must be comprehensive as well. Face-to-face networking and lobbying, responses to requests for proposals, unsolicited proposals, dissemination of publications, newsletters, news releases and press conferences, special events, and direct-mail marketing are all essential elements of fund-raising. Many fund-raising strategies assume that most funds come from certain, relatively elite, monied sectors of society. However, in the industrialized countries at least, the majority of funds raised comes from relatively small donations made by individuals. Effective campaigns target individuals across the socioeconomic spectrum. Further, special efforts should be made to reach out to, and be relevant to, demographic sectors in society that have traditionally been assumed to be insulated from broader campaigns. Specifically, immigrant communities that have established secure roots, especially in the industrialized countries, may have a strong interest in supporting preventative educational strategies.

Targeted Approaches

Another basic principle is that successful fund-raising involves matching specific activities in HRE with particular donors, that is, fund-raising approaches must be *targeted*. Donors have their preferences (though these frequently change over time) with respect to priority constituencies and types of educational activities. The responsibility of the fund-raising strategist is to ensure that all constituencies and all types of activities are supported by the different funders interested in each separate activity.[5]

Alliance-Based Relationships

Funders give money to people or organizations whose objectives they support. In a sense, all fund-raising transactions are the material expression of alliances between funders and fundees. Funders need to receive regular, timely feedback on whether the objectives for which they entered the alliance are being achieved. Funder relationships need to be nurtured for the long term, and good files must be kept on these relationships so there can be organizational continuity. Such alliances can, and often do, cross class, gender, and racial boundaries, and span the state and civil society.

In addition, there also must exist an alliance between the human rights educator and the fund-raiser for human rights education. This is a symbiotic relationship, and each party must be fully aware and appreciative of the needs and realities of the other. Usually human rights educators are obliged to act as fund-raisers as well, so a full appreciation of and skills in both functions are required for these personnel.

Alliances among funds-seeking groups themselves are also extremely important. While some "clean" competition in the field is rarely harmful, in these times of scarcer resources, collaboration and joint approaches are often very appealing to large funders and usually make practical sense. For the funds-seekers, joint approaches, consortia, or coalitions, often between formal educators and human rights nongovernmental organizations (NGOs)[6] can save valuable preparation time and can promote resource sharing, once funding goals have been achieved. Clearly, relations of mutual trust and compatibility in terms of ideology, values, and organizational culture are necessary for such cooperative ventures to succeed. Participating sectors must be able to share territory, funds, and accolades.

Social Entrepreneurship

All effective fund-raisers in HRE are successful entrepreneurs: social entrepreneurs. They sell—and they *do* sell—ideas, commitment, and change. And they sell aggressively and relentlessly, into their targeted markets. In some instances, special events or items such as books and handcrafts are being sold. Proposals, nevertheless, are usually the product that is being sold. Proposal production must be rapid and sophisticated and result in a relatively unique and recognizable output that will meet the "buyer's" needs. Above all, social entrepreneurs must be *credible*. No amount of businesslike efficiency will compensate for dubious commitment to the product being sold. Nor will funders respond positively, in the long run, to style-over-substance approaches.

Personal Relationships

The elitist model of "golf-buddy" fund-raising, where the "I'll-fund-your-pet-project-if-you'll-fund-mine" style ruled the day, has not completely vanished by any means. But more relevant are the lessons that emerge from that exclusive method. First, it is essential to establish a positive rapport and relationships of trust with funders, whether they are corporations, foundations, governments, small businesses, or individuals. This can be achieved by HRE fund-raisers undertaking detailed research on their potential funders, by establishing face-to-face contact, by keeping funders informed of project progress, by maintaining systematic and transparent administrative and financial records, and by providing constructive evaluations of the efforts they have supported. Nothing can replace the feeling of confidence that the funder needs to develop with regard to the people "on-site" who lead or participate in HRE activities.

Clear Mission and Objectives

It is not possible to overemphasize the importance of a very clear mission statement for the organization seeking funds and an equally clear set of goals and objectives for the project at hand. The investment of time and human resources in achieving these statements will be repaid over and over again. First, it ensures that the individuals who are selling the educational project or program share a consistent and sustained self-image. They, or you, know who you are and why you are doing this work. Second, you know how you differ from others who may also be competing for funds from the same source(s). Third, the donor can easily identify your group or initiative because you have established an image the donor can easily recall. Fourth, your clear self-image will be sufficiently strong that funder criteria cannot divert you inappropriately from your chosen goals and objectives.[7]

Fund-raising as an Educational Activity

Each approach to a potential donor can be seen as an educational opportunity in its own right. Provided with well-written and effective communications materials and illustrative examples, the donor becomes better informed about the project. The object is that the donor actually become personally interested in the goals of the work and takes some personal initiative, that the ground is being prepared for a possibly long-term relationship, and that the informed donor will be able to carry your message for support to other donors. Just as there are formal and informal networks among NGOs, teachers' associations, and government officials, there are also linkages among donor agencies, charitable foundations, and major corporate givers. If you establish a good rapport with one major donor, that contact becomes a positive "character" reference for the next, and so on. In the meantime, there will be a growing number of potential funders who know of your initiative and why it matters.

Emerging Techniques, New Strategies

The emerging techniques for HRE fund-raising described below have been developed and tested over the past decade in particular. These techniques have drawn on ideas and methods from the fields of business management, development finance, and communications, among others. Used in conjunction with the proven principles described above, these new techniques hold much promise.

Results-Oriented Accountability

Increasingly, funders expect to receive feedback on their investment in terms of what has been achieved. Whereas in the past the final project report often described the processes used for achieving the stated goals, now funders want to know whether the proposed strategies actually met the expectations. For example, if three thousand inner city school children studied and understood the Universal Declaration of Human Rights, then how did it affect their attitudes and behavior toward each other, and how did the children relate to the subsequent curriculum on anti-violence? In fact, did incidents of schoolyard violence drop, or at least were there more cases of attempted peacemaking? It is no longer sufficient to report that copies of the Universal Declaration were widely distributed or that the kids read the documents. The fact that grantees/funds-seekers are now accountable for results is a very good thing.

This shift is leading to some rethinking of assumptions and processes. Groups and organizations are entering into a period of *reengineering*.[8] Instead of looking at the way we do things, and making modifications and adjustments, we need to look at what we want to achieve and how we can best get there. If a video game will tell the story about rights and responsibilities much more effectively than traditional or even

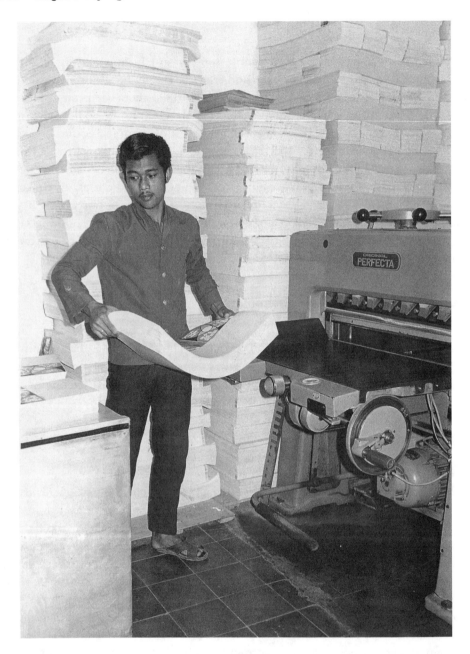

Figure 33.1. A worker in a printing factory in Indonesia prepares paper for the presses. Funding for the printing of textbooks for primary schools in Indonesia is partly supplied with support from the United Nations Children's Fund (UNICEF), supplemented with paper supplied by the Canadian government. International cooperation and the sharing of resources are essential to the development of human rights education worldwide. (UNPHOTO L. Groseclose/ps)

improved classroom methods, we had better get serious about figuring out how to design such a game and take it to "market." The effect of this shift is that organizations that have developed organizational conventions or culture are discovering that it may take more than moving people around to new portfolios to achieve the stated objectives. It may actually take total redeployment of personnel or even a complete overhaul of people and products. Every organization or initiative needs to question its educational and fund-raising strategies rigorously and regularly, in order to achieve more effective results with less costly methods.

Donors also require detailed financial accountability of their funds, and this applies whether the donor is a major foundation, government, corporation, or an individual giver. What specifically did they receive in return for their yen, mark, dollar, franc, or peso? How much money went to administration and travel for first-world persons? Is the program likely to be self-sustaining eventually? Was it ecologically sound? With advances in financial reporting technology, funders expect and deserve highly detailed, graphically presented, and up-to-date figures.

Market Rates of In-Kind Contributions

Donors from the corporate and government sectors are now requiring that a portion of the funds for a particular project be generated from a source or sources other than themselves. Historically, nonprofit groups have identified in-kind contributions from host institutions (such as university administration), pro bono work, time and effort of board members, and volunteer work, and have usually undervalued these types of contributions. Market rates are increasingly being applied to calculate the value of such contributions. In other words, if a retired teacher is volunteering her or his time, then the calculation should be made on the basis of the rate, per day or per hour, which she would earn as a professional in a similar capacity. This technique has two important effects: first, it appropriately acknowledges the value of the contributor of the in-kind work; and second, it usually enlarges the portion of the total budget generated from sources other than the principal funder(s). Further, if eventually the project is able to buy the services of those who previously were working pro bono, then their rate of pay has already been established at a fair market level.

New Donors: Corporate Social Responsibility

Shareholder activism, ethical investment, and boycotts all promote corporate social responsibility. Socially responsible corporations tend to be more open to funding human rights education. Perhaps the most dramatic case in point here is that of American companies operating in South Africa. Pressure from pension funds, other shareholders, consumers, workers, and public opinion forced many U.S. companies in the 1970s and 1980s not only to reform their labor and social practices in the workplace, but also to establish charitable giving programs for black education in South Africa. Some corporations set up new foundations expressly for this purpose on-site in South Africa. In 1988 there were twenty-five private, American grant-making organizations in that country. Together with foreign governments, these donors funded a wide range of human rights education activities that eventually contributed to the fall of apartheid.[9]

With multiparty, multiracial elections having been held in South Africa, what is the future of corporate responsibility elsewhere, on other issues? It is indeed certainly strong in such areas as the environment, women's issues, family and child care issues, and worker training, to name only a few. Overseas operations in such countries as Burma and China prompt serious concerns among socially responsible shareholders, employees, and consumers. The future of activism for corporate social responsibility is bright; it will not fade away.[10]

Nonprofit Business Revenue

During the past decade, in the North and South alike, more and more human rights groups and social movements have been setting up business ventures to generate additional income for their work. Amnesty International's marketing of shirts, calendars, posters, and other retail items supplements that organization's other fund-raising activities. The Bangladeshi NGO BRAC (Bangladesh Rural Advancement Committee) also operates a host of profitable business enterprises. Some nonprofits run their businesses as wholly owned, for-profit subsidiaries. Others set up separate, nonprofit community development corporations to serve as the umbrella for their business ventures.[11] Regardless of the form of enterprise, the experience of businesses sponsored by nonprofits shows that "hard" business skills and knowledge are essential to ensure commercial success which, in turn, results in the support of HRE. In small organizations, some human rights educators may also need to become business managers. Effective training in business skills is essential in this case.

Social Investment

Closely related to the trend toward nonprofit-owned businesses has been the growth of various forms of social investment, wherein institutional or individual investors use social or ethical criteria in evaluating investments as well as using financial criteria. Micro-credit programs pool and on-lend very small amounts of money to micro-entrepreneurs, who repay their loans to their "solidarity" peer group. Community loan funds, credit union loan funds, and pension and trade union equity funds targeted at job creation are other mechanisms for social investment.[12] So is debt-for-development conversion, where institutional investors buy a Southern country's debt at a discount and then use the local funds thus generated for sustainable development and social justice projects. Human rights educators should learn more about how these and other social investment methods might be used to fund HRE. In general, profits generated by social investment funds or the enterprises in which they invest can be channeled to support HRE activities.

Electronic Networking and Coalition Building

With 20 million users already on the Internet, the global electronic highway, it must be recognized that the twenty-first century will be one dominated by electronic communications. As Budd L. Hall[13] and others have shown, electronic networking, E-mail, and other forms of communication can enable NGOs to organize, build memberships, lobby for policy change, and transfer technology. Again human rights educators must "tool up" to be able to use these modes of communication effectively; they also must have the necessary equipment and power sources. Electronic networks then can be used to identify and pursue funding sources around the world. Having a global cadre of associates ready to solicit support from donors at each local "node" on the network would facilitate the use of this type of networking for fund-raising purposes.

Reallocation of Profit from Contracted Research

This is not an especially "new" technique, but it is emerging as a significant approach by virtue of its current large scale. As a result of the privatization, downsizing, and contracting out that took place in the governments of the North in the 1980s, much more consulting, or contract research, is carried out in the field of development. Consequently there are many more opportunities now than ten years ago, for example, for social organizations to take on contracted research and then retain a portion of the profit from such assignments for human rights education. Here strong skills in project management and budgeting are imperative. So are skills in marketing the services of the group to potential clients.

Recognition and Awards

In academia, in the North at least, it is increasingly common for universities and colleges to name entire schools in honor of major individual donors. Recognizing important donors by naming chairs, lectureships, and scholarships after them is a long tradition in postsecondary institutions, but the scale, as with contract research, of this phenomenon is unprecedented. Human rights educators can honor donors in this way, or they can honor, in particular, human rights leaders, and then solicit support from others in honor of those leaders.[14] To be sure, certain educational activities could be named for donors, but the interests and reputation of the donor being recognized would need to undisputably fit the activity in question.

Tithing

Religious organizations have been using the principle of tithing for centuries to secure their operations. Members of these communities are expected to contribute regularly, frequently, and as generously as possible, a percentage of their income to a variety of regular and special appeals. Borrowing on this "obligation" or tradition, many fund-seeking groups are devising means of accessing givers in systematic, repeated appeals. A number of well-known methods are automatic pay deductions, monthly bank debits by advance approval, and quarterly appeal letters or calls.

Some of the more recent strategies have been "penny-accumulation" methods; merchants and businesses advertise that one penny per dollar (or other currency) of a transaction will go to a charity. Use of specialized bank cards ring up pennies as well. Even more innovative are some of the techniques used by local projects; for example, teachers in one school district had a "dress-down" day per month. In exchange for the right to wear very casual clothes, they paid a dollar each time to generate funds for special projects. A teachers' federation or broad-based membership group, even students in some places in the world, could afford a token amount on a fairly regular basis. It sustains their awareness of the HRE project at hand while it gradually builds the coffers.

A final idea on the subject of tithing relates to regularly designating a certain minimum portion of *any* human rights project to HRE. In other words, educational activities are automatically built into any human rights activity. This would require considerable funder initiative or at least support in order to work.

Case Studies

To illustrate the many ways in which proven principles and new techniques can blend with each other to form new strategies for HRE fund-raising, we review several short case studies below. Space does not allow for a comprehensive survey of the hundreds, likely thousands, of such initiatives around the world. Yet these cases suggest the range of models and strategies that are possible.

The Human Rights Summer College

This program was offered for eight consecutive years (1985–93) by the Human Rights Research and Education Centre at the University of Ottawa, Canada. The Summer College was designed for adult human rights activists in Canada and abroad to consider the theoretical underpinnings of their frontline work, to gain access to greater knowledge about standards, legislation, and policy, to become more effective through the development of skills needed in their work, such as lobbying, using the media, and building coalitions, and finally to build linkages with other participants across a broad range of issues and perspectives. The program was an intensive, two-week residential training course with about fifty participants, most coming from NGOs. The learning methodology was grounded in adult education techniques, with a fully developed curriculum that was adapted each year based on input from evaluations. For the whole period of time it was offered, the Human Rights Summer College was the only annual program anywhere specifically targeted to address the needs of activists.

The principal source of funding was the Canadian Department of the Secretary of State, which had a mandate to foster human rights education generally and especially to provide opportunities to equality-seeking groups to develop their organizational capacity. The average annual budget was $60,000 Canadian plus the registration fees, which ranged from $300 to $900 over the years. In some years, the program received small grants from other sources, including a foundation for women's rights and a provincial government department.

This case exemplifies a number of the traditional features of funding for human rights education. First, the project was carefully conceived and developed with very specific goals and objectives. Relations with the funder were viewed as very important, and considerable time was spent maintaining open contact. Former participants were often the best advocates of the program and on several occasions pressed the government not to withdraw support.

Certain classic errors were also made in this case scenario. An overly dependent relationship evolved between the Human Rights Research and Education Centre and the federal department. This was not the result of naiveté, but rather for lack of other options. Nevertheless, when departmental priorities shifted to support for projects that could be self-sustaining after an initial period of investment, the Summer College was hit drastically. While the program itself was leading-edge and highly acclaimed, the managers were not able to generate sufficient funds through registration fees, corporate donations, sale of copies of the curriculum, and so on, to fill the widening gap left by government cutbacks. Efforts were being made by the Human Rights Centre to build a general-purpose endowment fund, but these efforts coincided with economic recession and donor fatigue. The Summer College was not offered in 1993.

On the other hand, there were several features of the funding aspect of this program that deserve mention. For example, some of the registration fees gathered in the first two years, when the program was well funded, were accumulated and made into a kind of "revolving loan fund" or bursary fund. Subsequently, participants in the program could apply for full or partial bursaries, including the forgiving of registration fees. In a related strategy, registration fees were graduated, with participants from government agencies paying a higher fee (i.e., nonsubsidized rate), and thus contributing to the lower rates for subsidized or bursary-supported participants. Since all this was fully transparent, it could be viewed as a type of cross-sectoral alliance.

Another sectoral alliance that could contribute to a reactivation of the program lies with organized workers. Trade unions in Canada are active in human rights education work and are constantly searching for suitable training. A negotiated arrangement between the Human Rights Centre and several unions, guaranteeing a certain number of places and one or more curriculum modules of specific interest, would secure a certain amount of funding. This was done on one occasion and was most successful.

The challenge for the future is to determine whether such training for human rights activists is a useful activity, either for the original host organization or some other. If so, how can it be delivered as inexpensively, yet effectively, as possible?

Canadian Labour's Humanity Funds

In recent years, four trade unions in Canada have created new vehicles for raising funds for overseas education and development projects with Southern trade unionists and NGOs. The Canadian Autoworkers Union (CAW), the Canadian section of the United Steelworkers of America (USWA), the Communications, Energy and Paper Workers Union, and the Canadian Union of Public Employees have all established nonprofit "humanity" funds, which mobilize, through local collective agreements, one-cent-per-straight-time-hour contributions from employers and/or union members, and match these contributions with grants from the Canadian International Development Agency (CIDA) and other external funders.

The two largest of these funds, run by the auto and steel unions, each presently generate some $1 million in employer (CAW) and employer/employee (USWA) contributions every year. The combined membership of the four unions is nearly one million unionists, and therefore the growth potential for these funds is very significant. The sponsoring unions support human rights education through seminars and struggle against apartheid and dictatorship, and economic alternatives to structural adjustment. Many of their current projects are implemented jointly with Canadian and Southern NGOs.

The funds managers are presently forming an institute for labor development to promote education and linkage projects on a broader basis around the world. This institute will serve as a mechanism to build the capacity of the funds to manage larger programs and projects and to draw down larger grants from CIDA and other funders as this capacity grows. The labor funds have thus blended the traditional approaches of nonprofit, NGO programming and structures with the new techniques, at least for Canada, of collectively bargained contributions to international cooperation.

Burkina Faso Schools Project

In the late 1980s, human rights educators in the African state of Burkina Faso launched an extraordinarily innovative strategy for bringing human rights to the young learners in that country. A cadre of eventually more than three hundred retired teachers from various regions volunteered to receive training in human rights concepts, principles, and relevance and were "unleashed," so to speak, in the schools. As a result, vastly more young students were exposed to human rights ideas than could have been achieved by even some much more elaborate strategy.

From the perspective of fund-raising, some initial (minimal) funds were received from an aid agency, and the project was sponsored by a national human rights NGO. But since the cadre of retired teachers were volunteers, delighted to be able to teach once again, and the use of print documents was minimal, the costs have remained very low. This project is traditional in the sense that it uses volunteer labor. However, it is remarkably innovative in seeking an inexpensive and participatory strategy with a wide impact.

International Endowment Fund for HRE

At the 1993 UN World Conference on Human Rights, the concept of launching a Decade of Human Rights Education was approved in principle, through incorporation in the Vienna Declaration. Subsequently the General Assembly resolved to proclaim a Decade of HRE and is currently processing this resolution. The NGO-based organizing committee for this Decade is now developing a major, global strategy to support the Decade, through the creation of an International Business Council and Endowment Fund for Human Rights Education.

The Organizing Committee is building on the fund-raising lessons learned from other major international projects, such as funding the NGO networking costs leading up to the Rio Conference on the Environment, and also the recent International Tribunal on Violence Against Women, held during the 1993 UN World Conference on Human Rights in Vienna. These major activities were funded in part first by developing a conscientization strategy among CEOs of major national and multinational corporations, and foundations and then eventually garnering their financial support.

The International Endowment Fund for Human Rights Education is in the preliminary stages of such a campaign; namely, to bring the importance and benefits of education for human rights and democracy into a more visible and prominent position among potential major funders; and then to build a consortium of interests to endow the fund. Eventually the fund is expected to secure a sufficient capital base to support HRE projects in many parts of the world, on the bank interest it generates.

This fledgling campaign reflects a number of the enduring and emerging strategies identified above, including targeted approaches, fund-raising as an educational activity, socially responsible investment, and coalition building among donors. As the groundswell for this fund grows, no doubt other fund-raising strategies will also emerge.

Conclusion

It will not be easy to raise money for human rights education in the future. However, the combination of proven principles and new techniques will, in fact, result in many innovative, vigorous programs and projects all over the world. Ultimately, though, the test of the success of these fund-raising initiatives is not how much money will have been mobilized, but whether the initiatives will have made a difference in the lives of the learners and in the societies to which they belong. Funding is and always will be a means, not an end. We must keep our eyes on the real prize: freedom, dignity, and peace for all.

The authors would like to thank the following for their inspiration and advice: Dal Brodhead, Bill Black, Iva Caccia, Budd Hall, Kalmen Kaplansky, Kate McLaren, Don McRae, William Pentney, Ed Ratushny, Murray Thomson, and Douglas Williams. This chapter is dedicated to the memory of Renate Shearer and Walter Tarnopolsky: human rights educators extraordinaire.

Notes

1. Douglas Williams et al., "Handbook on Fundraising for Human Rights Activities," Human Rights Research and Education Centre of the University of Ottawa and the Human Rights Unit of the Commonwealth Secretariat, unpublished paper: a hands-on manual about fundraising for human rights projects, intended to complement the *International Directory* (see note 5 below).

2. Magda Seydegart, with Iva Caccia, Rosalind Curry, Kate McLaren, and Susana Ponce, *The Global Classroom: Appraisal and Perspectives on Education for International Understanding, Canadian Country Report*, prepared for the Council of Ministers of Education, Canada (Toronto, 1994).

3. See, for example, Jeffrey Hollender, *How to Make the World a Better Place* (New York: William Morrow, 1990); L. Peter Edles, *Fundraising: Hands-On Tactics for Non Profit Groups* (New York: McGraw-Hill, 1993), a detailed, practical how-to manual on all the little and big steps that achieve funding objectives and at the same time build a strong organization; and Joan Flanagan, *Successful Fundraising: A Complete Handbook for Volunteers and Professionals*, rev. ed. (Chicago: Contemporary, 1990), which covers everything you need to know to raise money; well organized, with useful resource and reading lists.

4. Henri Lamoreux, R. Mayer, and J. Panet-Raymond, eds., *L'intervention communautaire* (Montreal: Editions Saint-Martin, 1984), chap. 9.

5. *Funding Human Rights: An International Directory of Funding Organizations and Human Rights Awards* (Ottawa: co-published by Internet: International Human Rights Documentation Network and the International Centre for Human Rights and Democratic Development, 1993; 2d ed., 1996). The Directory provides a descriptive listing of possible sources of funding, worldwide, for projects in human rights, defined broadly, and including concepts such as justice and peace, good governance and democracy. Intended as a companion volume to Williams (see Note 1 above).

6. Richard Pierre Claude, "Global Human Rights Education: Challenges for Non-Governmental Organizations," unpublished paper prepared for the Conference on Human Rights Education, Columbia University, New York, 1992.

7. Diane Borst and Patrick J. Montana, eds., *Managing Non-Profit Organizations* (New York: AMACON, 1977).

8. See Henry Mintzberg and James Brian Quinn, *The Strategy Process: Concepts and Contexts* (Englewood Cliffs, N.J.: Prentice-Hall, 1992).

9. Michael Sinclair and Julia Weinstein, *American Philanthropy: A Guide for South Africans* (Washington, D.C.: Investor Responsibility Research Center, 1988).

10. Peter D. Kinder, Steven D. Lyndenberg, and Amy L. Domini, eds., *The Social Investment Almanac* (New York: Holt, 1992).

11. Edward T. Jackson and Jane E. McNamara, *Voluntary Sector Enterprises: Factors Influencing Success* (Hull, Ontario: Voluntary Action Program, Department of Secretary of State, 1988).

12. Hollender, *How to Make the World a Better Place*; Kinder et al., *Social Investment Almanac.*

13. Budd L. Hall, *Learning Lessons: Global Networking and International Non-Governmental Organizations* (Hull, Ontario: Canadian International Development Agency, 1992).

14. Ken Wyman, *Face to Face: How to Get Bigger Donations from Very Generous People* (Ottawa: Voluntary Action Directorate, Multiculturalism and Citizenship, Government of Canada, 1993), a specialized, highly practical step-by-step guide to building endowments and large charitable giving strategies.

Epilogue:
THE NEXT STEP, QUALITY CONTROL

J. Paul Martin

Given the limited resources available for human rights education, it is important to assimilate the lessons of past and existing programs. Even though human rights education must be adapted to local conditions and involves a more overtly normative and a more social change-oriented content than other forms of education, there are general educational and human rights-specific criteria that must be used to assure cost-effective learning. In addition to the content of a program, the critical components include (a) overall design, (b) adaptation to local needs, potential, and motivations, (c) appropriate and responsive target groups, (d) planning for continuing institutional development, (e) proven educational, in addition to human rights, leadership, and (f) effective educational methods and evaluation techniques. Each of these categories contains visible, but also less obvious options. The more that these other options have been investigated at the planning stage, the more likely that it will be a successful program. This chapter provides a quality control checklist geared primarily to programs outside universities, especially to those in regions seeking new legal and democratic orders.

The recent rapid expansion and popularization of human rights education beyond legal training, as evidenced in this volume, call for evaluation and quality control. These various studies of human rights education indicate a wide variety of goals and strategies, the products of both different theoretical approaches and the need to adapt the programs to the unique conditions of their target populations.[1] Outside western democracies, these programs are often complicated by the fact that many, if not most, are planned, financed, and organized by external actors, often as part of more extended emergency, peacemaking, or peacekeeping operations. Each project is conditioned by the individual interests and abilities of the governmental and non-governmental organizations involved. The quantity of these operations now permits more critical evaluation, the possibility of developing cumulative knowledge, and also access to experienced personnel to plan and to run future programs. Assimilating this experience is critical if the limited resources normally available to these projects are to be used to their best advantage. This chapter defines some of the quality control parameters with a view to promoting more systematic planning evaluation of human rights education programs.

The Evaluation of the Educational Enterprises

Copious literature is available on the evaluation of education in general. It ranges from all-inclusive taxonomies to the careful measurement of the smallest of spatial factors, such as the size of a classroom or numbers of students in learning situations. At this stage the promotion of human rights education is still too rudimentary to be able to draw on these sophisticated studies. Evaluation must first focus on the basics, namely, goal setting, planning, and design, the determination of educational strategies and methods, and the anticipated achievements or benefits. The unique problems associated with human rights education stem from its normative content, the fact that the educational goals go beyond cognitive and factual learning to address attitudes and behavior.[2] In doing so, they risk challenges from social sectors with different perceptions of the meaning of human rights and the form that human rights education should take. Critics can be many and vocal: fellow teachers, school and system administrators, local and national politicians, as well as parents. To respond to their concerns, it is important to develop a coherent analysis of human rights education, one that goes beyond portraying any human rights education as equal to others.

Successful educational enterprises are built with multiple elements. As in the proverbial chain, weakness in any of them will jeopardize the whole project. Successful projects must have adequate financial and political support, adequate facilities, planning, and logistical support, qualified and effective personnel, a minimum of educational materials, and responsive students. Without any one of these components, the educational achievement will be jeopardized, putting in question all investment and human time commitments. On the other hand, each of the above elements is radically conditioned by local circumstances. A shady tree, for example, might be an adequate facility in one country, whereas an auditorium with a CD-ROM display system might be needed in another. The same variation is possible in each of the other categories. Thus while the actual details and form will vary from situation to situation, there are minimum conditions necessary to assure an effective learning process. The art of the educator is to bring them together in a way that fosters enthusiastic learning.

The Evaluation of Human Rights Education

Compared with other forms of education, human rights education reflects a conceptualization of social problems involving human rights violations suffered either by the learners or others. Education is geared toward providing knowledge and encouragement in the use of applicable international standards as means to assess the violations and to seek recourse. As common international standards of social justice, human rights are being integrated into the different forms of civic education around the world. Traditionally most countries have encouraged civic education as a way to emphasize loyalty to one's country and the knowledge and skills necessary for a citizen. In so doing, civic education has reflected a society's predominant political culture. In authoritarian or centralized societies, civic education has emphasized the contribution of leaders, past and present, to the well-being of the society and the correlative, largely supportive duties of the citizen. In a more democratic structure, civic education encouraged political participation and the accountability of governments.

Incorporating human rights into civic education brings an emphasis on the individual citizen's rights and claims against society, emphasizing the fact that no individual citizen or group of citizens should experience discrimination and that there are restrictions on the powers of government. It also links each nation's own experience with international reference points, a theme brought out in Richard Claude's contribution in this volume.

The values implicit in a country's civic education (to the extent it includes human rights education) pervade the public school curricula even when there are no formal programs in human rights or civic education. In its selection of themes and topics, the teaching of history, for example, very visibly transmits chosen values and ideals. In subtle ways, national values influence the whole educational system.[3] This systemic influence, coupled with traditional classroom teaching styles in Eastern Europe, for example, has proved the biggest challenge to those who would bring change.[4] In addition to the democracy-to-authoritarian spectrum, there is thus another range of variations, namely, the degree to which the goals of education are change-oriented or system-reinforcing. The recent expansion of civic and human rights education in the "new democracies" has been promoted as a means to encourage change in the direction of more participatory and democratic political structures and encourage concepts of world citizenship.

This social change-orientation, which characterizes many human rights and civic education programs, especially in those countries outside the traditional western democracies, raises many questions of political consequence. What are the changes being promoted? How deep are the changes to go? And, most important, Who sets the goals and decides on the priorities? Especially important for these educational initiatives is their relationship with the larger social setting, that is, What are their desired and their actual short- and long-term benefits? Will it work? Evaluation and quality control linked with planning and design seek to make the answers to these questions more precise.

The Steps Toward Quality Control

While the breadth of goals and strategies involved in most human rights and civic education projects appear to preclude easy measurement, there are some criteria that can form a checklist to evaluate a given program. This list is derived from personal experience acquired through seventeen years of organizing human rights courses and training programs in the United States, Africa, and Eastern Europe, as well as from discussions with, and analytical papers prepared by, graduate students in a research seminar taught at Teachers College, Columbia University, for the past five years. As such, this chapter is more conceptual than empirical, an invitation to others to carry out the more extensive fieldwork that is necessary if we are to benefit from the experience of others. I would like to propose nine primary evaluation categories, all of which are important components of the planning and design process.

1. The Overall Rationale

To be effective, any educational initiative has to work with other social forces. Educational design begins with an assessment of the social conditions that identify not only the need for the project but also of its educational potential, that is, the positive conditions that make the proposed educational step both possible and appropriate. A project rationale addresses such questions as: Are the goals and basic elements of the education project commensurate with the needs at this particular time? Are the strategies likely to attain the goals? Are they the best strategies? How does this project fit with other initiatives in human rights and democracy education? Does it reinforce or compete? The goal is to show how it will succeed and that it is based on the maximum understanding of local conditions, constraints, and opportunities. In sum, that it is the best way to use the funds available.

2. The Selection of a Target Group

Few people cannot benefit from some human rights and civic education. The problem is, given the limited resources available, choosing which group or groups who would benefit the most and how their education would benefit others. A project rationale needs to examine the options and reasons behind the eventual choice, the group's receptivity relative to other potential groups, anticipated individual and institutional benefits, and so on. In many human rights education programs, the participants tend to be heterogeneous, often with quite different needs. This reflects the fact that most human rights education is addressed to people with only a rudimentary knowledge. Greater internal coherence maximizes the participant need–course content ratio.

3. The Motivational Patterns of the Target Group

Anyone who has taught knows the difference between the motivated and nonmotivated student. The former can almost learn by his or herself. On the other hand, motivation is not a given. It can and very often has to be stimulated. Certainly it cannot be taken for granted or go unanalyzed by educational planners. No educational project will work unless it is cognizant of the motivational patterns of its target group. In some cases they may be highly motivated young teachers, seeking knowledge and skills that will lead to much-cherished personal fulfillment. In other cases, as illustrated in the case studies discussing the education of military personnel, a target group might see itself as utterly coerced and thus reluctant to respond. The design of a human rights and civic education program must therefore include an assessment of the motivation of the target group, asking questions that identify why the participants would want to learn about human rights, what their perceptions of the goals of the program are, and what benefits they could be persuaded to appreciate. Planning must be based on assessments of how the eventual program will be seen by the learners to benefit them. Rewards must respond to their needs. Thus many local human rights education training programs in Africa include funds for local transportation, lunch, and even a small stipend to make up for the few dollars the participants might otherwise have needed to earn to support their families. (These are all pennies when compared with the cost of the travel and accommodation for the international experts.) No matter how beneficial human rights education might appear to the potential participants, they need to feed their families, and for many of them this is a hand-to-mouth process. Understanding these constraints and planning accordingly results in more successful programs.

4. The Quality and Educating Experience of Leaders

Leadership is a factor in all social life, and the quality of the individual instructor makes a substantial difference to the educational process. Organizational ability and the capacity to motivate a work team are critical qualifications for any leader. In the field of human rights education, most activists are self-taught. There are only a few systematic training programs in human rights education, and most are only a few weeks in duration.[5] Most human rights educators have come to the field of education from a sense of the need to recruit more supporters. Moreover, the planning and design of human rights education programs in parts of the world where the need is greatest have so far been dominated by standards set by the external funding organizations, few of which have experienced educators on their staffs. Professional human rights educators, especially those with experience outside universities, are few in number.

If one is committed to cost-effective growth, the development of local leadership in human rights education is obviously the major task. The choice of local personnel to receive support—for example, educators, legal experts, organizers, and financial managers—makes a big difference to both long- and short-term goals. Experience shows the importance of new local nongovernmental organizations (NGOs) moving from a single committed leader to a team that can evolve and replace leaders and members as necessary. Today few countries lack qualified and human rights-committed individuals that can be drawn from different existing sectors: NGOs, legal, medical, teaching, and other professions, including government officials. Indeed, external re-sources might best be spent in the formation and support of this type of group rather than channeling all the resources to specific events. Certainly using qualified local personnel before bringing in "experts" from overseas is not only cost-effective, but it also develops the local pool of expertise. Much could be added regarding the per-sonal qualifications of the individuals involved.

External financial support is fraught with ambiguities. It is often an important lifeline for the staff of many organizations in developing countries. In their search for the funds needed to survive as an organization and as individuals, local groups often have to respond to priorities other than their own. At the same time the external funders see their funds being used in less than efficient ways and would like to see their supported projects become more independent. One feels that we could all do better studying and learning from the now wide variety of past experiences.

5. Institutional Actors and Support

The resources available to human rights education in most countries is minuscule compared to those committed to other national priorities. Few NGOs in developing countries have access to the resources necessary to educate to any substantial de-gree more than their own members, typically a very small percentage of those they would like to reach. To reach beyond the "converted," human rights education must be integrated into the existing education systems of primary, secondary, and tertiary education. Difficult though this will be, it is the only way to reach a relatively large segment of the citizens. While not always immediately possible, this goal should be integrated into any human rights education planning.

Again, based on the premise of limited available resources, the effectiveness of any program will be closely related to its capacity to mobilize institutional support ranging from governmental offices, local and international NGOs, and international and national funding to the local media and individual citizens. Frequently, with the exception of funding, expanding institutional support is an afterthought, whereas it should be integrated into basic planning and design.

Defining the role of government agencies and individual officials in human rights education is an especially difficult task. Much depends on local circumstances. Experi-ences vary widely. Generally some level of government cooperation will be necessary, if only to avoid petty administrative harassment. In the end, the important threshold is to convince governments that the promotion of human rights standards make for a better national polity and a better national economy. Each program must address this long-term goal in its planning and develop an appropriate strategy. As many human rights problems focus on the relationship between individuals and state power, educa-tion programs have increasingly tried to integrate units of government and individual officials into the learning experience. The format of this experience is important. It makes a big difference when the authority figures lecture and when they function in dialogue formats where participants can discuss openly, for example, the function of the police and the rights of citizens vis-à-vis a policeman, outside of the context of an altercation on the street. This interaction can be mutually beneficial.

A major problem in improving the planning and execution of human rights education programs has to be the institutional priorities set by external funding organizations. This is best illustrated by the fact that most funding for human rights NGOs in Africa comes from other governments or from the overseas private sector. I have encountered numerous instances where guidelines that make sense in the metropolitan headquarters do not respond well to needs in the field.

6. The Learning Strategies and Teaching Methods

Classroom teaching is usually seen as the central piece of an educational program,[6] but it is radically dependent on the other elements. As in the case of the other components, there are multiple choices involved, and all the options need to be investigated. Such an analysis must address format and physical location, as well as the specific human rights components. A large downtown hotel might make an excellent venue for a conference but be a very distracting location for more focused learning.

Modern educational theory is more familiar with the impact of the student-teacher relationship on learning. Teaching about justice and democracy, for example, requires a commensurate atmosphere in the classroom. Otherwise the students assimilate only a formalistic knowledge. Closely related to the emphasis on praxis and empowerment inherent in much of the human rights education discussed in this volume, especially in Latin America, is the need to encourage the learners to become active in both learning and life. This participatory approach is discussed in a number of chapters, notably those of Ellen Dorsey and Bernard Hamilton. Success in the active participation approach leads to the need to introduce the students to the human and material resources that can respond to the resultant emerging needs. Even more than the human rights content, changing teaching style has been a primary focus of civic education reform in the former socialist countries of Eastern Europe.

The actual strategies used depend on local needs and circumstances. Certainly there are many options, although only if researched and planned in advance. Generally I have found that participants who have been active in the field of human rights (whether they be peasants or professionals) come ready both to learn and to take home ideas and materials for later use. Programs should therefore be prepared to provide them with materials and equipment they can use at home both to deepen their own knowledge and to use to teach others. The educational strategy is thus more one of introducing ideas and strategies to be worked out later, rather than seeking immediate outcomes. The task therefore includes the choice and packaging of the materials (as also of the training itself) in ways most appropriate to later use.

A very different case is that of human rights education programs for less motivated persons such as members of the armed forces or the military (covered in the chapters by Marc DuBois, Michael Hinkley, and Edy Kaufman). In these cases much depends on the instructor's ability to relate to the participants as well as on the way in which they have been brought to the sessions. My own limited experience indicates that maximum attention has to be given to the training and experience of the instructors and to providing them with high-quality visual and other supportive materials.

7. The Selection of Subject Matter

Human rights education in universities and among international professionals is dominated by persons trained in law. Indeed the first phase of international human rights has focused on international standards, institutions, and enforcement. The second phase focused on monitoring and reporting of violations. Without leaving behind these activities and still using the major human rights documents to define the field of human rights, human rights activists, professional and otherwise, have now adopted a much broader agenda, calling upon an expanded range of professional expertise. The new fields include economic and social rights, the use of the media and public relations, education at all levels, extensive databases, NGO mobilization and development, and many special sector skills, notably with regard to the rights of women, minorities, indigenous peoples, refugees and displaced persons, and prisoners. A consistent general interest in the United States has always been human rights and foreign policy, but this reflects the peculiar positions of power of the U.S. and a handful of other countries in world politics and might not be a priority item for basic courses in human rights in other parts of the world. Given the issues actually covered by the major human rights instruments, this adds up to a huge set of options for a prospective program. Every curriculum in human rights imposes choices and therefore exclusions. The most important first step is to make the exclusions consciously.

The selection of material for a given program is conditioned by many factors, most notably the needs of the target group and the goals of the program. There is a fundamental distinction between human rights education for victims or potential victims and human rights education for others. In the case of the former, the education is designed to empower them or to help them overcome violations and achieve their rights. In the latter the goals are more diverse, most likely to teach them about human rights and to encourage them to promote them. I personally believe that any course should both seek to empower people to assert their own rights and to be more responsive to the ways in which they might be able to help others in the same task.

My own experience and reviews of existing curricula and training programs suggest that the core content of a human rights course should cover the following basic categories, adjustments being made for past education and experience:

1. Cognitive
   the definition of "human" and "rights"
   the development of the idea and practice of international standards

> national and international enforcement mechanisms
> the content of the major human rights documents
> the capacity to distinguish among rights and to relate them to different social
>   goals
2. Attitudinal
> a sense that these standards can and should affect daily life
> a sense that they make a desirable difference
> sympathy for and responsiveness to those deprived of rights (empathy)
3. Behavioral
> basic strategies and practice in social change and conflict resolution
> training in the use of some local implementation systems
> practice in specific skills

These elements should provide the core for both professional and general education training, including basic courses on civic education. The bulk of the time allotted to a given program will be devoted to the cognitive elements. The attitudinal and behavioral will be interspersed. As indicated above, as content, they are likely to raise some opposition on behalf of others. It is therefore important that the case for the choice of content be argued, and not simply relinquished or reiterated without argument. The core sets the stage for more specific problems. International human rights emphasizes the importance of general standards rather than individual violations. In addition to the core, each program would need to respond to the specific needs of the target group, each of which would require analysis and an eventual selection of course content.

8. The Anticipated Benefits

A survey of the literature on human rights education reveals a remarkably long list of anticipated outcomes.[7] Learning and the products of learning are difficult to attribute to any one factor. The success of a given educational initiative might depend more on external factors such as general political environment or choice of sponsors or location. Nevertheless, systematic planning and design based on desired outcomes are critical. The basic questions are: What is the program designed to achieve? Is this the best way to achieve those goals?

As in all educational activities, there are primary and secondary goals, short- and long-term goals, as well as benefits that only appear later. All programs aim to increase knowledge about human rights standards and institutions, and most seek to promote greater responsiveness and awareness. Many programs now focus on specific promotional skills such as data collection and management or forms of litigation. The benefits from these skill programs are more readily identified and measured. Quality control is thus easier to establish.

Even in specific skills training programs, but especially in programs designed to reach the general public, most human rights educators have a much broader goal in mind, which is the development of a societywide culture and politics of human rights. In this respect there are a number of additional benefits that, with due advance consideration, can be integrated and that can benefit any program. They include:

the degree to which a given program might encourage replication, or reaches multipliers, namely, those whose education will be directly relayed to others;

planning that foresees and results in other follow-up activities (e.g., creation of new materials), the promotion of new and old institutions, mechanisms and groups that will reinforce learning, or more generic human rights goals; and

the development of national and international linkages and support mechanisms.

9. Cost-Effectiveness

The basic test of any program is whether, assuming that available funds were in no way restricted, this particular project would be the best way to spend them. While there are many training and education models in use, most are adaptations of formats (conferences, workshops, seminars) developed in the industrialized countries. In the developing world and the former Eastern Europe, most training and education programs are ad hoc and irregular and depend to a large degree on international financing. Few programs described in this volume are permanent. Universities and schools in these countries offer courses which, in structure, timing and content, follow academic models based on western models, rather than designing educational units adapted to local life, needs, and resources. Cost-effectiveness is at the heart of the problem. Resources are limited.[8] It is not cost-effective for an agency to be willing to bring four experts across the Atlantic, for example, when one would have been enough, given the absorption capacity of the learners and the fact that many learners who wished to attend could not do so because they could not afford the modest fee (literally 1/12 of the cost of each international expert). One can recount numerous similar examples of agency funding sources distorting a cost-benefit approach.

Conclusion

Ultimately the challenge to human rights education is in its planning and design stage. Much is possible if it is foreseen and integrated into the program design. At issue is the degree to which the limited resources available can be used (a) to reach the largest segments effectively and (b) to create local personnel and institutions that can continue the work. This result should not be left to chance when it can be integrated into program planning. Equally important will be a revision of the distribution patterns of international aid in such a way as to encourage local initiative and long-term growth in the NGO sector. The more immediate task is more information and research on the effectiveness of existing programs, especially those that are taking place in regions seeking new legal and democratic orders.

Notes

1. A recent overview of the general problem faced by human rights groups can be found in *The Status of Human Rights Organization in Sub-Saharan Africa* (Washington, D.C.: International Human Rights Internship Program, 1994).

2. J. Paul Martin, "Human Rights: Education for What?" *Human Rights Quarterly* 9 (1987): 414–22.

3. "History-Social Science Framework for California Public Schools," California State Department of Education, Sacramento, 1988.

4. Felicia Tibbitts, "Human Rights Education in Schools in the Post-Communist Context," *European Journal of Education* 29, no. 4 (1994): 363–76.

5. The ideal regular program is the annual program of the Renée Cassin Institute in Strasbourg, France.

6. Ralph Pettman, *Teaching for Human Rights: Activities for Schools* (United Nations Human Rights Commission, 1984); and the chapter by Nancy Flowers and David Shiman in this volume. (Chapter 10).

7. Martin, "Human Rights Education for What?" and Susanne M. Shafer, "Human Rights Education in Schools," in *Human Rights and Education*, ed. N. B. Turner (Oxford: Pergamon Press, 1987).

8. For an overview, see *Teachers in Developing Countries: Improving Effectiveness and Managing Costs*, ed. J. P. Fanell and J. B. Oliveira (Washington, D.C.: World Bank, 1993).

Reference Documents

African Charter on Human and Peoples' Rights (Banjul Charter). Adopted 1981; entered into force Oct. 21, 1986. O.A.U. Doc. CAB/LEG/67/3 rev. 5:21 I.L.M. 58 (1982).

Convention on the Elimination of All Forms of Discrimination Against Women. Adopted Dec. 18, 1979; entered into force Sept. 3, 1981. U.N.G.A. Res. 34/180, 34 UN GAOR Supp. (No. 46), UN Doc. A/34/46 (1979).

Convention on the Rights of the Child. Adopted Nov. 20, 1989; entered into force Sept. 2, 1990, U.N.G.A. Res. 44/25, 44 UN GAOR Supp., (No. 49), UN Doc. A/44/49.

European Convention for the Protection of Human Rights and Fundamental Freedoms. Nov. 4, 1950, E.T.S. No. 5. Entered into force Sept. 3, 1953.

International Covenant on Civil and Political Rights. Opened for signature Dec. 19, 1966; entered into force Mar. 23, 1976. U.N.G.A. Res. 2200 (XXI), 21 UN GAOR Supp. (No. 16) 52, UN Doc. A/6316 (1967).

International Covenant on Economic, Social and Cultural Rights. Opened for signature Dec. 19, 1966; entered into force Jan. 3, 1976. U.N.G.A. Res. 2200 (XXI), 21 UN GAOR Supp. (No. 16) 49, UN Doc. A/5316 (1967).

United Nations Charter. Signed at San Francisco on June 16, 1945; entered into force Oct. 4, 1945. 1976 Yearbook of the United Nations, 1033.

United Nations Decade for Human Rights Education, GA 49/184 of 23 Dec. 1994.

United Nations Declaration on the Right to Development, U.N.G.A. Res. 41/128, 41, UN GAOR Supp. (No. 53), UN Doc. A/41/53 (1986).

Universal Declaration of Human Rights. U.N.G.A. Res. 217A (III), 3(1) UN GAOR Res. 71, UN Doc. A/810 (1948).

Vienna Declaration and Programme of Action. Adopted June 25, 1993 by the World Conference on Human Rights. New York: United Nations Department of Public Information, DPI/1394-39399-August 1993-20M.

Select Bibliography

Bibliographic guidance is provided in several chapters of this volume, for example, chapters 10 and 32. Several scholarly journals routinely publish useful book reviews by which to keep current regarding new publications. Book reviews in the field may be found in *Harvard Human Rights Journal* ("Book Reviews," Publications Center, Harvard Law School, Cambridge, MA 02138); *Human Rights Quarterly* ("Book Reviews," Johns Hopkins University Press, Journals Publishing Division, 701 W. 40th St., Suite 275, Baltimore, MD 21211); and *Human Rights Internet Reporter* (Human Rights Internet, c/o Human Rights Centre, University of Ottawa, 57 Louis Pasteur, Ottawa K1N 6N5, Canada). North American Partners for Human Rights Education has established a resource center with bibliographic search capabilities and services (K. Rudelius-Palmer, Human Rights Center, University of Minnesota Law School, 437 Law Center, 229 19th Ave. South, Minneapolis, MN 55455). Consistently reliable for announcements regarding new publications in the field of human rights education is *Human Rights Education: The Fourth R*, jointly published by Amnesty International USA's Human Rights Education National Steering Committee and Human Rights Internet. Concentrating on European announcements and publications is the *Human Rights Education Newsletter* (Margot Brown, ed., University College of Ripon and York St. John, Lord Mayor's Walk, York, Y03 7EX, UK).

The select bibliography below, multilingual and global in scope, emphasizes recent book-length publications and is divided (with subsections) into the following categories: (1) general; (2) formal education; (3) training of professionals; (4) nonformal education; (5) methodology.

1. General

Bernstein Tarrow, Norma, ed. *Human Rights and Education.* Pergamon Comparative and International Education Series 3. New York: Pergamon Press, 1987.

Center for the Study of Human Rights. *Twenty-Four Human Rights Documents.* New York: Center for the Study of Human Rights, Columbia University, 1994.

Development Education Centre. *Do It Justice: Resources and Activities for Introducing Education in Human Rights.* Birmingham, UK, 1988.

Eide, Asbørn, and Marek Thee, eds. *Frontiers of Human Rights Education.* Oslo: Universitetsforlaget, 1983.

Graves, Norman J., ed. *Teaching for International Understanding, Peace and Human Rights.* Paris: UNESCO, 1984.

Magendzo, Abraham K. *Curriculum, escuela y derechos humanos (Curriculum, School, and Human rights).* Santiago: Programa Interdisciplinario de Investigación en Educación, 1989.

Starkey, Hugh, ed. *The Challenge of Human Rights Education.* London: Cassell Education, for the Council of Europe, 1991.

United Nations. *Human Rights: Questions and Answers.* New York: United Nations, 1987.

UNESCO. *Congrès international sur l'enseignement des droits de l'homme (International Congress on the Teaching of Human Rights).* Paris: UNESCO, 1980.

UNESCO. *Human Rights Teaching.* Paris: UNESCO, 1986–87.

2. Formal Education

Primary

Amnesty International, Puerto Rican Section. *Our Rights! Series for Children and Youth.* Rio Piedras, Puerto Rico: Amnesty International, Puerto Rican Section, 1993.

Arab Institute for Human Rights, Amnesty International, Tunisian Section. *Human Rights for Children: The U.N. Convention.* Tunisia: ADHOUA, 1992.

Barker, Dan. *Maybe Right, Maybe Wrong: A Guide for Young Thinkers.* Buffalo, N.Y.: Prometheus Books, 1992.

Burr, Margaret, and Rachel Warner, eds. *We Have Always Lived Here: The Maya of Guatemala.* London: Minority Rights Group, 1991.

Hatch, Virginia. *Human Rights for Children: A Manual of Activities for Elementary Schools.* Washington, D.C.: Human Rights for Children Committee, Amnesty International USA, 1991.

Mogrovejo de Thissen, Sheila, and Nélida Céspedes Rossel. *Desde la vida de los niños (From the Lives of Children).* Lima: Tarea, 1992.

Selwood, Sara. *Free Expressions: The Amnesty International Art Education Pack.* London: Amnesty International UK, 1991.

Williams, Roy. *Children and World Development: A Resource Book for Teachers.* London: UNICEF-UK and Richmond Publishing Co., 1987.

Secondary

Amnesty International Austria. *Spiele zur Werterziehung: Für Schule und Erwachsenbildung (Games for the Education of Values for Schools and Adult Education).* Linz, Austria: Locker, 1988.

Amnesty International Belgique Francophone. *Vivre dans la dignité, c'est aussi un droit de l'homme: Education aux droits de l'homme, dossier pédagogique pour le secondaire (Living in Dignity Is Also a Human Right: Human Rights Education, Pedagogical Dossier for Secondary Schools).* Brussels: A. D. Quart Monde, 1988.

CEDHOSSAI. *Dossier pédagogique: Comment éduquer aux droits de l'homme et à la paix?* Dakar, Senegal: CEDHOSSAI, 1991.

Frankel, Marvin E., with Helen Saideman. *Out of the Shadows of Night: The Struggle for International Human Rights.* New York: Delacorte, 1989.

Hicks, David W. *Minorities: A Teacher's Resource Book for the Multi-Ethnic Curriculum.* Oxford: Heinemann Educational Books, 1981.

New York State Education Department. *Teaching About the Holocaust and Genocide,* Human Rights Series. Albany, N.Y.: State Education Department, 1985, 1986.

Reardon, Betty. *Educating for Human Dignity: Learning About Rights and Responsibilities: A K–12 Teaching Resource.* Philadelphia: University of Pennsylvania Press, 1995.

Selby, David. *Human Rights.* Cambridge: Cambridge University Press, 1988.

Shiman, David, et al. *Teaching About Human Rights.* Denver: Center for Teaching International Relations, 1988.

Smith, Lesley. *Dimensions of Childhood: A Handbook for Social Education at Sixteen Plus.* London: Health Education Authority and UNICEF-UK, 1988.

Walker, Jamie. *Violence et résolution des conflits à l'école (Violence and Resolution of Conflicts at School).* Strasbourg: Council of Europe, 1990.

Higher Education

Freedman-Apsel, Joyce and Helen Fein, eds. *Teaching About Genocide.* Ottawa: Human Rights Internet, 1992.

Cassese, Antonio. *Human Rights in a Changing World.* Philadelphia: Temple University Press, 1990.

Claude, Richard Pierre and Burns H. Weston, eds. *Human Rights in the World Community: Issues and Action,* 2d ed. Philadelphia: University of Pennsylvania Press, 1992.

Donnelly, Jack. *International Human Rights.* Boulder, Colo.: Westview Press, 1993.

Eide, Asbørn, et al. *Violations des droits de l'homme: Quel recours, quelle résistance? (Resistance Against Human Rights Violations).* Paris: Serbal, for UNESCO, 1984.

Forsythe, David. *Human Rights and World Politics.* 2d ed. Lincoln: University of Nebraska Press, 1988.

García, Edmundo G. *The Human Rights Reader.* Manila: National Bookstore, 1990.

Laqueur, Walter, and Barry Rubin, eds. *The Human Rights Reader.* 2d ed. New York: New American Library, 1989.

Olguin, Leticia, ed. *Educación y derechos humanos: Una discusión interdisciplinaria (Education and Human Rights: An Interdisciplinary Discussion).* San José, Costa Rica: Instituto Interamericano de Derechos Humanos, 1989.

Vincent, R. J. *Human Rights and International Relations.* Cambridge: Cambridge University Press, 1990.

World University Service. *Academic Freedom: A Human Rights Report,* vols. 1 and 2. London: Zed Books, 1990.

Adult and Continuing Education

Collins, Michael. *Adult Education as Vocation.* London: Routledge, 1991.

Jarvis, Peter. *Adult Education and the State: Towards a Politics of Adult Education.* London: Routledge, 1993.

Kirkwood, Gerri, and Colin Kirkwood. *Living Adult Education: Freire in Scotland.* Milton Keynes: Open University Press, 1989.

Lovett, Tom, ed. *Radical Approaches to Adult Education: A Reader.* London: Routledge, 1988.

Ouane, Adama. *Handbook on Learning Strategies for Post-Literacy and Continuing Education.* Hamburg: UNESCO Institute for Education, 1989.

3. Training of Professionals

Science, Health, and Social Work Professions

Annas, George J., and Michael A. Grodin. *The Nazi Doctors and the Nuremberg Code.* Oxford: Oxford University Press, 1992.

Centre for Human Rights. *Teaching and Learning About Human Rights: A Manual for Schools of Social Work and the Social Work Profession.* Geneva: United Nations Centre for Human Rights, 1992.

Dubé, Ginette, and Angela Smailes, eds. *AIDS and Human Rights: Sharing the Challenge.* Vancouver: Vancouver World AIDS Group, 1992.

Gruschow, Janet, and Kari Hannibal. *Health Services for the Treatment of Torture and Trauma Survivors.* Washington, D.C.: American Association for the Advancement of Science, 1989.

Hannibal, Kari. *Taking Up the Challenge: The Promotion of Human Rights. A Guide for the Scientific Community.* Washington, D.C.: American Association for the Advancement of Science, 1992.

Marange, Valerie, for the Amnesty International (France) Medical Commission. *Doctors and Torture: Collaboration or Resistance?* London: Bellew Publishing Company, 1991.

Randall, Glenn R., and Ellen L. Lutz. *Serving Survivors of Torture.* Washington, D.C.: American Association for the Advancement of Science, 1991.

Rasmussen, Ole Vedel. *Medical Aspects of Torture.* Copenhagen: Laegeforeningens Forlag, 1990.

Stover, Eric, and Elena O. Nightingale, M.D. *The Breaking of Bodies and Minds: Torture, Psychiatric Abuse and the Health Professions.* New York: W. H. Freeman and Company, 1985.

Legal Studies

Alston, Philip, ed. *The United Nations and Human Rights: A Critical Appraisal.* Oxford: Oxford University Press, 1992.

Brownlie, Ian. *Basic Documents on Human Rights.* 3d ed. Oxford: Oxford University Press, 1993.

Daes, Erica-Irene A. *Status of the Individual and Contemporary International Law.* Geneva: United Nations Centre for Human Rights, 1992.

Hannum, Hurst. *Guide to International Human Rights Practice.* 2d ed. Philadelphia: University of Pennsylvania Press, 1992.

Lillich, Richard B. *International Human Rights: Problems of Law, Policy, and Practice.* 2d ed., Boston: Little, Brown and Company, 1991.

Meron, Theodor, ed. *Human Rights in International Law,* 2 vols. New York: Oxford University Press, 1984.

Newman, Frank, and David Weissbrodt. *International Human Rights.* Cincinnati: Anderson Publishing Co., 1990.

Sieghart, Paul. *The International Law of Human Rights.* Oxford: Clarendon Press, 1983.

Steiner, Henry J., and Philip Alston. *International Human Rights in Context: Law, Politics, Morals: Text and Materials.* New York: Oxford University Press, 1996.

Vasak, Karel, ed., and Philip Alston, English edition, ed. *The International Dimensions of Human Rights,* 2 vols. Westport, Conn.: Greenwood Press, for UNESCO, 1982.

Public Officials

Human Rights Research and Education Centre, University of Ottawa. *Human Rights Training for Commonwealth Public Officials Manual.* London: Commonwealth Secretariat, 1990.

Security

Alderson, J. *Human Rights and the Police.* Strasbourg: Council of Europe, 1984.

Howard, Michael, George J. Andreopoulos, and Mark Shulman, eds. *The Laws of War: Constraints on Warfare in the Western World.* New Haven, Conn.: Yale University Press, 1994.

Laverrière, Jean-Marc, and Laurent Marti. *Soldier's Manual.* Geneva: International Committee of the Red Cross, 1972.

Meron, Theodor. *Human Rights and Humanitarian Norms as Customary Law.* Oxford: Oxford University Press, 1991.

Reisman, W. Michael, and Chris T. Antoniou, eds. *The Laws of War: A Comprehensive Collection of Primary Documents on International Laws Governing Armed Conflict.* New York: Vintage Books, 1994.

Reynard, A. *Human Rights in Prisons.* Strasbourg: Council of Europe, 1986.

United Nations. *Symposium on the Role of the Police in the Protection of Human Rights.* New York: United Nations (Doc.No. ST/HR/Ser.A/6), 1980.

4. Nonformal Education

NGOs, Community-Based Education, and Development Issues

Clark, John. *Democratizing Development: The Role of Voluntary Organizations.* London: Earthscan Publications, 1991.

Committee for the Protection of Democratic Rights (CPDR). *Know Your Rights: A Handbook for Political Activists, Social Workers, Trade Unionists.* Bombay: Kobad Ghandy, 1980.

Dembo, David, Clarence J. Dias, Ayesha Kadwani, and Ward Morehouse. *Nothing to Lose But Our Lives: Empowerment to Oppose Industrial Hazards in a Transnational World.* New York: New Horizons Press, in cooperation with the Asian Regional Exchange for New Alternatives, Hong Kong, and the Indian Law Institute, New Delhi, 1988.

Dias, Clarence J., ed. *Initiating Human Rights Education at the Grassroots: Asian Experiences.* Bangkok: Asian Cultural Forum on Development, 1992.

Freire, Paulo. *Pedagogy of the Oppressed.* New York: Seabury Press, 1973.

Gloppen and Lise Rakner. *Human Rights and Development: The Discourse in the Humanities and Social Sciences.* Fantoft-Bergen, Norway: Chr. Michelsen Institute, 1993.

Gordinne, P., ed. *Droits de l'homme, droits des peuples: Guide pour l'information et l'éducation (Human Rights, Peoples' Rights: Guide for Information and Education).* Brussels: Médiathèque de la Communauté Française de Belgique, 1989.

Graves, Norman J., ed. *Teaching for International Understanding, Peace and Human Rights.* Paris: UNESCO, 1984.

Timm, Richard W. *Training of Trainers in Human Rights.* Bangladesh: South Asian Forum for Human Rights (SAFHR), 1992.

Timm, Richard W. *Working for Justice and Human Rights: A Practical Manual.* Dhaka: Hotline Asia Oceania, n.d.

Women

Arnot, Madeleine and Gaby Weiner. *Gender and the Politics of Schooling.* London: Hutchinson and Open University, 1987.

Hazon, Winnie. *The Social and Legal Status of Women: A Global Perspective.* Westport, Conn.: Greenwood Press, 1990.

Kerr, Joanna, ed. *Ours by Right: Women's Rights as Human Rights.* London: Zed Books, 1993.

Tomaševski, Katarina. *Women and Human Rights.* London: Zed Books, 1993.

Weiner, Gaby and Madeleine Arnot. *Gender Under Scrutiny: New Inquiries in Education.* London: Hutchinson and Open University, 1987.

Multicultural Education

Council for Cultural Co-operation. *Compendium of Information on Intercultural Education Schemes in Europe: Education of Migrants' Children.* Strasbourg: Council of Europe, 1983.

Finkelstein, Barbara, Anne E. Imamura, and Joseph J. Tobin, eds. *Transcending Stereotypes: Experiencing Culture and Education in Japan.* Yarmouth, Mass.: Intercultural Press, 1991.

Lynch, James, Cilia Modgil, and Sohan Modgil, eds. *Cultural Diversity and the Schools.* Vol. 1: *Education for Cultural Diversity: Convergence and Divergence.* Vol. 2: *Prejudice, Polemic of Progress?* Vol. 3: *Equity or Excellence? Education and Cultural Reproduction.* Vol. 4: *Human Rights, Education and Global Responsibilities.* London and Washington, D.C.: Falmer Press, 1992.

Taylor, Charles. *Multiculturalism and the Politics of Recognition.* Princeton, N.J.: Princeton University Press, 1992.

Religious Groups

Bautista, Liberato, ed. *Human Rights: Biblical and Theological Readings.* Manila: Philippines National Council of Churches, 1988.

Capotorti, Francesco. *Study on the Rights of Persons Belonging to Ethnic, Religious and Linguistic Minorities.* Geneva: United Nations Centre for Human Rights, 1991.

Catholic Commission for Justice and Peace in Zimbabwe. *The Hit Kit.* Harare: Catholic Commission for Justice and Peace in Zimbabwe, 1989.

Horace Perera, L. H., ed. *Human Rights and Religions in Sri Lanka: Buddhism, Hinduism, Christianity, Islam.* Colombo: Lanka Foundation, 1988.

Livezey, Lowell W. *Nongovernmental Organizations and the Ideas of Human Rights.* Princeton, N.J.: Princeton University Center for International Studies, 1988.

Mayer, Ann. *Islam and Human Rights: Tradition and Politics.* Princeton, N.J.: Princeton University Press, 1991.

Rosenbaum, Alan S., ed. *The Philosophy of Human Rights: International Perspectives.* London: Aldwych Press, 1980.

Secretariado General de la Conferencia Episcopal Peruana. *Yo forastero y me recibieron: La iglesia frente a los hermanos desplazados (I Was a Stranger and They Received Me: The Church and Displaced People).* Lima: Conferencia Episcopal Peruana, 1990.

University of Botswana. *Human Rights and You.* Gaborone: Macmillan Botswana Publishing, 1989.

Vicaría de la Solidaridad. *Religion.* Santiago: Vicaría de la Solidaridad, Ediciones Paulinas, Manuales de educación en derechos humanos, 1991.

Zalaquett, José. *The Human Rights Issue and the Human Rights Movement.* Geneva: The World Council of Churches, 1981.

5. Methodology, Comparative Studies, Research, Evaluation

Claude, Richard Pierre. *Educating for Human Rights: The Philippines and Beyond.* Quezon City: University of the Philippines Press, 1996.

Fuente, Carmen and Mercedes Muñoz-Repiso. *Preparation for Life in a Democratic Society in Five Countries in Southern Europe.* Strasbourg: Council of Europe, 1982.

Green, Jennifer and Jack Tobin, *Guide to Human Rights Research.* Cambridge, Mass.: Harvard Law School Human Rights Program, 1994.

Jabine, Thomas B. and Richard Pierre Claude, eds. *Human Rights and Statistics: Getting the Record Straight.* Philadelphia: University of Pennsylvania Press, 1992.

Léonard, Massarenti. *Une pédagogie des droits de l'homme (Pedagogy for Human Rights).* Geneva: Editions Labor et Fides, 1991.

Ramsey, Patricia. *Teaching and Learning in a Diverse World.* New York: College Press of Columbia University of the City of New York, 1987.

Spirer, Herbert and Louise Spirer. *Data Analysis for Monitoring Human Rights.* Washington, D.C.: American Association for the Advancement of Science, 1993.

Starkey, Hugh, ed. *Socialization of School Children and Their Education for Democratic Values and Human Rights: Report of the Colloquy of Directors of Educational Research Institutes Held in Ericeira, Portugal.* Amsterdam and Lisse: Swets and Zeitlinger, 1991.

Torney-Purta, Judith. *Evaluating Global Education: Sample Instruments for Assessing Programs, Materials and Learning.* New York: Global Perspectives in Education, 1986–87.

UNESCO. *World Directory of Human Rights Teaching and Research Institutions.* Paris: Berg Publishers, 1988.

Contributors

George Andreopoulos, Assistant Professor of Government, John Jay College of Criminal Justice, City University of New York and Lecturer in International Human Rights, Yale University, USA

Roxana Arroyo,* Member, Central American Commission for the Defense of Human Rights, feminist attorney and activist, Codahuca, Costa Rica

Upendra Baxi, Professor of Law, Warwick University, UK

E. Débora Benchoam,* Teacher, Buenos Aires, Argentina

Audrey Chapman, Director, Program on Science and Human Rights of the American Association for the Advancement of Science, USA

Richard Pierre Claude, Professor Emeritus of Government and Politics, University of Maryland, College Park, USA

Matthew Cowie, Lecturer, Law Department, University of Nottingham, UK

Alexander von Cube, Former Research Associate, Institut für Bevölkerungsforschung, Wiesbaden, Germany

Clarence Dias, Director, International Center for Law in Development, USA

Ellen Dorsey, National Field Director, Amnesty International, USA and Adjunct Professor, School of International Service, American University, USA

Unity Dow, Director, Metlhaetsile Women's Information Centre, Mochudi, Botswana

Marc DuBois, Attorney, New Orleans, Louisiana, USA

Judith Dueck, Educator and Librarian, Winnipeg, Canada. Executive board member of the Human Rights Information and Documentation Systems International (HURIDOCS)

Lloyd S. Etheredge, Director, International Scientific Network (Internet) Project at the Policy Science Center, Yale University, USA

Nancy Flowers, Curriculum Coordinator for Amnesty International, USA

Dorota Gierycz, Social Affairs Officer, Sustainable Development and Policy Coordination, United Nations

Olivier Giscard d'Estaing,* Director, BUSCO—Association Mondiale des Entrepreneurs pour le Sommet Social, Paris, France

*Denotes an author who contributed a previously unpublished statement, comment, or analysis used in an editorial box or "sidebar."

Cosmas Gitta, Uganda Human Rights Worker and Fellow of the Center for the Study of Human Rights, Columbia University, USA

Lawrence Gostin, Professor of Law, Georgetown University Law Center and Professor of Public Health, the Johns Hopkins University School of Hygiene and Public Health, USA

Sofia Gruskin, Instructor, François-Xavier Bagnoud Center for Health and Human Rights of the Harvard School of Public Health, USA

Bernard Hamilton, President, Leo Kuper Foundation, London, UK

Kari B. Hannibal,* Education Coordinator, Physicians for Human Rights, Boston, USA

Donna Hicks, Deputy Director, Program on International Conflict Analysis and Resolution, Harvard University Center for International Affairs, USA

D. Michael Hinkley, U.S. Naval Legal Service, Yokosuka, Japan

Sin Kim Horn, Cambodian Coalition for Health and Human Rights, Phnom Penh, Cambodia

Rhoda E. Howard, Professor of Sociology, and Director, Theme School on International Justice and Human Rights, McMaster University, Hamilton, Ontario, Canada

Tokunbo Ige, Africa Programs Officer, International Commission of Jurists, Geneva, Switzerland

Edward T. Jackson, Associate Professor of Public Administration, Carleton University, Ottawa, Canada

Kozara Kati, Human Rights Documentation Center and Director of Aid Norway Albania, in Tirana, Albania

Edy Kaufman, Executive Director, Harry S. Truman Research Institute for the Advancement of Peace, Hebrew University, Jerusalem, Israel

Allen S. Keller, M.D., Department of Medicine, New York University Medical Center, USA

Shulamith Koenig, Executive Director, Organizing Committee of the Peoples' Decade of Human Rights Education, USA

Jana Kviečinska, Human Rights Education Program Director, Milan Šimecka Foundation, Bratislava, Slovak Republic

Zita Lazzarini, Visiting Lecturer, Department of Health, Policy and Management, Harvard School of Public Health, USA

Abraham K. Magendzo, Director, Programa Interdisciplinario de Investigaciones en Educación (PIIE), Santiago, Chile

Jonathan Mann, M.D., François-Xavier Bagnoud Professor of Health and Human Rights, Harvard School of Public Health, USA

Rita Maran, Human Rights Program Associate, Doreen B. Townsend Center for the Humanities, University of California, Berkeley, USA

Stephen P. Marks, Director, United Nations Studies Program, School of International and Public Affairs, Columbia University, USA

J. Paul Martin, Executive Director, Center for the Study of Human Rights, Columbia University, USA

Garth Meintjes, Associate Director, Center for Civil and Human Rights, and Assistant Professor, Notre Dame Law School, USA

Ligia Neacsu-Hendry, Former Director, Education Program (SIRDO), Bucharest, Romania

Edward L. O'Brien, Professor, Georgetown University Law Center, and Co-Director, National Institute for Citizen Education in Law, USA

Theodore S. Orlin, Co-Director of the Human Rights Advocacy Project of the Utica College of Syracuse University, USA

Gabriel Otterman, M.D., Physician, Center for the Study of Society and Medicine of the College of Physicians and Surgeons of Columbia University, USA

Anita Parlow, Executive Producer, "Bearing Witness," Public Broadcasting System, USA

Betty A. Reardon, Director, Peace Education Program, Teachers College of Columbia University, USA

George C. Rogers,* Attorney, Buenos Aires, Argentina

Magda J. Seydegart, Partner, South House Exchange (Management Group for Human Rights, Women's Rights and NGO Institution Building), Ottawa, Canada

David A. Shiman, Professor of Education, and Co-Director of the Center for World Education, University of Vermont, USA

Susannah Sirkin,* Deputy Director, Physicians for Human Rights, Boston, USA

Gopal Siwakoti,* Director, International Institute for Human Rights, Environment and Development (INHURED International), Kathmandu, Nepal

Sam Sopheap, Cambodian Coalition for Health and Human Rights, Phnom Penh, Cambodia

Paul Spector, Senior Associate, Institute for International Research, Washington, D.C., USA

Herbert Spirer, Professor Emeritus of Statistics and Business Administration, University of Connecticut, USA

Louise Spirer, Independent Statistical Consultant, USA

Sheryl Stumbras, Attorney, Metlhaetsile Women's Information Centre, Mochudi, Botswana

Maria Suarez-Toro,* Producer, Feminist Radio International Endeavor (FIRE), Santa Ana, Costa Rica

Sue Tatten, Director of the Legal Resources Project of the International Human Rights Internship Program, Washington, D.C., USA

Ivan Turek, Professor of Mechanical Engineering and Human Rights Educator, Methodic Centre, Presov, Slovak Republic

Caroline Whitbeck, Professor of Engineering Ethics, Massachusetts Institute of Technology, USA

Richard J. Wilson, Professor of Law and Director, International Human Rights Law Clinic, Washington College of Law, American University, Washington, D.C., USA

Index